Foreigners
in the
Union Army and Navy

CARL SCHURZ, 1829–1906

ELLA LONN

Foreigners
in the
Union Army
and
Navy

LOUISIANA STATE UNIVERSITY PRESS

Baton Rouge

To the memory of

the soldiers of the Union armies

and

the soldiers of the Confederate armies

who fought valiantly for the cause

which seemed to them right

Preface

This book is designed as a companion to the author's volume on *Foreigners in the Confederacy*. It did not require the suggestion of several reviewers that a study of foreigners in the Union services might well follow the Confederate study to turn her thought in that direction. Indeed, the former work had not yet gone to press before the author had decided that her attention would next be turned toward the foreigners and foreign-born in the Northern army and navy.

This piece of research has been the most laborious of the writer's entire experience, as the amount of material to be sifted, in both manuscript and printed form and in several languages, seemed absolutely without limit. Often when the search seemed to be nearing an end only to disclose fresh sources which could not be ignored, the writer was forced to wonder whether, like the work of the famous poet Tasso, her labors would consume ten years of her life and then not be finished. In moments of pessimism she also wondered if there would ever be any historians if each person realized that on entering his chosen field of history he was binding himself to a life of slavery. Nevertheless, it has been a pleasant task, filled with many thrills, especially when persistence enabled the writer to reach the goal of definitely determining the nativity of a certain person which had threatened to evade all pursuit; when the search disclosed in some obscure private or noncommissioned officer a future governor or senator; or when in a private she recognized a man who had already attained distinction in a foreign country. The writer could regret, when she saw some alluring book in Italian or Polish, that she had not mastered those languages, for these works might well throw additional light on her subject. There is one book in Russian in Peabody Library in Baltimore at which she still looks longingly for the possible data which she may have missed.

There may be a feeling on the part of some readers that a disproportionate amount of space has been devoted to the minor nationalities in comparison with the Germans, who streamed into the Union army in such enormous numbers. Always there existed the necessity to cut down the amount of space given to the Germans. There were two reasons: first, the Germans have been more adequately treated with some degree of scholarship, and many of the leaders (Schurz, Hecker, and Börnstein, among others) have left memoirs; and, secondly, it seemed highly desirable to emphasize the minor nationalities, such as the Scandinavian and Polish, in order to leave in the mind of the reader the varicolored picture of a composite army of many diverse nationalities. Furthermore, a writer is obliged to recognize the danger of piling up too many illustrations, too many characters, too much detail; so much strikes the mind that there is the possibility of nothing striking it clearly. This feeling led the author to exclude from the completed text many German colonels, who really, in her judgment, merited a place in the record by virtue of their contributions.

There remains the pleasant task of acknowledging the help of many persons in making possible this volume. First, the writer makes grateful acknowledgment to the Social Science Research Council for a grant which enabled her to take time off from her college teaching. The many librarians and custodians of archives of places where she has worked have been invariably helpful. In particular she feels indebted to the members of the staff of the National Archives, where she worked several months. The staff at Peabody Library allowed her many privileges which facilitated her work. She owes to the Society for the History of the Germans in Maryland the privilege of using its file of *Der Deutsche Pionier*. To Miss Ruth A. Carlson of Augustana College and to Mr. J. Hovde of Decorah, Iowa, she is indebted for help in translating a few Swedish and Norwegian passages when the going became too rough. She acknowledges with appreciation the help of Dr. Mina Kerr, for many years a professor of English at Milwaukee-Downer College, who has read the entire manuscript and made many valuable suggestions. Finally, the painstaking care shown by Mary Lamury McMinn and other members of the staff of the Louisiana State University Press in preparing the manuscript for the press is gratefully acknowledged.

Ella Lonn

Contents

Contents

CHAPTER ONE

Foreign Population in the North
in 1860

T HAT the foreign-born element in the population of the United States
  in 1860 was very large in proportion to the native-born is a truism.
Likewise, the fact that by far the greater part of that foreign element was
located in the northern states is as well known to Northerners as to
Southerners. However, the mere reiteration of these two striking facts is
insufficient for a clear perception of their significance in the fighting and
the winning of the Civil War.

By way of broad comparison between the two sections, North and
South, it may be noted that in 1860 there were scattered through the
states later constituting the Confederacy only 233,650 persons born under
a foreign flag, while there were 3,903,672 foreign-born in the strictly
northern states.[1] Of the whole number of foreign-born in the United
States, 86.60 per cent were inhabitants of the free states. To put it another way, for every white immigrant in the slave states, eight had settled
in the free states. It seems only fair to exclude from the calculation the
border states, as they did not constitute a source for foreign-born recruits
for the Confederacy, and except in Missouri they yielded comparatively
few for the Union army. It is also striking how greatly the pace of immigration had accelerated between 1850 and 1860. The total number
of foreign-born in the population of the United States in 1860 was
4,136,175. Over one half of that number, or 2,598,214, poured in during
the period 1850–1860, an astonishing rate of increase in the foreign-born

---

[1] *Eighth Census, 1860. The Statistics of the Population of the United States* (Washington,
1864–1866), xxix. These figures have been revised to exclude from the Southern count the
slave states which did not secede from the Union, since in each case the large numbers of
soldiers who marched off to join the Confederate army were drawn almost exclusively from
the native-born; on the other hand, sometimes a striking proportion of foreign-born joined
the Union army from those states, as was the case in Missouri.

The number whose birthplace was not stated is so small (51,883) as not to require consideration. *Ibid.*, xxviii. Adjustments have been made to allow for deaths and remigration in the
figure 2,598,214.

element in a single decade. Clearly, this significant increase had not escaped the attention of the Southern leaders and may partially account for their intransigent stand after Lincoln's election. If a definite stand was to be taken, it must be before the population of the North was given an even greater disproportionate increase by further influx of foreigners.

The largest element to migrate to the United States after the War of 1812 consisted of citizens of the British Isles and British North America. Great Britain and Ireland sent a population, as the census compilers declare, "for a kingdom," as it amounted to some two and three-quarters million. To this large number Ireland contributed at this early period rather less than a million while Scotland and Wales sent only the meager number of 56,000. The proportion from that part of the British Empire now called the Dominion of Canada was more numerous than may be generally recognized, for it increased the total British contingent by 117,142 for the same period of time, 1819–1860. Thus the total British addition to the population was 2,750,874—close to 3,000,000. Next in magnitude was the immigration from Germany, including Prussia, of more than 1,500,000 persons, according to the census returns, or 31 per cent of the population. Strangely enough, in the light of the well-known attitude of Frenchmen against emigration, the third largest contribution during the period of four decades, though dropping in number far below that of Germany, came from France. Her loss to America was almost 250,000 citizens.[2] The number added by the smaller European countries to the stream of immigration to the United States during this early period was, with some exceptions, too small and scattered to have any marked influence in determining the trend and action of the North. Whether these immigrants from small European countries provided an appreciable number of recruits for the Union army will be revealed in subsequent chapters.

Because a study of the numbers contributed by the various nationality groups to each northern state is dry and perhaps not sufficiently rewarding to justify inclusion in the text, this has been relegated to the notes.[3]

---

[2] Exact figures for the period from October, 1819 to May 31, 1860, are as follows:

Ireland (1820–1860)	967,366	Germany	1,486,044
England	302,665	Germany (Prussia included)	1,546,476
Scotland and Wales	55,825	France	208,063

Eighth Census, 1860. The Statistics of the Population, xxii. The reader must be cautioned in regard to the number recorded from Canada (117,142), as United States officials did not attempt to segregate those who were Canadian citizens from those who entered the United States via Canada. The author cannot reconcile the above figures for Great Britain, as the census is very confusing. *Ibid.,* xxi, xxii.   [3] See Appendix, Section A.

The states having the largest number of resident foreigners (arranged in descending order according to the respective sizes of their foreign-born population) were New York, Pennsylvania, Ohio, Illinois, Wisconsin, and Massachusetts. The greatest number of Irish were to be found in New York, Pennsylvania, Massachusetts, and Illinois, while the largest number of Germans were within the borders of New York (of course), Ohio, Pennsylvania, Illinois, Wisconsin, and Missouri respectively. On the other hand, the states with the smallest number of foreigners were Delaware, Oregon, Vermont, Maine, and New Hampshire.[4]

The large foreign population in the industrial centers made a distinctive contribution to, and presented an especial problem to, the northern section, just as it made one of the important contributions to, and brought many problems to, the army. From the earliest settlement, the Dutch and Quaker colonies on the Atlantic seaboard were composed of diverse ethnical elements. The condition was accentuated by the industrial revolution. The various unassimilated groups in the body politic were increasing year by year, particularly in the country's metropolis and in the mining sections of Pennsylvania. The unprecedented immigration of Irish into New York City during the last two decades before the war was transforming that city into a sort of New Ireland. These Americanized Irishmen asked only that they be allowed to earn a living, to take an active part in ward politics, and to hold fast their hatred of Great Britain. They opposed emancipation of negroes because of fear of competition in the labor market.[5]

A statistical study of the sixteen American cities having the largest populations in 1860 reveals that each of these cities had a much higher percentage of foreigners than had the state in which it was located. In New York City the population recorded as foreign reached the impressive figure of over 383,717 people out of a total of 805,651; Irishmen alone amounted to 203,740; Germans had brought their number to 119,984; and all groups formed 47.62 per cent of the population whereas in the state as a whole foreigners constituted only 25.73 per cent. The degree to which the metropolis had become a mélange of nationality groups was manifested in 1849, when mass meetings were held in various cities to express sym-

[4] *Eighth Census, 1860. The Statistics of the Population,* xxix, xxx.

[5] Shannon makes the comment that if the Irish had "been led to believe that Great Britain was whole-heartedly friendly with the South they would have been united in their loyalty to the Union." Fred Albert Shannon, *The Organization and Administration of the Union Army* (Cleveland, 1928), I, 20.

pathy for the Hungarian revolutionists. At one meeting in New York, attended by 30,000 people, three stands for speakers were erected—one for American, one for German, and one for French and Italian listeners. Philadelphia, the second largest city in the nation, with well over 500,000 inhabitants, counted her foreign population at over one-fourth of the entire population. Brooklyn, next door to our greatest port, had a huge foreign element of 39.22 per cent of its total population of 266,661. Baltimore, fourth in size, had a relatively lower percentage, 24.71, probably as a result of her location in a slaveholding state. Her percentage of foreigners, it will be noted, approaches that of the other chief centers of the slaveholding states—Charleston with 15.5 per cent (30 per cent of the white population), Mobile with 24 per cent, and Richmond with 13 per cent of the entire population of each of those cities, but fell far below the great port of New Orleans, with almost 40 per cent. The numerous Irish in Boston boosted the foreign proportion to 35.88 per cent.

Chicago, Cincinnati, and Milwaukee showed clearly the effect of the westward tide of immigration during the fifties. Almost half of the population of over 100,000 in Chicago consisted of Germans, Irish, and less numerous foreign elements—49.99 per cent, to be exact. In Cincinnati census takers reckoned the foreign element as 45.71 per cent, and in Milwaukee the strong German population raised the foreign proportion to over 50 per cent. Louisville, one of the largest of the cities south of the Ohio River, showed a surprisingly large German strain, twice the size of the Irish contingent, placing the foreign element in that border city at 33.73 per cent. The 50,500 Germans and almost 30,000 Irish in St. Louis formed an overwhelming part of the large foreign population of that city —59.76 per cent—and accounted, incidentally, for a large part of the foreign element in the entire state of Missouri. San Francisco was the only city with an appreciable number of Asiatics in her foreign population of over 50 per cent. Proportions of foreign-born varied in the other large centers from 46.44 per cent in Buffalo to 24.80 per cent in Providence.[6]

Comparison of the percentage of the foreign element of each city with that of the state in which it was located emphasizes that it was ever to the city that the newcomers were chiefly attracted. A few typical examples will

[6] *Eighth Census, 1860. The Statistics of the Population,* I, xxxi–xxxii; for the mass meeting in New York in behalf of Hungary, see Carl Wittke, *We Who Built America* (New York, 1940), 431; for foreigners in the South, see Ella Lonn, *Foreigners in the Confederacy* (Chapel Hill, 1940), 3, 4, 7, 9.

The foreign population of Washington, D.C., was surprisingly large (61,122—17.61 per cent) for a nonindustrial city. *Eighth Census, 1860. The Statistics of the Population,* xxxii.

substantiate that fact: New York City had a proportion almost double that of the entire state of New York; Chicago's percentage exceeded that of Illinois by almost three times; Cincinnati's proportion was triple that of Ohio; Philadelphia's was double that of Pennsylvania, despite the large numbers in the mining sections. Even in Wisconsin, where the large numbers of foreign-born on farms raised the proportion in the state as a whole, the discrepancy between the percentage for Milwaukee and that for the entire state was marked, although it was smaller than in other instances.[7] Probably California presents the largest variation from the rule, since the percentage for San Francisco, the state metropolis (50.09 per cent) exceeds that for the state as a whole (47.98 per cent) by only a few points.

That the foreign element from Great Britain and Canada was numerous through the states of the Atlantic seaboard was well known at the time, apart from statistics, but it has been less generally recognized that it was also scattered rather generously through the Middle West. Since neither language nor religion erected a barrier between this group and the masses of the native population, likewise basically of Anglo-Saxon blood, the British element rapidly merged with the native-born, almost without being regarded as foreign. Britishers tended to merge with New Englanders more easily than did any other group, and they shared in many respects the attitudes of the New Englanders, such as hostility toward slavery. There was accordingly no segregation nor were there any colonies of the British-born.

Aliens of other origins, however, tended—as was perfectly natural— to congregate in certain sections of a city or to acquire neighboring farms in a rural locality to which the name "German settlement," "Swedish settlement," or "Swiss colony" became attached. Concentration of the immigrants in compact settlements made these colonies, to all intents and purposes, outposts of the mother civilizations as much as Massilia and Syracuse were in ancient times outposts of Hellenic culture. Here the tongues of the European homelands were used almost exclusively, and newspapers in these languages also entered the homes. Settlers adhered to

---

[7] For the population percentages of foreigners in the states, see *Eighth Census, 1860. The Statistics of the Population,* xxxi. The percentages in the cities in relation to those of their states are as follows:

New York	47.62%	New York (state)	25.73%
Chicago	49.99	Illinois	18.97
Cincinnati	45.71	Ohio	14.03
Philadelphia	28.93	Pennsylvania	14.81
Milwaukee	50.49	Wisconsin	35.69
San Francisco	50.09	California	47.98

their old religious faiths, and since services were conducted in the tongues most easily understood, even religion constituted a bar to amalgamation. Likewise, members of each group tended to marry among their own people, so that in the main it was not until the third generation that intermarriage began to perform its normal part in the fusion of the racial groups. Old customs of the fatherland were transplanted to various parts of the New World; the methods of celebrating Christmas in a German or a Swedish home had the flavor of that part of Europe from which the immigrant hailed. Even semisocial cultural organizations assumed the pattern of the Old World rather than that of the New: thus, the Germans erected their choral societies and *Turnvereine,* the Swedes centered their social life about the church and *Svea* societies, and the Irish organized their Hibernian societies and erected their St. Patrick halls. Mental predispositions were cultivated and preserved. The two really sizable groups in 1860, aside from the natives of British origin, were the Germans and the Irish. Generally, when they passed by the seaboard cities, they followed the same routes in their westward migration and settled in the same general districts of the Midwest which had been chosen by the native northeasterners. Side by side with New Englanders and good Congregationalists, German and Norwegian Lutherans developed Illinois, Wisconsin, Iowa, and Minnesota. Teutonic peoples scattered widely, taking up lands in the West and populating the American wilderness. This wide settlement served to a certain extent to diffuse American ideals among these settlers.

THE GERMAN ELEMENT

In Germany a number of expulsive influences had been at work. The industrial revolution had disrupted the economic life of regions in which handicrafts had flourished, and had been accompanied by acute suffering during the process of adjustment; crop failures had depressed agriculture; failure had blighted the hopes of political reform in the abortive revolts of 1830 and 1848 and had driven many in Central Europe to despair of ever reforming the political ills. Under such conditions reports of the economic opportunities and of the hospitality of the American democracy became powerful attractions. The form of our government, with its promise of full participation by all citizens and its guarantee of perfect religious freedom, proved a powerful magnet to migration. These incentives were sufficient to bring to this country a class of Germans who, while distinguished for high moral standards and liberal political views, did not disdain to plow their own fields as they meditated on the philosophy of Kant or re-called passages of Goethe, and who sought their recreation in choral societies, which sang with taste the beautiful songs of Schubert and Von Weber. These men of substance, character, and social standing provided for years a leadership for the German element far higher than that existing for some other groups.

The Forty-eighters, who came to control the powerful German-American press, were mostly stanch crusaders who would not yield an inch on what they regarded as a matter of principle. They created for a time considerable friction between the "Grays," as the Germans who came before 1848 were called, and the "Greens," as the men who came after 1848 were dubbed. Many of the latter were radical reformers and revolutionists, who were determined to remake the world and who thought to begin by making the United States the center of a world of republics. Apparently, they expected to bring about the millenium. Some were even visionary enough to plan a separate German state in the West, where they could preserve their beloved *Deutschtum* and speedily bring to reality their utopian dreams. They could hardly be termed modest when their program proclaimed reform of slavery, American Puritanism, the Constitution, Sabbath observance, and Methodism, for many of them boasted of being freethinkers. To such minds, to find slavery firmly fixed and nativism widespread in a free republic stamped America as semicivilized. For the majority, hopes of a new German revolution had been crushed by 1854, and they had settled down to the thought of America as a permanent home.[8] They imparted a stamp of political idealism, social radicalism, and religious skepticism, which affected the attitudes of all the Germans toward the issues producing the war and the conduct of officers and men during the campaigns.

With this exalted idealistic group of Forty-eighters mingled others who came to a new home because it extended better hope of material reward for persevering industry. Although many remained in the eastern states and cities, thousands moved westward into the Mississippi Valley, while other thousands came up the river from New Orleans. Thrifty peasants, land-hungry for generations, came in great numbers to the rich, agricultural areas of the West, adding a strong German strain to the population of the western prairies. Those who found that their skill in shoemaking, cabinet making, brewing, and woodworking was greatly in demand in the

[8] Wittke, *We Who Built America*, 193–95.

new cities remained in the urban centers as artisans and petty tradesmen.[9] Artisans, thoroughly trained under the discipline of the old guild apprentice system of Germany, found a ready market for their skills. Throughout the Northern states there were around a million German-born settlers and an additional two hundred thousand were located in the four border states. No other nationality was so generally distributed over the United States as was the German.

Any exhaustive discussion of foreign colonies in the Northern states is precluded by the limitations of the subject, but a brief consideration of the locations of the chief settlements of foreigners is in order. Colonies or settlements of Germans were to be found in almost every Northern state. By 1860 the German section of New York City was inhabited by a hundred thousand Germans and extended from Chatham Square to Astor Place, as far as St. Marks—a section of the Old Bowery characterized then by beer gardens, bowling alleys, and numerous German societies. Within this area were located German schools, churches, bookstores, printing establishments, and even a German theater; and here by 1836 two German daily newspapers were in circulation.[10]

From New York City the Germans spread inland, generally along the Erie Canal. They had begun to settle in Buffalo as early as 1830; consequently, by the eve of the Civil War a strong Teutonic element had been added to the original New England strain, and a Continental type of life, quite alien to the puritanical ideas of the Yankees had appeared.[11]

Although a new German element was added to the old Pennsylvania Dutch element in Pennsylvania, it mingled little with it; for the new contingent concentrated in the cities, while the descendants of the colonial strain occupied the farms. So strong was this German element that by 1837 the legislature of the Keystone State was publishing the governor's messages and the laws in German translation, and a law was permitting German instruction in the schools. As early as 1840 the German vote of that state was felt important enough to warrant the printing in German of the biographies of Van Buren and Harrison. A movement arose for the promotion of a German press, a normal school to train German teachers, and a

[9] Wood Gray, *The Hidden Civil War. The Story of the Copperheads* (New York, 1942), 25–26. German exiles who read Homer in the original were to be found working on the railroads and in the shops.

[10] Wittke, *We Who Built America*, 198; Alvin Fay Harlow, *Old Bowery Days* (New York, 1931), *passim*. Germans clung to this section of the city until the nineties. "Little Germany," east of the Bowery, did not boom until after the Civil War. Harlow, *Old Bowery Days*, 370.

[11] Wittke, *We Who Built America*, 198.

German university, and for the shortening of the time required for naturalization. Though the teachers' seminary was short-lived, the movement proved a stimulus to the German press and to the founding of German literary and musical societies.[12]

Cincinnati had had prominent Germans among its inhabitants since the beginning of the nineteenth century and stood out not only in Ohio but also in the entire country as one of the most important of all the German-American cities. It even elected a German mayor in 1807; the first German newspaper in America, a weekly, appeared there in 1826; and three decades later one of the best German papers in the country, the Cincinnati *Volksblatt,* made its appearance. Most indicative of the size of the German colony is the fact that the area across the canal, where the Germans had settled, bore the name "Over the Rhine." [13] Thirty per cent of the population was German and constituted an influential element in the city. They cultivated the vine along the heights of the Ohio River. On Sunday evenings they congregated in the beer gardens with their pipes and steins to talk, argue, and sing songs of the Fatherland. The German tongue was heard on the streets, and numerous cafes and breweries bore German signs. Many inhabitants even appeared in the streets in peasant costume of black velvet with red vests and large silver buttons reminiscent of the Rhineland from which they had come.[14]

There were also sizable congregations of Germans at Columbus, Dayton, Toledo, and Cleveland before 1860. Toledo boasted both a German Lutheran and a German Catholic church and many German societies; and about one third of the population of Cleveland, seventy thousand people, was made up of Germans. At the smaller centers of New Bremen, Minster, Chillicothe, Xenia, Delphos, Piqua in Miami County, and Greenville in Darke County, there were German contingents. Canton, Sandusky, Massillon, Alliance, and Steubenville each had a considerable German group. German agricultural colonies were located in Meigs, Brown, and Stark counties; Auglaize and Henry counties had vigorous villages and rural centers of Germans, some of them centers of Catholicism;

---

[12] Gustav Körner, *Das deutsche Element in den Vereinigten Staaten von Nordamerika, 1818–1848* (Cincinnati, 1880), Chap. II; Wittke, *We Who Built America,* 199.

[13] The Old Miami Canal entered Cincinnati from the north, bending east toward the Ohio at Canal Street. North and east of the canal was the German section. Wittke, *We Who Built America,* 200.

[14] See Charles Mackay, *Life and Liberty in America* (2d ed.; London, 1859), I, 214–15; Fredrika Bremer, *The Homes of the New World. Impressions of America* (London, 1853), II, 359.

Union County, one of the best agricultural sections of Ohio, had from 1830 on drawn a large German-Lutheran farming population from Bavaria and Hesse-Darmstadt.[15]

In Indiana there were German colonies at Richmond and New Harmony, but the most important centers for these were Lafayette and Fort Wayne. In Illinois, by 1860, the German element numbered 130,000. Belleville in St. Clair County, the village of Waterloo,[16] Galena, Quincy, Alton, Peoria, and Peru had such settlements. Belleville, lying only fourteen miles southeast of St. Louis and really a suburb of St. Louis although in Illinois, was a pure German neighborhood, settled by a group of "Latin farmers" [17] and professional men. There were about eighty German families in the settlement—with culture of a type which could support a Schiller Festival a decade before the Civil War. Chicago not only had a large German colony but was definitely one of the cultural centers of the Germans; for it could sustain a German theater, an orchestra, bands, lodges, and singing societies. *Turnvereine* first appeared in Illinois in 1851 at Chicago and Peoria.[18]

German entrance into Missouri was already well advanced by the third decade of the century. This immigration, which spread along both banks of the Missouri from its mouth inland for 125 miles, gave the region a distinctly German character. The town of Hermann, laid out in the panic period of 1837, was still in existence in 1860. Viniculture was the chief industry of the area and soon won for the district a reputation for the quality of its wine. The town had a distinct German flavor with its Schiller, Goethe, and Mozart streets. It is worth remarking that the Continental Sunday at Hermann attracted many German excursionists from St. Louis up the river to "Little Germany." From 1848 until 1860 a theater guild was able to present German plays on Sundays without interruption, and a rationalist society managed to exist throughout the war—indeed, until 1902.[19] Settlements were made in Franklin, Morgan,

[15] Wittke, *We Who Built America*, 200–201.

[16] The Baltimore *Der Deutsche Correspondent*, October 4, 1861, alludes to Waterloo as mostly inhabited by Germans.

[17] A term used to designate highly educated Germans versed in Latin and Greek who had become farmers.

[18] Wittke, *We Who Built America*, 201.

[19] *Ibid.*, 202. Hermann had been sponsored by the *Deutsche Ansiedelungs Gesellschaft von Philadelphia*. See William G. Bek, *The German Settlement Society of Philadelphia and Its Colony, Hermann, Missouri* (Philadelphia, 1907), *passim*.

Warren, and Benton counties, and also at Warrenton, Dudenville, and St. Charles. But primarily it was St. Louis which gave Missouri its reputation as a German center. The Germans had occupied chiefly the southern part of the city. After their invasion the earlier French music, dances, and customs were said to have yielded to Teutonic music, recreation, and folkways. Perhaps a fairer statement would be that here an interesting mixture of French, Spanish, Irish, and German characteristics prevailed. As in any locality where Germans lived in numbers, liquor was consumed in large quantities; in some of the theaters the audiences smoked and drank beer served by German waitresses. In the *Lustgärten* scattered about St. Louis, German bands played light German music, while German families, including children, sat for hours drinking beer and listening to the music. Since no one individual consumed more than a limited quantity of beer, however, the gardens were orderly places.[20]

Wisconsin has claims to pre-eminence as an area of German colonization, and the reasons are not hard to find. Soil, climate, and products were similar to those of the homeland; in addition, state officials, to attract settlers for the development of the state, cordially welcomed Germans along with other immigrants. The first period of heavy German influx into the state was the last two decades before the war. Milwaukee became the nucleus from which new settlers scattered over the state; and with its music, drama, and other artistic activities, it became, in addition, a center of culture. Travelers honored it by calling it the "German Athens," in appreciation of the contrast between its culture and the crudeness of many other American frontier towns. For a picture of Milwaukee shortly before the war we are indebted to Fredrika Bremer, the writer. In a portion of the city called "German Town" she found German newspapers, typically German houses with German inscriptions and signs on the doors, and German music, dancing, and other diversions distinguishing the Teutons from the Anglo-Americans, who, especially in the West, according to Mrs. Bremer, knew no other pleasure than business. The Milwaukee bookstalls contained many foreign books and magazines. On the eve of the war the Germans seemed to have absorbed the other nationalities; for,

[20] Wittke, *We Who Built America*, 202–203; E. D. Kargan, "Missouri's German Immigration," in *Collections of the State Historical Society of Missouri*, II (1904), No. 1, pp. 23–24; Albert Bernhardt Faust, *The German Element in the United States, with Special Reference to Its Political, Moral, Social, and Educational Influence* (Boston and New York, 1909), I, 444–45. Part of this immigration was brought about by the famous report on this region by Gottfried Duden.

as in Cincinnati, German was heard upon the streets, and *Maiwein* and bock beer were widely advertised.[21]

The rural settlements tended to appear in the densely wooded areas of the eastern and north-central counties of Wisconsin. Many Germans bought partly cleared farms from American and Irish pioneers. The Teutons, with their fertilizer and diversification of crops, introduced intensive agriculture and better methods than had been used previously. For instance, they removed the stumps instead of cultivating around them, and they also developed dairying and stock raising.[22]

Iowa had few Germans until the fifties, although it is true that the *Deutscher Westlicher Ansiedelungs Verein* sponsored a settlement at Gettysburg, Iowa, in 1842. Strong colonies developed later in and around Davenport, Des Moines, and Dubuque with its lead mines, and these in turn planted daughter colonies. The infant territory of Minnesota presents us with only two distinctively German settlements: Henderson, on the Minnesota River, and New Ulm, proclaiming its parentage in its name. The *Land Verein* of Chicago helped to establish the latter in 1854 as a refuge for land-hungry German immigrants. It was also supported by the socialistic *Turnerbund* of North America and had certain socialistic features.[23] Numbers of Germans were, of course, to be found in St. Paul (enough to support a newspaper, the *Minnesota Staats-Zeitung*) and even at this early date they ranked first among the foreign population in the state which Scandinavian immigrants were later to mold into a New Sweden.

In addition to these German colonies scattered in the cities and through the countryside, there were communistic settlements, expressions of a movement which was at the height of its popularity about 1843. Only those which were in existence in 1860 and essentially foreign in customs and outlook will be noted. At Zoar, in Tuscarawas County, Ohio, was located one such communistic colony, created by German peasants from

---

[21] Wittke, *We Who Built America*, 201–202; Bremer, *The Homes of the New World*, II, 222–23.

[22] Körner, *Das deutsche Element*, 281–91; Faust, *The German Element in the United States*, I, 473–77, 479–81; Joseph Schafer, "The Yankee and the Teuton in Wisconsin," in *Wisconsin Magazine of History*, VI (1922–1923), 125–45, 261–79, VII (1923–1924), 3–20, 148–71.

[23] Wittke, *We Who Built America*, 203; Faust, *The German Element in the United States*, I, 461–62, 484–85; see also, on New Ulm, Minnesota, the anonymous article "Die deutsche Ansiedlung von New Ulm," in *Der Deutsche Pionier*, III (1871–1872), 13 ff.; and Alex Berghold, "Geschichte von New Ulm, Minnesota," in *Der Deutsche Pionier*, VIII (1876–1877), 122 ff., and IX (1877–1878).

Württemberg. With its broad acres and the small industries essential to a self-supporting community, Zoar resembled a typical German peasant village. Each member was assigned the tasks he was to perform for the common welfare, and in return he was provided from the common fund with daily necessities and two suits of clothing a year. The German pietist group first established at Harmony in Butler County, Pennsylvania, moved in 1815 to New Harmony, Indiana—the town which was later to become famous as the scene of Robert Owen's experiment—and finally settled down ten years later at Economy, Pennsylvania, on the Ohio River only about twenty miles from its first location. By the period of the Civil War this group had greatly declined from the five hundred souls who returned from Indiana, but it was probably at the height of its financial prosperity. It was German in customs and language and was held together until 1903 by the bond of religion.

Wisconsin had one such communistic colony, a Catholic settlement at St. Nazianz, where its founder, Father Oschwald of Baden, had led it in 1854 when friction developed in Germany with the Catholic hierarchy. On the colony's holdings of three thousand acres these German Catholics lived in peace; however, in 1890, long after the death of its founder, it was taken over by one of the Catholic religious orders. A fourth such venture was that at Bethel in Shelby County, Missouri, founded by a Prussian named Dr. Wilhelm Keil, who was regarded as a quack physician—*der Hexendoktor*. He enlisted a large following as an independent mystic at Pittsburgh and led some five hundred German farmers to Missouri in 1844. The Amana Settlement, which today comprises seven quaint villages along the Iowa River and covers a tract of 26,000 acres of the most fertile agricultural land in Iowa, was the fifth of these enterprises of communistic character. Born under German mysticism in revolt against military service and Lutheran formalism, it moved from Germany in response to "divine suggestion"—first, in 1842, to an old Seneca reservation near Buffalo, and then, in 1854, to Iowa. In 1860 its people were plain, quiet, peaceful German peasants and artisans, and even today a visitor can readily imagine himself in the Black Forest region of the Germany of 1840.[24]

[24] For Zoar, see Wittke, *We Who Built America*, 342–43; for the New Harmony group, *ibid.*, 343–47; for St. Nazianz, *ibid.*, 347–49; for Bethel, *ibid.*, 348–49; for the Amana settlements, *ibid.*, 352–55.

THE IRISH ELEMENT

Repeated crop failures, an oppressive land system, and suppressed aspirations for national independence had driven the Irish from their old homes in the "Emerald Isle." Most of them reached our shores in such dire poverty that a smaller portion of them than of the Germans succeeded in reaching the central West. Almost their only asset was physical brawn and the resulting ability to do manual labor. In the eastern cities industry afforded opportunity for prompt employment, while their scanty resources were insufficient to defray the cost of a journey to the interior immediately after an ocean voyage. In time many did go West—in many instances being recruited as laborers in constructing canals and railroads, and then, when such tasks were completed, settling down along the routes which they had helped to build. Thus, in the West also, they tended to settle in the great commercial centers and junctions, such as Joliet, where an Irish colony brought in for the digging of the Illinois Canal dominated local politics for many years. It is hardly strange that their unhappy experiences on the estates of Ireland under the absentee-landlord system, combined with their proverbial gregariousness, turned Irishmen, as a class, to the larger cities, East and West, North and South. As for the Midwest, they were less numerous than the German group in Chicago, but still even in 1860 they embraced nearly one fifth of the inhabitants, despite the huge numbers of Germans and Scandinavians; and they were the least numerous in Milwaukee, where they were outnumbered by the Germans five to one. All told, the sons of Ireland residing in the Middle West on the eve of the Civil War numbered some 320,000. Set apart by their Roman Catholic religion and by their humble social status, they, like the Germans, stood together and apart from their fellow foreigners, as likewise from the native Americans.[25]

The migration of the Irish across the Atlantic, sufficiently stimulated by forces in Ireland, was further stimulated by the need of American contractors for cheap labor to construct the internal-improvement projects which swept the various states of the Union like a plague. There was hardly a canal or railroad built without Irish labor. Then came the mushrooming of the New England mill towns, with their insatiable maw for laborers. The character of the immigration from the Emerald Isle changed after the famine of 1845–1848. The poor small farmer, who knew English

[25] *Ibid.*, 129–33.

and was proud of his economic independence, was succeeded by the farm laborer, who had to be financially assisted in his migration, who was ignorant of the English language, who possessed, moreover, a volatile temperament, and who found adjustment to the new environment difficult.

In the forties and fifties, little Dublins grew up almost overnight in the New England factory towns and in the Middle Atlantic states. The Irish population of Boston tripled in a single decade. In Rhode Island the first Irish millworkers were recruited from railroad laborers on the Providence-Boston Railroad. Miserable shantytowns began to appear. In the port towns and in the cities Irish crowded into tenements, twenty to thirty families living in one house. In South Boston in 1850, the Irish slums were tenements three to six stories high, where whole families lived in one room without light or ventilation, and even the cellars were crowded with human beings—and probably with rodents. The sanitary conditions were faithfully reflected by the high death rate among the children of the Irish. The immigrants in the hovels of the eastern and western sections of New York City were always attacked by cholera to a greater degree than were those in other sections. In these shantytowns secret societies of Irishmen arose, calling themselves "Connaughtmen" or the "Far Downs," and engaging in low, bloody brawls and riots, impervious even to the arguments of the priests. The Irish boardinghouses were particularly obnoxious —far worse than the German inns to be found in port towns—and were frequently condemned as "pigsties." The usual such boardinghouse was a brick building, with the inevitable grogshop on the first floor overflowing with runners and loafers of every kind. A saucer of free tobacco stood on the counter for the runners. The bedrooms on the upper floor were overcrowded and filthy. Irish leaders expressed alarm at the effect of these conditions on the Irish character. Native Americans feared the competition of Irish laborers, though they shunned the hard work performed by the latter. Friendly papers and individuals warned the Irish away from the canal and railroad construction. As wages were low—one dollar a day or less—and paid partly in liquor and overpriced merchandise, benevolent persons urged the Irish to work on farms or squat on government land in the West.[26]

A part of Charlestown, Massachusetts, inhabited by Irishmen, was

[26] *Ibid.*, 131–32, 133–35, 135–37. It is but just to point out that the Irishman usually came straight from the status of tenant without the thrift acquired by the man who owns his home or the soil he cultivates. He naturally lacked a sense of value and foresight as compared with the Scot, the Hollander, or the native-born Yankee.

known as "Dublin Row"; [27] the construction of Blackstone Canal produced Woonsocket, Rhode Island, an Irish-Catholic settlement; Pawtucket, Rhode Island, Lowell, Massachusetts, and Paterson, New Jersey, all had their Irish shantytowns.[28] Many were the Irish settlements in the coal regions of Pennsylvania, where conditions of low pay and "murderous neglect" of ventilation and of protection against accidents were deplorable. Similar conditions prevailed in the coal pits between Fall River and Newport.[29] Irish had settled in the coal and iron region of Ulster County, New York, and in the mining section around Dubuque, Iowa.

Though no reliable figures for farming communities of Irish are available for the period from 1845 to 1860, there is evidence to prove that they were known in the West. As indicated above, thousands who could tolerate the loneliness of the American farms settled as farmers along the railroads and canals they had helped to build, especially along the Illinois Canal, north of Peoria in Illinois. In McHenry County, for instance, there was an Irish farming settlement large enough to support three fairly large Catholic churches. The Irish workers on the Illinois Central Railroad exchanged the scrip with which they were paid for thousands of acres of Illinois land held by that railroad company. Many Irish settled on farms in Wills and LaSalle counties.[30] Some Irish-Catholic farm communities existed in 1860 in Allegan County, Michigan, and near Council Bluffs and at "Garryowen" in Jackson County, both in Iowa. The Trappist monastery near Dubuque became a center for Irish farmers who came in from the surrounding country to attend Mass.[31] The number of Irish in Wisconsin in 1860 was fifty thousand. Some seven hundred were living

[27] Boston *Traveller*, January 12, 1857.

[28] Wittke, *We Who Built America*, 137–38. Other workers did their best to make life so uncomfortable for the Irish workers and their children that they would leave, but the Irish stuck until dispossessed by the new immigrants of the nineties. *Ibid.*, 138.

[29] *Ibid.*, 139–40.

[30] John Francis Maguire, *The Irish in America* (New York, 1869), 246; Paul W. Gates, *The Illinois Central Railroad and Its Colonization Work* (Cambridge, 1934), 89, 95–97, 234, 252; W. J. Onahan, "Irish Settlements in Illinois," in *The Catholic World*, XXXIII (April–September, 1881), 157–62. Wittke regards the statement in the Springfield *Illinois State Register*, March 5, 1853, that three fourths of the Irish employed on public works in Illinois from 1833–1853 took up homesteads as probably exaggerated. He also states that the Irish Catholic clergy tried to keep their parishioners from going West in order to hold their parishes together and to protect them against heresy. Wittke, *We Who Built America*, 148–50.

[31] For Allegan County colony, see the Boston *Pilot*, August 4, 1860; for the settlement near Dubuque, see *ibid.*, November 20, 1852; August 26, 1854; November 3, 1855; July 14, October 13, 1860; and June 28, 1862. This paper occasionally printed requests for Catholic priests from Irish settlers in Iowa.

on farms in Kenosha County, and more than six hundred were in Racine County. In Ozaukee County, where Irish farmers settled among Germans, many learned to speak the German tongue.[32] Minnesota had its Shieldsville—named in honor of General James Shields, the Irish hero of the Mexican War—in addition to Kilkenny, Erin, and Montgomery townships, which stood as "little islands of Irish agricultural settlement" against the Scandinavian tide.

THE FRENCH ELEMENT

The French have become comparatively so negligible a factor in the American picture that despite the earlier statement that they ranked third numerically in the population of 1860, it is difficult for the American of today, unless he has studied the question, to realize the relative importance of the French element at that time. In 1851, when the German contingent for that year amounted to 72,482, the French immigrants entering the United States numbered 20,126. Some of these, like the Germans, were revolutionary refugees of the unsuccessful revolt of 1848, but many were what might be termed economic refugees. Most of the French entering after 1825 were of the working and professional classes, and both these groups settled in the cities. They found intelligent sympathizers among their countrymen, for the French resident here followed European politics closely. For instance, in 1850 the French Democratic Republicans of New York celebrated the anniversary of the birth of the French Republic with a banquet at the Coliseum and the Lafayette Guards present in full dress.[33] There was every sign of vigor in the French colony of New York. The mere existence of three French papers—of which the best, the *Courrier des États-Unis,* had been in existence since 1825—argues a strong colony,

---

[32] Joseph Schafer, from a study of four counties in Wisconsin, reached the conclusion that the Irish proved to be farmers as good as those of any nationality, but that they were likely to develop several farms during a lifetime rather than to stay put as did the Germans. Also he noted a tendency among the Irish to withdraw from communities where Germans predominated. See Joseph Schafer, *Four Wisconsin Counties, Prairie and Forest* (*Wisconsin Doomesday Book,* II [Wisconsin State Historical Society, Madison, 1927]), 100–101.

It should be stated that plans were projected for Irish farming communities in the West and in Canada to found an Irish state under the supervision of the Church, but all came to nought. Wittke, *We Who Built America,* 148.

[33] For the Lafayette Guards, see Chapter VI of text. For the figures on German and French immigration for 1851, see *Annual Report of the Commissioner General of Immigration, 1920* (Washington, 1921), chart following p. 276.

still cherishing the mother tongue. By 1861 enough Frenchmen had settled in Chicago to justify a French church and a French hotel there; a decade earlier Cincinnati could maintain a French military battalion and a French church with regular weekly service.[34]

Although the average Frenchman greatly preferred city life, a few rural colonies were successfully planted in the Middle West. One existed in Switzerland County in Indiana near the Swiss settlement in that vicinity. *Le Journal de l'Illinois,* first issued in 1857 at Kankakee, Illinois, and listing twelve hundred subscribers, argues a considerable French settlement in that neighborhood. Records show settlements of French Canadians established in 1852 at St. Anne, at Bourbonnais, and at Assumption, all in Illinois and all drawn there largely by the land policy of the Illinois Central Railroad Company.[35]

The single example of a communistic experiment by French immigrants was located at Nauvoo, Illinois, and bore the picturesque name of "Icaria." It was fashioned after the communistic views of Étienne Cabet, an editor and politician exiled from France in the thirties for his hostility to Louis Philippe. A group of more than three hundred Icarians proceeded in 1849 from New Orleans to Nauvoo, the deserted Mormon city in Illinois, probably because land and houses were cheap there. It prospered until by 1855 the colony numbered five hundred. In sharp contrast with the pietistic views of the German communistic communities, this French group was composed in majority of freethinkers. French wine and French joy of life prevailed. Lawyers and lawsuits were forbidden, together with all features of the capitalist profit system. When factional disputes rent the community, Cabet moved to Adams County, to build a new Icaria, housed in log cabins. He moved on a third time, however, followed by two hundred faithful disciples—this time to a location near St. Louis, Missouri, where he created a third communistic colony. Both of these later colonies, in Iowa and Missouri, continued in existence through the war.[36]

[34] The other two papers in New York were *Le Franco-Américain,* begun in 1846, and *Le Républicain,* first appearing in 1853. See Baltimore *Patriot and Commercial Gazette,* April 20, 1841, on French activities; see Boston *Transcript,* July 23, 1856, on the colony; for the celebration of 1850, see New York *Tribune,* April 19, 1850; for Cincinnati, see Cincinnati *Commercial,* April 3, August 7, 1851.

[35] Wittke, *We Who Built America,* 320, 325; Gates, *The Illinois Central Railroad,* 234–38.

[36] Wittke, *We Who Built America,* 359–60.

SCANDINAVIAN ELEMENT

The Scandinavian element, although negligible in comparison with the two largest nationality groups, was important locally and spiritually in its support of the Union cause. Scandinavian immigration began in appreciable volume in the forties but never exceeded ten thousand in any one year until the closing year of the war. As the large influx of Scandinavians did not set in until after the Civil War, there were in the United States in 1860 only 72,582 of these immigrants, and they had come chiefly from Norway and Sweden. The story of the Scandinavian immigrants has been aptly called the "saga" of the conquest of the rolling prairie—of moving West in covered wagons, of breaking the tough grass of the prairies, and of living in dugouts and sod shanties until the comparatively luxurious days of the log cabin came at last. The Scandinavians almost always accepted migration as a permanent removal to a new home. They had to meet all the obstacles against which the other settlers of the West contended—droughts, storms, and grasshopper and locust plagues—yet their attitude was different. Whereas others yielded to these discouragements, the hardy men and women of the Northland buckled on the armor of their steadfast wills and deep religious zeal and resisted appalling hardships, ultimately to win success. They had been well conditioned to hardship in the homelands. Most of these immigrants came from the lower class; they were peasants who had worked their small farms or leased plots of stony, unproductive soil. Life was just one round of unceasing toil with little recompense, and the tales of 160-acre farms at $1.25 an acre were romantically alluring to persons living close to the margin of existence. A succession of poor harvests and hard times in Norway, which depressed wages but only increased the burden of taxes, gave great impetus to the exodus of these people with large families and pitifully small incomes. It might also be recalled that over 40 per cent of the soil of Sweden is unproductive, while nearly 60 per cent of Norwegian land is mountainous. The economic crisis of 1864–1865 in Norway and Sweden probably explains why even the war could not halt the stream from this part of Europe. Political and religious movements in both Norway and Sweden, especially in the early decades of the century, were contributing, if not significant, causes of emigration. There was a considerable reaction against the formalism of the state church and a marked increase of dissenting sects, the members of which were usually not too kindly treated. The Danes, relatively more fortunate and prosperous, migrated in comparatively smaller numbers; for Denmark has always been able to support a denser population than her Scandinavian sister countries.[37] Furthermore, the Dane lacked the adventurous and pioneering instinct of the Swede and the Norwegian.

Each Scandinavian group is proud of its individuality and eager to preserve it; hence, each group will be accorded separate treatment here.

Norwegian Settlements

The Norwegians, who were the first to set the tide of migration, began to come in the forties, reaching five thousand annually around the close of the Civil War. A strong democratic tradition and a highly developed national consciousness preserved a group solidarity stronger than that of either of the other two northern nationalities. By 1860 Norwegian migration was larger in proportion to the population than that of any other group, always excepting the Irish.[38] The overwhelming majority of Norwegians settled in Wisconsin, Iowa, Illinois, and Minnesota, though their numbers were meager in the last-named state until after the war. There were over four thousand in Illinois, mainly in the region around Chicago and in the Fox River section to the south. This first Norwegian colony in the central West was in LaSalle County and attracted enough settlers by virtue of its cheap land [39] to make it a large and prosperous community. New arrivals in 1836, two years after the original settlement, found lands immediately to the northeast and northwest. Despite a decided trend to the northwestern states beyond, the area referred to as the Fox River colony continued to grow so that finally it embraced parts of five counties. Even as early as 1843, when Johan Reiersen, the journalist,[40] visited the settle-

---

[37] The law of primogeniture, which forced younger sons to leave the ancestral estates to gain a living, contributed its part to the migration. Wittke, *We Who Built America*, 264.

[38] For accounts of the earliest ventures at settlement of Norwegians in America, see Theodore C. Blegen, *Norwegian Migration to America, 1825 to 1860* (Northfield, Minn., 1931), I, Chaps. II and III; Carlton C. Qualey, *Norwegian Settlement in the United States* (Northfield, Minn., 1938), Chap. II. Cleng Peerson first came to America in 1821, but made a brief trip home in 1824 to arrange for the coming of the immigrant band later the next year. They located in New York in the northern half of Murray Township, later set apart as Kendall Township, whence the colony has been generally known as the Kendall settlement. Qualey, *Norwegian Settlement*, Chap. II. Almost all of the colony moved to Illinois.

[39] One Kendall settler was able to buy an entire section of land in Illinois for the amount brought by this small farm in New York. Qualey, *Norwegian Settlement*, 24.

[40] This Reiersen is the man who founded the first Norwegian settlement in Texas. See Lonn, *Foreigners in the Confederacy*, 21. Before long the Fox River settlement became the mother

ment, he found that it had passed the initial stage, so that its six hundred inhabitants were in comfortable circumstances.

The Norwegian immigration to Chicago coincides with the early mushroom-like growth of the city itself. Chicago was the natural point of entry—whether by railroad or by the lake route—to the Northwest. The bouncing infant of the West attracted thousands of Norwegians, who stayed on as laborers, shopkeepers, sailors, and professional men. Certain individual Norwegians had been present in the population since 1836 and had located on the north side at a point then known as "The Sands," on Pine Street near Chicago Avenue. This colony trebled during the decade prior to the war and numbered 1,573 in 1860.[41]

The Norwegian colonies established during the first phase of the north-westward advance into Wisconsin took root—after the Black Hawk War had eliminated the danger of Indian forays—with the establishment of the Jefferson Prairie settlement in Rock County. This quickly expanded across the state line into the northern tier of Illinois counties, so that this entire area is properly regarded as one colony. By the eve of the war the settlement had ceased to expand and was a Norwegian farming community. A second Norse settlement lay at Rock Prairie, a name justly applying to the entire region on both sides of the state line and extending into Winnebago County, Illinois. Together these two settlements included a total of almost four hundred families in 1860.[42] Not far to the southwest of Milwaukee lay a third colony in Waukesha County, which took its name from Lake Muskego but expanded into Racine County around Wind Lake. From being a point of first importance where immigrants halted, it declined during the fifties; but on account of its proximity to Milwaukee [43] it still existed as a small colony in 1860. Centering in Dane County in a rich agricultural region lay the most important, certainly the most prosperous, of early Wisconsin colonies, Lake Koshkonong settlement. So rapidly did the fame of the region spread that settlers

---

of a colony in Shelby County, Missouri, led by the ever-pervasive Cleng Peerson; but it disintegrated within three years. Another daughter colony, Pontiac or Rowe Settlement in Livingston County, south of La Salle, also belongs to the prewar period. Qualey, *Norwegian Settlement*, 32–34.

[41] Qualey, *Norwegian Settlement*, 37–38.

[42] For Jefferson Prairie settlement, see *ibid.*, 44–46; for Rock Prairie, *ibid.*, 46–47.

[43] The land about Muskego Lake proved unfavorable, as it became swampy in the spring; the colony therefore shifted southward to Wind Lake in Racine County. *Ibid.*, 48–49. It never became large like those at Rock Prairie and Koshkonong, though it remained a living name to Norwegians because of the help and advice extended there to newcomers.

streamed in from all directions and even directly from Norway until, at the moment of our study, the population numbered 3,699 persons. A fifth colony, an overflow from Koshkonong, was located in north Dane County and southern Columbia County, and was composed of several smaller settlements which bore names well known at the time—Spring Prairie, Bonnet Prairie, and Sand Prairie settlements. A much larger colony, extending from northwestern Dane County southward into the northwestern tip of Illinois, constituted a sixth area of settlement. This was the largest and densest Norwegian settlement in the state; the northern part was generally known as the Blue Mounds settlement, and the southern part as the Wiota settlement. This location reflects credit on the judgment of the foreigners, for it is a region of rare fertility of soil and great beauty of scenery.[44] In Manitowoc County along the western shore of Lake Michigan, a fairly large seventh colony developed; its population of 1,500 in 1860 was largely concentrated in the city of Manitowoc and the surrounding countryside. Waupaca and Portage counties in central Wisconsin constituted another large area of settlement. Toward the close of the fifties a settler in Waupaca County claimed that Scandinavia township was two-thirds peopled by Norwegians—whence, no doubt, the name—and that two other townships were half populated by the same nationality. By 1860 there were 1,620 Norwegians living in this settlement.[45]

The decade of the fifties was the pioneer period for the development of an extensive area of settlement in western Wisconsin, where 5,658 Norwegians were scattered over 15 counties in 1860. The colonies centered in largest numbers in Vernon (with its famous Coon Prairie colony), La Crosse, and Trempealeau counties, with the Trempealeau Valley a unit of Norwegian settlement two hundred square miles in extent.[46] By 1860 the Norwegians in this state numbered 29,557 or 3.8 per cent of the entire population. From the first they were the most numerous of the three Scandinavian peoples in the state, and they were outnumbered by only one foreign stock, the Germans, who amassed in this state the impressive figure of 123,879.[47]

The fact that good land near the Norwegian settlements in Wisconsin was largely pre-empted in 1850 turned many new Norwegian immigrants

---

[44] For Koshkonong settlement, see *ibid.*, 52–54; for the other two settlements, *ibid.*, 57–59.

[45] For Manitowoc, *ibid.*, 63–64; for Waupaca and Portage counties, *ibid.*, 66–67.

[46] For the colonies in western Wisconsin, see *ibid.*, 69–73. For the way in which older settlements became the parents of the new in western Wisconsin, see Blegen, *Norwegian Migration*, I, 141, 364 n.

[47] Qualey, *Norwegian Settlement*, 40.

to Iowa and Minnesota. In 1839–1840 some Norwegians—whom Cleng Peerson, the pioneer in Norwegian migration to the United States had recruited for the short-lived colony in Shelby County, Missouri—moved on to the new Territory of Iowa to take out land on Sugar Creek. By 1860 the Norwegians constituted a very thin trickle in the population of this state—5,688 in a total of 674,913. Already the concentration of the descendants of the Vikings in the northeastern corner of the state had begun to manifest itself, a trend which was vastly accentuated in the sixties. The two northern tiers of counties were preferred because of the fertility of the soil and the presence of adequate resources of wood and water. It should be noted that while this settlement is adjacent to Norwegian areas of settlement in Minnesota, it is in no sense a part of those colonies. The settlement in Allamakee County in the extreme northeastern corner of Iowa was made by Wisconsin Norse and bore the picturesque name of Paint Creek settlement. The colony stretched from a point near Lansing westward for about fifteen miles. The number of Norwegians in this county reached 1,187 before the war. The county just to the west of Allamakee, Winneshiek County, drew the largest number of this nationality. The town of Decorah, later a center of Norwegian culture and religion, was begun as early as 1853.[48] By the time the census was gathered in 1860 the Norwegians in this county mustered 4,207, and it is a conspicuous fact that the larger number had been born in Norway. For the entire northeastern section of Iowa, embracing six counties, the number rose from the negligible figure of 241 in 1850 to 6,403 in 1860.

One of the most interesting settlements in Iowa was that founded by the Danish pastor-editor, the Reverend Claus L. Clausen, in Mitchell County, west of Winneshiek, on the Big Cedar River, to which he led some forty families from Rock Prairie, Wisconsin, in 1853, with the village of St. Ansgar as the nucleus. Prior to the war there were no less than five hundred Norwegians in this area. Also in this same general region were the three hundred Norwegians living in the next two counties to the west of Mitchell. One of the most famous settlements by this people in America, located in Story County in almost the exact center of the state but overlapping into the counties to the north and south, had almost five hundred settlers by 1860. In general, except for the large number in the north-

---

[48] This importance was partly owing to the location there of Luther College, founded in 1861 and moved to Decorah the next year. Its seminary is the oldest Norwegian theological school in the United States. It also supported a normal department to train teachers especially to teach Norwegian. In 1861, 80 per cent of the instruction was in Norwegian; sixty years later, only 8 per cent. Wittke, We Who Built America, 291.

eastern corner and a goodly number in Sioux City, the Norwegian influence in Iowa was scattered and relatively unimportant.[49]

The tremendous tide which has virtually turned Minnesota into a New Scandinavia did not begin to roll in until after the Civil War, but its beginnings are clearly discernible before the opening of the war. It seems hardly credible that whereas only nine Norwegians were recorded by the census of 1850 as having taken out land in Fillmore County, Minnesota, the tide could have swept in 8,356 during only ten years. The decade of the fifties saw pioneering only in the southern counties. Scandinavians, as well as other settlers, had only a brief period to take up claims before the war, since the public land was not open for settlement until completion of treaties with the Sioux and Mendota Indians in 1851. The agricultural value of the land was known to many, so that when the first block of land was opened for sale in 1855, thousands poured into the new area.

In the early period of invasion, two large areas of Norwegian settlement were marked out in southeastern Minnesota and a number of small scattered settlements were begun in the north-central counties. The larger area spread through the two southern tiers of counties extending from the Mississippi River west for perhaps a hundred miles and into Brown County of the third tier of counties. The second area began in Goodhue County, which was east of the third tier of counties, and spread into the adjoining counties to the west and north. Pioneers flocked into the southeastern corner, which might roughly be described as a triangle enclosed by the Mississippi and Minnesota rivers and a line drawn from the southern bend of the Minnesota south to the state line. The area thus enclosed was densely populated by Norwegians.[50] Urban centers of Norwegian life crystallized at St. Peter, Wanamingo, and Spring Grove. Hence, the new settlements soon enjoyed signs of prosperity.[51] The only large colony established in the central portion of the state was the Norway settlement in northwestern Kandiyohi County, and it lost most of its settlers in the Sioux War of 1862.

The Norwegians who settled in the Twin Cities in the early period were

[49] Qualey, *Norwegian Settlement*, 88–92, for Claussen's settlement; for that west of Mitchell, Worth-Winnebago settlement, *ibid.*, 92–93; for the Story County colony, *ibid.*, 94.

[50] See the map constructed by Qualey, *ibid.*, 113. Note also his maps for Illinois, 35; for Wisconsin, 65; and for Iowa, 79. See also 114–19.

[51] A report of H. A. Stub, a pioneer clergyman to Norwegians, appeared in 1857 in Christiania (Norway) *Morgenbladet*, June 3, 1857. A report by the Reverend Laurentius Larsen, pastor of the Rush River settlement in Pierce County, Wisconsin, on organizing congregations, is illuminating. See Madison *Emigranten*, August 14, 1858. Norwegians were scattered throughout the southeastern counties as well as in the areas described.

not numerous, but there were enough of them in 1858 to warrant organizing a congregation in St. Paul. Their presence in the young cities is further
evidence that not all Norwegians migrated to rural areas, for many of them
took advantage of the demand for labor in a growing urban area. The
wages furnished bread and butter for thousands who arrived with empty
pockets and also enabled them to build up a competence with which to
purchase government land further west, and so to secure the farm for
which every immigrant's heart seemed to yearn.

Although this period had scarcely seen the beginnings of the tide which
was to pour into the Dakota Territory the large number of Norwegians
who ultimately settled there on free lands, we cannot ignore the embryo
settlement of about 150 Norwegian and Danish families located on farms
around the town of Vermillion and up the Missouri River in Dakota, according to an immigrant's letter written on December 7, 1860, and
published in the Madison *Emigranten* of February 18, 1861. In 1860,
Norwegians were scattered about, mainly in small numbers, in all the
states and territories of the Union except Vermont and Delaware.[52]

Swedish Settlements

Swedish migration to the United States in the nineteenth century did
not really begin until modification of the Swedish immigration laws allowed citizens to leave that country without special permission from the
king. Intolerable economic and political conditions drove certain intellectuals—including military men and some university students—together
with some landless peasants, to America in search of a more liberal environment and better financial opportunities. Religious dissent, which expressed
itself in open opposition, was rigorously suppressed in the nineteenth as
in the eighteenth century. Headed by Gustaf Unonius, a small group
from Upsala University founded the first Swedish colony in the West in
1841—on the lands bordering beautiful Pine Lake in northwestern Waukesha County, Wisconsin, about thirty-five miles northwest of Milwaukee
—and christened it New Upsala in honor of the Swedish university.

[52] The following table, listing only the Norwegians born in Norway, shows their location
in 1860 by states, arranged in descending order as to size of their Norwegian population:

Wisconsin	19,758	(Half of all Norwegians in the country)
Minnesota	8,356	
Iowa	5,353	
Illinois	4,130	(The number had doubled during the previous decade)
California	715	(Small but larger than in Michigan or Missouri)

Qualey, *Norwegian Settlement*, Appendix, 219–47.

However, within only two years came a large group of Norwegians, who in time outnumbered the Swedes. By 1850 the settlement had spread beyond its original county into Dodge, Washington, and Jefferson counties. Another group of Swedes from the other Swedish university, Lund, under the leadership of a distinguished scientist, Thure Kumlin, joined the Norwegian settlement at Koshkonong Lake—also, it will be recalled, in Wisconsin [53]—where he contributed to the botanical knowledge of the Middle West. The settlement at Pine Lake is of historic interest primarily as the pioneer of Swedish colonies in the United States, for the letters to Sweden from this colony stirred many other Swedes to migrate. Pepin County in the same state was largely settled by Swedes.

The Swedish movement toward America, starting just a little later than the Norwegian, opened a flood toward the Middle West which descended upon Illinois in 1849. Around 150 persons under their pastor, the Reverend Lars Paul Esbjörn, founder of the Swedish Lutheran Church in America, began the colony at Andover in 1849. By the eve of the war, Swedish settlements were scattered over the Illinois prairies in a broad band from east to southwest, from Lake Michigan to the Mississippi. The important urban centers were located at Rockford, Andover, Galva, Knoxville, Rock Island, Moline, DeKalb, Galena, Galesburg, and Swedona. In 1858 a thousand Swedes were living in Galesburg, congregated in "Swedetown." Rural areas were dotted with humble log cabins planted close together to justify the term "settlement" in Henry and Kane counties.[54]

The Bishop Hill settlement in Illinois merits special attention, as it was the best known of religious communities among Scandinavian immigrants. Like so many of the German communistic movements, it was the material embodiment of a reaction against the rather formal practices of the Swedish state church and represented an effort to capture the simplicity and sincerity of early Lutheranism. The movement was sponsored by Eric Janson, a peasant and a prophet, who in 1846 led his followers to Illinois and founded the Bishop Hill colony, whither disciples followed him until, all told, they numbered fifteen hundred. Communism was established in the colony rather as an expedient to save the colony than

[53] *Ibid.*, 55–56. It is of passing interest that Unonius, known in Sweden as a radical, established in Chicago the first Swedish Episcopal Church. Nels Hokanson, *Swedish Immigrants in Lincoln's Time* (2d ed.; New York and London, 1942), 16–17. Hokanson seems to claim incorrectly the founding of Koshkonong by Swedes, as he speaks of Kumlin as "Head of the Koshkonong colony." Hokanson, *Swedish Immigrants*, 17.

[54] Hokanson, *Swedish Immigrants*, 49, 57.

from conviction as to its merits. By thrift and devotion these Swedish pietists finally wrested prosperity from the cold Illinois soil, so that by 1848 a
number of buildings dotted the prairie. Internal difficulties, which almost
disrupted the colony, and business reverses ended in a revolt which deposed
the successor to Janson and brought division of the communal property in
1861. However, the colony still continued as a Swedish settlement through
and beyond the war years. In 1850 another religious group, known as
"Luther-Readers" or "Hedbergians," dissenting from the state church,
settled in Illinois and Minnesota. A group of Mormons, including 107
Swedes, 225 Danes, and 18 Norwegians, were on their way to Utah in
1859.[55]

At this date Chicago was the geographical and cultural center of
Swedish America; and, while it was far from being a Swedish city, it had
a large Swedish section. Swedish could be heard on the streets in parts
of the north side, as on North Halstead and Calumet streets.[56] Thus,
Chicago became a center for news, education, and the preservation of the
Swedish language and culture.

These were the days when, after an ocean voyage of four or five months
on freighters, the Swedes, like the Norwegians, were likely to arrive nearly
destitute in New York. Agents—social workers we would call them today
—from the Bethel Ship Mission often met the immigrant ships and tried
to direct the new immigrants westward by canal or railroad to Chicago and
then into the upper Mississippi Valley. If the immigrant was destitute,
he went to work as a farm hand or, more likely, with pick and shovel as a
member of a railroad construction gang. It was not at all unusual for the
Swedish laborer, like his Irish counterpart, to settle on the land along the
route of the railroad which he had just helped to construct, for his driving
ambition was to secure a farm.

In the fifties the Illinois Central was already trying to tempt Swedes
and Norwegians to settle on its lands. It had received in 1851 the first grant
made by the Federal government to any railroad, a grant of 2,500,000 acres
in eastern and central Illinois, on both sides of its right of way. Oscar
Malmborg, the well-known agent of this road, returned to Sweden to
travel extensively and to obtain publicity in the newspapers for the Illinois
Central lands. He made such trips in 1854 and again in 1860. Although

---

[55] Wittke, *We Who Built America*, 349–51; Jonas Olson, successor to Janson, continued
to preach to a small group until 1898. For the Hedbergians, see Hokanson, *Swedish Immigrants*,
16.

[56] Hokanson, *Swedish Immigrants*, 49; Wittke, *We Who Built America*, 269.

it is impossible to establish a close connection between his work and the immigration, it is hard to believe that his propaganda was without effect; for a number of Swedes and Norwegians began to settle in Illinois early in the sixties. The settlements at Neoga and Big Springs, Shelby County, 180 miles south of Chicago, were made in the early sixties and were followed a short time later by those at Peru and Paxton. The last-named place became a center for settlement, partly because the Illinois Central was active in obtaining the location of a Swedish-Lutheran college there in 1863. Another link between this railroad company and the Swedish Lutheran Church is too interesting to be omitted. The company offered the Swedish church leaders a commission on all land sales at a time when they needed every possible penny, with the result that those church leaders sold over 36,000 acres for the Illinois Central Railroad. The majority of the new settlers, along with a mere handful of Norwegians, located in Ford County and at other points in eastern Illinois. The small settlement in Kankakee County lay within the region of the railroad land grants.[57]

Indiana, too, had its settlements of Swedes. By 1855 there were about five hundred Swedes located near Lafayette, while about that same period a small rural settlement began to grow up some seven miles from La Porte in the northwestern portion of the state. Attica had a large enough community of Swedes for a Swedish-Lutheran church; Calumet evidently had a small number; and Lake and Porter counties had small groups of Swedes in 1860.[58]

The first Swedish settlement in Iowa was the work of Peter Cassel, whose New Sweden, founded in 1842 in Jefferson County, enjoys the distinction of being the first permanent settlement by Swedes in the nineteenth century. Within six years a Swedish-Lutheran congregation had been organized. By 1854 the population of this inland place had grown to five hundred, many of whom owned fair-sized farms. Only a few years later, in 1846, a second Swedish settlement in Iowa—revealing its origin by its very name, Swede Point—was established in Boone County.[59] In hilly Wapello County a group of Swedes found a pretty location, which no doubt reminded them of their homeland, and settled there in 1848, calling it Bergholm's settlement. The soil proved fairly good for corn and rye, and by 1862 twenty to thirty Swedish families had hewed out their

[57] For the Illinois Central Railroad grants, see Qualey, *Norwegian Settlement*, 36–37.

[58] Wittke, *We Who Built America*, 269; Hokanson, *Swedish Immigrants*, 20, 112.

[59] Wittke, *We Who Built America*, 269; Hokanson, *Swedish Immigrants*, 18; O. N. Nelson, *History of the Scandinavians and Successful Scandinavians in the United States* (Minneapolis, 1893–1897), I, 65–66.

farms from woods and prairie—sizable farms, some three hundred to four hundred acres in size. Lansing in Allamakee County was claimed as a Swedish colony.[60]

From the Illinois settlements went some of the pioneers, soon augmented by direct immigration from Sweden, to found the first Swedish communities in Minnesota. We are indebted to a church paper for the knowledge of various early settlements. Around thirty families were living about 1861 at St. Peter, Nicollet County; Red Wing had a number of Swedish families; Spring Garden in Goodhue County, situated eighteen miles southwest of Red Wing, consisted of thirty-seven Swedish families. Carver was first an early Swedish center in Nicollet County, but Norwegians penetrated into it as early as the period 1852–1855; Vasa, also in Goodhue County, Marion, and Chisago Lake are all claimed as Swedish centers.[61] Some Swedes had penetrated into Kansas as early as 1855. Many of the earliest colonizers worked first on the Union Pacific and Santa Fe railroads and with their earnings bought land along the routes. A few had trickled into Nebraska even before the Union Pacific offered employment in its shops.

Oddly enough, the colonies in the East followed rather than preceded those of the western prairie. Sixty skilled workmen settled in Brockton, Massachusetts, in 1844 and became the nucleus of the Swedish element in the shoe industry. By the following year a fairly large Swedish group was perceptible in the mills and factories of Jamestown, New York. At Worcester, where there was a considerable colony a decade later, Swedes were just beginning to arrive. On the Pacific coast in the Golden Gate city they had already begun to arrive in sufficient numbers to justify organization of a church of their own.[62] Illinois, Wisconsin, and Iowa were receiving the largest numbers; but scattered groups were settling in Pennsylvania, Michigan, and Indiana. Almost seventeen hundred Swedish immigrants were arriving yearly during the decade of the fifties, a movement little more than checked by the first years of war.

The strength of the Swedes, like that of the Swiss, may be roughly estimated by the Swedish organizations. The Swedish gymnastic movement was something like the German *Turnerbund,* in that it took its

[60] Chicago *Hemlandet,* January 3, 1862. In the issue of February 19, 1862, Lansing is listed as a Swedish center in the West.

[61] *Ibid.,* February 19, 1862; Blegen, *Norwegian Migration,* I, 363. The inclusion of Norway Lake in Kandiyohi County in this list hardly seems justifiable. See Qualey, *Norwegian Settlement,* 125. Carver had about fifty Swedish and Norwegian families.

[62] Wittke, *We Who Built America,* 269–70; Hokanson, *Swedish Immigrants,* 17–18.

rise from the same general feeling of national humiliation incident to the Napoleonic conquests. Singing societies arose in many Swedish communities. In native costume, the Scandinavian National Quartette toured Wisconsin and Minnesota before the war. The musical societies were preceded by the organizations for benevolent and welfare purposes, among them *Svea,* which started in Chicago in 1857.[63]

Aside from a few liberal intellectuals, as noted above, the Swedes who came during this period were drawn from the better element of the Swedish working class, 50 per cent of whom were skilled tradesmen, laborers, farmers, or servants. Carpenters, masons, painters, tailors, blacksmiths, shoemakers, gardeners, and watchmakers, who owned their own tools, made up the bulk of the number. Of paupers and criminals there were none, largely because there are few in Sweden, and because Sweden did not export this type of product. There were few of the liberal intellectuals comparable to the Forty-eighters who were driven out of Germany.

Danish Settlements

Danish immigration, small even during the greatest period of Scandinavian migration, was almost negligible during the forties and fifties, when the Norwegian and Swedish tides were beginning to come in. It did not even begin until after the middle of the century, when reports of the favorable economic opportunities in America began to seep in from Germany and Norway. The usual letters and pamphlets began to circulate, and missionaries sent to Denmark by American religious sects encouraged immigration. By 1860 about two thousand Danes had been attracted to Great Salt Lake by Mormon missionaries. Despite the meagerness of Danish immigration, there is record of the establishment of a Danish settlement in 1847 in Waukesha County, Wisconsin, and of a large Danish settlement in Franklin County, Iowa. Denmark's comparative indifference to the economic opportunities open in the United States has a logical explanation in her greater prosperity as compared with her Scandinavian sisters. With her dairying and cattle-raising industries, for which England and Germany offered a ready market, her people did not sound the depths of the poverty of Norway or even of the poorer peasants of Sweden.

---

[63] Wittke, *We Who Built America,* 272–73. Svea is the embodiment of Sweden as a nation, just as our Goddess of Liberty typifies to us the American union.

SWISS ELEMENT

In general, the Swiss who migrated to the United States spoke a Swiss-German and represented an essentially German culture. Hence they tended to intermingle with the already existing German communities to such a degree that it is not always easy to identify them as separate communities. Likewise, when the Swiss came from the French-speaking cantons, they often merged with a French colony in America. This same tendency manifested itself again when these same Swiss took up arms for the defense of their adopted fatherland, so that we shall see them enlisting often with a German regiment or helping to fill up a French company. However, groups of Swiss immigrants were settled in various parts of the United States in more or less closely integrated bodies. What might be called colonies existed in many of the cities of the East. The largest body of urban Swiss was to be found, as might be expected, in New York; it was large enough to provide at least one full company of sharpshooters for Berdan's regiment, and several other companies, to be duly chronicled in the proper place. A large body of Swiss seems to have been located in a western section of the metropolis called "Blumenthal." Swiss congregated also in the lesser cities, such as Boston, Buffalo, Rochester, Newark, Philadelphia, Baltimore, Washington, Cincinnati, and Minneapolis.[64]

In addition to these groups of Swiss in the large cities there were in the middle-western states aggregations of Swiss to which the word "colony" applies with particular appropriateness. The colonies at Vevay and Tell City in Indiana proclaimed by their very names their Swiss origin. The settlement at Vevay arose primarily from the efforts of the Dufour family to promote the development of viniculture in Switzerland County in the Ohio Valley; it dates back to 1813, when they obtained 3,700 acres from the government and laid out the town. Even though many early settlers forsook it for Cincinnati,[65] it managed to survive up to the war. Tell City,

[64] The formation of certain societies proves the existence of a considerable number of Swiss in the various large cities of the United States and justifies the writer in according them the status of colony. Among such societies were the *Grütliverein*, the *Wohlthätigkeits-Gesellschaft* (Swiss Benevolent Association), the *Schweizer Männerchor*, and the *Helvetia-Verein*. Steinach treats these organizations fully in connection with each city. See Severin Alderich Steinach, *Geschichte und Leben der Schweizer Kolonien in den Vereinigten Staaten von Nord Amerika* (New York, 1889), *passim*.

[65] The county in which Vevay is located (Switzerland County, Indiana) was organized

located 125 miles above Louisville on the Ohio River, on some six thousand acres purchased by a Swiss colonization society with headquarters in Cincinnati, was actually begun in 1858. Swiss came to the new settlement from all parts of the United States, so that by 1861 it had a population of slightly over a thousand and could be regarded as an important Swiss colony.[66]

Highland, Illinois, and New Glarus, Wisconsin, were really significant Swiss colonies. Despite the fact that Highland had only a scanty population in 1861, about one half of its two thousand inhabitants were Swiss. More important, it was the center of an area of farms and hamlets extending for perhaps fifteen miles—in which area most of the farms belonged to Swiss—so that the population of the neighborhood was actually approximately eight thousand. The first settlers had wisely chosen for the location of their new home the so-called "Looking Glass Valley"—often termed the garden spot of Illinois—where the good black soil promised rich reward for toil, while the accessibility of St. Louis—only twenty miles away—offered a certain market. The first group of perhaps fifteen persons arrived from Switzerland after a trying journey of 118 days. Their nostalgia appears in the name bestowed on their infant settlement, Helvetia, a name retained until its incorporation in 1884. The usual story of hardship and distress must be registered. Festivities, naturally enough, modeled themselves on the national festivals of Switzerland and became fairly numerous. The *Helvetia Schützen,* the singing societies, the *Turnvereine,* and even an amateur theatrical troupe—all founded before the war—assumed significant roles. The citizens were employed as farmers as well as in the vineyards and in a local brewery. The Swiss organizations, especially those encouraging shooting practices, came to their highest development in Highland, where in 1860 *Helvetia,* the shooting association of Highland, had already been founded. Years of practice in shooting had preceded the idea of a society for contests and must certainly have been a factor in training the soldiers from Highland in precision shooting.[67]

---

in 1814. The touch with the mother country was manifest by the fact that the classical school, established in 1816, and a short-lived library were supported by the Literary Society of Old Vevay in Switzerland. See Wittke, *We Who Built America,* 302–303, and Perret Dufour, *The Swiss Settlement of Switzerland County, Indiana* (Indianapolis, 1925), *passim.*

In 1825 the Swiss Artillery Company of Vevay marched seventy miles to share in the reception accorded an old friend of America, the distinguished Frenchman Lafayette. The action of this group reflects the interest of the entire colony in Lafayette's visit.

[66] Steinach, *Geschichte und Leben,* 224–27; Wittke, *We Who Built America,* 303.

[67] Steinach, *Geschichte und Leben,* 247–51.

Among the numerous Germans in Wisconsin was tucked away one of the essentially large Swiss colonies, New Glarus, its name proclaiming the loyalty of the founders to the old Swiss canton. When an economic crisis gripped this part of Switzerland, a colonization society, encouraged by the Swiss government, sent two agents to the United States to seek a favorable location for prospective Swiss immigrants. They bought twelve hundred acres of fields and eighty acres of woodland among the roughest hills of Green County, Wisconsin, about twenty miles southwest of Madison. This area was divided into twenty-acre plots. Only about half of the two hundred Swiss who set out for the New World in 1845 went on to Wisconsin, and the colony probably would not have survived without occasional contributions from the homeland. The community adhered to the Swiss Reformed Church until the coming of itinerant preachers led to the founding of an Evangelical church. After the usual years of hardship the settlers gradually met better conditions. The colony in 1859 was still following the old Swiss customs for marriage, baptism, and burial. That the first school, opened in 1847, was taught by an Irishman was probably a concession to necessity; Swiss-German was spoken almost exclusively in all school and city meetings, at the polls, and even in the court. A stranger visiting the community in 1850 might well have thought that he had entered a part of Switzerland. Swiss had appropriated almost the entire township, half of the city of Washington, a great part of several other towns, and the southern part of Dane County. Altogether in 1860 they numbered not far from three thousand, or about one seventh of the total population of Green County.[68] In the entire state they numbered almost five thousand.

In Iowa there were small groups of Swiss in Dubuque, Burlington, and Davenport; but it was only in Benton County that there was a small colony, calling itself Lucerne.[69] In the frontier state of Minnesota, strangely enough (although the first Swiss settlers had penetrated to Fort Snelling as early as 1826), the one settlement which may be described as Swiss was Bern, laid out in 1856 in Dodge County, by some Swiss families from old Bern. In 1860 a visitor might have counted some forty or fifty families almost wholly from Glarus and Bern. Also a small Swiss colony, which bore the suggestive name of "Helvetia," was to be found in Carver County. Many Swiss settlers intermingled with the Scandinavians and

[68] *Ibid.*, 288–92, 295.

[69] The Swiss who first settled in Davenport, Iowa, came as early as the period 1844–1849, and were almost entirely from the Oberland, St. Gall; the first Swiss came to Dubuque in 1834. *Ibid.*, 261–62, 269–70, 271.

Germans in settlements such as Winona and New Ulm. Even in distant San Francisco enough Swiss could be found in 1856 to form a Swiss Mutual and Benevolent Society to help the poor Swiss in California; and the Swiss Rifle Club organized in September, 1860, was one of the oldest in the Union.[70]

DUTCH SETTLEMENTS

The Dutch element, while few in numbers and relatively late in arriving—with the exception, of course, of the old Dutch element settled in the Atlantic states during colonial days—contributed one more strain to the racial mixture that flowed into America. Besides the economic impulse toward emigration there was religious dissent. Under royal patronage irregularities were allowed to creep into church practice and dogma until dissenters reached the point of rupture with the state church. The eighteenth-century phenomenon of Dutch migration to the New World under the leadership of their pastors reappeared in the nineteenth. These dissenters settled in the largest numbers in Michigan, Wisconsin, and Iowa. A group of these pietists settled around the Black River in Michigan near Kalamazoo and Grand Rapids, led by a pastor who added to his religious zeal the typical shrewdness and practicality of his nation. By the eve of the war the colony had grown to over four thousand and had expanded into seven villages, reflecting the homeland by their names—Holland, Groningen, Zeeland, Vriesland, Overissel, Graafschap, and Drenthe.[71]

In Iowa also the Dutch settled by religious groups in clannish farming communities. Pella, Orange City, and Muncie promptly became—and to this day remain—the centers of Dutch influence in that state. Since the Hollanders brought property with them, they met with a friendly welcome from state authorities and generally from neighbors. Their leader had secured title to not less than eighteen thousand acres in the northeastern part of Marion County; and here the groups, six hundred strong, settled in August, 1847, to erect their dugouts and sod houses. Advertisements in Holland soon brought additional immigrants, who usually created home-

---

[70] *Ibid.*, 311, 312, 339–40, 343; Wittke, *We Who Built America*, 302.

[71] Aleida J. Pieters, *A Dutch Settlement in Michigan* (Grand Rapids, 1913), 18. This work is regarded by Wittke as the best account of early Dutch settlement. Wittke, *We Who Built America*, 306–309.

steads beside the lakes or water courses. Few Dutch sought the wheat and corn belt but, as in Michigan, devoted themselves to truck gardening and dairy products, for which they found a ready market.[72]

Small Dutch colonies arose elsewhere. One pastor, the Reverend P. Zonne, led his followers into Wisconsin on Lake Michigan only twenty miles south of where Sheboygan now stands and in this area established the villages of Cedar Grove and Osnaberg. In 1850 Dutch settlements were to be found in Illinois at South Holland, Roseland, and Chicago. Numbers of immigrants remained behind in the eastern cities, as manifested by the activity of Dutch societies and churches.[73]

In most of these settlements, certainly in the religious agricultural communities, the villages had been erected on a stern Calvinistic foundation, making for separation from the native Americans. Dancing, cards, theaters, and liquor were forbidden. The children attended parochial schools and church services, which were prolonged sessions; music, except psalms, was not encouraged; recreations were very few indeed. The Dutch language was practically the only medium of communication in the home, the church, and the newspapers. Unquestionably, the churches were barriers to assimilation. Books and magazines entered but rarely the homes of Dutch farmers. In those early days the people clumped about in wooden shoes. The very diet, with its Edam cheese, smoked beef, rusks, rye and currant bread, and delicious pastries, reflected that of Holland. By 1861 Americanization had made little inroad on the 13,000 residents in Dutch communities; yet these Dutchmen had come to stay, as was clearly indicated by the promptness with which they took out naturalization papers.[74]

WELSH COLONIES

Of a few other small nationality groups which must be briefly mentioned, the Welsh will be considered first. Before the Irish supplanted them, the Welsh supplied the labor in the anthracite coal mines of Pennsylvania; and by 1861 they were not yet feeling the competition of the Irish. In 1843 a Welsh society was formed in New York City to further benevolent purposes, to preserve the purity of the Welsh language,

[72] Henry S. Lucas, "The Beginnings of Dutch Immigration to Iowa, 1845–1847," in *Iowa Journal of History and Politics*, XXII (1924), 483–531.

[73] New York *Times*, October 19, 1877; S. F. Rederus, "The Dutch Settlements of Sheboygan County," in *Wisconsin Magazine of History*, I (1917–1918), 246–265.

[74] See Wittke, *We Who Built America*, 309–10, 307.

to celebrate Welsh holidays, and to protect Welsh immigrants. The publication of three magazines in Welsh in New York state in the early forties attests to the presence of a not-negligible body of Welshmen in our body politic. It is surprising to read that the Association of Welsh Congregational Churches of New York included in 1861 no less than twenty-two churches. In that same year, the first Eisteddfod (a Welsh importation to promote singing and literary competition) west of the Rockies was held by Welsh gold miners in North San Juan, a fact attesting to participation by men of that nationality in the gold rush to California. During the two decades between 1830 and 1850 the men of Cornwall and a few Welshmen went into the lead-mining region of Wisconsin in the southwestern part of the state, until by the latter date they had reached the considerable number of 7,000 in this area.[75]

ITALIAN ELEMENT

Although Italian immigration up to the period of the war and even for several decades afterwards was hardly more than a trickle compared with the Anglo-Saxon and Teutonic migration, there is ample evidence of the presence of an appreciable group in the population of 1860. It consisted largely of vendors of plaster statuary, organ-grinders, and a few hundred political refugees of the *Risorgimento*.[76] By 1860 *L'Echo d'Italia* had already appeared as the organ of the Italian population in New York; an Italian church had been erected in Philadelphia in 1852; and a Boston paper in 1857 had commented on the Italian organ-grinders in such a way as to suggest that they must have been fairly numerous there. Italians in New York and Cincinnati obviously retained a keen interest in their homeland, for they sponsored meetings in 1859 to celebrate the victories of the Sardinian and French armies in the war for unification. An effort to raise a Garibaldi regiment in 1861 for the American Civil War becomes explicable when we realize that New York City alone harbored a colony of perhaps two thousand Italians.[77]

[75] Louis A. Copeland, "The Cornish in Southwest Wisconsin," in *Wisconsin Historical Society Collections*, XIV (1898), 301–34. Even at present the language used by the older inhabitants in this district shows a strong Celtic influence. In 1860 there were about three hundred Welsh in the district. Joseph Schafer, *Wisconsin Lead Region* (Madison, 1932), 290–98.

[76] Garibaldi, it will be recalled, worked for a time in Antonio Meucci's candle factory on Staten Island. Wittke, *We Who Built America*, 436.

[77] Giovanni Schiavo, *The Italians in America before the Civil War* (New York, 1934),

HUNGARIAN ELEMENT

There were only about three thousand Hungarians in the United States when the war broke out, but they furnished, as we shall see, a disproportionately large number of officers. The majority, "Kossuth exiles," as they were often called, left their homeland for America after the revolt of 1848, in response to the congressional offer of a home in America to Kossuth and his followers. Although during his visit to this country Louis Kossuth conferred with the secretary of agriculture concerning the territory to be given to the Hungarian emigrants, he did not wish to stay, because he still had faith in the success of his cause in Hungary. He even felt that those who did migrate to America must not do so with too serious thought of a permanent residence. A band of these Hungarian patriots eventually founded the community of New Buda in Decatur County in south central Iowa, adjoining the Missouri line. Count Ladislaus Ujházy, who led them, was made postmaster of the newly established post office there by the United States government. A number of Magyar aristocrats in the group proceeded to build a large log "castle" with implements and funds secured from sympathizers in St. Louis. In 1858 Congress accorded the members of the community the opportunity to buy the land at the usual price of $1.25 an acre without having to pay interest from the date of their arrival. Count Ujházy had, however, long before moved on with some of his followers to San Antonio in the hope of finding a warmer climate and land better suited to the cultivation of the grape. In his group were several picturesque characters whom we shall encounter later as officers or privates in the war. Most of the members proved impractical farmers, amusing their neighbors, who were realistic frontiersmen, by their ignorance of practical farming. The colony, with its tiny population of seventy-five at its largest, has little more than a historical interest; but was still in existence in 1860. For years the little band of exiles had their

---

212, 224. Schiavo claims that between 1836 and 1856 more than two hundred exiles came to the United States from Italy; he mentions Marconcelli, who lived in Philadelphia but died in New York in 1846. For the appearance of *L'Echo D'Italia*, see New York *Tribune*, June 27, 1850; for the dedication of the Italian church in Philadelphia, see the Boston *Pilot*, October 30, 1852. It was the Boston *Traveller*, April 3, 1857, which suggested putting Italian organ-grinders to work with shovels to fill in the Back Bay region. For meetings to celebrate the victories of the French and Italians, see Cincinnati *Enquirer*, March 27, July 15, 1859. See also Arthur C. Cole, *The Irrepressible Conflict, 1850–65* (A *History of American Life*, VII, New York, 1934), 126.

faces turned toward Europe, keeping up a steady correspondence with Kossuth; but in the Civil War their energy and idealism for a cause found a new outlet.[78]

BOHEMIAN ELEMENT

The impetus to migration among the Bohemians came only after the failure of the revolutionary movement of 1848, after which a number of the liberals fled to the United States. The rush to California in 1849 brought other Bohemians of an entirely different type. From 1848 to 1865 over forty thousand Bohemians came to this country, mostly from the backward, southern districts of the homeland. It is probably safe to say that there were around forty thousand of this nationality in this country in 1861. Racine, Wisconsin, and Cedar Rapids, Iowa, were the chief centers for distribution of the immigrants from Bohemia into the agricultural Northwest. In the fifties they came to Wisconsin, where they became successful, reliable farmers—indeed, among the state's best. It is significant that the first Bohemian newspaper in America, printed probably of necessity in German type, was published at Racine. Bohemians were among the early foreigners to take out homesteads in the upper Mississippi Valley; and they added to that section a neat, industrious, and intelligent peasant class, who, eager to preserve their own language and customs, established themselves in colonies. Settlements appeared, such as Wilbur, the county seat of Saline County, Wisconsin, and a little Bohemia in Minnesota. Urban aggregations began to develop in the larger cities—on the Lower East Side of New York and in St. Louis, where they had settled in numbers large enough to form a fraternal society and a church parish in 1854. Little English was heard on the streets of the rural Bohemian settlements, and the farmers ate their lunches in saloons much like the old Bohemian beer gardens.[79]

[78] Among the more important members were Francis Vargas, who rose to public office in Iowa and Ignace Haimer, who held the chair of modern languages at the University of Missouri. George Pomutz, having turned typical "promoter," advertised New Buda with "Kossuth Place," "Bohm University," and a system of public parks—all of which existed only in his imagination. He actually sold lots as far east as Hoboken. By such means he induced some Germans to come to the colony. Edmund Vasvary, *Lincoln's Hungarian Heroes; The Participation of Hungarians in the Civil War, 1861–1865* (Washington, 1939), 18; Wittke, *We Who Built America*, 431–32; New York *Tribune*, April 29, June 19, 1850; New York *Times*, May 3, 1861; Lilian M. Wilson, "Some Hungarian Patriots in Iowa," in *Iowa Journal of History and Politics*, XI (1913), 479–516.

[79] Wittke, *We Who Built America*, 410, 414, 416. The oldest lodge in the United States is the C.S.P.S. (Bohemian Slavonian Protective Association), referred to in the text. *Ibid.*, 413.

POLES

Americans are sufficiently conscious of the Poles as a part of the "New Immigration," but for purposes of this study we must realize that there were Poles living in the United States in 1860. After the abortive Polish revolt of 1830 there came to the United States some 350 exiles to whom Congress made a grant of land in Illinois. Likewise, after the unsuccessful revolts of 1848 and 1863, Polish political refugees fled to the "land of the free." Despite the fact that most of them were peasants, they congregated in the cities because their resource for a living was their brawn. Enough Poles had settled down in New York City by 1853 to celebrate the anniversary of the revolt of 1830, and it was marked by speeches in Polish, German, and Italian. Even earlier, in 1845, a similar celebration had occurred, with the representatives of all the important foreign groups participating in the program. More dramatic was the commemoration in Cincinnati in 1859 of the Warsaw uprising of 1830, an affair arranged by the Polish exiles, with two of the actual participants in the uprising present at the banquet as guests of honor.[80] Settlements of Poles were begun in Texas and Wisconsin before the Civil War. Polonia, located in Portage County, Wisconsin, was founded in the fifties. It was planted among existing German, Irish, and French communities. In 1863 a separate Polish Roman Catholic church was built in this community. The opening of a Polish church in Milwaukee in 1865 indicates the degree to which Poles had been settling in that city prior to and during the war.[81]

Such was the composition of the population of the United States in 1861—a conglomeration of almost every European nationality: German and Irish, Scandinavian and Welsh, Dutch and Polish, Swiss and Hungarian. A good third of all the human beings who lived in the United States had been born abroad and still in many ways preserved the customs and ideas of the homeland in their hearts. In many villages and in many sections of our cities, a visitor could readily believe that he was in a Rhenish city or had dropped into a Dutch village, so faithfully was the atmosphere of the homeland reproduced. Many tongues were spoken here, and many

[80] For the New York celebration in 1853, see Boston *Transcript,* December 1, 1853; for that of 1845, see New York *Weekly News,* December 6, 1845; for the event in Cincinnati, see Cincinnati *Enquirer,* November 30, 1859. See also Miecislaus Haiman, *Polish Past in America,* 1608–1865 (Chicago, 1939), 72–73, 78.

[81] Wittke, *We Who Built America,* 422. Poles were settled in Texas as early as 1856, but that does not belong to this story. See Lonn, *Foreigners in the Confederacy,* 19.

persons neither spoke nor understood any tongue other than their native speech. From these diverse elements was to be drawn a very considerable portion of the Northern volunteer army which was to defend the Constitution drawn up by Anglo-Saxon Americans, and to fight and die for American ideals. The miracle is that it proved possible.

CHAPTER TWO

Attitude Toward the War Issues

THE attitude assumed by the various foreign-born groups toward the issues presented by the War of Secession was of the first importance. The inclination of the German, Scandinavian, and other foreign-born groups to settle in compact communities tended to make them react as units—with exceptions, of course—on public questions. Until after the firing on Fort Sumter the Irish were stanchly Democratic in politics, valuing past favors of that party to their race and fearing that any interference with the slavery question might result in the freeing of the negroes. Such action might eventuate in the negroes' flooding the North and becoming the economic competitors and even the social equals of the Irish laborers. Irish longshoremen were employed at the docks in all the leading ocean and lake ports. They resented the introduction of negroes into this field of labor, as their entry depressed the wage scale. This economic competition largely explains the opposition of the Irish to the abolition movement and also partly explains the draft riots of the war period. It certainly is paradoxical to find the Irishmen, who bitterly denounced the bondage imposed upon Ireland by England, now voting in squads at the polls against "every proposal to give equal rights to the colored race," and shouting outside the polls, "Down with the Nagurs! Let them go back to Africa, where they belong!" [1] Everywhere the Irish were doing the hard work, wielding the pick and shovel and bending their backs to heavy loads of the porter; but they were enjoying a monopoly in this field and were utterly unwilling to renounce it. When negroes were brought in to the larger seaports and lake ports to break the strikes of the longshoremen during the Civil War, riots resulted.[2]

Influential Irish leaders, even among the clergy, interpreted the agitation for abolition as radicalism, a radicalism which they feared, with the example of Europe before them, might easily be turned against the Catholic Church. They leaned, therefore, toward rigid obedience to the law

[1] The New York *Tribune*, May 11, 1850.
[2] Wittke, *We Who Built America*, 137.

and strict interpretation of the Constitution of the United States with its guarantee of slavery.[3] It happened occasionally that an Irish bishop made little show of support for the Union, as was the case with Bishop James Duggan in Chicago, who wielded his due influence with the large Irish group in his diocese. Even Archbishop John Hughes, that valuable supporter of the Union cause, opposed emancipation, although he urged support of the war. As late as the fall of 1861—after the outbreak of war— he could say, "We despise, *in the name of all Catholics, the 'Idea' of making this war subservient to the philanthropic nonsense of abolitionism.*" Some few exceptions to the rule with respect to the Irish attitude were to be found, as in Iowa.[4]

Furthermore, to many Irish the ascendancy of the "abolitionist Republicans" seemed to connote a revival of detestable New England Puritanism. When it came to the election of 1860, the Irish were dubious as to Lincoln's qualifications for leadership of the country, an attitude in which they did not differ from many of the native Americans. Such aspersions as the following, printed in the Boston *Pilot* of October 13, 1860, were frequent with the Irish: "Very good men have made their mark, Lincoln has made his—with an axe." There were a very few Irish Republicans, but most of the Irish undoubtedly voted for Stephen A. Douglas. At the actual outbreak of war, the *Pilot* urged its readers to respond to the call to preserve the Union and to support their President.

The Irish responded immediately to the firing on Fort Sumter. On April 16 the Irish residents of Boston assembled in great numbers at their Jackson Club Room in Hanover Street to express enthusiastically their affection for their adopted country, their firm determination to support the President, and their detestation of the rebellious southern citizens who were inciting civil war. No group could have voiced more patriotic sentiments:

> Resolved by us, the adopted citizens of Boston, of Irish birth and parentage, in this the most dangerous and threatening crisis through which our beloved adopted country has yet passed, that it is the solemn and sacred duty of every citizen and of every man who participates in and enjoys the inestimable blessings and privileges of our

[3] *Ibid.*, 168.

[4] See New York *Herald*, October 8, 1861, in which a long article by Archbishop John Hughes of New York is quoted from his organ, *The Metropolitan Record*. It has not been possible for the author to locate the issue of the *Record* containing the original speech. For exceptions in Iowa, see F. I. Herriott, "Iowa and the First Nomination of Lincoln," in *Annals of Iowa*, VIII (April, 1907–January, 1909), 198.

free government, to cast aside all party distinctions and unite as one man in support of the national administration, and in defence of our common country, its flag and its freedom. . . .

Resolved, that we call upon every adopted citizen of Irish birth to stand true to the country which has become the home of so many millions of our race and of the oppressed of the Old World, and not permit the liberties for which Washington fought and Montgomery died to be trampled under foot by the slave oligarchy of the South.[5]

By 1862 the *Pilot* was advising election of a Democratic Congress; furthermore, though still glorifying the heroism of the Irish soldiers, it was even urging an armistice.[6] This was hardly supporting the executive in the war.[7] In other words, the Irish shifted rather quickly to their prewar position in politics, though this did not affect their ardor for war or the stubbornness with which they fought on the field of battle. As was to be expected, from their fear of negro competition in the labor market, many Irish opposed the Emancipation Proclamation and became more outspoken in their criticism of the President after it was issued. While the feeling of the Irish during the draft riots was not without some justification, the fact must be admitted that the Irish were the worst offenders and that the rioting assumed the form of a serious antinegro demonstration. The *Irish-American* in New York printed the list of the drafted men in its issue of September 12, 1863, with heavy black lines between the columns as token of mourning. This was probably done to express the feeling that draft officials were drawing unduly on Democratic wards of the city.

The affiliation of the immigrant with the Democratic party was natural, and Democratic politicians were quick to see their opportunity to garner new votes. The very name "Democrat" smacked of liberality, whereas the name "Whig" carried so little appeal that leaders of that party considered changing the name. Democratic newspapers flattered the foreign-born voters, denounced the Whigs for their nativist sympathy, and supported suggestions to print official documents in German. Tammany and other political clubs won and held much immigrant support by their timely charities. Hence, it was only natural for the majority of the German voters to resist Whig efforts to win their favor and to believe that the party

[5] Mrs. J. Blakeslee Frost, *The Rebellion in the United States; or, the War of 1861* . . . (Hartford, 1862–1864), I, 144. Richard Montgomery, an Irish-American general, fell in the assault on Quebec in 1775.

[6] Wittke, *We Who Built America*, 169–70; Boston *Pilot*, October 4 and 11, 1862.

[7] Boston *Pilot*, March 16, August 24, 1861; August 9, 1862.

of Jefferson and Jackson was the true friend of the laborer and of the immigrant. A large block of Germans, particularly Roman Catholics, were suspicious of the new Republican party and of its large Know-Nothing and Puritan elements, recognized as the foes of immigrants. A considerable number of these Catholics clung to the Democratic party because they regarded as bitter enemies the Forty-eighters of their own nationality, many of whom were radical freethinkers and atheists now turning Republican, and because they regarded the entire Republican party as compounded of temperance fanatics, abolitionists, and defilers of churches.

It was not until the late fifties, when the slavery question became the great issue, that they wavered in their allegiance. German-Americans were deeply shaken by the Kansas-Nebraska Bill of 1854, which revived the slavery controversy, by the battle over homestead legislation, which must necessarily hold especial interest for land-hungry immigrants, and—most of all—by the increasing control of the Democratic party by its Southern wing. It should be clearly recognized that the majority of the German immigrants were not radical abolitionists; they were not disposed to drive slavery out of the states where it existed but were definitely opposed to its extension into the territories. The *New Yorker Staats-Zeitung* in 1850 still regarded slavery with equanimity; and Dr. Carl F. W. Walther, the patriarch of German Lutherans in America, defended it—as did Southern clergymen—on Biblical grounds.[8] If Douglas had not reopened this issue by his Kansas-Nebraska Act, it is probable that the Germans might not have deserted the Democratic party; but this move aroused the Germans to the point of protesting by mass meetings and by hanging Douglas in effigy.[9]

The radical Forty-eighters, who had lost none of their idealism, thus found a new cause on which to expend their reform aspirations; but many of these radicals who crossed the party line on the antislavery cry were so temperamental and egotistical that they were not dependable for long-term support of the Republican party.[10] Some Germans supported John C. Frémont for President in 1856, so that the desertion of the Democrats by the Germans was already well under way. Turner societies endorsed Fré-

[8] Ernst Bruncken, "The Political Activity of Wisconsin Germans, 1854–60," in *Proceedings of the Wisconsin State Historical Society*, 1901, p. 197.

[9] Wittke, *We Who Built America*, 244–45; F. I. Herriott, "The Germans of Chicago and Stephen A. Douglas," in *Jahrbuch der Deutsch-amerikanischen historischen Gesellschaft von Illinois*, XII (1912), 399.

[10] Gray, *The Hidden Civil War*, 30; Robert Rombauer, *The Union Cause in St. Louis in 1861* (St. Louis, 1900), 103.

mont with this slogan: "Free speech, free press, free soil, free work, and a free Kansas." [11] The small group of educated political liberals among the Germans rejoiced in the idealism of the Republican movement, urging their fellow countrymen to join them in their desertion to the new party. By 1860 the Republicans had already cut deeply into the ranks of the formerly Democratic Germans.

In the convention and the campaign of 1860 politicians of both parties wooed the German vote and, only a bit less fervently, that of the other foreign-born nationality groups. At the Republican convention in Chicago, leaders made every endeavor to convince the German delegates—and there were many—that nativism did not control the party. Foreigners occupied places of prominence. Carl Schurz, for instance, was chairman of the Wisconsin delegation and a member of the Committee on Resolutions and hence was able to write into the platform a plank opposing any change in the rights accorded to immigrants.[12] The other issue on which Republican leaders knew the German vote could be marshaled was that of free homesteads for settlers. Southerners were generally opposed to, and stigmatized as class legislation for foreigners,[13] any such law as had been defeated in 1854 by Southern votes and in 1860 by the veto of a Democratic President. Northern and Western Republicans in Congress, on the other hand, generally supported the Homestead Bill.

Under the general direction of Schurz, who was a member of the Republican National Committee and in charge of the foreign department, a phalanx of foreign-born campaign orators, German, Scandinavian, and Dutch, set out to corral the foreign vote. Gustav Körner, Francis Lieber, Friedrich Hassaurek, Frederick Münch, and Judge Krekel of Missouri, all German-born leaders, took up the cudgels for Lincoln. Schurz traveled the enormous total of twenty-one thousand miles to the leading German centers in the East and the West to persuade his countrymen to cast their ballots for the Republican candidate. Two of his speeches enjoyed wide circulation as campaign literature, along with the Homestead Law printed

[11] In the political campaign of 1856, German leaders, such as Friedrich Hecker, Friedrich Hassaurek, Gustav Körner, Friedrich Fröbel, and Carl Schurz, spoke in many cities for the Republicans. Lincoln campaigned for Frémont in the German city of Belleville, Illinois. Wittke, *We Who Built America*, 245–46. The Republicans carried the strongly German city of Milwaukee in a local election in 1858. See New York *Tribune*, September 2, 1856, for further details on the Germans in the election of 1856.

[12] Gustav Körner, *Memoirs of Gustav Körner, 1809–1896* (Cedar Rapids, Iowa, 1909), II, 87; Wittke, *We Who Built America*, 247.

[13] For views of Southerners expressed in Congress, see *Congressional Globe*, 31 Cong., 1 and 2 Sess., 482–84, 522–24, 583–86; 33 Cong., 1 Sess., Pt. 2, p. 944.

in several languages and sponsored by the Republicans.[14] The Germans were probably flattered by the thought advanced by some of their number, especially by Schurz, that they held the balance of power in the Midwest and therefore perhaps in the election. Some students of this election have reached the conclusion that the foreign-born vote in the Northwest decided the outcome of the election and that one vote in twenty cast the other way would have tipped the scales for Douglas. Joseph Shafer, however, after a scientific study of the Wisconsin vote, challenges this conclusion and arrives at a belief that "the assignment of a dominant influence to the foreign-born" contingent in the election of 1860 is wholly erroneous.[15] The natural conservatism of the mass of the Germans caused a shift in their party faith not clearly perceptible until the Lincoln campaign. It is possible that uneasiness over the party association with the Irish was a contributing factor, for there had long been an antipathy between the two races.[16] Many Germans unquestionably shared in the election of Lincoln, but they were probably not the determining factor, as has so often been claimed.

To imagine, however, that the Germans deserted the Democratic party en masse would be a serious misapprehension. The number of German Republicans was large; but many, including some distinguished Germans, clung to the Democratic party throughout the period of the war. The *National Zeitung* of New York City under German editorship was denouncing Lincoln as a military dictator before the close of 1861.[17] Such prominent Germans as Charles Reemelin of Cincinnati, the writer Anton Eickhoff, Jacob Reinhard of the Columbus *Westbote,* Christian Kribben of St. Louis, and Judge Wilhelm Lang of Tiffin, Ohio, remained stanch Democrats.[18] The *Volksfreund* of Buffalo denounced the "Black Re-

[14] Wittke, *We Who Built America,* 249. In the distribution of patronage after the Republicans had won the election, the Germans were recognized more generously than they had ever been.

[15] See William E. Dodd, "The Fight for the Northwest, 1860," in *American Historical Review,* XVI (1910–1911), 774–88; Donnell V. Smith, "The Influence of the Foreign-Born of the Northwest in the Election of 1860," in *Mississippi Valley Historical Review,* XIX (1925–1926), 192–204. Schurz had a tendency to exaggerate the importance of the Germans. For Joseph Schafer's discussion, see his article "Who Elected Lincoln?" in *American Historical Review,* XLVII (1941–1942), 51–63.

[16] That the Know-Nothing Party had opposed Catholicism affected some Germans, but the Whig proposal to require a residence of twenty-one years before citizenship was possible affected every German and every foreign-born person. See Rombauer, *The Union Cause in St. Louis,* 104.

[17] New York *Times,* September 3, 1861. The *Times* gives some excerpts—valuable because no file of the *National Zeitung* seems to have survived.

[18] Körner, *Das deutsche Element,* 132, 226, 287.

publicans" roundly, and the *New Yorker Staats-Zeitung* went so far as to support Governor Horatio Seymour.[19] The New York *Journal* was the organ of the German Copperheads. In some of the rural sections of Wisconsin, Germans volunteered but slowly for the field, as they remained antiwar Democrats. There were antidraft riots among the Germans in Ozaukee and Washington counties, as there were among the Irish in the East. Milwaukee County, with its large percentage of German residents, gave a majority to George B. McClellan in the presidential election of 1864. Slowly, however, the Forty-eighters educated the German farmers, who had been apathetic and uninterested in abolition or the constitutional question, to a realization of what the war meant. German slackers in Milwaukee gave the authorities some trouble.[20] Even in loyal Belleville, an antiwar Democratic paper, the *Volksblatt,* was published by a German.[21] The Germans in the communistic settlements at Amana, Iowa, held true to their conscientious opposition to war and consequently suffered some persecution from angry and self-righteous neighbors. Though they furnished no volunteers, they did hire substitutes and contributed money and clothing for the soldiers worth thousands of dollars.[22]

German and Scandinavian Republican clubs were formed in all the cities to explain in the native tongue the stand of the Republican party on various questions. "Wide-Awake Clubs," the semimilitary clubs which were a marked feature of the campaign of 1860, were organized among the foreign-born wherever feasible, as branches of the general association. Wide-Awakes were organized among the Germans in Washington and had in three days over fifty members from among the most respectable Germans of the city, a large part of whom were Jews. The Swedish Wide-Awakes were especially active in Illinois, where they marched in parades, bore banners with mottoes in Swedish, and arranged for young Swedish women representing, for instance, the states and Kansas to ride in coaches in the parades. The Wide-Awakes in Baltimore included a large number of Germans and evoked the usual plug-ugly tactics for which that city was notorious. A big Republican meeting in November in that city was pre-

[19] New York *Tribune,* July 23, 1863.

[20] Schafer, *Four Wisconsin Counties, Prairie and Forest,* 158–68; Shannon, *The Organization and Administration of the Union Army,* II, 235.

[21] The office was visited by persons unknown and was thrown into disorder. Frank Moore (ed.), *Rebellion Record: A Diary of American Events, with Documents, Narrative, Illustrative Incidents, Poetry, etc.* (New York, 1861–1868), VI, Pt. 1, p. 52.

[22] Wittke, *We Who Built America,* 355; Bertha M. H. Shambaugh, *Amana That Was and Amana That Is* (Iowa City, 1932), 147–48.

ceded by a torchlight parade, during which the paraders were attacked by stones and assailed with vitriol, so that some Wide-Awakes were wounded. The German speakers declined to speak, as they were assailed by the most shameful insults and their voices would have been drowned more completely than were those of the American speakers.[23]

Perhaps the general shift in the attitude of the majority of the Germans may be best stated in the following terms: Before 1850 they saw in the Democratic party the best exponent of the liberties for the sake of which they had exiled themselves from a beloved Fatherland. But when the issue of secession or union became the compelling question, the Germans recognized the whole befogged question for what it was—freedom or slavery for a certain class of people—and swung over to the party which stood for the freedom of all classes in the Union. They looked at the public question from the point of view of the common welfare and voted for what they regarded as principle rather than for those who had hitherto been their friends.

By no better method can the reader grasp the views of the German element toward the war than by scanning excerpts from the German newspapers, the number of which was legion during the period just preceding and following the outbreak of the war. The position of the *Illinois Staats-Zeitung* was clear from the beginning and never wavered. Strong language was necessary to express the depth of its feeling. It coined a word for the Confederate flag, the *Klapperschlangenflagge* (rattlesnake flag); and it alluded to the New York *Day Book* as the "most infamous Secession sheet in the North—this prostitute supported by the South." This paper had had the temerity to say that "the Allmighty himself has not the power to destroy American slavery." This sentiment so enraged the editor of the Chicago paper that he expressed his wonder that "the thunderbolts of Heaven did not strike down the rascal who had written that sentence as they will later annihilate the cause which he supports." [24] That editor seemed to feel a special rage and humiliation over the German papers in New Orleans for supporting the Southern cause:

> The good-for-nothing Concern, named "the New Orleans German Newspaper" interests us, if one may say so, by the unusual audacity with which it toots the horn on the side of the Secession-swindle;

[23] Hokanson, *Swedish Immigrants*, 59–60; Washington *Tägliche Metropole*, October 29, November 27, 1860.

[24] "Auf Eine solche Götterdämmerung gibt es keine Antwort, wir wundern uns nur, dass die Donnerkeile des Himmels dem Schuft nicht treffen, welcher diesen Satz geschrieben hat, so wie später die Sache zusammenschlagen werden, die er unterstützt," Chicago *Illinois Staats-Zeitung*, August 8, 1861.

it is actually in love with high treason, and while it belabors the German citizens for the secession movement, it seems to sustain itself by that philosophy which asks villainously: "For what purpose are the ranks there than to be sworn?"

The *Louisiana Staatszeitung,* which is only less bad than its colleague in the yellow fever city, spreads in the one column a paragraph of rage against the subscribers and in the other an article as stupid as it is infamous for its sins against the free press.[25]

This same Chicago paper expresses clearly how the surrender of Fort Sumter affected the German-born citizen: "So the government must, in order to make apparent to the weakest eyes that the last remedy lies in the sword, begin with the imperfect means at her command the unequal conflict against a disproportionate superiority, which has all the advantages of position, and the result was to be foreseen, as soon as the rebels could go so far in their madness as to fire on the flag of their own land." That had happened, and the Stars and Stripes had been forced to yield to the flag of treason.

But the matter had therewith also entered an entirely different status: "The people of the North arise now with all their strength and stand with the administration, which has given such evidence of moderation and which finally has reached for the decisive means which duty demands." [26] The article declared that the Germans also felt the disgrace as deeply as the native Americans. Would they do less to wash it away? This editor began at once to clamor for a German regiment—in order not to allow Cincinnati to surpass Chicago—and for an armory in Chicago, predicting that the war might last longer than many could then imagine. He saw that such

[25] "Das nichtsnutzige Concern, 'New Orleans Deutsche Zeitung' Genannt, interessiert wenn man so sagen kann, durch die ungewöhnliche Kechheit mit welcher sie zu Gunsten des Secessionsschwindels in die Trompete stosst, sie ist förmlich verliebt in den Hochverrath und indem sie die deutschen Bürger für die Sonderbundesbewegung bearbeitet, scheint sie sich auf jene Philosophie zu stützen, welche nau-schurkisch fragt: 'Wozu sich dis Mannreihe denn da, als um geschworen zu werden?' " *Ibid.,* February 27, 1861.

[26] The editor seemed to feel that the New Orleans *Louisiana Staats-Zeitung* was a Judas to the Union. For a coarse diatribe against the New Orleans *Deutsche Zeitung,* see *ibid.,* May 24, 1861. But see also the praise bestowed on *Die Union* of Galveston, *ibid.,* December 28, 1861.

On March 19, 1861, the Chicago paper estimated the strength of the Confederate army at eleven regiments altogether, or about 11,000 men, commanded by four brigadiers; and it estimated the strength of the Confederate navy at 600 marines with four commodores and four captains.

The editorial closed with two lines of poetry:

> Reisst die Kranze aus der Erden,
> Lasst die alle Schwerter werden.

And then it added, "What the poets sing, the German people can accomplish." *Ibid.,* April 16, 1861,

a regiment would probably be welcome to the Americans because the experience which many German-Americans had had in the revolution of 1848 would be an advantage; that German leaders in Illinois to command the regiment would not be lacking; and that they could thus assure for the Germans who participated in the war a share in making the peace.[27]

The editor of this paper seemed to feel impelled to vindicate his nationality; for he declared a few weeks later that the Germans who were serving voluntarily under the rebel flag were very few and that the scoundrels who had sold their pens to preach treason in the German tongue against their second Fatherland were, "God be praised," only a few individuals. Every nation produces mercenaries for which it cannot be held responsible.[28]

The organ of the Germans of St. Paul and Minneapolis, the *Minnesota Staats-Zeitung,* was just as determined in support of the Union. It became oratorical in its first issue after the fall of Sumter:

> When dishonored the glorious banner of the republic sank on Fort Sumter's walls, there sank also, thanks to our good fortune, the banner of party strife in the free realm of the North. The Southern traitors had counted on help from the Northern Democrats, but honor prevented. . . . warm thanks are due from every patriotic heart to the Democrats; honor to its [*sic*] leaders! They have extended their hands to their Republican brothers; and shoulder to shoulder in closed ranks we now offer defiance to the hordes of traitors. Defiance, defiance in battle for victory or defeat!
>
> Never, never will the time come, when—so has the tycoon of the breeders of slaves boasted—the flag of treason will wave on the dome of the capitol; for united is the mighty North; there are no longer parties, except patriots and traitors, and the patriots stand with the administration.[29]

Near the border, except in the national capital, a spirit of caution, if not hidden sympathy with the Southern point of view, was manifest. Dur-

[27] *Ibid.,* April 20, 1861. "Die Deutschen in Cincinnati haben ebenfalls bereits die Errichtung eines vollständigen deutschen Regiments beschlossen, und Chicago wird nicht zurückstehen wollen." The paper was ready with the name of a leader to command the regiment— August Mersey, who had been active in organizing the militia in Belleville, Illinois, and who attained some distinction in the war. He had served in the army of Baden but went over to the revolutionists in 1848. For the army and prediction of a war of some length, see *ibid.,* May 2, 1861.

[28] *Ibid.,* May 7, 1861.

[29] St. Paul *Minnesota Staats-Zeitung,* April 20, 1861.

ing the election campaign of 1860, the *Tägliche Metropole* of Washington did not fear secession. "Will then the élite of the South in this case [Lincoln's election] separate from the North? No, certainly not. In the threats of the South there does not lie half the irritation and earnestness which one met everywhere before the last election, in their speech [*i. e.,* that of the Southerners] as in the press; they have gradually accustomed themselves to the thought of seeing the reins of control of the Union sometime in other hands and to find the cry of separation silenced. Desire for the dissolution of the Union on the part of the South, for abolition on the part of the extremists of the North and of all sorts of extremism will fall into the background, and the extreme parties will continue to exist in the Union in a peaceful way, even if with a certain mistrust." [30] On October 30, this paper stated its position, which was indeed that of most Germans: "We Germans are no friends of slavery, but it by no means follows that we shall become sectional fanatics. What we are and what we have—our freedom, our existence as independent men and citizens, we owe to the Union; the future of our children depends on the Union; without the Union no more immigration! With the Union breaks down the last asylum of the oppressed of the entire globe. And therefore must the Germans in the northern tiers of [Southern] states stand for the united and undivided Union." [31] On November 17, this paper reluctantly admitted that all the letters from the cotton states left no doubt that they would secede, "with the possible exception of Louisiana." [32]

Nowhere in the foreign-language press appears a finer plea than in the columns of this paper early in December, 1860: "Let us lay down our

[30] The Washington *Tägliche Metropole* was against slavery and for Lincoln. "Wir haben so viel Vertrauen zu der Einsicht der Anführer der Republikanischen Partei, dass wir nicht befürchten, dass sie die Dinge so auf die Spitze treiben würden, um den Süden zu zwingen, aus dem Staatsbund auszuscheiden." *Ibid.,* October 13, 1860. See also the issue of October 6, 1860.

[31] On October 29 the *Tägliche Metropole* printed a number of belligerent excerpts from Southern papers: Charleston *Mercury,* St. Augustine *Examiner,* Montgomery *Georgia Republican,* and Montgomery *Daily Mail,* all breathing defiance in regard to the election. The next day it printed extracts from Northern papers: Washington *Commercial Advertizer,* Cincinnati *Gazette,* St. Louis *Democrat.* It rejoiced in being able to say that with a few exceptions the German press, fighting Northern fanatics as well as Southerners, was following a peaceful path favorable to the Union. It wished to hold fast to the constitutional principles on which the founding fathers had planted the republic. Washington *Tägliche Metropole,* October 29, 30, 1860.

[32] Why Louisiana should be regarded as an exception does not appear, but *Der Westbote,* of Columbus, Ohio (September 7, 1861), seemed to think it could have been saved to the Union if the Republicans in Congress had met Louisiana in a spirit of conciliation.

previous political dissensions on the altar of the Union. Let us forget that we were Democrats or Republicans; let us be American citizens who love the happiness, the welfare, the greatness of this land and especially the foundation of all these blessings—the Constitution and Union—above everything and we shall have fulfilled our duty as human beings and freemen, as sons of the greatest republic, the terror of the despots of the old world, to the satisfaction of ourselves and of posterity." [33]

Another Washington paper, *Washingtoner Intelligenzblatt,* sees the role of the foreign-born as important: "We immigrant [*eingewanderte*] citizens have the holy duty to throw ourselves into the breach and to preserve the Union and the Constitution, these great legacies of the Revolution, for the future. The native Americans are demoralized physically and spiritually. Love, true attachment for this land is entirely lacking. They are unworthy of the freedom, the inheritance of their fathers. They do not understand free institutions, because to them the difference between freedom and despotism is unknown. To us immigrants it is reserved to save this land from destruction. And we will do it!" [34]

There were definitely two points of view reflected in the eastern part of Maryland—that is, in Baltimore. This study is not concerned with descendants of Germans who had been born in this country, such as the Maryland Germans living in the western part of the state. Since Baltimore represented the southernmost outpost of Republicanism, it was the home of some of the most ardent adherents of that party, including Germans. But the sharp focus of the border also turned German Democrats into some of the most radical secessionist members of that group. The cleavage of the Germans came along sociological lines. The wealthy Germans, usually long resident here and bound to the South by business ties of the tobacco trade, were often Southern sympathizers; but immigrants, recently arrived from Germany, usually of the middle or lower stratum of society and likely to be associated with the Turner movement, generally identified themselves with the cause of the Union.

The two German newspapers of Baltimore reflect these divergent views: *Der Deutsche Correspondent,* founded in 1841 by Friedrich Raine, a man so thoroughly rooted in the Democratic party by 1861 that he never forsook it, states the conservative view; *Der Wecker,* founded by Carl Hein-

[33] Washington *Tägliche Metropole,* December 6, 1861.

[34] *Washingtoner Intelligenzblatt,* July 7, 1860. But a little later the paper declared that it was madness to console oneself that the Southern states could be preserved in the Union by force of arms; if affairs once went so far, the republic of free citizens had ended, and the period of military rule and dictatorship had begun. *Ibid.,* July 21, 1860.

rich Schnauffer and continued after his death in 1857 by his family, is the spokesman for the Unionist sympathizers. The latter insistently advocated "preservation of the Union" and held that adopted citizens must do their share for its preservation. The editor—though originally inclined, like most German editors, toward William H. Seward—consistently supported Lincoln from his nomination to his death and advocated the freeing of the slaves, but to avoid endangering the only progressive sheet in Maryland, he imposed on his pen moderation in his editorials.[35]

The editor of the *Correspondent,* somewhat like Germans of the Confederacy, was cautious. While loyal to the Union, he deplored the cry of irrepressible conflict, repudiated both parties, and wanted restoration of the Constitution as founded by the fathers. Early in the war he expressed the view that no state had the right to secede, but he classed in that same category for prohibition that "aggressive, fanatical and sectional political theory" which had contributed so much to the existing danger. More explicit is this statement a few months later:

> The German adopted citizens of Baltimore and Maryland regret the war and the teaching of the irrepressible conflict; they stand, however, after the present situation had become unavoidable, on the side of loyalty and follow without bitterness the lamentable scenes which the drama of war unrolls before our eyes. They wish peace under guarantees of a better future; they advocate freedom and the Constitution as they were founded by the fathers of our republic and look toward the New Year with hopes of reconciliation, of a rescue from the fate which threatens to prepare for the American people the same fate as for the oppressed of the old world. On the old parties, as they exist up to the present time, rests a curse; therefore we adhere to neither, but we shall always honorably dedicate our strength to that which is beneficial for conservation, that which maintains but does

[35] For the views of the editor of the Baltimore *Wecker* toward the Union, see issues of that paper of January 28, April 12, August 31, 1861. For attitude toward Lincoln, see issues of May 16, May 18, November 1, 1860; June 13, 1864; April 15, 1865. For opinion on slavery as sanctioned by the Bible, see the issue of January 14, 1864. The clear note of support of Lincoln struck by this editor at the second election must have been a solace to Lincoln, if he ever saw the editorial: "Eins bleibt unbestritten—seine Ehrlichkeit, seine Festigkeit und seine nie schwankende Hingebung für die Sache der Union und der menschlichen Freiheit." *Ibid.,* June 13, 1864.

The freethinking so characteristic of many Germans at that time comes out in his editorial on Walther's defense of slavery on Biblical grounds. He answers Walther, he states, not because *"wir auf eine Beweisführung aus der Bibel irgend welches Gewicht legten,"* but because there are Lutheran servants of the Gospels who do not shun to justify the rape of men. He also states flatly that an abolitionist could not be a Lutheran. *Ibid.,* January 14, 1864.

not destroy, that which saves the nation and nationality, but does not turn them into a football of ambition and corruption and finally annihilates them.[36]

Der Westbote of Columbus, Ohio, an ardently Democratic sheet, supported Douglas and, on October 11, rejoiced over the victory of the entire Democratic county ticket and over the Democratic local victories in the southern part of the state. "Each patriot must," it declared on October 25, "regard the election of a sectional president, whereby the peace of the land—yes, the stability of the Union—would be injured, as a great misfortune, and he must do his utmost to avert such a threatening storm from our beloved land. We believe that the friends of the Union in Ohio can thwart the election of Lincoln on November 6 if they unite their strength at one point." [37] It did not conceal its disappointment at the result of the election; but it hoped that the South, which had brought about this result, would for the most part resign itself to the inevitable and await quietly and calmly the development of affairs. It reminded Southerners that the Republican regime in any case could not last more than four years.[38]

Immediately after the election, the *Westbote* was inclined to blame the North for the situation, accusing it of violating the law for rendition of runaway slaves, an act which thus made Northerners the practical nullifiers and disunionists. Also, it condemned abolition as "an illness—a swindle, which overpowered at the last election the heads of our formerly intelligent people." [39] Of its devotion to the Union, however, there can be no question. As early as November 22 it proclaimed that "it is the duty of

[36] Baltimore *Der Deutsche Correspondent,* August 10, 1861. This paper was the first German paper in the United States to adopt the make-up of the American press.

[37] This paper spoke very sharply against the German leaders who supported Lincoln. It commented on how Hecker, who had campaigned for Frémont, had remained advisedly at home in 1860 and interpreted this action as indicating that he had no taste for the "Republican humbug politics." On Carl Schurz it poured out much scorn. "Der jetzt der Herrgott der deutschen Republikaner ist, und neben dem es gar keine anderen Götter giebt," Columbus (Ohio) *Westbote,* November 1, 1860. Earlier it had stated, "Wir wissen nicht, wer diesen Karl Schurz das Recht gegeben hat, zu behaupten, dass die Deutschen bereit sind, mit der Muskete auf der Schulter den Yankee-Fanatikern in ihrem Kreuzzuge gegen den Süden beizustehen, aber das wissen wir dass eine solche, durchaus unbesonnene und unpassende Sprache im Munde eines Deutschen wohl geeignet ist den schlummerden Know-Nothinggeist wachzurufen." *Ibid.,* October 25, 1861.

[38] *Ibid.,* November 8, 1860. The editor of *Der Westbote* was Jacob Reinhard.

[39] "So sprachen die gemassigten Leute im Süden und man muss gestehen, dass sie das Recht auf ihrer Seite haben." *Ibid.,* November 29, 1860. See also issues of November 8 and 22, 1860.

every patriot to do all in his power to avert the danger and extinguish the brand, which threatens to destroy the Union of free and independent states and to bury the hopes of millions under its ruins." It declared that the mass of the German citizens were true to the Union "to the last breath"; and it felt that the number of crazed fanatics and demagogues who would lure the Union to its grave, "in the North as in the South," was very small.[40] As late as April 25 it showed still a trace of faint hope that the South might be deterred from secession; it felt that the inspiring response of the North to the call to arms would exert "a highly wholesome and chilling influence on the South, if it were not entirely deluded." [41] It urged all Democrats, as citizens and sons of the republic, to do their duty, as "party labels have at this moment no meaning." [42] Beginning with the issue of October 9, 1861, this paper displayed on page two the American flag as an emblem and the country surrounded by waves to symbolize a storm. This emblem of loyalty appeared in each number until March 27, 1862.

The *Volksfreund,* a Cincinnati sheet, professed not to be disturbed by the turn of events in the winter of 1860–1861 and predicted that South Carolina, like Texas, would soon weary of its single lone star. By April it had to recognize the fact that war had begun; this it did with the Latin phrase, "Jacta est Alea," though it distributed the blame. "So the extremists of the North and South have finally succeeded in reaching the goal toward which they have so long and zealously striven," it commented. "War has begun, begun by the South itself with insolent hand. When and how it will end, rests in the dark bosom of the future. May its days be shortened! May the Union and freedom, which dwells in its shadow, happily survive this crisis and soon again stand in its full integrity, in its old splendor of victory and may a wholesome lesson proceed out of a sad, even now unknown past." [43] Then the paper showed its horror of the

---

[40] For faith in the Union, see *ibid.*, December 13, 1860. On December 20 it printed a poem entitled "Die Union jetzt! Die Union für immer!"

[41] The editor appended a note which said that since the above had been written, sad news had arrived and that a "deadly war seemed inevitable." It concluded, "Nun, mit Gott für die Constitution, die Union und Sternenbanner gegen alle Rebellen und Feinde," *Ibid.*, April 25, 1861.

[42] *Ibid.* "Wir sagen Allen, die etwas darauf gezweifelt haben mögen—und wir sagen es aus Überzeugung—dass die Demokraten in dieser trüben Stunde, als Bürger, als Söhne der Republik, ihre Pflicht thun werden. Sie werden die Regierung in allen constitutionellen Unternehmungen zur Erhaltung der Union, zur Behauptung der Constitution, zur Vertheidigung der Bundes-Hauptstadt unterstützen." *Ibid.*

[43] Cincinnati *Volksfreund,* January 1, April 13, 1861.

act which had just occurred in Charleston Harbor. "How shall one designate the unheard of audacity, the shocking defiance, the unexampled brutality of this attack? Even moderation and patience, which formerly so well clothed the stronger as opposed to the weaker, have their limits, which they may not overstep, without shaming themselves. The dignity of the federal government, the security of the free citizens and the insulted majesty of the law demand satisfaction and punishment, and then—not in blind revenge, we hope—the entire remainder of the Union will stand of one mind as one man." [44]

It is, of course, impossible to ignore so influential a paper as the *New Yorker Staats-Zeitung* under the editorship of Oswald Ottendorfer. It will be recalled that this paper had not been at all disturbed over the slavery question in 1856. Although Ottendorfer resigned from the National Democratic Committee in 1860, thus breaking with his party, he was not a converted Republican, and was very gloomy in the opening days of the year 1861. Unfortunately, no issues of this paper for this critical period seem to have survived; but we are able to catch a reflection of its attitude through a quotation from it in the Cincinnati *Volksfreund* of January 3, 1861: "How do matters now stand? If a favorable turn does not appear in a few days, which one scarcely any longer dares hope, then before the Republican administration takes the rudder, the South will stand opposed to it as a unity armed for battle, while the people of the North are divided and disunited. The Republican politicians and their tools, who protest at every compromise, will find that they have miscalculated lamentably —and we all, regardless of which political faith we have or had, must suffer under it." While the New York editor seemed to support the Union, he was never sympathetic to the administration and finally went over to Governor Seymour. It is probably to the credit of New York Germans that they were so little influenced by the views reflected by this leading editor.

It will be sufficient, in connection with the attitude of the French element of the population, to study the views of the *Courrier des États-Unis,* though it did not in truth reflect the views of a majority of the Frenchmen living in the United States, if we are to judge them by their deeds. The editor, understandably enough, had no patience with the inaction of the Buchanan administration and cried out in disgust:

> This which is happening in the United States must be a subject of profound astonishment and very little flattering to American renown.

[44] *Ibid.,* April 13, 1861.

What judgment is to be passed, in fact, upon a government—rather upon a purely political organization—which passively allowed itself to be invaded, to be overrun by revolution, without even knowing how to look it in the face?

Since the 8th of November—that is to say for more than two months—the same dilemma presented itself each morning: either to deal with the disunionist movement or to repress it.[45]

This editor was, however, irrevocably opposed to war. After war had actually come, he wrote: "The honor of the flag, irrevocably involved, makes war a necessity today; that we comprehend. But we are among those who submit to it without approving it because, in our opinion, it was not inevitable; because, above all, the deplorable struggle which is beginning is fatally condemned to produce only bitter and sterile results. On whichever side victory aligns itself, we see in perspective only sorrow for the whole world without joy to anyone, without hope of a better future for the price of the sacrifice encountered and the blood spilled." [46] In July the same paper expressed the view that far from repulsing the idea of a convention, which had been proposed, "the government and its friends ought to be the first to desire it, to solicit that assembly. Convinced, as they are, that their politics correspond to the view of an immense majority, they ought not to have any embarrassment to dread from an assembly which will be necessarily the organ of that same majority." [47] On July 24, a few days after the Battle of Bull Run had been lost by the Union forces, it expressed its profound conviction that the South would never be reduced by force of arms. It attributed the same opinion to the leaders of the party conducting the war and concluded that they did not wish any such idea to penetrate to the masses because the nation would then refuse to follow them. Hence arose maneuvers to blind the people to the real proportions of the war. The paper recurred to the view that the government should have ready propositions of peace and compromise for the seceded states.[48]

Such views, when coupled with insistence on freedom of speech, naturally brought criticism. The New York *Tribune* attacked the *Courrier des États-Unis* on August 23, declaring that it was pleading the cause

[45] New York *Courrier des États-Unis*, January 12, 1861.

[46] *Ibid.*, April 16, 1861.　　　　　　　　[47] *Ibid.*, July 3, 1861.

[48] "As our government has been founded and maintained by a system of compromise, it could never be dishonorable for an administration to seek to reestablish the government by the same means." *Ibid.*, August 10, 1861. See also issue of August 22, in which freedom of speech was demanded.

of secession. Its reply was to defy the *Tribune* to cite a single article which could be called traitorous. Thereupon, a petition for the suppression of the *Courrier,* for Copperhead sympathies, signed by over a hundred Frenchmen, and published by the *Tribune,* made its appearance. The *Courrier* rejoiced that the right of petition had not been lost! [49] An exchange of letters between the editor, E. Masseras, and the proprietor, Charles Lessale, in which the former proposed that the paper be reduced to printing only the news, closed the incident. The editor's last letter bears the terse remark, "J'opte pour le silence"; and therewith he withdrew temporarily from the paper.[50]

Meanwhile, however, the French residents of New York City had expressed themselves emphatically immediately after word of the attack on Fort Sumter had penetrated through the country. A number of French residents, among whom Messrs. Frémont, Quesne, and Faidu were prominent, held a conference preliminary to a general meeting of French citizens for their organization to participate in the war. Frémont offered resolutions tendering the support of French citizens to the Federal government and expressed the hope that the government would guarantee total extinction of slavery.[51]

In the Norwegians we encounter a strong, resolute, stubborn people. It was almost inevitable that they, as determined individualists and lovers of freedom, would uphold the Union cause against the secessionists once the issue became clear. In January, 1861, one of the leading Norwegian papers was already boldly referring to the disturbances in the South as "Rebellion in the South." The file of the Madison *Emigranten,* the most important of the Norwegian papers of this period, may be scanned for the attitude of at least one prominent Norwegian editor, C. F. Solberg, and indirectly for the views of many Norwegians.[52]

Faedrelandet, published in La Crosse, Wisconsin, by Frederick Fleischer and Johan Schroder, throws light on Norwegian opinion for the later period of the war, as it issued its first number on January 14, 1864. In that

[49] See New York *Tribune,* May 18, August 31, and September 2, 1861; and the New York *Times,* May 3, 1861.

[50] This terse phrase, which rang down the curtain, appeared in the New York *Courrier des États-Unis,* September 2, 1861. Masseras repeated gloomily what he had said earlier, "J'ai la conviction que la guerre ne sauvera pas l'Union et qu'en revanche elle perdre la Republique."

[51] Moore (ed.), *Rebellion Record,* I, Pt. 1, p. 48.

[52] Between 1850 and 1860 no less than eight Norwegian papers made their appearance in this country (all but two were published in Wisconsin), but none survived long. Fortunately, an almost complete file of the *Emigranten* is available at Luther College Library, Decorah, Iowa.

first number it declared itself an independent Union paper, standing for truth and justice, and, at the time, for the policies of Abraham Lincoln and "nothing else." In other words, it stood for the preservation of the Union and the freeing of the slaves. The instant reaction of the *Emigranten* to the attack on Fort Sumter was recognition of the necessity of forgetting partisanship and party strife.[53] Nowhere in the American press was the war brought home more insistently to its readers. The issue of April 14 carried Lincoln's call for 75,000 men in bold type; the issue of April 22 stated dramatically: *"Landet er i Fare! Krig! Krig! Till Vaaben, till Vaaben!"* [54]

This same issue carried Governor Alexander W. Randall's proclamation of April 16 in Norwegian to Wisconsin's loyal citizens. It carried also a stirring editorial appeal to Norwegians to do their part:

> Countrymen! almost before we know it, we are plunged into the midst of the most significant war that has ever been waged in any land. The rebels have not permitted themselves to hold back because of the patience and forbearance of the Union. They have struck the first blow and they neither could nor wished to halt before they either laid the Union in ashes or are themselves brought to naught. There is no question of party power or principle. It is the country's safety, preservation of our popular form of government, preservation of our civic and religious freedom and in consequence also our temporal welfare that is at stake. Every enlightened man in the North feels that, and everyone with a heart in the right place knows also what his duty is. Countrymen! Shall we Norse do our part of this duty or shall we remain merely onlookers, while our American, German, or Irish fellow-citizens do it for us and spare us from what belongs to all of us. . . .
>
> To arms, you young men, if there is the spirit of the Fatherland in you; the Union demands that. The foe stands not at the door; he is in the house itself. Do not fear, lest your cause is not just, for if ever a war was righteous, then is this one; if God were ever with the fighter, then He is with the American soldier in this war, for this is a war with traitors, a war for all that is good, right, and true in America, a war for self-defense.[55]

---

[53] The press of this paper was halted Sunday afternoon, April 14, to add late news. The appeal to eliminate partisanship appeared in the issue of April 22 with the declaration that there were only two parties after the attack on Fort Sumter—patriots and traitors.

[54] "The country is in danger! War! War! To Arms! To Arms!"

[55] The entire editorial is stirring and well worth quoting. One additional excerpt may appear here in the notes: "In our settlements in the Northwestern states there are hundreds of

Like the *Westbote,* the *Emigranten* displayed at its masthead, so to speak, a small American flag. This appeared, beginning April 27, 1861, on the second page at the head of the war news, and continued to appear every day throughout the war and even later.

Oddly enough, while the Norwegians have always been recognized as one of the peoples most devoted to freedom, the American-Norwegians became involved in a bitter dispute over the position assumed by a Professor Larsen and some of his colleagues at Concordia College, the German-Lutheran theological seminary in St. Louis, regarding the position taken on the question of slavery and secession. Here Norwegian students were then being trained for the Lutheran ministry. Influenced possibly by the presentation and defense of the Southern attitude to which they were exposed in the border state of Missouri, a group at the seminary reached the conclusion that though every rebellion is sin, they did not know whether secession was rebellion. Larsen held that if the governor of Wisconsin asked him to serve in the South as a soldier, he would do it to prove his obedience to authority.

At the conference of the north Wisconsin synod of the Norwegian Lutheran Church at Rock Prairie from June 26 to July 2, 1861, the entire question of slavery and secession was discussed and left in deeper confusion than ever, since the members of the committee which had been considering the situation at Concordia Seminary were divided in their report. The three clergymen on the committee would have preferred to have students from the Wisconsin synod continue their work at St. Louis, but the five laymen on the committee voted to begin instruction of their own even before the synod's building was ready. By a refinement of reasoning which the lay members did not pretend to understand, the clergymen held that slavery was no sin, a decision shortly afterwards revised to the statement that "slave-holding is not in itself a sin, but a great wrong." [56]

---

stout, strong, young men, who without depriving any family of its support or stopping any public business can shoulder their muskets and place themselves at the government's disposal. Let these go first, and if more should be needed, then let the older men lay aside the plow and spade and fill the ranks. Our country is, indeed, not the one in which we were born but it is not the less now our Fatherland, and shame on him who does not regard it with filial affection." Madison *Emigranten,* April 22, 1861.

[56] This controversy occupied much space in the *Emigranten.* See issues of June 13, 15, 1861. The *Hemlandet* was naturally interested in this controversy which tore a fellow Lutheran synod. The Swedish paper reported with much amusement an incident in connection with the marriage of the foremost Norwegian clergyman in Wisconsin. On the evening following his wedding a crowd of unruly youths gathered outside his home and started a frightful noise.

The editor of the *Emigranten,* however, shared with many of his readers an unhesitating opinion on the question of slavery. Flatly he stated
that "American slavery is dishonorable." "The worst of slavery, our greatest civic wrong, is that it is an absolute foe of republican institutions, and
that is ground enough to place it first in the reckoning among the things
against which we contend. Naturally, human sympathy and conviction
that the use of slavery here in this land has always been in ninety out of a
hundred cases in a high degree harmful both for the slaves and for the
country increase the strength of the opposition." Then the editor goes on
to deny the right of any man to bind for life another man and his descendants to him and his descendants "without sinning." Yet this paper also
says that the Republican party was not necessarily founded on the idea
that slavery as an abstract conception was sin.[57]

While the country moved into war, the thought of the Norwegians—
of privates and civilians as well as of officers and leaders—crystallized into
a definite, clear-cut conviction that the Union must be upheld, the Constitution maintained, the old Union—the Union as established "by Washington"—preserved, and the laws executed over the whole land. Norwegians were frequently reminded by their leaders and papers that as
citizens they had obligations to discharge as well as privileges to enjoy.

In general there was little difference in the attitude of the Swedes and
that of the Norwegians toward slavery and secession. Serious, with a deep
religious sense, which often partook of the puritanical attitude as compared with the laxity of German Lutheranism, even though they were
affiliated with the same creed, the Swedes were naturally deeply and
thoughtfully affected by the slavery controversy. Indeed, they found it
difficult to understand any position other than one of opposition. In addition they were unusually adaptable to American conditions; and as they
acquired a stake in the government by their acquisition of property, they
felt themselves a part of America and under obligation to share her
problems and the burdens of citizenship. Much as the Swedes loved the
land of their birth, they wished to share in the election of officials and
would probably have sought naturalization even without the impetus of
the Homestead Law, which required citizenship in order to take up a land

---

Offended and indignant, the pastor hurried out to denounce it as an outrage and a sin. "No,
Herr Pastor," replied the crowd, "not a sin, but a great wrong." Chicago *Hemlandet,* February 26, 1862.

[57] Madison *Emigranten,* June 13, 1861. In one construction the translation is not literal
but conveys the meaning.

claim. Industrious, law-abiding, and clear-thinking, they considered the secession question so integrally related to the slavery question as to be essentially one question. With an innate integrity which could not evade the slavery issue, they faced it squarely and lined up almost solidly against it.

The high rate of literacy among them, a heritage from the homeland, made them readers of their own outstanding papers, especially their religious paper, *Hemlandet* (The Homeland), so that there was no dodging the issue. This paper was founded and edited, first at Galesburg, Illinois, and then at Chicago, by a Swedish Lutheran pastor, the Reverend T. N. Hasselquist, a politically-minded man who had firm convictions and believed in letting them be known. This paper was stanchly antislavery and was influential, without doubt, in leading the Swedish element of the population into the newly created Republican party before the war.[58] Oddly enough, *Hemlandet* had justified the attack of the Know-Nothing party on the "wild Irish," on Catholicism, and on the "irreligious Germans," who desecrated the Sabbath with their beer gardens and merrymakings. It was natural as breathing for the Swedish immigrant to favor that party which advocated free homesteads, for he too came here land-hungry.

These factors accepted, it followed as a matter of course that the vast majority of Swedes would support Lincoln for President. Some Swedish churches actually flew American and Swedish flags from their spires in the presidential campaign of 1860. Just as to the German mind the name "Democrat" connoted a certain pleasing liberalism, so to the average Swede the name "Republican" meant opposition to monarchy and special privilege and seemed to reflect his own political faith. Although an initial gesture toward the Democratic party had been made by the earliest settlers, the Swedes forsook that party when it advocated extension of slavery. By denouncing any change in the naturalization law, the first Republican platform won the Swedish vote for Frémont.

---

[58] A Swede who had always voted the Democratic ticket expressed gratitude to the editor in a letter which was printed in the Chicago *Hemlandet*, January 16, 1861: "Yes, I think it a shame for Swedish nationals, almost each one of whom will acknowledge that he has been reared in what one calls sound christianity and has learned the difference between freedom and thraldom," to come over to America when grown and vote for the extension of slavery.

He felt that Swedes in the homeland who read about it would think that his countrymen had become wholly mad since arriving in America.

When a Swede in Mississippi wrote the *Hemlandet* a letter published in the issue of January 16, 1861, condemning as lies what appeared in the North about slavery, the editor merely marveled that "our friend does not wish to be a slave."

Lincoln, as a man of the soil who had toiled with his hands, had an understandable appeal for Swedish laborers. The Swedes with their Wide-Awake Clubs, campaigned vigorously for the Republican party and under their own political and religious leaders helped to put Abraham Lincoln in the White House.[59] Likewise, in 1864 Swedes lined up almost solidly for Lincoln's re-election. Some idea of their unanimity is indicated by the fact that at Moline, Illinois, the naturalized Swedish citizens met on election day in 1864 to cast their votes unitedly for Lincoln and the Union. From Red Wing, Minnesota, came the report that Scandinavians had voted for "Freedom, Right and Truth, and Swedish Honor." At the Swedish settlement of Vasa, Minnesota, only 7 Democratic votes were cast, 5 Irish and 2 Swedish; at Cannon Falls, which was full of Copperheads, Swedish farmers saved the day; and at Holden, settled by *Nörrman* (Northmen or Norwegians) only 1 Democratic ballot was cast out of 141 votes.[60] In all likelihood the Swedish vote was too small to contribute much to Lincoln's first victory, but it probably was a somewhat more important factor in 1864.

The Swedish paper exulted over Lincoln's victory in 1860 in the following words: "There is still hope for freedom, uprightness, and purity. Let fears and mistrust be banished. Let every friend of the fatherland fan the flames that now rise from freedom's altar in his fatherland. Let people cry with joy, the battle is fought and victory won." [61] By the close of the month this paper was frankly facing the fact of possible disunion: "The zeal with which these disunionists seize on Lincoln's election as a pretext

---

[59] The Reverend T. N. Hasselquist, strong supporter of the Republican party, served as vice-president at a Republican mass meeting at Galesburg, Illinois, on June 7, 1856; the Reverend J. Johnson was one of the campaign speakers in 1860. Hokanson, *Swedish Immigrants,* 57, 59. Swedish clergymen did not eschew politics. The *Hemlandet,* beginning with the issue of October 17, 1860, through the remainder of that month printed the full Republican ticket. On October 31, it cried, "Kom ihåg waldgen Tisdag (Remember the election next Tuesday)." In an editorial it emphasized the fact that the choice lay between Lincoln and Breckinridge, North and South, as Douglas was no longer in the race.

[60] For the election of 1864, see Hokanson, *Swedish Immigrants,* 63–64; Chicago *Hemlandet,* December 7, 1864. Of course, the Swedes did not unanimously support Lincoln any more than did the Germans. A Democratic club was formed among Swedes in Chicago in March, 1863, under the leadership of Captain E. G. Lange, and was promptly rebuked by the editor of the *Hemlandet* and by some Swedish soldiers. A Democratic club was also organized among the Swedes in the Bergholm settlement in Rapello County, Iowa, to be in its turn anathematized by Chicago Swedes at a meeting of July 19, 1860. Hokanson, *Swedish Immigrants,* 63, 67.

[61] Chicago *Hemlandet,* November 7, 1860. A meticulous enumeration of the vote in the different states appeared in this paper, so that it differed little at this time from a political paper. The editor could not refrain from a fling at Douglas, his paper reporting that the "poor man" had carried the state of Mississippi in the election. *Ibid.*

to secede from the Union and the fact that they thus immediately, at least in South Carolina, set the game in motion, prove that far from being averse to dissolving the federation, this should appear far more their dearest desire." But the editor deceived himself in believing that only the states with slavery would join South Carolina, probably only Alabama.[62] By January he, like many others, was thoroughly disgusted with the existing administration: "Nothing of all that has happened during this period presents such an extraordinary appearance as that the government in Washington, both the president and his cabinet, knowingly play into the hands of the rebels all they are able. When did one ever see a government fight thus against itself?" [63] *Hemlandet* took the news of the war calmly, remarking that while war, and especially civil war, was nothing over which to rejoice, the certainty of war was better than the torture of uncertainty.[64] Lincoln's first call, translated into Swedish, appeared in the same number.

The Swedes took the debacle of Bull Run in their stride. The defeat should serve merely to awaken a deeper love of country and put the armies under better discipline, to dispel overconfidence, to remove incompetent officers, and to improve the arrangements for supplying the army. When these preparations should have been made and the armies moved forward under a leader gifted with youth and genius, who had received his command more for ability than age, the victories of the republic would commence.[65]

As the war dragged on unsuccessfully, however, this paper which had been so ardent for Lincoln's election did not cavil to criticize him. "But this [the inactivity of McClellan] is evidence of an extraordinary weakness and lack of independence in President Lincoln, who himself is ex-officio the army's highest commander,—that he lets McClellan carry on unchecked the command over an army of 600,000, which first and foremost is too large for him, and, in the second place, should not be handled as is now the case. Furthermore, the government's war politics are so vacillating and uncertain that each general can act almost as he wishes." [66]

The attitudes of the lesser nationality groups may be quickly summed up. During the fifties many of the Hollanders of Michigan, originally

[62] *Ibid.*, November 28, 1860.   [63] *Ibid.*, January 4, 1861.

[64] *Ibid.*, April 17, 1861.

[65] *Ibid.*, August 7, 1861. When a Swedish brig fell into United States hands for trying to run the blockade, the *Hemlandet* merely remarked that it served the owner right. *Ibid.*, August 27, 1862.

[66] *Ibid.*, February 5, 1862.

Democrats, shifted slowly to the Republican party. In 1860 Douglas carried Holland township over Lincoln by the tiny margin of twenty-three votes. The Reverend Albertus Van Raalte had urged his followers to vote Republican largely because of the slavery issue, despite the fact that Hollanders, like the Germans, entertained suspicions concerning the alleged affiliation between Republicans and Know-Nothings. It is said that as a result of rapid decline in numbers, the Dutch Democratic Club of Grand Rapids in a Democratic parade in 1860 had to ride in a coach with the Irish.[67] The Dutch of Pella, Iowa, however, were and remained consistent Democrats, despite the fact that Henry P. Scholte, the leader who had brought them to their promised land, served as a delegate to the Republican convention in 1860.[68]

When it is recalled that the Hungarian aristocrats had freed their serfs in 1848 and had then fought side by side with them for the liberation of Hungary, their mystification over the American situation is intelligible. They could not understand the continued existence of slavery in the free and democratic United States nor the phenomenon of millions of Americans fighting for its preservation. The few exiles who came to the United States in response to our invitation did not care to settle in the slave states. Their attitude regarding slavery was clearly stated by David Black, one of their pioneers, who settled in Cleveland on the eve of the war. Black said that Hungarian aristocrats had given up their rights and property for the freedom of all Hungarians, while in America the southern rebels were ready to fight to prevent the liberation of their slaves.[69] The Hungarians thus add one more bit of evidence that the foreign nationality groups knew what Lincoln stood for and admired him for it. All—Irish, German, Scandinavian, Hungarian, and Dutch—were sufficiently devoted to the cause of the preservation of the Union to be willing to fight for it.

[67] Wittke, *We Who Built America*, 308.

[68] *Ibid.*, 309–10.

[69] Vasvary, *Lincoln's Hungarian Heroes*, 36. The reader is reminded that Ladislaus Ujházy was an exception, for after the death of his wife he moved from Iowa to Texas. See Chapter I. Eugene Piványi, *Hungarians in the American Civil War* (Cleveland, 1913), 8. There were also a few exceptions in Missouri and Louisiana.

CHAPTER THREE

Motives of the Foreign-Born

W E NOW come to the consideration of the precise motives which prompted these foreign-born in our midst to be willing to make the supreme sacrifice of their lives for the Union cause. The motives actuating them were many, varied, and sometimes mixed. Relatively seldom was wholly undiluted devotion to the ideal of liberty the motive, though comparatively seldom, at least during the early years of the war, was that motive entirely absent.

That idealism embraced two clear-cut objectives—preservation of the Union and liberation of the slaves. Many sincerely and intelligently felt that the United States must be preserved "one and inseparable," as Webster had proclaimed, though that phrase was translated into terms of the psychology and background of their separate nationalities. "At last the North was awakened from its slumber," wrote Hans Christian Heg, the Norwegian-born state prison commissioner of Wisconsin, "cast all political differences to the winds, and all are as one in crying: 'To arms for the defense of the old Union, established by Washington. Of the outcome there can be no doubt.' " [1] Although written in connection with the presidential campaign of 1864, a letter from a Norwegian leader to the editor of the Madison *Emigranten* breathes a spirit of devotion to Lincoln because of the ideals he represented: ". . . I prefer to die with the conviction that I have not been unfaithful in time of distress to the oath of allegiance I made my adopted country." [2] Even when thoroughly tired of the war and longing for peace, a Norwegian officer could write on February 28, 1863, that the freeing of the slaves and the preservation of the "best form of government on earth," for present and future generations was a great purpose.[3]

---

[1] We shall meet Heg as colonel of the Scandinavian Regiment, the Fifteenth Wisconsin. See Chapter VI. The above excerpt is from a letter sent to Norway and quoted in a Norwegian paper at Stavanger, Norway.

[2] From a letter from Knut Langland. Printed in the Madison *Emigranten,* October 24, 1864.

[3] This officer was Captain Hans Hanson. He had more to say on the subject: "For my part I

The Germans felt a special compulsion to maintain the unity of their adopted country in its integrity because of the evil effects from disunion under which they had suffered in their homeland. R. A. Witthaus, a German leader in New York, attributed to this factor the spontaneous response of the Germans to the call to the field: "They know too well, from experience in their dear fatherland, what it is to have a country torn asunder and divided into many small kingdoms and principalities; they know full well the insurmountable difficulties to move the commerce, practical [sic] science, manufactures, and agriculture as with one united effort, and while this their adopted country has done for them all in time of prosperity, the German cardinal virtues, 'honesty and gratitude,' prompt them to do all in their power now in its time of need." [4] Many, very many, of the Germans had gone through the hard school of revolution in Europe and knew better than many natives how to treasure the blessing of free institutions. Thus, the German stood opposed to the idea of state rights.

The great majority of the immigrants, and especially their leaders, felt the existence of slavery in the free United States to be a reflection on America; even those Germans who would have tolerated it where it already existed were sternly opposed to its extension.

This same idealism was reflected by practically every nationality represented in the North. It appears in the words of the Scotchman James Todd to the governor of Ohio, "This is the Country of my adoption, and I am ready to sacrifice my life or all I possess in protecting the honor of my Country." Likewise, while sojourning in Libby Prison, the Hungarian Emery Szabad wrote in his diary that he had come to America to fight for the Union, the destruction of which would cause joy to none but tyrants and despots.[5] It is striking indeed to encounter the exalted sentiments expressed by the eighteen-year-old Knute Nelson, who was destined

---

am tired of the whole business and I look with longing eyes to the day when peace shall be declared—not the kind of peace which the so-called Peace Democrats want, but peace won by our armies, which I believe will be the only lasting peace." Waldemar Ager (ed.), *Oberst Heg og hans Gutter ved Waldemar Ager* (Eau Claire, Wis., 1916), 165.

[4] These sentiments were uttered by Witthaus on the occasion of his presentation of flags to the De Kalb Regiment, which he had equipped. Printed in Moore (ed.), *Rebellion Record*, II, Pt. 2, p. 400. See also the New York *Herald*, June 20, 1861. The translation of his speech leaves much to be desired in the way of English.

[5] For Todd's letter to Governor William Dennison, April 16, 1861, see Executive Correspondence of the Governors of Ohio, March–April 15, 1861, Ohio Historical Society, Columbus, Ohio; for the Hungarian's statement, see Emery Szabad, "Diary in Libby Prison," in *Every Saturday*, V (1868), 422.

to fill the gubernatorial chair in Minnesota, in a letter written to his parents: "Gladly will I lay my contribution in my country's lap. If the land flows with blood and lives, so shall it be freed by the same means. That is the best that I can give it. The cause is good and he who dies in a good cause is indeed fortunate. . . . Do not grieve for me; do not take it for certain. Thank God that you could give a life for the country's protection. As the church earlier, so also our country will become greater and stronger in this war." [6] Nowhere is the devotion more touching than in the account of the Swedish youth William P. Esbjörn, who ran away to join the army and sought to conciliate his father, the Reverend Lars P. Esbjörn, father of the Swedish-Lutheran church in America, with the following words: "I had come to the conclusion lately to try to do something *for my Country* and for the poor African race there is news that I think a man of your principles would delight to hear. . . . I think this cause is just and a righteous war and should I meet my Death on the battlefield I feel that I am dying in a glorious cause." It should be recorded that the lad fell at Lexington within five months of the date of this letter. [7]

A righteous indignation seethes through the words of a Canadian who evidently felt his motives impugned. "Why should it be treated as a crime for Canadians to enter the American service? . . . Is not the cause of the United States the cause of civilization and free government? Has any struggle so largely affecting the welfare of mankind in general taken place in any other country on the face of the earth within the present or any former age?" The expressions "holy cause" and "death for right and truth" came glibly to the lips and pens of many soldiers. Fortunately, the adopted sons realized that freedom recognizes no nationality. [8]

Closely related to the idealistic motives which prompted men to fight for the abstract principle of preservation of the Union because that Union represented ideals of freedom was the feeling that the foreign-born must be willing to accept not only the privileges which American citizenship conferred but also its duties, however painful. The editor of *Emigranten,*

[6] For Knute Nelson's letter to his parents, Camp Uttey, Racine, Wisconsin, July 9, 1861, see Knute Nelson Papers, Minnesota Historical Society, St. Paul.

[7] For William E. Esbjörn's letter to his father, April 23, 1861, see Esbjörn Collection, Augustana College Library, Rock Island, Illinois.

[8] This Canadian's name was Arthur Rankin. Moore (ed.), *Rebellion Record,* III, Pt. 2, p. 188. The letter from Knute Nelson to "Good Friend Lars," October 12, 1861, says briefly that he rejoiced to hear that one of his boyhood comrades "goes hand in hand with me in this holy war. He does a service which the land and the country's welfare will thank you for." Knute Nelson Papers.

for instance, wrote in the issue of August 31, 1861, "This brings in remembrance that we must defend the land just as much as our native-born fellow citizens, that we in each relation meet the same privileges as they, and that we therefore also have the same duty to protect the land against inner and outer enemies." Again and again foreigners were told that the Union was in danger of destruction, that only a tremendous effort could save it, and that all those benefiting from its liberality must share in that great effort. Colonel Heg's call upon his fellow Scandinavians to form a Scandinavian regiment in September of 1861 voiced the same feeling:

> The necessity demands stronger efforts than hitherto have been made. . . . In other words, duty becomes more and more imperative and decided for each individual citizen of the large community to take an active share in the defense of the Fatherland. Scandinavians! Let us understand our present position, our duty and our responsibility as we ought to understand them.
>
> We have as yet far from borne our share of war's burdens in respect to delivering troops, which the large proportion of the Scandinavian population here in the country lays upon us as a duty. Individuals among us have gone out with companies from our neighborhoods, but hitherto not in great strength.

Colonel Heg pointed out that the Germans and the Irish had sent whole regiments to the field while the Scandinavians of the West had not sent out a single entire company. He declared that in the future men would ask where the Scandinavians were when men saved the Union.[9]

Integrally linked with the abstract idealism of a love of freedom went the active motive of gratitude. *Der Westbote* expressed this feeling when in 1861 it uttered as its New Year's wish the hope that in the future, as in the past, this republic might afford for the entire globe an asylum in which the persecuted son of the Old World might erect his cottage and dare to cry exultantly: "Hier bin ich Mensch, hier kann ich's sein!"[10] Again and again the foreign-born volunteer, officer or private, voiced his sense of gratitude for the opportunity which he had found in America. Especially was this the case with foreigners in the West, for they were well aware of the friendly attitude assumed by the meagerly populated

---

[9] This view of the hard school of European experience was expressed in the Washington *Tägliche Metropole*, October 29, 1860. For Heg's call, signed by several other Scandinavian leaders, see Madison *Emigranten*, September 30, 1861. For other calls, see Madison *Emigranten*, October 7, 1861.

[10] Columbus *Westbote*, January 2, 1861.

western states toward immigrants. This welcome to immigrants had been expressed in many ways during the decade before the war—during the very period when nativism in the form of the Know-Nothing party had flourished in the East. The West was not, of course, altogether free from nativism; but this attitude was not offensively obvious. Men with the frontiersman's mind and hardihood were welcome; Germans and Scandinavians were regarded as good material. Wladimir Kryzanowsky, a German Pole who appears as an officer in the war, boasted that the flag was loved no more deeply by native than by adopted sons and that the latter would spill their blood to save every star. This boast was made good by many of the foreign-born.[11] General Alexander Asboth reminded his fellow Hungarians of their debt to the Stars and Stripes.

A spirit of adventure motivated some of the foreign-born—far less, of course, than it did their countrymen in the home armies who came seeking experience and the means of advancement upon their return. Still, it inevitably made its appearance with a certain type of bold, half-reckless young man. This was the young man who was free of the family ties and obligations which operate to hold a man home from war until the call is too imperative to be disregarded or a draft settles the conflict in his mind. As already mentioned, there was a decided preponderance of males of military age among practically all immigrant groups. The promptness with which many Turner societies enlisted as a body can probably be accounted for in part by this spirit of adventure. In addition, they took pleasure in a certain type of drill, knew that they were partially trained—at least to respond to commands in unison—and realized that it was but a step from gymnastic drill to military drill. To go out together, before anyone realized what war meant, with a large number of their friends appeared a frolic. The effect of example operated powerfully, no doubt. When one young man saw his best friend volunteer, he responded in order not to be left behind or outdone; when most of a given Turner society or other organized band signed the muster roll, even the reluctant, perchance unwilling, felt compelled to manifest equal bravery, or were persuaded by friends to make the enlistment of the group "unanimous."

Strong appeals were successfully made to the national sentiment of the German, the Swede, the Irishman, the Frenchman, and the Swiss. This was an appeal to the love of the old homeland to serve the new. Every change was rung upon this motif: the obligation to respond numerically

---

[11] This boast was made at Baltimore on the occasion of the presentation of a flag by the German Republican Club to the Wide-Awakes. Baltimore *Wecker*, November 27, 1860.

as well as, or better than, other nationality groups, to fight as daringly and tenaciously, to do so in order to sustain the name of German or Swede, or, in other words, to maintain the honor of the old homeland. Appeals were made which revived the memory of the glories of the fatherland. One of the most elaborate and dramatic was the call issued by the Swede Axel Silfversparre to the Swedes and Norwegians of Illinois:

> Have you forgotten the heroes who for your religious freedom fought and fell on Lützen's bloody field? Has their blood thinned in your veins, that you without blushing allow apostles of traitors to arise among you?
> Swedes! Have you forgotten that the enlightenment of humanity and freedom has always found Swedish people among those zealous guarantors? Norsemen! Have you forgotten truth and that you swore for a free constitution in dear old Norway? That it was our pride to say that among Scandinavians are found no traitors! [12]

The Irish sought to inspirit their countrymen with memories of the fame of Irishmen in the American Revolution as well as of the victories won on other battlefields. Especially were Irishmen never allowed to forget the glories won by the band of exiles who fought for France under the fleur-de-lis. Even the Scotchman, merged though his land had been with England for over 250 years, recalled ancient Scotia as a rallying cry for Scotchmen in America. Said one Scot, offering his services to Ohio, "You will find all the Scotchmen firm and ready to strike hard blows, even though enough follow the traitors. . . . 'If you strike me, I will strike you again,' is Scotland's motto. Not a field in her border but has been black with her children's blood. Rise artillery men, Sappers and Miners, get strength, the mind is willing, now is the time to do or die." [13]

The Germans were no whit behind the Swedes in efforts to stir Teutonic pride, but the appeal was sometimes more subtly couched in the suggestion of superiority to praise: "Brave Germans! Let us show, unconcerned about praise or censure on the part of the other nationalities, that we are *Germans* and in German loyalty are prepared to defend our Amer-

[12] Chicago *Hemlandet*, March 6, 1863. See Appendix, Section B, for the entire text of the long call.

[13] For evidence of Irish eloquence, see William F. Fox (comp.), *New York [State] Monuments Commission for the Battlefields of Gettysburg and Chattanooga. Final Report on the Battlefield of Gettysburg* (Albany, 1900), II, 487. (Hereinafter cited as *New York at Gettysburg.*) For the Scotch, see Todd's letter to the Governor of Ohio, April 16, 1861, Executive Correspondence of the Governors of Ohio, March–April 15, 1861.

ican home as the blessed place of freedom." [14] Again, listen to Friedrich Kapp, as he presented a sword to Colonel Max Weber: "A German soldier has a double fame in this war. He enters for his adopted country, and he has to do honor for the German name. He will show the world that the German stands in the foremost ranks of fighters for freedom." [15]

Allied to this motive as an impetus to enlistment was the inducement held out of joining companies or regiments composed of men of a certain nationality, of serving under officers of their own nationality, and of having their army service facilitated by the issuing of commands in their own tongue. In the call which appeared in the *Emigranten* of October 7, Colonel Heg offered this additional motive for a Scandinavian regiment as he stressed the question of the language to be used in commands. The officers were to be men who spoke Norwegian, a fact which would afford an opportunity for Scandinavians who could not yet speak English to enter the service.

The offer of automatic citizenship, without the formalities otherwise required, to all soldiers who entered the Union armies was certainly extended to the foreign-born, but it is questionable how great an inducement to enlistment it proved. A judicious evaluation would probably place it among the rewards of service.

The desire for rank and recognition was indubitably an inducement to many foreign-born leaders who aspired to a commission. Our system of recruitment at the time must surely have stimulated the ambition of anyone who thought he could rally a group about him. Everyone knows that in the early days little regard was paid to military training. Almost anyone who could persuade eighty, or sometimes fewer, men to enlist could secure a captain's commission; almost anyone who could raise a regiment could attach the title of colonel to his name. This motive operated powerfully on the native and no less powerfully on the foreign-born. For instance, we know that Colonel Heg became commander of the Fifteenth Wisconsin Regiment largely by his own efforts and ability as a recruiting officer; without his personal efforts and arguments with his fellow countrymen, that regiment would probably never have become a reality. Perhaps a desire not to lose the captain's commission explains why a company originally intended to be composed only of Italians embraced in the end also Frenchmen, Germans, and Irishmen. As will soon appear, this lure of a commission was held out to Swedish Hans Mattson. Americans knew

[14] St. Paul *Minnesota Staats-Zeitung*, May 4, 1861.
[15] Chicago *Illinois Staats-Zeitung*, June 5, 1861.

how to play upon this string when striving to secure the influence of certain foreign-born citizens among their fellow countrymen. The glitter of a title must have appeared the more possible of attainment because so many of the foreign-born had had more or less military training, and that gave them at the outset a substantial advantage over most Americans.

From General Philippe Régis de Trobriand down to a humble Pole we find evidence of that motive. The distinguished Frenchman wrote that he wondered if the fate which had deprived him of the heritage of his father's sword in France, where his father had held a distinguished position in the army, might perchance be reserving for him in America in the volunteer army some compensation in fighting for a cause which had immortalized Lafayette. G. L. Scherer put his sword at the disposal of Governor William Dennison of Ohio—a sword on which was engraved, "Never drawn without cause, never sheathed without honor." Though he did not stipulate officer rank, his emphasis on six years in a cadet school in the old country and conversance with tactics, fortification, and infantry and artillery exercises leaves little doubt that he expected a commission. V. M. Degerfeld of Sandusky, who had been "ranged," according to his strange phraseology, in his sixteenth year as a cadet in a regiment and had "stood" in active service for ten years, earnestly begged the governor to "range" him somewhere as an aide of a brigadier. Max Polachek in addressing Brigadier General Charles W. Hill assured him that he asked for a situation "only from the purest patriotism, to serve my adopted country," because his business paid at least twice as much as he could get in the army and as a noncitizen he would be exempt from the draft. He was evidently seeking a commissioned post.[16]

An inducement held out as the war got under way and certain regiments or batteries became recognized as having enviable reputations was that of joining such a superior organization or of enjoying the advantage of superior equipment. The Ninth Massachusetts Regiment heralded its virtues in the following terms: "Let the ranks of the glorious Ninth be at once manned by heroes, worthy successors of those who have fallen, and fit companions of the veterans still eager for the fight. That regiment is yours. Its history—its glory, its past—its future is yours, and sheds a luster not on you only, but on the Irish Race." The veteran Battery H in

[16] Régis de Trobriand, *Quatre Ans de Campagnes à l'Armée du Potomac* (Paris, 1868), I, 61; for Scherer, see Executive Correspondence of the Governors of Ohio, March–April 15, 1861; Degerfeld to Adjutant Henry B. Carrington, April 19, 1861, *ibid.*, April 16–24, 1861; for Max Polachek to General Hill, see letter dated August 15, 1862, *ibid.*, August, 1862.

the First Illinois Artillery, for instance, declared in an advertisement for recruits that although it had fought and bled in all the battles of Generals Grant and Sherman for twenty-six months, it still had more serviceable men than any other regiment which had entered the service even one year later. It also held out the inducement that its battery was equipped with the best cannons to be had in the world, twenty-pounder Parrotts, and that the battery was regarded as one of the best-drilled in the service. Sometimes a short term of service was mentioned as an added inducement —though this was a promise likely to be unfulfilled. In the advertisement previously mentioned, the Ninth Massachusetts pointed out that it had already served sixteen months of its three-year term; consequently, men joining then would have only twenty months to serve, as they would be discharged with the regiment. This could readily have its appeal for men who feared the already threatened draft for a full three-year term.[17]

The leaders also felt a desire to help assuage the resentment of Americans at the hesitation on the part of the foreign-born to enlist. There was some bitterness in different areas when men on whom America had bestowed citizenship, with its opportunities and privileges, held back from assuming also its responsibilities. Pressure was brought to bear upon them. If flattery failed, bitterness was not slow to make itself felt. Their American brothers called them "greenhorns" and cowards; their fellow countrymen in the ranks besieged them with threats and sometimes even with beatings. The more intelligent among the foreign-born recognized a potential danger to their national groups and felt that enlistment was necessary to prove that adopted sons, actual and potential, were willing to bear their share of the burdens of citizenship. Often this incentive was expressed as "raising the Scandinavian name in America." [18]

Among all the motives perhaps one of the strongest was that manifested by some Irishmen—and not merely by the more ignorant among their number. Many enlisted in the hope of being enabled somehow to strike a blow at England; they were greatly disappointed that none of the crises in Anglo-American affairs at that time led to an armed conflict with Britain. The presence of the green flag with so many Irish regiments was evidence of this feeling. Michael Corcoran, a chief officer in the Fenian Brotherhood, fearing the distraction of the Irish from the cause of Ireland by entry into the Union army, implored all nonmembers of the state

17 For the Ninth Massachusetts, see the New York *Irish-American*, August 2, 1862; for the Illinois battery, see the Chicago *Hemlandet*, February 3, 17, March 30, April 13, 1864.

18 This motive is abundantly illustrated in Hans Mattson, as will be seen later in this chapter.

militia to hold aloof in order to reserve their lives for the cause to which they were pledged. If, however, any brother Fenians were still determined to go to the war, he preferred them to go with their own countrymen rather than have their national identity lost among strangers. He later voiced the view that they would not be the worse for a little practice. Thomas Francis Meagher, however, felt it the duty of every liberty-loving citizen to help preserve the Union—a duty to Ireland as well as to America: ". . . I hold that if only one in ten of us come back when this war is over, the military experience gained by that one will be of more service in a fight for Ireland's freedom than would that of the entire ten as they are now." [19] With such views in the minds of the leaders, it is not strange that the quick Celtic imagination led many in the ranks to look upon the war as nothing more than a favorable opportunity for preparing to crush England.

Finally comes the motive which we may designate as mercenary. From the start, that was undoubtedly one reason why the Irish volunteered so readily. An Irishman of the Tenth Tennessee was asked what had taken the Irish into the "rebel" ranks. "Our poverty and friendliness" was his prompt answer. We may know well that the same factor brought its pressure to bear on the Irishman of the northern states. As the day of bounties arrived—and it came early in the war—we see the pecuniary inducement operating strongly. Sometimes it was quite openly avowed, as in the case of Bersven Nelson, a Norwegian immigrant who had arrived in Wisconsin in the summer of 1861. After working in a sawmill for a few weeks, he encountered a Norwegian sergeant recruiting for the Scandinavian regiment of Wisconsin. "Yes, and then there was a bounty of a hundred dollars, and thirteen dollars a month, free clothes, and free food. This seemed good enough to me, and furthermore [revealing still another incentive], I would have an opportunity to travel and to see a great deal." [20] The most offensive aspect of this inducement—the presence at the docks in port cities of recruiting officers and runners, who took advantage of, and even abducted, foreign immigrants as they came off the ships—will be discussed in a later chapter.[21]

Of course, not every immigrant yearned for the smell of powder, and this became more manifest with the entry of the draft. Carlton C. Qualey

[19] Michael Cavanagh, *Memoirs of Gen. Thomas Francis Meagher, Comprising the Leading Events of his Career Chronologically Arranged . . .* (Worcester, Mass., 1892), 370–71, 369.
[20] Ager (ed.), *Oberst Heg og hans Gutter,* 15–16.
[21] See Chapter XV.

quotes a letter from an immigrant in Dodge County, Minnesota, to someone in Norway. "It is not good to be in this so-called wonderful America just now. You can see by this how we live! On the one hand there is prospect of becoming cannon fodder for the South, and on the other the impending danger of becoming a prey of the Indians." [22] Among some of our foreign-born there was great decency in meeting the problem of the draft, even when they wished to escape it. In Chicago a society was organized among the Swedes, in a Swedish-Lutheran church, to create a common treasury by the payment of one hundred dollars by each of the twenty or more members who might be drafted.[23]

Probably nowhere is to be found a clearer statement of the motives which actuated some of our foreign-born to enlist than that penned by Hans Mattson of Red Wing, Minnesota, in a letter to his wife. Its value to the modern reader is greatly enhanced by the fact that it reveals with clarity the complex motives so often present, for the source of our actions is more often a maze than one single golden thread. Evidently his wife had been reproaching him for leaving her for the war, and in a long letter he attempted to set forth his reasons.

> I have not been . . . endowed with the characteristics . . . which I have . . . in order to spend an inactive life and, after a few years, die and be forgotten, without particular good resulting for myself, my children, or humanity. I had already reached an important position, and the best men in our country had already turned their attention to me. You and I had already enjoyed great advantages from their and our country's favor. I was already noted as a leader here, and especially as the leader among our own people. I also had a little military education. . . . I had in a few years . . . brought my family almost from dire want to ease and affluence. I was believed to

[22] This was, it will be noted, about the time of the Sioux uprising which took place in Minnesota during the Civil War. This pessimistic letter was printed in Christiania *Morgenbladet,* November 22, 1862. See Qualey, *Norwegian Settlement,* 104–106.

[23] The name of the organization was "Philadelphia," adopted, no doubt, because of its Greek meaning, "brotherly love." The treasurer was P. L. Hawkinson, vice-consul for Norway and Sweden. He had an office in the *Hemlandet* office. See the issue of that paper for September 7, 1864. It will be noted that the *Hemlandet* had moved from Galesburg to Chicago.

The action of a father who evaded the draft by consenting to the enlistment of his seventeen-year-old son may have been less selfish than it sounds: "I am in the mercantile business and have a son 17 years old he wants to enlist in a company being raised in our Town for the three-year service. I am willing for him to do so provided that you or the war department can Exempt me a draf while he is in the service. My business is such that we cant both leave." John Riech to the Governor, August 11, 1862, Executive Correspondence of the Governors of Ohio, August, 1862.

possess courage and a strong sense of honor. People had often heard the expression, in speech and writing, of my liberal and liberty-loving opinions,—The War came. Our free land was threatened with destruction. The ideas I had so often expressed to my own advantage were put to a hard test. Half a million men were needed for the defense of our country, and of those three to four hundred ought to come from our own county. Almost one-third of the people there were my countrymen. I waited to see what would be done. The Americans sent out one company in the First and one in the Second Regiment from our county, and among them were five Scandinavians. A little hatred had previously existed between our people and the Americans: now there was more reason for it. People began to ask, Why don't you do anything for the defense of your country and yourselves? . . . Are you too cowardly or too indifferent to defend yourselves and us? People said to me, Why, you are a soldier, with more knowledge of war than anybody in our country. You have profited at the expense of the country. You have often spoken of how your people were loyal to their new country and to the party of freedom. You have great influence and your example is good for a hundred men. . . . Our government and we will repay you. We will let you keep your office; [24] and you will also be able to get a good position in the army, —you will not need to go as a simple private with small pay. Go, you are worth a hundred men.— At the same time I felt my duty in my own heart. . . . The honor of our nation was at stake in this state, and it lay in my power to save it. . . . I meditated long; I prayed for God's guidance, I partly realized the sacrifice I should be making for myself and for you. And I made my decision—and here I am. . . . The one hundred men have followed me. . . . The difference between us and the Americans will disappear so much the faster. I have peace of conscience. . . . I shall go bravely forward on the path of danger but also of duty and of honor. . . .[25]

So far, it is the sentiments of leaders which have found expression. It is suitable, however, and necessary that the motives of humbler foreigners

[24] Mattson held at the time of enlistment the office of county auditor.

[25] This letter to his wife, dated Fort Snelling, October 3, 1861, was written in Swedish, as were many of his letters to her, and was addressed to "My own beloved Cherstie," evidently a pet name. His letters breathe a very great devotion to her, as the final paragraph of this letter will show. "But I am glad that I did not realize how great the sacrifice and the sorrow of parting was. . . . Sometimes I almost wish that we did not love each other so well, then the parting would not be so bitter. . . ." None of the letters written by Mrs. Mattson to her husband are to be found among the manuscripts in the Minnesota collection. Hans Mattson Papers, Minnesota Historical Society, St. Paul.

be sought. Probably the motive which usually swayed the common soldier among the foreigners as a whole was the desire to extirpate slavery; this gave the struggle a moral aspect and turned the war in a sense into a holy crusade. The contact of the foreign-born soldier with slavery during the war only deepened his feeling against it.

If the reader were asked to identify the writer of the following letter, he would doubtless insist that he was a grandson of some New England Revolutionary hero, so completely had he identified himself with the American causes and arguments: "Let our countrymen remember that this war is waged for our children and grand-children, just as our fore-fathers fought in the Revolution against England to assure us freedom, we now justly are proud of, so it is our holy duty now to take up arms to preserve this splendid gift for our descendants. Let us remember that if this Union is divided, then it is ended with all hopes for freedom in Europe; then tyrants can with full justice point to this ill-fated attempt at popular government as proof of the impossibility of creating a free Re-public." It is only in his exhortations to his Norwegian countrymen that we can recognize him as a son of Norway: "And therefore forward Scandi-navians! Let us show our fellow-citizens of other nationalities, that when it concerns fighting for a holy cause, the Scandinavians are just as patriotic as any other class of naturalized citizens." [26]

The utter simplicity of Torsten Christian Nyhuus in setting forth the motives which took him to camp rings with a genuineness which makes the reader feel that he is looking into the heart of many a foreign-born private:

> When I saw the danger in which our dear Union stood, I believed that it would not be right for me to lay my hands in my lap, but must do what I could, to be helpful to defend the laws, which should as-sure our lives and our property. I turned first, after I had consulted with God about my duty, to my wife; she was at first not willing to let me go; then after further consideration she felt that perhaps it might be her duty to let me go, since there was a call from the authorities for help, and God's word teaches that we should be obedient to the authorities. With prayer to the Almighty for his protection, our families and friends stood praying as we left those who are our second selves, and with moved hearts we took our departure from our dear ones.[27]

[26] Letter from a soldier in the Fifteenth Wisconsin at Camp Randall to the editor of the Madison *Emigranten*. It appeared in the issue of December 23, 1861.

[27] This letter was addressed to "Relatives and Friends," and is dated Camp Randall, Janu-ary 27, 1861. See *ibid.*, February 3, 1862.

This chapter may well close with a bit of idealism from the son of another liberty-loving country. Rudolf Aschmann, a native of Switzerland, who saw three years in the Army of the Potomac with Berdan's Sharpshooters, wrote: "It is beautiful to fight for an idea that is to bring freedom to all men; attractive is the satisfaction which each brave soul brings with him out of the hot combat to have contributed his bit to the success of a beautiful cause. Most of the Swiss may have found this the cause for their participation in the great work." [28]

[28] Rudolph Aschmann, *Drei Jahre in der Potomac Armee, oder Eine Schweizer Schützen-Compagnie im Nordamerikanischen Kriege* (Richtersweil, Switzerland, 1865), iii.

CHAPTER FOUR

The Regular Army of the United States in 1861

SMALL as was the regular armed force upon which the American citizen of 1861 expected the Federal government to depend for the suppression of rebellion, size is not the only consideration which should arrest the attention of the modern reader. In fact, in its composition and distribution the Regular Army presents striking peculiarities, which require at least brief consideration. In the first place, the army was organized under the three divisions conventional at the time—the infantry, the artillery, and the cavalry. In all, there were nineteen regiments distributed among the three arms as follows: ten regiments of infantry, each company in each regiment consisting of 82 men; four regiments of artillery, each light battery consisting of 64 men; one regiment of *carabinier à cheval* or mounted infantry; two regiments of cavalry; and two regiments of dragoons, each comprising ten companies of about 60 men each. If the regiments had all been full, they would have constituted an army of about 19,000 men; but, as indicated above by the incomplete numbers in the companies, the force represented at best a scantier army than that.

The regiments of the army were often not as respectable as those of the New York militia, which sometimes attained 850 men. Foreign visitors, as evidenced by François Victor Adolph de Chanal, were prone to quote the American army as consisting of about 15,000 men, to which must be added 1,098 officers.[1] This brings the Frenchman's estimate fairly close to the official figures of Secretary of War John B. Floyd in his annual report of 1860. In that report, Floyd gave the actual numbers of troops as 16,006, as of December 1, and stated that they were "chiefly employed in the West to hold in check marauding Indians." [2] This is as near as we can come to

[1] François Victor Adolph de Chanal, *The American Army in the War of Secession* (Leavenworth, Kans., 1894), 15. The organization above was given in the New York *Courrier des États-Unis,* January 29, 1860.

[2] "Report of the Secretary of War," 1860, in *Senate Executive Documents* (Washington,

the size of the army at the opening of hostilities on April 15, 1861. One year later the number, including the new enlistments under the act of July 29, 1861, had risen to 20,334; but by the spring of 1865, it had actually sunk to 13,880.[3]

More important, as it happens, than the actual number was the distribution of the troops. In December, 1860, Floyd declared that the country was divided—ostensibly for defense—into six departments: the Departments of the West, Texas, New Mexico, Utah, California, and Oregon. This, of course, left the East and the Gulf Coast wide open to attack, though according to the report of a loyal newspaper on November 20, 1860, there were eight batteries of artillery stationed at Fortress Monroe; two at Fort Moultrie, South Carolina; and one each at the arsenals at Fayetteville, North Carolina; Augusta, Georgia; Key West; Barrancas Barracks, near Pensacola; and Baton Rouge.[4] Public opinion in the North virtually forced the sending of one company of marines on January 6, 1861, to hold Fort Washington on the Potomac, fourteen miles from the national capital. This fort had not been garrisoned for some years, and marines were stationed there now to satisfy the public that the fort would not be occupied by the Southerners. Troops were sent about that time from Fort Leavenworth—not to a Southern point, however, but to Fort McHenry in a border state.[5]

It is clear, therefore, that the dependence of the government for the preservation of the Union rested perforce on the state militia. The only evidence that the Federal government was interested in, or even concerned about, the state of the militia was the appropriation of $1,202,645, allocated for the year ending October 30, 1860, for arming and equipping the militia with Sharps carbines, Colt rifles and pistols, cavalry sabers, artillery swords, cartridge boxes and belts, bayonet scabbards, and pistol holsters. Secretary of War Floyd did urge in his report the sale at cost of ammunition and spare parts from the arsenals to the states and territories as a means of promoting militia service, "as some of the articles of good quality could

---

1861), 36 Cong., 2 Sess., No. 1, p. 213; also in *Messages and Documents*, 1860 (Abridged, Washington, 1860), 182. Undoubtedly the effective strength was below that—by 1,700 or more, according to De Chanal.

[3] See "Report of the Secretary of War," 1861, in *Senate Executive Documents*, 37 Cong., 2 Sess., No. 1, p. 13; "Report of the Secretary of War," 1865, in *House Executive Documents*, 39 Cong., 1 Sess., No. 1, pp. 49–50.

[4] Washington *Tägliche Metropole*, November 22, 1862.

[5] New York *Courrier des États-Unis*, January 7, 1861.

be had only from the national arsenals." [6] At no time during the war did the so-called "regulars" constitute more than 3 per cent of the armed forces.

Some leaders of opinion in America felt that the fact that a leading country like the United States was unable to defend itself against a civil rebellion was a matter of deep humiliation. "These circumstances," wrote Brigadier General Theodore B. Gates, "revealed a state of affairs humiliating to a just national pride, and endangered for a time the very life of the Republic. To see a government of thirty-eight millions of people, rich in all the resources that tend to make them great and powerful, ranking second to no nation of the earth, so denuded of its proper martial puissance that it could not set a squadron in the field, even to save its capital from capture, was unspeakably humiliating." He asked with much pertinence, "Does any man believe that the war of the rebellion would have been fought if this Government had had an adequate, a loyal and efficient army in 1861?" [7]

Europeans criticized us, naturally enough, for our methods and our delay. Said one observer:

> In Europe we should have set to work to increase the army by enlarging its organization and incorporating recruits. An army of sixty thousand regulars would have done more than double or triple the number of volunteers; but in America they do not know this, and besides, they do not wish to know it. It would involve renunciation of the general and deeply rooted creed, that every American, when he wishes to do a thing, may find within himself, without any apprenticeship, the power to do it; and, consequently, there is no volunteer who, when he puts on the uniform, does not at the same time put on the qualities of a soldier. [8]

There was an aspect in the situation, however, which Europeans did not sense; here was an early example of appeasement, mistaken then, undoubtedly, as it was to prove nearly a century later in international affairs. Jacob Cox, member of the Ohio legislature in 1861, later noted that "in the powdery condition of affairs it was not thought politic to agitate the

---

[6] "Report of the Secretary of War," 1860, in *Senate Executive Documents*, 36 Cong., 2 Sess., No. 1, p. 964.

[7] Theodore B. Gates, *The "Ulster Guard" (20 N.Y. State Militia) and the War of the Rebellion* (New York, 1879), 19. Gates served first as colonel of this regiment.

[8] The Prince de Joinville, *The Army of the Potomac: Its Organization, Its Commander, and Its Campaigns* (New York, 1862), 12–13.

question of a better military organization"; but for more than a year before the war he had been giving such leisure as he could to the study of tactics and military history, and he was "sure many others had been doing the like." [9]

Foreign-born men were to be found among the officers of the Regular Army, though, as might be expected, not in great numbers nor in high-ranking positions. The highest rank (at least, the highest encountered by the writer) held by a man of foreign birth in the "old army"—as the Regular Army as it existed before the Civil War was often designated—was that of lieutenant colonel. This officer, Timothy Andrews, was an Irishman who had left his post of paymaster temporarily to lead a regiment to the Mexican War. After that war he returned to his task of paying the army, in which post he attained the rank of lieutenant colonel in 1851. Another Irishman, Daniel H. Hastings, held the rank of captain of First United States Dragoons by January, 1860. He was made superintendent of Mounted Recruiting Service and commanded the Cavalry School at Carlisle Barracks from 1861 to 1864, but did not attain the rank of major until 1863—and then only as a result of his Civil War service. A German by the name of Theodore Fink was the only other foreigner discovered by this writer to attain even the modest rank of captain; the fact that he had been breveted second lieutenant during the Mexican War in January, 1848, shows how slow promotions were for foreign-born soldiers. Fink was obviously a man of ability, for he had served as Acting Regimental Quartermaster and Commissary of Subsistence as early as 1848. This rank had come only after many years of service in the army. [10] Several lieutenants turned up in the search, but only second lieutenants: an Englishman who rose from the ranks in the United States Mounted Rifles and who had distinguished himself in the conflict with the Mogollon Indians in New Mexico; and several Irishmen, such as one Edward Treacy, who closely paralleled the career of the Englishman in the same organization of the Mounted Rifles, [11] and James A. Hearn, who after service in the Mexican War reached a lieutenancy ten years later in 1858. [12]

[9] Jacob D. Cox, "Why the Men of '61 fought for the Union," in *Atlantic Monthly*, LXIX (1892), 391.

[10] Guy Vernon Henry (comp.), *Military Record of Civilian Appointments in the United States Army* (New York, 1869–1873), II, 35 (for foreign-born colonels in the Regular Army); II, 158 (for majors); II, 88–89 (for captains).

[11] *Ibid.*, I, 171, 183. The Englishman was Christopher McNally.

[12] *Ibid.*, I, 334. The last-mentioned was brevetted major for meritorious services in the Civil War.

This study of foreign officers in the old army professes no claim to completeness; there probably were certain other foreign-born officers in the old army who attained commissioned offices, but the point is well substantiated that very few of the foreigners entering United States military service ever received a commission. Part of the reason undoubtedly lies in the fact that they were of humble station and had enjoyed little education.

Noncommissioned officers of foreign origin were more numerous; many served as first sergeants or sergeant majors, some of them after long years of service in the army. One Scotchman who enlisted in 1854 and was assigned to the First United States Artillery saw service against the Indians from 1855 to 1857 in Florida, and rose to the rank of first sergeant.[13] It was a second Scotchman on whom General John Gibbon bestowed the encomium "the best first sergeant I ever saw in the service." An Englishman who entered our service in 1854 came up the hard way from private through the grades of corporal and sergeant to become regimental quartermaster sergeant just prior to the war. It is not surprising to learn that he won several brevets for meritorious service during the Civil War.[14] The search for foreign-born officers reveals several Germans and a number of Irishmen as sergeant majors.[15] The latter seem to have been fairly common as first sergeants and as ordnance and commissary sergeants.[16]

The rank and file of the old army had been for the most part composed of Germans and Irishmen. This should not surprise the reader, for the

[13] James Chester was his name. He was brevetted second lieutenant of the United States Artillery in February, 1863, and became acting Assistant Inspector General for North Carolina. *Ibid.*, I, 196–97. He rose to the command of the post at Beaufort, South Carolina.

[14] For the encomium, see John Gibbon, *Personal Recollections of the Civil War* (New York, 1928), 13 and note; for the Englishman, see Henry (comp.), *Military Record of Civilian Appointments*, I, 198.

[15] The Germans were William Falck, who had enlisted in 1858, and Gustavus Urban, who had enlisted in 1855 and who rose to be regimental quartermaster sergeant. Henry (comp.), *Military Record of Civilian Appointments*, I, 307, 184, respectively. The Irishmen were Thomas Drury, who had enlisted in the army in 1842 and who became an ordnance sergeant; John Fitzgerald, who had served in the artillery since 1856 and had served as commissary sergeant in Dakota Territory just prior to the war; and Robert Howard, who had become a sergeant major in the Fourth United States Artillery in 1853 after four years service (which covered the entire Mexican War). *Ibid.*, I, 203, 210, 301, respectively. It is interesting that Howard was brevetted lieutenant colonel during the Civil War.

[16] *Ibid.*, I, 212, 227–28; II, 127–28, 160; for an Irish ordnance sergeant, see *ibid.*, I, 301; for a commissary sergeant, see *ibid.*, I, 203.

same situation which partly explains their presence in the volunteer army of the Civil War period was operative earlier. Great numbers of foreigners of these two nationalities were pouring into the United States during the decades of the forties and fifties; and when other opportunities for work did not open for them, many drifted inevitably into a field which was not crowded. Because native Americans scorned service in the armed forces except as officers, the military service was an open field. Service in the army also had an influence on the loyalty of these foreign-born regulars in 1861. They viewed the political questions from their European backgrounds, as did their civilian fellow countrymen.

Furthermore, they felt no compulsion of state ties; and, indeed, the great majority in the Regular Army had enlisted from northern states. Hence, when the army was being more or less disrupted by the resignation of Southern-born officers, the foreign-born, mainly noncommissioned officers and privates, stood firmly by the Union. Added to the fact that the Union government, and not the newly created Confederate government, represented the authority which they recognized as the legal government in the United States was the practical consideration that they did not care to desert their source of livelihood.[17] At least one German sergeant major, who was surrendered with the Seventh United States Infantry in New Mexico in July, 1861, joined the Army of the Potomac in October, 1862,[18] as soon as an exchange of prisoners had effected his release.

This influx of foreigners into the army was noticeable as late as January, 1861; the Baltimore *Der Deutsche Correspondent* commented on the presence of 625 recruits at Governor's Island, three fourths of whom were Prussians and Englishmen.[19] In order to establish some authoritative figures, the writer took a sampling of several different periods from the manuscript register of enlistments in the United States Army for 1857–1858 and for 1859. In a group of slightly over 1,000 soldiers, 507—almost exactly one half—were foreign-born; in another group of 500 men, 363

[17] See G. F. R. Henderson, *Stonewall Jackson and the American Civil War* (London and New York, 1898), 127; New York *Tribune*, September 4, 1861.

[18] Henry (comp.), *Military Record of Civilian Appointments*, II, 80.

[19] Baltimore *Der Deutsche Correspondent*, January 17, 1861. "Auf Governor's Island bei New York sind jetzt 625 Rekruten, von denen drei-Vierteile aus Fremden, namentlich Preussen und Engländern, welche schon in der Armee gedient haben, bestehen. Die Kasernen in Fort Columbus und Castle William sind überfüllt und die Soldaten exerzieren täglich, haben aber leichte Dienst."

—or over two thirds—had been born under another flag. While the pre-dominance of those from Germany and Ireland held strikingly true here, England as the country of origin ranked third in both groups.[20]

It is noticeable that after the term of service of three years, these soldiers of foreign origin frequently re-enlisted; it is even more striking that re-enlistment came sometimes—and not infrequently—after an interval of several years. The natural inference is either that the men had become adjusted to army life and on the whole preferred it or that they had not been able to adjust to civilian life and employment. The experience of Frederick Robinson, who was a son of the Emerald Isle, is a case in point. He enlisted and was assigned to the Fourth United States Artillery in 1849. Discharged in 1854, he did not re-enlist in the Regular Army until August, 1858; but he was caught in the service by the Civil War, during which he rendered gallant service in the United States Fifth Artillery. It is interesting that between his two periods of military service he acted as a schoolteacher in Illinois but evidently did not find teaching to his liking. There were, of course, many other instances of re-enlistment, sometimes during the Civil War itself.[21]

Military service before the war could be decidedly active. One Irish-man, enlisting in the Second United States Dragoons in 1854, engaged in the Sioux Indian expedition of 1855, the Kansas riots during 1856–1857, and the expedition of 1857–1858 into Utah, where he was located in 1861.[22]

Naturally, the foreign-born were scattered, as previously shown, through all branches of the service—the artillery, the infantry, and the dragoons—and represented many nationalities, although the larger num-ber were, as already indicated, Irish and Germans. An occasional English-man turned up in the ranks and usually found the travel and adventure he craved. For example, a man who bore on the records the common label of John H. Smith, after his enlistment was sent first to Florida to scout Indians, then to Boston Harbor for a term of duty, then to Minnesota for more contact with hostile Indians, and then to the Artillery School of

[20] Register of Enlistments, U.S. Army, A-Z, October, 1857–1858, War Records Division, The National Archives, Washington. Register of Enlistments, 1859.

[21] For Robinson, see Henry (comp.), *Military Record of Civilian Appointments*, I, 223. For other instances of re-enlistments, see *ibid.*, II, 90, 119, 144–45, 155, 166.

[22] *Ibid.*, I, 166. A German, Edward Myers, had lively service in New Mexico, on the Pacific Coast, and against hostile Indians in the Southwest, after he enlisted in 1861. *Ibid.*, 173. For further examples of Germans in the old army, see *ibid.*, II, 94, 95, 118, 131–32; of Irishmen, *ibid.*, II, 115–16, 159.

Practise at Fortress Monroe, where the outbreak of war found him.[23] A Russian rendered service in the Second Dragoons from 1855 to 1860. Isaac D'Isay, despite his French name, actually hailed from the Netherlands.[24] An occasional Scotchman, Swede, or Pole could be encountered in the service also.

The reaction of these foreign-born in the service of the United States Army to the political questions agitating the people at that time is interesting and important. Fortunately, an expression of opinion from one Ph. Schweenfurth—who was a member of Company D, Second United States Infantry, serving in "Dacotah" Territory in May, 1861—to the Illinois *Staats-Zeitung* has been preserved. He gives a clear statement of the composition and attitude of the members of his company toward the big issue of secession:

> Our company counts at this time 72 men, of whom 20 are German, 10 Americans, the remainder Irishmen, also several Englishmen and Scotch. Among Companies A and B, which are here with us, are to be found likewise many Germans. Naturally, there rules as a consequence of the events in the states considerable sensation. The opinion among the 70 Germans is unanimous for the legal government, to which we are pledged, as is that of the Americans, while many voices among the Irishmen, of whom we may well have here the scum, favors [*sic*] the rebels. There are naturally daily quarrels over it and the Irish slip around morosely, since they see the Americans and the Germans united. A few days ago, moreover, certain of the Irishmen began to see clearly, and it is to be desired, that orders to march to the states will soon arrive; if they are confirmed, we shall convert all of them . . . if we smell a rat with our Irishmen, or generally with those who favor the rebels, we are almost decided to exterminate them. As remarked, we Germans here are solidly for the Union and Republicans besides. . . .[25]

The length of service of these foreign-born, together with their frequent re-enlistment, suggests that once they were in the American army, the service tended to become a profession for them. Many enlistments of foreigners date from the late forties and the fifties, but some definitely antedate the Mexican War. Some soldiers became veterans of that conflict by virtue of enlisting with the volunteer group of a given state, and

---

[23] *Ibid.*, I, 225–26. Instances of Englishmen and Scotchmen have been noted.
[24] See *ibid.*, II, 40–41, for the Russian, Charles Benzoff; I, 295–96, for the Dutchman.
[25] Chicago *Illinois Staats-Zeitung*, May 21, 1861.

then offered themselves as recruits to the national army.[26] One soldier hailing from the Emerald Isle went into the artillery in 1839 and must have loved fighting, for after the Mexican War he participated in the Utah expedition and won honor in the Civil War.[27] The most outstanding case is that of the Englishman James R. Hansham, who joined the First Light Artillery as second lieutenant in January, 1805, and commanded it as captain in 1811 and until it was disbanded in 1815. He thus presumably fought against his native land in the War of 1812. As military storekeeper, he seems to have been stationed at various arsenals from 1838 to 1858, then to have been awaiting orders for several years, and finally to have been discharged in 1862 after fifty-seven years of service and after overlapping all three American wars of the century. The only other person who approaches him in length of service is the Irish paymaster alluded to earlier, who enlisted in 1822, served through the Mexican War with distinction as colonel of *Voltigeurs,* returned to his paymaster job, and finally retired in 1864 of his own volition after forty years of constant service.[28]

Some index to the proportion of foreign-born in the "old navy" may be gleaned from the statistics of beneficiaries at the Naval Asylum at Philadelphia. The recipients of this care would presumably be privates and noncommissioned officers. The number which appeared on the roll on January 1, 1860, was 146. Of this number, 38 had been born under a foreign flag, a relatively small proportion; but, as it would appear that the foreigners tended to drift back home after leaving the service, these statistics may not be a wholly safe index.[29] As should be expected, foreign-born soldiers who were injured in the line of duty later drew pensions just as did the natives.[30]

---

[26] This was the case with one Thomas Britton, who served in Mexico as drummer in the Fourth Pennsylvania Volunteers under General Scott. Henry (comp.), *Military Record of Civilian Appointments,* II, 51–52.

[27] *Ibid.,* I, 210.

[28] For Hansham, see *ibid.,* II, 103; for the paymaster, Timothy P. Andrews, see *ibid.,* II, 35.

[29] Stated in the "Report of the Secretary of the Navy, 1860," in *Messages and Documents,* 258.

[30] A letter from the British ambassador to Secretary Seward, November 4, 1863, proves clearly that pensions were so received by foreign-born. Lord Lyons brought to Seward's attention the case of one Thomas Grimes Roberts of Coventry, England, who had enlisted in the American military service and been in a hospital in Savannah. He had last been heard of at the office of the pension agent at Jackson, where he had told the agent that he was thinking of returning to England. Lord Lyons surmised that he had been shipwrecked, as no one had

A very sizable proportion of the members of the old army, privates as well as officers, were drawn upon to help direct the volunteer army when the war of 1861 created an unprecedented demand for officer personnel. The value of the discipline and experience already received by these officers differs in no wise from the value of such training received by officers in all armies, and so calls for no extended discussion. It will, however, be considered in the proper place when the relation of that training to the service of our foreign-born is evaluated. To cite a single illustration, however, the reader might well recall the operations off Hatteras Inlet and the siege of Fort Macon, North Carolina. Battery C, First United States Artillery, was stationed at Beaufort, South Carolina, and Morris Island. The experienced soldiers who composed this battery performed the laboratory duties, mounted the guns, and rendered similar expert services. Much of the success of the Union operations against Forts Sumter, Wagner, and Gregg was attributable to the experience of the men of that battery and their skillful captain, an Irishman named Michael Leahy.[31]

The reaction of these foreigners who sought service in the United States Army to the conditions prevailing in the old army holds interest, to say the least, for the modern reader. Fortunately, an expression of the opinion of a German has been preserved; unfavorable as it is, it is illuminating. He wrote to a German consul from Fort Riley, Kansas, probably in late September, 1860, and explained how he came to enlist: "I was in St. Louis without work for several weeks. I was led with my comrade to the employment bureau, where service in the army was mentioned, and it appeared to me rather good and so I enlisted as better than to hunt still longer for work." He complained that the fare, to which he was not accustomed, made him ill for a month. He was in a company which was praised by no soldier and from which, during his period of service, twenty men had deserted. "I hardly believe I can spend five years in such circumstances. And so I beg you to bring about my release. I will return the expense gratefully." He was not yet twenty-one when he enlisted.[32]

---

heard of him since 1859. Lord Lyons was seeking further information about him in 1863. Notes from the British Legation, LVI, Division of State Department Archives, The National Archives.

[31] Henry (comp.), *Military Record of Civilian Appointments*, II, 127–28.

[32] Washington *Tägliche Metropole*, October 4, 1860.

CHAPTER FIVE

Military Units of Germans

IT IS discouraging to the scholar when he has to admit that despite the most laborious research, no claim can be made for complete accuracy of the data presented. In the first place, proper primary data on which to base statistics regarding the foreign-born companies and regiments do not exist for the first year of the war, as the place of nativity was not recorded in early enlistments. It was not until organization of the provost marshal general's office that these highly important data began to be entered. Of 2,500,000 men in the army of the United States, the nativity of only 1,200,000 could be ascertained from records by Benjamin A. Gould at the time that he made his study, *Investigations in the Military and Anthropological Statistics of American Soldiers.* By personal inquiry he established, apparently to his satisfaction, the nativity of another 293,000 soldiers; he then assigned the nativity of the remainder of the soldiers according to the proportions established by the known data.

Even the above statement does not, however, cover the difficulties. On a few rolls (these are rolls contained in the Descriptive Books and not mere muster rolls) all the spaces provided for the entry of birthplace are blank; the vast majority of rolls have many blanks on this point; and it is a rare roll indeed on which nativity has been entered for every soldier recorded. Gould admitted that the birthplace of 75,000 soldiers is unknown—a lamentably large proportion of the army.[1] The actual number is even larger.

---

[1] These blanks are easily explained: an American scribe may often have experienced difficulty in understanding a foreign accent; in fact, he may have been unable to understand an interpreter, whose dialect might have bothered even a fellow countryman. The vagaries of translating "Preussen" into "Russian," and the scribe's weakness in orthography ("Pohland" for Poland, "Brownsweg" for Braunschweig, or "Biren" for Bayern—presumably—or even "Iryeland" or "Mariland") arouse considerable distrust as to the perfect accuracy of the record. Again, the clerk, always hurried, may have deliberately left the entry blank, hoping to achieve greater accuracy later, when he could work at his leisure—the leisure which never came.

It was sometimes possible for the writer to obtain the data as to nativity from the "Jacket," a folder into which the War Department has gathered from all available sources the data on

Finally, the personnel of companies and regiments was constantly being changed by death, resignation, expiration of term of enlistment, and the addition of new recruits. Therefore, statistics on the proportion of foreigners in a given company or regiment can be true only for a specific brief period, the exact date of which does not appear on the page but must be ascertained by other means. The ideal procedure would call for scrutiny of the composition of a regiment at the moment it was sent to the field and then comparison of its composition at frequent intervals until disbandment. This is manifestly impossible; indeed, the scholar is forced to be grateful for what has been recorded in the Descriptive Books in our National Archives and for the many regimental histories and memoirs which help to give a record of a given regiment at the time of its organization. Even the nativity of the commissioned officers was seldom entered.

The basis for the organization of the Union army might at first appear to have been nationality groups. True, that was a most important basis, but it was far from the only basis on which regiments and companies were constructed. Organization was sometimes based on geographical lines, as the One Hundred and Fourteenth New York State Volunteers, representing the Twenty-third Senatorial District; sometimes on occupational principles, as in the Sixteenth New York Regiment, recruited from butchers and farmers, or the Eleventh New York Regiment, composed of musicians; and sometimes on a political relationship, as in the Forty-second New York Infantry, raised by the Democrats of the Tammany Society of New York and led to the field by the Great Sachem. Sometimes the concepts at the base were fantastic and even freakish. A pugilist set to work to fashion a company of pugilists; an admirer of Frederick William I tried to form a battalion of grenadiers, each six feet or more in height; a group of theological students applied for the right to form a company of fellow students; a temperance regiment was actually organized in Iowa, with the purpose, no doubt of forwarding the temperance cause by the demonstration of superiority on the field of battle as a result of abstinence; and the Ironsides, the One Hundred and Twenty-sixth New York Regiment, doubtless prompted by the Cromwellian tradition, was organized on religious principles under the auspices of the Young Men's Christian

each soldier. The birthplace was sometimes supplied by a comment by an officer, sometimes by a letter which had crept into the folder, and occasionally by the "bed ticket" which was tied to the head of the bed of a patient in some hospital, presumably for identification in the event of death.

Association.[2] The volunteer fire companies of New York dropped their proverbial rowdyism long enough to form the two well-known regiments of Fire Zouaves.

The type of organization, however, which was most prevalent and had the deepest influence on the composition of the army was that based on racial groups. Our foreign-born displayed remarkable enthusiasm for forming companies, regiments, and even divisions among their fellow countrymen. Efforts were sometimes made, as will appear, to organize a regiment from a nationality group too small to sustain it. The war fever swept every class in the foreign element, just as it did every class in the native population—every profession, every occupation, from the well educated to the humblest workingman, from the Irish laborer of the seaboard city to the remote Scandinavian farmer of the western frontier. It swept into the army an illiterate minority consisting chiefly of European immigrants.[3]

As recruiting got under way, it became evident that many of the immigrant citizens of the Union preferred to serve in regiments made up of their own countrymen and under officers of their own blood. This desire brought a sympathetic response from high officials in Washington. When the call of August, 1861, came to Wisconsin for five additional regiments, Governor Randall requested officially that one of these regiments might be composed of Germans; and the Ninth Wisconsin Regiment resulted. This served as an impetus to the patriotic of other nationalities. If it was natural for foreign-speaking recruits to seek to enter a company or regiment composed largely of their countrymen, that tendency was encouraged by other factors. When alien army officers discovered that foreign officers were not welcome in native units, they promptly sought permission to organize special companies among their countrymen in America under the promise of an officer's commission. These volunteer recruiting officers advertised in foreign-language papers, addressed meetings of their countrymen, and dispatched agents to urge immigrants to enter their proposed commands. Promising better conditions and special favors, they even

[2] For regiments of butchers and farmers, musicians and pugilists, even of so-called "Grenadiers," see New York *Courrier des États-Unis*, April 24, 1861. The New York *Irish-American*, October 11, 1862, published with much gusto the fact that the officers of the Ironsides Regiment had been arrested on a charge of defrauding Brooklyn of the $360 bounty by pretended enlistments of bogus recruits.

[3] It might be remarked in passing that the idea of military units based on nationality was not new, for it had appeared in the Mexican War. The Cincinnati *Volksblatt* of May 21, 1846, had carried a statement by August Moor announcing the formation of a German battalion from Cincinnati Germans for service in the Mexican War.

called upon men already enlisted to desert their companies in order to join new ones.[4] Almost at the doors of Castle Garden were planted two recruiting tents, with placards holding out as bait large bounties for recruits and active recruiting agents trying in their own tongues to persuade immigrants to enlist under the Federal banner.

The Federal hosts were, accordingly, not recruited from one continent alone. The speech of almost every European nation might have been heard in the camps of the Army of the Potomac. There were brigades of Irish and divisions of Germans. There were those who had fought with the Red Shirts of Garibaldi, and some who had followed Kossuth into rebellion. Canada sent her contingent of keen-eyed riflemen. The call to war issued from Washington gathered under one flag a motley assemblage. Motivated, as we have seen, by honor, by a desire for emoluments (including the promised bounties), or by sheer love of adventure, the soldiers came —patriot (whether native or foreign) and hireling, foreign prince, knight-errant, and soldier of fortune—to range themselves under the Stars and Stripes. It was such a cosmopolitan assemblage, of Germans and Irishmen, of Frenchmen and Italians, of Poles and Scandinavians, of Hungarians and Dutchmen, as had never been gathered together since the Thirty Years War. In the early days it was not difficult to recognize, under the Federal uniform, the former British soldier by his excellent carriage and the polish on his arms, the Prussian soldier by his precision of movement, the Scandinavian by his prompt obedience. It was a safe venture to predict that many would soon become drill sergeants or even, if able to read and write, commissioned officers. To the commanding general was assigned the stupendous task of welding out of this heterogeneous mass an organized and efficient force and, above all, of preserving its morale through four long years of war.

For the purposes of clarity the contingents will be handled separately as nationality groups and by states. The reader must bear in mind that from most states, especially those with large cosmopolitan cities, went many different nationality units at the same time.

---

[4] Numerous advertisements could be cited from the Chicago *Hemlandet,* the Madison *Emigranten,* and the many German newspapers—for example, Baltimore *Der Deutsche Correspondent,* and others.

DISTINCTIVELY GERMAN UNITS

New York

Since the Germans sent the largest number both absolutely and relatively in proportion to their population, they will be discussed first. In New York City alone, thousands of Germans tendered their services at the firing of the first gun on Fort Sumter. During the entire war there went out from New York ten almost solidly German regiments: three regiments in which one half or more were of that nationality, five German artillery batteries, and two cavalry regiments in which fully one half the men were Germans. The ten purely German regiments, with two others more than one half German, were all organized in 1861, the first six under Lincoln's first call. In addition the Fifth New York Militia, the oldest and perhaps the best of the regular German militia regiments, was one of the first to leave New York under Colonel Christian Schwarzwälder for the defense of the capital.[5]

As distinctive German regiments the following should be recognized: the Steuben Rifles (Seventh New York), organized by Colonel John Bendix and reorganized under Colonel George von Schack; Colonel Ludwig Blenker's Eighth New York, with which also was identified General Julius Stahel as lieutenant colonel, and Prince Felix Salm-Salm; the United Turner Rifles (Twentieth), under Colonel Max von Weber; the Astor Rifles (Twenty-ninth), under Colonel Adolf von Steinwehr; the De Kalb Regiment (Forty-first), under the famous Leopold von Gilsa; the German Rifles No. 5 (Forty-fifth), often termed the Platt Deutsch Regiment, under the command of Colonel George von Amsberg; the Frémont Regiment (Forty-sixth) under Colonel Rudolf von Rosa and later under Colonel Joseph Gerhardt; the Sigel Rifles (Fifty-second), named, of course, for the German general, a prime favorite among Germans in America, and led by Colonel C. F. Freudenberg; the Schwarze Jäger (Fifty-fourth), under Colonel F. Gellman and later under Colonel Eugene Kozlay; and German Rifles No. 3 (One Hundred and Third), which went out under Colonel Fred W. von Egloffstein.

The Steuben Rifles was composed of German riflemen, many of whom had already served in the armies of Europe. At a later period, when the

---

[5] New York *Courrier des États-Unis*, April 23, 1861.

records showed the place of birth, there was in the companies an admixture of many other nationalities and of Americans, some of whose names did not indicate German ancestry. The regiment, however, was overwhelmingly foreign in composition and still so predominantly German as justly to be assigned to the quota of that nationality. The bestowal of a flag upon the regiment by descendants of Germans who had come from Germany before the American Revolution indicates the sentiment still attaching to the land of their ancestral origin. Steuben valued highly the Cross of the Order of Fidelity, indeed the only one of his decorations that he always wore, and so the women who made the flag copied this cross from his portrait in the City Hall and embroidered it into the flag.[6]

All told, there were 1,046 men in the Eighth Regiment, known also as the First German Rifles, commanded by that picturesque semisoldier of fortune, General Louis Blenker. Although the lieutenant color sergeant of the regiment was Hungarian, and several other nationalities were scantily represented in the ranks, this might be termed an *echt* (genuine) German regiment. Several of the captains and subalterns are recorded as having been born in Germany and as having seen actual service in war, while many of the privates were European veterans. Some of the characteristics which distinguished Blenker's division appeared first in his regiment, but they must be reserved for later discussion.[7] After the regiment had arrived in Washington, General Winfield Scott and President Lincoln held a review of it before the White House, at which time the former pronounced it the "best regiment we now have here." [8] A corps of pontoniers was attached to this regiment.

[6] The proportion of Germans in the companies, even after nativity was being recorded, ran four fifths, seven eighths, three fourths, eight ninths, and so on. The nativity of the officers is unfortunately not recorded, but names indicate men born in Germany or of German parentage: Chau, Krager, Weise, Meyer, Brand, Sternberg, all captains. Company Descriptive Book, Seventh New York Infantry, War Records Division, The National Archives.

[7] The data on Blenker's regiment have been compiled from several official records. A queer compilation entitled "Guard Report, Sick Report—Memo., Co. A—Descriptive Book, Companies A, E, G, H. Clothing, Cos. E, G, and Order Book, Cos. A, E, G, H, Eighth New York Regiment," affords data on the four companies named. In Company A there were only eight non-Germans; in Company E, only five; in Company G, seven; and in Company H, only six —this in the third year of the war. Unless otherwise stated, all Descriptive Books are located in The National Archives. Bound with the large book is a small hand-ruled book, in which the clothing record is entered with comments (in crabbed German script) such as *"Desertiert mit Gewehr, Degen, und sämtlichen Kleidungsstücken," "Das alte Gewehr abgeliefert."* Even the regimental orders are entered in German. For unusual characteristics in this regiment see Chapter XIII.

[8] Chicago *Illinois Staats-Zeitung*, June 13, 1861.

The Twentieth New York Regiment, or United Turner Rifles, was organized in April, 1861, from among the various *Turn* societies in that city. German citizens provided the money for its expenses, and a committee of women called "Turner Sisters" supplied many necessities. The regiment was recruited by Max von Weber, a former officer of the German army, who naturally became its colonel. It is interesting that it was to this body of Germans that the Swede Baron Ernst von Vegesack was later sent as commander.[9] The regiment drilled daily at the *Turnhalle* and in Harmony Garden.

The Astor Rifles was composed almost exclusively of Germans when it first went to the field. As was true with all these regiments, replacements brought a small infiltration of other elements; but the organization retained its overwhelmingly German character, and the infiltrations were almost entirely of Europeans. In the absence of records for six companies, the historian can merely point to allusions in the papers which refer to the regiment as composed "exclusively of Germans." All the officers had had military training in European military academies.[10]

Few of the German regiments enlisted more attention than the De Kalb Regiment, or the Forty-first New York. This is attributable not only to the fact that it was recruited under special authority of the War Department but also to the fact that it received material help from R. A. Witthaus, a patriotic and wealthy German citizen. About 700 of its 1,040 members, as well as its commander, had fought in the Prussian Army against the Danes in 1848–1849; and 23 of its 33 officers were veterans who had seen service in European campaigns. Its commander, Colonel Leopold von Gilsa, has already been indicated; the choice for second in command fell on Emil Duysing, a former lieutenant of the army of Hesse-Cassel, a soldier fresh from the Danish war. Company G was recruited in Philadelphia, Company H in Newark, and the rest of the companies in New York. Company F was permanently detached in November, 1861, to be reor-

9 Joseph Rosengarten, *The German Soldier in the Wars of the United States* (Philadelphia, 1886), 114–15; Thomas W. Hyde, *Following the Greek Cross; or Memories of the Sixth Army Corps* (Boston, 1894), 89. See also Chapter XI of text.

10 The official record in The National Archives gives the personnel of only four companies (A, C, F, and G), and is recorded in a book labeled "Court Martials, Company Descriptive Book, Clothing, Twenty-ninth New York Infantry." The record of Company C shows how many other nationalities were represented by only a few men. There were fifty from Germany, twelve natives of America (many of them with German-sounding names), and one each from France, Belgium, Bohemia, Holland, Switzerland, Alsace, Austria, and Poland. See also New York *Courrier des États-Unis*, May 10, 1861. For the statement as to the training of the officers, see the New York *Times*, May 3, 1861.

ganized as the Ninth New York Independent Battery. Company A had been organized before the war as the De Kalb Zouaves and lent its name to the entire regiment. A fine band of twenty-five pieces with a drum corps of twenty members was attached to the command.[11]

The Forty-fifth New York probably enjoyed the name of the Platt Deutsch Regiment because it was recruited among North Germans. In most of the cases where the nativity of the commissioned and noncommissioned officers is given, it proves to be German, though one Hungarian attained a captaincy, as did one Austrian. Participating in many battles, some companies of this regiment lost heavily, so that one company seems to have been enlisted *de novo* in 1864 and another recruited after 1861 about one third (chiefly native-born) [12] of its total numbers. The Forty-sixth New York functioned under two colonels during its history; and the Fifty-fourth, which may have gone to the field almost wholly composed of Germans, showed a strong admixture of native Americans and other Europeans in three of its companies by the time that birthplace was being recorded.[13] This last colorful regiment will appear often in this story.

The Fifty-second New York State Volunteers was organized at Staten Island in the fall of 1861 by the consolidation of four companies of the Sigel Rifles, which gave the name to the entire regiment, with six companies of the German Rangers. It formed part of the Third Brigade under General Sumner. In October, 1864, a tiny remnant of the original regiment, five officers and thirty-five men, returned to New York.[14] In July, 1865, it was finally mustered out with only a small proportion left of the total inscribed on its rolls. It is impossible to determine exactly the composition of German Rifles, No. 3, or the One Hundred and Third New York Regiment, except in May, 1863, when Wilhelm Heine became its colonel, the third to command it. Except for one company, which was composed almost exclusively of native-born, it was at that time still pre-

---

[11] The writer was unable to locate any descriptive books for this regiment or for the Turner Regiment. See, however, Fox (comp.), *New York at Gettysburg*, I, 304–306; Rosengarten, *The German Soldier in the Wars of the United States*, 115; New York *Courrier des États-Unis*, May 6, 1861.

[12] Company Descriptive Books, Forty-fifth Infantry, except Company G, which was supplied by the Regimental Descriptive Book, War Records Division, The National Archives.

[13] No Company A appears in the Company Descriptive Book for the Fifty-fourth Regiment. The three companies with large admixtures of non-Germans were Companies H, I, and K. On the other hand, thirty-three additional recruits in Company D were chiefly Germans. This last statement is added to give a glimpse of the composition at a later period.

[14] Rosengarten, *The German Soldier in the Wars of the United States*, 115–17.

dominantly filled with men born abroad, the greater part of them in Germany. The first colonel of the regiment organized an elite company constituted entirely of former German officers, who were promised rapid advancement and who wore a special emblem on their uniforms.[15] This unit saw such hard service that despite three separate recruitments, it could present only three companies at the muster-out.

The Sixty-eighth, although it had one company in which Germans constituted only one third in a mixed group, should be fairly classed as half German. It was recruited in New York City during July and August, 1861, and was named the Cameron Rifles in honor of Simon Cameron, the secretary of war. A majority of its members had resided in the United States for a number of years; and it constituted as good fighting material as could be found, for many of its officers had seen service in the German and Austrian armies. In late August, with the regulation strength, it left for Washington, where it was soon assigned to Blenker's division. By June of the next year it was serving in Von Steinwehr's division in Sigel's corps, and by the time of the Gettysburg campaign it had been transferred to Von Gilsa's brigade in Barlow's division.[16] The Fifty-eighth and the One Hundred and Nineteenth constitute the other half-German regiments from New York.

The Germans contributed several batteries of artillery from this state: Louis Schirmer's battery; Emil von Sturmfels' battery; and, above all, Michael Wiedrich's battery of light artillery, recruited in Buffalo. This last-named, originally a militia battery attached to the Sixty-fifth New York State Militia, was composed of German-Americans. Although the men had been actively perfecting their organization for months, it was not until August 21 that the government sanctioned their request to be assigned to Frémont's command, which was then in Missouri. Colonel William P. Carlin of the Regular Army, who had been stationed at Buffalo and thus knew Wiedrich, made an urgent request for the battery to be sent to him in Missouri; but in mid-November it was sent to Wash-

---

[15] Company Descriptive Book (except for Company D, which was supplied from the Regimental Book). See also Wilhelm Kaufmann, *Die Deutschen im amerikanischen Bürgerkriege* (3d ed.; München and Berlin, 1910), 494.

[16] We owe to Arnold Kummer the account of this regiment, published in Fox (comp.), *New York at Gettysburg*, II, 568. In Company D—the company referred to as the exception in the regiment—Germans and Irish each constituted just about one third of the total number, other nationalities making up the other third. Company Descriptive Book, Sixty-eighth New York Infantry.

ington, where it was attached to Blenker's division. Michael Brickel's artillery, also organized in Buffalo and composed of four batteries, all manned by Germans, constituted the First New York Independent Battalion of Light Artillery. After Antietam, where Major Arndt, acting commander of the battalion was killed, the batteries were made independent, and were numbered Twenty-ninth, Thirtieth, Thirty-first, and Thirty-second Independent Batteries. As in so many of the organizations, there was a slight admixture of many other nationalities in the Thirtieth Battery under Captain Adolph Vögelee; and many American-born Germans served in the Thirty-first Battery. The Twenty-ninth was afterwards consolidated with the Thirty-second under Captain Charles von Kusserow, an old officer of the Prussian army; and ultimately the Thirtieth was merged with the Thirty-first. To this group should also be assigned the Fifteenth New York Heavy Artillery, which, except possibly for one company, was largely made up of Germans.[17]

The Fourth Cavalry under Christian F. Dickel as nearly approaches a German cavalry as any New York could boast. It should probably be classified as a mixed, or half-German, unit, but the roster for Company A, according to the Company Descriptive Books entered in 1862 or later, recorded all except two—a Swiss and a Dane—as having been born in Germany. Company H had only eight non-German members; and three fourths of Companies C and I were Germans. Moreover, the fact that this regiment was assigned to Blenker's division argues that it was thought of as German. The four companies of Germans in the First Regiment New York Cavalry were all old cavalrymen; recruited by Carl Schurz at the very outset of the war, they constituted one of the many contributions to the Union cause by this great leader of the Germans. His appointment as minister to Spain prevented his acting as colonel of this, the first regiment of volunteer cavalry raised, but it is associated indissolubly with his name. It must be noted that only some of the members of the regiment were Germans and that almost all came from New York.

---

[17] For Wiedrich's battery, see Frederick Smith, "Historical Sketch," in Fox (comp.), *New York at Gettysburg*, III, 1245; for Brickel's artillery see Rosengarten, *The German Soldier in the Wars of the United States*, 125–26. Company books were found for Batteries Thirty and Thirty-one but not for the other two. The Company Descriptive Book for the Fifteenth Heavy Artillery is complete and records a regiment enlisted in 1863–1864. Company M has been rejected from the list of German-American groups because the names of the 136 men born in America do not sound German. The captains of Brickel's batteries were Henry Dietrich, Adolph Vögelee, John Knieriem, and Charles von Kusserow.

New England

Before proceeding to the discussion of Germans from Pennsylvania who served in the Union forces, the reader should note the presence in the Sixth Connecticut Regiment of a company of Germans made up from New Haven, Norwich, and Waterbury, and commanded at first by Captain Daniel Klein; and of a second company drawn from Bridgeport, Meriden, and New York under Captain Henry Biebel. Captain W. C. Moegling also commanded a company of Germans in the Eleventh Connecticut till he rose to be lieutenant colonel of the regiment. Likewise, in two German companies recruited in Boston by May, 1861, one in the Seventeenth Massachusetts Regiment and one in the Twenty-ninth, there were several officers and nearly thirty privates trained in the German armies.[18]

Pennsylvania

For purposes of this study it is proper to ignore the numerous regiments of infantry and artillery which the Pennsylvania Dutch put into the field. They represented American-born of German descent, often several generations removed. Furthermore, the writer found few Pennsylvania regiments composed wholly of Germans. The Twenty-seventh, under Colonel Max Einstein and later under Adolphus Buschbeck; [19] the Seventy-third, under Colonel John A. Koltes; the Seventy-fourth, under the well-known Alexander von Schimmelfennig; the Seventy-fifth, commanded by Colonel Heinrich Bohlen and later by Franz Mahler; and the Ninety-eighth, formerly the Twenty-first, were all so strongly German in composition that they may justly be classified as German. The entire field and staff of the first-named appear to have been German, and many of the noncommissioned officers were born in Germany; but not one company without repre-

[18] See Rosengarten, *The German Soldier in the Wars of the United States*, 133, for the Connecticut units; for the Boston companies see the Boston *Pilot*, May 18, 1861. The Boston companies were supported by several of their countrymen who could ill afford the expense involved. George H. Gordon, *Brook Farm to Cedar Mountain in the War of the Great Rebellion, 1861–1862* (Boston, 1863), 11. It might be noted that Rifle Company B, First Connecticut Volunteers, which went out for the first three months campaign, was composed of foreign-born. Records in the office of the Adjutant General of Connecticut. The two German companies in the Sixth Connecticut Regiment were Companies B and H.

[19] Only the Regimental Descriptive Book for the Twenty-seventh Pennsylvania and the Company Descriptive Books for some of the companies have been preserved at The National Archives.

sentatives from other countries than Germany was to be found by the time the data were being recorded.

The active spirits for early military organization among Philadelphia Germans were John F. Ballier, Wilhelm Binder, and Heinrich Bohlen, whom we shall meet again; surpassing even these in zeal was John A. Koltes, whom we shall meet later as a general. Koltes drilled the Männerchor Rifle Guards for home service and, in addition, recruited a regiment, the Seventy-third, for the war. Two companies of Pittsburgh Turners, who had gone out April 16 as Companies B and K in the Fifth Pennsylvania Volunteers for the three months service, formed the nucleus of the Seventy-fourth Pennsylvania, organized a few months afterwards. Command of the regiment was given to Colonel von Schimmelfennig, a brilliant Prussian officer, who made of the regiment a model organization in drill and discipline. Companies H, I, and K were largely German in personnel even in 1863. Colonel Bohlen, previously referred to as one of the leaders in stimulating military organizations in this state, became colonel of the Seventy-fifth Regiment, which he equipped at his own expense. The fourth of the leading spirits, John F. Ballier, organized the Twenty-first Regiment, later to be reorganized as the Ninety-eighth Pennsylvania, and was rewarded with its command. Mention should not be omitted of the four companies of Philadelphia Turners who joined their comrades in the Twenty-ninth Regiment, organized in New York, when they could not be placed in any of the Pennsylvania German regiments.[20]

New Jersey

The German contingent in New Jersey can be quickly disposed of. No purely German regiment was formed until 1864, when the Third Cavalry was raised in Hoboken. There were, however, few regiments without German companies. Many Germans from this state served, as was natural,

[20] The full list of officers of the Seventy-fourth Pennsylvania, given in the Regimental Book as of 1864, would seem to indicate that they were Germans or American-born Germans. For the Turner companies, see "Address of Cap. Paul F. Rohrbacker," in John P. Nicholson (comp.), *Pennsylvania at Gettysburg. Ceremonies at the Dedication of the Monuments erected by the Commonwealth of Pennsylvania* (Harrisburg, 1891–1893), I, 432.

For officers of the Seventy-fifth Pennsylvania, see H. Nachtigall, "Account of the Part taken by the Seventy-fifth Regiment Pennsylvania Volunteers in the Battle of Gettysburg, July 1, 2, and 3, 1863," *ibid.,* I, 438; for the Ninety-eighth Pennsylvania Volunteers, see Kaufmann, *Die Deutschen im Bürgerkriege,* 186; for the four Turner companies of Philadelphia, see Rosengarten, *The German Soldier in the Wars of the United States,* 113. For discussion of the officers named, see Chapters VIII and IX of text.

in New York and Pennsylvania regiments. Battery A of the First New Jersey Artillery was at first entirely German,[21] while Batteries B and C were distinctively German.

Ohio

Ohio Germans sent to the field no less than six regiments. The first of these was the Ninth Regiment, composed of the stanch, well-drilled Turner companies of Cincinnati and headed, oddly enough, by Colonel Robert L. McCook, an American who spoke no word of German but was immensely popular with his Germans and knew how to infuse those phlegmatic Teutons with excitement. So great was the bond between him and his men that when he was offered a brigadiership, he did not accept the commission. When—ill and with his command sadly divided —he was being transported in an ambulance, a band of Confederate guerrillas, discovering his helpless condition, fell upon the escort, overturned his ambulance, and shot him in cold blood. His regiment, upon visiting the scene, avenged his death by hanging some of the guerrillas and destroying their homes.[22] As McCook had been later promoted to command of a brigade, Gustav Kämmerling commanded the regiment during most of the war. The Twenty-eighth Ohio was an equally interesting regiment. Known as the "Second German Regiment," it was organized at Cincinnati during April and May, 1861, and mustered into the United States service at Turner Hall on June 13 for three years, or the duration of the war. It was commanded by Colonel August Moor, a veteran of the Mexican War. The Thirty-seventh Infantry, drawn from Cleveland, Toledo, Sandusky, and northern Ohio, bore the label of "Third German Regiment"; it was overwhelmingly, though not exclusively, German. The colonel in command by 1862 was Edward Siber; he was succeeded by Colonel Ludwig von Blessing, who was, like Siber, a former Prussian officer. The One Hundred and Sixth, despite an American commander, was designated as the "Fourth German Regiment"—a classification justi-

---

[21] Kaufmann, *Die Deutschen im Bürgerkriege*, 186. Rosengarten lists such companies in the First, Second, Third, and Fourth regiments. *The German Soldier in the Wars of the United States*, 145.

[22] Robert McCook was a member of the famous family and had, besides his father, seven brothers in the Union service. Several of the family, including the father, died in the service. For the account given above, see W. J. Tenny, *The Military and Naval History of the Rebellion in the United States with Biographical Sketches of Deceased Officers* (New York, 1866), 731–32. For the Ninth Ohio, see Oberst Gustav Tafel, "Die Neuner," *Eine Schilderung der Kriegsjahre des 9ten Regiments Ohio Vol. Infanterie, vom 17 April 1861 bis 7 Juni, 1864* (Cincinnati, 1897). See also Chapter IX of text.

fied by its German lieutenant colonel, Gustavus Tafel, as well as its German captains, noncommissioned officers, and privates. The One Hundred and Seventh Ohio, which served under Colonel Seraphim Meyer,[23] indubitably belongs to the roster of German regiments from this state; and the One Hundred and Eighth, under Lieutenant Colonel George T. Limberg, partly merits its title of the "Sixth German Regiment."

In instant response to the call, the citizens of Ohio also sent individual companies to the defense of the Union. The "Steuben Guards," a militia company of Columbus, representing the best element among the Germans of that city, was ready to move within a very few days after the first call. A company from St. Marys mustered fifty Germans. To the credit of the Germans is generally assigned the Third Ohio Cavalry, though it was composed only partly of Germans. There were three German batteries from Ohio. Louis Hofman's battery of Cincinnati, the Fourth Ohio Battery, consisting mostly of old cannoneers from Baden, Germany, went to the defense of the Unionists in Missouri on August 22, 1861. Louis Markgraf's battery from Cincinnati was half German; and a third German battery from Ohio, sent out from Cincinnati under William von Dammert but commanded from 1862 by Hubert Dilger, won undying fame. Other regiments which were led by Germans and the ranks of which were from one-half to three-fourths German were the Forty-seventh, under Colonel Friedrich Poschner; the Fifty-eighth Ohio, under Valentine Bausenwein; the Seventy-fourth, under Alexander von Schrader; and the One Hundred and Sixty-fifth, under Alexander Bohländer.[24]

[23] In addition to the Company Descriptive Books for these Ohio regiments, see for August Moor's regiment, D. Cunningham and W. W. Miller (comps.), *Report of the Ohio Antietam Battlefield Commission* (Springfield, Ohio, 1904), 71 ff. Judging by the actual enrollment officially recorded, it is rather difficult to follow the classification made by Kaufmann, though he may be correct for 1861: eleven Ohio regiments called German but only four pure German regiments. In the Descriptive Books, none were found with only Germans enrolled; there were six regiments which could be justifiably regarded as German regiments.

The second German regiment was raised under authority given by the President to the Honorable John A. Gurley. See General Joshua Bates to Governor William Dennison, Camp Dennison, July 11, 1861, Executive Correspondence of the Governors of Ohio, May 16–July 11, 1861.

[24] For the prompt response in Ohio, see the Columbus *Westbote*, April 25, 1861. For Hofman's battery, see Chicago *Illinois Staats-Zeitung*, August 22, 1861. The author is aware that she differs here again from Kaufmann in her classification of Ohio regiments. She cannot admit as German a regiment like the Ohio Seventh, of which by 1862 only one third of the members were of that nationality. Kaufmann, *Die Deutschen im Bürgerkriege*, 186–87. That it could completely change its composition in a year seems strange.

Indiana

The response of the Germans from the central West was generous. The outstanding regiment of Indiana Germans was that assembled as the Thirty-second Indiana, under Colonel August von Willich. Since Von Willich carried over into the Indiana regiment the surplus from the Ninth Ohio, this regiment was accordingly always recognized as the sister regiment of the Ninth Ohio. The Germans Albert Lange and Johann B. Lutz did much for the organization of troops in this state. The One Hundred and Thirty-sixth, recruited in Evansville, was, like the Twenty-fourth Indiana, half German; it later won glory by its march through Georgia. Friedrich Behr's battery, recruited in Indianapolis, and Martin Klauss's battery, recruited in Evansville—the Sixth and the First Independent respectively—were both recognized as wholly German organizations.[25]

Illinois

The presence of many Germans in Illinois and the fact that this state was the residence of several distinguished German leaders ensured the creation of several regiments drawn from the German element of the population there. These included the Twenty-fourth, Eighty-second, and Forty-third Illinois regiments—the last not strictly admissible here as it was recruited from second-generation Germans. At the President's first call, companies, later fitted into existing regiments, instantly sprang up in Chicago. The Union Cadets, a Turner company, stepped forward under Captain Gustav Kowald; the Lincoln Rifles, organized by Captain Géza Mihalotzy in January, 1861, was promptly in camp at Cairo; Union Rifles No. 1 and No. 2, under Captain P. H. Lippert and Captain Anton Iten respectively, were soon to find themselves parts of larger units; companies of the Washington Light Cavalry under Captain Frederick Schambeck, consisting of men trained in Germany, appeared. By April 19, fifty-four Illinois companies had already been accepted by the government.[26]

The regiment first named above, the Twenty-fourth Illinois, was the first Hecker Jäger Regiment; named for Friedrich Karl Franz Hecker, the distinguished leader of the Baden Revolution of 1848, it stood com-

---

[25] Kaufmann, *Die Deutschen im Bürgerkriege*, 188–89. The Regimental Descriptive Book gives somewhat fuller information on the Thirty-second Regiment than does the Company Book.

[26] Chicago *Illinois Staats-Zeitung*, May 20, 1861. Many of the Illinois companies could not be accepted by the government.

pleted by May, 1861, its members pledged for three years service. A large number of the members had rendered military service in Europe; and the names selected for the various companies, such as Schwarze Scharf-schützen, Chicago Jägers, and Pioniere, show how the thinking of these Germans harked back to the Fatherland. The company raised by the Hungarian Géza Mihalotzy was added to this regiment, and Mihalotzy became at first lieutenant colonel and, by December, colonel. A German company, fully armed, materialized from Bloomington and from Ottawa. On May 21 notices began to appear for recruits to report for drill every Monday, Wednesday, and Saturday evening at seven-thirty at Kinzie Hall in Chicago. On May 25 Hecker gracefully accepted the proffered command. Though the ranks were filled overwhelmingly by Germans and the officers were of that nationality, some other nationalities were represented, as is sufficiently attested by the presence of Mihalotzy and his company.[27]

The Eighty-second Illinois Regiment might properly be termed the "Second Hecker Regiment," since the enthusiasm of the Germans of Hecker's adopted state also produced it. Hecker, who withdrew from the command of the Twenty-fourth because of internal politics, took the field as colonel of the Eighty-second Regiment, a more purely German command. The members of his entire staff of the Eighty-second, including the lieutenant colonel, Edward S. Salomon (not a member of the distinguished Salomon family of Wisconsin), are recorded as having been born in Germany. The nativity of but three of the captains was recorded (on a date subsequent to the organization of the regiment): two were Germans and one was an Austrian. Not all the lieutenants were German, for two were registered as Bohemian and Danish respectively. While many of the noncommissioned officers had been born in Germany, there were also many of other origin—Swedish, Swiss, English, Hungarian, French, Bohemian, and Scotch. In the ranks the intermixture of other nationalities was so slight that it is proper to consider this a German regiment. It is interesting that one of the companies was a Jewish unit—the wealthiest of the entire army, for the Chicago Jews had raised a large sum to aid it. The members of this unit, who joined Hecker's regiment in acknowledgment of his well-known liberal attitude toward the Jews,

[27] These details on the organization appear in the Chicago paper. Only the official record for Company D is to be found, and it appears in the Regimental Descriptive Book. At the time this record was made, all the sergeants and corporals were still of German birth, but twelve representatives of other countries had crept into the ranks.

definitely brought honor to the name of their race. It was from the ranks of this company that Edward Salomon rose to command the regiment. One Swiss company was to be found in this regiment,[28] as will appear in the next chapter.

The Forty-third Illinois was in great part organized by the famous Gustav Körner from among Germans of the second generation in the German colony of Belleville. Both of its colonels, Julius Raith and Adolf Engelman, had served in the Mexican War.[29] In addition, Battery E of the Second Illinois Light Artillery was almost entirely German in composition; Company B of the Twelfth Illinois Cavalry was German except for seven stragglers of four other nationalities. Christian Thielmann's company of dragoons, a Cook County organization, had been completed by July 26, 1861. The captain, by whose name the company was known, had been a *Rittmeister* and, with his two lieutenants, had already learned military science in his homeland. The company had enlisted only well-read persons; two thirds of them had rendered military service in Germany, and some of this portion had smelled powder. At first it was put, with the Coles County Company and the Montgomery County Company, into the First Illinois Cavalry Regiment; but ultimately it became Company A of the Sixteenth Cavalry Regiment.

Kaufmann rates as half German or more than half German the following Illinois regiments: the Ninth, a three months regiment, the Thirty-sixth, Forty-fourth, Forty-fifth, Fifty-seventh, and Fifty-eighth Infantry regiments, the Thirteenth and Sixteenth Cavalry, and the batteries of artillery of Stollemann, D'Osband, and George C. Gumbart.[30] To these the writer would add the Twenty-seventh Infantry Regiment.

[28] The names of the officers of this regiment and the nativity of most of them can be ascertained from the Regimental Descriptive Book; those of the privates and of the officers below the rank of captain, from the Company Descriptive Book, which has no blanks. The writing is very German. For the Jewish company, see Kaufmann, *Die Deutschen im Bürgerkriege,* 188–89. For the Swiss company, see Chapter VI of text.

[29] Kaufmann, *Die Deutschen im Bürgerkriege,* 495, 540; Rosengarten, *The German Soldier in the Wars of the United States,* 231. Körner was a close friend of President Lincoln.

[30] For the battery of the Second Illinois Light Artillery, see Regimental Descriptive Book; for Company B, Twelfth Illinois Cavalry, see Company Descriptive Book; for Thielmann's dragoons, see Chicago *Illinois Staats-Zeitung,* July 26, 1861. For the groups classed as half German, see Kaufmann, *Die Deutschen im Bürgerkriege,* 189. Gumbart appears in John J. Fallon (comp.), *List of Synonyms of Organizations in the Volunteer Services of the United States during the Years 1861, '62, '63, '64 and '65* (Washington, 1885). This compilation was made under the direction of Brigadier-General Richard C. Drum. Gumbart is listed therein in Battery E, Second Illinois Light Artillery.

Missouri

In no other state was the share of the Germans so great as in Missouri and in no other state did their participation prove so crucial.[31] The First Regiment of Missouri Volunteers was full by April 23. As it consisted largely of Germans and German-Americans, it was expected that a German, probably Franz Sigel, would command it. The officers conceived the view that an influential American must be at its head; and so the command fell to Francis P. Blair, a purely political choice strongly opposed by the privates, who felt that a military man was necessary. It was into this regiment that the three Turner companies of St. Louis were incorporated. One company consisted almost entirely of loyal Irishmen.[32] The Second Missouri Regiment stood in the arsenal fairly complete on the same date, April 23. Composed also of German-born or descendants of Germans, it had an Austrian for its colonel, Heinrich Börnstein of the *Anzeiger des Westens,* a good choice but one received with shrugs in many American quarters because he was so little known. A few days later the Third Missouri, likewise a German regiment, was in service under Colonel Franz Sigel. Note should be made of the fact that a company from Belleville, Illinois, organized by Adolf Dengler, a Forty-eighter, was led by Dengler to St. Louis, where it joined Sigel's regiment.

Special interest attaches to the Fourth Missouri, as its members chose for their name the Black Jägers, a name susceptible of misinterpretation by Southerners. This group, consisting chiefly of immigrants, had its origin in a hunting and rifle club of many years standing. Its leader in 1861 was Nicholaus Schüttner, a carpenter who compensated for lack of education by a resolute patriotism. In some of the companies there were a few native Americans and in one company a great many Bohemians. Armed and accustomed to handling rifles, this group was of special consequence in preserving Missouri for the Union. The original society was composed largely of men who had seen military service in Europe. When the Union flag was planted on the southeast corner of Broadway and Pine Streets in St. Louis opposite the Minute Men's secession ensign, Captain Schüttner instantly mounted guard for its protection with a company of about forty men from the Jägers.

[31] The aid given to Missouri by other states at the outbreak of war will be briefly discussed on p. 147 and note. See also pp. 220–21.

[32] By 1862, although some companies remained preponderantly composed of Germans or of German-Americans, two (Companies D and I) definitely should not be called German, according to the Company Descriptive Books.

Although these four regiments filled the state's quota, General Nathaniel Lyon decided to allow organization of a fifth regiment. As its colonel, this unit chose Karl Eberhardt Salomon, the third member of the distinguished family which had fled to this country after participation in the German Revolution of 1848 to serve the Union cause.[33] The members of this regiment came chiefly from the southern part of the city and from Carondolet and St. Louis counties. The slower organization—it was not organized until May 18—resulted from the fact that the first four regiments had filled Missouri's quota, and the mustering of the Fifth Regiment of Volunteers became legal only after the President increased the Missouri quota to ten thousand men. The Fifth Missouri Regiment was formed by the consolidation of a company of sappers and miners under Captain J. D. Vörster, a pioneer company under a Captain Geisler, a pontonier company under Captain Louis Winkelmeyer, and seven companies of the Fifth United States Reserve Corps.

Members of these five regiments were all three months volunteers. After completion of three months, the First Regiment was changed into an artillery regiment; and three of the other regiments were reorganized for three years service. In addition, a battery of light artillery under Major Franz Backhoff and at least six regiments of a reserve corps or Home Guard had been enlisted. All of these regiments had been raised almost entirely in St. Louis, and the Germans of that city had furnished four fifths of the men. In view of the fact that the Home Guards were in charge of part of the communication lines and were kept in active service against the aggressive hostility of Confederate partisans till the time for which they were enlisted had expired, it is obvious that they rendered harder war service than most of the volunteers in other parts of the country during their three months of service.[34]

[33] Friedrich Schnake, "Der Ausbruch des Bürgerkrieges in Missouri," in *Der Deutsche Pionier,* XI (1879–1880), 194–96. After the three months service with Missouri troops, Salomon became colonel of the Ninth Wisconsin. For Company F, Second Missouri Infantry, see Order and Company Descriptive Book. Comments which yield some light also appear, as, "Has his parents living in Germany." The Company Descriptive Book for the Schwarze Jäger is disappointing, as there are many blanks in the nativity column and no record at all for Companies G, H, and I. The most helpful secondary source on the Jägers is Robert Rombauer, *The Union Cause in St. Louis,* 198. For the Belleville company see Kaufmann, *Die Deutschen im Bürgerkriege,* 491. For the other Salomons, see p. 198, below.

[34] For the statement as to the Missouri regiments, artillery, and pioneer companies, see *Adjutant General's Report* on Missouri State Militia, 1862, pp. 6–7. See also, Chicago *Illinois Staats-Zeitung,* July 11, 1861, which reproached the Germans for their jealousies and bickerings. For the Fifth Missouri Regiment, see Robert Rombauer, *The Union Cause in St. Louis,*

Also to the Germans must be attributed the Twelfth Missouri, organized under Peter J. Osterhaus and commanded (after his promotion to command of a brigade) by Hugo Wangelin, who made a reputation for himself and his soldiers. A few companies were recruited outside St. Louis in 1861, nine companies in the midst of a German settlement of Union sympathizers in Benton County, and a company in St. Geneva. All of these combined to perfect a regimental organization in June, 1861.[35] Another Turner regiment, the Seventeenth Missouri, under Colonel Franz Hassendeubel, incorporated a company from Philadelphia and strong detachments of Turners from Cincinnati, Detroit, Milwaukee, Davenport, Peoria, Keokuk, and Gutenberg, although the Turners of St. Louis formed the core of the regiment.[36] Company K, in the Eighteenth Missouri Regiment, and Company I, in the Seventh Infantry were purely German companies. The Thirty-ninth, Fortieth, and Forty-first regiments also consisted preponderantly of Germans when they went to the field.

There are many irritating blanks as to names and nativity of the members of the Second Missouri Light Artillery, evidently recruited rather late in 1861 and mustered out of service in 1863. It must be put down as a German organization, however, for according to the data available, the officers were overwhelmingly of German birth, and from four fifths to seven eighths of the privates were German, while a fraction were of nationalities other than native-born American. There were various batteries commanded by Christian Essig, Charles Mann, J. Albert Neustädter, Martin Wölfe ("Welfley" in official records), and Klemens Landgräber, the last-named also known as the "Flying Dutchman" of the First Independent Battery.

The discussion of the Missouri contingent of German troops can be closed with mention of the cavalry regiments. The Fourth Missouri Cavalry bore the name of Frémont Hussars. One group of Germans had come from Wisconsin to constitute Company M in this unit. The colonel and adjutant general were native Americans, but most of the officers and

---

198–99. The record in The National Archives is particularly disappointing. The idea of Home Guards, a literal translation of the Hungarian word *honvéd*, originated with three Hungarians, Anselm Albert and two of the Rombauer brothers. Pivány, *Hungarians in the American Civil War*, 16.

[35] Wiley Britton, *Memoirs of the Rebellion on the Border, 1863* (Chicago, 1882), 41–42. The record for this regiment in The National Archives is in the same volume with the Clothing Record and is badly bound, several pages having been misplaced.

[36] Regimental Descriptive Book. See also Kaufmann, *Die Deutschen im Bürgerkriege*, 188.

the great majority of the rank and file were Germans. Many of them were old officers who soon learned to adapt their old military experience to the problems of war in a new country. From the lieutenant colonel, Gustav von Helmrich, for twenty-eight years a cavalry soldier in Germany, down to the Swiss trumpeter, all were imbued with that military spirit which marks the typical German soldier. Its band of twenty-two pieces was constituted of Germans with but three exceptions, and two of those were Swiss. The buglers were almost all Germans.[37]

Finally, Company A of the First Missouri Cavalry was made up of so many Germans that it may be put down as a German company.[38] Perhaps it will not seem strange that all these regiments were drawn from the German population when one recalls that eight tenths of the unconditionally Union men in St. Louis consisted of the foreign-born—chiefly Germans.

Wisconsin

Turner societies had, of course, arisen in Wisconsin. A Turner Schützen Corps consisting of eighty-six men had been organized in Milwaukee. After much doubt and delay, this corps finally decided to enter the war under Captain William Behrens, was assigned to the Fifth Wisconsin Militia Regiment, and was sworn in on June 12, 1861. This was a natural arrangement, as that regiment was overwhelmingly German and had no company with less than two thirds of its members of that nationality.[39] The Ninth Wisconsin Regiment, named the Salomon Guards in honor of the governor, raised by one of his brothers, and commanded by another, was appropriately a German regiment. Its ranks were filled almost completely with men of that nativity, though through replacements it later became a mixed regiment.[40] The second German regiment to be formed

---

[37] Rosengarten, *The German Soldier in the Wars of the United States*, 94–95. The Regimental and Company Books do not agree. The Regimental Book has been used, as it seems the earlier record. Kaufmann, *Die Deutschen im Bürgerkriege*, 511, identifies Helmrich with the Fifth Cavalry; but see Fallon (comp.), *List of Synonyms*, 70. For a Swiss bugler in this regiment, see Chapter XII of text.

[38] Company Descriptive Book, First Missouri Cavalry.

[39] For the Turner Schützen, see Chicago *Illinois Staats-Zeitung*, June 13, 1861; for the Fifth Wisconsin, see Company Descriptive Book. Governor Randall himself gave the farewell to the Turners.

[40] As with practically all regiments by 1862, there was infiltration of other nationalities; but the proportion of Germans ran high (nine tenths—and in one company all except less than five per cent). The records for Companies E, F, and G are missing from The National Archives.

became the Twenty-sixth Wisconsin Infantry, under Colonel Wilhelm Jacobs and after his resignation under F. C. Winkler. The Forty-fifth Wisconsin, while containing a slightly smaller proportion of Germans than either the Ninth or the Twenty-sixth, was still decidedly a German regiment in private and officer personnel. With the addition of the Second Wisconsin Independent Battery of Light Artillery as a German battery, the Twelfth Wisconsin Battery, recruited in Sheboygan and known as a "Platt Deutsch" battery, and Company F of the Sixth Infantry, the German contribution of the Badger State was complete.[41] There were also a few regiments more than half filled with Germans—the Eighteenth, Twentieth, Twenty-third, Twenty-seventh, Thirty-fourth, and Thirty-fifth. Several companies in the Second, Third, and Fourth Cavalry regiments could be identified as German.

Iowa, Nebraska, Minnesota, West Virginia, and Kansas

The story of the German companies from Iowa, Nebraska, and Minnesota is soon told. Companies B, G, and K, attached to the Sixteenth Iowa Infantry, were about half German in composition; and over two thirds of the men in Company F, one company of the Fifth Iowa Cavalry enlisted at Dubuque and Burlington, were of that nationality. The effort to constitute a regiment of Germans never materialized. Nebraska had at least one cavalry regiment—the First Nebraska under Colonel Wilhelm Bäumer —which was reported by Kaufmann as consisting one half of Germans. For no Minnesota regiment can the claim of a purely German regiment be advanced; for none seemed to have a much larger proportion of men of that nationality than one third. However, individual companies of the First, Second, Fifth, and Sixth regiments were largely filled by Germans, while Henning von Minden's company of cavalry, organized in 1861,

[41] The Descriptive Books of the Twenty-sixth Regiment are complete. Every man in Company B except one Hollander was German-born; all in Company E except five, whose names suggest second-generation Germans. Company A in the Forty-fifth Regiment had only six non-Germans and four of these were probably German-Americans. Company I had all Germans except two—one Scot and one Irishman. Company Descriptive Book. The names of the regimental officers would indicate that they were either Germans or American-born Germans. The record proves that the captains and lieutenants of the Second Wisconsin Light Artillery were German-born, and that most of the noncommissioned officers and five sixths of the privates were likewise born in Germany. See Clothing, Letter, Order, Descriptive, and Morning Report Book. Hense-Jensen does not claim such a high proportion of native-born Germans in the partly German regiments as does Kaufmann. See Wilhelm Hense-Jensen, *Wisconsin's Deutsch-Amerikaner bis zum Schluss des neunzehnten Jahrhunderts* (Milwaukee, 1910), I, 192.

consisted one half of Germans. Emil Münch's battery, later known as Wilhelm Pfänder's, was made up exclusively of former Cincinnati Turners from New Ulm. A German company in St. Paul became possible only because a group of nineteen vigorous men from New Ulm, understanding that a German company was being formed in that city, arrived and declared their desire to join it. Under this fresh impulse a meeting of Germans was called to lay the foundation of a German company. In a few days the signing of thirty recruits seemed to justify the beginning of drill under a German citizen. This company had to wait for the second call. In this frontier community where few were unemployed, it is not strange that foreign companies were slow in materializing; even the First Minnesota Regiment of native-born was slow in forming. Finally, the loyal Virginians who separated to form the state of West Virginia dispatched to the Union forces a battery manned by Germans.[42] Kaufmann asserts that the First and Second Kansas regiments were half German.

Maryland and Kentucky

Several German companies were raised in Maryland, notably the Color Company of the Public Guard Regiment, or the Fifth Maryland; two wholly German companies were also formed in the state just before the Battle of Gettysburg was fought; and several German companies were authorized for the Third Maryland Regiment. In the fall of 1861 *Der Deutsche Correspondent* was filled with advertisements for recruits: Colonel Wladimir Krzyzanowski was seeking recruits for his Fifty-eighth New York as far away as Baltimore; in fact, advertisements appeared in this paper in the issue of October 9, 1861, for no less than nine different companies—not all for German companies.

German as well as Swedish officers seeking enlistments could indulge in perfervid oratory, as did Captain Otto Linde in the following flight: "Citizens! A man who cannot obey can also not command. Let us take to heart this motto of our great Schiller. Let us with all strength and in

---

[42] The Company Descriptive Book for the Fifth Iowa Cavalry gives the data only for Companies F–M. See also Kaufmann, *Die Deutschen im Bürgerkriege*, 190. On the Minnesota companies see St. Paul *Minnesota Staats-Zeitung*, April 20, May 4, 6, 1861. Colonel Wilhelm Bäumer, writing to the St. Louis *Westliche Post*, claims that the company, which was recruited in Omaha, Council Bluffs, and St. Joseph, Missouri, was exclusively German. Quoted by the Chicago *Illinois Staats-Zeitung*, July 1, 1861.

While we should not, of course, refer to West Virginia as a separate entity until after June, 1863, the western portion of Virginia is so designated in this work as a matter of convenience.

arms move against those traitors who have brought unspeakable misery to this land and our families.

"Shall we let our families perish entirely? I say no! To arms! So long as blood still flows in our veins, so that we can show ourselves worthy of those great men who fought for freedom in 1776 with their blood."

From another border slave state, Kentucky, came two half-German Regiments, the Fifth and the Sixth; both were organized in Louisville, and the Sixth ranked as one of the best of the state. The Second Cavalry and Stone's battery had many Germans, though they cannot properly be classified as German units.[43]

DEMAND FOR LARGER GERMAN UNITS

Regiments of Germans sprang up spontaneously in many parts of the North. No sooner was a company formed than someone conceived the idea of a German regiment. As soon as a regiment was attained the cry arose for a brigade. When the brigade became a reality, then a division became the objective. With the completion of a division, ambition soared still higher, so that there were Germans who aspired to a corps or even an entire army of Germans. It has been estimated that six thousand Germans in New York, and four thousand in Pennsylvania—probably including many rather remote descendants of Germans—responded to Lincoln's first call for volunteers. Scarcely six months after the declaration of war, six thousand Germans from Illinois were in the army; as late as 1864 it was still possible to recruit an entire regiment from among the Germans in and around Chicago. The regiments which are usually classified as German—though it is not always correct to call them purely German regiments—amounted to 36,000 men and might comprise divisions, but hardly such a grand military unit as a corps or an army. The administrative authorities had to improvise an army—to organize the units at hand according to pressing needs into brigades, divisions, and corps. They could hardly accede to the wishes of Germans or Irish in the grouping of German or Irish divisions.

It is possible that in the assembling of large masses of Germans, such

[43] The first advertisement for a cavalry company appeared in this Maryland paper, August 10, 1861. See also issues of October 4, 1861, and January 3, 1862. For the companies formed for the Gettysburg campaign, see the issue of June 30, 1863. The appeal of Captain Linde appeared in this newspaper October 4, 1861. For the regiments from Kentucky, see Kaufmann, *Die Deutschen im Bürgerkriege*, 190.

as did occur, chance played a big role. Although the one grand unit, Blenker's division, seemed to become a reality as if in response to German ambitions, it is more likely that it came into existence because just at the beginning of the war it happened that ten German regiments of infantry were formed in New York and four in Pennsylvania. The German division under Blenker's command was hence probably the result of the fact that so many regiments of the same nationality sprang up in contiguous areas, rather than of a determination to create a division of a given nationality.

Kaufmann has justifiably pointed out that in the West a second division could easily have been formed from the German regiments recruited in Ohio, Indiana, Illinois, and Wisconsin, but that was not done. He has offered the explanation that the Germans themselves did not cherish the idea—that many of the Forty-eighters considered that they should not set up provincial bodies of troops. Such catholicity of view may have existed among some Germans of the West, but it certainly did not find frequent expression. On the contrary, the writer did find editors arguing for the large nationality units as a means of winning recognition for their nationality. After the defeat at First Manassas, Gustav Körner, then lieutenant governor of Illinois, proposed to the President the organization in Illinois of a German brigade of experienced soldiers. Lincoln recommended the project to the War Department, but it failed because of the indifference of Secretary Cameron.

The editor of the *Illinois Staats-Zeitung* had much to say in August, 1861, about a German division to be under the command of Sigel. This was a modification of an earlier cry for a German army corps, for, as early as May 8, he had written:

> The idea has been suggested to assemble a German army corps and indeed under German command; this is also the wish of the German fighters, as well as of the Irish, to form a separate corps. . . . A further advantage would be that many more Germans would share in the struggle, that the unity of the command would attain greater results. After peace is attained, a German Corps (which must have its own general staff) would be a mighty reservoir of Germans against the efforts of nativism. Never again could haters of foreigners raise their heads and aliens could with more force press for the granting of equal rights. Hitherto foreigners have been only the bootblacks of Americans.

As a matter of fact, in Missouri a German brigade was formed which persisted, under a regrouping known as the Osterhaus Brigade, even after the dismissal of the three months volunteers; it was commanded by Wangelin throughout the war. The Second Brigade of the Third Division, Twentieth Corps, under Colonel Bernard Laiboldt, affords a third example of a German brigade. This consisted of the German Second and Fifteenth Missouri regiments, of the Forty-fourth and Twenty-seventh Illinois regiments—which were only half German—and of the German Missouri Artillery under Gustav Schüler. This brigade saw hard service under Sheridan's command.[44]

General Sigel did, of course, command the Eleventh Army Corps until he was relieved March 31, 1863, but this corps was never composed exclusively of Germans. Sigel was appointed to this important command on June 26, 1862, with the thought that his appointment would conciliate the Germans and encourage enlistments. Formed originally on the nucleus of Blenker's division, into which much confusion had crept, the corps was at that time constructed principally of German regiments. Its division and brigade commanders were almost all foreigners, with the two noted exceptions of Generals Robert Schenck and Robert H. Milroy. The corps numbered then about 10,800 infantry and 900 artillery.[45] At Chancellorsville, General Oliver O. Howard had command of this corps, with Schurz, Steinwehr, and one American, Charles Devens, in command of the three divisions. At Gettysburg, when General John F. Reynolds fell and Howard had to take his place, command of the Eleventh Corps fell to General Schurz.[46] However, separate nationality divisions involved many inconveniences, so that they tended to be abandoned; and the German contingent melted slowly into the American army of 1,500 regiments consisting of 1,500,000 men.

[44] Ibid., 181–83. The Illinois Staats-Zeitung, July 13, 1861, boosted Sigel's divisions: "In einer anderen Spalte findet der Leser interessante Details über die glänzenden Operationen Sigels und seiner heldmutigen Deutschen. Die Thaten und Verdienste eines Sigels kann die Anglo-amerikanische Presse nicht todtschweigen." On Körner's desire for a German brigade, see Chicago Illinois Staats-Zeitung, August 13, 1861. See Kaufmann, Die Deutschen im Bürgerkriege, 183; Chicago Illinois Staats-Zeitung, May 8, 1861, on the desire for a German corps.

[45] Charles F. Horton, Virginia Campaigns of 1862 under General Pope (Papers of Military Historical Society of Massachusetts, No. 2), (Boston and New York, 1895), II, 36, 37. One authority gives the number of Germans in the corps as far less than half—only 4,500 of the 10,000; another makes the entire corps number 11,500. This subject will be more fully discussed in Chapter XVI.

[46] W. R. Livermore, The Story of the Civil War (New York, 1894–1913), III, Pt. 1, p. 128. (Vols. I and II by John Codman Ropes.) For the list of German companies and regiments, see Appendix, Section C.

CHAPTER SIX

Military Units of Irish and Other

Nationalities

IRISH

WHEREVER on the battlefield the green flag with the harp of Erin emblazoned on it was waving, the beholder might know that an Irish regiment was fighting. Though New York (and that meant virtually New York City) sent forth the most numerous Irish regiments, Americans have become so accustomed to thinking of Boston as the home and fountainhead of the American Irishmen that Massachusetts seems the only suitable starting point for the discussion of the Irishman's part in our Civil War. The Old Bay State contributed two entire Irish regiments besides numerous individual Irishmen in various companies.

New England

The Ninth Massachusetts, recruited in Boston and its general neighborhood and usually referred to simply as the "Irish Ninth," was the third three years regiment to leave Massachusetts for the seat of war. Amid the general excitement engendered by the outbreak of war, Captain Thomas Cass, then head of the Irish Columbian Association, proposed to the governor the formation of an Irish regiment for three years or the duration of the war. Upon the governor's acceptance, recruiting officers appeared in all parts of the state and aroused an ardor which caused many robust young Irishmen to tramp miles to enlist. Many men who were of good family and who were comfortably situated joined this regiment because of patriotism and affection for a government they considered liberal. Though they did not love the Stars and Stripes as dearly as their native green, they could and would fight for it. Recruiting was not then the dreary routine it afterwards became, for the existing excitement brought rapid enlistments. By April 22, five companies had been raised in Boston, a sixth in Salem, a seventh in Milford, an eighth in Marlboro, and a ninth in Stoughton. On May 11 the requisite ten companies were in camp on Long Island in Boston Harbor, where one month later they were mustered into the service.[1] The second regiment, the Twenty-eighth Massachusetts, is properly deferred for later discussion with the Irish Brigade, of which it was a part. The Emmett Guards of Worcester, a militia company which went out for the three months service at the first call, was in New York by the end of April.

In other parts of New England arose three regiments which, though under a strict classification properly regarded as mixed, were clearly held to be Irish by their contemporaries and so find their place here, contrary to the writer's conscience. The first hailed from rockbound Maine, which, even in 1861, was thought to represent pure Anglo-Saxon stock. From Aroostook and Washington counties in the extreme northeastern corner of the state, a regiment of Irish-Americans, the Fifteenth Maine, under Colonel John McCluskey, rose to defend the land of their adoption. The presentation of a silk flag by the ladies of Aroostook on February 22, 1862, marked the recognition of the unit as an Irish organization. Amid the usual ceremonies—the formation of the regiment in a hollow square and fervid speechmaking—the flag was unfurled. On one side it bore the arms and motto of the state, surmounted with a single star—the Star of the East; on the reverse appeared the harp and shamrock of Ireland. Said the speaker, with reference to the Catholic Church: "I love to see Americans and Irishmen fight side by side in this momentous contest. As long as the shamrock remains inscribed upon this beautiful flag, as long as that church looks down upon this bard of Erin—that church whose standard Columbus first erected on your wild and savage shores—no countryman of mine shall desert it."[2]

It was, of course, pure coincidence which bestowed on Connecticut's lone Irish regiment the same number that Cass's Massachusetts regiment bore. To this regiment, composed mostly of Irishmen, Norwich furnished a large part of Company H, named the Sarsfield Guards. Oddly enough, this regiment was sent, at the governor's request, to Camp Chase at Lowell, Massachusetts, for instruction. The governor feared that, owing to the

---

[1] Michael H. MacNamara, *The Irish Brigade in Bivouac and Battle in Virginia and Maryland Campaigns* (Boston, 1867), 14–16, 20; William H. Powell, *The Fifth Army Corps (Army of the Potomac). A Record of Operations during the Civil War in the United States of America, 1861–1865* (New York, 1896), 16. Descriptive Books, both Regimental and Company, are missing for this regiment. The Boston *Pilot* published many articles on this regiment, as was to be expected. See issues of March 15, May 3, June 14, August 2, 1861.

[2] New York *Irish-American*, March 8, 1862.

exuberant and turbulent character of its recruits, it could not readily be disciplined at a home camp. On November 18, 1861, General Benjamin H. Butler reported it as "doing very well" and as being ready to embark on the *Constitution* the next day.[3] While there was a varying admixture of other nationalities in every company and some American-born, whose names were suggestive of Irish parentage by the time nativity was being recorded, the Irish were still the predominant element in every company. One of the few records on which the birthplace was recorded for an officer was that of a Scottish captain. Since Captain John Healy's birthplace was given as Connecticut, the inference is almost inescapable that his father or grandfather was born in the Emerald Isle. The nativity of the noncommissioned officers was usually recorded and as a rule proved Irish or American. A third Irish regiment which was claimed for New England was the Tenth New Hampshire Infantry. In addition, two odd companies must be noted: Andrew Mahoney's Company E of the Nineteenth Massachusetts Regiment, and the Emmett Guards of Burlington, Vermont (Company A of the Thirteenth Vermont), composed largely of Irishmen. The members of the latter company were given a handsome send-off by the citizens of Burlington.[4]

New York

Into New York, especially into the great metropolis, had poured Irishmen during the decades just before the war—many, because of their initial poverty, to remain in that port city. Into Irish regiments streamed those same Irishmen and their sons during the early war years. The first organization of Irish to leave New York for the defense of the Union was

[3] Malcolm McGregor Dana, *The Norwich Memorial; The Annals of Norwich, New London County, Connecticut, in the Great Rebellion of 1861–65* (Norwich, 1873), 49; James A. Marshall (ed.), *Private and Official Correspondence of Gen. Benjamin F. Butler during the Period of the Civil War* (Norwood, Mass., 1917), I, 280; Thomas Hamilton Murray, *History of the Ninth Regiment, Connecticut Volunteer Infantry, "The Irish Regiment," in the War of the Rebellion, 1861–65* (New Haven, 1903), 32–34, 37.

[4] In only one company of the Ninth Connecticut (Company G) did the Irish constitute only one third of the whole, a number which was not increased to one half by counting every American-born soldier as Irish by descent. Company E of the Ninth Connecticut was overwhelmingly Irish. For the Burlington company, see the New York *Irish-American*, October 11, 1862. Companies B–F of the Tenth New Hampshire are missing in the Company Descriptive Books, but can be supplied from the Regimental Descriptive Book. The chief officers of this regiment, as given in the Boston *Pilot*, August 2, 1862, were Colonel Michael S. Donahoe, Lieutenant Colonel John Coughlin, and Major Jesse F. Angell. The first two were sons of Irishmen. It is clear from the article that second-generation Irishmen were regarded as Irishmen.

the well-known Sixty-ninth New York Militia, composed almost entirely of Irish and Irish-Americans. Their commander, Colonel Michael Corcoran, had always been popular with his countrymen, but that popularity had been greatly enhanced when he scored a victory over the government. As an officer in the Regular Army of the United States, he naturally faced court-martial when he refused to parade his militia regiment in honor of the Prince of Wales on the occasion of the latter's visit in 1860. When the Sixty-ninth offered its services, the court-martial was dismissed. No sooner had Corcoran issued a call for volunteers than his recruiting office was besieged by men eager to serve in this regiment and under this leader. He could have furnished a brigade with less trouble than a regiment. Within a few days he had enrolled 6,500 men and had to refuse thousands, all of whom had passed the medical examination.

The scene presented at the departure of the regiment attested the ardor of the Irish patriotism. By an early hour the militiamen and their friends had taken complete possession of Prince Street, where the regiment's armory was located. For several hours there had been waiting on Broadway an assembly of men, women, and children so vast that it had driven every vehicle from that street. Housetops and windows were crowded with enthusiastic Irishwomen, who waved their handkerchiefs incessantly to the crowd below. Several Irish civic societies about two thousand strong, with waving banners, had formed as an escort. The march down Broadway was a triumphal procession. Arriving at the North River, the crowd pressed onto the pier, forcing soldiers out of the ranks till they had to fight their way to the gangplank. Some citizens were trampled underfoot while soldiers lost muskets or caps and faced the danger of being themselves trampled, but eventually all got aboard.[5] To the everlasting credit of the members of the Sixty-ninth, it should be recalled that though their term of service expired July 20, 1861, the entire regiment, after a stirring appeal from Colonel Corcoran, decided to see the issue through the impending battle. They behaved with great gallantry at the First Battle of Bull Run, although their commander, Colonel Corcoran, was lost as a captive to the Confederates.

Next in order comes Meagher's Irish Brigade. Its origin presents a rather complicated story. On the very day that the Sixty-ninth Militia returned

[5] For the number offering to enlist, see the New York *Courrier des États-Unis*, April 24, 1861; for the scene at the departure of the Sixty-ninth, see Moore (ed.), *Rebellion Record*, I, Pt. 2, pp. 142–43. The records of Companies E and F are lacking in the Regimental Book, and the names of members of the other companies do not synchronize in the two books, but the fact of nativity of the men as Irish is well established.

to New York from the battlefield of Bull Run, the Irish patriots Thomas F. Meagher and Robert Nugent conceived in the regiment's armory the idea of forming an Irish Brigade with the trained Irish officer General James Shields as its commander. Owing, however, to the absence of Shields and their inability to reach him, the command devolved on Meagher. The Sixty-third New York Regiment was already organized. The Sixty-ninth New York Regiment was formed by the officers and men of the Sixty-ninth Militia, who had served in the three months campaign and, in a spirit of patriotism, desired to serve their country during the war. This new formation was necessary because the officers of the Sixty-ninth Militia had voted at a meeting of the officers against tendering the services of that organization to the government for three years or the duration of the war. As a sort of footnote, it might be added that the motion to continue in the service was defeated largely by the vote of a large number of officers who had been commissioned by the state but had remained at home during the three months campaign. Furthermore, the casualties and captures at Bull Run meant the loss of the vote of certain officers who otherwise would probably have voted for the motion.[6] The Sixty-ninth Regiment New York Volunteers was assigned this number in order to indicate its identity with the militia regiment from which it had originated and to recognize the distinction it had won at Bull Run.

With these two was associated the Eighty-eighth, together with two batteries of artillery, which, owing to the exigencies of the service, were separated from the infantry. The name applied to the Eighty-eighth New York Infantry, "Mrs. Meagher's Own," probably came from the fact that its colors were presented to the regiment not long before its departure for Washington by Mrs. Meagher in front of the archiepiscopal residence on Madison Avenue. It was also sometimes called Connaught Rangers, in reference to the Eighty-eighth British Infantry regiment, and sometimes Faugh-a-Ballaghs ("Irish Fourth," an appellation long appearing on the guidons of the regiment), in reference to a Gaelic origin. This regiment was practically an alien organization, as comparatively few of its members were citizens by birth. Fully a third were old British soldiers, many of whom had seen service in the Crimean War and the Indian Mutiny. A few spoke only Gaelic when they enlisted from the very gates of Castle Garden. The officers were at first nearly all former officers or noncommissioned officers

6 For the data on the origin of the Sixty-ninth New York Regiment, the writer is indebted to the article by James J. Smith, "The 69th Regiment Infantry," in Fox (comp.), New York at Gettysburg, II, 506–507.

of the Sixty-ninth Militia, who had faced battle at Bull Run. There was, accordingly, a touch of the veteran about this regiment from the very start, so that it is scarcely surprising that its steadiness excited the warm admiration of grim old General Edwin V. Sumner.[7]

These three regiments went to the front in the late fall and early winter of 1861 with their full complement of officers and men, the best physically that Irish brawn could furnish, and all of them eager for the fray. They were soon assigned to General Sumner at Camp California, Virginia. Nugent commanded the brigade until February, 1862, when he was relieved by Meagher, who had been made a brigadier general on February 3. The Twenty-eighth Massachusetts, organized originally for the Irish Brigade at Cambridge and Boston in December, 1861, and made up largely of Irish, came to join it on December 1, 1862. Finally, the fifth and last of the Irish regiments which made up the brigade, the One Hundred and Sixteenth Pennsylvania Cameron Dragoons, joined it at Harpers Ferry in October, 1862, and remained with it until October, 1864, when it was replaced by the Seventh New York Heavy Artillery, not an Irish unit so far as the author has been able to ascertain.

By May, 1862, the Sixty-ninth New York had added to a contingent of 350 men leaving New York to join that regiment a company of Zouaves, elegantly equipped and armed, according to the New York *Tribune* of May 23, 1862. A correspondent of the *Irish-American* from Philadelphia said in the issue of March 8, 1862, that the One Hundred and Sixteenth Pennsylvania would soon be able to take the field: "It is composed of the choicest material of Irishmen who I think will vie with their gallant countrymen and brothers, the 69th, in action."

The Irish Brigade originally numbered about five thousand men; but the losses in its many battles so reduced the ranks as to necessitate large additions of new recruits, so that from first to last it enlisted not less than seven thousand men. Yet when it returned to New York at the close of the war, its roll call did not disclose as many as seven hundred.[8]

[7] On the Eighty-eighth Infantry, see W. L. D. O'Grady, "88th Regiment Infantry," in Fox (comp.), *New York at Gettysburg*, II, 510–11.

[8] "Address of General Robert Nugent" and "Historical notes on the Irish Brigade," in Fox (comp.), *New York at Gettysburg*, II, 475–76, 487; and "Oration of Denis F. Burke," *ibid.*, II, 490. The Sixty-ninth Regiment left New York on November 18, the Sixty-third on November 28, and the Eighty-eighth on December 16, 1861. The Descriptive Books sustain the claim that these regiments were very largely Irish except for the One Hundred and Sixteenth Pennsylvania Regiment, in which the proportion is much smaller—so small that to have considered it Irish as late as the date the Descriptive Books were compiled seems unjustified. The Twenty-ninth Massachusetts Regiment was temporarily attached to the Irish Brigade,

Enthusiasm for the war was still high when Meagher returned to New York in July, 1862, to recruit for the brigade. A meeting was called for July 25 in the armory of the Seventh New York State Militia, over Thompkins Market—then the largest room in the city. Long before Meagher's appearance it was packed with over five thousand Irish-Americans; whenever a few left because of the suffocating heat, their places were taken by others. Each of the two platforms, erected midway on opposite sides of the room, was decorated with flags, while the national colors ornamented the walls and ceiling. A band played Irish and American national airs during the evening. The reporter declared that the wildest outburst of applause and enthusiasm he had ever witnessed greeted Meagher's appearance. When Meagher stated that Nugent's regiment had been reduced from 750 to less than 300 he caused a sensation. "I ask for recruits," he declared, "I ask for them alone." "We will, we will," shouted back voices in the crowd. "You shall have all you ask," cried one voice. Meagher was ready to pin down Irish exuberance. "Shall I have you?" he asked. "I take you at your word. Suppose you come forward and give me your name and residence." The voice subsided, but hisses and groans silenced a man who asked why the Black Republicans did not go.[9]

At Fredericksburg the Irish Brigade was almost wiped out. When it became apparent to the leader that there was no prospect of their being allowed to recruit new members for the New York regiments of the Brigade, it was decided to consolidate the three regiments with perhaps three hundred effective men into a battalion of six companies and to muster out supernumerary officers. General Meagher had previously asked leave to resign, as his brigade no longer existed except in name. After endless futile efforts to persuade the War Department to relieve the Irish Brigade of the severe duties for which its strength no longer was adequate, Meagher felt that it was a mockery to keep up a brigade with the few men left and a great wrong to consolidate regiments that had attained great renown. Although the Sixty-third served through the Wilderness Campaign—its ranks being recruited by the addition of three new companies and by augmentations—as a distinctive Irish organization it may be regarded as nonexistent after Meagher's resignation.[10]

June to November, 1862; but by the latter date it was replaced by the Twenty-eighth Massachusetts.

[9] New York *Irish-American*, August 2, 1862.

[10] John F. Dwyer, "63rd Regiment Infantry," in Fox (comp.), *New York at Gettysburg*, II,

The best known of all brigades was probably the Irish Brigade, since it experienced the hardest fighting of the war and made an unusual reputation for dash and gallantry. The remarkable precision of its maneuvers under fire, its desperate attack on the impregnable wall at Marye's Heights, its never-failing promptness on every field, and its long-continued service in the field all made for it a name inseparable not only from the record of the Civil War but from the history of the Irish race.[11]

After Colonel Corcoran was finally released from a Confederate prison camp in 1862—he had sampled several such camps after his capture at Bull Run—he was made a brigadier general as a partial solace. Immediately he began to organize among his fellow countrymen another unit, which resulted in the Corcoran Legion. When completed, this legion consisted of five regiments, all recruited in the Empire State: the One Hundred and Fifty-fifth, One Hundred and Sixty-fourth, One Hundred and Seventieth, One Hundred and Seventy-fifth, and One Hundred and Eighty-second New York regiments. These units all had, naturally, a predominately Irish composition in both officer and private personnel, although they also had a sprinkling of men from most of the European countries. That many of the American recruits recorded under Irish-sounding names were descendants of Irish fathers seems a common-sense assumption. It is worth noting that even this Legion had to have its regiment of Zouaves, the so-called "Phoenix Regiment," which became identified as part of the One Hundred and Sixty-fourth Regiment. Usually the Irishmen loved to don uniforms of Hibernian green, but evidently even they could not resist the lure of the baggy trousers and the eccentricity of the fez. However, from the colonel to the drummer boy, the Corcoran Legion was genuinely Irish as it went to the field.

Interesting, and indicative of the way in which nationality groups tended to become blurred as the war moved on, is the fact that in one company of the One Hundred and Fifty-fifth at a late date Germans were more numerous than Irishmen. There was also an infiltration of other nationalities among the noncommissioned officers. Scottish and Swedish sergeants appeared, while German, Spanish, and Swiss corporals rubbed shoulders with the Irish. By 1863 "Irish Legion" seems to have been some-

---

502–503. See also New York *Irish-American*, October 11, 1862; May 16, June 20, 27, 1863. Meagher resigned shortly before May 16, 1863.

[11] William F. Fox (author and comp.), *Regimental Losses in the American Civil War* (Albany, 1889), 118.

thing of a misnomer for Companies C and K of the One Hundred and Seventy-fifth Regiment, as those two companies were almost entirely German.[12]

There remains only to name a few scattered regiments of the Empire State. The Irish Rifles, otherwise known as the Thirty-seventh New York, was organized with John Burke as lieutenant colonel. Burke was so thorough a tactician that he was "stolen" by the Sixty-third Regiment for its colonel. The One Hundred and Fifth New York Volunteers came into existence by consolidation of two projected Irish regiments in upstate New York. Howard Carroll, a native of Ireland, had joined the Irish Brigade and was acting as quartermaster when he heard that an Irish regiment was being formed in his home city of Albany. He promptly returned to aid in its organization. Eventually, it was consolidated with an embryo Irish regiment in Rochester as the Western Irish Regiment. Entering this as lieutenant colonel, Carroll succeeded to the command upon the resignation of his superior.[13] However, by 1862 only Companies G, H, and I could justly be termed Irish. There was occasional mention of the fact that the Irish miners in the coal and iron region of Ulster County constituted the Ulster Guard, originally the Twentieth New York Militia; but the officers of this unit were native-born Americans, and the proportion of Irish in the ranks cannot be determined from the rolls. After its three months period of duty it was remustered as the Twentieth New York State Militia to preserve the old rank for the officers. Finally, the First Fire Zouaves, the Eleventh New York, was decidedly Irish in composition.

Pennsylvania

For data on the Irish contingent from Pennsylvania we are largely dependent on John T. Fallon's *List of Synonyms of Organizations in the Volunteer Service of the United States* . . . and the various Descriptive Books of the Union army. Irishmen of that state recruited the following: the Twenty-fourth Infantry Regiment, enlisted for the first three months service; a second Irish regiment, named the Sixty-ninth Infantry to honor the famous New York regiment; Company F in the Thirteenth Regiment

---

[12] Both the Regimental and Company Descriptive Books have been preserved for the One Hundred and Sixty-fourth and One Hundred and Eighty-second New York regiments. Nativity for members of Company I, One Hundred and Sixty-fourth Regiment, can be ascertained only from the Regimental Book. No record exists for Companies F–I in the Company Book of the One Hundred and Seventy-fifth Regiment. The company with more Germans than Irishmen was Company D, One Hundred and Fifty-fifth New York.

[13] New York *Irish-American*, October 11, 1862,

of Reserves; and the Hibernian Target Company, which became Company C in the Second Regiment Reserves. It should, of course, be recalled that James A. Galligher's battalion of Irish dragoons became Companies A to E and, with other companies, constituted the One Hundred and Sixteenth Pennsylvania Regiment in Meagher's Irish Brigade, later becoming a part of the Thirteenth Cavalry Regiment.

Central West

In the central West, despite the presence of many Irish in the cities and on some farms, Irish regiments were not as numerous as they were in the East. The best that the Irish of Ohio seem to have been able to muster was one regiment, the Tenth Ohio, and a few companies—the Hibernian Guards, Company B of the Eighth Ohio Regiment, which volunteered for the early three months service, and two companies in the Sixty-first Ohio. The Seventeenth Wisconsin Infantry Regiment was apparently the only completely Irish regiment from that state, though the Eleventh Wisconsin was chiefly Irish.[14] Indiana claimed credit for sending two Irish regiments to the war, the Thirty-fifth and Sixty-first regiments, the latter becoming ultimately part of the Thirty-fifth. Missouri, apparently teeming with Germans, was able to produce at least one Irish regiment, the Irish Seventh Infantry. Michigan's Irish regiment might be so classified only by courtesy (even though it was raised by the Irishman Edward Doyle), for the Twenty-seventh Michigan was only in part composed of men of the Emerald Isle.

The Irish organization in the West which surpassed all others in importance was Mulligan's brigade, which, though classified as the Twenty-third Illinois Infantry, was recruited by James A. Mulligan in several of the western states. In addition to companies raised in Illinois, it included a company from Detroit; Patrick Naughton's dragoons, enrolled at Jefferson City, Missouri, and afterwards in the Fifth Iowa Cavalry; the Oconto Irish Guards, an artillery company from Wisconsin; and John Rourke's battery, also from Wisconsin. Mulligan's brigade met an undeserved fate in opposing the Confederates at Lexington, Missouri, on September 20, 1861, when, after a valiant defense, the lionhearted young commander was obliged to surrender his exhausted garrison to a vastly superior force because of lack of support from the Union forces.[15] The

[14] The Seventeenth Wisconsin Infantry was known as the Irish Brigade. See Fallon (comp.), *List of Synonyms*, 170.

[15] See also discussion of Mulligan in Chapter IX. On May 30, 1861, the officers of his

Irish Legion was the name assumed by the Ninetieth Illinois Regiment, recruited and organized at Camp Douglas and christened by a Father Dunne, who had largely been instrumental in its organization. With few exceptions, the roster of its commissioned officers sounds like a roll call held in Ireland. The rank and file of the companies were largely Irishmen.

FRENCH

Recalling the relatively large proportion of the French element in the population as compared to other nationality groups, the reader will naturally expect a large showing of French companies and even regiments in the Union army. He will be disappointed, for only one completely French regiment materialized and only one was, so to speak, at hand. After the surrender of Fort Sumter the French of New York City met very promptly at the Steuben House for the purpose of organizing a regiment of French volunteers to support the Union.[16] Already, however, the French militia regiment, the Gardes Lafayette (the Fifty-fifth New York), had taken steps for action. All officers were summoned to meet on April 20 to consider the position of the regiment and adopt measures to defend the flag and to maintain order in the city. The assembled officers decided on measures to double the effective strength by recruitment and to furnish uniforms at a minimum price—in a word, to put the regiment on a war basis for early departure. They also accepted the offer of a subscription among the French population to equip more completely the organization and its company of Zouaves. The size of the subscription, $6,500 by May 2, attests the interest of the French colony in New York City in a French regiment.[17]

Advertisements for recruits began to appear in the *Courrier* on April 23 and specific requirements were set up: men for the artillery company might be French or German, but must be acquainted with the service of that arm and must have served two years in an artillery in France or Germany; members who aspired to join the regiment must be of proper age

---

regiment had sent a bitter protest to the Chicago Council for the niggardly economy which had denied them proper equipment. See Chicago *Illinois Staats-Zeitung*, May 30, 1861.

[16] Wittke, *We Who Built America*, 322.

[17] The notice of the meeting of the officers appears in the New York *Courrier des États-Unis*, April 19, 1861. One of the subscription lists was kept in the office of the *Courrier*. See issues of April 27, 29, May 2, 1861.

and furnish references. It is certainly interesting that Company A of the artillery was organized under one Theodore Lichtenstein![18] The companies were rapidly filled up, each to a hundred men, and some companies were temporarily encamped at the Battery by May 1, awaiting orders for departure.[19] Then began a tedious period of waiting that all but disrupted the organization. By June 1 a state of insubordination existed; more than half of the men had deserted to enroll in other companies with better prospects of getting to the front. One day an entire company, with drums beating, passed over to the Fourteenth Regiment at Brooklyn. After having vainly sought to secure the dispatch of the regiment, Colonel Eugene Le Gal finally resigned, since the officers blamed him for the delay.[20]

After some weeks of searching for a new commander, the regimental officers on July 21 hit upon a happy choice, Régis de Trobriand, a well-known writer who had had military training and experience in France.[21] Two days later, the day after the defeat at Bull Run, the War Department telegraphed acceptance of the services of the regiment. The new commander promptly opened a recruiting bureau to fill the gaps. Old members whose engagements elsewhere were not obligatory returned, and new recruits came in by squads, so that within four weeks the number was increased by more than four hundred.[22] Consequently, by August 28 the regiment was strong enough to take the field, fully armed and equipped

[18] See card in New York *Courrier des États-Unis,* April 25, 1861.

[19] New York *Franco-American Advertiser,* May 1, 1861. This paper predicted departure of the Gardes Lafayette before the end of the week and manifested much pride in the four hundred companies already enrolled in the state. This paper is not extant, but it was quoted by the New York *Courrier des États-Unis,* May 8, 1861.

[20] New York *Courrier des États-Unis,* June 1, 1861. Le Gal inserted a long letter of explanation, dated June 5, which appeared in the issue of June 7. In order to expedite the departure of the regiment he had even made a trip to Albany to see the governor.

[21] De Trobriand's name was suggested by the only person in the regiment who knew him personally, a lieutenant who had served in the army in France. De Trobriand tells of his interview with the major and three of the captains of the regiment: "It was not difficult for us to reach an understanding. The condition for my candidacy was that I should lead the regiment to war; the condition for my acceptance was that the regiment should follow me to war." He was elected unanimously. De Trobriand, *Quatre Ans de Campagnes,* I, 75.

[22] It should be recalled that the old regiment had been on the basis of militia numbers. It had had only the minimum required for the militia—320 men, not a war footing, but enough for parades, funerals, and maneuvers. Naturally, De Trobriand advertised in the New York *Courrier des États-Unis* for recruits. See issue of August 6, 1861. When information came that several Frenchmen in Philadelphia wished to join the Gardes Lafayette, they were advised through the press to address themselves to Captain Baudier or Lieutenant Arosjean (*ibid.,* August 17, 20, 24, September 2, 1861)—advice which suggests that there were recruiting officers in Philadelphia.

and better trained in the handling of arms than most of the other volunteer regiments. De Trobriand led only nine companies from New York, as the tenth was to join him later in Washington.

As in so many of the regiments called French or Irish or German or Spanish, the nationality lines were blurred in this regiment, though the French were in a majority in over half the companies. In recruiting, it had proved desirable to open the ranks to all nationalities. After the French, the Germans were the most numerous; almost all the companies counted Germans in their ranks, and Company H was composed exclusively of them. Company K was made up wholly of Irishmen, commanded by three American officers drawn from the Seventh New York Militia. There was also in the regiment a small number of Spaniards, intelligent, reserved, and of good bearing, and a few Italians, whom De Trobriand stigmatized as poor soldiers. Finally, when the tenth company came, it proved to be composed of Americans, disciplined but little and drilled hardly at all; this company was distinctly inferior to the other companies and never rose above that relative inferiority, though it constituted, in the eyes of its commander, a special case. He considered a company of Zouaves (an inheritance from the militia days which was injected into the regiment) to be an anomaly. The regiment was a medley of French, Germans, Americans, and Irish, with no one element predominating.[23]

The passing of these foreigners through Baltimore did not provoke a repetition of the sad experience of the Sixth Massachusetts, but it did reveal clearly the Southern sympathies which still existed in that city. No one followed the column marching to the sound of the drums, which, according to French fashion, strongly accented the beat, but all bystanders watched it pass. Here and there queries in French were hurled at the marching men: "What are you going to do in Washington?" "The war does not concern you." "To go to kill Americans! Thanks!" "What have the people of the South done to you?" The men of the Fifty-fifth did not reply, as discipline forbade talk from the ranks; but they retaliated by assuming joking airs and making gestures "more eloquent than polite." [24]

By July, 1862, the Gardes Lafayette had already been reduced by its hard service to less than four hundred men; the rest, apart from a certain number of deserters, were dead, confined in Confederate prison camps, or

[23] The writer could find no Descriptive Books for the Fifty-fifth New York Regiment, but the gap is more than compensated for by De Trobriand's specific statements, from which were drawn the above details as to the composition of the Fifty-fifth. De Trobriand, *Quatre Ans de Campagnes*, I, 83–85.

[24] *Ibid.*, I, 78.

lying spent in hospitals. The regiment's career ended with the close of the year 1862. At the Battle of Fredricksburg there could be placed in line only slightly over two hundred men. Faced with the impossibility of filling the gap by fresh recruits, the War Department adopted the only means of restoring effectiveness, that of consolidating the weakest regiments with the strongest; and so the Fifty-fifth was incorporated into the Thirty-eighth New York Regiment. When the term of the Thirty-eighth expired in June, 1863, the remaining men of the Fifty-fifth were transferred to the Fortieth New York, formed of the remnants of six different organizations.[25]

Individual French companies were scattered through various regiments. It has already been indicated that some impatient members of the Gardes Lafayette marched off. Some formed a company, which became known as the Anderson Zouaves, in the Sixty-second New York Regiment. An advertisement in the *Courrier des États-Unis* made a command of the French language a requirement for enlistment. This Zouave company seems, in turn, to have experienced insubordination, for on August 16, its officers inserted a call to members who had left camp "several days ago" to return the uniforms "if they do not wish to be prosecuted by the law as deserters." Since the company appeared in final government lists as a part of the regiment indicated above, it must actually have served in the war. Many French served in the Garibaldi Regiment, but only one company was wholly French; it will be discussed later in this chapter in connection with the regiment.[26]

SCOTCH UNITS

The Scotch citizens of America sent to the war one regiment, the Seventy-ninth New York, which made much history, good and bad. It had previously been a part of the New York militia and was usually referred to as "Cameron's Highlanders" because it was commanded by

[25] *Ibid.*, II, 49–50.

[26] The card appeared in the issue of the *Courrier* of May 27, 1861. The government list particularly referred to here is that compiled under the direction of Brigadier General Richard C. Drum, to which reference has already been made. Fallon (comp.), *List of Synonyms*, 98.

It would be, of course, purposeless to discuss the companies which were projected but failed to materialize, such as La Compagnie Française des Chasseurs à Pied, which, according to the *Courrier des États-Unis* of May 11, 1861, had the necessary numbers by that date. The writer has found nothing further concerning this company and so concludes that it was never accepted and that hence it was disbanded.

Colonel James Cameron, brother of the secretary of war in the Lincoln cabinet, and part owner of the New York *Times*.[27] It was composed largely of Scots and descendants of Scots. It consisted of three hundred men organized in six companies. Immediately after the news of the surrender of Fort Sumter spread, the regiment tendered its services to the government; and active recruiting without regard to nationality began in order to bring the ranks to a war standard, for many of the original members were debarred from enlisting because of age. On April 24 Captain Maclary received orders to enter service at once, but the membership of the regiment was so small that stronger regiments were first sent out. The Highlanders had to watch regiment after regiment pass through the city to Washington while they were left behind.[28] Finally, however, the day came for departure, and the Seventy-ninth was escorted to the train by the Caledonian Club, nearly half of whose members were in its ranks. The regiment then numbered eight hundred men exclusive of the band and drum corps. The band, consisting of fourteen musicians, was one of the best in the city and had volunteered with the regiment for service in the war. Already the infiltration of the Irish, which was later to make them outnumber the native Scots in most of the companies, must have begun; [29] for the intoxication which was the chief cause of their undoing in the mutiny about to be discussed is more frequently associated with the Irishman than with the Scot.

The event for which the regiment became notorious was the mutiny of August 14, 1861. The regiment was encamped in the suburbs of Washing-

[27] This bit of information came from the Chicago *Illinois Staats-Zeitung*, January 11, 1861.

[28] See William Todd, *The Seventy-ninth Highlanders, New York Volunteers in the War of the Rebellion, 1861–1865* (Albany, 1886), 1–2; see New York *Courrier des États-Unis*, April 25, 1861, for the order to enter the service.

It is interesting that at this early period the foreign units received particular attention from the American press. The Buffalo *Daily Courier* (not extant), for instance, printed in its issue of May 20 a poem dedicated to the "Highland Guard," entitled "Step to the Front, Sons of the Heather."

[29] A few samples from the Company Descriptive Book will substantiate the statement in the text. In Company A there were forty-five Irish-born, thirty-two Scotch-born, and thirty Americans (Only if every one of the thirty Americans had been of Scotch descent would the two groups together have outnumbered the Irish). In Company B there were thirty-four Irishmen, only nineteen Scotchmen, and twenty Americans (Here, if the twenty Americans had been added to the Scotchmen the two would have outnumbered the Irish). In Company C there were thirty-four Irish and only five Scots. In Company D there were twenty-five Irish and one Scotchman, as compared with thirty-four Germans. In Company F, there were eighty-nine Irish, sixty-two Scotchmen, and eighty Americans. In this last company the record obviously includes replacements.

ton and was ordered to march into Virginia that morning to join General Daniel Sickles' brigade. It positively refused to obey. The Scotch seemed intractable in disposition; they had lost their commanding officer, Colonel Cameron, and several of their best officers at First Bull Run; and, worst of all, many were intoxicated, as they had just been paid off. Desertions had also occurred until 140 men were missing. When Colonel Isaac I. Stevens could not restore peace, McClellan ordered discipline restored. Colonel Andrew Porter was sent with a battalion and a battery of regulars, who drew up in front of the mutineers and prepared to mow them down if necessary. The ringleaders were arrested and put in irons, and the rest of the men marched into Virginia in accordance with previous orders. In an impressive ceremony they were deprived of their colors. The independence of the Scotch and the early lack of discipline are well indicated in this episode, for when the order for surrender of the colors was read, a private cried out in broad Scotch, "Let's keep the colors, boys!" No response, however, came from any other man.[30] The colors were restored after a month, and the Highlanders completely retrieved their reputation later in the war. It was of them that the Charleston *Mercury* said, after a desperate charge by the Scotch regiment, "Thank God, Lincoln has, or had, only one 79th regiment; for there is only a remnant left to tell the tale." [31]

SCANDINAVIAN UNITS

Now comes the story of the Scandinavian companies and regiments. There were a few individual Swedish and Norwegian companies, but the big contribution, the Fifteenth Wisconsin, was a joint enterprise. The first company to be raised among the Scandinavian element of the population was a New York company which was incorporated in the First New York Volunteers on April 25, 1861; this was called the Scandinavian Company of New York, an appropriate name in view of the fact that its

[30] By way of partial excuse it was stated that the men felt that the order to join General D. E. Sickles was in violation of previously given assurances of an opportunity to recruit and prepare for the coming campaign. These promises may never have been authorized, but may have been given by subofficers. See Frost, *The Rebellion in the United States*, II, 331–32; Shannon, *The Organization and Administration of the Union Army*, I, 181. For the episode at the withdrawal of the colors, see P. F. Mottelay and T. Campbell-Copeland (eds.), *The Soldier in Our Civil War: A Pictorial History of the Conflict, 1861–1865* (New York, 1890), I, 129. The soldier was fortunate in that no officer was able to identify him. As will be seen later, this was not the only instance of mutiny in the army.

[31] Todd, *The Seventy-ninth Highlanders*, 80, 163.

eighty members were drawn equally from natives of all three of the northern countries. On August 10, the very day that its members took the oath, they were stationed in Tompkinsville, Staten Island, where they stayed a month. Five days before their departure, there occurred an officers' ball; and at this affair the women of New York gave the members of the company a large, handsome American flag, in defense of which they swore to offer life and blood. Shortly before this they had received a drum, on which they had vowed to write the donor's name in the enemy's blood.[32]

It was to be expected that Wisconsin, which had a larger Norwegian population than any other state in the Union, would produce a Norwegian company promptly. Before April 22, the governor of the state named T. I. Widney as lieutenant, giving him orders to raise a company—principally among the Norwegians in Dane County, probably, for they were especially numerous there. Many Norwegians in Madison, the county seat of Dane County, had already volunteered, partly for the projected company and partly for other companies. Sixty-five men, largely Norse, had by May 11, in advance of any call for more than three months of service, pledged themselves for three years or the duration of the war.[33] This company, known as the Dane County Guards, served under an American captain who had been in the Mexican War, while Widney took second place. The company left Madison on June 12 for the camp of the Third Wisconsin at Fond du Lac, where it became Company K. From this camp it moved to the front. After the Battle of Cedar Mountain not many of the old Norwegians of the company were left to carry on the fight.[34] Porter C. Olsen, American-born son of one of the Norwegians who came over in the first sloop in 1825,[35] raised a company consisting chiefly of

[32] The officers were well known among the Scandinavians in America. The captain had fought in 1848 in the Danish war, and the first lieutenant, Banker C. T. Christenson, was especially well known. Madison *Emigranten*, August 10, 1861. This does not appear in Fallon's list.

[33] Even more had presented themselves, but many dropped out at the prospect of three years of service. Widney became first lieutenant, while there were three Norwegians who became sergeants and two who became corporals. See Madison *Emigranten*, April 22, June 29, 1861.

[34] The captain was William Hawley. *Ibid.*, June 29, 1861. The number of Norwegians was given as forty-one on June 29. The Norwegian officers appear in the same issue of the Madison *Emigranten*. The loss at Cedar Mountain is recorded in the issue of August 18, 1862. This company appears in Fallon (comp.), *List of Synonyms*, 168.

[35] The first Norwegian immigrants came over in the *Restaurationen*, a tiny, thirty-eight-ton sloop which means to the Norwegian element of our population what the *Mayflower* means to the descendants of the Puritans.

Norwegian-Americans from the Fox River colony in Illinois and, as its captain, led it to join the Thirty-sixth Illinois Volunteer Infantry, a Fox River unit.[36]

It is possible to turn up records of a number of primarily Swedish companies, though the Swedes were numerically fewer than the Norwegians. The "Galesburg Light Guards" was a Scandinavian militia group existent in Illinois in 1858. All but two of the group were Swedes or Norwegians and those two were Germans, so that this was another company whose members were wholly foreign-born. They left Springfield with, and took their place as Company G in, a regiment almost entirely German-American, the well-known Forty-third Illinois, under the German Colonel Julius Raith. Oddly enough, the captain of this Scandinavian company, Captain H. M. Starkloff from Galesburg, was a German and therefore doubtless known to many of the company, a fact which probably explains his acceptability to them. However, the lieutenants and all the noncommissioned officers were Scandinavians.[37] In 1864, Swedish draftees or substitutes were bidden to join this "veteran Swedish" company, since they had the right of choice. They were assured that they would be welcomed and would receive much good advice relating to camp life.[38] There was a second Swedish company in this regiment, Company E.

One of the earliest Swedish companies to get under way was an artillery company of Chicago which duly became Battery G in the Second Illinois Light Artillery. The Swedish organ *Hemlandet* showed great satisfaction over a Swedish organization and urged the joining of such a company by all the Swedish countrymen who felt called on to volunteer to defend the country's freedom. By April 24, 1861, fifty of the requisite eighty had already enrolled. Others intending to join were urged to act with the greatest speed, especially as instructions had already begun under Captain Charles J. Stohlbrand, an experienced officer from Sweden. The majority of the members were Swedes, and the rest were Norwegians and Danes. This unit was organized in Chicago with the aid of the Swedish consul, G. J. Sundell, but it was not accepted because the quota had already been filled. Undaunted, Stohlbrand recruited a second group at Sycamore and

[36] Olsen was killed at the Battle of Franklin. See Blegen, *Norwegian Migration to America*, II, 390; Rasmus B. Anderson, *The First Chapter of Norwegian Immigration, Its Causes and Results* (Madison, 1907), 113–14.

[37] The Chicago *Hemlandet* published, with additional data, the entire list of officers in its issue of October 9, 1861; see also issue of October 21, 1861. The Madison *Emigranten*, July 26, 1856, commented on this militia company as a Swedish company.

[38] Chicago *Hemlandet*, September 21, 1864.

De Kalb in the course of the same year. This was mustered into service in September and became Battery G (previously mentioned) of the Second Illinois Light Artillery.[39]

The Bishop Hill settlement in Illinois, a Swedish communistic venture in its early days, raised a company in 1860, the *Svenska Unionsgardet,* with about fifty enrolled. Although not yet recruited to the full number, it was in camp at Princeton under Captain Eric Forsse by September 30, 1861. Forsse had been an officer and had had twelve years experience in Sweden. This company went into the Fifty-seventh Illinois Regiment.[40]

Meanwhile the Swedes in Minnesota were being stimulated by Hans Mattson of Red Wing to raise a company. He appealed for recruits outside his home state through the two chief Scandinavian papers of the West. In *Hemlandet* he cried: "It is high time for us, as a people, to rise with sword in hand, to fight for our adopted country and for liberty. This country is in danger. A gigantic power has arisen against it, and at the same time against liberty and democracy in order to crush them." [41] *Emigranten* on September 16 carried an advertisement calling attention to the organization of one or possibly two companies in Goodhue County, Minnesota, for the Third Minnesota—obviously referring to Mattson's company. Recruiting seems not to have been too easy; but by October 18 Mattson had seventy-four enrolled, so that he no longer greatly feared that the company which he was already drilling at Fort Snelling would be broken up to fill other companies.[42] By November 26 this company had been incorporated as the Scandinavian Guards (Company D) in the Third Minnesota. Mattson's heart was overflowing with such affectionate pride in his men that he boasted that he had the "best drilled and disciplined Company in the Regiment." [43] A muster roll proves the rightness of classifying this as a Swedish company, since about two thirds of the members were of that nativity; but it is more accurate to designate it as Scandinavian because almost all of the other third were Norwegian.[44] Even the three who were not Norwegian were clearly Scandinavian of the second generation.

[39] *Ibid.,* April 24, 1861. Listed also in Fallon (comp.), *List of Synonyms,* 23.

[40] *Ibid.,* October 16, 21, 1861. Not listed by Fallon.

[41] Hans Mattson, *Reminiscences: The Story of an Emigrant* (St. Paul, 1891), 60.

[42] See Mattson to his wife, October 17, 18, 1861, Mattson Papers. The whole care of the company rested on his shoulders, he complained, as all the rest were so "green." *Id.* to *id.,* October 16, 1861, *ibid.*

[43] *Id.* to *id.,* November 26, 1861, *ibid.* Listed in Fallon (comp.), *List of Synonyms,* 63.

[44] Contrary to the usual practice, this muster roll serves all the purposes of a Descriptive Book. It is preserved in the Minnesota Historical Society.

Early the next year Axel Silfversparre, an artillery officer who had served in the Svea Artillery Regiment in Sweden for almost ten years and had but recently come to America to offer his services, was busy creating another battery of light artillery among the Swedes. He had secured leave of absence from Frémont to organize a battery in December, 1861. He had been authorized to introduce various improvements in artillery tactics. Because he wished the honor of a superior battery to go to Swedes in Illinois, he had refused various offers. To fill his company, he announced meetings in Altona, Princeton, Galesburg, Andover, and Moline for the last week in January, 1862—since recruiting had to stop for a time with the current month.[45] Recruitment must have proceeded slowly, for it was not until March 3 that he received orders to take his battery to St. Louis. Even then his numbers were not complete, and he was urging last-minute enlistments. At Camp Douglas, Chicago, he then had seventy men—forty of them Swedes.[46] The group had already been mustered in on February 20 as Battery H, First Illinois Light Artillery, under Silfversparre as captain.

Unfortunately, the commander of the battery involved himself in difficulties; in May, complaints against him began to make themselves heard, and rumors that his command would be taken from him floated about among his men. The heavy work even on a light battery might have accounted in part for the complaints, and the captain's state of health may have been partly responsible, as one soldier stated in a letter to *Hemlandet* of July 16. Silfversparre felt aggrieved that the editor should "do him harm." He pointed out how the raw recruits in his battery had worked up from complete ignorance to equality with the members of any other battery. He felt that he had always dealt uprightly, honorably, and fairly with every member.[47] After the Battle of Shiloh this battery was transferred to

[45] For Axel Silfversparre's announcement, see Chicago *Hemlandet*, January 3, 22, 1862. Listed in Fallon (comp.), *List of Synonyms*, 22.

[46] He based his appeal of March 3, 1862, largely on mercenary motives. "Krig ar Måhända slut om en liten tid; och du kan, om du gar med, ha dina $100 (The war will perhaps be ended in a little while; you can, if you go out with us, have your $100)." Each prospective recruit would receive reimbursement for his travel expenses in case there was no time to telegraph for a pass. As the men already in his company had received permission to go home to say goodbye, any new recruit could travel back with them from western Illinois to Chicago. Chicago *Hemlandet*, March 3, 1862.

[47] The discontent with Silfversparre arose while the company was stationed with Halleck's Army at Pittsburg Landing. A letter from one Seth, a member of his company, detailing the rumor alluded to above, was printed in the Chicago *Hemlandet* on May 7, 1862; and in a separate section the editor added that he had heard other complaints. One "N.W.," in a letter which appeared in the issue of May 14, wrote about the work on the battery being heavy. The

Sherman's division, where it served with the Fifty-fifth Illinois till the close of the war. Early in 1864 it was advertising in *Hemlandet* for replacements—for young, strong, and active volunteers. Mention should also be made of the fact that several Swedish home-guard companies were organized in New York and Chicago in 1863 to preserve order during the draft; the one in Chicago adopted the name of the Svea Guards.[48]

By all odds the most significant contingent sent to the field by the Scandinavian element of the population was the Fifteenth Wisconsin Regiment, a dream come true of an entire regiment composed so largely of citizens of the northern European peninsulas as to justify its name of Scandinavian Regiment. Though the Norse was by far the largest element, the dream of a wholly Norwegian regiment did not materialize.

A movement, inspired probably by Governor Randall's bid for a German regiment, was launched during the first months of the war for a Norwegian regiment in Wisconsin. Hans C. Heg, prison commissioner of Wisconsin, had already offered his resignation to the governor and declared to friends his intent to go to the war. On September 25, 1861, a meeting of Scandinavian leaders was held at the state capital, where it was formally decided to raise a regiment. A letter petitioning for the appointment of Heg as colonel was sent to the governor. In a few days Heg and nine other Scandinavian leaders called on their countrymen to support the proposed unit, stressing the unique opportunity for them to serve under officers and with comrades who spoke their own native tongue. In a later issue of *Emigranten,* which had carried this appeal, appeared Heg's first call to his fellow countrymen. In forcible language he told them that the government of their adopted country was in danger. What they as free men had "learned to love in their old fatherland—their freedom— their government—their independence . . ." was menaced by arrogant ambition. "Does it not concern us as brave and stout citizens to give help to defend our new Fatherland's rights and our families' homes. Fellow-countrymen—that behooves you to answer!" The call by the ten leaders revealed that Chicago had promised two companies for the regiment, and in recognition of this contribution the governor of Wisconsin had accorded the position of lieutenant colonel to Kiler K. Jones of Quincy, Illinois,

---

remark about Silfversparre's health was printed in the issue of May 17, 1862. For Silfversparre's reply, see *ibid.*, July 16, 1862.

[48] *Ibid.*, February 3, 7, March 30, April 13, 1864. In the issue of February 10 it was pointed out that the Swedish society *Svea* aided Swedish soldiers. For the Home Guards, see Hokanson, *Swedish Immigrants*, 98, 115.

formerly of Manitowoc. Heg announced that, with the completion of the enrollment of a thousand men, he would organize the unit as the First Scandinavian Brigade.[49]

Just as the German *Illinois-Zeitung* and *Hemlandet* had supported moves for German and Swedish companies, so the *Emigranten* lent its support to the Norwegian project. This paper stated in an editorial that it was authorized to assure its readers that the Wisconsin government not only consented to the undertaking but would do everything possible to bring the regiment speedily into the field. In addition *Emigranten* made up a special number, a small one-sheet issue, composed of articles dealing with the Fifteenth Wisconsin and the Civil War in general, from its issues of October 7 and 14. This was distributed widely and was probably used as a circular among possible recruits.[50]

Recruiting officers were chosen and promptly began work in Norwegian settlements. Effective aid was given in English as well as Norwegian papers. Heg himself was the chief recruiting officer. Throughout the fall he wrote several different calls and spread them broadcast. He appealed to all Scandinavians—not merely to Norwegians. He stressed the fact that the officers would be men who spoke the Scandinavian languages. He visited Scandinavian settlements in Wisconsin, Iowa, Minnesota, and Illinois. Everywhere he went he inspired, and appealed to, the patriotism of his fellow Scandinavians.[51]

The regiment finally brought together at Camp Randall, Madison, in December was about nine hundred strong; it departed for the South on

[49] For the appeal of the ten leaders, see Madison *Emigranten*, September 30, 1861. It was addressed "to all Scandinavians capable of bearing arms, Countrymen and Fellow-Citizens." Notice the loose use of the word "brigade." Heg's first personal call appeared in the same paper on October 7, 1861. The first suggestion for a Scandinavian company seems to have come from J. A. Johnson. See *ibid.*, September 2, 1861.

[50] This editorial appeared in the same issue as did the appeal by the ten leading Scandinavians. The special issue contained, among other things, an article on Colonel Heg, one on the foreign officers in the Union service, and excerpts from Wisconsin and Chicago papers. A facsimile of this special edition can be found in Theodore C. Blegen (ed.), *The Civil War Letters of Colonel Hans Christian Heg* (Northfield, Minn., 1936), opposite p. 22.

[51] Madison *Emigranten*, October 7, November 18, 1861. For a general account of the regiment, see Blegen's introduction to *Civil War Letters of Colonel Heg*, 20–42; also Ager (ed.), *Oberst Heg og hans Gutter*, 7–8, and Introduction. See also P. G. Dietrichson, *En Kortfattet Skildering af det Femtende Wisconsin Regiments Historie og Virksomhed under Borgerkrigen* . . . (Chicago, 1884). The best account, however, of the history of this regiment is John A. Johnson, *Det Skandinaviske Regiments Historie* . . . (La Crosse, Wis., 1869). The Chicago *Journal*, October 5, 1861, refers to it as a "brigade." For a meeting in Manitowoc County, where Lieutenant Colonel Jones was to speak, see Madison *Emigranten*, October 7, 1861.

March 2, 1862. One captain was a Dane; another, a Swede who had been in the Mexican War as a volunteer. Lieutenant Colonel Kiler K. Jones was an American; but his wife was Norse, and he could speak Norwegian well enough to make himself understood. The major was a Dane, as were the adjutant and the chaplain, Claus L. Clausen. A Lieutenant Seigel, although of German descent, had been born and reared in Norway; Lieutenant George Wilson, who was to rise to be lieutenant colonel, was born of English parents in Hamburg, but grew up in Christiania. Otherwise, 90 per cent of the personnel was Norwegian, as is sufficiently evidenced by the names chosen for the companies, such as Wergeland Guards, Odin's Rifles, Norway Bear Hunters, and St. Olaf Rifles. Some of the privates were immigrants who had first stepped on American soil only a few weeks earlier. Company K was largely recruited from Minnesota and Iowa, Company A from Chicago and Illinois.[52] For the account of the journey of this regiment to St. Louis we are indebted to A. F. Solberg, the editor of *Emigranten,* who entrusted his editorial duties to a subordinate in order to act as reporter for his own paper.[53] That these Scandinavians rendered good service in the war will be shown in a later chapter.

SWISS, WELSH, DUTCH, AND MEXICAN UNITS

The roll of the lesser nationalities—the Swiss, the Mexican, the Welsh, and the Dutch—is soon called. The Ninth New York State Militia had a company composed almost exclusively of Swiss. At the outbreak of the war it hastened to fill its ranks so that it could render its share of service for the defense of the country. The Swiss of the Indiana colony at Tell City furnished two companies of descendants of Swiss, led by Captain Louis Frei and a Captain Bleisch, according to the chronicler Steinach; Captain Emil Frey's company of sharpshooters from Highland, Illinois, entered Hecker's Eighty-second Illinois Volunteers. Probably, however, the best-known Swiss company and the one which rendered the most

[52] Ager (ed.), *Oberst Heg og hans Gutter,* 7. See also Madison *Emigranten,* October 14, 21, 1861. To indicate how very Norwegian was the composition of the regiment, the *Emigranten* pointed out that it boasted 128 "Ole's." For further details, see *ibid.,* December 23, 1861; January 20, February 3, 10, 1862; see also Introduction to Blegen (ed.), *Civil War Letters of Colonel Heg,* 52–53. Wergeland was one of Norway's most distinguished poets; St. Olaf is revered in a Protestant country for having introduced Christianity into Norway in 1015.

[53] For the presentation of the flag to the regiment in Chicago, see Chapter XVIII; for the captains of the regiment, Chapter X.

distinguished service was the Swiss company from Wisconsin in Berdan's regiment of sharpshooters. Its record was partly attributable to the fact that the commander of the company, Colonel Kaspar Trepp, was himself a native of Switzerland. The careful historian certainly cannot accept Kaufmann's statement that this Swiss company organized in Wisconsin soon grew into a regiment consisting two thirds of Swiss *and* Germans, and so call it either a German or a Swiss regiment. He can, however, readily accept Company G as a Swiss company, at the same time chronicling sadly that when it was mustered out in August, 1864, it numbered a mere dozen. The Fifteenth Missouri may have consisted largely of Swiss when it was recruited, but it soon changed its character.[54] When the reader recalls the Mexican companies in the Confederate services,[55] he will not be surprised to read that Uncle Sam also reached out for some soldiers of that nationality to swell his ranks. He managed to muster only one regiment from New Mexico under Colonel Miguel E. Piño (which rendered little service, for the Mexicans were easily thrown into a panic), and several guerrilla bands, dignified as three months militia companies, under Mexican leaders.[56] Research has turned up but one Welsh company; this was recruited and led by Captain Richard Jones as Company E of the Ninety-seventh New York, one of three regiments raised in Oneida County.[57] The last of the nationality groups to be represented by a separate military unit was the Dutch of Michigan, who sent a contingent into the Second Michigan Cavalry as Company D.[58]

[54] For the company in the New York Ninth Militia Regiment, see New York *Courrier des États-Unis*, April 23, 1861; for the companies from Tell City, see Steinach, *Geschichte und Leben*, 225. In this book there is a story of how, when the first Freischutzen festival was held at Highland, Illinois, on July 4, 1863, a small group of Captain Frei's company sent a contribution of fifteen dollars for the prize gift. *Ibid.*, 254. For the Swiss company in Berdan's regiment, see Kaufmann, *Die Deutschen im Bürgerkriege*, 558. See also Charles Augustus Stevens, *Berdan's United States Sharpshooters in the Army of the Potomac, 1861–1865* (St. Paul, 1892), 486. By 1862–1863, "Swiss Rifles" as the name of the Fifteenth Missouri Regiment seems something of a misnomer, as there were but a few Swiss recorded in the Descriptive Books.

[55] See Lonn, *Foreigners in the Confederacy*, 126–28.

[56] This was the Second Regiment New Mexico Volunteers. See Latham Anderson, "Canby's Campaign in New Mexico," in R. Hunter (ed.), *Sketches of War History, 1861–1865* (Cincinnati, 1888–1890), II, 372, 374, 383. The leaders, captains of Mexican companies, bore conventional Mexican names—Gaspar Ortiz y Alarid, Nestor Gonzales, José Ignacio Martinez, Francisco Perea. Antonio Vigil had a band of cavalry. Fallon (comp.), *List of Synonyms*, 97.

[57] Franklin B. Hough, *History of Duryée's Brigade during the Campaign in Virginia under Gen. Pope* . . . (Albany, 1864), 180–81.

[58] Marshall P. Thatcher, *A Hundred Battles in the West, St. Louis to Atlanta. The Second Michigan Cavalry* . . . (Detroit, 1884), 23.

MIXED UNITS

Finally, we come to a group of mixed regiments—composed, it is true, of foreign-born but of different, and often of many, nationalities, and usually labeled by misnomers. Sometimes these false names arose from a desire to send a regiment representative of a particular nationality to the field, a laudable ambition but one unfulfilled, since other nationalities had to be admitted to make the regiment itself a reality.[59]

The Garibaldi Guard, the Thirty-ninth New York, invites the imagination; however, though it certainly was a picturesque set of men, it was not an Italian organization, as one might expect from its name. The reader might assume that Hungarians constituted a majority of the men under the command of the Hungarian Colonel George Utassy, but his men were from all known and unknown lands, from all possible and impossible armies: Zouaves from Algiers, men from the French Foreign Legion, Cossacks, Garibaldians, Sepoys, English deserters, Turks, Swiss, Croats, Bavarians, and Platt Deutsch. Such a mixture was probably never seen in the same regiment before, perhaps not even among the free lances of the Middle Ages. The regiment was truly remarkable for the large number of countries represented in its ranks and companies: there were three companies of Hungarian hussars, three of Germans, one of *Bersagliere* Italians, one of Swiss, one of French *chasseurs à pied,* and even one of Spaniards and Portuguese. Many of these men had served in Europe before coming to America; some had had combat experience; and many of the officers had served in more than one campaign. The officers represented the same mélange as the men: the colonel was a Hungarian, the lieutenant colonel an Italian, the major an American, and the surgeon a German—presumably. Altogether the regiment counted 350 men and officers.

This was the first regiment from New York to enlist for three years and

---

[59] It is worth noting that the British residents in New York City and its environs began immediately after April 15 to recruit a British regiment, using the office of the British consul as headquarters. Five companies had been enrolled by May 9, and the regiment, the Thirty-sixth New York, was completed by the addition of companies from Albany, Troy, Boston, and Jersey City by May 13, 1861. However, a note from the British Legation to the State Department, October 7, 1861, transmitting a letter from R. A. Davis to Lord Lyons, reveals that this British regiment was never accepted but was disbanded. Notes from the British Legation, XLII, Division of State Department Archives, The National Archives. For its formation, see New York *Courrier des États-Unis,* April 21, 24, May 6, 10, 13, 1861.

also the first of the fourteen regiments which the President authorized the Union Defense Committee to organize and equip from New York City. With the first call to arms, recruiting began among many nationalities— among the best Italian carabineers, the Hungarians, and the Swiss. As it became apparent to the separate groups that alone each could not muster a regiment, they decided to unite their companies into a regiment with the name "Garde di Garibaldi," a title retained throughout the war. The regiment had eight companies by April 29, and by May 3 they were transferred from their quarters in Volk's Theater to barracks. On May 23 at Lafayette Place the Hungarian companies were given a handsome flag and a richly embroidered Hungarian standard with the red, white, and green stripes, bearing within a wreath the motto *Vincere aut Morire;* the regiment was given a flag which had been borne triumphantly by Garibaldi's men in 1848–1849 and planted by the hero with his own hand on one of the battlements of Rome.[60] It was not until May 28 that the regiment was mustered into the United States service.

This organization underwent a mutiny such as had occurred in the New York Highlanders. On July 9, 1861, its members defied orders and started for the Long Bridge on their way to Washington. They succeeded in crossing the bridge, but an hour later they found themselves surrounded by five thousand infantry; thereupon they laid down their arms and were marched back to Alexandria. They afterwards rendered good service in many battles.[61]

Great stress was laid in the regiment during the early months of its existence on the fact that seven nationalities were represented by its ten companies; but by the time its personnel was being recorded in the Descriptive Books, far more than seven nationalities were appearing in almost all the companies.[62] During December, 1863, and January, 1864, the

[60] The description of these flags given in the New York *Courrier des États-Unis* of May 24, 1861, and that in "The Garibaldi Guard and its Services," in Fox (comp.), *New York at Gettysburg,* I, 283, do not agree. The writer accepts the latter as more authoritative than a hasty newspaper report. At Spotsylvania the regiment lost its colors.

[61] For the mutiny, see Charles Carlton Coffin, *Four Years of Fighting: A Volume of Personal Observation with the Army and Navy, from the First Battle of Bull Run to the Fall of Richmond* (Boston, 1886), 11–13. The service of these companies is discussed in Chapter XVI. For a list of these foreign companies and regiments, see Appendix, Section C.

[62] As a matter of fact, the Descriptive Book of this regiment reveals only one company which does not show a highly mixed composition as to nationality. This was Company B, which was almost wholly German. See Regimental Descriptive Book, Order Book, and Clothing Book. For the changes of 1863–1864, see "The Garibaldi Guard and its Services," in Fox (comp.), *New York at Gettysburg,* I, 286.

regiment experienced a still greater change in personnel; recruits in numbers sufficient to organize six new companies, most of them Irish or Americans, completely altered its character. When the original term expired and the small band of survivors was mustered out, one-year recruits enabled the Thirty-ninth New York to continue as an organization, but the picturesque Garibaldi Guard no longer existed.

A regiment named "Enfants Perdus" might be assumed by the reader to have been French, but it had companies in which Frenchmen were only an appreciable element and others in which they were outnumbered by other nationalities. Unfortunately, the official record of the regiment is not complete, lacking all data for five of the companies; but there is enough evidence to establish it clearly as a foreign regiment and a mixed one. To understand the choice of this name for the regiment, it is necessary to understand that in military parlance it meant men appointed to some exceedingly hazardous duty from which their chances of returning were almost nil. Perhaps the best English equivalent of *enfants perdus* is not "lost children" but "forlorn hope," for the selection of the name represents a certain bravado on the part of the men, many of whom were black sheep and soldiers of fortune who would readily take desperate chances. Under those circumstances a smile is perhaps permissible when we read that a daughter of General John Tyler gave them their flag and that a clergyman presented it. The lieutenant colonel, Felix Comfort, was a Frenchman; but the name of the major, Michael Schmidt, suggests a German, while that of the surgeon, Benjamin F. Harrison, seems to be Anglo-Saxon. Only one of the companies, Company D, could by any fair appraisal be termed French; but here the names of the captain, Charles Daillet (who resigned March 23, 1862), and the lieutenants certainly suggest that they were Frenchmen, while the noncommissioned officers with but two exceptions are definitely entered as Frenchmen.

Of the privates in Company D, fifty-eight were recorded as having been born in France; to these might be added three Canadian French, thus yielding sixty-one French in a company of seventy-eight, or a proportion of about seven ninths. Company E must be put down as a foreign unit, though not as a French one. This element constituted only about one fifth of the entire company; generous representation of a number of other nationalities made it about two thirds foreign. Company C, officers and men, must be pronounced a German company with about seven tenths of its membership of that nationality. Company F, likewise, must count as German, with Swiss running a close second; all its elements combined made it almost a solidly foreign company. Again in Company G the foreign element constituted decidedly more than half. It must be recognized that, as formed in August, 1861, the regiment might have been more strongly French or even more pronouncedly foreign than appears upon the record.[63]

Next to be entered as a misnamed organization is D'Epineuil Zouaves, which unlike the Enfants Perdus did bear a number—the Fifty-third New York. Since the Descriptive Books are incomplete and no regimental history exists, the writer can only reveal her initial impression that this was another French regiment. The advertisements carried in the *Courrier des États-Unis* through August, 1861, justify in every way the expectation of a French organization. The prospective recruit was informed that the uniform was blue like that of the French Zouaves; the cloth and the tailors came from French workshops and factories; and the tactics to be followed were those of the French Zouaves. The superior officers of the regiment were French, as was the organization; but drill was to be in both English and French.[64] The regiment was sent to camp on Staten Island on August 23 but left for Washington only on November 18, 1861. French at first but later decidedly mixed in composition, this unit must be classified as at least foreign, since in each of the three companies for which data exist foreigners counted about one half of the whole.[65] It is of interest that one company consisted of Indians from the Tuscarora Reservation; it served only until March, 1862.

Perhaps no braver hope arose than the Polish Legion (otherwise known as the Fifty-eighth New York Infantry), and probably no military unit was more inaccurately named. Polish volunteers, quartered at the Park Barracks in New York, began to talk before April 18 of a Polish regiment. Their appeals, like those of all the other nationality groups, harked back to their history: "Rally around our banner, under the wing of the Polish white eagle. The spirit of Pulaski and of Kosciusko will sustain us. Dis-

[63] In the National Archives each company is entered separately in a leather-covered book, but books exist only for Companies C-G. The manuscript book for Company F is labeled "Compagnie F," and names are entered in a foreign hand with elaborate flourishes.

[64] This advertisement appeared in the New York *Courrier des États-Unis*, August 10-15, 19, 20, 23, September 3, 4, 1861.

[65] The advertisement was addressed to "Hommes de Bonne Volonté sans Emploie." Descriptive Books were found at the Archives only for Companies D, F, and G. Frederick Phisterer (author and comp.), *New York in the War of the Rebellion* (Albany, 1890), 414, states that its members were mostly Frenchmen recruited from New York City and other parts of the state. See also New York *Tribune*, April 21, 1862.

tinguished officers will lead us, and the sentiment to serve the holy and just cause of liberty will be our honorable recompense." [66] By May 4 several companies had enlisted, but then the project halted. In August Colonel Wladimir Kryzanowski, a Polish officer who had seen service in the last Polish revolt, was authorized by Secretary of War Cameron to recruit a regiment among all the Poles of the Union. He succeeded in enlisting about four hundred men, whom he christened the United States Rifles. Colonel Frederick Gellman under the same authority recruited part of a regiment, the Morgan Rifles, which had been formed by consolidating with a group bearing that name other groups known respectively as the Polish Legion, the Gallatin Rifles, and the Humboldt Jägers. The consolidation of the Morgan Rifles and the United States Rifles resulted, by October, 1861, in the Fifty-eighth New York Infantry, the former furnishing six companies and the latter four. Wladimir Kryzanowski became colonel, while Frederick Gellman took the second place; the name "Polish Legion" was preserved.

While the regiment was emphatically not composed wholly of Poles, having few if any Poles recorded as such in its various companies, it was definitely filled with foreign-born recruits, many of whom were certainly Poles entered on the records as other nationalities. It is necessary to recall that many of the privates hailing from the portions of Poland which had been absorbed by Prussia and Austria probably reported themselves to the enrolling clerks as Germans or as Austrians, so that we have no accurate way to measure the number of Poles. However, a Pole captured the first place in the regiment; Anthony Zyla, the chaplain's name, sounds as if a Pole was serving in that capacity; and one captain, the commander of Company G, and several of the noncommissioned officers were certainly Polish. Almost all the countries of Europe were represented in the ranks of this regiment, but in some of the companies Germans were present in preponderating numbers. In Company A, for instance, in which 165 men were enrolled from first to last, 141, or two thirds of the total number, gave their birthplace as Germany. The same proportion held true for Company C, and an even higher proportion existed for Companies D and F.[67] Cer-

[66] New York *Courrier des États-Unis*, April 24, 1861. It was addressed to old officers and soldiers.

[67] Company Descriptive Book. August Kzaculsky recorded himself as having been born in Germany, but it is hard to escape the conviction that it was in German Poland. The same holds true for Captain Berwicki, Captain Ludwig Galeski of Company H, and Lieutenant Whaluski of Company I. None of these appear in *War of the Rebellion: A Compilation of*

tainly, in this regiment Poles were more generously promoted to officer-ships than they were in other regiments. The regiment left New York in November, 1861, and proceeded to Washington, where it was assigned to Bohlen's brigade of Blenker's division, a division composed almost wholly of soldiers of foreign birth. There were also some companies in the Thirty-first New York made up almost entirely of Poles.[68] An effort to organize a Polish cavalry regiment, the United States Lancers, was only partially successful, but it helped to form the Ninth New York Cavalry. Scattered here and there through the various regiments were separate foreign companies, reserved for discussion here because many of them were of mixed nationalities. Company D of the Eighty-ninth Illinois, the Railroad Regiment, is a case in point: in this the number from any given nationality was small—the largest, that from Germany, consisting of fourteen members—but altogether the foreign-born numbered fifty-six in a company of fifty-seven.[69] Other illustrations are Company E of the First New York Cavalry, largely, but not exclusively, German; Company H of the Ninety-seventh New York Regiment; a Jäger company from Erie, Pennsylvania; two companies from Milwaukee in the First Wisconsin Regiment; and a company from the Sixth Connecticut, in which foreigners constituted three fourths of the entire company.[70]

---

the *Official Records of the Union and Confederate Armies* (Washington, 1880–1901). (This work is hereinafter cited as *Official War Records.*)

[68] Haiman, *Polish Past in America*, 110.

[69] The record for Company G, Eighty-ninth Illinois Infantry is missing from the Company Book.

[70] For Company E, First New York Cavalry, see Company Descriptive Book; for Company H, Ninety-seventh New York Regiment, see Hough, *History of Duryée's Brigade during the Campaign in Virginia under Gen. Pope,* 181; for the company from Erie, Pennsylvania, see Chicago *Illinois Staats-Zeitung,* May 7, 1861; for the Milwaukee companies, see Chicago *Illinois Staats-Zeitung,* May 6, 1861. See Appendix C. The Connecticut company was Company C.

CHAPTER SEVEN

The Rank and File

THE long list of companies and regiments of foreign-born recorded in the preceding chapters by no means exhausts the story of the foreign-born in the ranks of the Union forces. Indeed, to leave the account at that point would be to give the reader a false impression. We must take note of the many companies in which members of a given nationality constituted from one fourth to two thirds of the whole; companies in which they constituted less than one fourth but still a not negligible part of the whole; the innumerable companies in which were scattered just a few Germans or a few Irishmen; and, above all, the vast number of companies in which a mixture of nationalities enlivened the roll call.

The heterogeneity of the northern army was one of its most marked characteristics—a heterogeneity so great that one is almost overwhelmed by the diversity of races and nationalities. The ubiquity of the Germans has been shown. Not one of the three hundred regiments which marched out from New York was without one or more Teutons. Besides the companies of Germans from Cleveland, men of that nationality from that lake city served in twenty-two mixed Ohio regiments of infantry and in many Ohio cavalry and artillery regiments, as well as in regiments of Michigan, Missouri, Illinois, Indiana, and Pennsylvania, and in the American fleet.

Likewise the total raised in Missouri for the three months service was well over ten thousand, of which Germans constituted nearly nine thousand. From first to last, this state sent thirty-one thousand German soldiers to the field, so that almost every second man in the Missouri forces was a Teuton. As the German population of the state was hardly ninety thousand, this contribution must be admitted to be striking. It has been argued that many Germans in the state enlisted because they were safer in the army than at home at the mercy of Confederate sympathizers; there may be a grain of truth in the argument, for the hatred that Missouri Confederates felt for the Germans was frightful, especially after Germans from St. Louis had nullified the Confederate attack on Camp Jackson. As is well known, the German farmers were shot down, their fields laid waste, and their houses burned. Colonel Sigel brought over a thousand fugitives from southern Missouri to St. Louis; and this number was greatly augmented by the German fugitives from the Confederate states, especially from Arkansas, Texas, Louisiana, and Tennessee. Several thousand of these fugitives served in Missouri regiments, while thousands of Germans poured in from neighboring states to hold the Confederates in check.[1] Germans were found in nearly every regiment of infantry, in almost every battery of artillery and in almost every regiment of cavalry—often in officers' posts but more frequently as privates. Even the Engineers and Mechanics Company of the First Michigan Infantry, which one might logically expect to find composed of native Americans, contained some Germans.

The Irish proved in the end to be equally pervasive. Before the outbreak of war they were inclined, as has been stated in an earlier chapter, to be pro-Southern or, at least, definitely antiabolitionist. In such a pivotal city as St. Louis the Irish constituted a real menace to every Union man. A very small number of Irish joined the first ten Union regiments from Missouri; in fact, there were regiments in which there was not a single Irishman.[2] As events revealed to them—as they thought—the true spirit of disunionism in the Confederacy, they forsook the cause of the South and began to enter the Union armies. Before long, Irishmen were present everywhere in the Northern regiments. In view of the Irishman's predilection for politics, it should surprise no one that citizens originally from the Emerald Isle were numerous in the Tammany Regiment, though it could not be classified as a strictly Irish regiment. Likewise, the Third New Hampshire Regiment, though composed in large measure of native-born sons and men from states immediately adjoining New Hampshire, still had a considerable number of Irishmen.[3] Only in a very few native regiments and the most occasional company was there "niver a paddy."

Scandinavians were scattered about in most western and even some eastern regiments. In the camp of the Western Cavalry Regiment near Chicago, for instance, sixteen Swedes were to be found in October, 1861;

[1] It is thought that two thousand Germans from Illinois alone and one thousand from Wisconsin served in Missouri. Others came in from Indiana, Kentucky, and Iowa. This was natural, as Missouri was the first area in the West to be threatened by the Confederates. Kaufmann, *Die Deutschen im Bürgerkriege*, 187–88; *Report of the Adjutant-General*, Missouri, 1863 (Jefferson City, 1864), 13–14.

[2] Robert Rombauer, *The Union Cause in St. Louis*, 258–59.

[3] Daniel Eldredge, *The Third New Hampshire and All About It* (Boston, 1893), 22.

in July small numbers of Swedes were reported in many companies in the Nineteenth Illinois—nine in the Moline Rifles, four in the Chicago Zouaves, and one in a Chicago infantry company. Of course, Swedes were scattered through the Minnesota companies, and there was a wholly Swedish company in the Third Minnesota. On January 14, 1863, fourteen Swedes were reported in Company C, thirteen in Company I, and three in Company K of the Second Minnesota Regiment. The interest in his fellow countrymen expressed by the editor of *Hemlandet* reveals the presence of certain Swedes in several companies from Pennsylvania and of six soldiers of that nationality in the Ninth New York Cavalry. A letter from a cavalryman to that same paper proves the presence of at least one Swede in the Ninth Illinois Cavalry. Even in 1864, after the Fifteenth Wisconsin had absorbed many Swedes, twenty-one were reported from Tennessee as enrolled in Company A of the Eleventh Minnesota Volunteers.[4]

Similarly, Norwegians drifted into many regiments other than the Fifteenth Wisconsin. Driblets of one, two, three, four, and even nine appeared in each of eight of the ten companies of the Eleventh Wisconsin. There were thirty-one Norwegians in the Sixth Iowa Cavalry when it was stationed at Camp Hendershott near Davenport in January, 1862. The *Emigranten* reported five in the Eighth Kansas, five in the Thirteenth Iowa, forty-six in Company G of the Twelfth Iowa, and eleven in Company H of the Fourth Minnesota. A Norwegian of the Third Wisconsin in camp near Arlington, who used a period of convalescence to visit the adjoining regiments, reported with joy that he had not found one regiment without Scandinavians. "If all the Scandinavians, who are now in the United States service were together," he concluded, "there would be many regiments, but the thing is, they are scattered over the whole army, and when the war is over, it may perhaps not show that Scandinavians were along." Small groups of from three to seven Norwegians and Danes had been reported the preceding July in the companies of the Third Wisconsin.[5] In June, 1861, while the First Minnesota Regiment lay at Fort

---

[4] We are indebted to the Chicago *Hemlandet*, July 17, October 9, 1861, for the careful recording of individual Swedes in various companies all over the country. For the cavalryman's letter, see *ibid.*, January 29, 1862; for the Swedes in Pennsylvania and New York regiments, see *ibid.*, January 14, 1863; for the Eleventh Minnesota, see *ibid.*, March 28, 1864. The Moline Rifles do not appear in Fallon (comp.), *List of Synonyms.*

[5] The Madison *Emigranten* is the source of information on these scattered Norwegians. In the Eleventh Wisconsin, the only companies with no Norwegians were H and I. *Emigranten*, November 11, 1861. For the Sixth Iowa Cavalry, see *ibid.*, January 9, 1862; for the Kansas

Snelling, around fifty Norwegians were reported in that regiment. Seventeen Norwegians were scattered through the companies of the Second Wisconsin, while nine Swedes served with the eleven Norwegians in Company H, Fourth Minnesota. Nearly all the able-bodied men in the Norwegian settlement of Trempealeau Valley in Wisconsin enlisted in the course of the war. Most of the Norwegians from Iowa who enlisted during the war hailed from the northeastern corner of the state, while the Swedes came from all over the state.[6]

Swiss, likewise, were scattered rather widely, if thinly, through the ranks. Over three hundred citizens from Highland, Illinois, served in the war; many Swiss fought in the Fifteenth Missouri Regiment; over one hundred Swiss from New Glarus, Wisconsin, participated also; and the Swiss colony in Dodge County, Minnesota, delivered a significant contingent for defense of the Union. Besides the Swiss Company, there were several individual Swiss scattered around in Berdan's sharpshooters.[7]

All the major European countries were represented; we have heard of Irish, German, French, Scotch, British, Mexican, Welsh, and Dutch contingents. There were individual Belgians, Russians, Austrians, Poles, Hungarians, and Bohemians. The contingent of the Latin races was completed, though but little increased in number, by a handful of Spaniards, Portuguese, and Italians. Such unusual groups as Slavs, Magyars, Turks, and Icelanders were represented. There was, in fact, hardly a corner of the globe, however remote or obscure, which was not represented. Often, as will be later illustrated, there could be assembled in a single company an almost incredible number of nationalities. Although the list of Hungarian officers included many highly distinguished men, the actual number of that nationality in the country were too few and too scattered to organize a regiment. Kossuth himself, as is well known, wielded no influence on Hungarians in respect to the American Civil War; but two leaders of the March uprising in the Hungarian Revolution, five sons of his two sisters, and four of his faithful bodyguard fought in the Union ranks.[8] The num-

---

and Iowa companies, see *ibid.*, February 2, March 30, 1863; for the letter from the convalescent soldier, see *ibid.*, December 16, 1861. See issue of July 13, 1861, for small groups of three to seven Norwegians and Danes in four companies of the Third Wisconsin Regiment.

[6] For the First Minnesota, see *ibid.*, June 1, 1861; for the Second Wisconsin, see *ibid.*, August 10, 1861; for Company H, Fourth Minnesota, see *ibid.*, February 10, 1862; for the enlistment from Trempealeau Valley, see Qualey, *Norwegian Settlement*, 73.

[7] See Steinach, *Geschichte und Leben*, 252, for Highland; for the Swiss in Berdan's regiment outside the Swiss company, see *ibid.*, 143–44.

[8] The two leaders were Philip Figyelmessy, a Hussar who had also fought for Italian liberty,

ber of Czechs in relation to the entire army was quite negligible, but after the fashion of minority races they tended to seek out each other. A handful of Czechs in Blenker's Eighth New York lined up by the roadside when the Twenty-eighth Wisconsin passed through Hunter's Chapel, because they had heard of the enrollment of many Czechs in that regiment. One New Yorker recognized several friends in the Wisconsin regiment. A Lieutenant Landa was in the group, and with him were about sixty Czechs.[9] Although occasionally a Pole won recognition as an individual and became a low-ranking officer, Poles to the number of several thousand were to be found in the ranks.[10]

Although Canada was neither remote nor obscure, it was nevertheless one of the lesser countries from which Union soldiers hailed. The insistence of its citizens on the geographical subdivisions fascinates the modern reader. Not British America, as the whole of Canada was then termed, but rather New Brunswick or Nova Scotia was the place of origin commonly given by the Canadian soldier. Newfoundland and Prince Edward Island were also repeatedly listed as places of birth.

Union soldiers had come from the most distant points of the globe— from Persia in the Near East and from Cape Colony in the southernmost part of Africa; from the isle of St. Helena and from the island of Islay off Scotland; from Jamaica and from the East Indies; from the Ionian Islands and from Ceylon; from the Isle of Man and from Guernsey of the Channel Islands. One soldier—apparently ignorant of the fact that he could record his citizenship as that of his father—reported himself as born on the Atlantic Ocean; another declared that he had been born on "God's Five Seas!" Probably no one company had brought together more men from very remote corners than Company C of the First New York Cavalry; its members hailed from Capetown, Persia, Barbados, the East Indies, Cuba, Jamaica, Chile, Bombay, and Surinam.[11] Surely, if one had been seeking merely to form a company representing as much geographical territory as possible, one could scarcely have done better. Every one of

---

and Matthias Rozsafy, who had left a seminary for the priesthood to follow Kossuth; the five sons of his two sisters were Albert Ruthkay and the four Zsulavsky brothers, and his bodyguard members were George Grechowski, Stephen Kovács, Joseph Németh, and Gustav Wagner. Vasvary, *Lincoln's Hungarian Heroes*, 26.

[9] Thomas Capěk, *The Czechs in America* (Boston, 1920), 156–57.

[10] Maurice Kraszynski, a private in the First Connecticut Infantry in April, 1861, rose to be captain in 1864 and served through the war. Henry (comp.), *Military Record of Civilian Appointments*, II, 124–25.

[11] See Company Descriptive Book, First New York Cavalry.

England's greater dominions, including Australia and New Zealand, was represented in one company or another. General C. Armstrong, the son of American missionaries, was born in Wailuku, Hawaiian Islands. It is interesting to note that one private had been born in the Sandwich Islands, although his name, Theodore F. Forbes, suggests that he might have been the child of an American father who had stayed temporarily in the islands.[12]

Unquestionably the most interesting place name turned up in this study was Dea Tristan, which called for some geographical research in its own right. It proved to be a tiny volcanic island claimed by England, and its location can best be established by the statement that a parallel drawn between Montevideo and Cape Town would strike it. One private came to join the Seventeenth Massachusetts from this tiny island, which today is occupied by 130 inhabitants and visited once a year for mail.[13] The Civil War proved to be a serious blow to these islanders, as whaling vessels ceased to stop there; but the record makes no interesting connection between whalers and the enlistment of this one islander in the Northern army.

To examine all the batteries or regiments in which a given nationality constituted from one fourth to one half the total number would be not only tedious but fruitless—if, indeed, it were possible. Suffice it to cite a few examples and to state that such units existed everywhere in the Union army, East and West, and that such small concentrations existed for many different nationalities and often with a mixture of nationalities. To find all through the companies of many New York regiments a proportion of foreign-born amounting to one fourth or one third to one half should occasion no surprise. This was the case in the Tenth New York Regiment, where the Irish predominated among the 25 per cent of the foreign-born prevailing through all the companies. It was true also in several companies of the Second New York Infantry; in the One Hundred and Second New York Infantry, where the proportion rose even to one half; and in the One Hundred and Forty-sixth New York, where the proportion of foreigners increased with the recruits of 1864.[14] Certainly one might expect to

---

[12] For General Armstrong, see Ezra D. Simons, *A Regimental History. The One Hundred and Twenty-fifth New York State Volunteers* (New York, 1888), 174; for Forbes, see Henry (comp.), *Military Record of Civilian Appointments*, I, 312.

[13] In the Company Descriptive Book, the place of birth is recorded as Dea Cust, Isle of Trist, but the proper name is Dea Tristan. The soldier, Richard H. Fullen, did not enlist until December, 1863.

[14] See Company Descriptive Books A-F, I, Tenth New York Infantry; Company Descriptive Books B-E, G, H, and I, Second New York Infantry; Company Descriptive Books A-F, G-K,

find the third regiment of Fire Zouaves, recruited from among the firemen of New York, largely an Irish regiment; as a matter of fact, its proportion of foreigners was mixed—certainly by 1863—and ran only from one fourth to one half, rising in one company to two thirds and increasing notably toward the close of the war.[15]

Various New England regiments belong in this class, having had one or more companies with from one fourth to one half foreign-born. Company A of the First Maine Infantry showed almost half born outside the United States, with Canadians constituting the largest element; and this large proportion is probably to be explained by the fact that many had been drafted or hired as substitutes by the time the record was made. The Sixth Connecticut Infantry had one company in which three fourths of the men were foreigners, with the Germans leading numerically; another company in which the Irish were the largest group of foreigners; a third company in which a more widely mixed group made up the foreigners; a fourth and a fifth which, except for a very small number of men, were German and were so classified in an earlier chapter; and a sixth company in which two thirds of the men were from foreign countries.[16]

A sampling of the artillery shows the same proportions in many regiments. In the first five companies of the Third Heavy Artillery of Rhode Island the foreign-born showed percentages of 25 to 33 per cent. Although the contingent of foreigners was also about one third in the very large Third Battery of Light Artillery of Connecticut, that group was made up almost entirely of Irish. In the Second Illinois Regiment of Light Artillery, known as Adolph Schwartz's battery, the monotonous proportion was varied in Company E, as has been noted, for with the exception of nine members the battery was solidly German. The last sampling, taken from the Thirteenth Independent Battery of Michigan Light Artillery, had 59, or about one fourth, in a battery of 214.[17] In these large units the

---

One Hundred and Second New York Infantry; Company Descriptive Books A-E, F-K, One Hundred and Forty-sixth New York Infantry.

15 In Company I, the one two-thirds foreign in composition, the Irish outnumbered other nationalities. Company Descriptive Books A-E, F-K, One Hundred and Fourth New York Infantry (Fire Zouaves; so designated in the Descriptive Book). Not in Fallon (comp.), *List of Synonyms*.

16 The companies in the Sixth Connecticut were Companies C, E, G, H, and I. Regimental Descriptive Book (Regimental Letters Received, and Endorsements, Clothing Book, Non-Com'd Staff and Band), Sixth Connecticut Infantry. For the German companies, see p. 100 of this volume.

17 Company Descriptive Books A-E, Third Rhode Island Heavy Artillery; Clothing, Order, Descriptive, and Morning Report Book, Third Connecticut Battery of Light Artillery;

record undoubtedly was made continuous for the period 1862–1865, showing all replacements.

A scanty sampling of cavalry regiments is desirable for completeness of the picture. Only Companies L and M of the First New York Cavalry (Lincoln Cavalry) were still foreign around 1862: except for five Europeans of other nationalities, Company L was still solidly German; Company M was largely an Irish company, though perhaps one third came from foreign countries other than Ireland. The Western Cavalry, or Ninth Illinois Cavalry, showed a slightly greater variation in proportion of foreign-born, for two thirds of the members of Company F had been born outside the United States, the largest number of these in Germany. The companies of the Twenty-fourth Michigan Cavalry had nearly one half foreign-born members, while Company D in the Sixteenth Illinois was one fourth Irish in composition.[18]

Of course, there were many companies where the proportion of the foreign-born was less than one fourth but still an appreciable element—one sixth, one seventh, or even one eighth. A foreign group might, however, make itself felt in the company as a socially unassimilated group or even as an obstacle because of the unpredictability of its actions, owing perhaps to inadequate familiarity with the English language. Illustrations of these smaller groups of foreigners intermingled with the native-born are the following: one company in the First Maine Infantry and one in the Second Maine, notable because their presence in this formerly rock-ribbed Anglo-Saxon state proves the all-pervasiveness of the foreign influence in the United States by 1861; Company A in the Thirteenth Maryland Infantry, in which some Irish and Germans with a sprinkling of English constituted a fifth of the whole and reflected the importance of this foreign element in forming Union regiments in a border state; several companies of the Fifteenth Cavalry Regiment of Kansas, in which state, despite the invasion of New England abolitionists to save the territory from slavery, the presence of some foreigners is manifest; the Hundred and Twenty-fourth New York, in which, though the ratio of foreigners to the natives

Regimental Descriptive Book, Second Regiment Illinois Light Artillery. Companies of the same proportions of foreign-born to American-born are found in the First Illinois Light Artillery, but the Company Book has preserved the record only for Companies I-M. See also Order, Descriptive, and Morning Report Book, Thirteenth Independent Battery, Michigan Light Artillery.

[18] Company Descriptive Books B-C, E-H, L, M, First New York Cavalry; Company Descriptive Books, Ninth Illinois Cavalry. A provisional company in this regiment, recorded as late as April 18, 1865, showed a higher foreign proportion—over one half.

was small in almost every company, still one ninth to one third or slightly more in each company were foreign; and finally, the Seventh Michigan, in which the number of foreigners in no company save one rose to more than one fifth.[19]

There were also, of course, regiments and companies which consisted almost exclusively of native Americans. When one recalls that this was an American war and that it was waged legally on an abstract constitutional question, it becomes a matter of surprise that there was hardly a regiment or a company to be found in which there were no foreign-born. It would be incorrect to think that purely American units were nonexistent, for the writer has encountered records of a few companies in which every individual was registered as having been born under the flag for which he was fighting.[20] Some of these instances occurred in companies raised in border states and in Tennessee and Alabama after they had been wrested from Confederate control. Hence, it is but just to point out that such volunteers were apt to be Union men from principle and therefore less likely to be other than sons of the soil.[21]

In some companies could be encountered the lone Englishman, the single German or Irishman, the stray Hungarian, and the man from Martinique, who, though resident in the Confederacy, found themselves out of sympathy with the Confederate cause.[22] Even here there was the

[19] These companies were Company C, First Maine Regiment, and Company H, Second Maine Infantry; Company Descriptive Books. For the Maryland company, see Company Descriptive Books A-H, K, Thirteenth Maryland Infantry; Company Descriptive Books A, D, F-I, Fifteenth Kansas Cavalry. The one exception in the Michigan regiment was Company F. Regimental Descriptive Book, Order, and Casualty Book, Seventh Michigan Infantry.

[20] For instance, there were Company D, One Hundred and Fortieth Ohio Infantry; Company F, Fourth Indiana Cavalry; Companies G and H, Fifty-sixth Illinois Infantry. See Company Descriptive Books for the first two companies and Regimental Descriptive Book for the last two.

In the hundreds of Descriptive Books examined, the writer did not encounter one complete regiment with only native sons enrolled. Of course, instances may have been recorded in those books not examined, or regiments for which records are missing may have been completely native-born.

[21] Company D, Third Union Kentucky Infantry, and Company A, First Alabama Cavalry, were among those groups organized after the Union had assumed control. There were other groups recorded from outside Kentucky, but all were from Southern states. The Alabama group had entered the Confederate army under compulsion and declared themselves glad to escape. The First Tennessee Cavalry was almost solidly native except for one German in Company C, but the record is missing for three companies.

[22] In the Second Union Florida Cavalry there were four Englishmen; in Company B of the First North Carolina Infantry (Union), one Irishman; in Company F, one German; in Company C, one Englishman and one Irishman; in Company G, one Englishman and one man born in Martinique; in Company L, two Irishmen. See Regimental Descriptive Books.

inevitable exception, however, for in some of the companies of the First Tennessee Light Artillery there were a number of foreigners—especially in Company A, which had thirty-four Irishmen and a sprinkling from other foreign countries.[23]

Much would be lost from this aspect of the subject should the reader fail to realize how conspicuous one or two foreigners could be in a company. A chronicler of the Fifty-second Massachusetts Regiment, for instance, alluded to a stray foreigner in Company D in the following terms: "Alongside in the line of file closers, go . . . and lisping, light-haired Wiebel, the German"; or "Pat O'Toole, our wild Irishman, tearing through the camp, after having shot eight cows, without his hat, screaming to the boys to coom after his coos afore thim spalpeens of batterymen had tuck thim entirely." [24] The number of foreigners in the service increased greatly as the war dragged on. A chronicler of the Twentieth Massachusetts reported that two or three days before the Battle of Reams Station, in late August, 1864, that regiment received two hundred German recruits who could not understand English.[25]

From the preceding pages it should be clear that those minority portions of companies did not usually represent just one nationality but were more often mixtures of several nationalities. It is necessary to stress, moreover, the great variety of nationalities which might be assembled in one regiment—indeed, in one company. In the first place, regiments might be mixed; that is, in certain regiments one or more companies might have both foreign-born and native-born in their numbers, or, again, some regiments might consist of wholly native companies side by side with wholly foreign companies. There might also be wide variation in the composition of the foreign contingent, as it might represent largely one nationality, consist of two or three nationalities, or have just a few of many different nationalities. The Eleventh Illinois Cavalry presents such a mixture: while in most of its companies only a small proportion (one twelfth to one third) were foreign-born, Company E had almost two thirds foreign-born, among whom the English, Irish, and Germans competed for superiority in numbers. Whereas the other companies of the Forty-fifth Illinois Infantry did not offer striking numbers of foreign-born

[23] Company B had no foreign-born; Company D had seven; Company E had fourteen. See Company Descriptive Books. The Second Kentucky Cavalry also had a number of foreigners, Company Descriptive Book.

[24] James K. Hosmer, *The Color Guard. Being a Corporal's Notes of Military Service in the Nineteenth Army Corps* (Boston, 1864), 25, 104.

[25] C. W. Bardeen, *A Little Fifer's War Diary* (Syracuse, N.Y., 1910), 35,

in their ranks by 1862–1863, Company C had drawn over half its members, and Company F two thirds of its members, from the Irish. A like situation obtained for the Fifth Missouri State Militia Cavalry except that over one half of Company A and over two thirds of Company C were composed of Germans.[26]

There were doubtless various reasons for the great mixture of nationalities in some companies. Some units, although their leaders had intended them to be of one nationality, were obliged to admit men of other nationalities in order to effect an organization. Furthermore, units of Irish, Germans, or French were, naturally, more easily organized in cities, where numbers of those nationalities were congregated, than in rural sections. This partly explains the many mixed regiments in the West, where German farmers and German tradesmen from the small towns often could not enter German regiments. Except in Missouri and Ohio, relatively few purely German regiments were formed in the West; moreover, among the German population residing in the country few national connections existed.[27] Hence, if men felt moved to volunteer, the best they could do was to enroll in a German or Irish company or in a company in which they knew certain of their countrymen to be already enlisted.

To begin with the artillery, in the Fifth New York Independent Battery, commanded by Captain E. D. Taft, were a highly mixed group of artillerists who had come originally from almost all of the European countries—the British Isles, Germany, France, Switzerland, and Sweden—as well as from Canada, Cape Colony, and the West Indies. All these countries were not, of course, represented in equal numbers; for Ireland led, Germany contributed only one less, and each of these two groups constituted about one fifth of the whole. The greater number of this battery recorded their birthplace as one of the states of the Union; but were one to admit those of the second or third generation, many of the names would swell the number of the Irish and Germans.[28] The Thirty-fourth Independent Battery of New York Light Artillery was also a highly diversified group: in this, men born in this country were most numerous; the Germans next most numerous; the Irish only about half as numerous as the Germans; the English, the French, the Danes, and the Swiss present in

[26] See Company Descriptive Books B-C, D-H, I, M, Eleventh Illinois Cavalry; Company Descriptive Books for the Forty-fifth Illinois Regiment; and Company Descriptive Books for the Fifth Missouri State Militia Cavalry. This last regiment lacks the record for Companies H-K.

[27] Kaufmann, *Die Deutschen im Bürgerkriege,* 183–84.

[28] Order and Descriptive Book, Fifth New York Independent Battery.

small numbers; and the Scotch and Hungarians represented by one man each. The entire foreign group comprised more than half the battery, while the Germans alone constituted rather less than a third of the whole.[29]

The First Battalion Light Artillery of Maine offers no exception to the rule of the presence of foreigners in the organizations of this state. Of a total of slightly over two hundred men, forty-seven were foreign-born; only four countries, England, Canada, Scotland, and Ireland, were represented, with the last-named leading in numbers. In all, the foreigners combined equaled somewhat over one third of the whole.[30] In Thomas Vaughn's light artillery of Springfield, Illinois, twelve foreign countries were represented, over half of them by a single individual.[31] To take a single sampling of the cavalry from another section of the country, Brackett's Independent Battalion of Minnesota cavalry showed a decided mixture of race origins in its three companies. If the three companies are considered as a unit, it can be seen that no less than eighteen countries were represented in its ranks; also present were a considerable number of native-born Americans. As in so many other units, the German delegation in one of these three companies constituted about one half of the whole number, while other nationalities were sparingly represented—by only one individual in the case of certain small countries, such as Poland, Holland, and Austria.[32]

In the infantry, the number of regiments and companies which had enrolled in their ranks a varied mixture of nationalities was legion. A mixture of seven or eight different nationalities, in addition to the preponderating number born in the United States, was common. This was true in a regiment of the District of Columbia, where the reader would probably have expected more purely native companies. The Irish led the number of foreigners in this in every company except one, Company I, and there the Germans outnumbered the Irish more than two to one.[33]

---

[29] Order and Descriptive Book, Thirty-fourth New York Independent Battery.

[30] Muster and Descriptive Roll, First Maine Light Artillery, Battery A. Again, this large number doubtless represents the full list of recruits for the entire war period, or at least from 1862 to 1865.

[31] Order and Descriptive Book, Vaughn's light artillery; Mulligan's regiment of artillery, First Illinois Regiment Light Artillery, still a fourth Illinois artillery, did not show such great diversity of foreign nationalities in its companies, and was certainly not an Irish organization, as one might suppose.

[32] Company Descriptive Book, Brackett's battalion of cavalry. In Company C there was only a small proportion of foreign-born to native-born (one fourth to one fifth).

[33] In Company E there were a considerable number of Irish. Company Descriptive Books, Second District of Columbia Regiment.

It is worthy of note that the Mozart Regiment (otherwise the Fortieth New York), which one might assume to have been German or Austrian, was a mixture of many nationalities and had many Americans in its ranks. Company E, which was constituted two thirds of foreign-born, contained members of French, Polish, Italian, Swiss, and Belgian nativity, in addition to the more conventional members of British, Irish, German, and Canadian origin.[34] The Twenty-ninth Massachusetts was outstanding for the many nationalities represented in each of its companies; its heterogeneity was a reflection of the alien elements which had crowded into the manufacturing centers of the old Bay State. Among the men in this regiment were representatives of nationalities less frequently encountered—Russian, Belgian (in unusual numbers), Hungarian, Italian, Danish, Cuban, and Polish.[35]

Company C, Twenty-seventh Michigan Infantry, might be cited as illustrative of how highly mixed a company might be; it contained 22 Canadians, 16 Irishmen, 38 Germans, 20 Englishmen, 2 Frenchmen, 1 Swiss, 3 Scotchmen, and 1 Welshman, in addition to 55 native Americans. Thus, this company was two-thirds foreign. On the other hand, Company K of the One Hundred and Seventy-fifth New York affords an extreme example of variety of nationalities, though the company must have been at all times overwhelmingly German. No less than fifteen different countries were represented. The greatest number—166—had come from Germany; 26 from Ireland; 23 from New York State (of which group, relatively few names suggest Germans of the second generation); 4 each from France and England; 3 from Russia; 2 each from Austria, Sweden, Holland, and Spain; and one each from Scotland, Demark, Norway, and Switzerland. The total of foreign-born other than German amounts only to 50 out of a total of 239. The unusual size of the company can probably best be explained, as stated earlier, by assuming that the roll recorded all who were ever enrolled in the company and did not indicate its size at any given period.[36] It should also be noted that this was part of the Irish Legion.

Typical, perhaps, of the private born abroad who helped fill the ranks of the Union army was a Swede who came to this country with his father

[34] Company Descriptive Books A-E, G-K, Fortieth New York Infantry.

[35] The Company Descriptive Books of this regiment are unusually interesting. Companies B and K included many Belgians; in fact, they come as close to being Belgian units as any the writer has encountered.

[36] Company Descriptive Book, Twenty-seventh Michigan Infantry; Company Books, One Hundred and Seventy-fifth New York Regiment.

in 1853. He spent his first winter in America (1853–1854) with an American family, working for his board and attending school for four months, thus becoming conversant with the English language. The next spring he went to St. Paul, Minnesota; there he apprenticed himself to a bookbinder, with whom he remained until 1860. The war found him in New York, where he promptly enlisted in one of the Zouave regiments of that state. This volunteer, Charles Frederick Johnson, who has himself recounted his story, is typical of the sturdy, capable immigrants, of whatever nationality, who helped fight our battles until the ranks—too greatly depleted—were filled by the hired foreign substitute, the kidnapped foreign sailor, or the later immigrant. It is definitely to the credit of foreign-born soldiers of this earlier type that they so often re-enlisted in a hard service.[37]

A second instance of a foreign-born soldier and noncommissioned officer involves another Scandinavian, a Norwegian who was a mere lad of seventeen when he volunteered for the service. Deprived of his father at three, he was brought by his mother to the United States in 1850. She located in Wisconsin and gave him a stepfather, toward whom he manifested much filial affection. While a student at Albion Academy, Wisconsin, he enlisted in May, 1861, with several fellow students. A lad of his age naturally started as a private, but he retired as a corporal in July, 1864. By that date he had become convinced that his duty lay at home, looking after his ailing stepfather and caring for his mother and younger brothers. Already he had known the hard experiences of war, having been wounded and captured in the siege of Port Hudson, Louisiana. No one could read his letters to various members of the family—breathing love and solicitude for his mother, respect for his stepfather, and a sense of almost paternal responsibility toward his younger brothers—without recognizing an unusual maturity, good sense, and stability. The promise of future success which such traits of character suggest was not unfulfilled, for this lad was Knute Nelson, later governor of Minnesota for two terms and United States senator for eighteen years.[38]

It is also a conspicuous fact that a number of these private soldiers had served in wars abroad for varying periods. That most of the Europeans (unless they had come over before attaining military age) had had to undergo the usual military training and learn the rigors of its discipline

[37] He has told his story in an interesting book, *The Long Roll* (Aurora, N.Y., 1911).

[38] See Knute Nelson Papers, Letters of November 13, 1861; July 8, 1862. See also note on Nelson's life filed with the Papers.

is a foregone conclusion, but a goodly number had actually experienced genuine warfare. A few had been professional soldiers, and a smaller number had served as officers in European armies. Two obscure records picked up at random from the Descriptive Books seem so admirably to illustrate this point that they are reproduced: Robert Kimber, England, Company B, Fourth New York Cavalry, had served in the British army; Jacob Christ, France, Company G, Sixty-eighth New York, was by occupation a soldier.[39]

The number who had seen service in the field was so great that any attempt at an estimate would be impossible. However, a few illustrations will emphasize the point. Repeatedly the histories of particular regiments or batteries refer to previous military experience of individuals in the ranks. Notice was accorded such soldiers in the Fourth New York Heavy Artillery in the following words: "A large number of the men [at the Battle of the Wilderness] had seen service, many in two years' regiments and some in foreign wars." Again, "Our regimental color-bearer was an Englishman, who had his discharge from the *Light Brigade* that made the famous charge of Balaklava during the Crimean War. . . ." A member of the Christian Commission told of encountering in the sick tents at Yorktown an old Irish soldier who had served twenty years in the British service in the East Indies and had fought America's foes in Mexico.[40]

Furthermore, there were many former officers who enlisted in the ranks as privates. Count Piper, minister from Sweden, brought to the attention of Secretary of State Seward the case of an "excellent military man" of the Swedish army who had entered Brickel's light artillery battalion as a private in the hope of speedy promotion from the ranks. He, however, had found his path blocked on account of his ignorance of the English language.[41] Charles J. Biggs, born in Bristol, England, had served for almost ten years as a lieutenant in the British army and had been wounded in the Crimean War. He enlisted as a private in the One Hundred and Fourteenth New York Volunteers in August, 1862, and, having no

[39] Copied directly from the Company Descriptive Books for the companies concerned.

[40] For the old soldiers in the Fourth New York Heavy Artillery, see Hyland C. Kirk, *Heavy Guns and Light: A History of the 4th New York Heavy Artillery* (New York, 1890), 161; for the Englishman, see Joseph A. Joel and Louis Stegman (authors and comps.), *Rifle Shots and Bugle Notes* (New York, 1884), 538; for the Irishman, see Edward P. Smith (author and comp.), *Incidents among Shot and Shell* (New York, 1866), 20–21.

[41] Not many were so fortunate as Count Piper's Swede, for Captain Dahlgren promised Minister Piper to employ the Swede at the Navy Yard as soon as he got his discharge, as he was a good carpenter. Piper to Seward, January 7, 10, 1862. Notes from the Swedish Legation, IV, General Records, State Department Archives, The National Archives.

language barrier, rose quickly to the rank of a noncommissioned officer. One Fidel[ius] Schlund, who had taken part in the Baden Revolution and languished long in Kempten Fortress, came with his four sons to serve under the American flag.[42]

Strong nationality feeling could lead men to forsake a unit in which they were already enlisted for an organization composed of their fellow countrymen. For instance, an Irish sergeant, who had taken a squad of fourteen Irishmen from the Twentieth Massachusetts Volunteers outside of camp to bathe, was induced by an agent of the New York Irish Brigade to desert with eleven of his men in order to join the Irish organization; however, the group was promptly arrested. On another occasion Colonel Charles W. Le Gendre was raising a regiment to be called the New York Rifles (Fifty-first New York Volunteers); and Colonel Enrico Fardella, an Italian, was raising a regiment of his countrymen nearby. Although the recruiting which was going on actively was arousing jealousy, it was not producing open friction until Colonel Le Gendre learned that a company of his men were about to be turned over by their captain, one Cresto, to Colonel Fardella's command. Before the plot could be carried out, Colonel Le Gendre ordered Captain Gossamer and Lieutenant Georgeo of his command to take charge and to order every man to his quarters. Unfortunately, the accidental discharge of a pistol produced excitement in which two men were killed and several wounded.[43]

Any group entertained respect for an able officer or patriotic comrades. Sherman, for instance, had the wholehearted confidence and support of the Swedish soldiers, who declared they would follow him wherever he went. The reason was obvious in the comment often made of him, "He was always with us when there was any fighting going on." Germans, on the other hand, were devoted to General Frémont.[44] The *Courrier des États-Unis* voiced the spontaneous admiration of Frenchmen for the immediate response of the Germans to the call to arms: "German ardor grows from day to day. Alone it could furnish the full quota for New York.

[42] For Biggs, see Elias P. Pellet, *History of the 114th Regiment New York State Volunteers* . . . (Norwich, N.Y., 1866), 363; for Schlund, see Kaufmann, *Die Deutschen im Bürgerkriege*, 550.

[43] See George A. Bruce, *The Twentieth Regiment of Massachusetts Volunteer Infantry* (New York, 1906), 7, for the desertion of the Irishmen; for the rivalry between Le Gendre and Fardella, see Mottelay and Campbell-Copeland (eds.), *The Soldier in Our Civil War*, I, 132.

[44] See Hokanson, *Swedish Immigrants*, 72, for the feeling of the Swedes toward Sherman; for the attitude of the Germans toward Frémont, see T.E.C. ("An English Combatant"), *Battlefields of the South* . . . (London, 1863), I, 190–91.

Those who are part of the regular militia gather around some officer and form a detached corps." [45]

Probably the first thing noticed by a visitor to one of the many regiments embracing recruits of several different countries would be the multiplicity of tongues spoken. In a single regiment a half dozen or more languages could be heard, and the efforts at conversation among soldiers of different nationalities presented a ludicrous scene. Utassy says that he had fifteen nationalities in his regiment and commanded them in seven languages. At first, in regiments composed almost exclusively of one foreign nationality the commands were given in the mother speech of the group; thus, French was used in the Gardes Lafayette, German in the De Kalb Regiment, and Norwegian in the Fifteenth Wisconsin. Presumably, the War Department allowed this rather remarkable phenomenon within an English-speaking country [46] on the theory that orders would be better executed if fully comprehended and that foreign regiments could thus by their example in discipline and precision render a finer service to the native regiments.

In July, 1861, however, "General Order No. 45," an order from the War Department prohibiting acceptance into the service of recruits who did not speak English, caused much apprehension—not to mention indignation—among the foreign-born. Declared the *Illinois Staats-Zeitung*:

> The German *Turner* in Washington had affixed to their cannon a plaque with the words, "Here German is spoken," and at Carthage under Siegel's command the cannon have not merely spoken German but [have] spoken in the dialect of Baden and in truth so clearly that the rebels leaped head over heels from their horses and rolled bleeding in the sand and at the arrival of each at the gates of Heaven is reported to have said to St. Peter that they had died in learning the German speech. And now indeed everyone must first pass an English examination before he can receive permission to let himself be shot for the Union. . . . The stupidity would be too great for even "General" Cameron.[47]

The order was soon explained as not applying to those companies in which the men and the officers spoke the same tongue; it was intended

[45] New York *Courrier des États-Unis*, April 29, 1861.

[46] It should be pointed out that this was not unprecedented, for in Napoleon's army during the Russian campaign, Italian, German, Dutch, Polish, Hungarian, and Bohemian, as well as French, were spoken, and commands were given in these different languages. Chicago *Illinois Staats-Zeitung*, July 23, 1861.

[47] *Ibid.*

to prevent the foreign-born from enlisting under English-speaking officers, whom they could not understand, and to induce them to enlist under officers whom they could understand. "The government desires, that regiments be formed of their own nativity groups, and they will be welcome to fight for the Union," Cameron declared. The German paper just quoted called the modification the "Recall of Cameron's Know-Nothing Order." [48] Finally, to relieve all misapprehension, the order was rescinded. What the rule ultimately meant was that foreign groups might be commanded in their own tongues if their officers understood English commands. Slowly, as misunderstandings and difficulties from allowing plural languages for command manifested themselves more and more, the practice was discarded. It was felt, for instance, that the skirmish on the Weldon Railroad (which resulted when the Confederates attacked General Winfield Scott Hancock) was lost because the breach was made in a section of the line being held by recruits commanded in part by officers who could not speak a word of English.

Another difficulty arose from the enlistment of officers who were under the misapprehension that commands could be given in their own tongues, and their consequent resignations. One John Mohr is a case in point. He submitted his resignation as second lieutenant to Colonel Seraphim Meyer of the One Hundred and Seventh Ohio Regiment on the ground of "a lack of sufficient knowledge of the English language." When he had received his recruiting commission, the oath had been administered in German, whence he had deduced the idea that commands were to be given in that language. Even the lieutenant colonel of the French Fifty-fifth resigned because of lack of familiarity with English, and, as De Trobriand adds, education "incompatible with such an elevated rank." [49]

The lay reader, accustomed from childhood to think of the navy-blue uniform and the dark-blue cap with black visor as the distinguishing dress of the Federal soldier—just as he has associated the Confederate gray with the Southern soldier—will be surprised at the type and variety of dress

[48] *Ibid.*, August 6, 1861. Some wrote the editor that this order was a weapon in the hands of the foe, who were busy everywhere in the North to keep the people from enlisting. And the editor asked if each patriot did not owe it to the Union to tear such weapons from the foe. *Ibid.*, August 9, 1861. See also the comment in that same issue on the modification of the order as "reasonable."

[49] For the skirmish on the Weldon Railroad, see Rossiter Johnson, *The Fight for the Republic* (New York, 1917), 349–50; for Mohr's resignation, see letter in Mohr Jacket, The National Archives; and for the French lieutenant colonel, see De Trobriand, *Quatre Ans de Campagnes*, I, 327.

which appeared in the Northern camps early in the war. The drab word "uniform" scarcely applies to the colorful, sometimes bizarre, costume affected by many regiments.

First, a few words about the Zouave regiments, for they had the most romantic costumes. The reader needs to be correctly informed about the various Zouave regiments because they are likely to be confused and also because there were few regiments of the Zouaves in which there were not some foreigners. The comment of the editor of the *Courrier des États-Unis* on May 16, 1861, "Il pleut des Zouaves," seemed almost literally true. First, one may seek the cause for the extravagant popularity of the idea of the Zouaves. While many countries have furnished a nationalized type of soldier—as the Scotch the Highlanders, the Germans the Grenadiers, and the Russians the Cossacks—the French have eclipsed all in their Zouaves. It was partly the valor of the French Zouaves in Algeria and elsewhere [50] and partly the picturesque, vivid, utterly alien type of dress which fascinated the American soldier. He seemed to seize upon it with childish enthusiasm. Everything in New York was "à la Zouave." The observer could note more Zouave uniforms on the streets of New York than on the streets of Paris. Some companies were really composed of French who had served more or less in the field and who regarded all other soldiers—American, German, or Irish—from the heights of Solferino and Malakoff; but most Zouave companies were imitations, devoid of Frenchmen. Everywhere through the country "literally scores of companies, and many regiments" assumed this name. Differences of opinion arose as to the regulation uniform, but all agreed on the necessity of baggy Turkish trousers, a fez, and flashing colors in which red dominated. The making of fezzes became an industry.[51]

To none of the many Zouave companies does there seem to have been more frequent allusion than to Billy Wilson's Zouaves. Colonel William Wilson, who had been one of the first to offer his services to the government, had recruited from the rowdy and criminal classes of New York City a regiment of nearly twelve hundred volunteers—men drawn to-

[50] The name "Zouave" was first taken from a tribe of Kybeles in Algeria, whose fighting qualities had been noted for generations throughout North Africa. After the French occupied Algiers in 1830, a body of these troops was incorporated into the French army with French officers, French discipline, and French arms. The corps of three battalions became noted in the many conflicts preceding the final conquest of Algeria. Long before this the native element had been eliminated, and after 1840, the Zouaves were simply European troops uniformed as Arabs.

[51] Shannon, *The Organization and Administration of the Union Army*, I, 43.

gether by the amazing cry "Death to the Plug Uglies of Baltimore" and by the appeal to punish those guilty of the attack in Baltimore on the Sixth Massachusetts Regiment. In this unit—a mixed, partly foreign group—were to be found hardened veterans of many wars in many parts of the world alongside the dregs of the city.[52] In addition, there were the Anderson Zouaves; the Zouaves Imperieux; the famous Fire Zouaves, two regiments strong, recruited by Ellsworth at Lincoln's request among the firemen of the metropolis, and including, naturally, many born in Ireland or here of Irish parents; D'Epineuil Zouaves, discussed in an earlier chapter; Abram Duryée's Zouaves; and Rush C. Hawkins' Zouaves, or Ninth New York Volunteers, which contained many Irish and a sprinkling of other nationalities.[53] Outside of New York City there were the Zouaves d'Afrique of Philadelphia, composed, it was reported, of soldiers who had all served in the Crimean War; the Boston Tiger Fire Zouaves, or Company K of the Nineteenth Massachusetts Infantry (a mixed regiment if ever there was one, for all told it embraced seventeen nationalities, with Irishmen predominating, and consisted from one third to three fourths of recruits born abroad); and the Sprague Zouave Cadets of Cleveland, a company in the Seventh Ohio which went out for three months service.[54]

The most striking feature of the uniform of the Federal army was its extraordinary variety. To encourage enlistment, each new military organization was given the freedom to choose its own uniform, until one foreign officer cried in his bewilderment, "God knows whether fantasy gave itself free range!" [55] All sorts of costumes were seen—from the plain dress of the United States regulars to the gaudy outfit of the Zouaves, which could not even be designated as neat. The colors ran through the various shades of red, navy blue, gray, sky blue, yellow, green, and black;

[52] On Wilson's Zouaves, see Mottelay and Campbell-Copeland (eds.), *The Soldier in Our Civil War*, I, 81–85; the Comte de Paris, Louis-Philippe-Albert d'Orleans (Louis F. Tasistro, tr.), *History of the Civil War in America* (Philadelphia, 1875–1888), I, 178–89. Since the original of these ponderous volumes was not readily available to the author, the translation was used. Wilson's Zouaves were opposed to a similar group from New Orleans, Wheat's Tigers. Theodore Gerrish and John Hutchinson (authors and comps.), *The Blue and the Gray. A Graphic History of the Army of the Potomac and that of Northern Virginia . . .* (Portland, Me., 1883), 105–106. For Bob Wheat's Tigers, see Lonn, *Foreigners in the Confederacy*, 105–106.

[53] For the Fire Zouaves, see New York *Courrier des États-Unis*, August 12, 1861.

[54] This was Company B. For the Boston Tiger Fire Zouaves, see Company Descriptive Books, Nineteenth Massachusetts Infantry. For the Cleveland Zouaves, see A. W. Pease to Governor Dennison, Executive Correspondence of the Governors of Ohio, April 16–24, 1861.

[55] De Trobriand, *Quatre Ans de Campagnes*, I, 66.

the materials varied from drill to fine wool with satin for trimming; and hats and caps were of every variety of pattern and material. Nothing is more astonishing, however, than the fact that gray, today almost invariably associated with the Confederates, was widely used in the early period of the war by the Federals and often referred to as the "standard" gray. A few regiments wore blue from the beginning and appeared in that color at the First Battle of Bull Run; these included some of the New York regiments, the Twenty-second Pennsylvania, and the first and second companies of the Vermont Volunteers. The members of the Thirteenth Massachusetts wore blue, but they introduced variety by having their jackets of dark-blue flannel and their trousers of light blue.[56]

In the First Massachusetts Volunteers the uniform was furnished by the state and described as the "standard gray"; Townsend's men of the Third New York wore "the gray uniform." Most of the companies of the First Vermont Volunteers, wore gray; the Indiana regiments had a uniform like that of the Georgia troops, gray with black facings; the First Iowa had a uniform closely resembling that of the Louisiana troops; Maine, Kansas, and Nebraska troops affected the gray uniform, though in the last-named the uniform was designated as "provisional" and had a satin-decorated blouse and gray-drill trousers.[57] In July, 1861, a Norwegian described the Wisconsin uniform as consisting of two pieces, one of dark-gray wool and the other of blue drill like a farmer's work shirt; the parade dress permitted shirts of blue flannel.[58] Rhode Islanders must have presented a somewhat striking appearance on the march, with their gray pantaloons, loose blue blouses, and large red blankets strapped diagonally across their backs. The men of the Boston Rifle Company wore light-blue trousers, red shirts, dark gray overcoats, and fatigue caps. A Brooklyn company, who were all firemen, had felt hats, black fire coats, drab

[56] Charles E. Davis, Three Years in the Army. The Story of the Thirteenth Massachusetts Volunteers, from July 16, 1861, to August 1, 1864 (Boston, 1894), xxxv.

[57] For the First Massachusetts Volunteers, see Moore (ed.), Rebellion Record, I, Pt. 1, p. 107; for the Third New York, see Matthew J. Graham, The Ninth Regiment New York Volunteers (Hawkins' Zouaves). Being a History of the Regiment and Veteran Association from 1860 to 1900 (New York, 1900), 59; for the Vermont uniform, see Moore (ed.), Rebellion Record, I, Pt. 1, p. 65; for the uniform of the Indiana regiments, see Henry W. Benham, Recollections of the West Virginia Campaign . . . (Boston, 1873), 685; for that of the Iowa troops, see Der Deutsche Pionier, XII (1880–1881); 123 n.; for the Nebraska dress, see Chicago Illinois Staats-Zeitung, July 1, 1861.

[58] Knute Nelson Papers. Common sense would indicate that the garment of wool was the trousers and that the garment of drill was the shirt, although Nelson does not make this distinction.

trousers, and red shirts—affording a sharp contrast with the gray uniform of the main portion of their regiment.[59]

The Berdan sharpshooters (among whom, it will be recalled, there was a company composed of Swiss and a number of other foreign-born individuals) wore dark-green coats, broad-brimmed felt hats, light-blue trousers (later exchanged for green ones), and leather leggings. Their knapsacks were of hair-covered calfskin with cooking kits, regarded as the best then in use, attached. Their distinctive dress—deliberately chosen in order to distinguish them from the Regular Army, by this time clothed in navy blue—won for them the appellation of "Green Coats." [60]

Diverse and striking as these uniforms were, those among the foreign regiments were often even more so. The men of Blenker's regiment (the Eighth New York) were uniformed in short gray coats with wide sleeves and wide backs which could by means of buttons be made narrower, deep-gray shirts, gray trousers trimmed with green stripes, and gray caps which were striped with green. Each officer appeared in a narrow gray coat and a red cap with one, two, or three gold stripes, according to rank. It was a practical dress and one suggestive, according to an informed writer, of the regular Prussian uniform.[61] The German Turners of the Twentieth New York were distinguished by their high, conical hats, which, when the men broke and ran—as they did at the Battle of White Oak Swamp— dotted the battlefield far and wide. The Black Rifles or Schwarze Jäger, as the men of the Fifty-fourth New York called themselves, wore uniforms of black and silver like those of the regiment after which theirs was named, Lutzow's Schwarze Jäger, and carried, besides the Stars and Stripes, a black flag on which a skull and crossbones were embroidered in silver. This flag, however, was not sanctioned by the authorities and was afterwards discarded. After April, 1862, the regiment was reuniformed by General William S. Rosecrans.[62] It was certainly a far cry from the black and silver of the Jägers to the vivid blue and yellow of the Uhlannen, a battalion of New Jersey Cavalry composed of Germans and called "the butterflies" on account of their colorful uniforms.[63]

The reader might expect to be told that the Irish Brigade was uniformed

[59] On the Rhode Islanders, see Moore (ed.), *Rebellion Record*, I, Pt. 2, p. 125; on the Brooklyn company, *ibid.*, I, Pt. 2, p. 144.

[60] Aschmann, *Drei Jahre in der Potomac Armee*, 6.

[61] Chicago *Illinois Staats-Zeitung*, May 20, 1861.

[62] Hyde, *Following the Greek Cross*, 73–74; Francis J. Werneck, "Historical Sketch," in Fox (comp.), *New York at Gettysburg*, I, 402–403, for the uniform of the *Jägers*.

[63] Hyde, *Following the Greek Cross*, 216–19.

in green, but it contented itself with gray trousers, a green collar, and green shoulder straps on its blue jacket. This uniform had the additional virtue of being very inexpensive, for it cost only $7.25. The Zouave company of Meagher's brigade enjoyed the privilege of wearing special gold-embroidered green vests; at least one soldier wore his constantly—so that if he fell in battle, he might die with the color of his fatherland over his heart.[64] The Gardes Lafayette retained the colors of the uniform of the old Fifty-fifth Militia, the light blue of the French army adorned with black on the sleeves and the red cap. When on parade, the Scotch Highlanders of New York wore kilts; but their undress or fatigue uniform consisted of a blue jacket, Cameron tarlatan trousers, and a cap. The companies of the Thirty-first New York, made up almost entirely of Poles, wore the traditional Polish quadrangular caps of red and white.[65]

After the period of playing at war by fancy dressing passed, some approximation to a simple and useful costume was inevitable. The Garibaldi uniform, consisting of a red flannel shirt with a broad falling collar, blue trousers held in place by a leather belt, and a soft felt hat, was found practicable and was extensively copied. With the addition of some sort of overcoat and a good blanket in an improvised knapsack, a soldier was not badly outfitted. The Garibaldi Guard adopted this dress, of course; the broad, flappy, black felt hat with the round crown and the cock feather, and the trousers tucked into the boots gave these soldiers an appearance of readiness for business which other regiments lacked. The warm scarlet color of the shirt, reflected upon the men's faces as they stood in line, made a picture which never failed to impress the reviewing officer.[66] Their Hungarian leader, Utassy, however, continued to wear the uniform of the Hussars.

For really bizarre dress, one must turn to the various Zouave companies whose uniforms varied from the standard red breeches, fancy jackets, and long tasseled caps. The Zouaves of Salem, Massachusetts, preferred blue jackets and trousers trimmed with scarlet braid. The Hawkins Zouaves

[64] Chicago *Illinois Staats-Zeitung*, June 25, 1861; Cavanagh, *Memoirs of Gen. Meagher*, 455.

[65] De Trobriand, *Quatre Ans de Campagnes*, II, 101; Todd, *The Seventy-ninth Highlanders*, 1; Haiman, *Polish Past in America*, 110.

[66] Jacob D. Cox, "War Preparations in the North," in Robert Underwood Johnson and Clarence Clough Buel (eds.), *Battles and Leaders of the Civil War* . . . (New York, 1887–1888), I, 91; Chicago *Illinois Staats-Zeitung*, June 5, 1861. The fact that a regiment embarking at Fort Snelling wore the red shirts is indicative of how widespread was the use of this costume. Jane Grey Swisshelm, *Half a Century* (Chicago, 1880), 213.

used army-blue trousers, only slightly full and pleated at the waist, with magenta braid down the outer seam; jacket and vest with magenta trimmings; a wide sash of the same vivid color encircling the waist; white leggings; and a red fez with blue tassel to complete the costume.[67] Probably the most fantastic, brilliant, and *outré* of all was the dress of the Zouave regiment raised by the French officer Colonel Lionel J. D'Epineuil, which organization ultimately proved a failure and had to be disbanded.[68]

Almost immediately, however, these fantastic fancy-dress costumes had to be abandoned for a practical, common-sense uniform. Governor Edwin D. Morgan promptly recognized their impracticability and childish nonsensicalness and announced as early as May, 1861, that no officer in New York whose confirmation depended on military authority would be commissioned until his men had accepted the regulation uniform.[69] Furthermore, on the battlefield Massachusetts Zouaves could scarcely be distinguished from Louisiana Zouaves, so that both sides came to recognize the desirability of a regulation uniform. Thus the bizarre variety of uniform yielded to the sensible dark-blue recognized as the label of the Federal army.

The flags carried by the different regiments were as varied as the uniforms, and in the melee of a battle it was difficult to distinguish them from the Confederate flags. The regimental flags interspersed with the Stars and Stripes made great splashes of color, particularly those which were of one solid color with legends or figures inscribed on them. The Hawkins Zouaves, for instance, carried a flag made of rich red silk and bearing simply the words "Ninth Regiment New York Volunteers, 'Toujours Prêt,'" though just why the last words should have been in French is not apparent. It can be asserted without qualification that to no nationality unit did the flag as a symbol mean more than it did to the Irish. It meant the cause for which they were fighting, but it also meant much more. When it was first unfurled over the vessel on which the Ninth Massachusetts was sailing from Boston, wild cheers rang from a thousand throats

[67] For the Salem Zouaves, see Moore (ed.), *Rebellion Record*, I, Pt. 1, p. 61; Graham, *The Ninth Regiment New York Volunteers*, 47. The fatigue uniform of the Hawkins Zouaves was a blue flannel fatigue dress, which a private pronounced very comfortable in summer. Johnson, *The Long Roll*, 10.

[68] Silas W. Burt, *My Memoirs of the Military History of the State of New York during the War for the Union, 1861–1865* (Albany, 1902), 58.

[69] For Morgan's decree, see New York *Courrier des États-Unis*, May 3, 1861; Otto Heusinger, *Amerikanische Kriegsbilder* (Leipzig, 1869), 4.

and many a tear-dimmed eye gazed at it reverently. The sight of the green flag of old Erin, with the harp and sunburst emblazoned on it, had an almost electrical effect, adding fresh vigor to the courage of many an Irish regiment on the battlefield. Here was "the nostalgia of the exile for his native land." On December 14, 1862, at Fredericksburg the three old regiments of the Irish Brigade went into action for the first time without their green flag; they had sent the tattered remnants to New York the day before. While the brigade was drawn up in line of battle in one of the streets of Fredericksburg, General Meagher ordered a sprig of evergreen boxwood placed in each soldier's and officer's cap in order that his men might still carry the colors of the Emerald Isle into their bloodiest fight.[70] The green flag came to bear a special significance for the foe also—one of hard, bitter fighting. Nothing expresses better the effect of the Irish flag on the enemy than the remark of a Confederate soldier which has come down through the years: "There comes that damned green flag again." The distinguishing feature of the Irish Brigade may be said to have been the red trefoil, its green feather, and the green flag. The distinctive Hungarian flag carried by the Garibaldi Regiment with its red, white, and green stripes has already been described.[71]

Another striking feature of the Union army was the presence in it of former officers from European armies as noncommissioned officers, as well as of persons conspicuous for one reason or another among the privates of the rank and file. Repeatedly, the research revealed an older officer. One such illustration was Felix Vogeler, who was fifty-one years old and who had been in the French cavalry service for fourteen and one-half years. He served from the day of his enlistment in the American service as a noncommissioned officer and soon took a place on the staff of a general in the Western Department. The Swedish vice-consul at Cincinnati, James P. Melines, entered the military service of Ohio as a private. In Company K, Fifteenth New York Heavy Artillery, were found several assumed names, the reason for which is in some cases apparent. A Mr. Hitz, consul general of Switzerland in Washington, took the name of Albert Baehr; Albert Bonestrel of the *Spielberg Amt* of Durlach, Baden, preferred to enlist under the name of Carl Bittner. Just why Andrus Boder should enroll himself as "Mr. Bahr" is not apparent. Hitz we shall meet again.

[70] MacNamara, *The Irish Brigade in Bivouac and Battle*, 79; Cavanagh, *Memoirs of Gen. Meagher*, 466. The Twenty-eighth Massachusetts was the only regiment of the Irish Brigade able to carry its colors into battle.
[71] See Chapter VI.

Records of the occasional scholar who enlisted in the Union army prove interesting. The story of a young Swede in a Maine regiment, who unfortunately must remain nameless, certainly justifies this assertion. He had taken a degree at the University of Lund and could converse readily in five languages besides knowing Latin and Greek. Upon being asked, as he lay wounded in a hospital, in what language he would like a Testament, he requested one in English, as he was not familiar with that language. When he was pressed to tell why, with his education and in his circumstances, he had come to this country to enlist in the Union army, his reply was simply, "Why, I heard there was a war over here and I came." He found the realities of war what he expected but the care of the soldiers better: "I have looked into these things a great deal at home, and in Germany, and I think no government and no people ever took such care of their soldiers. . . ." His patience under the discomforts of his severe wound and the coarse fare was unceasing marvel to others.

The usual tales of noblemen incognito in the ranks have been told also of the Union army. In Kaufmann's list there are several men of title who seem to have served merely as privates. Two of them, Eugen von Kielmannsegge and Vincent E. von Körber, served in Kentucky cavalry regiments, and both fell in 1864 in Grant's Wilderness Campaign. Somewhat more intriguing is the story of Axel Mauritz Day, who on September 2, 1863 was mustered into Company I, Sixteenth New York Regiment, as a private. The report spread later that he was a Swedish nobleman who had reached New York in the June preceding his enlistment. Mere rank in this case did not impress the War Department, for the minister of his country recommended him in vain for a commission. More genuine seems the record of the presence of the Swedish poet, Thorwaldsen, in the Sixteenth Ohio Volunteers at Camp Potomac in August, 1862; for it was reported to a newspaper in Göteborg, Sweden, by a young Gothenberger who was serving in the same company.[72] Thrilling also are the tales of officers of high distinction who were willing to enter the service for Uncle Sam as mere privates, but whose military talents were not long allowed to be so wasted, men like Osterhaus, August von Willich, Hecker, Von Wangelin, and Von Vegesack.

[72] For the two German noblemen, see Kaufmann, *Die Deutschen im Bürgerkriege*, 519; for Axel Mauritz Day, see Hokanson, *Swedish Immigrants*, 102; for Thorwaldsen, see *Swedish Immigrants*, 104. There is a record of a Martin Thowaldsen in Company C, Twenty-eighth Ohio. Index, War Records Office, The National Archives.

Myriad are the tales which have come down about individual Irishmen and Germans who furnished amusement to their American fellow soldiers. While a sober treatise on history should not be loaded with anecdotes, a splash of color now and then may well enliven the narrative. Three oddities—all, as it happens, involving Irishmen—may suitably conclude this chapter.

The first story is of a type of soldier seldom encountered among the "fighting" Irish. The "Professor," so dubbed by the regiment itself and found, of all places, in the Ninth Massachusetts, generally managed to fall out as the regiment was approaching an engagement. The day after the Battle of Gettysburg, he was charged by his commanding officer with absence from the ranks the preceding day. The Professor gave the customary salute with unusual dignity and explained: "When within about two miles of the historic field, I fell out by the roadside for the purpose of recuperating my exhausted energies. After five hours unruffled slumber I awoke, startled by the roaring of many batteries of artillery, and, Colonel, in the weakness of my judgment, and under all the painful circumstances, I deemed it prudent to remain in the rear." [73]

In sharp contrast stands the conduct of the Professor's fellow countryman at the same battlefield. One Michael Broderick, who had been detailed to the Fourth New York Battery and placed as a driver on a battery wagon, left his team when the fire from the Confederate riflemen sheltered behind a large boulder became especially annoying to the artillerists; picking up an infantryman's musket, he was soon engaged with one of the enemy behind the boulders. Seemingly oblivious to the bullets flying about, Mike kept his eye glued on his man, but he also sought the protection of a large rock. When his strange antics attracted the attention of his commanding officer, who promptly took him to task for leaving his team, he begged, "Let me stay here, Captain, sure there are plenty back there to look after the horses." Mike again began to dance first to one side of the boulder and then to the other, challenging his opponent to come out and face him; he would dodge back only to jump out again, shouting, "Come on now, if you dare, bad luck to ye." That night Mike was reported missing, but early on the third of July, he turned up with a Confederate musket and cartridge box. He had been captured and placed in a belt of timber; but, watching his opportunity to escape, he had found a belt and musket and began to march up and down as if he were a Con-

[73] MacNamara, *The Irish Brigade in Bivouac and Battle*, 198–99.

federate guard. The ruse had worked and Mike had soon rejoined his company.[74]

The third character typifies the drolleries of the drunken Irishman—unfortunately, one of many. One frosty morning he was seen near the guardhouse with his feet fettered and his body encased in a barrel, above which his eyes were twinkling. "Me bould Major," he saluted a passing officer, "a man is a man if he is in a barr'l," whereupon the major had him released. That same evening somebody scratched for admission at the colonel's tent and Dennis Mahoney's head appeared, much the worse for abuse. "Me gallant Colonel," said he with a magnificent bow. "Sergeant of the guard, arrest this man," ordered the colonel. "Ye poor little grass-hopper,— to h——l wid ye!" returned Dennis with the height of disdain. This hit the colonel in a tender spot, since he weighed only about a hundred pounds. Back to the guardhouse went Dennis to sleep off his inebriation and his victory, for he had spoken his mind about the colonel directly to that officer's face.[75]

[74] James E. Smith, *A Famous Battery and its Campaigns, 1861–'64* (Washington, 1892), 111–12.

[75] Hyde, *Following the Greek Cross,* 32–33.

CHAPTER EIGHT

Foreign-Born Generals *

THE patriotic uprising of April, 1861, brought to the aid of the government millions of heads, hearts, and hands, eager to do and to serve; but the great problem of how to perform the task had to be learned, and there were pitifully few to show the way. There were thousands of well-disposed, wholly inexperienced patriots who honestly believed that making an efficient fighting machine out of a thousand entirely raw recruits from the free and independent citizenry of a republic would be an easy process. It was in reality a Herculean task, especially since it was perforce undertaken without the aid of an adequate nucleus of regular troops and of educated, trained officers upon which to build by expansion and from which to draw trained officers.

The people of the North, ignorant of military operations, regarded with superstitious and undiscriminating deference all men of military education and especially those with combat experience. The United States possessed, comparatively speaking, only a handful of men who had served in the brief Mexican War. Northerners, therefore, at the commencement of the war were inclined to look upon the foreign-born participants in the revolutionary movements of Europe and the foreign officers who came streaming to America as a godsend. In truth, the outbreak of the war proved a godsend to some of the Germans whose careers had been wrecked by the revolutions of 1848, especially those from Prussia. They had been soldiers, and even the most imperfect knowledge of affairs military was then of the highest value to Americans, who understood nothing at all of military

---

* A statement in regard to the rank accorded each officer is in order because foreign-born writers, in their zeal to claim honor for the country of their birth or ancestry, have been prone to designate officers by their brevet rank, regularly calling a particular officer "general," when, in fact, he appears in government records as "colonel." Officers are listed according to their linear rank and not according to their brevet rank in *Official Army Register of the Volunteer Forces of the United States Army for the Years 1861, '62, '63, '64, '65* (Washington, 1865–1867). (This work is hereinafter cited as *Volunteer Army Register.*) It is furthermore provided in army regulations that brevet rank shall take effect only when an officer is assigned to some special service that accords with his brevet rank.

science. The military chiefs of the revolutions of 1848, whose importance and military talents were usually overrated by their countrymen in the United States, rose at once to high rank. Just as England at the outbreak of the Crimean War granted rank to foreigners in its army according to the rank previously held by them in the home countries, so the government of the United States acknowledged the military rank which foreigners in its army had held in the revolution.

As every American knows, the rank of lieutenant general was accorded only to Grant, but in the lower ranks foreigners were well represented. The number of major generals was relatively small, and the Northern authorities were almost as parsimonious as the Southern authorities in bestowing this rank on any but native citizens. As a matter of fact, there were only six men of foreign birth, if Philip Sheridan is included, who attained this high rank. It is interesting to note how the honor was used by Union authorities as a means of recognizing nationality groups for their response to the call for troops and their devotion to the Union cause. First came the recognition of the German element, which clamored insistently for appointment of a German to this high rank. It may be fairly stated that the promotion of Franz Sigel to a major-generalship was intended as a recognition of the entire German element in the army, and that he was practically the choice of his fellow countrymen. The exaltation of Carl Schurz to such military rank was doubtless partly motivated by the same consideration, but political exigencies also weighed with President Lincoln in honoring a man who had contributed so much to his election. The promotion of General Osterhaus seems to have been actuated more largely by military merit.

Two Irishmen attained the rank of brigadier general, but it is difficult to feel that their promotion was prompted by a desire to please or conciliate the Irish element in the country. It is possible that had not General Meagher resigned shortly after the Battle of Fredericksburg in protest at the treatment of the Irish Brigade and thus broken the continuity of his service, promotion to a major-generalship might have been given him in recognition of the valuable service of the Irish. Certainly, General Robert Patterson was Irish, and no question as to his nativity entered in any way into his war record. The advancement of Sheridan—and doubt certainly exists as to whether he should be classified as Irish-born—was entirely the result of his military achievement. The fact that he was constantly referred to as the "Little Irishman" indicates that both the Irish and those of other nationalities were conscious of the country of his origin and considered some of his qualities characteristic of the race.[1] Whether or not the governmental authorities were conscious of the nationality of Julius H. Stahel, one major-generalship went to this native of Hungary.

Of course, George Meade, though he had been born in Spain in 1816 while his father was the American naval agent at Cadiz, does not enter this story; for it did not require the presence of the American flag floating over the house at the time of his birth to establish his status as an American citizen. The same statement holds true for General Jacob Dolson Cox, who was born in Montreal, Canada, while his father, a building contractor, was engaged in the construction of the roof of the Church of Notre Dame; he was descended from English and German stock which had come into the United States in the seventeenth and eighteenth centuries.

Though Schurz undoubtedly became the most prominent political figure among German Americans and achieved a highly respectable position as a military personage, it seems suitable to begin the discussion of German officers with General Franz Sigel, admired by most Germans in the country almost to the point of obsession.[2] Born at Sinsheim, Baden, on November 18, 1824, he received his military education at the academy at Karlsruhe. He entered the army of the Grand Duke of Baden, in which his promotion was so rapid that by 1847 he had attained the rank of chief adjutant and was regarded as one of the best artillerists in Germany. When the revolutionary movement of 1848 arose, he had already resigned from the army; and, as an associate of Friedrich Hecker, he took part in the revolution. He was soon appointed to the chief command of one of the armies of the Liberals; and when a revolutionary government succeeded

[1] According to Sheridan's own statement, he was born in Albany, New York; the date of his birth is usually given as 1831. However, when he registered at West Point on July 1, 1848, he gave his age as eighteen years and one month. That would place his birth date on June 1, 1830. The whole question then would turn on how early in 1830 his parents arrived in the United States. It must also be recognized that the youth may have felt that it was to his advantage in seeking an appointment to the military academy to represent himself as native-born. Allen Johnson and Dumas Malone (eds.), *Dictionary of American Biography* (New York, 1928–1944), XVII, 79.

This is one of the few instances where the author has departed from the strict rule of admitting to these pages only bona fide foreigners, concerning whose nativity there can be no question.

[2] An illustration of the esteem in which Sigel was held by the German-Americans is seen in the Baltimore *Der Deutsche Correspondent*, July 22, 1864; a paragraph on Sigel had to be dragged in, although it certainly had little significance. As this study is in no sense a dictionary of biography, there is no reason to supply full details of the lives of the foreign-born who appear as officers in the Union army. Where, however, facts in the previous experience help to explain the appointment to a given rank or shed light on the careers in the American army, the writer has not hesitated to indicate them.

in establishing itself the next year, he became minister of war in the insurgent government. He took part again in the unsuccessful campaign against the Prussians, distinguishing himself in many engagements; in one instance with only thirty thousand men he opposed troops nearly eighty thousand in number and effected a retreat without loss of any men or artillery. Despite a large opposing army, he withdrew successfully to Switzerland, where he remained until he was expelled by the Swiss government in 1851, whereupon he came to America after a brief sojourn in England. It was the generalship displayed in these brief campaigns which gave him his immense prestige with the Germans in this country.

In New York he became for a few years a teacher of mathematics in an academy and served at the same time as major of the Fifth New York Militia. In 1857 a call to a teaching post in the German-American institute in St. Louis, which brought him to Missouri at a time of crisis, afforded him his opportunity. Responding instantly to the call of his adopted country at the outbreak of the Civil War, he soon organized one of the first regiments of volunteers raised in the state and also a battery of artillery. Sigel was urged by the Germans of New York to become general of a brigade, but he refused on the plea that Missouri presented a wider field of usefulness and that he did not care to desert the loyal Germans of his adopted state.[3] He gave proof on various occasions during the war in Missouri not only that he was versed in the military art but also that he possessed aptitude for command. After helping General Lyon to save St. Louis with its arsenal for the Union and to capture Camp Jackson, he participated in the battles of Carthage [4] and Wilson's Creek and conducted the retreat from Springfield, thus proving himself to be quite a master of military science. Very shortly afterwards he sought to withdraw from the army, largely because of unpleasant relations with General Halleck, who was bitterly antagonistic toward him,[5] but partly from resentment at the

[3] Robert Tomes, *The Great Civil War. A History of the Late Rebellion with Biographical Sketches of Leading Statesmen and Distinguished Naval and Military Commanders* (New York, 1862–1866), I, 426.

[4] The Battle of Carthage (where Sigel, with only twelve hundred men, inflicted a heavy loss upon five thousand Confederates even though he was obliged to retreat) won for him one of those sudden reputations which were made in the first year of the war but obscured by the greater events of later years. Rossiter Johnson and others (eds.), *Campfire and Battlefield* (New York, 1894), 41. He did, however, ensure the safety of the baggage train in excellent fashion and made a junction with General Lyon at Springfield.

[5] The New York *Tribune* took up the cudgels strongly in Sigel's favor. The issue of January 13, 1862, said: "We lose Gen. Sigel because he was sent to a post which he could not accept with honor. On the contrary we have no general in this department who conducts himself

size of the command to which he had been assigned. As brigadier general of volunteers he commanded two divisions under General Frémont in southern Missouri; he was especially conspicuous for his bravery and skill at Pea Ridge, on March 7–8, 1862, where he contributed greatly to winning the decisive Union victory which settled the fate of this border state.[6]

He was later summoned to Washington, promoted to a major-generalship to date from March 21, 1862, and placed in charge of troops at Harpers Ferry. Succeeding to the command of General Frémont's army corps, the First Corps, he served under Pope in Virginia and took a prominent part in the Second Battle of Bull Run. In September, 1862, his corps was transferred to the Army of the Potomac as the Eleventh Corps; later, under General Ambrose E. Burnside, Sigel was given the Reserve Grand Division, consisting of the Eleventh and Twelfth Corps. He gave up his command temporarily in the spring of 1863 on account of his ill health; he returned to duty in the summer, but only to a subordinate command. In March, 1864, he succeeded to the command of the Department of West Virginia; but after his humiliating defeat at New Market by the brigade composed partly of cadets from Virginia Military Institute and less than half the size of his force, he was relieved and assigned to the Division at Harpers Ferry. When General Jubal A. Early threatened Washington the following July, Sigel was able to hold out for four days, as we shall see later, against a greatly superior force. However, the authorities were convinced that he was not sufficiently aggressive, and so they

---

with greater and more delightful modesty, but if one denies the acknowledgement which is openly his due, and if one takes away from him the troops, who expressly took up arms to serve under him and which he had recruited, and gives him others, and if he is placed under officers who are far behind him in experience (not to speak of ability), that must not only wound the pride of the general, but even his personal honor." His resignation was never acted upon by the authorities.

Halleck wrote General Curtis on March 19, 1862: "I was by no means surprised at General Sigel's conduct before the battle of Pea Ridge. It was precisely what he did at Carthage and Wilson's Creek. After your expedition started, I received documentary proof from Generals Sturgis, Schofield, and Totten, and a number of other officers, in regard to his conduct on those occasions, which destroyed all my confidence in him." Cyrus Bussey, *The Pea Ridge Campaign Considered* (Military Order of the Loyal Legion of the United States, Commandery of the District of Columbia, *War Papers*, No. 60), 23–24.

[6] Many accounts of this battle appear: J. T. Headley, *The Great Rebellion: A History of the Civil War in the United States* (Hartford, 1866), I, 304–305, 311; Kaufmann, *Die Deutschen im Bürgerkriege*, 243–55; Willard Glazier, *Battles for the Union: Comprising Descriptions of Many of the Most Stubbornly Contested Battles in the War of the Great Rebellion . . .* (Hartford, 1875), 72–79; Mottelay and Campbell-Copeland (eds.), *The Soldier in Our Civil War*, I, 251.

removed him from his command, though he did not resign his commission until after the close of the war.[7]

As a general, Sigel was prompt to decide upon and to take action, and his manner of dealing with Confederate property was severer than that of any native American.[8] At the outbreak of the war, Sigel was the rallying point of the Germans of Missouri and of the Northwest. His popularity was undeniable, if a little puzzling, not only among the Germans in the Army of the Potomac but among Germans throughout the country. "I fights mit Sigel" was a shibboleth of German-Americans. The men who fought with Sigel in Missouri were always told in St. Louis, "Pytem! you pays noting for your lager." [9]

This uncritical enthusiasm for Sigel continued long after the war, but a fairer estimate is reflected by Kaufmann. As commander of a grand division, Sigel could not prove himself capable. It is difficult to comprehend the exalted position in which his fellow countrymen insisted on placing him. His name lives even yet in German circles, while one hears almost nothing of the other German generals. After all allowances are made for his misfortunes—and he was always a *Pechvogel,* as the German designates an unlucky person—Sigel does not emerge as a towering figure. He could not escape his evil genius, General Halleck. When he allowed himself to be transferred to the eastern theater, Halleck was immediately summoned to Washington as chief of staff. It must be realized that Sigel's military fate lay in the hands of Secretary of War Edwin M. Stanton and Halleck.[10] He was naturally overshadowed by other officers in the East, but it must also be frankly acknowledged that officers trained at West Point showed deep-seated resentment at seeing one of the few major-

[7] For details on his life, see Johnson and Malone (eds.), *Dictionary of American Biography,* XVII, 153–54; Kaufmann, *Die Deutschen im Bürgerkriege,* 449–66; Mottelay and Campbell-Copeland (eds.), *The Soldier in Our Civil War,* I, 253.

Sigel was sharply criticized for delay in bringing up his men at the Second Battle of Bull Run. George H. Gordon, *History of the Campaign of the Army of Virginia under John Pope* . . . (Boston, 1880), 207, 208, 209–10. Halleck was hard on Sigel, as always, in connection with his campaign in the Valley to aid Grant in his Wilderness campaign. See Charles Willis Thompson, *The Fiery Epoch, 1830–1877* (Indianapolis, 1931), 176; see also Henry M. Coppée, *Grant and his Campaigns: A Military Biography* (New York, 1866), 275; Horace Greeley, *The American Conflict: A History of the Great Rebellion in the United States of America, 1861–'64* (Hartford, 1867), II, 599–600. For his stand against Early, see pp. 541–42 of text.

[8] George Alfred Townsend, *Campaigns of a Non-Combatant, and his Romaunt Abroad during the War* (New York, 1866), 233.

[9] *Ibid.,* 232–33.

[10] Rossiter Johnson and others (eds.), *Campfire and Battlefield,* 41.

generalships assigned to a foreign-born citizen. This was something which could render difficult the path of any officer outside the magic circle. West Pointers were certain to view him as an interloper in their midst, to be treated as the outsider that he was. He offered his second withdrawal at just the wrong moment, when his corps (the First) of only five thousand had been strengthened (as the Eleventh Corps) to over twelve thousand men. He left just when his unquestionably superior knowledge of tactics would have given him a splendid opportunity at Chancellorsville, for he would never have committed Howard's blunder in the drawing of the defensive lines.

Sigel's entire manner and bearing made him unsuitable to the task of working with West Pointers. "He was the type of cosmopolitan German scholar who hád no eye for his surroundings and went his own way. He resembled far more the research German school-master than the dashing soldier. On horseback the small, thin man with the fixed, death-like expression gave no impression of the heroic." He lacked the gift of spreading warmth about him and of winning new friends; rather he seemed to repel strangers. One needed to be a German to know and value him. His West Point comrades saw no occasion to thaw this "block of ice," as they called him. Even his life-long friend, Carl Schurz, recognized these unfortunate qualities. It seems not unfair to charge that the German-Americans were blinded by his record in the Baden revolt, and that once they had made him their choice for the major-generalship to be accorded a German they could not admit an error in their choice and therefore a shortcoming in their idol.[11]

Carl Schurz, politician, statesman, and soldier, was born in a small village on the Rhine near Cologne in 1829. He received his formal education at the Gymnasium at Cologne and the University of Bonn. Because he engaged in the abortive revolutionary movement of 1849 in Baden and the Palatinate, becoming a lieutenant and staff officer and sharing in the final battles, he was compelled, like so many of the Forty-eighters, to seek refuge in Switzerland. It was not, however, until 1852, after expulsion

---

[11] Kaufmann gives an exhaustive discussion of the question of Sigel's merits. *Die Deutschen im Bürgerkriege,* 451–66. The comment of Carl Schurz is well worth quoting: "Siegel besass nur wenig von den liebenswürdigen Verkehrsformen, welche Ubelwollen entwaffnen und in gute Kameradschaft umwandeln können. Seine Unterhaltung entbehrte sehr der sympatischen Elemente. Es war etwas Reserviertes, wenn nicht gar Abstossendes in seinem Wesen, was eine freundschaftliche Annäherung eher erschwerte als förderte," 461. The passage translated in the text occurs on p. 460. *The Reminiscences of Carl Schurz* (New York, 1907–1908), II, p. 350.

from France and a brief residence in England, that as a twenty-three-year-old youth he came to the United States. After a few years in Philadelphia and after rather extended travel through the East and Midwest he settled on a farm in Wisconsin, where he began to study law and practice politics.

Though Schurz had been originally a Seward man, Lincoln appointed him minister to Spain at the outbreak of war, in recognition of his services during the election of 1860. Schurz was then engaged in forming a cavalry regiment—the first for the Union army—and was expecting to lead it. He accepted the diplomatic post, but his soul craved military action; consequently, he returned to America in January, 1862, resigning his ambassadorial post a few months later. He succeeded in winning from the President a commission as brigadier of volunteers, and later a major-generalship. For this action he was scorned in the German-American press—though unjustly, as is proved by a letter to Lincoln in which he renounced the promotion unless it also be given to Stahel.

The Forty-eighters looked on him as a rival of Sigel. They called him "Zivilist Schurz," denied that he had military talent, and treated him as an interloper who wished to usurp the place from a German professional officer. Schurz's war record affords little justification for the above charges. His skill in military tactics was almost as exceptional as his ability in the field of statesmanship. At Second Manassas he commanded a division of the First Corps of Frémont's army, covering the final retreat; at Chancellorsville his division of the Eleventh Corps bore the brunt of Jackson's attack. At Gettysburg he temporarily had command of the Eleventh Corps and on the first day for a second time took the brunt of the attack against the right wing (which again had been badly placed by higher officers); under Howard's orders he was forced to retire to Cemetery Ridge in some disorder, leaving nearly half his men dead or wounded. He was then transferred with his corps to the Western field in the fall of 1863, so that he took part at Chattanooga. He was attached to Sherman's corps at Missionary Ridge and stood in reserve during the chief portion of the battle. He was denied a part in Sherman's march to the sea because he had charge of a corps of instruction at Nashville. During part of 1864 he laid down his sword, at Lincoln's express wish, to participate directly in the latter's second election campaign. At the very close of the war he served as chief of staff to General H. W. Slocum in Sherman's army.

Schurz had prepared himself for his military career. At Madrid he devoted all his leisure to studying military campaigns and tactics, a subject which he had pursued ever since his German experience. The German professional officers who served under Schurz had great respect for him after they saw how he led his troops in the frightful eight hours at Second Manassas; and he won the regard of General Sherman, General Hancock, and many other high-ranking Union officers. Schurz's suggestions at Chancellorsville, had they been heeded, could undoubtedly have been his greatest contribution to the war. He repeatedly begged his superior, General Oliver O. Howard, to take precautions against a surprise and proposed the drawing up of the entire Eleventh Corps on the open fields of Hawkins' Farm, as he thought that area best adapted for the use of artillery; but he had to be content to bring his three regiments into the proper position to check the enemy.[12]

The third German in the trio of Teutonic major generals was Peter Joseph Osterhaus, a Prussian. Born in Coblenz in 1823, he attended a military academy in Berlin and served as a volunteer in the Twenty-ninth Infantry regiment. His participation in the revolution of 1848 necessitated his flight to America, and in 1861 he was residing in St. Louis, serving as bookkeeper for a wholesale hardware firm. In April he entered the Second Missouri Regiment as a private, but he soon became its major. Upon reenlistment he was commissioned colonel of the Twelfth Missouri. In this rank he led a brigade in the Army of the Southwest, and at Pea Ridge he commanded a division. He saved Sigel on the occasion of that officer's retreat from Bentonville and independently led one of Sigel's two divisions in that important battle. It was he who discovered the position from which Sigel's decisive attack was later made. After Sigel's artillery had caused the enemy to waver, Osterhaus stormed the foe's chief position at Elkhorn Pass. His ability there won him promotion to the rank of brigadier general. He then commanded a division of the Thirteenth Corps on the Little Red River in the northern part of Arkansas, where he participated in a most honorable way in the siege of Arkansas Post.

During the Vicksburg campaign, Grant entrusted to Osterhaus an independent command on the Big Black River in order to prevent reinforcements and supplies from reaching Vicksburg—a task requiring constant, painful activity. During the siege of Vicksburg, the Osterhaus Division penetrated the outer works on May 22, 1863. While his comrades won laurels at Fort Donelson, Shiloh, Corinth, and Murfreesboro, Osterhaus

---

[12] For fuller accounts, see Johnson and Malone (eds.), *Dictionary of American Biography*, XVI, 466–68; Kaufmann, *Die Deutschen im Bürgerkriege*, 468–70; Schurz, *Reminiscences*, II, 407–41; III, Chaps. I and II. He was practically shelved when he was put in charge of a training station.

had only thankless, difficult tasks to perform without opportunity for winning distinction. He assisted Grant down the Mississippi from Vicksburg in the incessant battle against the foe and against malaria and yellow fever. Truly, during the first two years of war, Osterhaus received few favors from the God of War; but in November, 1863, he had his chance when he marched with Sherman in the Chattanooga campaign. As his division could not cross the swollen Tennessee, he reached Hooker's corps instead of Sherman's and became the real hero of the battle above the clouds. He led the advance from Lookout Mountain to the south side of Missionary Ridge, climbed to the summit, helped drive the foe from the crest, and directed the pursuit of the Confederate army. At Ringgold he fell upon the rest of the fugitives, independently directed a bloody battle, and reaped the significant result of the destruction of the foe. In July, 1864, he rose to the rank of major general and as such made the march through Georgia with Sherman. It was Osterhaus who broke through at Marietta and thereby made Johnson's position at Kenesaw Mountain untenable. He participated honorably at Jonesboro, as well as in the decisive battle of Peachtree Creek and the many battles around Atlanta. In September, Osterhaus was placed in command of the Fifteenth Corps, led it through Georgia to Savannah, and directed his troops in their assault on Fort Mc-Allister, which protected Savannah from the landside; thus he made possible Sherman's famous Christmas dispatch to Lincoln, "Savannah is ours." He was present at the surrender of General E. Kirby Smith (in the capacity of Confederate chief of staff) to General Edward R. Canby.

Osterhaus could never have brought any political pressure to bear and did not enjoy, as did Sigel, the support of his fellow-countrymen. His military training in Prussia was very limited, and so he was largely a self-made general. Each achievement and each promotion of his eventful career was the proof of merit and the revelation of leadership. He possessed in high degree adaptability to American conditions. He was first and foremost—in contrast to many of his fellow Forty-eighters—a military officer and not a crusader; and although he criticized the management of the war, he could see that an improvised "people's war" waged by an unmilitary nation could not be conducted according to European rules and usages. Hence, he was always at peace with his Anglo-American comrades and superiors, who all spoke of him with the highest respect. Only once was any nativism exhibited against Osterhaus and that was on the part of General Howard, who protested when Osterhaus replaced General John A. Logan in command of the Fifteenth Corps. He did not lay down his sword until January, 1866. He had been under arms almost five years, had been in thirty-four battles, and had never sustained a defeat when he led independently. In his case, merit seems to have won its just reward, for he was one of the few foreign-born to attain the next highest rank to that reserved for Grant.[13] Possibly the encomium of Emil Mannhart was not extravagant: he said that the foe had given Osterhaus the nickname "the American Bayard." [14]

The fact that Robert Patterson must be classified with the outstanding stars of the Civil War is a tribute not to his achievements in the Civil War but to earlier accomplishments. He was, in truth, a holdover from the Mexican War (and even the War of 1812) who lingered on for a few months into the Civil War and must be accorded his place in the record. The place of his birth was Tyrone, Ireland, and the date, 1792. He became an American citizen by accident when his father, because of participation in the revolt of 1798, was sentenced to exile. The eight-year-old lad naturally accompanied his father when he emigrated to the United States and settled on a farm in Pennsylvania. He entered a countinghouse in Philadelphia at the age of fifteen, took part in the War of 1812, and was mustered out as captain of the Thirty-second United States Infantry. Between this war and the Mexican War he engaged in commercial pursuits in Philadelphia. From the Mexican War he emerged as a major general of volunteers, honorably mentioned by General Scott for the capture of Jalapa by his cavalry. Apparently, despite his business interests, he never lost his military connections, for during the long years between 1833 and 1861 he commanded a division of Pennsylvania militia and functioned as a good Democrat. In 1861 he was mustered into the Federal service for three months as a major general of volunteers—apparently on the theory that a little military experience, however ancient and however aged the possessor (Patterson was then almost seventy) was better than none. Governor Andrew G. Curtin appointed him to command the Pennsylvania three months volunteers. He was later assigned to command the military department of Pennsylvania, Delaware, Maryland, and the District of Columbia. In mid-July he was ordered to prevent the forces of General J. E. Johnston, then near Winchester, from reinforcing General P. G. T. Beauregard at Bull Run while General Irvin McDowell advanced into

[13] See Kaufmann, *Die Deutschen im Bürgerkriege,* 445–49; Johnson and Malone (eds.), *Dictionary of American Biography,* XIV, 88–89; Schnake, "Der Ausbruch des Bürgerkrieges in Missouri," in *Der Deutsche Pionier,* XII (1880–1881), 57 n.; Francis Trevelyan Miller (ed.), *The Photographic History of the Civil War* (New York, 1911), X, 221–22.

[14] Kaufmann, *Die Deutschen im Bürgerkriege,* 445 n.

Virginia; but he failed to engage the Confederate general, a blunder which he tried to explain on the basis of the absence of orders from Scott to attack. In view of this failure, for which he was severely criticized, and of his advanced years it is not surprising that he was mustered out of the Federal service at the expiration of his commission on July 27, 1861.[15] It is doubtless incorrect to accept the claim of his opponents that but for his disregard of orders this first battle would have been a victory and the war reduced to a matter of months.

Every schoolboy knows the great trio of the Union army—Grant, Sheridan, and Sherman. To recapitulate the events in the life of Philip Sheridan seems almost a work of supererogation. It is desirable here only to emphasize the qualities which he probably owed to his ancestry. Born either just before or just after the arrival of his parents in this country, he was the typical Irishman, imbued with a genuine love of a fight, cool-headed and calm in the midst of battle, functioning at his best in the heat of conflict. Assiduous for the health and comfort of his men, endowed with the magnetic personality often found in the Irishman, he won the complete confidence of his subordinates, who were always ready to follow their dashing, brilliant leader. There are conflicting statements not only as to the date of his birth but even as to the place, Ohio and New York contending for the honor. According to the general himself, it was Albany, New York, where he arrived as the third of six children born to his immigrant parents. The father soon moved his family to Ohio, where he went to work on the roads and canals, while his brilliant son acquired in the village school his rudimentary education, interrupted when he went to work as a clerk in a country store at the ripe age of fourteen. It is typical of the fighting Irishman that he was bitterly disappointed that he was too young to go to the Mexican War; his disappointment was partially allayed, however, when he won an appointment to West Point. He illustrated the Irish temperament when by his impetuosity and pugnacity he involved himself in such difficulties with a cadet officer at the academy that he was suspended for one year. It was well for the Union cause that he was allowed to return and graduate, for thus trained military skill was added to the dash and intrepidity which otherwise would undoubtedly have swept him into the war as a volunteer.

[15] Johnson and Malone (eds.), *Dictionary of American Biography,* XIV, 306–307; "Report of the Joint Committee on the Conduct of the War," *Senate Reports* (Washington, 1863), 37 Cong., 3 Sess., III, No. 108, gives the findings of the Congressional committee on Patterson.

He began his war career with the rank of captain, serving as quartermaster and commissary of United States troops in the southwestern part of Missouri. His aggressive spirit naturally chafed at the restrictions of staff duty, so that he welcomed appointment as colonel of the Second Michigan Cavalry in May of the second year of the war. The quality of his fighting ability is sufficiently indicated when it is recorded that little more than a month later he won the star of a brigadier general for a signal victory at Booneville, where he led a brigade. He won a further promotion to major general in December, 1862, as a reward for his service at Perryville and Stone River. By his stubborn resistance in the latter battle, he saved Rosecrans' army. Chickamauga and Missionary Ridge only added to his laurels and won Grant's favor. When that leader went to take command in the East, he made Sheridan commander of all cavalry in the Army of the Potomac, a corps of ten thousand men, which, with characteristic energy, he completely reorganized in a month. As commander of the Army of the Shenandoah, he defeated General Early and laid waste the fertile valley; for this victory he was rewarded with a brigadiership in the Regular Army. His famous twenty-mile ride to Winchester about a month later to wrest victory from defeat brought him a major-generalship in the Regular Army, as well as the thanks of Congress. It was in the East, as a cavalryman, that he proved his real brilliance.[16]

Short and slight, Sheridan was of unprepossessing, even ungainly, appearance. He always sought to take the offensive, a fact which doubtless contributed to his success. It does not detract from his merit to say that his greatest victories came near the close of the war and were wrested from a foe decidedly inferior in numbers and equipment. A fitting and probably merited tribute was that which styled him "the Marshal Ney of the American army." [17]

No more fascinating personality turned up in the entire research for this book than the Hungarian General Julius Stahel, believed by McClellan to have been a Count Serbiani. Among the relatively numerous Hungarian officers, he alone attained the rank of major general. He was born at Szeged in the Hungarian Lowland. After receiving a classical education in his native town and at Budapest, he entered the Austrian army as a private. He had reached the rank of a commissioned officer when the Hungarian

[16] Johnson and Malone (eds.), *Dictionary of American Biography*, XVII, 79–80; *Personal Memoirs of P. H. Sheridan* (New York, 1888), *passim*; Joseph Hergesheimer, *Sheridan, A Military Narrative* (New York, 1931), *passim*.

[17] Joel and Stegman (authors and comps.), *Rifle Shots and Bugle Notes*, 528.

revolution of 1848 opened, whereupon he immediately resigned and threw in his fortunes with his fellow countrymen. As lieutenant-aide on the staffs of General Arthur Görgey and General Richard D. Guyon, he rendered effective, even brilliant, service; but the Austrian forces, aided by the Russians, finally triumphed, and he was forced to flee. After residing for some years in Berlin and London, where he earned his livelihood as a teacher and journalist, he came to the United States in 1856 and settled in New York City. Until the outbreak of the Civil War he was on the staff of an influential weekly German newspaper. The call to arms was a clarion bugle call to him, and so he entered the Federal army as a volunteer, soon becoming lieutenant colonel of Blenker's Eighth New York Regiment. At the First Battle of Bull Run, where he covered the retreat and won praise from Lincoln for his brave demeanor,[18] he commanded this regiment and soon afterwards became its colonel. As early as November, 1861, he was promoted to brigadier general of volunteers and designated leader of a brigade in Blenker's German division. He made the chief attack at the Battle of Cross Keys, which miscarried because of the bad advance of Colonel Francis Wutschel.

Stahel was in the campaign of 1862 under General John Pope and fought with distinction at Second Bull Run, covering Pope's retreat with Schurz's division. In September he captured Warrenton, where he took more than a thousand Confederate prisoners. Barely two months later, while on a reconnaissance against General Stonewall Jackson, he drove the foe across the Shenandoah to Sperryville and won a second victory, capturing two flags, several hundred prisoners, and great booty in the form of food, horses, and cattle. In January, 1863, he received the command of the Eleventh Corps but soon yielded it to Schurz. In the following spring he was assigned to the cavalry, the arm of the service for which he was especially adapted. He was one of those who reorganized the badly led Federal cavalry and finally made it an effective weapon of attack. Generals Joe Hooker and Samuel P. Heintzelmann pronounced Stahel's cavalry regiments the best that they had ever seen, and at Lincoln's request the defense of the nation's capital was entrusted to these troopers. By March, 1863, and at the same time as Schurz, he had attained the highest rank possible, that of major general. Toward the end of the year he was transferred to the Department of the Susquehanna, where he organized

---

[18] Testimony of his firm stand at Centreville comes from both sides. Lincoln and General Scott sent for Blenker and Stahel to express their gratitude for the protection of the rear of the army.

the scattered cavalry for the defense of the capital of Pennsylvania. By the spring of 1864 he was directing the cavalry in the Department of West Virginia and leading General David Hunter's advance in the battles down the Shenandoah Valley. While he was leading the charge in the Battle of Piedmont he was badly wounded in the arm. Even after being wounded,[19] he led a brilliant attack, breaking through the defenses and bringing about annihilation of the Confederates; for this gallant feat he was awarded the Congressional Medal of Honor. This exploit, however, ended his active service; for after his recovery he was assigned to recruiting duty at Harpers Ferry and Martinsburg and later served as president of a general court-martial until his resignation from the army in February, 1865. In his American military career, he rose rapidly, passing from lieutenant colonel to major general in less than two years, and from the command of a regiment to that of an army corps. He seems to have enjoyed the confidence and respect of his superiors equally with that of his subordinates. It is no exaggeration to pronounce as brilliant his work on several occasions.[20]

The government was far less niggardly in bestowing on foreign-born citizens the rank of brigadier than in bestowing on them a higher rank, and in most cases the honor seems to have been well earned. Because the Germans were more numerous and more distinguished than the officers of this rank from other nationality groups, the story will again open with the Teutons. We are concerned with nine men in all. Louis Blenker was so essentially the swashbuckling soldier of fortune that the temptation to classify him with the soldiers of fortune was almost irresistible, but since it seems to have been Bavarian loyalty that sent him, with a group of other youths, to Greece in 1833 with the newly elected King Otto, it seems just to assign Blenker to the group of German-American citizens who served their adopted country. Certainly he gave color to the whole group. Born in Worms, in the grand duchy of Hesse-Darmstadt, he was apprenticed

[19] While Stahel was in the surgeon's hands, General Hunter expressed disappointment, as he wanted Stahel to charge the foe's flank while he attacked the front. Stahel had his wound partly dressed, led the charge (though his left arm was useless), dislodged the enemy, and created a general stampede. Piványi, *Hungarians in the American Civil War*, 39–40.

[20] *The National Cyclopaedia of American Biography* (New York, 1893–1947), IV, 352; Johnson and Malone (eds.), *Dictionary of American Biography*, XVII, 493; Kaufmann, *Die Deutschen im Bürgerkriege*, 475–76; Piványi, *Hungarians in the American Civil War*, 36–40. It is worthy of note that even in the Hungarian revolt he was awarded the Cross of Bravery. The Reminiscences of General Julius Stahel-Szamvald, MS in The National Archives.

The Germans seemed to feel that Stahel, in allowing his command in the Eleventh Corps to pass to Schurz, joined in an intrigue to prevent Blenker from receiving a major-generalship. See "General Adolph Steinwehr," in *Der Deutsche Pionier*, IX (1877–1878), 23.

in his youth to a jeweller; but he enlisted in the Bavarian Legion raised to accompany King Otto, who—as a Wittelsbach—drew many Bavarians to Athens. There Blenker rose from private to sergeant, and when the legion disbanded in 1839, he received with his discharge the rank of lieutenant. After his return to his native land, he attended medical lectures with the purpose of becoming a professor of medicine, but he soon turned to commercial pursuits. In 1849 he became a leading member of the revolutionary government in Worms, was made commander of the national guards, and took an active part in the revolutionary wave which swept Europe at that period. After the movement had been crushed, he retired to Switzerland, was ordered to leave that country, and so embarked at Le Havre for the United States.

After a brief residence on a farm in upstate New York, he moved to New York City, where he was engaged in commerce until 1861. At the outbreak of war, he raised the Eighth Regiment, a group of German volunteers, and was commissioned as its colonel. The regiment was soon incorporated with others into a brigade, of which Blenker was appointed commander; the brigade was attached to General McDowell's army as a portion of the Fifth Division. At the First Battle of Bull Run his division, as has been stated, did effective service in covering the retreat of the Union forces. The general opinion was that Blenker had conducted himself excellently. For his military efficiency on this occasion he was made brigadier general of volunteers on August 9, 1861. At the opening of the Yorktown campaign he was ordered from the Army of the Potomac to western Virginia. He shared in the Battle of Cross Keys on June 8, 1862, but was shortly relieved of his command to be succeeded by Sigel. He was ordered to Washington where he remained some time; but after a brief, hectic career, he was mustered out of service on March 31, 1863, out of favor because there had been mismanagement of regimental funds, though he was not thought personally corrupt.[21]

Among the Germans who became brigadier generals, August von Willich easily tops the list. His initial appearance in the armed service was as a private in what was started as the first German regiment of Cincinnati, officially known as the Ninth Ohio Regiment.[22] Von Willich became at once the first adjutant to the commander of the regiment, Colonel Robert

---

[21] Tenny, *The Military and Naval History of the Rebellion in the United States*, 769; Kaufmann, *Die Deutschen im Bürgerkriege*, 483–84.

[22] Within three days after the roll was opened, 1,500 men stood ready for muster. Since under regulations only 974 could be accepted, August Moor had a start of 526 for his regiment, which became the Twenty-eighth Ohio.

McCook. The task of drilling the raw recruits devolved on him [23] by virtue of his European experience as an officer and participant in the revolution. In the fall, when Governor Oliver P. Morton appointed him colonel of the Thirty-second Indiana Regiment, he resigned from the Ninth Ohio and organized the new regiment always recognized by the Ninth Ohio as a sister regiment. Von Willich made both into brilliant fighting units.

He was born in 1810 in the province of Posen—not of the Hohenzollern family, as was often reported, but of an old noble family. He came by his military interest naturally, for his father was a *Rittmeister* in a Hussar regiment and in the Napoleonic wars had received a wound which rendered him incapable of further service. When the young Von Willich was less than three years old, he and his slightly elder brother came into the house of the famous theologian, Friedrich E. D. Schleiermacher, probably because Schleiermacher's first wife had been related to Von Willich's family. At the age of twelve he entered the cadet house at Potsdam and three years later, the military academy in Berlin. When he was scarcely eighteen, he received his commission as second lieutenant of artillery and by 1841 had advanced to a captaincy.

The liberal ideas of young Germany found in Von Willich an ardent response, so that when in 1846 a conflict arose between a part of his brigade and the government, he tendered his resignation. Instead of accepting it, the government removed him from the restless Rhine province to a garrison in Farther Pomerania. He refused to go and in the end addressed an open letter to the king; the consequence was that he found himself before a court-martial, which—oddly enough—declared in his favor, so that his resignation was accepted. At the age of thirty-six he turned to the carpenter trade (a "disgrace" for which his relatives would not forgive him) and took special satisfaction in marching past the assembled officers on the parade ground with his ax on his shoulder. He joined heartily with Karl Marx in the communist movement [24] and once led the mob in Co-

[23] Robert L. McCook, who humorously exaggerated his own lack of military knowledge, used to say that he was only "clerk for a thousand Dutchmen," so completely did the care of equipping and providing for his regiment engross his time and attention. Jacob Dolson Cox, *Military Reminiscences of the Civil War* (New York, 1900), I, 36. This member of a famous Irish-American family, all nine of whom were in the war, was so popular with the Germans of Cincinnati that he was chosen colonel of a purely German regiment though he could not speak a word of German, the reader is reminded.

[24] Marx ridiculed Von Willich as a "spiritual Communist and Knight of the noble conviction." Kaufmann, *Die Deutschen im Bürgerkriege*, 472 n. Von Willich became a friend of

logne in an attack on the city hall. He remained loyal to communist ideas.

Hurrying to Baden at the first news of the revolt in 1848, he co-operated with Hecker, Von Schimmelfennig, and Blenker, and with them escaped to Switzerland at the collapse of the revolt.[25] From Switzerland he went to London, where he soon belonged to one of the reddest of the radical clubs. He landed in New York in 1853 with a wild plan to gather an army to march against Hamburg. He was soon earning his bread at his old trade of carpentry in the Brooklyn Navy Yard, but his military and mathematical knowledge shortly thereafter brought him a post in the Coast Survey. Before long the workers' organization gave him the editorship of *Der Deutsche Republicaner* of Cincinnati, which post he was filling in 1861.[26]

Out of this background and experience came one of the best officers in the Union army—and one of the sternest disciplinarians. All commands were given by trumpet signals. American officers watching Von Willich's troops as a battle unfolded and seeing the brilliant results—soldiers with one month's training conducting themselves like veterans—were amazed. Everyone knows of the rebel yell at the attack, a bright, shrill yell. Von Willich's German regiment also had a special war cry. His men used a short but loudly uttered "Hurra," not the "Hör–rah—rah" in a flickering, long-drawn sound. At first, soldiers laughed at the elderly man, especially because he spoke a bookish English with a strong accent. He mastered English theoretically, but since his harsh East Prussian tongue could never command colloquialisms, he often used expressions found only in literature.[27] Ridicule soon ceased, however, especially after men saw him in battle. He was always in the advance, where the bullets whistled thickest. He proved the real "Marshal Forward" of that war as Kaufmann has aptly termed him. Apparently, he had never learned fear; if his soldiers manifested an impulse to waver, he would ride to the front and issue his commands for arms drill in the midst of battle, and then would follow a parade formation and drill as far as the terrain permitted. He did that repeatedly in the thickest rain of bullets—at Shiloh, Perryville, and Chickamauga— and his men responded. This performance never failed to draw American officers as spectators.

Judge John B. Stallo in Cincinnati, who sought in vain to eradicate his communistic ideas. *Ibid.*, 472.

[25] "General August Willich," in *Der Deutsche Pionier*, IX (1877–1878), 445.

[26] *The National Cyclopaedia of American Biography*, XIII, 65.

[27] Kaufmann, *Die Deutschen im Bürgerkriege*, 473.

With less than five hundred men, Von Willich routed Terry's Texas Rangers at Munfordsville; for brilliant service in the siege of Corinth and at Shiloh, he won promotion to a brigadier's rank in July, 1862. He met with most of the personal vicissitudes of war: He was captured at Murfreesboro—his horse killed and he himself surrounded by the foe—but was exchanged within four months. Then he took Liberty and Hoover's Gaps (passes in the Allegheny Mountains) and by the seizure of these passes made possible the advance of Rosecrans' army on Chattanooga. He fought at Chickamauga, where he commanded a brigade, and gave his finest performance at Missionary Ridge: without waiting for orders, he allowed his nine regiments to climb the heights, carrying the neighboring troops with them. In an attack on the enemy's works in the Battle of Resaca, at the beginning of Sherman's march through Georgia, a bullet hit his right shoulder and rendered him incapable of service after May, 1864. The reader will feel no surprise that he rose to be brigadier; indeed, the surprising thing is that he did not become a major general. As brigadier, he commanded a division but led independently only once during his three years at the front. Later, he was named commander of the district of Cincinnati, at which post he remained until the summoning of his corps to Texas. Here he served until October, 1865, when he left the service with the final honor of a brevet major generalship.

Von Willich was an eccentric character, according to Friedrich Hassaurek, who, however, was no admirer. He certainly had peculiarities and odd habits, which often caused his best friends to call him a *närrischer* (mad fellow); but he also possessed traits which raised him above the level of the ordinary. Among these were, above all, his remarkable bravery, his firmness and circumspection in danger, and his unquenchable curiosity, which last drew him to academic lectures while he was visiting Berlin during his old age. The American war led him back to a military career—which must be regarded as his proper sphere, for he was essentially the soldier. The old war horse could not resist the lure of combat; therefore, he offered his services to Prussia in the Franco-Prussian War in 1870, but his offer was declined on account of his age. Among the thousands of idealists who came to this country after 1848, Von Willich stands in the front rank. A friend called him "personified unselfishness." He belongs among the most appealing personalities of the war; his most devoted and articulate admirers were the American officers who served under him.[28]

[28] On Von Willich, see *ibid.*, 451, 472-75; "General August Willich," in *Der Deutsche Pionier*, IX (1877-1878), 439-45; *The National Cyclopaedia of American Biography*, XIII,

A second scion of a German noble family who served under the Union flag was Adolph Wilhelm August Friedrich, Baron von Steinwehr, born September 25, 1822, at Blankenburg in Brunswick. The love of the military was in his veins; for his grandfather, as a lieutenant general in the Prussian service, was in the campaign against Napoleon, and his father served as a major in the army of the Duke of Brunswick. True to the family tradition, the son was reared to be a soldier. After a single semester at Göttingen, he entered the Brunswick military academy; upon leaving this, he entered the ducal service as a lieutenant. There was a touch of the soldier of fortune about him for in 1847, under leave of absence for a year, he came to the United States to tender his services in the Mexican War. As he found it difficult to get a commission in the Regular Army, he accepted service as an officer in an Alabama volunteer regiment. After the war he sought in vain a post in the Regular Army; but with the aid of a southern officer he secured an appointment as engineer in the Coast Survey and, oddly enough, served under United States commissioners to settle the new boundary line on the Mexican frontier. At the end of 1849 he went with the Engineer Corps to Mobile to help survey the port of Mobile and Mobile Bay. Here followed his marriage to an Alabamian, a relationship which normally should have cemented his ties with the South. Discouraged at his inability to secure an army commission despite his new American citizenship, he took his family to Germany. There he definitely broke his ties with Brunswick by resigning his commission in the Brunswick army and returning in 1854 to settle on a Connecticut farm as a "Latin farmer."

At the outbreak of the Civil War, he entered the Union service as colonel of the Twenty-ninth New York, recruited among Germans and organized largely through his efforts. Immediately after the arrival of his regiment in Washington in late June, it was attached to Blenker's brigade, which consisted of Stahel's Eighth New York, Von Steinwehr's Twenty-ninth, Utassy's Thirty-ninth, and Max Einstein's Twenty-seventh Pennsylvania Regiments. Von Steinwehr had barely time to drill his men before they were ordered to the battlefield of First Bull Run. Though these German troops begged to be led to the fray, they were held in the reserve division and, with the other three regiments, covered the retreat. Von Steinwehr proved himself in this affair a cautious and brave officer. His promotion to the rank of brigadier general came early, his commission bearing the date of October 12, 1861. He was assigned to command the second brigade of Blenker's division, composed, as we know, almost wholly of men of German birth or parentage. At the opening of the spring campaign of 1862, he was ordered to the Shenandoah Valley to join Frémont's army; he made the terrible march with Blenker's division and took part in the Battle of Cross Keys, though his brigade was there led by Colonel Koltes.

When Pope organized the Army of Virginia, he placed Von Steinwehr in command of the Second Division in Sigel's corps. He participated prominently at Second Bull Run, but in Sigel's headquarters rather than on the field. At the reorganization of Sigel's troops into the Eleventh Corps, Von Steinwehr still retained his command of the Second Division, and thus he shared in the defeat at Chancellorsville and in the victory at Gettysburg. At Chancellorsville his able hand was seen in the preparations. He built the ramparts to which Buschbeck's brigade fled and in which it then could so brilliantly defend itself. At the first shots heralding Jackson's attack, Von Steinwehr hurried to the field and arranged Buschbeck's new position but left to him the direction of the defenses—and the fame subsequently connected therewith.[29] It was not until Gettysburg that Von Steinwehr's military genius found an opportunity, and then it expressed itself in a brilliant way. He discovered the strength of Cemetery Hill as a defensive position and effectively defended it—but the vote of thanks by Congress went to Howard. To this hill he brought the remaining divisions of the Eleventh and First Corps and made the defense of July 2 and 3. He then went to Chattanooga and shared in the night battle of Wauhatchie, where his troops made a great contribution to the Union victory. Again, however, he had little opportunity to win recognition, and the glory of the victory went to his brigadier officer, Buschbeck.

Of the German officers in the army, Von Steinwehr was probably the most thoroughly trained. He possessed, furthermore, an exact knowledge of the nature of the American military organization and was highly regarded by many West Point officers. If knowledge, experience, and military ability had determined the selection of a supreme commander of the German troops in the East, he would probably have received the distinction. There was little time to hunt out the most capable men among the numerous candidates, and at the same time the rivalry among place-hunters

---

[29] Von Steinwehr was not mentioned in the reports of the battle, not even by Augustus C. Hamlin in his book *The Battle of Chancellorsville*.

was bad—not the least among the German officers. Von Steinwehr was never a contender for place and so in the lottery for the higher rank he drew a blank. His interest and ability, we are told, lay less in the realm of troop leadership than in that of general-staff functions.[30]

In Brigadier General August V. Kautz one meets one of the most brilliant cavalry leaders of the war. He was born in Ispringen, Baden, in 1828, and emigrated to America with his parents, while still a small child.[31] The family settled on a farm in Ohio, near Ripley. We know, however, that as an eighteen-year-old youth he enlisted at the outbreak of the Mexican War as a private in the First Ohio Volunteers and served during the first year of hostilities. He had evidently found his field, for he entered West Point, graduating in 1852. He gained some distinction as an Indian fighter in Washington and Oregon Territories during the next few years; this was followed by travel in Europe during 1859–1860, which widened his experience. On his return he was appointed captain in the newly organized United States Cavalry, where he was to make his real contribution. He served during the Civil War as lieutenant colonel under General Abner Doubleday with the Second Ohio Cavalry and became one of the leaders who by 1863 had brought this hitherto neglected arm of the service to great significance. From December, 1862, to April, 1863, he had command of Camp Chase; he then became commander of a brigade of cavalry which took part in the capture of Monticello, Kentucky, and was engaged in the pursuit and capture of the Confederate raider John Morgan.

By April, 1864, he was brigadier general of volunteers in command of a cavalry division of the Army of the James engaged in cutting the railroad communications of the enemy. On June 9, 1864, he attacked Petersburg successfully with his small cavalry force, for which deed he was brevetted lieutenant colonel in the Regular Army. Toward the close of the war, he commanded the first division of the Twenty-fifth Army Corps, shared in the movements which led to the final surrender, and entered Richmond at the head of his division of colored troops with General Godfrey Weitzel on April 3, 1865. On one of the final days of the war, he was brevetted

[30] For Von Steinwehr, see Kaufmann, *Die Deutschen im Bürgerkriege*, 470–72; for the quotation, see *ibid.*, 470–71; Schnake, "Der Ausbruch des Bürgerkrieges," in *Der Deutsche Pionier*, XI (1879–1880), 19; "Gen. Adolph von Steinwehr," in Fox (comp.), *New York at Gettysburg*, III, 345–46.

[31] The writer encountered difficulty as to the year in which the family came to the United States. One authority states merely that young Kautz was a child, another that the family came over in the year of his birth. Compare Kaufmann, *Die Deutschen im Bürgerkriege*, 477, and *The National Cyclopaedia of American Biography*, XIV, 142. Kaufmann gives the place of his birth as Pforzheim.

major general in both the volunteer and regular services. His achievements emerge less sharply than the performances of infantry leaders, for the cavalry seldom found opportunity to attack in mass. Yet Kautz, as a cavalry leader, made a name for himself which deserves to rank, not with that of Sheridan, of course, but with that of George A. Custer. He fought in more than a hundred combats. During the long time that his cavalry remained at Petersburg—from June 9, 1864, until Richmond fell—his troops exactly reversed the situation of the early part of the war by incessantly harassing the Army of Northern Virginia with constant raids, by cutting its communications, and by attacking its supply trains.[32]

A successful cavalry raid requires a judicious selection of routes, rapid marches, short halts, and sudden, unexpected blows. In this type of service General Kautz was "the right man in the right place." His blow against one railroad in Virginia illustrates this fact. At half-past two o'clock on one afternoon when he had marched a distance of seventy miles, he struck the Weldon Railroad just in time to intercept a body of rebel troops on their way to Petersburg. "A thunderbolt from a clear sky could hardly have been more astounding to the enemy. Instantly he was attacked. In an incredibly short time the action was over, the enemy was whipped, the railroad was cut, the public buildings were in flames, and the gallant Kautz was again on his march, with some sixty prisoners in his train." [33]

Alexander von Schimmelfennig must be regarded as one of the German victims of the war, for, owing to the hardships and exertions of the campaigns, he survived the close of the war by only a few months. He was pursued by misfortune to the end, for by his death he was denied the opportunity to complete a book which he had begun on the Civil War. He, too, brought the experience of a Prussian officer to the aid of the Northern government. Born in 1824, he was a young man in his twenties when he engaged in the Schleswig-Holstein war, and later in the revolution in Baden. He came to America, not merely as a refugee from his government for his participation in a revolutionary movement, but also as an educated, trained military man, largely free from the idealism and

[32] For further details, see Johnson and Malone (eds.), *Dictionary of American Biography*, X, 263–64; *The National Cyclopaedia of American Biography*, XIV, 142; Kaufmann, *Die Deutschen im Bürgerkriege*, 477; Rosengarten, *The German Soldier in the Wars of the United States*, 67, speaks of him very briefly.

[33] This account of Kautz's tactics appears in the work of a Maine chaplain, Samuel H. Merrill, *The Campaigns with the First District of Columbia Cavalry* (Portland, 1866), 235–36. Twenty-four hours had not elapsed before the division moved again on another raid, one of the most hazardous and effective of the war. See *ibid.*, 237–42.

crusading spirit of most of the Forty-eighters. He marched to war as colonel of the Seventy-fourth Pennsylvania Regiment; recruited among the Germans of Pittsburgh, this was one of the elite regiments of the Army of the Potomac.[34] Not unnaturally, he was assigned to Blenker's German division and fought with distinction at Cross Keys. He then shared in Pope's Peninsular campaign of 1862 under General Sigel. At the Second Battle of Bull Run he fought with special distinction, as his brigade pushed over the railroad jetty and hurled Jackson's main troops back. It was probably as a reward for this feat that he was nominated for the rank of brigadier general.

At Chancellorsville he fought under Schurz at the Hawkins Farm— in the ramparts defended by Buschbeck but built, it will be recalled, by Von Steinwehr. The proud old Prussian officer felt his honor assailed when the West Pointers and the native press made the Eleventh Corps the scapegoat for the errors of the high command. He sent to his superior officer, General Schurz, a letter expressing the indignation of the German officers; General Schurz published the letter. On the first day at Gettysburg, Schimmelfennig led a division of the Eleventh Corps commanded that day by Schurz. Schimmelfennig was struck down on the first day of battle by a blow from a gun, but he recovered sufficiently to seek shelter in a neighboring stable, where he awaited the outcome of the battle; two days later the strains of "Yankee Doodle" assured him of safety. After this battle he had himself transferred to the Carolinas, since he no longer wished to serve in the Eleventh Corps, but the siege in the swampy territory about Charleston brought on malaria. However, he had the honor to be the first to march into Charleston at the head of his troops, and by a coincidence it was to this German general that Johann Wagener, the German general in Confederate service, was forced to capitulate. There are many evidences of the skill of the Prussian-trained Schimmelfennig. Schurz learned much from him, especially in reference to the direction of troops.[35]

[34] According to the Chicago *Illinois Staats-Zeitung* in its issue of April 22, 1861, there was talk of this regiment's being a flying corps composed of German veterans of revolutionary experience from Baden, Holstein, and Prussia. Rumors of this type were thick about that time.

[35] Kaufmann, *Die Deutschen im Bürgerkriege*, 549–50; John Howard Brown (ed.), *Lamb's Biographical Dictionary of the United States* (Boston, 1900–1903), VI, 635. For the episode of Schimmelfennig's escape from threatened capture, see Moore (ed.), *Rebellion Record*, VII, Pt. 3, p. 52; compare the statement in Frank Moore (ed.), *Anecdotes, Poetry and Incidents of the War: North and South, 1860–1865* (New York, 1866), Appendix, Selection 3, which

Friedrich S. Salomon, the most important of four brothers who came from the village of Ströbeck near Magdeburg, Germany, to Wisconsin in 1848, attained the rank of brigadier general and of titular major general. He was the victor at Fort Helena in Arkansas on July 4, 1863. He had built the fort, and on the date designated he repelled in a brilliant manner an attack on the fort by twelve thousand Confederates. General Benjamin M. Prentiss, his superior, received credit for this victory; but it appears that during the battle he was on a cannon boat on the Mississippi out of range, looking on from afar. The Confederate loss was 1,200 dead and wounded, while Salomon lost less than 150 dead and wounded. When the foe had been driven away, Prentiss came and claimed the victory.[36] In another small action, that of Jenkins Ferry, Salomon again had independent command and directed with distinction. He participated also in many skirmishes and battles; but as he fought almost always in remote theaters in the West and Southwest, it was not vouchsafed to him to play the role of a leader in the decisive battles.[37]

The second brother,[38] Carl Eberhard Salomon, might conceivably have emerged from the war with the rank of brigadier general if such title had not already been bestowed upon his brother. As it was, his linear rank was that of colonel, and consequently he must be discussed in the next chapter.[39]

One might suppose that the man selected to head the Turner Regiment, the Twentieth New York, was a colorful personality; and the supposition is justified. Max von Weber, born in Acharn, Baden, in 1824, was one of the German refugees who had fought as colonel under Sigel in the Baden revolution and, furthermore, had previously been an officer in the Baden

---

said he found refuge in a stable, with Schurz's statement that he hid in a pigsty. Schurz, *Reminiscences*, III, 35-37.

[36] Kaufmann rendered a tardy justice to Salomon in his book and related that a number of officers who participated in the struggle signed a paper stating that Salomon had conducted the fight independently, but that Grant suppressed this paper. See Kaufmann, *Die Deutschen im Bürgerkriege*, 389, 389 n.

[37] Comparatively little has been written on General Salomon. He was duly recorded in Francis B. Heitman (comp.), *Historical Register and Dictionary of the United States Army from its Organization, September 29, 1789 to March 2, 1903* (Washington, 1903), and was discussed in Kaufmann, *Die Deutschen im Bürgerkriege*, 545.

[38] One brother, Edward S. Salomon, was governor of the state of Wisconsin and hence could readily accord command of a regiment to his brothers, as, in fact, he did.

[39] See Chapter IX. The reader cannot fail to remark how rich was the contribution made by the three brothers of a single family of German refugees.

army. He had had a fine military education, for he had studied at the Polytechnic School and then graduated from the Karlsruhe Military Academy in 1843. After his arrival in New York he conducted a well-known hotel on William Street. This became the headquarters of the exiles from South Germany; to many of them he was a sort of foster father. He organized and served as colonel of the Turner Regiment until his promotion to a brigadiership in April, 1862. At the beginning of the war the intention of the leaders was to attach the Turners to Blenker's brigade; but since Von Weber did not wish to serve under Blenker, he protested, and so the regiment was sent to the Peninsula. Von Weber was for a time commandant at Fortress Monroe and distinguished himself in the battles at Norfolk. He won his greatest fame at Antietam, however, where his brigade held its position at Rulett's house after General John Sedgwick's left had collapsed; his force stood its ground under a murderous fire until finally another brigade came to its rescue. He repeatedly hurled the foe back, yielding only when the Confederates brought four more batteries into action. In this battle he was severely wounded, losing the use of his right arm; consequently, he was not able to join Sigel in the Shenandoah Valley until May, 1864. Since he had only eight hundred men, he could no longer operate effectively, though he defended Harpers Ferry against General Early in July of that year.[40]

General Heinrich Bohlen fell relatively early in the war, but not before he had rendered a service to his adopted country. Born in Bremen in 1810, he had, strangely enough, no share in the revolution of 1848, despite a strong predilection for the military calling. He shared in the siege of Antwerp in 1832, went to the Crimean War as an observer,[41] and served honorably in our Mexican War as an officer. Meanwhile, he had established himself in Philadelphia as a prosperous merchant and highly respected citizen. In 1861 his patriotism led him to raise a regiment of his German fellow countrymen, the Seventy-fifth Pennsylvania, which he organized at his own expense and led to the war to serve in Blenker's division. Among a galaxy of colorful officers, Bohlen was certainly not the

[40] For Von Weber, see Kaufmann, *Die Deutschen im Bürgerkriege*, 561–62; *The National Cyclopaedia of American Biography*, XII, 264; Brown (ed.), *Lamb's Biographical Dictionary of the United States*, VII, 527–28.

[41] During the Belgian revolution of 1830 the Dutch general David Henri Chassé held the citadel of Antwerp for two years against the citizens of the city until forced by a French army to surrender. Bohlen hurried to the Crimean War, but decided after his arrival that there would be no fighting and so started off up the Danube only to return to the Crimea when it was too late to share in the war.

least colorful. William Howard Russell, the British war correspondent, pictured him as dressed in a uniform and cap decorated with eagles flying amid laurel leaves and the letters "U.S." in gold, and mounted on a steed caparisoned with a splendid war saddle and brass stirrups and holsters—all worked with eagles. Before the close of the year he was promoted to the rank of brigadier and attached to Frémont's department. He distinguished himself at Cross Keys, but on August 21, 1862, at Freeman's Ford on the Rappahannock, he was killed while bravely leading his troops forward to resist Jackson's attempt to cross at that point. He was one of the most beloved officers of the entire corps.[42]

The name of Karl Leopold Matthies of Iowa has been almost completely forgotten. An officer of the Prussian *Landwehr* (militia) in Germany, he emigrated to Iowa in 1849. Before the outbreak of the war he had already organized a company which Governor Samuel J. Kirkwood had accepted on January 9, 1861. As lieutenant colonel, Matthies led the Second Iowa Regiment (a half-German regiment) at the Battle of Wilson's Creek, and soon thereafter he became its colonel. Though he did not attain the rank of brigadier general till late in 1862, at Iuka he led a brigade and later a division of the Seventeenth Corps; however, the tremendous exertion made him incapable of further service after May, 1864.[43]

Far more famous than the German brigadier generals were several Irishmen of this rank, notably Generals Corcoran and Meagher. After Colonel Michael Corcoran's refusal to parade his regiment for the Prince of Wales,[44] his name was a talisman in Irish homes and something of a scandal in American homes—until the war brought forth his call to his regiment to stand by the Union and the consequent suppression of his court-martial. Corcoran was born in County Sligo, Ireland, in 1827, a descendant through his mother of the Earl of Lucan, whose family title

---

[42] Kaufmann, *Die Deutschen im Bürgerkriege,* 484–85; Tenny, *The Military and Naval History of the Rebellion in the United States,* 732. Because he had been hit in the back a rumor arose that he had been shot by his own men in an act of revenge, but this was vehemently denied by General Stahel and members of the Seventy-fifth Regiment. Tenny, *The Military and Naval History of the Rebellion in the United States,* 732. For Russell's comment, see William Howard Russell, *My Diary North and South* (London, 1863), 585.

[43] It has been impossible to find much data on this German-born brigadier from Iowa. Kaufmann had a few words about him in *Die Deutschen im Bürgerkriege,* 531, and Heitman (comp.), in his *Historical Register and Dictionary,* recorded him. A medallion relief of him adorns the war memorial in Des Moines.

[44] This regiment was the Sixty-ninth New York State Militia, of which Corcoran had been colonel since 1859. See p. 119.

and estates had been confiscated in the seventeenth century. An Army career was rather in the family tradition, since his father had seen military service in the West Indies as an officer in the British army. After a thorough English education, young Michael entered, and remained three years in, the Irish constabulary establishment. As a sort of protest against Ireland's wrongs, he resigned this service in 1849 to emigrate to the United States, where New York City became his home. His military career here began with his enlistment as a private in Company I, Sixty-ninth New York State Militia. He displayed some military talent, and so he advanced rapidly—until by 1859 he had been elected colonel of the regiment. It was with this rank that he entered the Civil War; his career was promptly interrupted, however, when he was captured at the First Battle of Bull Run, where his regiment took a leading part. Because he refused release at the price demanded—that he would not take up arms against the foe— exchange was not effected in his case for almost a year; [45] on his return journey from war imprisonment, he was the object of many attentions; indeed, a company from New York met him at Philadelphia to serve as an escort, and at the Battery the mayor and a large procession of militiamen and firemen gave him a warm welcome home.

He soon organized and led to the field the Irish Legion, whereupon he was made a brigadier general of volunteers—the rank to date from the day of his capture. The Irish Legion took part in the battles of Nansemond River and Suffolk during April, 1863, and was added in the following August to the Army of the Potomac. On December 22, 1863, on an occasion when General Meagher had paid a visit to Corcoran, the latter decided to accompany his friend to Washington. He mounted Meagher's horse only to be thrown; the horse landed on top of him, and he died, apparently without gaining consciousness.[46] Obviously, his role in the war was a restricted one.

Possibly an even more distinguished leader among the Irish was Thomas Francis Meagher. Born in 1823, he was, like Corcoran, a native

[45] Corcoran was imprisoned in Richmond and Charleston, retained as a hostage for some Confederate privateersmen condemned by the North as pirates. During his captivity he was offered a post as harbor master, to which he had been nominated by Governor Morgan; he declined it because he desired to serve his adopted country as a soldier. New York *Irish-American*, January 14, 1862.

[46] For additional information about Corcoran, see *Appletons' American Annual Cyclopaedia and Register of Important Events* (New York, 1862–1875), 1863, p. 331; Tenny, *The Military and Naval History of the Rebellion*, 771; Mottelay and Campbell-Copeland (eds.), *The Soldier in Our Civil War*, I, 369.

son of Ireland; but unlike his countryman, he had a large part in the struggle prior to the rebellion of 1848. As a stripling he took issue with the renowned Daniel O'Connell at a political meeting and divided the latter's applause. Participation in the rebellion of 1848 brought about Meagher's arrest for sedition. The trial resulted in his condemnation to execution, a sentence commuted by the English government to banishment to Tasmania; but three years later, in 1852, he effected his escape to California. He soon moved on to New York; there he became an advocate and pleader of the Irish cause, until his fierce, impassioned oratory made him the darling of the "Young Ireland" group in his new home. After the outbreak of war he organized a company of Zouaves, later a part of the Irish Sixty-ninth Militia under Colonel Corcoran. Although he was offered a position on the staff of Frémont as aide-de-camp with the rank of colonel, he would not leave the Sixty-ninth, just as he had previously declined command of a new Irish regiment, later the Sixty-third New York Volunteers, and a part of the Irish Brigade.[47]

He fought in the First Battle of Bull Run as a major, and after the Sixty-ninth Militia Regiment refused to enlist beyond the three months tour of duty, he organized in the winter of 1861–1862 the Irish Brigade, of which he became colonel. He very soon rose to the rank of brigadier. He led his brigade through some of the hottest battles of the war and was associated with it in some of its most brilliant episodes. None was more brilliant or hopeless than the charge on Marye's Hill at Fredericksburg. When he was denied the opportunity of filling his decimated ranks and the Irish Brigade, as a nationality unit organized to bring glory to Ireland, was threatened with extinction, he resigned his position. He felt that it would be perpetuating a deception if he were to retain the brigadier rank and nominally command a unit when it was no more. On May 19, 1863, in a most affecting scene, he bade farewell to his troops with more than usual fervor and eloquence. He then passed down the whole line in dead silence, shaking the hands of the officers and of many of the men. Many of the soldiers were weeping, while General Meagher himself stood in the twilight with head bared and tears streaming down his face.

One last war service Meagher was called upon to perform. Lincoln appointed him with the rank of brigadier general to an important position in the Provisional Division of the Army of the Tennessee with instructions to report to General James Blair Steedman at Chattanooga. When the latter was called by General George H. Thomas to Nashville, Meagher

[47] *Appletons' American Annual Cyclopaedia*, 1862, pp. 409–10.

commanded the military district of Etowah during Steedman's absence, a position which involved the direction of twelve thousand infantry, two regiments of cavalry, and the defense works of Chattanooga. Confronted then with the obligation to join Sherman, Meagher went the following January to Savannah, where he was mustered out with the coming of peace.[48]

General Meagher's hold on his men derived in large part from his personality and temperament. He possessed a large, corpulent, and powerful body; his face was plump and ruddy with a firm mouth and piercing blue eyes; he had brown hair, mustache, and eyebrows. His regulation uniform was plentifully trimmed with gold lace, as were indeed the uniforms of his entire staff. Customarily, he wore Hessian boots with spurs on his small, aristocratic feet. In general he was intensely sanguine; at times he was impulsive, as was attested by his movements; and he was also liable to moments of peevishness, even to fits of melancholy. His fierce oratory had proved sufficient to draw his factious Irish into the war. He was in real life "the counterpart of some rash, impolitic, poetic personage" from Irish poetry or fiction. Without having had previous military experience he led the Irish Brigade into battle and wrested many a victory from fate. He was ever thoughtful of the interests of his men. His magnetism in inducing many Irishmen, in addition to the five regiments of his brigade, to flock to the defense of the Union was worth thousands of men. He was, it must be admitted, of a jealous nature; consequently, his men often suffered from his coldness and sometimes did not receive the advancment they had fairly earned.[49]

The prominence of a man after his death is not always the measure of his importance at the time of his activity in a given cause. The name of Thomas A. Smyth, an Irishman, was declared to be as familiar in the Army of the Potomac as that of McClellan himself. "How can I find

[48] See also St. Clair A. Mulholland, *The Story of the 116th Regiment Pennsylvania Infantry* . . . (Philadelphia, 1899), 123–24; Cavanagh, *Memoirs of Gen. Meagher, passim;* Johnson and Malone (eds.), *Dictionary of American Biography,* XII, 481–82. In the late summer of 1861 Meagher delivered five magnificent addresses (which were among his greatest) in as many weeks before immense assemblies in Boston, Bridgeport, Brooklyn, and New York. These addresses were published in every leading paper in the North with tremendous effect for the Union. It was claimed that the number of Irishmen he influenced to enroll was ten times the number he commanded in the Brigade. Cavanagh, *Memoirs of Gen. Meagher,* 413.

[49] For personality and character, see Townsend, *Campaigns of a Non-Combatant,* 129–30; O'Grady, "88th Regiment Infantry," in Fox (comp.), *New York at Gettysburg,* II, 513. Only one medal of honor was bestowed in the Eighty-eighth Massachusetts, outside of the two accorded to officers.

language to depict to you his brilliant service? Suffice to say that General Thomas A. Smyth was one of the grandest soldiers of our race." [50] In his youth he emigrated to this country and engaged in coachmaking in Wilmington, Delaware. At the opening of the war he raised a company in that city and led it to Philadelphia to join a three months regiment which saw service in the Shenandoah Valley. On his return he was made major of a Delaware regiment and rose through the various grades till he was made brigadier general of volunteers as a reward for gallant conduct at Cold Harbor in October, 1864. During the absence of General John Gibbon he commanded the Second Division of the Second Corps in a number of important engagements, always so creditably that he won from General Hancock the highest praise.

"If there was any formidable position to be stormed, in which daring and skill were requisite, General Smyth with his brigade was always selected for the undertaking." Dashing and soldierlike in appearance, he never failed to secure the entire confidence of his men, and when with true Irish impetuosity he lifted his cap and at the head of his column swept upon the foe, his purpose was certain to be achieved. He commanded a brigade at the Battle of the Wilderness and at Spotsylvania, adding in both battles to his reputation as a soldier. Though two days before the surrender of Lee he fell mortally wounded at the hand of a Confederate sharpshooter near Farmville, Virginia, he lingered three days before he died, the last Union general to fall in the war.[51] Two days before his death his ability was rewarded with a brevet major generalship.

Another Irishman who was a part of the Regular Army and served his adopted country in several wars was Brigadier General Thomas William Sweeny. Born in County Cork, Ireland, about 1820,[52] he followed his widowed mother to New York in 1832 after she had satisfied herself as to the prospects offered in America. Here he served an apprenticeship to a leading law-publishing firm. His warlike interest led him to join the crack

[50] This was the evaluation of Denis F. Burke, speaking at the dedication of a monument at Gettysburg in 1888. See "Oration of Denis Burke," in Fox (comp.), New York at Gettysburg, II, 481.

[51] Wilson and Fiske (eds.), Appletons' Cyclopaedia of American Biography, II, 141; Tenny, The Military and Naval History of the Rebellion in the United States, 799; see Edmund N. Hatcher (comp.), The Last Four Weeks of the War (Columbus, Ohio, 1892), 184, for the quotation.

[52] The National Cyclopaedia of American History, XI, 228, and Johnson and Malone (eds.), Dictionary of American Biography, XVIII, 242. The latter gave the date of his birth as 1820, which the writer accepts as more authoritative than the New York Irish-American, April 26, 1861, which gives 1822.

militia corps of the city, the Independent Tompkins Blues, later known as the Baxter Blues. This was one of the first companies to volunteer for the Mexican War; Sweeny was at once elected second lieutenant of Company A, First New York Volunteers, which was assigned to Shields's brigade. He participated in all the important engagements of the campaign, losing his right arm and incurring face wounds, the scars of which he bore to his grave.[53] In recognition of his services he was given a commission as second lieutenant in the Regular Army, with which he saw arduous duty in the West against the Indians for a long time.

The outbreak of the Civil War found him in command as captain at the St. Louis arsenal until the arrival there of General Nathaniel Lyon. After Lyon was disabled, Sweeny also conducted the negotiations for the surrender of Camp Jackson, but his chief service was as agent for organization of the three months volunteers. He was chosen commander of these volunteers and dispatched to aid Sigel in the southwestern part of Missouri. He so impressed that officer with his views before the Battle of Wilson's Creek that Sigel acted on them—with resulting success. When the three months men were disbanded, Sweeny was mustered out; but he returned to volunteer service as colonel of the Fifty-second Illinois in January, 1862, and served under Grant in the capture of Fort Donelson. He won outstanding credit from Sherman for helping to save the day at Shiloh by defending a gap in the line at a critical moment. Here he received two bullets in his remaining arm and won the admiration of the army for his refusal to leave the field until the close of the battle. He rendered praiseworthy service in the battles of Corinth and Kenesaw Mountain, and before Atlanta. As early as the close of 1862, he received the commission of brigadier general of volunteers, and he was discharged from the volunteer service only in August, 1865. Although bold, as are most Irishmen, nimble of mind, and aggressive in action, he apparently lacked coolness and sound judgment. He was so ardent an Irish partisan that he became a leader in the Fenian invasion of Canada in 1866, but that episode did not prevent his reinstatement in service in the Regular Army.[54]

[53] It is interesting that on Sweeny's return from the Mexican War the printers of New York gave a grand ball in his honor at Castle Garden, and that he was brevetted captain by the governor and presented with a silver medal by the city government, New York *Irish-American*, April 26, 1861. It is also interesting that he later received a sword from the city of Brooklyn for his services in the Civil War.

[54] In addition to the references already cited, see Johnson and Malone (eds.), *Dictionary of American Biography*, XVIII, 242. At the battlefield of Shiloh he had to remain afoot in his wounded condition, as his horse had been killed under him. New York *Irish-American*, April 26, 1862.

Among the group of Irishmen, there remains to be mentioned one other brigadier general of the Regular Army. The record of James Shields is not such as to make him one of the outstanding figures of the war. Born in County Tyrone in 1806, he received a good classical education in Ireland, together with training in tactics and sword play. He emigrated to the United States when he was about twenty years old and settled in Illinois, where in a varied career he taught French, read law, fought in the Black Hawk War, and "practised Democratic politics." His profession of the law opened the door, as it so often does, to the state legislature and a little later to a seat on the supreme bench of the state. High rank came easily to him in the Mexican War, for he entered the service with the commission of a brigadier general of Illinois volunteers and was brevetted major general for gallantry at the battle of Cerro Gordo.

Subsequently, he was sent to the United States Senate from Illinois. At the conclusion of his term he settled in Minnesota on lands awarded for his army service, and on the admission to the Union of that western state, he represented it in the federal Senate for the short term. He next made California his residence. Then for a brief period his home was in Mexico, where he was part owner of a mine. It was from that country that he offered his services to Washington when the attack on Fort Sumter precipitated war. His appointment as brigadier general of volunteers followed shortly, whereupon he succeeded General Frederick W. Lander to the command on the upper Potomac. Shields enjoyed the distinction of administering a decisive defeat to Stonewall Jackson's forces at Winchester in the spring of 1862. For this victory and for his defense at Port Republic, even though he there sustained defeat, Shields and his division won the congratulations of General Nathaniel P. Banks. The resignation of General Shields in March, 1863, and his retirement to San Francisco are not readily explained, for, like most Irishmen, he was at his best in a fight.[55]

In the list of brigadiers appear only two Frenchmen. Philippe Régis de Trobriand, son of Joseph, Baron de Trobriand, would have stood as a dis-

[55] W. H. Condon, *Life of Major-General James Shields, Hero of three Wars and Senator from Three States* (Chicago, 1900), *passim;* Evart Duyckinck, *National History of the War for the Union, Civil, Military, and Naval* . . . (New York, 1861–1865), II, 333; Johnson and Malone (eds.), *Dictionary of American Biography*, XVII, 106. Mention of Brigadier General John McNeil is hardly justifiable, for, though born in Halifax, Nova Scotia, he was the son of American parents. In 1820 he moved to Boston, where he thoroughly identified himself with the Union cause.

The author hastens to state that she has used the work of the old historian Duyckinck in a very few instances—and then only for details which seem reliable and which have escaped later writers.

tinguished Frenchman without his war experience as commander of the Gardes Lafayette. It is certainly of interest that he could trace his family history to Irish warriors who settled on the continent early enough to accompany William of Normandy on his conquest of England, but who returned to France before the fifteenth century. He was born at his father's château near Tours and enjoyed the advantages of wealth and position, even though his father, hostile to Louis Philippe, resigned his position as general and left the army. The son graduated from the Collège de Tours in 1834 and graduated in law three years later from the same institution. Then he promptly occupied himself with duels and literature. On no more substantial basis than a dare he came to the United States in 1841, made the customary tour of the country, met prominent people, and married an heiress. After a period of residence in Venice, he returned to New York to make his permanent home and to become a member of a literary group.

In the summer of 1861, after he had been elected colonel of the Gardes Lafayette, officially known as the Fifty-fifth New York Volunteers, he became an American citizen. He saw much service and proved a valued and sagacious officer throughout the war. In the Peninsular campaign he was engaged at the siege of Yorktown and in the Battle of Williamsburg; and at various times he also commanded a brigade, as he did from Portsmouth to Fredericksburg. Early in 1864, he attained the rank of brigadier general, commanding the garrison and defenses of the city of New York from May to June, though he craved a position near the battle front. He rose to the command of a division in the operations which terminated with the surrender of General Lee. For "highly meritorious services" during the final campaign he was accorded the rank of brevet major general of volunteers. It is striking that in July of the year following the war he was named to the colonelcy of a regiment in the regular infantry, actually commanding a post in Dakota Territory. As a final recognition of his war service, he received the rank of brevet brigadier general of the United States Army.[56]

The second Frenchman who served in this rank in the Union army was Alfred Nattie Duffié, who brought to the service such a varied experience that one is tempted to think of him as a soldier of fortune—but is precluded from thus classifying him by the fact that all his previous experience had been under the flag of his native France. After studying at several

---

[56] De Trobriand did not escape the bickering which went on constantly for the high-ranking posts. As early as September, 1862, his position had been questioned by a colonel who wished to replace him in the Fifty-fifth New York Regiment.

military academies in Paris, he graduated at St. Cyr in 1854. Actual service in Algiers and Senegal preceded his combat in the Crimean War, where he was promoted from second to first lieutenant of cavalry. He took part in the campaign in Italy against Austria, winning several medals of honor. The outbreak of the American war found him already in the United States, where he had arrived the preceding year. He promptly accepted a captaincy in a New Jersey cavalry regiment, but he was soon promoted to the rank of major in the Harris Light Cavalry of New York. From this post he proceeded in July, 1862, to the colonelcy of the First New England Cavalry, thus designated because it had been authorized to recruit in the different states of New England, though the greater part of its effective strength came from Rhode Island. A few months sufficed for Colonel Duffié to transform it from its pitiable inefficiency to such a condition that it was regarded as one of the best and most dependable regiments in the division. A splendid tribute to Duffié comes from the pen of his countryman, De Trobriand, after a visit to his camp: "I found him in his tent, surrounded by officers to whom he was giving a course in tactics. We inspected together his camp where all breathed order, neatness and a perfect understanding of the last details of the service. The horses were in good condition, men in excellent deportment, the equipments irreproachable." [57] In June, 1863, Duffié attained the rank of brigadier general of volunteers, in which rank he served through the remainder of the war.[58]

A single Spaniard claims attention briefly by virtue of an interesting personality as well as by his service. Edward Ferrero was born in Madrid in 1831 of Italian parents and was brought to the United States a year or two later. Inheriting a military inclination, he entered a New York militia company as soon as his age permitted, becoming a field officer in the Eleventh Regiment. In the summer of 1861 he recruited the Fifty-first

[57] De Trobriand, *Quatre Ans de Campagnes*, I, 330. De Trobriand rejoiced in this favorable aspect of the cavalry and declared that the time was approaching when the superiority of the enemy in cavalry would be changed into inferiority. *Ibid.*, I, 331.

[58] In addition to De Trobriand's work, see Wilson and Fiske (eds.), *Appletons' Cyclopaedia of American Biography*, II, 247–48. Fox (comp.), *New York at Gettysburg*, III, 1108, accorded him a few words. Heitman's work made him colonel of the First Rhode Island Cavalry which became Companies I-M of the New England Cavalry.

Duffié considered himself an eloquent speaker, but his efforts at rhetorical display combined with his French accent greatly amused his men. He used to harangue them as if they were about to enter a sanguinary battle. The old stone walls of the peaceful farm were pictured as bristling with the enemy's bayonets, and the boys were called on to charge at the hidden foe and capture him. John Algernon Owens, *Sword and Pen; Ventures and Adventures of Willard Glazier* (Philadelphia, 1883), 120–21.

New York Volunteers and, as its colonel, led it with dash and effect at the battles of Roanoke Island and New Bern. He soon won promotion to the command of a brigade, distinguishing himself at Second Bull Run and the next day at Chantilly in covering the Union retreat. After the death of General Jesse Lee Reno at the Battle of South Mountain, Colonel Ferrero had command of a brigade, and at Antietam he was handed his promotion to the rank of brigadier general. As this appointment expired by the adjournment of the Senate without confirmation, Ferrero was reappointed to this rank on May 6, 1863. He shared in the desperate fight at Fredericksburg and was present in the reserve with his brigade at the attack on Vicksburg, as the Ninth Corps had joined Grant in the West. He pursued and defeated General Joseph E. Johnston at Jackson, Mississippi, and was the one to plant his brigade colors on the dome of the capitol. At Knoxville, where he commanded a division under General Ambrose E. Burnside, he resisted the assault of General James Longstreet's veterans against Fort Saunders.

He returned to the Army of the Potomac in the spring of 1864 and received command of a newly formed division of colored troops at the siege of Petersburg. It had not been intended by Union leaders that these untried men should lead the assault at the crater, but Ferrero's division, pushing through the front, actually delivered the assault on the heights beyond and was repulsed with great slaughter. Ferrero was held partly responsible for the failure, as he was charged with exercising little command over his troops, a charge somewhat similar to the one made against his conduct at the siege of Knoxville, where the gallant defense of his division occurred without orders from him. He seemed incompetent to command so large a body as a division in action. In the memory of many soldiers of the Ninth Corps, Ferrero was associated with Burnside because of their Catholic devotions on the eve of a battle. Ferrero was made a major general by brevet during the activities before Petersburg. His services during the latter part of the war were in connection with the defense of Bermuda Hundred.[59]

The brigadier generals, Asboth and Schoepf, are certainly among the

---

[59] Johnson and Malone (eds.), *Dictionary of American Biography*, VI, 338–39; Mottelay and Campbell-Copeland (eds.), *The Soldier in Our Civil War*, II, 249. Ferrero had continued the successful and fashionable dancing school established in New York by his father and had also taught dancing at West Point, where he had instructed General McClellan and other regular officers. This led to the charge that these officers had recommended him as brigadier over more meritorious officers. Charles A. Cuffel, *Durell's Battery in the Civil War Independent Battery D, Pennsylvania Volunteer Artillery) . . .* (Philadelphia, 1900), 87.

galaxy of foreign-born fighters in the American war who are best remembered. Alexander Sandor Asboth came from a family prominent in the
history of Hungary. Desiring from childhood to pursue a military career
as his elder brother had done, he permitted his mother to persuade him
to study engineering. Through his period of service in the Austrian army
he had already made a national reputation for ability in military affairs
when the Hungarian Revolution of 1848 brought an abrupt change in his
career. He immediately enlisted with the revolutionary army and was
made a colonel in the engineering corps and later an aide to Kossuth. After
the crushing of the revolt, he shared his commander's exile and intern-
ment, followed him to Kütahya, Turkey, and then accompanied him to
America aboard a United States frigate in 1851.

In 1861, by that time an American citizen, he was prompt in his offer
to defend his adopted country, and that country was not slow to avail itself
of his military experience. General Frémont, who had known Asboth in
New York, selected him for his chief of staff. When the former was appointed to the Western Department, he made Asboth a brigadier general.
The Senate, however, refused to confirm the appointment on the ground
that it was irregularly made. His gallantry and skill with his artillery at
Pea Ridge in March, 1862, were proved in action at the head of a division
despite a wound of the previous day. After the Missouri campaign he was
assigned to the command at Columbus, Kentucky; in 1863 he became
commander of the District of West Florida with headquarters at Fort
Pickens near Pensacola. In September, 1864, after a stubborn resistence,
he captured Marianna, with its considerable store of arms and supplies. In
the battle, he was severely wounded, one bullet shattering his right arm
while another lodged under his right cheek. He never fully recovered from
the effects of his wounds though he remained in the service through the
end of the war. He left the army with the well-earned brevet of major
general.[60]

Asboth was a tall, well-built man, with firm yet kindly expression and
a disposition tinged with melancholy. He was fundamentally a man of
action, who enjoyed and exulted in hard, physical exertion. He was an
excellent horseman; at the age of fifty he still loved to urge his horse to
utmost speed, so that other riders were often unable to keep up with him.
An evidence of his hardihood was his terse comment when the men complained of lack of tents: "In Hungary we make a winter campaign—we

[60] Johnson and Malone (eds.), *Dictionary of American Biography*, I, 379; *National Cyclopaedia of American Biography*, IV, 413; Vasvary, *Lincoln's Hungarian Heroes*, 44–47.

sleep without tents, our feet to the fire,—sometimes our ears did freeze." [61]

Another political refugee who proved of great service, a Pole by birth, was Albin Francisco Schoepf. Born at Podgorze near Cracow in 1822, he was still a young man—only twenty-six—at the time of the Hungarian Revolution, but he already possessed considerable experience as an asset. He had had a thorough military education at an Austrian academy in Vienna, had emerged as a lieutenant of artillery in 1841, and before the insurrection had won promotion to a captaincy on the field. At the beginning of the independence movement, he left the Austrian service to enlist as a private in one of the Polish legions but soon became a captain and later a major. After the suppression of the revolt, he was exiled to Turkey, served under the Hungarian General Josef Bem against the insurgents at Aleppo, and then became instructor of artillery in the Ottoman service with the rank of major. He arrived in America in 1851 without resources or friends; hence, he took a job as porter in a hotel in the national capital. His military bearing attracted the attention of Joseph Holt, who was then patent commissioner, with the result that Holt procured for him a minor drafting position in the patent office. When Holt became secretary of war under Buchanan, Schoepf was transferred to the War Department, where in recognition of his capacity as an engineer, he was sent to Virginia to conduct a military survey.

It was probably through Holt's influence that he was appointed a brigadier general in September after the opening of the war and sent to Holt's own state, Kentucky. General Felix K. Zollicoffer, after a series of successes against the Kentucky home guards, attacked Schoepf's fortified position in the hills of Rock Castle County; Schoepf defeated him [62] but had to sacrifice the prestige he had thus gained by a precipitate retreat which had been ordered by his superior officer. Schoepf's brigade led the pursuit of the foe after its defeat at Mill Springs. At Perryville he commanded a division in the Third Army Corps but resigned soon afterwards, partly because of a wound which had caused him deafness and partly because of disgust at the intrigues revealed at the court-martial of General Don Carlos Buell. In 1863 he became commander of Fort Delaware, located near New Castle and used as a federal prison, where he seems to have served during the remainder of the war.[63]

[61] Jessie Benton Frémont, *The Story of the Guard: A Chronicle of the War* (Boston, 1863), 44–45.

[62] For an account of Schoepf's fight at Wild Cat Camp, see Headley, *The Great Rebellion*, I, 169–71.

[63] Piványi, *Hungarians in the American Civil War*, 31–32; Robert Tomes, *The Great Civil*

An arresting figure was General John Basil Turchin, often called the "Russian Thunderbolt," whose American career ran the gamut from brilliant victories to a court-martial and what amounted to vindication by President Lincoln. He was born in the valley of the Don in 1822. Graduating from the Imperial Military School at St. Petersburg, he received a lieutenant's commission in the horse-artillery service, where his talents soon won him promotion to the rank of captain on the general staff. He returned to the Imperial School for three years of further training in the theoretical part of his education. At the opening of the Crimean War he won a post on the staff of the Crown Prince, a post corresponding to assistant adjutant of a corps commander. He had the honor of having his plans for the defenses of the coast of Finland adopted and superintended their execution. The resulting works were regarded as among the most elaborate scientific specimens of military engineering of that time.

For some reason he wanted to go to America and managed to leave Russia in 1856 on the plea that he wished to make a journey. The ways of free government seemed to please him, for he settled in Chicago, where he found employment in the engineering department of the Illinois Central Railroad. As soon as the war broke out, he secured a commission as colonel of the Nineteenth Illinois Regiment, a Zouave unit celebrated for its excellence of drill and *esprit de corps*. His brigade always distinguished itself in those battles in which it was led by its intrepid commander. Turchin's capture of Huntsville, Alabama, in early 1862; the last charge of his brigade at Chickamauga; and the scaling of Missionary Ridge at the extreme left of the Army of the Cumberland, where no less than nine guns were captured and the foe driven north—all were feats worthy of a heroic leader. Several times he commanded a division of the cavalry corps of the Army of the Cumberland. Although his method of treating rebel property, including slaves, was possibly that of an experienced European soldier, it was disapproved by his superior officer. When his men dashed into Athens, Alabama, in 1862, they were charged with misconduct, and their commander was court-martialed and dismissed from the service by General Buell.[64] Before the sentence could be promulgated,

---

War, II, 23; Wilson and Fiske (eds.), *Appletons' Cyclopaedia of American Biography*, V, 423; Haiman, *Polish Past in America*, 129–32. The facts concerning his career before coming to America are hard to establish.

[64] The story of the treatment of Athens, as told by Joseph G. Vale, is worth repeating. When Turchin's advance of two companies entered the town and the rebel cavalry evacuated it, the citizens began to fire indiscriminately on the Union soldiers. Turchin formed his com-

however, the Russian's plucky wife hurried to Washington and won from the President not only an order to set aside the court-martial but also Turchin's promotion to the rank of brigadier general. He thereupon returned to the front to be assigned to a brigade in the army.

Turchin possessed a delicate sense of humor, inflexibility of will, and a resolute purpose. Without question, he was impulsive, thinking and acting quickly; and he possessed the resourcefulness to meet emergencies. His treatment of Colonel Oliver Perry (?) Hazard of the Thirty-seventh Indiana, a West Point graduate, illustrates his firmness. Turchin had sent his own brigade physician to the camp of this regiment in order to remedy the frightful handling of the sick, for several soldiers had died from the use of medicine given them by the regimental doctor. When Colonel Hazard tried to drive the brigade doctor from his camp, Turchin arrested the colonel. For a foreigner to commit this action was probably tactless, but his intervention aroused general rejoicing in the brigade.[65]

There remains for consideration only the lone Swede who attained the rank of brigadier general, Charles John Stohlbrand. Born in 1821 near Kristianstad, he entered the Royal Vendes Artillery as a cadet at the age of eighteen. During 1848–1850 he participated with part of his regiment in defense of Denmark in the Schleswig-Holstein campaign; hence, to this degree he was a soldier of fortune. At the close of that war he came to the United States, settled in Chicago, and took a prominent place in Swedish circles. When the call for volunteers went out in July, 1861, he organized a company of artillery; however, it could not be accepted, as the quota had been filled. Nothing daunted, before the end of the summer

---

mand in the center of the town and addressed his soldiers. In referring to the attack on his advance guard, he concluded pointedly, "Now, boys, you stops in this rebel town dis night, and I shuts mine eyes for von hours." In about an hour he called his adjutant to learn if the town were yet burned down. It was not. "Vell, vell, tell de boys I shut mine eyes for von hour and a half." The boys understood, and Athens was soon a group of wrecked and plundered buildings. Joseph G. Vale, *Minty and the Cavalry. A History of Cavalry Campaigns in the Western Armies* (Harrisburg, 1886), 28. Turchin's name was widely execrated by the Confederates, who declared that the conduct of the citizens of Athens in joining their troops against the Northern troops was done only under "violent provocation." See also for this episode, Duyckinck, *National History of the War for the Union*, II, 436–37. Mary A. Livermore, *My Story of the War: A Woman's Narrative of Four Years Personal Experience* . . . (Hartford, 1887), 615, differs in some unimportant details.

[65] Chicago *Illinois Staats-Zeitung*, January 16, 1862. For other references on Turchin, see *National Cyclopaedia of American Biography*, XII, 241; J. Henry Haynie, *The Nineteenth Illinois* (Chicago, 1912), 131–34; Chicago *Hemlandet*, July 17, 1861. See also the publisher's preface to John B. Turchin's own book, *Chickamauga* (Chicago, 1888), 5–6; for the account of how his men stood at the Battle of Chickamauga, see Turchin, *Chickamauga*, 77–78.

he had brought together a second company at De Kalb and Sycamore, as has been related in an earlier chapter, which was mustered into service under his captaincy as Battery G, Second Illinois Light Artillery. Promotion came promptly, for on the last day of the year he was made a major, later becoming chief of artillery under General John Logan and also sharing in the movements against Corinth. In 1863, when General Logan succeeded to the command of the Fifteenth Corps, Stohlbrand was transferred to head its artillery brigade; thus, he assumed virtually the duties of a brigadier general, although he was not accorded the rank until February, 1865. About the middle of May, 1864, during the Atlanta campaign, he was captured by the Confederates and sent to Andersonville prison; he escaped twice—the second time, successfully—and rejoined his command in October. After being made a brigadier, he was assigned first to a brigade in the Fifteenth Corps and then to one in the Seventeenth.

The story of Stohlbrand's promotion is especially interesting. Displeased with his failure to receive a promotion in recognition of his services, he offered his resignation; but Sherman, who wished to retain him in the service, asked him personally to deliver a dispatch to the President. After Lincoln had studied the papers which Stohlbrand handed him, the President extended his hand with the words, "How do you do, General?" Stohlbrand naturally corrected him but the President assured him that there was no mistake. "You are a general, and I need you in the Carolinas." It will be noted that thus Stohlbrand leaped over several ranks.[66] The promotion was undoubtedly owing to Sherman's high opinion of him, summed up in the words, "A braver man and a better artillery officer than General Stohlbrand could not be found in the entire army." [67]

[66] Hokanson, *Swedish Immigrants*, 160–61.

[67] *Ibid.*, 112–13; Wilson and Fiske (eds.), *Appletons' Cyclopaedia of American Biography*, V, 699. In one of his early advertisements for recruits he makes his position with regard to excessive fondness for liquor unmistakably clear. "In order not to mislead any one, let me here say that such as are accustomed to worship Bacchus above their obligations are not available to enter Battery De Kalb." Chicago *Hemlandet*, September 11, 1861.

CHAPTER NINE

Foreign-Born Colonels

THE ironic comment of the Comte de Paris with regard to the American method of bestowing the title of colonel was applicable even to foreign regiments: if a man by influence, time, and money raised a regiment, "he became colonel of that regiment by right." [1] When a foreigner could not secure a commission through the regular channels of the State and War Departments, he occasionally undertook, as we have seen, to raise a company or regiment among his fellow countrymen residing in the United States.

The number of Germans who were allowed to add the title of colonel or lieutenant colonel to their name was large, but that fact is less significant than that a goodly proportion of the number had already previously won considerable distinction. Adolf Eberhard Buschbeck may acceptably head the list, for there were many who felt that the only rank worthy of his merits would have been that of major general. Certainly none who saw him in action denied that he was a brilliant fighter. The obituary in *Der Deutsche Pionier* sums up his standing in the army: "An able officer, faithful and brave, esteemed by his superiors, honored and loved by his soldiers." [2] He brought to his American post a rich background of training and tradition, for his father was an officer in a Prussian battalion at Coblenz when he was born. At the tender age of eleven he was sent to the cadet house in Berlin, from which he passed after six years into the Prussian army as standard bearer. His ability, especially in mathematics, soon attracted the attention of his superiors, notably of General Adolf von Steinwehr, with the result that he served at the cadet school at Potsdam as a teacher from 1847 to 1852. Why he came to America is not clear, but the fact remains that he settled in Philadelphia in 1853 to become a teacher in a girls' school. The raising of the Twenty-seventh Pennsylvania Volunteers in 1861 was largely a result of his zealous efforts. Although he entered the regiment only as second in rank, he took over the command in a few

---

[1] Comte De Paris, *History of the Civil War in America* (New York, 1867–1870), I, 186.

[2] "General Adolph Eberhard Buschbeck," in *Der Deutsche Pionier*, XVI (1884–1885), 216.

months when Blenker complained of the colonel, Max Einstein. Upon the arrival of the regiment in Washington in June, 1861, it was added to Blenker's brigade, with which it stood in the reserve at the First Battle of Bull Run. In the fall Buschbeck was assigned to General Stahel's brigade. Buschbeck distinguished himself at Cross Keys; he was recognized as the hero of the Eleventh Corps at Chancellorsville; he fought bravely at Gettysburg as well as at Missionary Ridge, where he was especially praised by Sherman for his fight at Tunnel Hill. He made the march through Georgia with Sherman and performed his hard part at the bloody battles of Peachtree Creek and Ezra Church. He was constantly at the front and contributed to many decisive victories.[3]

Among the Germans in the country, Doctor Friedrich Hecker was a figure with which to conjure long before the war. Of noble birth on his mother's side, reared in court circles and university-trained in law, he early became a leader in the liberal movement for parliamentary government in Baden. As an impractical idealist, it was inevitable that he should become involved in the uprising of 1848. In the hope of raising funds to support the revolution, he went to America, where he was received as a conquering hero; but upon being recalled by the revolutionary government the following January, he returned to Germany. Before he arrived there, the revolt had collapsed, and consequently Hecker returned to America to become a Latin farmer near Belleville. Such a leader could not stay out of politics; and so it is no surprise that with his liberal, humanitarian views, he became one of the early Republicans.

So great was his confidence in Sigel as a military leader that after the fall of Sumter had shaken the German citizens, he, together with his stepson, promptly entered the ranks of Sigel's Missouri regiment as a mere private. Very shortly Hecker was summoned back to Illinois to assume command of a regiment of Germans organized in that state. His first reaction was to decline with the declaration that he had no higher ambition than to serve as a private under his friend Sigel, but he finally yielded to the demands of his Illinois admirers and returned to take command of the Jägers, known officially as the Twenty-fourth Illinois Regiment. His appearance in Chicago and his acceptance of the command stimulated the activity and enlistment of German men and youths like an electric shock. German zeal for the cause had suffered a decline by June because Germans felt that Illinois troops, especially those from Chicago, had not been properly treated. Emphasis was laid upon the fact that Hecker was using the interval before his assumption of command to study military tactics. The call which he inserted in the *Illinois Staats-Zeitung* for the few needed to complete the regiment reveals the type of person he was: "Only men, who wish truly to defend the fatherland and to fight for the highest good, freedom, need to enroll themselves. The regiment does not go out for a game but the gravity of the times calls it to arms and only men who grasp this seriousness are welcome." [4]

Unfortunately, dissension arose between him and the officers of this regiment, so that he withdrew from it in anger; however, the second Hecker regiment was soon recruited for him, appeared on the rolls as the Eighty-second Illinois, and indeed, became (as the *Illinois Staats-Zeitung* predicted of the Jägers) one of the best in the West.[5] Hecker fought well at Chancellorsville, where he was wounded; but as the bullet had rebounded from a large silver snuff case which he always carried, he was able to take the field again in a few months. He participated also in the fighting at Wauhatchie, at Chattanooga, and at Missionary Ridge, his three chief engagements. He so resented the fact that he had not been promoted that he resigned his commission early in 1864.[6] Hecker lives in American history rather for his winning personality, magnetic oratory, and devotion to a cause which he believed right than for any contribution he made on the field of battle.

Among the foreign-born who came to the front at the first call to arms and around whom their countrymen rallied was Leopold von Gilsa. Though severely tenacious of the articles of war, he found the profanity clause the one article of the orthodox military faith which he was incapable of observing. A former Prussian officer who had had combat experience as a major in the Schleswig-Holstein War, he found it easy to exchange earning his livelihood by lectures—or singing and playing the piano in the

---

[4] The call appeared in the June 4, 1861, issue of the Chicago *Illinois Staats-Zeitung*. This paper was enthusiastic for Hecker, hailing him in the following terms: "Energische Männer mit stahlhartem Charakter und eisenfester Seele bedürfen wir, und ein solcher Mann ist Friedrich Hecker." It was also sure that his regiment would prove an "elite Corps." *Ibid.*, June 3, 1861.

[5] Baltimore *Der Deutsche Correspondent*, June 10, 1862, revealed that he was wary of undertaking formation of a new regiment. He insisted on guarantees against intrigues and turmoil.

[6] See also Johnson and Malone (eds.), *Dictionary of American Biography*, VIII, 493–94; Robert Tomes, *Battles of America by Sea and Land with Biographies of Naval and Military Commanders* . . . (New York, 1878), I, 426; Wilson and Fiske (eds.), *Appletons' Cyclopaedia of American Biography*, III, 156; Körner, *Memoirs*, I, 518–20, 528–30; II, 150–52, 193–94.

music and beer halls of the Bowery—for the colonelcy of the Forty-first New York Regiment, better known as the De Kalb Regiment. This German unit contained a goodly number of soldiers who had served with him in Holstein. He distinguished himself at the Battle of Cross Keys, but the battle with which his name is inseparably connected is that of Chancellorsville. He had command of the brigade of the Eleventh Corps which was obliged to receive the first wave of Stonewall Jackson's attack, and he succeeded by his resolute exertion in rallying the retreating columns and checking, for a short time at least, Jackson's deluge.[7] He was also in the heaviest of the fighting at Gettysburg. In the fall of 1863 he was sent with his brigade to the Carolinas and saw fighting at the siege of Charleston. He accompanied his regiment to New York when it was mustered out in 1864 but set to work in the following winter to organize a new regiment; this, however, never saw combat service. It seems a pity that this capable and daring officer left the service after four years of fighting with the same rank with which he had entered—possibly because of the machinations of Princess Salm-Salm, between whose husband and Von Gilsa ill will existed.[8]

Hugo von Wangelin is usually referred to as a general by virtue of a brevet brigadier generalship which he received. As befitted the scion of a noble family—especially of an old Mecklenburg family—and the son of a man who had made the Russian campaign in the Napoleonic wars and whose brothers were lieutenants in the Prussian army, Wangelin had a military training, first at the cadet school at Kulm and then at the military academy at Berlin. He had been at the latter institution only about a year when his mother, long since widowed, took her children to America and settled on a farm near Cleveland. Hugo, however, moved in 1839 to St. Clair County, Illinois, in order to settle on a farm near friends in the Latin

---

[7] There is a thrilling story of how he saved the remnants of his brigade. He returned from an unavailing request for re-enforcements to find what was left of his brigade maintaining the hopeless conflict and in danger of being entirely surrounded. After dispatching two captains in succession to recall it, both of whom were shot down, the intrepid commander at full gallop dashed up to his command and thundered, "Wollt ihr denn all' in die Hölle sein? Züruck!" Then, recognizing tactical propriety, he shouted, "Herr Major, commandiren sie in retreat, marsch!" Owen Rice, "Afield with the Eleventh Army Corps at Chancellorsville," in R. Hunter (ed.), *Sketches of War History 1861–1865* (Cincinnati, 1880–1890), I, 384–85. Ever after, any allusion to this disaster stirred his spirit to stormy emotion. *Ibid.*, 379.

[8] A story which will bear repetition relates how on the retreat from Chancellorsville Von Gilsa met General Howard, who was generally felt to be responsible for the defeat. Howard reminded the German officer to depend on God, whereupon the latter poured out a stream of barrack oaths in German until Howard thought him mad. Kaufmann, *Die Deutschen im Bürgerkriege*, 503–504. For Von Gilsa, see also Fox (comp.), *New York at Gettysburg*, I, 304.

settlement. Faced suddenly with the alternative of having an inheritance in Germany confiscated or serving a year in the Prussian army, he chose the latter evil, thus adding experience as a lieutenant to his equipment for approaching responsibility. After his return to Illinois, he sold his farm in 1845 to settle in Belleville and later in Lebanon.

In 1861 he entered the Twelfth Missouri Regiment as a volunteer but was at once elected major. When Colonel Osterhaus was promoted to the rank of brigadier general, Wangelin was advanced to the colonelcy of the regiment. In this rank from the fall of 1863, he constantly commanded the brigade which had originally been Osterhaus'. His regiment was complimented by Governor Gustav Körner of Illinois as one of the best in the army. To enumerate the battles and skirmishes in which Wangelin participated is virtually to call a roster of the battles fought in the West—more than fifty in all. At Ringgold he lost his left arm. Hardly had he been furloughed home when General Sterling Price invaded Missouri and Lincoln issued a call for volunteers for one hundred days. Men streamed from all the western states, and the command over these new troops was entrusted to Von Wangelin, although he was disabled. He returned to his command in March, 1864, in time to be present at the battles before Atlanta. Here he brilliantly held the hill from which Union troops had earlier been driven and, though again wounded, he stayed with his troops. During the four years of war, he was constantly at the front without furlough except for the brief period previously mentioned. As a fighter his record should probably place him with General von Willich.[9]

There was a small group of naturalized German citizens who had already given proof of their devotion to their adopted country by enlistment for the Mexican War. One of these was August Moor, colonel of the Twenty-eighth Ohio Regiment, who merits consideration more for his venerable record in the Seminole and Mexican wars than for his achievements in the Civil War.[10] Franz Hassendeubel, a well-trained engineer, hastened back from a visit to Germany at the first news of actual hostilities to enter Sigel's regiment as lieutenant-colonel; his greatest service, however, lay in planning the ten forts for the defense of St. Louis. John A.

[9] See the article "General Hugo Wangelin," in *Der Deutsche Pionier*, XV (1883–1884), 408–10; also Kaufmann, *Die Deutschen im Bürgerkriege*, 561; Rosengarten, *The German Soldier in the Wars of the United States*, 111–13.

[10] *Der Deutsche Pionier*, XVI (1884–1885), 482; Kaufmann, *Die Deutschen im Bürgerkriege*, 534. It is indicative of General Moor's character that in order to keep certain promises to recruits regarding fare and equipment he sold his property to cover the debts he had incurred for the regiment.

Koltes, who had taken an active part in the militia since his return from the war in 1848, now raised and led to the field the Seventy-third Pennsylvania Infantry; his promising career was cut short at Murfreesboro.[11] Bernard Laiboldt acquitted himself brilliantly against General Wheeler twice when he had the opportunity at independent command. Friedrich Schäfer, who with little training for the field commanded a brigade at Murfreesboro, was pronounced by Osterhaus one of the best regimental leaders of the western army.[12] Adolf Engelmann, son of the famous botanist and physician, led the flower of the Belleville youth in the Forty-third Regiment after Julius Raith, its first colonel, fell at Shiloh.[13] All these had served in the Mexican War.

There was a group—a relatively large group—of German-Americans who had served as officers in the various provinces of Germany and thus brought to their commands trained skill. Conspicuous among them was Joseph Conrad, a man especially identified with the German-Swiss Fifteenth Missouri who conducted himself outstandingly at Murfreesboro, Chickamauga, and Missionary Ridge (where he was one of the first to press into the rebel works on the heights) and who shared in the eleven battles around Atlanta. Toward the very close of the war, he was brevetted brigadier general for his services in the Atlanta campaign.[14] Also to be recognized in this group is Baron Fred von Egloffstein, who, after ably leading his distinguished unit, the One Hundred and Third New York Regiment, was obliged by the intrigues of his lieutenant colonel to leave it; however, he was later exonerated and advanced to brevet brigadier general. Adolf Dengler, who organized one of the companies of second-generation Germans at Belleville and led it through the battles in Missouri

[11] Rosengarten, *The German Soldier in the Wars of the United States*, 140, gave the essential facts of Hassendeubel's career, but the best account was by Schnake, "Der Ausbruch des Bürgerkrieges in Missouri," in *Der Deutsche Pionier*, XII (1880–1881), 215–16. The best account of Koltes is found in Tenny, *The Military and Naval History of the Rebellion in the United States*, 733. See also Rosengarten, *The German Soldier in the Wars of the United States*, 13, and Kaufmann, *Die Deutschen im Bürgerkriege*, 520–21.

[12] At the close of 1863, Laiboldt brought a valuable train through from Chattanooga to Knoxville. With only a hundred men, he warded off an attack by fifteen hundred men under General Wheeler, a feat which he repeated against the same Confederate officer in August, 1864, at Dalton, Georgia, against slightly fewer odds. Sheridan, *Personal Memoirs*, I, 522–25; "Deutsch-amerikanische Nekrologie," in *Der Deutsche Pionier*, XV (1883–1884), 171. When Wheeler called on him to surrender, he replied, "I have been placed here to hold this post, not to surrender it."

[13] See Kaufmann, *Die Deutschen im Bürgerkriege*, 495, for Engelmann; see *ibid.*, 540, for Raith.

[14] *Ibid.*, 489.

and Arkansas only to fall in the great assault on Vicksburg on May 22, 1862, had fought in the revolution of 1848. Joseph Gerhardt, another Forty-eighter, rose from captain of a company of Turners from the national capital to colonel of the Frémont Regiment of New York; his services were recognized with a brevet brigadiership. Fritz Anneke, an able Prussian artillery officer of the Baden revolt, was colonel of the Thirty-fourth Wisconsin; but because he could not refrain from criticizing the blunders of his superior officers, especially in the face of injustice to German officers of his regiment, he was court-martialed and dismissed. Ludwig von Blessing, a former Prussian officer, commanded the Thirty-seventh Ohio after Edward Siber's resignation and became a brigadier by brevet.[15] Carl Eberhard Salomon, who fought first in Missouri under Sigel as colonel of the Fifth Missouri at Wilson's Creek, Pea Ridge, and Sarcoxia, and later under his brother, General Salomon, as colonel of the Ninth Wisconsin, should be mentioned as another officer who had had a war record in Germany and whose courage won for him the rank of brevet brigadier general.[16]

Next to be considered are a group of civilians of German birth who reached the rank of colonel without special training: one of these is Edward S. Salomon, the other Salomon—no relative of the distinguished Salomon family—who rose from raising and commanding a Jewish company in Hecker's regiment to the command of that regiment and to a brigadiership by brevet for hurling back the foe repeatedly at Bentonville.[17] Others of the group are Louis Wagner, who though he led the Eighty-eighth Pennsylvania honorably at Second Bull Run and Chancellorsville, attaining a brevet brigadiership at the youthful age of twenty-seven, probably rendered his best service in training fourteen thousand colored soldiers while invalided at William, Pennsylvania; [18] William C.

[15] For Von Egloffstein, see *ibid.*, 494–95; for Dengler, see *ibid.*, 491; for Gerhardt, see "General Joseph Gerhardt," in *Der Deutsche Pionier*, XIII (1881–1882), 282; for Anneke, see Hense-Jensen, *Wisconsin's Deutsch-Amerikaner*, 202–205, and Kaufmann, *Die Deutschen im Bürgerkriege*, 478–79. Anneke had first been colonel of artillery on General McClellan's staff. For Blessing, see Kaufmann, *Die Deutschen im Bürgerkriege*, 484. This Blessing is not to be confused with Franz Blessing, major of the Seventy-fourth Pennsylvania Regiment. For Colonel Siber, see Chapter XI, "Knights-Errant and Soldiers of Fortune."

[16] Kaufmann said that Salomon was colonel of the Third Missouri Regiment, but according to Heitman, he was colonel of the Fifth Missouri Regiment. See Heitman (comp.), *Historical Register and Dictionary*, I, 857.

[17] Kaufmann, *Die Deutschen im Bürgerkriege*, 545–46. He commanded the division after Hecker was wounded at Chancellorsville.

[18] Wagner ran the gamut of war experience: severely wounded, he was picked up by the

Küffner, who was mustered out as a brevet brigadier, and who, exemplifying the loyal Germans of Texas, fled to join the Union army and amassed the longest single record of combats encountered in this study—110 engagements; and, finally, Albert Sigel, a colonel of the Fifth Missouri Militia who commands attention as the brother of General Sigel.[19] Wilhelm Heine and Konrad Krez stand out as artists in differing fields who could also prove themselves capable military men. Heine was a painter and writer of Dresden who had been forced to flee to America after participating in street fighting: in his efforts to earn a livelihood, he departed widely from most of his countrymen by joining the American fleet and making himself a capable sailor and engineer. Oddly enough, he entered the Civil War as an engineer in the army but rose to a colonelcy and even a brevet brigadiership.[20] Krez was regarded as the most gifted German poet in America; his inspiring song "An mein Vaterland" belongs among the finest examples of German poetry. He saw service at Vicksburg, in Arkansas, and against Mobile as commander of the Twenty-seventh Wisconsin and emerged as brigadier by brevet for his services at Mobile.[21]

It seems fitting to close the discussion of the German colonels (it is certainly unnecessary to treat each of the fifty-seven unearthed by the research) with the record of an especially brave soul. George W. Mindel, who hailed from Frankfurt am Main, became colonel of the Twenty-seventh New York Regiment shortly after enlisting and served as a staff officer for McClellan and later for Philip Kearney. He commanded a brigade of five regiments in the Ninth Army Corps. An officer who won

foe from the battlefield of Bull Run and exchanged; but after Chancellorsville, the badly tended wound broke out afresh, so that he was sent to a Pennsylvania camp, where he recovered sufficiently to take the field again in the Fifth Army Corps. *Ibid.*, 560.

[19] Küffner had migrated from Mecklenburg to Texas as a youth, but he could not share the views of the Confederates; hence, he enlisted after making his way North with the Ninth Illinois. He was wounded four times—severely at Shiloh and Corinth; after his last wound he entered the Veteran Corps but recovered enough to become colonel of the One Hundred and Forty-ninth Illinois and serve in Prince Salm-Salm's brigade to the end of the war. *Ibid.*, 523; Heitman (comp.), *Historical Register and Dictionary*, I, 609. For Albert Sigel, see Kaufmann, *Die Deutschen im Bürgerkriege*, 553, and testimony from his daughter, Miss Lena Sigel.

[20] Kaufmann, *Die Deutschen im Bürgerkriege*, 510; Rosengarten, *The German Soldier in the Wars of the United States*, 71. Heine's chief service was in the engineer corps, but he led the German One Hundred and Third New York toward the end of the war.

[21] Heitman (comp.), *Historical Register and Dictionary*, I, 609; Johnson and Malone (eds.), *Dictionary of American Biography*, X, 505–506.

a brevet major generalship and was awarded two medals for bravery—one for the skill with which his command broke through the center at Williamsburg, silencing the Confederate artillery, and the other for services on the march through Georgia—was no ordinary soldier. An early death after the war—attributable, doubtless, to the hardships which he had endured—was sad reward for his devotion.[22]

Among the group of Irishmen who were entitled to call themselves colonel were many who were well known at the time and whose names may still live among the Irish descendants of Civil War veterans. Among these should certainly be reckoned Colonel Patrick Kelly, who succeeded General Meagher in command of the Irish Brigade, though still with the title of colonel. He had early won a brevet majority for gallant action at Shiloh. He was with the brigade from its inception, as lieutenant colonel and then as colonel of the Eighty-eighth New York. Meagher's mantle fell on one worthy to wear it; Kelly shared in all the weary marches and fighting—through the tragedy of Fredericksburg and the victory of Gettysburg to Petersburg, where he fought his last fight. On that June afternoon in 1864 as he advanced with the colors of his old regiment in his hand to storm the entrenchments of the city at the head of his command, a shell struck down one of the bravest soldiers of the Army of the Potomac.[23]

Of the colonels of the regiments of the Irish Brigade, almost all of whom were Irish-born, Robert Nugent was one whom all New York Irishmen knew and one of the relatively few of this brigade who survived Fredericksburg. He went out in April, 1861, as lieutenant colonel of the Sixty-ninth New York Militia, but when that body declined to re-enlist after termination of its three months enlistment, he became captain of a United States company. When Meagher organized the Irish Brigade, Nugent transferred to the command of the new Sixty-ninth Regiment and continued with it until it was mustered out late in 1865. He could not look on while other men were fighting, and so he remained in command of the same regiment through its consolidation into a battalion in 1863 and its expansion by the addition of new companies in 1864. He early began to accumulate brevet titles for bravery in various battles and crowned his long

[22] The name also appears spelled "Mindil." See Kaufmann, *Die Deutschen im Bürgerkriege*, 533–34.

[23] Mulholland, *The Story of the 116th Regiment Pennsylvania Infantry*, 126; "Oration of Denis Burke," in Fox, (comp.), *New York at Gettysburg*, II, 481.

and honorable career in March, 1865, with the title of brevet brigadier general.[24] The Irish colonel Richard Byrnes as a mere lad joined the Regular Army, in which by the opening of the Civil War he had risen to the post of sergeant major of the First Cavalry. In October, 1862, he was commissioned by Governor John A. Andrew as colonel of the Twenty-eighth Massachusetts. He commanded the brigade after the departure of General Smyth until he was mortally wounded at the Battle of Cold Harbor in June, 1864.[25]

Colonel Thomas Cass earned his command of the Irish Ninth Massachusetts by long service in the militia of that state, progressing from private to commander of the "Columbia Artillery." He fell relatively early in the war at Gaines's Mill in the Peninsular campaign.[26] Colonel Thomas W. Cahill of the Ninth Connecticut Volunteers saw service in the Southwest in the operations of the army of General Benjamin F. Butler which resulted in the capture of New Orleans. In the battle at Baton Rouge after the death of General Thomas Williams, the command devolved on Cahill, who was able to force the Confederates to abandon the ground they had won.[27]

The third post in the Tenth Ohio, raised among the Irish citizens of Cincinnati shortly after the President's first call, was filled by an Irishman, though the two highest positions were held by natives. Major Joseph W. Burke, born in County Mayo, Ireland, found himself so opposed to British policy that he joined the revolutionary movement of 1848 and renounced all thought of government service, even though four of his brothers had reached high rank in the army and he himself had been educated for the service. He emigrated to America, where he devoted himself to the study and practice of the law. He began his military career as chief of staff to Colonel W. H. Lytle, assisting that officer in organizing some of the finest

[24] It is passing strange that none of the encyclopedias carry an account of Robert Nugent and that there was only the most incidental mention of him in Cavanagh's book on Meagher. The author has had to rely on Heitman (comp.), *Historical Register and Dictionary*, I, 754.

[25] "Oration of Denis Burke," in Fox (comp.), *New York at Gettysburg*, II, 461. Tenny mentioned that a Matthew Murphy went out with the Sixty-ninth Militia as a private and that on the regiment's return he was elected colonel of it. After its reorganization he is said to have led it to the field as part of the Irish Brigade, but the author found no mention of him in Heitman's work or elsewhere except in the New York *Irish-American*, November 15, 1862; and there was no certainty that the person there referred to was the same, as the name is not uncommon. Heitman has given a person of that name in the One Hundred and Eighty-second New York Regiment.

[26] Powell, *The Fifth Army Corps*, 16–17. It was the third three-year regiment to leave the Old Bay State.

[27] Miller (ed.), *The Photographic History of the Civil War*, II, 133.

regiments sent by Ohio to the field. The Tenth Ohio was one of the first to leave for the campaign in western Virginia. When Lytle was wounded at Carnifex Ferry, the command devolved on Burke, who directed his troops with the utmost obstinacy until night put an end to the carnage and afforded the Southern commander an opportunity to retreat. Upon Lytle's promotion to the rank of brigadier general, Burke became colonel of the regiment and soon gained the confidence of his keen-sighted general. In March, 1865, almost nine months after he had been mustered out, he won the brevet of brigadier general.[28]

An unusual Irishman in more ways than one was Colonel James Gwyn, who was both well educated and a Protestant, though both points are explicable in an Irishman from Ulster. The war found him settled in Philadelphia. As promptly as April 18 he entered the service as captain of a company in the Twenty-third Pennsylvania, in which he saw service on the Peninsula. In July, 1862, he resigned to accept the lieutenant colonelcy of the Corn Exchange Regiment. After sharing in the battles of Fredericksburg, Chancellorsville, and Gettysburg he was promoted to the command of the regiment. Though seriously wounded in the Battle of the Wilderness, he was able to rejoin his regiment in front of Petersburg. For gallantry in the engagement of Poplar Spring Church he was brevetted brigadier general; and for his services at the Battle of Five Forks, major general.[29]

Seldom have the merits of a young officer commanded recognition as did those of Patrick Henry O'Rorke, who was brought to this country when but a year old. His school record was so distinguished that he was offered a scholarship, which he had to decline to go to work. But a few years later he won an appointment to West Point, from which he was precipitated almost immediately into the war on the staff of General Daniel Tyler. As an engineer officer he showed rare skill and talent in constructing the batteries on Tybee Island. In 1862 he accepted the colonelcy of the One Hundred and Fortieth New York Volunteers and found good material on which to expend his efforts. In the Chancellorsville campaign, at the ripe age of twenty-five, he was temporarily in charge of a brigade. He lives in history especially for his quick perception of the importance of Little Round Top at Gettysburg. The story of the saving of that strategic point to the Union will be told in some detail in a later chap-

[28] John Fitch (comp.), *Annals of the Army of the Cumberland* (Philadelphia, 1864), 239–42.

[29] *History of the Corn Exchange Regiment, 118th Pennsylvania Volunteers from its First Engagement at Antietam to Appomattox* (Philadelphia, 1888), 639. This was officially the number of the Corn Exchange Regiment.

ter. It will suffice here merely to state that he led his men gallantly up the hill, seizing the colors himself to encourage his troops when the storm of fire struck them at the crest, but falling dead as his men responded to his example. His promotions were remarkable: he rose in the short span of two years from brevet second lieutenant to brevet colonel in the Regular Army, the last promotion accorded posthumously for his feat at Gettysburg.[30]

A quartet of Irish-born colonels deserve brief mention. Though an engineer by profession, Colonel Howard Carroll served for a time as quartermaster in Meagher's brigade but became second in command when the One Hundred and Fifth New York was formed by consolidation, succeeded later to the command, and led the brigade until he was mortally wounded at Antietam.[31] Because Michael K. Bryan's unit, intended for the Corcoran Legion, was not full, it was left behind and then diverted to General Banks at Port Hudson. Its leader fell in one of the battles in Louisiana in 1863.[32] More important was William Joyce Sewell. Arriving in the United States at an early age, he grew up with a strong loyalty to the Union which prompted him to recruit a company for the Fifth New Jersey Volunteers at the first call for three years troops; this action brought him a captain's commission. By January, 1863, he was commanding the regiment, and had succeeded in infusing steadiness into it under trying conditions. He was awarded a medal of honor for having assumed command of a brigade at Chancellorsville, where he rallied around his colors a mass of men from other regiments and led them brilliantly through several hours of desperate battle. Though himself badly wounded, he inspired them by his presence and the bravery of his example. For this feat he was also brevetted brigadier general; a brevet major generalship was awarded him for gallantry during the entire war.[33] Andrew Patrick

[30] Wilson and Fiske (eds.), *Appletons' Cyclopaedia of American Biography*, IV, 591; Francis Marshall [Pierce], *The Battle of Gettysburg. The Crest-Wave of the American Civil War* (New York, 1914), 158. The Comte de Paris described the Gettysburg episode in detail. *History of the American Civil War*, III, 614–18.

[31] Hough, *History of Duryée's Brigade during the Campaign in Virginia under Gen. Pope*, 181–82.

[32] New York *Irish-American*, September 26, 1863. M. K. Bryan was recorded in Heitman's book merely as colonel of the regiment noted in the text, the One Hundred and Seventy-fifth New York.

[33] Though Sewell was kept from active service for some time by wounds received at Gettysburg, he returned to the field, only to be prostrated by exposure during the Wilderness campaign. When forced to resign in July, 1864, he still accepted the colonelcy of the Thirty-eighth New Jersey Regiment for its short period of service—two months in the fall of 1864. See

Caraher, entering service as a captain in the Twenty-eighth Massachusetts, was so severely wounded at Fredericksburg that he was retired as major to the Veteran Reserve Corps in September, 1863. He attained the rank of colonel at the very end of the war when appointed to command the Second United States Volunteers.[34]

One other Irishman of the volunteer service appears today to be less well known than his merits deserve. General St. Clair A. Mulholland, who had emigrated with his parents from Ireland to Philadelphia, became active in local militia organizations. As a lieutenant he was active in helping to form the One Hundred and Sixteenth Pennsylvania Volunteers for the Civil War. By June, 1862, he had received appointment as lieutenant colonel of the regiment, and by December he had received his first wound as he charged up Marye's Heights at Fredericksburg with the Irish Brigade. As a consequence of the consolidation of his regiment into a battalion, he was mustered out and had to accept the lower rank of major in order to continue as an officer. At Chancellorsville he distinguished himself by recapturing some lost guns of a Maine battery and by brilliantly holding the enemy in check all night, thus covering the withdrawal of the army over the Rappahannock, a feat which won for him the official commendation of General Hancock and years later the Congressional Medal of Honor. At Gettysburg he led the One Hundred and Fortieth Pennsylvania Volunteers but returned to his own regiment as its colonel on its reorganization in May, 1864. For his gallantry in action in the Battle of the Wilderness he was later brevetted brigadier general. October 15, 1864, he assumed command of the Fourth Brigade, First Division of the Second Corps, and shared in all the operations around Petersburg. His last honor, that of brevet major general, was accorded for gallantry in capturing the Confederate fortification at Boydton Plank Road on October 27, 1864.[35]

Colonel James A. Mulligan was so completely identified with the Irish, raising practically singlehandedly the Twenty-third Illinois Regiment, the Irish Brigade of Illinois, that the reader would probably not forgive his exclusion from these pages, even though he was born a few years after his

Samuel Toombs, *New Jersey Troops in the Gettysburg Campaign from June 5 to July 31, 1863* (Orange, N.J., 1888), 371; Wilson and Fiske (eds.), *Appletons' Cyclopaedia of American Biography*, V, 474. The *Cyclopaedia* gave date of his accession to a colonelcy incorrectly, according to a check with Heitman's work.

[34] Heitman (comp.), *Historical Register and Dictionary*, I, 281.

[35] Johnson and Malone (eds.), *Dictionary of American Biography*, XIII, 318–19; Mulholland, *The Story of the 116th Regiment Pennsylvania Infantry, passim.*; David Powers Conyngham, *The Irish Brigade and its Campaigns* (New York, 1867), *passim.*

parents had migrated from Ireland to Utica, New York. Graduation from a Catholic university, travel and experience with John Lloyd Stevens on his expedition to Panama in 1851, study of the law, and editorship of a Catholic weekly paper constituted legitimate claims to leadership among the Chicago Irish. He became famous throughout the country for his splendid defense of Lexington, Missouri, from July till September, 1861. He stubbornly held the besieged town for nine days, but was finally obliged to surrender his little band of 2,600 to an overwhelming force of 24,000 under General Price. After two months' imprisonment (for he refused a parole) he was exchanged—to return to Chicago as a hero.

After reorganizing his regiment, he had command of Camp Douglas and participated in several hard-fought engagements in Virginia. His loyalty to his regiment led him to decline a commission as brigadier general. Even in his death he was a dramatic figure. Fatally wounded during a charge on the Confederate lines at the Battle of Kernstown, he forbade his men to carry him from the field while the brigade colors were endangered; before they could return for him, he was carried off to die in the hands of the foe. Colonel Mulligan possessed the type of courage we associate with the best of the Irish. He offered at Lexington to take a position on a level spot of ground and give General Price the odds of four to one in a fair and open fight, but no attention was paid to his offer. When Mulligan surrendered his sword, Price asked for the scabbard; Mulligan replied that he had thrown it away. Price returned the sword with the remark that he disliked seeing a man of his valor without a weapon. The defense at Springfield constitutes one of the thrilling chapters in American history, for deeds of desperate valor were performed; but that story belongs rather to military history than to this account.[36]

There remain to be noted a few colonels of this nationality in the cavalry. Colonel Robert H. G. Minty of the Fourth Michigan Cavalry, subsequently commanding the First Cavalry Brigade, had served under his father for five years in the British army in the West Indies, in British Honduras, and on the west coast of Africa; but in 1853 he had retired from the service on account of a malady contracted before he came to Michigan. On the call for cavalry regiments he joined the Second Michigan as major, but before that regiment left the state he was made lieutenant colonel of

[36] *The National Cyclopaedia of American Biography*, V, 329; Brown (ed.), *Lamb's Biographical Dictionary of the United States*, V, 618 (a somewhat fuller account); Tenny, *The Military and Naval History of the Rebellion in the United States*, 786–87. For the episode of Mulligan's offering odds of four to one and the inability to surrender the scabbard, see Frost, *The Rebellion in the United States*, II, 379, 381.

the Third Michigan Cavalry. This command had an active part in the capture of New Madrid and Island No. 10. By July, 1862, Minty had led the regiment in thirty-six battles and skirmishes, every one a success; he left it to assume command of the Fourth Michigan Cavalry. The following November he was ordered to Nashville to report to the chief of cavalry, only to find himself assigned to the First Brigade under Colonel McCook. Just before the close of the war he was named brevet brigadier general and brevet major general for meritorious service during the war, and twice he received the thanks of Congress.

The opinion of his merits expressed by General James H. Wilson must not be omitted: "He was in every respect a modest and obedient officer, an excellent disciplinarian, and as good a leader as Murat himself." [37] In General Hugh J. Kilpatrick's raid around Atlanta and in Wilson's final raids through Georgia and Alabama, Minty commanded a division. There were those who felt that if he had been made a brigade commander in the Tennessee campaign, he would have been, by virtue of his rank, in a position to strike a blow with the cavalry which would have changed the character of that fierce struggle from one of defense and uncertainty to one of bold offense; in any case, he was everywhere the active leader—at Stone's River, Shelbyville, and Chickamauga. At the last-named battle he gave timely warning of General Braxton Bragg's plans against Chattanooga; without his services in the neighborhood of Ringgold, Rosecrans' army would never have found the road to Chattanooga open to it after the morning of September 19.[38]

The personality of Colonel George Gray, who commanded the Sixth Michigan Cavalry, was complex and erratic. A lawyer of brilliant parts, he was a good type of the witty, educated Irishman. Though generally suave, he displayed at times an irascible temper. His wit was tart and not always palatable to those against whom it was turned. Though not trained at West Point or in the army, he was something of a martinet in discipline. In the school of instruction which he set up in his tent, the officers had to assemble nightly to recite tactics, and no mercy was shown to anyone who failed in his "lessons." Nothing was so offensive to him as untidiness of dress or shabbiness of habiliments.[39]

[37] James H. Wilson, *Under the Old Flag. Recollections of Military Operations in the West for the Union* . . . (New York, 1912), II, 171–72.

[38] Fitch (comp.), *Annals of the Army of the Cumberland*, 205–209; Johnson and Malone (eds.), *Dictionary of American Biography*, XIII, 33. See also Vale, *Minty and the Cavalry;* Thatcher, *A Hundred Battles in the West, St. Louis to Atlanta*, 301–303.

[39] J. H. Kidd, *Personal Recollections of a Cavalryman with Custer's Michigan Cavalry*

The Hungarians who wore the insignia of colonel are astonishingly many in proportion to their numbers. It is not unduly exalting Géza Mihalotzy to put him first, for his name is perhaps the most widely known of this group. Born in Pesth, he enjoyed conditions favorable to the acquiring of a military education and took part in the Hungarian Revolution of 1848–1849. At the collapse of the revolution he came to the United States in 1850, settled in Chicago, and began the study of medicine. As has been related earlier, he helped to organize the Lincoln Riflemen more than two months before Lincoln's initial call for troops. Hardly had he left for Cairo with the first group dispatched from Chicago under General Swift, when his friend and fellow exile Julian Kuné was besought by a group of Germans to organize a regiment, which materialized into the Twenty-fourth Illinois Volunteers. The Lincoln Riflemen, recalled by special permission of McClellan, were incorporated in the Twenty-fourth Illinois; Mihalotzy became first lieutenant colonel and later, upon the resignation of Colonel Hecker, he became colonel with Kuné as major. The Hungarian led his regiment through all the several battles in Tennessee and stood high in the estimation of his superiors as regimental commander. He was shot through the hand at Chickamauga while waving his sword. About midnight on February 24, 1864, he went to the front at Buzzard Roost Gap in accordance with his custom of personally inspecting the picket line; on this occasion he was wounded severely by a single shot—so severely that he died about three weeks later.[40]

Equally well known is the name of Frederic George Utassy, an old Hungarian officer who organized and became colonel of the Garibaldi Regiment, or the Thirty-ninth New York, with its mixture of nationalities. Whatever may have been Utassy's faults, lack of courage was not among them. For instance, at Harpers Ferry, where he commanded a brigade, the Unionists found themselves out of ammunition with the Confederate batteries so arranged as to enfilade them; although doomed by a council of war to surrender, Utassy, who had voted never to surrender, requested permission to cut his way out. A few months later the same intrepid officer was found guilty of malfeasance for the misappropriation of over three thousand dollars, and was court-martialed and sentenced to

---

Brigade in the Civil War (Ionia, Mich., 1908), 51–52. It seems unnecessary to devote space to one John Murphy, an Irishman who had enlisted in the cavalry of the regular army in 1855 and who rose during the war to a colonelcy by July 1, 1864.

[40] Pivány, Hungarians in the American Civil War, 15, 32–33; Tenny, The Military and Naval History of the Rebellion in the United States, 774; Kaufmann, Die Deutschen im Bürgerkriege, 533.

the penitentiary. His dismissal from the service followed as a matter of course. Truly, he departed, as Kaufmann said, in no honorable way.[41]

There were a number of Hungarians who, though little known, yet served the Union well and who all were brevetted brigadiers. Eugene Kozlay, originally an Austrian officer, came to America with Kossuth as his adjutant, remained here, and became colonel of the Fifty-fourth New York Regiment, popularly known as the Black Jägers. His regiment belonged to Blenker's division; toward the end of the war he was commander of the port of Charleston.[42] Frederic Knefler rose rapidly from first lieutenant of the Eleventh Indiana to colonel of the Seventy-ninth Indiana and to a brevet brigadiership, bestowed probably for conspicuous bravery at Chickamauga. It is especially interesting that he was a Hungarian Jew and one of the few of his race to attain this honor.[43] George Pomutz turned his experience in the Hungarian army to the advantage of his adopted country by going out from his farm as first lieutenant in the Fifteenth Iowa. He rose only to the lineal rank of lieutenant colonel, but he won the brevet title of brigadier for meritorious service and possibly for bravery at Shiloh.

Among the fifteen colonels of Hungarian nationality, the following also deserve a few details. John T. Fiala, one of the ablest engineers of Hungary, was educated at the Austrian military academy at Gratz, joined the revolutionary army in 1848, and attained the rank of major. After the death of his chief, whom he followed to Syria, he became a refugee to America in 1851. Here he made the first large topographical map of Missouri and suggested to General Lyon the St. Louis forts subsequently built under Frémont. He entered the military service as lieutenant colonel of the Second Missouri Reserve Corps but soon became chief topographical engineer with the title of colonel on Frémont's staff. That general again had him appointed to his staff as colonel aide-de-camp when Frémont took command of the Mountain Department in 1862. In that region Fiala was attacked by a dangerous disease which necessitated his retirement from the service in June, 1864. He was praised by Sigel as an extraordinarily

---

[41] On his dishonesty, see Henry S. Alcott, "The War's Carnival of Fraud," in A. K. M[cClure] (ed.), *The Annals of the War* (Philadelphia, 1879), 711; Piványi, *Hungarians in the American Civil War*, 43, 60; Kaufmann, *Die Deutschen im Bürgerkriege*, 558. He resigned his commission on March 18, 1863, but was reappointed colonel on March 19, 1864.

[42] "Nekrologie," in *Der Deutsche Pionier*, XV (1883–1884), 421; Kaufmann, *Die Deutschen im Bürgerkriege*, 521.

[43] This name should more properly be spelled "Knöpfler." Piványi, *Hungarians in the American Civil War*, 32, 52.

capable officer.[44] Nicholas Perczel, who had played a prominent role in the Hungarian Revolution, not only as a colonel in the Honvéd army, but also as a legislator in the Diet, organized and led the Tenth Iowa. He even commanded a brigade in the western campaign.[45] Colonel Gustave Wagner, who had been a major of artillery in the Honvéd army and had accompanied Kossuth to Kütahya, was sent by McClellan to Cairo as instructor of artillery to bring order and discipline to the artillery branch there. When Wagner joined Frémont's staff as chief of ordnance, Grant wrote that his loss would be felt. Wagner later commanded the Second New York Artillery. He distinguished himself especially at Fairfax Court House in Pope's campaign, but he resigned before the close of the war.[46] Ladislaus Zsulavszky may have owed his high rank to his relationship to Louis Kossuth, for he was a nephew; in any case, as colonel, he was allowed to organize the Eighty-second United States Colored Infantry at Port Hudson, Louisiana, and to command the first brigade in the District of West Florida. It is of passing interest that two other officers of the same name, possibly his brothers, served in the same regiment as lieutenants.[47] Lastly, Robert J. Rombauer, the eldest of a distinguished family, had been an artillery lieutenant in the Honvéd army. When the revolt was crushed, he stayed on in his native land, convinced that it would be impossible for Austria to seek vengeance on every subaltern officer. His confidence was misplaced, for he was seized and pressed into the Austrian army as a private; after ten months his mother succeeded in rescuing him. He then joined the rest of the family on a farm in Iowa. The war found them all in St. Louis, where Robert took a leading part in organizing the home guards for the three months service. He re-enlisted for three years, serving with the rank of colonel of the First United States Reserve Corps of Mis-

[44] *Ibid.*, 21, 55; Kaufmann, *Die Deutschen im Bürgerkriege*, 497; Vasvary, *Lincoln's Hungarian Heroes*, 52. Despite the fact that physicians despaired of his life, Fiala recovered to settle to a useful life in California.

[45] Perczel did not get on well with the American officers, for he complained of the drunkenness among his superiors. Vasvary, *Lincoln's Hungarian Heroes*, 69–70. See also Piványi, *Hungarians in the American Civil War*, 34, 57; Rosengarten, *The German Soldier in the Wars of the United States*, 132. His full name was Nicholas Perczel de Bonyhad.

[46] He evidently came by his courage honestly, for his mother, at great personal danger, returned from Turkey in disguise under a false passport in order to effect the escape of Mrs. Kossuth. Piványi, *Hungarians in the American Civil War*, 15–16, 55; George B. McClellan, *McClellan's Own Story. The War for the Union* . . . (New York, 1887), 45. See also Vasvary, *Lincoln's Hungarian Heroes*, 85.

[47] Piványi, *Hungarians in the American Civil War*, 34–35. The two lieutenants referred to in the text were Emil and Sigismund, the latter of whom died in the war. Vasvary, *Lincoln's Hungarian Heroes*, 88, 89.

souri.[48] The name of one Hungarian, that of Charles Zagonyi, early gained wide currency by virtue of his famous cavalry charge at Springfield, Missouri, in October, 1861. Introduced by Asboth, he was charged by Frémont with organization of the famous Body Guard. He became commander of cavalry in Frémont's new command in the Mountain Department and was holding the rank of colonel when he resigned in 1864.

Among the naturalized Austrians, Henry Börnstein merits first place, not because of his military service—which was, indeed, slight—but because of his personal influence through his enlistment. Though he was known as the gifted editor and owner of the St. Louis *Anzeiger des Westens,* his appointment as colonel of the Second Missouri Regiment was not entirely without justification, as was so often the case, for he had formerly for five years been an Austrian officer. He participated only in the first battles in Missouri, since he was soon sent by Lincoln to Bremen as consul. His real service to the cause was his leadership in the uprising of the Germans in St. Louis and the example he set by the prompt formation of the Second Missouri Regiment.[49]

Although Kaufmann classified with the Germans the two lone Poles of the rank of colonel—and logically, when he wrote [50]—today a separate classification must be made for the Polish revolutionist of 1846 Wladimir Krzyzanowski, colonel of the Fifty-eighth New York Regiment, and for Joseph Karge. The former, obliged to flee after the short-lived Polish revolt of 1846, settled in America and became a civil engineer. At the outbreak of the Civil War, he himself organized his unit, in which there were several companies of German Poles. He was sent to Blenker's division and shared in its fortunes; during Pope's campaign in late 1862, he became commander of a brigade in Schurz's division. Schurz always cherished a warm friendship for this brave, intelligent, and capable officer, and after

[48] Kaufmann, *Die Deutschen im Bürgerkriege,* 543; Vasvary, *Lincoln's Hungarian Heroes,* 86–87. Some other Hungarians of this rank in the Union army were the following: Anselm Albert, who had been in the engineering corps of the Honvéd army and had served as chief of staff to Frémont with the rank of colonel (Piványi, *Hungarians in the American Civil War,* 54); Cornelius Fornet, originally an engineer in the Hungarian army who ultimately organized the Twenty-first New Jersey Infantry and became its colonel (*ibid.,* 47–48); Joseph Németh, whom we shall meet as a soldier of fortune (*ibid.,* 57); and Gabriel de Korponay, a Honvéd officer and colonel of the Twenty-eighth Pennsylvania (*ibid.,* 56). All these Hungarians have been checked as to rank against *Official War Records.*

[49] Börnstein was another of the Forty-eighters. See Kaufmann, *Die Deutschen im Bürgerkriege,* 485. His outstanding qualities were exactly those needed at the time—strong emotion, daring courage, and an iron will. See Chicago *Ilinois Staats-Zeitung,* August 23, 1861.

[50] Kaufmann's book was published in 1911, before the resurrection of Poland which followed World War I.

his death gave one of the eulogies to his old war comrade. "Kriz," as he was universally called in the army, fought with recognized distinction at Second Bull Run, Chancellorsville, Gettysburg, and in the West at Chattanooga and Knoxville. He died soon after the war as a result of the war strain. Schurz declared that the reason he did not attain the general's rank was that when his promotion was before the Senate for confirmation, none of the senators could pronounce his name.[51]

Joseph Karge—born, as was "Kriz," in Prussian Poland—was recognized as one of the best cavalry leaders in the Union Army. He enjoyed the benefit of an excellent education at German universities and also saw service in the Prussian army. He was fortunate enough to escape from the prison where he was incarcerated after participating in the Polish Revolution of 1848. In New York by 1851, he was successful in establishing a private classical school. He entered the war as lieutenant colonel of the First New Jersey Cavalry. He repeatedly distinguished himself by his promptness, energy, and dashing bravery. At Brandy Station his gallantry saved his regiment from annihilation by Stuart's cavalry and he captured Warrenton with a large booty. Even a wound received at Fredericksburg which had forced his resignation could not prevent him from organizing a second New Jersey cavalry regiment. He made a similar record in the West. He took part in seven large expeditions and in scores of minor engagements from which he nearly always emerged victoriously. He was constantly in command of larger bodies of troops than his rank would have demanded. He made an excursion into Missouri against Price, shared in Benjamin H. Grierson's raid through Mississippi, and dispersed the Confederates in several minor engagements. Karge's victory at Bolivar against an overwhelming enemy was the only successful incident of the Union expedition against the Confederate cavalry leader Nathan B. Forrest in early May, 1864. General Samuel D. Sturgis in his second expedition expressed appreciation of the valuable services of the "excellent and dashing officer, Colonel Joseph Karge." Official recognition of Karge's ability came late; it was in March, 1865, that Lincoln nominated him brigadier general by brevet. For each successive service he was selected as the man especially qualified for the emergency.[52]

It is regrettable that the services of "General" Edward D. Baker must be

[51] Kaufmann, *Die Deutschen im Bürgerkriege,* 523; Brown (ed.), *Lamb's Biographical Dictionary,* IV, 507. As his appointment as brigadier general expired early in 1863, his linear rank reverted to colonel, and ultimately he ranked as brigadier only by brevet.

[52] The best account of Karge is in Haiman, *Polish Past in America,* 123–28.

described here, for his merits entitled him to much greater rank. Many qualities and events combined to make him a popular favorite and later to endear his memory: his humble origin; his successful struggle against poverty; his record in the Mexican War as colonel of an Illinois regiment, in which post he proved himself a valiant officer; his attainment first of a seat in the lower house of Congress as representative of an Illinois district and then of the distinguished position of senator from Oregon in the upper house; his self-reliance, which led him ever farther to the new West; his fervid rhetoric, which wooed men into the army; his readiness to take up arms again for his adopted country; and, finally, the gallant sacrifice of his life. He had settled down to the practice of law in Springfield, a member of the brilliant circle around Abraham Lincoln. Immediately upon the declaration of war in 1861, he helped to raise a regiment in New York and Pennsylvania, called rather irrationally the First California Volunteers, and led it to the field. He was soon placed in charge of a brigade and might have had the rank of brigadier or major general of volunteers, but since he could not have accepted the proferred honor without resigning as senator from Oregon, he had to decline the brigadiership. He was notified of his appointment as major general just before he entered battle; it is difficult to believe that he would have rejected such an honor. However, he fell at Balls' Bluff in October of the first year of the war, and so it was with, technically, only a colonel's rank that he died. Few deaths cast more of a pall over Washington and the country than did the death of this Anglo-American.[53]

A second English colonel was Edward L. Molineux, who, early after his arrival in the United States, identified himself with the New York Militia by joining the celebrated Brooklyn City Guard. His work in promoting the One Hundred and Fifty-ninth New York Regiment for the

[53] He held his brigade in a camp near the capital so that he could alternate the duties of senator and military commander. He was regarded as one of the best defenders of the Union cause. His last utterance in the Senate was a reply to Breckinridge, when he met the Kentucky senator with weapons keener and brighter than his own. Tomes, *The Great Civil War*, I, 586–88; James A. Logan, *The Great Conspiracy: Its Origin and History* (New York, 1866), 351–55; Johnson and Malone (eds.), *Dictionary of American Biography*, I, 517–19; John D. Baltz, *Hon. Edward D. Baker* (Lancaster, Pa., 1886), 13–16. It is of passing interest that his first military experience was in the Black Hawk War. Heitman listed Baker with the rank of major general though he never accepted his appointment.

Stone's official report cast on Baker the entire blame for the disaster at Ball's Bluff, charging him with recklessness and disobedience of orders, but in the congressional enquiry the charges seem hardly corroborated by the facts. The disaster resulted chiefly from Baker's being greatly outnumbered and from insufficiency of transportation.

Civil War was recognized by his appointment as lieutenant colonel; from this post he rose quickly to a colonelcy. Under General Banks he saw action at Port Hudson and Irish Bend, where he was so severely wounded that he was long assigned to such duties as inspector general, acting provost marshal–general, and commissioner for exchange of prisoners. In 1864 he was given command of all the Union forces north of the Red River; in August he reinforced Sheridan with a provisional division and shared in all the battles of the latter's Shenandoah campaign. For conspicuous gallantry in several battles he was made brigadier general by brevet in October, 1864, and major general the next year.

Still a third Englishman of this rank was James Ashworth, who lived, after his arrival in America in 1838 at the tender age of two, in Pennsylvania. Although in 1861 he fought informally in Maryland, it was not until August, 1862, that he joined the One Hundred and Twenty-first Pennsylvania in time to share in the battles of Fredericksburg, Chancellorsville, and Gettysburg. At Gettysburg he was so desperately wounded that he was honorably discharged with the rank of colonel. Subsequent service in the Veteran Reserves in Louisiana did not alter his ultimate status.[54]

One Scotchman, named, oddly enough, David Ireland, and one Canadian, with the name of Joseph R. Scott, also held the rank of colonel. The former entered the service as adjutant in the Scottish regiment, the Seventy-ninth New York; became colonel of the One Hundred and Thirty-seventh New York in 1862; and distinguished himself at the battles of Lookout Mountain, Missionary Ridge, and Resaca, where he was severely wounded. At the time of his death he commanded a brigade. The Canadian, who had come to this country when only twelve years old, manifested interest in the militia by forming the "National Guard Cadets" in Chicago, afterwards famous as the United States Zouaves. In this company he modestly accepted a lieutenancy under Elmer E. Ellsworth as captain. When, with the outbreak of war, he succeeded to the command of the Nineteenth Illinois, he was, at twenty-three, one of the youngest colonels in the army. His handsome, distinguished, and soldierly appearance was no detriment to his promotion. At the reorganization of the Nineteenth Illinois as a three years regiment, he yielded the command to Colonel Turchin, though he was the choice of the men, and later succeeded to the command on Turchin's promotion to brigadier general. At the battle of Stone's River he fell, seriously wounded, at the head of his column and died from the effects some months afterwards.[55]

The French colonels were few. The only one even fairly well known before the war was Charles W. Le Gendre, who came to the United States in 1854 after his marriage to an American in Brussels and became a citizen of his adopted country. He helped to recruit the Fifty-first New York Regiment and was rewarded with the rank of major. His record in the war was one of conspicuous bravery. Twice wounded, the second time seriously when he lost an eye at the Battle of the Wilderness, he was honorably discharged in October, 1864. By March, 1863, he had already attained the rank of colonel, but after his discharge he received a brevet of brigadier general.[56] Colonel Charles A. de Villiers, in command of the Eleventh Ohio Regiment, brought rich experience to the service, for he had been an officer in the French army and was a trained physician. At the beginning of the war, even before First Bull Run, he was taken prisoner in western Virginia and sent to Richmond. There about mid-September after his capture, he became an assistant to the physician in the hospital and thus won some liberty; he finally succeeded in eluding the guards. Disguised as an old mendicant Frenchman, decrepit and nearly blind, he secured the permission of the commandant at one point to go to Fortress Monroe under a flag of truce in order to embark for France. By late October he had rejoined his regiment and continued in the service until the close of the next April, when he received his discharge and did actually embark for his native France.[57] The third of the trio is Nikolas Greusel, who as an Alsatian may properly be classified as French in nationality as of 1861, though the name suggests German blood and ancestry. Before the Civil

[55] For Ireland, see Tenny, *The Military and Naval History of the Rebellion in the United States*, 789; for Scott, see Haynie, *The Nineteenth Illinois*, 134–36, one of the best accounts.

[56] The obstinacy of Colonel Le Gendre made him very unpopular in his own regiment and in the entire brigade. On one occasion while the regiment was waiting for the completion of a bridge, he held the men in the hot sun (though there was a thick growth of trees only a few yards away) and refused to let other officers bring their regiments up for shelter, because it was unmilitary to march one regiment past another. Thomas H. Parker, *History of the 51st Regiment of the P. V. and V. V. (Pennsylvania Volunteers and Veteran Volunteers)* (Philadelphia, 1869), 342–43. See also *The National Cyclopaedia of American Biography*, XXV, 79, and Johnson and Malone (eds.), *Dictionary of American Biography*, XI, 145–56.

[57] For the full account of his escape, see Moore (ed.), *Anecdotes, Poetry, and Incidents of the War*, 154–55. For a brief account of his career see Wilson and Fiske (eds.), *Appletons' Cyclopaedia of American Biography*, II, 156.

War he had already seen service in the Mexican War as captain in a Michigan regiment, so that it was with experience in officership that he went out in 1861 as major of the Seventh Illinois. Before long he became colonel of the Thirty-sixth Illinois, with which he served until he was honorably discharged because of illness in February, 1863. A fourth Frenchman, J. Lionel d'Epineuil, of the Fifty-third New York, also became a colonel.[58]

Though few in number, the representatives of the Swiss nationality in this rank were men of ability. Hermann Lieb had been born in Switzerland but was residing in Illinois when war broke out. He entered the Eighth Illinois Infantry as a private in Company B for the three months service, was selected its first captain after re-enlistment, and then became major of the regiment by the close of the second year of war. By 1863, he was transferred to the command of the Fifth United States Colored Heavy Artillery. On May 6, and in the following January, crowned with two victories, he independently led an expedition against Marion, Arkansas. In the generous bestowal of honors on March 13, 1865, he was the recipient of a brigadiership by brevet for meritorious service during the war.[59] A second Swiss, Brodbeck, whose Christian name does not appear in extant records, had settled in Dubuque. He organized, and was commissioned colonel of, a regiment which fought boldly in the western theater, according to Kaufmann and Steinach. Arnold Suttermeister, a third Swiss, organized the Eleventh Indiana Battery in Fort Wayne in the spring of 1861 and led it to the field. His scene of action was in the West, where he distinguished himself at Corinth, Chickamauga, and Missionary Ridge. His battery made the march through Georgia and both Carolinas and fought honorably in many battles of that campaign. He commanded a brigade of reserve artillery in the army of General Thomas and was mustered out with the title of colonel of artillery. Steinach claimed as a fourth Swiss of this rank one "Moesch," apparently Joseph A. Mösch, colonel of the Eighty-third New York Infantry. Kaufmann seems to have overlooked the promotion of John H. Kuhn, a fifth Swiss, from major in the Ninth Illinois to colonel of the One Hundred and Forty-fourth Illinois Infantry.[60] He was badly wounded at Shiloh.

[58] Kaufmann, *Die Deutschen im Bürgerkriege*, 505.

[59] *Ibid.*, 527; Heitman (comp.), *Historical Register and Dictionary*, I, 632. Kaufmann incorrectly said Lieb commanded the Fourth Colored Infantry, but see *Official War Records*, Ser. 1, XXXIX, Pt. 2, p. 69.

[60] For Brodbeck, see Kaufmann, *Die Deutschen im Bürgerkriege*, 486; for Arnold Suttermeister, *ibid.*, 555. It is possible that the person referred to was Samuel Brodtbeck of the Twelfth Iowa Infantry, given in Heitman (comp.), *Historical Register and Dictionary*, II,

The Scandinavian contingent of colonels is impressive for its quality rather than for its numbers. Colonels Hans Christian Heg and Hans Mattson will seem to the reader to be old friends, but Colonels Oscar Malmborg and Ernst Holmstedt will be new acquaintances. With Colonel Heg we touch vividly the pioneer days of the Norwegians in Wisconsin, for with his parents as a lad of ten he had arrived at Muskego in 1840. The quality of leadership had appeared in his father; for the elder Heg emerged at once as the acknowledged leader of the community, while his farm became for hundreds of his countrymen an immigrant station on the road to the farther West. At the ripe age of twenty-two young Heg entered the political arena, a thorough Democrat but a free-soiler, and offered himself unsuccessfully for a seat in the Wisconsin assembly. By 1861 he was already known as a farmer and a businessman; elected to office as state prison commissioner, he first displayed his executive ability in this post. He thought of military service at the first call for troops. By September, 1861, Heg received authorization, as has been stated earlier, to recruit for a Scandinavian regiment; he set the machinery in motion all over the Northwest, and by the close of the year he had achieved his quota.

Heg was a young man, less than thirty-four when he was killed. He was tall and straight, strong and vigorous, giving an impression of greater age because he wore a heavy beard. His demeanor was quiet, even to taciturnity; this, combined with disciplinary sternness, sufficed to conceal the boyish ardor for danger and adventure and the desire for glory with which he went to war. He had genuine resources of courage, the confidence of the frontiersman in his own competence, and a strong sense of responsibility toward his men which led him to participate cheerfully in all their sufferings and privations. More than once he deferred requests for leave of absence for fear that his absence might lead to demoralization in his companies. His tendency to boast, which is marked in his letters to his wife,[61] can be overlooked when one notes that his services did not escape

---

83, in which case his rank was only that of major. Though Kaufmann was always anxious to give his characters the highest rank possible, he almost always indicated that the rank was by brevet only, if that was the case. It will be noted also that Heitman spelled Brodtbeck's name differently, although it is a rather common name. Since the *Official War Records* yields only "Major Brodtbeck," the writer is inclined to think Kaufmann in error. For Mösch, see Steinach, *Geschichte und Leben,* 43. He is also identified in Heitman (comp.), *Historical Register and Dictionary,* II, 130. Kuhn appears in *Official War Records* with this rank. Ser. 1, XLVIII, Pt. 2, p. 49.

[61] Attention should, in all fairness, be drawn to the fact that Heg was constantly trying to encourage his wife, who seemed to have a premonition that he would not return from the war. See his letter of September 5, 1862. In his letter of April 1, 1862, he says, "Everybody

the appreciative notice of his superiors; he received praise, for example, in the reports of General William P. Carlin, who called him "the bravest of the brave." [62] He saw service through the West until he was placed in command of a brigade in the First Division of the Twentieth Corps, to which his regiment was transferred. As acting brigadier general he fought at Chattanooga and at Chickamauga, where he fell on the second day of the disastrous battle.[63] The verdict of the *Emigranten,* that he was the best of all the Norwegians to undertake the organization of a Scandinavian regiment and then to lead it, was doubtless correct.

In Colonel Hans Mattson we encounter a political and military leader among the Swedes not only of Minnesota but of the entire Northwest as well. Though he had been born a Swede and had come to America in 1851, he had already emerged before the war as an organizer for the Republican party in Minnesota and chairman of the branch in his home city of Red Wing. As captain, he led a company of Scandinavians to the Third Minnesota Regiment; in a letter of June 19, 1862, he informed his wife that after having "acted as major for a long time," he had received his commission as major—which document he was sending her for safekeeping.[64] He announced his promotion to a colonelcy on June 12, 1864, to his wife in the following terms: "I have just had a pair of eagles put on

---

says that this Regiment would not be worth anything under anybody else." Blegen (ed.), *Civil War Letters of Colonel Heg,* 73.

[62] A letter from "N. H." after the battle of Murfreesboro to the editor of Madison *Emigranten* is an index to the feeling of his men toward him: "I cannot close these lines without telling about our stout colonel. Wherever the danger was worst, there he was, always gay and friendly and at the same time cheerful and calm. It is a marvel that he came through unhurt. Many a warm clasp after the battle showed how dear he had become to us in the relatively short time we have been together. But not only we under officers love him; also superior officers know how to treasure and value him." Printed in the issue of February 2, 1863. For accounts of Heg, see Fitch (comp.), *The Annals of the Army of the Cumberland,* 231–33; Blegen (ed.), *Civil War Letters of Colonel Heg,* 4–6, 27–30; Chicago *Hemlandet,* October 16, 1861; Tenny, *The Military and Naval History of the Rebellion in the United States,* 766–67.

[63] Carlin, in bestowing praise on Heg and Colonel J. W. C. Alexander, said, "If men like them commanded more brigades, we would have been spared the shame of seeing our troops driven back." Madison *Emigranten,* February 2, 1863. See also issue of October 7, 1861, of the same paper.

[64] He explained that he could not send money in that letter as he had to buy a field officer's uniform, horse, and saddle, etc. He said that he had a beautiful horse which would belong to her when the war was over, if he could bring it home safely. He would receive $180 a month pay, but his expenses would also be greater, as he would now mess with the colonel and would have to have an extra servant to care for his horse. Mattson Papers.

my shoulders and feel rather proud." [65] On June 29 of the same year he spoke of commanding the whole right wing, consisting of five battalions, three batteries of light artillery, and two squadrons of cavalry. In October he was given command of a brigade of the Seventh Army Corps for one month, until the return of Colonel Frank Graves.[66] Caught in a backwater of the war in Arkansas, Mattson did not rise above the rank of colonel.[67]

The qualifications of Oscar Malmborg to command a regiment were many: he had been educated at the Karlberg Military Academy and had served eight years in the Swedish army. He might fairly be termed a soldier of fortune of the Mexican War, for he came to the United States to volunteer as a private for that service; however, he won promotion and became an American citizen. At the outbreak of the Civil War he was serving as vice-consul for Sweden and Norway in Chicago. As a resident of that city, he was given the task of training the Fifty-fifth Illinois by Colonel David Stuart. It was not until the advance on Corinth, when he had charge of the strategic movements of the entire division, that Malmborg had an opportunity to win recognition; by his able management on this occasion he gained the praise of both General Thomas and General Grant. It was not, however, until January 1, 1864, that he was commissioned colonel of the regiment. He published quarter-page advertisements in *Hemlandet* in 1864, calling for recruits for the Fifty-fifth Illinois. The Chicago *Tribune* commented favorably on Malmborg's bravery and military capacity at the same time that he was also especially praised by the state government.[68] At a later period he served as colonel of the Second United States Veteran Volunteers.

Colonel Ernst Holmstedt shared several characteristics other than nativity with Malmborg. Both had gained experience in the Mexican War, and this fact probably helped both to win commissions when they offered themselves for service in the Civil War. After completing a com-

[65] Letter of June 13, 1864, *ibid*. He stated in this letter that he had gone up to Little Rock on June 13 to be mustered in as colonel. As early as October 24, 1862, he had written of being in command of the regiment, presumably during an absence of Colonel Everett W. Foster.

[66] Letters of June 29 and October 24, 1864, *ibid*.

[67] Mattson's letters to his wife furnished the best information on him. An explanatory note inserted with his letters by the Minnesota Historical Society recorded the main facts of his life. Hokanson, *Swedish Immigrants*, 72, 112, 116, gave the military facts briefly.

[68] Data on Malmborg is scanty. Some comments are found in Chicago *Hemlandet*, October 23, 1861, January 20, 1864; Chicago *Tribune*, June 15, 1864; and Hokanson, *Swedish Immigrants*, 113.

mercial course in Sweden, Holmstedt had emigrated to America and had found work with a firm in New York. In the Civil War he won sufficient distinction to become lieutenant colonel of the Forty-first New York Regiment, later included in Blenker's division, and finally to become colonel of the Seventy-fourth United States Colored Infantry.[69] Daniel Anderson entered the war as a member of the First Iowa Cavalry, rose to be its colonel, winning notice for his services at Bayou Meto, Arkansas, on August 28, 1863, and finally commanded a post at Little Rock with the same rank. Still another Swede, Colonel Adolphus J. Johnson, was colonel of the First, and later of the Eighth, New Jersey Regiment.[70]

One does not search in vain even for Italian colonels, despite the paucity of Italian privates for them to command. Unquestionably, the outstanding Italian was Count Luigi Palma di Cesnola, born in 1832 at Rivarole near Turin of a family originally Spanish but resident in Piedmont since the opening of the twelfth century. Intended for the priesthood, he left college when war broke out between Austria and Sardinia to enter the Sardinian army as a volunteer. The youngest commissioned officer in the Sardinian army at the time, he was promoted in February, 1849, for bravery at Novara, to a lieutenancy in the Queen's royal brigade. At the conclusion of the war he was sent to the royal academy at Cherasco to complete his military education, later serving in the army several years and taking part in the Crimean War. He was no soldier of fortune, for he came to New York City in 1860 and there, the next year, married the daughter of a captain in the United States Navy. With his military background it is not surprising that he secured a commission at the opening of the war as lieutenant colonel of the Eleventh New York Cavalry Regiment, nor that he won promotion to the position of colonel of the Fourth New York Cavalry in 1862, nor that he afterward led a brigade of cavalry during the greater part of the war. For heroic conduct in a cavalry charge at Aldie on June 17, 1863—for leading the regiment in a wild charge when it hesitated, even though he was without arms because he was under arrest and without a command—General Hugh J. Kilpatrick praised him and presented him with his own sword.[71] In the next charge Di Cesnola, desperately

[69] Hokanson had some references to Holmstedt, *Swedish Immigrants*, 103, 104, 109, 136.

[70] Heitman (comp.), *Historical Register and Dictionary*, 112, gave the above scanty facts for Anderson; for Johnson, see *ibid.*, II, 115; Hokanson, *Swedish Immigrants*, 109.

[71] Di Cesnola forgot that he was without a command and flew to the head of the column to reassure the men. The general, who witnessed the gallant act, released him from arrest and handed him his own sword, saying, "Here is my sword, wear it in honor of this day." Glazier, *Battles for the Union*, 250.

wounded, was taken prisoner and languished in Libby Prison for nine months. He was released, however, in time to be with General Sheridan throughout the Shenandoah Valley campaign. Upon the expiration of the term for which his regiment had enlisted, he himself, at the request of the commanding general, remained at the head of a brigade and almost constantly in combat. President Lincoln bestowed on him the brevet rank of brigadier general in one of the closing days of the war.[72]

It is strikingly true, though perhaps without special significance, in view of the great number of German troops, that a very large proportion of the foreign-born lieutenant colonels identified were Germans. Not infrequently an officer of this rank succeeded to the command or was called from the lieutenant-colonelcy of one regiment to head another; in such a case, he was considered as of the lower rank. It will suffice to call attention to a few of the more striking personalities of this group. Among them was Carl Gottfried Freudenberg, who was born in the famous university city of Heidelberg. He early entered the German military service as a cadet in the Karlsruhe school. The revolt of 1848 found him there, but although only a lad of fifteen, he took the field with the insurgents and actually faced battle near Mannheim. He forswore his brilliant prospects and came to the United States, and a few years later the Civil War afforded him another opportunity for a military career. At the call for volunteers, he responded by raising a company—as captain of which he entered the Fifty-second New York Regiment in August, 1861. Having attained the rank of major by the following November, he was severely wounded at Fair Oaks. About a year later he bore the rank of lieutenant colonel and commanded his regiment at Chancellorsville and Gettysburg. At Gettysburg he was so desperately wounded that he was forced to resign. He accepted a commission, however, as major in the veteran reserve corps, organized the Twenty-third Regiment, bore the rank of lieutenant colonel again in April, 1864, and served as commandant in the Bureau of Refugees at Milwaukee.[73] He received the rank of brevet colonel for gallant service.

Having suffered dire poverty before the war in a land where he was a foreigner, Alexander von Schrader seized his opportunity when it was presented by the war; and then his gallantry and efficient training told. Soldiering was in his blood, for his father had fought his way up from the ranks to a lieutenant-generalship and by his bravery had won admis-

[72] *The National Cyclopaedia of American Biography,* I, 422.

[73] Rosengarten, *The German Soldier in the Wars of the United States,* 118–19; Kaufmann, *Die Deutschen im Bürgerkriege,* 500.

sion to the nobility. He entered his son at the early age of fourteen in the Prussian army as a cadet. After two and a half years the younger Von Schrader entered the service of the Duke of Brunswick and served three years as cadet and ensign, either on active duty or at hard study. By 1841 he had attained a second lieutenancy in the bodyguard of the duke, the famous regiment known as the Schwarze Jäger. In 1852 the young lieutenant left Germany to settle in America. He spent the following decade in various pursuits and places, but the opening of the war found him in Cincinnati. For a time he acted as drillmaster to the Eighteenth Ohio Regiment at Camp Dennison; and afterwards, to the Seventy-third Ohio at Chillicothe. In December, 1861, he was commissioned lieutenant colonel in the Seventy-fourth Ohio and was mustered into the service from that state. His soldierly capacity here attracted the attention of his commanding officer, General James S. Negley. When the latter assumed command at Nashville, Von Schrader received appointment as division inspector and served with unusual skill and fidelity in that capacity during the investment. It is probably no exaggeration to say that he was one of the most able engineer officers of the army. He sacrificed an arm in the Battle of the Wilderness. Corinth, Murfreesboro, Chickamauga, and the march through Georgia were some of the scenes of his fighting.[74]

Lieutenant colonels who had been born in Germany, like German-born colonels, were usually to be found in German regiments.[75] Some foreign-born lieutenant colonels, however, were found in nonforeign regiments, doubtless because of their superior qualifications by virtue of foreign training or experience. A few striking illustrations will suffice: George F. Leppien, whose experience as a Prussian officer undoubtedly commended him to the First Maine Artillery, and who later commanded the artillery in the second division of the first corps of the Army of the Potomac; W. C. Mögling, whose captaincy of a German company would not necessarily have commended him as lieutenant colonel to the other (native) companies of the Eleventh Connecticut; and Knut Oskar Broady, a

[74] Kaufmann, *Die Deutschen im Bürgerkriege*, 551; Fitch (comp.), *Annals of the Army of the Cumberland*, 67–69; Fitch misspelled the name. The Schwarze Jäger of Brunswick was the model of the regiment of the same name in New York: its uniform was black with a skull and crossbones as a distinctive badge. The organization was maintained in memory of Frederick William, Duke of Brunswick, who had sacrificed all his possessions to raise and equip the thousand troops in this fashion. Fitch (comp.), *Annals of the Army of the Cumberland*, 67.

[75] Numerous examples can be found in the biographical portion of Kaufmann's book, and have been checked against Heitman (comp.), *Historical Register and Dictionary*, 483, 484, 490, 493, 495, 517, 532, 534, 535.

Swede who acted as lieutenant colonel in the Sixty-first New York.[76]

Lieutenant Colonel Francis Peteler merits separate consideration, as he was second in command of Berdan's famous Sharpshooters. Born in Bavaria, he came alone at twelve years of age to the United States in 1840. He secured experience in the Mexican War, serving under General Scott. He raised in Minnesota, where he had been residing since 1853, the company of Sharpshooters which became Company A in the Second Regiment of Sharpshooters and was mustered in at Fort Snelling on October 5, 1861. After his arrival with the company at Washington, he became lieutenant colonel of the regiment.[77]

There were a few Austrians who held this rank in the Union army. Leopold Markbreit, a native of Vienna, was a half brother of Fritz Hassaurek, editor of the Cincinnati *Volksblatt*. He was chiefly known at the time for the questionable honor of having been selected by lot (along with Emil Frey and several other Union men then in the hands of the Confederates) to be shot if the Unionists should kill three captured rebel officers as spies.[78] Ernest F. M. Fähtz, a former Austrian officer who had seen service as a revolutionist in 1848–1849 in Austria and Baden, also rendered aid to the Union cause as lieutenant colonel of the Eighth Maryland Regiment.[79]

A singularly interesting character was Káspar Trepp, who came to the United States from the Swiss Federation to settle in Wisconsin. He organized in that state the Swiss company of Sharpshooters, which soon inspired the formation of a regiment, and left a brilliant war record. Except for the fact that as a Swiss he naturally could shoot, nothing in his artistic background as an architect indicated him as specially competent for sharpshooter work. When he was promoted to the rank of major, there was deep concern among the men of his company because his successor did not command their confidence. Unfortunately the ill-feeling between Trepp, now second in command, and Colonel Berdan grew to such proportions that both were placed before a court-martial; from this Trepp emerged to better advantage than his superior. Trepp was killed in battle at Mine Run while he was observing the movements of the foe from one

---

[76] See *ibid.*, 527, 534, for the first two lieutenant colonels; for Broady, see Hokanson, *Swedish Immigrants*, 106–108.

[77] C. A. Stevens, *Berdan's United States Sharpshooters in the Army of the Potomac*, 534.

[78] Kaufmann, *Die Deutschen im Bürgerkriege*, 530. Frey will be discussed in the next chapter.

[79] *Ibid.*, 497; "Deutsch-amerikanische Nekrologie," in *Der Deutsche Pionier*, XIV (1882–1883), 113. Fähtz had become a director of a college at Elkton, Maryland, by the late fifties.

of the trenches out of which they had just been driven and while he was preparing for a further push forward. Though he lived long enough to be carried to a hospital, where his wound was washed and bound, he survived only until midnight.[80]

As the reader would suppose, there were representatives of almost every nationality. A Frenchman conspicuous among his countrymen both in his native France and in America was Lieutenant Colonel Joseph A. Vigier de Monteil. The son of an officer of the army of Napoleon, he had passed his life from boyhood in the military service of his country, in which he had attained the rank of first lieutenant of artillery. He was compelled to flee to New York after the Revolution of 1848 because of his republican opinions. At the first call of his adopted country, the old soldier responded and went out as lieutenant colonel of the D'Epineuil Zouaves. When the regiment was sent back from Hatteras, he remained behind to accompany the army to Roanoke Island. On the day of the battle he seized a rifle as would a common soldier, joined the ranks of the Hawkins Zouaves, and was among the foremost, cheering the men in the assault. There his career ended, however, on February 8, 1862. His last words, according to Colonel Hawkins, were "Charge, *mes enfants;* charge, Zouaves." [81] The second in command in the Enfants Perdus was Felix Comfort, who resigned early, in May, 1863. Associated with Colonel de Trobriand in the command of the Gardes Lafayette was Lieutenant Colonel Louis Thourot, an old non-commissioned officer of the French army, who rendered good service at the battle of Williamsburg and moved about calmly, encouraging his men.[82]

Five Scandinavians attained the rank of lieutenant colonel—four Swedes and one Norwegian. Except the colonel, the only officer in the Forty-eighth New York who seemed to have had any formal military education was Lieutenant Nere Albert Elfving of Company B, a skillful swordsman, whose service with the regiment was long and conspicuous. Though a graduate of the Karlberg Military Academy and hence pre-

[80] See Kaufmann, *Die Deutschen im Bürgerkriege,* 558, for a brief paragraph on Trepp. The best data is found in Aschmann, *Drei Jahre in der Potomac Armee,* 116–17, 155–56. Trepp's men had to bury him in the lot of John Minor Botts, as an attack seemed impending; but one of his officers secured a three days furlough to take the body to Washington, from which point it was sent to New York for burial by the Swiss of that city. Aschmann, *Drei Jahre in der Potomac Armee,* 156–58. Kaufmann listed him as colonel, but Heitman as only lieutenant colonel. Heitman (comp.), *Historical Register and Dictionary,* II, 155.

[81] De Paris, *History of the Civil War in America,* I, 585; Duyckinck, *National History of the War for the Union,* II, 250.

[82] This praise of Thourot appears in De Trobriand, *Quatre Ans de Campagnes,* I, 197.

sumably a man with a career open before him in Sweden, he nevertheless chose in 1855 to come to the United States, where he found employment in the Geodetic Corps of the Coast Survey. He participated in General W. T. Sherman's expedition in 1861 in the occupation of Port Royal, in the battle of Fort Pulaski, and in the assault on Fort Wagner in 1863. By this time he had won three promotions, so that he shared in the expeditions against Fort Fisher in 1865 as lieutenant colonel, though he was in command of a brigade. At the Battle of Wilmington he was so unfortunate as to receive a knee wound which necessitated amputation of the leg. It is only fair to say that it was owing to his energy and discipline that his company made its good record.[83] Fabian Brydolf, the second Swede, was a landscape painter in his native Östergötland until his emigration in 1841 to the United States, where to some extent he continued his profession. In 1847 he enlisted in the Fifteenth Regiment of the Regular Army and fought in several battles of the Mexican War. In 1861 he was living in Iowa and serving as captain of a militia company which he led into an Independent Regiment in June, 1861. The loss of his right arm at Shiloh did not end his military career, for promotion to a lieutenant-colonelcy brought him to the Twenty-fifth Iowa, with which he served until the capture of Vicksburg, when he was appointed commander at Sherbourne Barracks at Washington. The third officer of Swedish birth was J. G. Gustafson, who was promoted from the Third Minnesota to the post of lieutenant colonel of the One Hundred and Twelfth United States Colored Regiment. This post carried its own special dangers in view of the hostility of the Confederates to white men leading negro troops.[84]

The story of Captain Knut Broady is so unusual that it merits at least brief recapitulation. When only fifteen years of age he joined an artillery company in Stockholm and at twenty shifted to the Swedish navy as subaltern. In 1855, shortly after his arrival in New York in 1854, he entered Madison University (now Colgate) as a special student to study for the ministry. At the outbreak of war he consented to drill some of the students; the resulting company, filled up to requisite numbers by the young men of the town, volunteered for service. With a captain's commission Broady entered the Ninety-first New York Regiment and saw action in thirty-

---

[83] He spent many hours teaching sword exercises to the officers of the regiment. When the surgeon told him that he must lose a leg, he replied, "Well, one pair of boots will last me now as long as two pairs will you." Abraham J. Palmer, *The History of the Forty-eighth Regiment New York State Volunteers in the War for the Union, 1861–1865* (Brooklyn, 1885), 8, 188, 204; Hokanson, *Swedish Immigrants,* 108.

[84] See Hokanson, *Swedish Immigrants,* 117, 136, for Brydolf; see *ibid.,* 116, for Gustafson.

five engagements, including such significant battles as Gettysburg, Mine Run, and the Wilderness. In the last battle named he was transferred to the Sixty-first New York with the rank of lieutenant colonel. He served under General Hancock and was entrusted with the command of three brigades at the Battle of Reams Station, where he received a wound in his leg. Upon his recovery he submitted his resignation, as the war was near its end and he was eager to resume his theological study. Hancock, who had already recommended him for a brigadiership, was disappointed and urged him to remain, but Broady insisted on his decision. An unusual honor was accorded him by President Lincoln: he was given the rank of colonel in the Regular Army with the right to retain that rank after the close of the war. The Norwegian was Ole C. Johnson, second in command of the Scandinavian Regiment, who was captured at Chickamauga and conveyed to Libby Prison, from which he escaped and made his way to his regiment. Throughout the rest of the war he had command of the Scandinavian Regiment, though without the rank of colonel.[85]

[85] For the fullest account of Broady, see *ibid.*, 106–108. For Johnson, see Blegen (ed.), *Civil War Letters of Colonel Heg*, 42; but the best account by far is in J. A. Johnson, *Det Skandinaviske Regiments Historie*, 109–11. He was far better educated than most of his fellow soldiers, as he had attended Albion Academy and Beloit College.

CHAPTER TEN

Lower-Ranking Officers

To ATTEMPT to enumerate all the foreign-born majors of the various services who fought in the Civil War would be tedious to the reader and unrewarding. Hence, only a few examples of each nationality, who for one reason or another were outstanding, will be brought forward. As usual, the Germans far outnumbered all others. A hasty count indicates about fifty majors of German nativity alone, but this is probably far from complete. Sometimes an officer came from a distinguished family, as was the case with Major Karl Schäfer von Bernstein of the Fifth Iowa Cavalry, whose father was a minister of war in Hesse-Darmstadt and who had himself been a military officer. Another member of the titled class from Prussia, Anton von Puchelstein, served on Blenker's staff and became a favorite member of his round table. Christoph von Degenfeld—who was, like Von Puchelstein, a former Prussian officer—carried on the family tradition by receiving a military education in Germany and applying it in the civil strife of another country, to which he had come in his youth with several adventurous friends. The members of the Twenty-sixth Ohio, of which he was appointed major, were selected from the entire state with extraordinary care, and experienced officers were sought in order to make the men ready for battle in the minimum of time. The rapid advance in military training made by this regiment was ascribed to the efforts of Major von Degenfeld. After a year under Rosecrans he laid down his commission to enter, as captain, the Twelfth Ohio Cavalry, an arm of the service more to his taste.[1] A wound received at Saltville, Virginia, in October, 1864, after causing him long suffering, proved fatal.

Klemens Landgräber, who rose to be chief of artillery of the Osterhaus Division, was a bold, brave man and one of the best artillerists of the West; he bore universally the nickname of "Flying Dutchman," a title which

---

[1] For Von Bernstein, see Kaufmann, *Die Deutschen im Bürgerkriege*, 547; for Von Puchelstein, *ibid.*, 539; for Von Degenfeld, *ibid.*, 491. A part of a key which the last-named carried in his pocket was driven into his body with the bullet, and neither could be extracted. See also, "Major C. M. Degenfeld," in *Der Deutsche Pionier*, X (1878–1879), 223–24. Von Degenfeld appears in *Official War Records*, Ser. 1, XII, Pt. 1, p. 904.

he acquired in May, 1863, at the siege of Vicksburg.[2] Louis P. Henning-hausen was one of the Germans living in Richmond before the war; but when he was threatened with imprisonment for teaching a mulatto to read, he moved to Baltimore, where he helped to organize the Turner companies of Baltimore and Washington. When war came, he served as major of the Forty-sixth New York Frémont Regiment. The number of German officers serving in the Union artillery and cavalry is strikingly large.[3] Major Andrew Brickel, commander of the Battalion of Light Artillery raised in Buffalo, fought through the entire war and was one of the best-known artillerists in the Army of the Potomac. One lone Pole, Ladislaus E. Koniuszewski, held the rank of major. The writer Miecislaus Haiman classifies him as a captain, but the evidence to the contrary in the *Official War Records* is indisputable. He went to the field as commander of Company A in the First Missouri; but by September 21, 1862, he was serving as major in the Twenty-sixth Missouri, and he was twice referred to by that title by his commanding officer.[4]

The Swiss major, who was distinguished for organizing in Highland, Illinois, the Swiss Sharpshooter Company of Hecker's Illinois regiment, is one of the most interesting and dramatic of the foreign figures in the Union army. Starting as a lieutenant in the Twenty-fourth Illinois, Emil Frey became a major in the Eighty-second Illinois—partly, perhaps, because he was an intimate friend of Hecker. He fought with distinction at Chancellorsville, in recognition of which service he was promoted to a majority on the battlefield; and he led a part of the regiment at Gettysburg, where he was captured by the foe. He was, however, most widely known for his long imprisonment at Libby Prison and his unfortunate selection by lot as one of three Union prisoners to be held by Jefferson Davis' order as hostages for three Confederate officers who had been condemned to death as spies by a Union court-martial. In case of execution of the three

---

[2] His batteries planted on a height, Landgräber saw that he could seize an excellent position if he advanced along the narrow ridge of the hill; but the enemy had trenches there, and furthermore, the line was covered with batteries. He asked his men if they dared to move against the dangerous stretch. "If you will ride ahead, we will follow," was the reply. On the one side the hill rose steeply; on the other lay the trenches of the foe. Landgräber got possession of the desired position and then was able to send his cannon balls into the backs of the foe. As he later passed the Thirty-sixth Iowa, which had been saved by his bold stroke, the entire regiment gave three cheers and a tiger for the "Flying Dutchman." Kaufmann, *Die Deutschen im Bürgerkriege*, 525–26.

[3] See *ibid.*, 511–12, for Hennighausen.

[4] See Haiman, *Polish Past in America*, 112. Compare with *Official War Records*, Ser. 1, XVIII, Pt. 1, pp. 102, 104.

Confederates, no power on earth, they were assured, could save them from a like fate. Other Southern officers were placed by the United States in solitary imprisonment in reprisal, but ultimately the matter of the execution was dropped. Though they were incarcerated in July, 1863, it was not until January 14, 1865, that their exchange was at last effected.[5]

The number of Hungarians holding the rank of major, just as was true of the number of Hungarians holding the various other ranks, was far beyond the proportion to be expected, considering how few there were of that nationality in the entire army. There were no less than fifteen Hungarian majors in the Union volunteer army. In this group were several names to which there has been occasion to refer earlier. A majority of them had had experience in the Honvéd army. Julian Kuné will be recalled as the Hungarian who was induced to help organize the Twenty-fourth Illinois, chiefly among Germans, and then found himself maneuvered into third place as major, although he had had experience in the field in Hungary and had been awarded a medal for his services while still a youth not yet twenty years old. Ordered with the regiment to Alton, Illinois, he soon found an opportunity to go to St. Louis to organize a company of mounted infantry and resigned his position of major toward the end of 1861 with an insignificant American war record.[6]

Albert Ruttkay was a nephew of Louis Kossuth, son of the latter's sister Louise. In the American war he served under General Asboth as major of the First Florida Cavalry. In September, 1864, he took part with Asboth and a cousin, Ladislaus Zsulavszky, in the fighting near Choctawhatchee Bay, where the Unionists took many Confederate prisoners. He won praise for his share in an expedition from Barrancas in the following November. By late spring of 1865 he was ordered to the Department of the Gulf to the staff of General Nathaniel P. Banks. Though, unlike his elder brothers, Raphael Rombauer had been too young for service in the Hungarian Revolution, he served in the National Guard at the outbreak of war in his new country. He then became a major of artillery of the First Illinois Light

[5] Kaufmann, *Die Deutschen im Bürgerkriege*, 498–500. Emil Frey published an article entitled "My American Experiences," in *North American Review*, CLVIII (1894), 129–39. So far as the author's researches have been able to reveal, A. G. Studer of the Fifteenth Iowa was the only other Swiss of this rank. See Kaufmann, *Die Deutschen im Bürgerkriege*, 555; *Official War Records*, Ser. I, X, Pt. 1, p. 289.

[6] Vasvary, *Lincoln's Hungarian Heroes*, 63–64; Pivány, *Hungarians in the American Civil War*, 33, 56. Kuné had had a truly romantic career after the Hungarian revolution, in Turkey, where he was forced to become a Mohammedan.

Artillery in the West Tennessee District, where he commanded seven batteries.

Charles Mundee is in all probability identical with the Captain Mándy of the Sixth Hussar Regiment in the Hungarian army. Enlisting as a captain in a Kansas regiment on August 24, 1861, he was promoted to the rank of major just a year later for bravery in several battles. For distinguished service at the Battle of Petersburg, where he led the division with disregard of personal danger and contributed to the victory by his example and by the skill with which he handled the command, he was brevetted brigadier general in April, 1865.[7] It speaks well for the Germans of the Fifty-eighth Ohio, a regiment composed largely of men of that nationality, that they were willing to accept a Hungarian for their major because of his experience as an officer in the Hungarian revolt. The same was true in the case of Andrew Gálfy-Gállik, a man who had been a merchant prior to the revolt and who had settled in Cincinnati after his flight to America. He saw unusually varied service in the American war, was taken prisoner at the battle at Chickasaw Bayou, and after he was exchanged, took service on the gunboat *Mound City*.[8]

Among the Scandinavians who attained the rank of major, there were none whose names would be readily recognized by the average American reader. Probably the name of Charles M. Reese has faded largely from the memory even of descendants of Danes in the country, though he is one of the very few of this nationality who rose to any prominence in the Civil War. He probably attained his rank partly by virtue of his experience in the Danish War of 1848, and partly by virtue of a wide acquaintance with Scandinavians as editor of *Nordstjernen* (North Star) and later of *Folkbladet* (People's Paper) in Chicago. At the outbreak of the war he organized an infantry company among Scandinavians in Chicago; but, like Stohlbrand's artillery company, it was not accepted. He then served as adjutant in Hecker's Jägers until he was named major in the Scandinavian Regiment of Wisconsin. Unfortunately, this Dane seems to have

[7] For Ruttkay, see Piványi, *Hungarians in the American Civil War*, 58, and Vasvary, *Lincoln's Hungarian Heroes*, 79–80; for Rombauer, see Vasvary, *Lincoln's Hungarian Heroes*, 75–76, and Piványi, *Hungarians in the American Civil War*, 58; for Mundee, see Vasvary, *Lincoln's Hungarian Heroes*, 68–69. See also Julian Kuné, *Reminiscences of an Octogenarian Hungarian Exile* (Chicago, 1911), *passim*.

[8] Vasvary, *Lincoln's Hungarian Heroes*, 55. Gálfy-Gállik appears in the American records merely as "Gallfy." He attained the rank of major only late in the war, for as late as March, 1864, he is listed as captain. See *Official War Records*, Ser. 1, XXXII, Pt. 2, p. 303. For the fact of capture, see *Official War Records*, Ser. 2, V, p. 856. Only Zsulavszky fails to appear in the *Official War Records*.

been a misfit with his Norwegian and Swedish cousins, and so it was, apparently, with satisfaction that Colonel Heg viewed his departure.[9]

Swedish writers have asserted that there were four Swedish majors, but only one seems to have been officially recorded. Eric Forsse, who led the company of Swedish Union Guards of Bishop Hill into service in September, 1861, as Company D of the Fifty-seventh Illinois, rose to be major of the regiment.[10]

As might be expected from their general record, the Irishmen of the rank of major were comparatively numerous and manifested the usual Celtic dash. Outstanding among them was Henry O'Neill, who came to the United States in 1860 after twelve years service in the East India Company (including service throughout the Sepoy Rebellion). He became major in the Corn Exchange Regiment of Philadelphia and attained a lieutenant-colonelcy by brevet. Patrick F. Dyer, commissioned captain at the early age of twenty-three, made good his escape from Salisbury Prison Camp to serve as major in the Thirteenth Tennessee Cavalry from its organization to its muster-out. Thomas Connolly, who became major of a native New Hampshire regiment, was made a brevet captain in the United States Regular Army for his services at the siege of Port Hudson, Louisiana. Another son of Ireland, John H. Donovan, of the Sixty-ninth New York, engaged in many battles, suffered the loss of an eye and capture by the Confederates at Malvern Hill, and rejoined his regiment only to be wounded again at Fredericksburg and relegated to the Veteran Reserve Corps as early as August, 1863. In the Battle of Fredericksburg he secured the rank of major, but later he also received, in recognition of his

---

[9] Madison *Emigranten*, February 3, 1862; Chicago *Hemlandet*, January 29, 1862; Blegen (ed.), *Civil War Letters of Colonel Heg*, 125.

[10] For Forsse, who appears in Heitman's work, see Hokanson, *Swedish Immigrants*, 115. Hokanson also named as major John Swainson, a Minnesota Swede, who, Hokanson claimed, became quartermaster with the rank of major; Eric Bergland; and John V. Ahlström, son of a Swedish composer, who had had military experience in a Swedish military academy and in the Upland Dragoons before coming to New Jersey in 1850 to open a music shop in Red Bank. As organizer of Company G, Fourteenth New Jersey Regiment, he had special claim to office but did not become even a lieutenant until July, 1862. Ahlström is recorded as becoming major in the Third New Jersey Cavalry. *Ibid.*, 114, 116, 108–109. Chicago *Hemlandet*, October 23, 1861, reports that L. R. Holmburgh was rewarded with a major's commission after the siege of Lexington, Missouri. Heitman is not, of course, infallible, but the writer finds no evidence in this book or in the *Official War Records* that any of the above except Forsse saw service as major during the war. Bergland joined the Regular Army after the war and attained the rank of major, but not until 1895. See Heitman, *Historical Register and Dictionary*, I, 213. Swainson held no officer's rank, for he appears on the records of the Adjutant General's Office in Minnesota as a private in Company K, Second Minnesota Cavalry, serving from January, 1864, to May, 1866.

gallantry, a colonelcy by brevet in the general passing-out of honors in March, 1865. Joseph O'Keefe, major in the Second New York Cavalry, fell in the desperate charge on the enemy's breastworks at Five Forks, but he had the satisfaction of receiving a brevet lieutenant–colonelcy on March 13 before his death on April 2 from wounds sustained in the battle.[11]

Thomas J. Barry, major in the Sixteenth Michigan Infantry, and Major (B. W. C.?) Massett, who entered the army with the rank of major of cavalry after the death of his son at Fair Oaks, are examples of Englishmen who attained this rank. The latter, contrary to the usual practice of British, had long before become an American citizen.[12] Of peculiar interest is George Wilson, who combined, as it were, several nationalities in his one person. Born in Hamburg of English parents, he followed an elder brother to Christiania, where he grew up, attended school, was confirmed, and became to all intents and purposes a Norwegian. In 1858 he came with some friends to America, and at the outbreak of war entered the Scandinavian Regiment as a second lieutenant. He rose in rank until he was serving after Colonel Heg's death as lieutenant colonel, though he was enrolled only as major because the regiment did not have the requisite numbers for the full complement of officers.

Major Francis Yehl of the Gardes Lafayette, who was a model of *sang-froid* at the Battle of Williamsburg, and Edward G. Mathey, who rose from first sergeant and engaged in many actions as major with the Eighty-first Indiana Regiment, had both been born in France. The name of Felix Agnus is not altogether unknown to students of this period of history. Living in New York in 1861, he enlisted in the Fifth New York, took on the duties of sergeant at once, and rose rapidly to be a major in the One Hundred and Sixty-fifth New York by September, 1863. He received three brevets on the same date on the eve of the close of the war: a lieutenant-colonelcy for gallantry at Gaines's Mill, a colonelcy for gal-

<hr/>

[11] For O'Neill, see *History of the Corn Exchange Regiment, 118th Pennsylvania Volunteers,* 641; for Dyer, see Samuel W. Scott and Samuel P. Angel, *History of the Thirteenth Regiment, Tennessee Volunteer Cavalry, U.S.A. . . .* (Philadelphia, [1903]), 276; for Connolly, see Henry (ed.), *Military Record of Civilian Appointments,* I, 280, and for Donovan, p. 297; for O'Keefe, see Willard Glazier, "The Harris Light," in Fox (comp.), *New York at Gettysburg,* III, 1108.

[12] Barry is found in the Regimental Descriptive Book and is duly recorded in Heitman's work; for Massett, see Tenny, *The Military and Naval History of the Rebellion in the United States,* 758, 759. Lieutenant Colonel W. C. Massett, recorded by Heitman, was apparently his son; a Benjamin W. C. Massett, English-born, became a paymaster in November, 1862. The similarity of initials suggests that this is the father referred to in the text. Heitman (comp.), *Historical Register and Dictionary,* I, 695. This man died in July, 1863.

lantry at the Battle of Port Hudson, and a brigadiership for meritorious service during the entire war.[13]

The record of the foreign-born who assumed the responsibility of directing companies in return for the honor of being called captain may appropriately begin with our Anglo-Saxon cousins, if with them may be joined, for once (by virtue of their being fellow subjects of the British crown), the turbulent Irish. Frequently the Union benefited from their experience in the British army. Captain Robert Loudon, who had served eight years in the English cavalry, distinguished himself with the Harris Light Cavalry in a hundred actions and, with a battalion, cut his way through the columns of Stuart, Lee, and Wade Hampton on the plains of Brandy Station.[14] Another such Englishman who had had several years in the British army was William A. Berry, who enlisted among the first in a Connecticut company for the three months campaign; he was then induced to enter the Second New York Artillery as a lieutenant, from which post he rose to the captaincy while on garrison duty at Washington. His regiment was not called to the front until early in 1864; then it participated in one of the battles near Petersburg, where Berry fell, a sacrifice to his adopted country.[15] Frederick Hurst, after serving thirty days with the Seventh New York Militia, proved a capable recruiting officer for the Forty-eighth New York regiment, in which he promptly became captain of Company K. A daring officer, he was so severely wounded in the assault on Fort Wagner that he died a few days later in Charleston in the hands of the foe.[16] English-born but long resident in Philadelphia, Alfred Macqueen enlisted in the One Hundred and Eighteenth Pennsylvania at its formation, taking part in every battle and skirmish in which the regiment was engaged.[17] One Scotchman of this rank merits mention. Captain John Scott, who had emigrated from Glasgow to Pennsylvania and learned the carpentry trade, entered the service as a private in the

[13] For Yehl, see De Trobriand, *Quatre Ans de Campagnes*, I, 196; for Mathey, see Henry (comp.), *Military Record of Civilian Appointments*, I, 169. "Jehl" does appear in Heitman's book, but De Trobriand would not be mistaken about the spelling of the names of his field officers. Agnus appears in Heitman (comp.), *Historical Register and Dictionary*, I, 154.

[14] Fox (comp.), *New York at Gettysburg*, III, 1108–1109. See also *Official War Records*, Ser. 1, XLIII, Pt. 1, p. 978.

[15] Dana, *The Annals of Norwich*, 241–42.

[16] Palmer, *The History of the Forty-eighth Regiment New York State Volunteers*, 208, 308; *Official War Records*, Ser. 1, LIII, p. 77.

[17] *History of the Corn Exchange Regiment, 118th Pennsylvania Volunteers*, 642. Philadelphia had been his home for eighteen years. Macqueen does not appear in the *Official War Records*.

Corn Exchange Regiment and passed through the various grades to the captaincy of Company I. He fell at Dabny's Mill at the very close of the war, February 6, 1865.[18]

Several Canadians attained the rank of captain: George A. Gale, who moved to New York when only six years old and who after the three months tour of duty re-enlisted in Company G of the Thirty-third New York, of which he became captain by December, 1862; George Be[ar]id, who was promoted from second lieutenant of Company I to captain of Company A, Sixteenth Michigan Infantry; and Hiram Andres, possibly a French-Canadian, who by August, 1864, held rank as captain in the commissary department and later won a brevet majorship for efficient service.[19]

None covered themselves with more glory than the young captains who had come from the Emerald Isle, and among this valiant band of men, those who led the companies in the Irish Legion and the Irish Brigade were outstanding. Patrick F. Clooney enlisted as a private in the famous Sixty-ninth Militia almost immediately after his arrival in New York in July, 1861. After the return of this regiment from Bull Run, he organized a company for the Irish Brigade and received a captain's commission in the Eighty-eighth New York. He was present at all the battles on the Peninsula, but he fell at Antietam, where although injured he had insisted on remaining on duty until the fatal bullet entered his body.[20] Captain D. Shanley of Company D, Sixty-ninth New York, was another officer who died of wounds received at Antietam, after having been captured with Colonel Mulligan at Lexington, Missouri, and then exchanged, only to join Meagher's brigade and share in many hard-fought battles before Antietam.[21] A prime favorite with General Meagher was Captain Maxwell O'Sullivan of the Eighty-eighth, whom the general regarded "as the *beau ideal* of the dashing, cultivated gentleman" and whom he delighted to have about him for his fund of wit and anecdotes and his rich, mellow voice; the older man seemed to find O'Sullivan's inexhaustible animal

[18] Scott's body fell into the hands of the enemy and was never recovered. *History of the Corn Exchange Regiment, 118th Pennsylvania Volunteers,* 644.

[19] For Gale, see David W. Judd, *The Story of the Thirty-third N.Y.S. Vols.; or Two Years Campaigning in Virginia and Maryland* (Rochester, 1864), Appendix, 18–19; for Beaird, see Company Descriptive Books A–E, Sixteenth Michigan Regiment; for Andres, see Heitman, *Historical Register and Dictionary,* I, 165.

[20] New York *Irish-American,* October 11, 1862. Since Clooney did not arrive in New York until July, 1861, it is possible that he should be classified as a knight-errant, but data is lacking for a clear classification.

[21] *Ibid.,* October 16, 1862.

spirits peculiarly refreshing.[22] In the One Hundred and Sixteenth Pennsylvania, Captain John O'Farrell (who commanded the Color Squadron in, and was so determined to share the fate of, Company I that he declined several promotions) and Timothy Hennessey (who had left a lucrative law practice in Philadelphia to lead Company G of this same regiment to the war, and who was recognized as a scholar-soldier) were outstanding. Frank Welpley, who had been first sergeant in one of the companies of the Sixty-ninth New York Militia, first rose to prominence and popularity for his work in the Fenian Brotherhood and was sent to Ireland to represent the Phoenix Brigade at the funeral of Terence McManus. When Corcoran organized the Irish Legion in the fall of 1862, Welpley was appointed a captain, and he participated in every battle of the Legion until he was killed at the Battle of Reams Station in August, 1864.[23]

Personal popularity often enabled a foreign-born, as it did the native, to rally a sufficient number of his countrymen for a company. Such was the case with Thomas O'Neil, who belonged to a family of fighters and who had just demonstrated his fearlessness in the three months campaign; for when his name was announced as captain for a company for the Twenty-fifth Massachusetts to be recruited in Worcester among the Irish, many of his countrymen rushed to his standard. When told by the surgeon that he could not survive the wound he had received at Cold Harbor on June 3, 1864, he regretted that he had not two lives to give for his adopted country.[24]

As pointed out earlier, frequently foreign regiments had foreign-born officers. This was true also with companies, and thus we find Colonel

[22] "Max" died of wounds caused by a fire in his tent. The reporter "Gallowglass" gives a vivid picture of O'Sullivan. Born into a good family, he was educated for the law and practiced it for several years in Ireland. He also became a member of various musical societies in Cork and Dublin, as he had a fine voice. He had come to New York in 1860, and by the beginning of the Civil War he was connected with the choir of St. Bridget's Church, acting as leader of the Harmonic School attached to it. He had served faithfully with the Sixty-ninth Militia during the three-month campaign; when Meagher tendered him a captaincy for the Brigade, he promptly organized a company, so that at the departure of the Brigade he paraded the best-drilled company. New York Irish-American, April 19, 26, 1862.

[23] See Cavanagh, Memoirs of Gen. Meagher, 407–408, for Welpley. This Hennessey is not to be confused with Major Timothy Hennessey of the Fifth Pennsylvania Cavalry. He died in San Francisco on January 15, 1861.

Terence McManus was one of the many Irish exiles in America. In order that he might influence his native land even in death, the Fenian Brotherhood put his remains on a ship leaving New York on October 19 and sent them back to Ireland to be buried there.

[24] Abijah P. Marvin, History of Worcester in the War of the Rebellion (Worcester, Mass., 1880), 126–27. O'Neil's uncle James fell at the battle of Talavera, and his father was wounded at Waterloo.

Stephen J. McGroarty starting his rather remarkable career by commanding a company in the Irish Tenth Ohio; Captain James O'Reilly heading Company C in the Sixty-ninth Pennsylvania, another Irish regiment; Patrick McGraw, who had served in the British army a total of fourteen years, serving as captain of Irish Company K in the Thirty-third New York and remaining with the regiment till the close of its two years campaign; and Lawrence O'Connor, as captain of the Fifth New York Cavalry, seeing service in many raids and battles under General Sheridan up to the time of the surrender at Appomattox.[25]

But there were also foreign-born serving as officers in native companies who had had, apparently, no special military training. Cases in point are the following: Captain Daniel B. Sullivan of Company I, Sixty-seventh New York; John W. Sweetman, who rose from a noncommissioned post to a captaincy in the Fourth New York Heavy Artillery; and John Quay, who had come to the United States from northern Ireland at the tender age of six months and who commanded in the One Hundred and Twenty-fifth New York, losing his life in one of the last battles of the war.[26] Sometimes Irishmen became captains by rising to the post in the service of the Regular Army. In this category are Captain Robert E. A. Crofton, who was appointed captain in the Sixteenth United States Infantry in May, 1861, and, despite hard battles and meritorious service, never rose to a higher rank except by brevet; and George McGown, who likewise received, during the war, promotions only from second lieutenant to captain, although he had been in the United States Army since 1858.[27]

Research has revealed that there were thirty-four Swedish captains, counting soldiers of fortune and knights-errant who were of this rank. There is hardly a name in the list which will strike a responsive chord in

[25] McGroarty was severely wounded while rallying his men around the colors at Carnifex Ferry. Moore (ed.), Rebellion Record, III, Pt. 2, p. 42; for O'Reilly, see Nicholson (comp.), Pennsylvania at Gettysburg, I, 405; for McGraw, see Judd, The Story of the Thirty-third N.Y.S. Vols., Appendix, 23; for O'Connor, see Henry (ed.), Military Record of Civilian Appointments, I, 174–75.

[26] For Sweetman, see Kirk, Heavy Guns and Light: A History of the 4th New York Heavy Artillery, Pt. 2, 473–74; for Quay, see Simons, A Regimental History The One Hundred and Twenty-fifth New York State Volunteers, 282–83.

[27] Henry (ed.), Military Record of Civilian Appointments, I, 287, 389. Of all the Irish captains noted, only the following are identified as captains in the Official War Records: Patrick F. Clooney, Ser. 1, XIX, Pt. 1, p. 201; Frank Welpley (in Official War Records, Francis Welpley), Ser. 1, XLII, Pt. 1, p. 132; Lawrence L. O'Connor (with the Fifth New York Cavalry), Ser. 1, XXV, Pt. 1, p. 43; Daniel B. Sullivan, Ser. 1, XI, Pt. 1, p. 901 (died of wounds received at the Battle of Fair Oaks, ibid., 1076); John Quay, Ser. 1, XLVI, Pt. 1, p. 598; and Robert E. A. Crofton, Ser. 1, XLIX, Pt. 2, p. 540.

the mind of the average reader, but a few names might be selected as suggestive of the group. Captain Eric Johnson represents the type of leader who was politically minded. The following story about him is possibly worth retelling, though Hokanson, from whose book it was taken, failed to give his authority for it. The Illinois Democrats took advantage of the absence of many Republicans at the front to frame a new constitution containing several proslavery clauses, which they submitted to the voters. The commission sent to the field to take the vote of Illinois soldiers sought to confuse the simple-minded and foreign-born voters with such questions as, "You do not want you sister married to a Negro when you return home, do you?" The inevitable "No" was recorded as his vote. When the Swedes of Company D of the Fifty-seventh Illinois realized that they were being tricked, they requested Captain Johnson to vote first in order to guide them; he voted against the pro-slave proposals with such consequent effect on his men that one of the commission re-marked of Company D that it was the "da—st black abolition company in the service." Captain Carl Arosenius of Company C, Forty-third Illinois, seems to have been another politically minded officer, for he reported to *Hemlandet* the results of the voting among some Swedish soldiers of the presidential election in 1864.[28]

Captain Charles E. Landström was elected second lieutenant in recognition of his work in helping to organize Company B, Fifteenth Iowa Volunteers. However, he was the sort of man who naturally forces promotion by the quality of his service, and so he became a first lieutenant by his distinguished work at Shiloh and in the advance on Corinth and was advanced to captain by virtue of his share in the expedition against Vicksburg. George F. Jocknick probably won his captaincy of Company I in the Third New York Cavalry by the recognized Swedish qualities of reliability and attention to duty through three years of service. G. F. Lindquist, who gave up his restaurant in New York City to enlist in the volunteer army, rose from the ranks to a captaincy in the Fifth New York Volunteers. His promotions, which were achieved by gallantry in action, were certainly well earned, for he took part in no less than thirty engagements. Although it is only natural for the reader to assume that several Swedes were captains in the Scandinavian Regiment of Wisconsin, there was, as a matter of fact, but one, as stated earlier—Captain Charles Gustaveson, of Company F, a Wisconsin farmer. As a soldier who had seen service in the Royal Life Guard for three years in his native country,

[28] Hokanson, *Swedish Immigrants*, 62. For Arosenius, see *ibid.*, 64.

and also as a volunteer private in the Mexican War, he was an acceptable choice to head Company F—a choice which might also constitute a bid for Swedish enlistments. He was soon regarded as the best swordsman in the regiment. He was another of the many captives taken at Chickamauga but was released in time to rejoin his company in 1864, before Atlanta.[29] Captain Charles Corneliuson headed a company in the Twenty-seventh Wisconsin Regiment.

In the Scandinavian regiment were congregated the largest number of Norwegian captains—in fact, with a few exceptions, the only ones. Andrew Torkildsen of Chicago had been largely instrumental in recruiting Company A from among his Norse countrymen in that city and so to him went the honor of leading it; the choice was a natural one, especially in view of the fact that he had had almost seven years of experience in the Swedish-Norwegian army. The Norseman who headed Company B, Ole C. Johnson, was destined to rise to the rank of lieutenant colonel and ultimately—after Colonel Heg's death and his own release from a Confederate prison—to head the regiment. Frederick R. Berg served as captain of Company C only until June 12, 1862, when he resigned; he was succeeded by Hans Hansen, of Norway, Wisconsin, who died in the hands of the Confederates from wounds received at Chickamauga. The captain of Company E, John Ingmundsen, hailed from Neshonoc, Wisconsin; he fell at Murfreesboro, the first officer of the regiment to be killed. Company I retained its first captain, August Gasman of Waupun, only until April, 1862, when Reynard Cook took his place. Company K, which was recruited in Minnesota and northern Iowa, elected—not unnaturally—a Minnesota man for its first officer, the well-educated Mons Grinager of Freeborn County. He served continuously through the entire war except during a convalescence from severe wounds sustained at Murfreesboro and during the winter of 1864, when he was detached for recruiting duty.[30]

[29] For Landström, see *ibid.*, 117–18; for Gustafson, *ibid.*, 119; for Jocknick, *ibid.*, 99; for Lindquist, *ibid.*, 101. For Gustafson, usually spelled Gustaveson in *Official War Records* and by the Norwegians, see also Blegen (ed.), *Civil War Letters of Colonel Heg*, 52, 53 n., and J. A. Johnson, *Det Skandinaviske Regiments Historie*, 124. See Appendix, Section D, for the full list of Swedish captains. See Chapter VI of text.

Of the seven captains named in the text, the following are identified in the *Official War Records:* Karl Arosenius, Ser. 1, XXIV, Pt. 2, p. 434; Charles Gustaveson (killed at Chickamauga), Ser. 1, XXX, Pt. 1, p. 534; and George F. Jocknick, Ser. 1, IX, pp. 343–44.

[30] For the Norwegian captains in the Fifteenth Wisconsin Regiment, see Blegen (ed.), *Civil War Letters of Colonel Heg*, 52, 53 n. The best account is found in J. A. Johnson, *Det Skandinaviske Regiments Historie*, 118–19, 120–21, 122–23, 125–26 (for Berg and Gas-

One other Norwegian of this rank might be mentioned: Asgrim K. Skaro was, according to the editor of *Hemlandet,* the first Norwegian to organize a company in Minnesota. He served for a long time in one of the state regiments, being active, apparently, at St. Peter, Minnesota, during the Indian uprising among the Sioux of that state in the fall of 1862. He later became captain of Company D of the Ninth Minnesota and in that capacity led it, on December 15–16, 1864, at the Battle of Nashville, where he was killed.[31]

The only Dane found to have borne the title of captain was one Joseph Mathiesen, promoted from a lieutenancy to the post of second captain of Company B in the Scandinavian Regiment. Upon his promotion, one notes, each of the Scandinavian countries was represented in the headship of the companies, thus justifying the name chosen for the regiment.[32]

Among the twenty-five captains of Hungarian birth, Theodore Majthenyi stands head and shoulders above the rest; he was, moreover, probably the only Hungarian of this rank whose name was well known to his American contemporaries. Zagonyi's gallant lieutenant and his father, Baron Joseph Majthenyi (a member of the landed nobility and of parliament, and a prominent refugee) came to their new home in America in 1851—first to New Buda and then to a farm near Davenport, Iowa. The younger Majthenyi enlisted for service in the Civil War as a sergeant in the Second Iowa Infantry, which was sent to Frémont's army; there he remained until August, 1861, when he became lieutenant and adjutant in Frémont's Cavalry Guard, of which Zagonyi was commander. He was the only Hungarian, besides his leader, who participated in the famous cavalry charge at Springfield. After the Guard was disbanded, he obtained a commission in April, 1862, as captain of the First Indiana Cavalry, with which he served until December, 1864.[33]

Also outstanding among captains of Hungarian birth were two members of a very prominent family, Roderick and Roland Rombauer, both of

---

man, see Appendix, 8, 22). Three appear in the *Official War Records:* Ole C. Johnson, John C. Ingmundsen, and August Gasman.

[31] Chicago *Hemlandet,* February 8, 1865. Skaro's home was in St. Peter, Minnesota. See *Official War Records,* Ser. 1, XIII, pp. 644, 772, for his command during the Indian uprising in that state in 1862.

[32] J. A. Johnson, *Det Skandinaviske Regiments Historie,* Appendix, 5.

[33] Shortly after the war he returned with his father to Hungary, taking with him his American wife. There he became an officer in the newly reorganized Hungarian army. He returned to America without his family in 1875, from which time all trace of him seems to have been lost. See Vasvary, *Lincoln's Hungarian Heroes,* 65–66. Piványi, *Hungarians in the American Civil War,* 26, 57.

whom had served in the Hungarian revolt. Although the family was wretchedly poor, as he states in his autobiography, Roderick managed somehow to study law at Harvard and then to settle about 1858 in St. Louis, where he was a struggling lawyer at the outbreak of the war. He enlisted as a private in the First Missouri Infantry and then became a captain in the United States Missouri Reserves. His company took part in the capture of Camp Jackson and rendered some service in southwest Missouri. After his recovery from a violent attack of camp fever, he served on Frémont's staff in West Virginia for several months in 1862; but after 1863 he dropped out of the war to pursue his personal career. Roland was twenty-four years old when he enlisted as sergeant in the First Missouri Infantry. He served as captain in the First Florida Cavalry under General Asboth and was appointed provost marshal of the District of West Florida by that commander.[34] As would be expected in a unit commanded by a Hungarian, several men of that nationality served as captains in the Garibaldi Guard: Victor Chandory, who had to leave the service early because of his health; Francis Takács, who served in the Garibaldi Guard only from May 25 to November 19, 1861, when he was discharged; and Anthony Utassy, who rose from the rank of lieutenant to that of captain in the Guards by September, 1862. M. E. Rozsafy was an artillery captain.[35]

The number of Poles who attained the rank of captain (some of them rising from the ranks) is astonishing; the research has revealed no less than twenty, and because of the failure during the war to record the nativity of commissioned officers, this number cannot be regarded as definitive. Among those who organized companies at the first call to arms were

[34] For Roderick Rombauer, see Pivány, *Hungarians in the American Civil War*, 58; Vasvary, *Lincoln's Hungarian Heroes*, 76; for Roland Rombauer, see Vasvary, *Lincoln's Hungarian Heroes*, 77; Pivány, *Hungarians in the American Civil War*, 19, 58. See also Roderick Rombauer, *The History of a Life* (St. Louis, [1903]), *passim*.

[35] For Chandory, see Vasvary, *Lincoln's Hungarian Heroes*, 49; for Takács, *ibid.*, 84; for Anthony Utassy, *ibid.*, 84. Several other captions of this nationality were George Grechenek, Gustav Kovacs, and Matthias Rozsafy, *ibid.*, 55–56, 62, 77–79.
The story of Rozsafy's activities in the Hungarian revolt reads like the wildest romance. He left school at twenty to enlist in the revolutionary movement. In his home town of Komárom he helped publish a daily paper, which contributed powerfully to sustaining the morale of the town. After the surrender of the fortress at Komárom he refused to accept a safe-conduct offered the soldiers, but went to Italy, where with several other emigrants he worked out plans for a new insurrection in different parts of the Austrian empire. They finally secured Kossuth's approval of these plans, Rozsafy and Colonel Joseph Mack even visiting Kossuth in Kütahaya to talk over the plans. Mack traveled into Hungary disguised as a Rumanian peasant with a dancing bear. He was accompanied by Figyelmessy, who was disguised as an orthodox Jew, and by Rozsafy, who posed as a French traveling salesman, though he could not speak French! When the conspiracy was discovered, the three were captured, but all succeeded in escaping. Rozsafy escaped only one day before he was to be executed. *Ibid.*, 78.

the following: Captain Adelbert Morozowicz, who organized and commanded the Ninth Independent New York Light Artillery; Lucas Soboleski, who collected the men for the Independent Company of Lancers of Missouri; Bernard J. Stampoffski, a veteran of the Mexican War who responded to Lincoln's call with Company F of the Ninth Illinois Cavalry, from Chicago; Thaddeus C. Hulanicki, who organized his own Battery L of the Second Illinois Light Artillery; and Stanislaus Mlotkowski, whose Pennsylvania battery took its name from him but was officially the Pennsylvania Independent Battery.[36]

Because of his heroic death at Belmont, there is justification for singling out Captain Alexander Bielaski. When Grant attacked the Confederate encampment at that point on November 7, 1861 General John A. McClernand's young Polish aide-de-camp, who had dismounted because his horse had been several times wounded, was shot down as he was advancing with the flag in his hand and encouraging his men to follow.[37] The example of the famous Thaddeus Kosciusko as a military engineer was honorably followed by Captain William Kossak of Missouri, who was on General Grant's staff. General Sherman considered Kossak's map of the battlefield at Shiloh the best he had seen; at Corinth Kossak supervised the construction of the Union fortifications, which were pronounced "very excellent" by Sherman; and at Vicksburg he erected new casemates to replace some which were unsatisfactory. The service of Captain Baron Wladislas Leski, aide to General McDowell, called forth from McDowell the following encomium, bestowed jointly on Leski and Captain Howard Stockton: "[They were] constantly at the front, exerting themselves with a zeal and intelligence that accomplished much for the army." [38] Captain Peter Kiolbassa was one of those foreign-born Confederate soldiers whose

[36] Most of these Polish captains merit consideration, but their comparative obscurity does not warrant extended discussion. For Morozowicz, see Haiman, Polish Past in America, 111–12; for Soboleski, Stampoffski (also spelled "Stempowski"), Mlotkowski, and Hulanicki, see ibid., 112. The writer has had to lean heavily on this work for captains, since Heitman did not record officers of so low a rank except for a special reason; and, it must again be pointed out, the Descriptive Books rarely record the nativity of commissioned officers. Haiman must have been in error in giving the Sixteenth Illinois Cavalry as the regiment in which Stampoffski served, unless he was transferred and no record of the transferal was preserved. The writer found him listed as captain of Company F in the Western Cavalry, Ninth Illinois Cavalry, in the Regimental Descriptive Book. See Appendix, Section E. Hulanicki and Mlotkowski can be found in the Official War Records.

[37] For Bielaski, see Haiman, Polish Past in America, 133–34. General John A. McClernand mentioned his death. Official War Records, Ser. 1, III, p. 277.

[38] Sherman's praise of Kossak's map is to be found in a report of April 10, 1862, ibid., Ser. 1, X, p. 254; McDowell's praise of Captain Leski, ibid., Ser. 1, XII, Pt. 2, p. 329. See also Haiman, Polish Past in America, 134–36, for Kossak; and p. 136 for Leski.

heart was not in the Southern cause, and so when he was captured he promptly enlisted as a private in an Illinois regiment and rose at length to the captaincy of the Sixth United States Cavalry.[39] In the signal service Captain Joseph Gloskowski of the Twenty-ninth New York rendered valuable service and won recognition in the official reports. At Antietam he sent "many important messages, one of which saved General Burnside from being cut off"; at Fredericksburg, "though constantly exposed to the fire of the enemy's batteries," he performed his dangerous duties; and at Chancellorsville his signals were the only means of communication between General Joseph Hooker's staff and parts of his army.[40]

The only French captains about whom we glean information are those mentioned by General de Trobriand as being in the Gardes Lafayette: Captains John J. Four, Louis Battais, Louis Demazure, and Philip Meyer —all solid men, the general declared, who sustained their companies at Williamsburg "without effort." He paid special tribute to Captain Four, who had learned war with the Chasseurs Vincennes. Mounted on the trunk of a tree, Captain Four directed with his voice and gestures the fire of his men at each point where the enemy penetrated into the barricade. Captain Battais, abandoned by his lieutenants and a dozen men who followed them, continued to command with Breton tenacity as at drill.[41] A Captain Henry J. Draime brought with him a rich background of experience when he enlisted as a private from Palmyra, Ohio, in Company B of the Thirty-third New York Volunteers. He had come with his parents from France in 1832 and had settled in Canton, Ohio. Seven years later he enlisted in the Fifth Regular United States Artillery, was soon made a noncommissioned officer, and remained in the service five years. Immediately after enlistment in 1861 he was elected second lieutenant and ultimately reached a captaincy.[42]

Several Swiss held the rank of captain. Johann Rudolf Fellman was already in his thirties when he came to this land. He was conducting a bookshop in Rochester when the war came. Enlisting in a New York regiment, he participated in the battles of Antietam, Fredericksburg, and Chancellorsville, showing such bravery that he was recommended for a captaincy. At Gettysburg a cannon ball crushed his leg, but he served in

[39] Haiman, *Polish Past in America*, 137.

[40] *Ibid.*, 134. For the other captains of this nationality see Appendix, Section E.

[41] De Trobriand, *Quatre Ans de Campagnes*, I, 197. The Christian names have been secured from the *Volunteer Army Register*.

[42] Judd, *The Story of the Thirty-third N.Y.S. Vols.*, 12–13.

the Veteran Reserve Corps to the end of the war. Leo Schumacher, who had come to Davenport, went out with the Sixteenth Iowa Volunteers and returned with a captain's commission. The most important Swiss of this rank was Rudolf Aschmann, a captain in the regiment known as Berdan's Sharpshooters, who, though forced by the loss of a leg to drop out after the Wilderness campaign,[43] nevertheless made a contribution to history by his book.

Also holding the rank of captain were a lone South American and one Italian. Louis Beirel was born in Valparaiso, Chile, but his record of devotion could scarcely have been surpassed by a native-born American citizen. He tendered his services to the government and raised—mainly by his own exertions—a full company, composed entirely of New York men; it became Company G of the First California Regiment and won an enviable reputation at Ball's Bluff. Captain Beirel avenged General Baker's death by instantly shooting his leader's assailant, and to prevent the general's body from falling into the hands of the foe, he carried it off the field under a shower of bullets. He took part in many other battles of the war and survived them all. Singularly interesting is the Italian, Achille di Vecchi, captain in the Ninth Independent Battery of Massachusetts Light Artillery, who resigned January 24, 1863, on the plea that he had been recalled to his post in the Italian army after an eighteen months absence. This writer harbors a suspicion that he was using a pretext to resign and that he really left from pique.[44]

The captains who had been born in Germany were legion; they undoubtedly ran into the hundreds. The writer identified, in a not-too-precise count, three score and ten. Of this large number, only a very few will be singled out for special mention. One meets the expected array of officers who had participated in, and gained experience from, the German revolutions of 1830 and 1848 or the Schleswig-Holstein War. Captain Bernhardt von Buggenhagen, a former officer in the Prussian Garde du Korps, who fell at Fredericksburg, led one of the companies in the Steuben

[43] For the first two mentioned, see Steinach, *Geschichte und Leben*, 117, 263; for Aschmann, see Kaufmann, *Die Deutschen im Bürgerkriege*, 479–80. Aschmann has left a good record of the military action of his company in *Drei Jahre in der Potomac Armee*, although unfortunately he has given only meager information about the personal activities of himself and his men. The first two Swiss appear in the *Official War Records*, Ser. 1, XLIII, Pt. 1, p. 981, and Ser. 1, XLIV, p. 851; and Kaufmann, *Die Deutschen im Bürgerkriege*, 479–80.

[44] For Beirel, see Mottelay and Campbell-Copeland (eds.), *The Soldier in Our Civil War*, II, 383; for Di Vecchi's resignation, see Jacket for Achille di Vecchi, in National Archives. See also for Di Vecchi the chapter on knights-errant and soldiers of fortune (Chapter XI).

regiment. Anton Vallendar, who after having been educated at a German military school had had excellent experience as a lieutenant in the Danish war against the duchies of Schleswig and Holstein, and also in the revolution of 1848, commanded a company in the Thirty-seventh Ohio Regiment.[45]

The European ties of the Old World held over into the New, as is illustrated in the case of Captain Christian Essig: he had been Sigel's adjutant in the Baden revolt, and in the Civil War he commanded a battery in Sigel's division during the campaign in Missouri; but his career was ended sadly when he drowned in the Mississippi.[46] In the German or partly German regiments was found the usual complement of German officers: Captain Charles Joseph in Company A and Frederick Schröder in Company D of the Ninth Ohio; Joseph B. Grünhut, who distinguished himself in Hecker's Eighty-second Illinois at Chancellorsville; Nicholaus Grumbach, captain of Company B in the half-German One Hundred and Forty-ninth New York, who commanded the regiment with credit at Gettysburg after all his superior officers had fallen; Theodore W. von Hencke, a renowned cavalry captain in both the German and the Union army; Ernest F. Herzberg, battery chief in the Second Wisconsin Artillery; and Oscar von Meusel of McClellan's staff, who probably paid the most bitter price exacted of any soldier, being burned in the forest at Chancellorsville. The number could be greatly extended. The captains produced their full quota of daring fighters.[47]

One might naturally suppose that the number of foreign-born holding the lowest commissioned office, that of lieutenant, would increase in pro-

[45] For Von Buggenhagen, see Kaufmann, *Die Deutschen im Bürgerkriege*, 487; for Anton Vallendar, see Executive Correspondence of the Governors of Ohio, January–May, 1862. Vallendar had to resign from the United States service because of a serious illness in March, 1862, but was soon soliciting a new commission from Governor Dennison of Ohio. He appears in *Official War Records*, Ser. 1, XLV, Pt. 1, p. 519, as captain on the staff of General Charles Crupp in January, 1865.

[46] For Captain Essig, see Kaufmann, *Die Deutschen im Bürgerkriege*, 496. His given name was secured from *Official War Records*, Ser. I, III, p. 17.

[47] For the two officers of the Ninth Ohio Regiment, see Company Descriptive Books; for Grünhut and Grumbach, see Kaufmann, *Die Deutschen im Bürgerkriege*, 505–506; Von Hencke served in the Fourth Missouri Cavalry and returned to Germany in 1870 to the very regiment in which he had served originally, only to fall in one of the battles at Metz. *Ibid.*, 511. For Herzberg, see *ibid.*, 512; for Von Meusel, see *ibid.*, 533. It was possible to check all these officers (except Grünhut) for rank by means of the *Official War Records*: Grumbach, Ser. 1, XXXVIII, Pt. 2, p. 203; Charles Joseph, Ser. 1, VII, p. 94; Frederick Schröder, Ser. 1, VII, p. 94; Von Meusel, Ser. 1, XXV, p. 638; Von Hencke, Ser. 1, XLVIII, Pt. 1, p. 1109; and Herzberg, Ser. 3, I, p. 991.

portion to the greater total number of lieutenants. As there were in the whole army rather more than twice as many lieutenants as there were captains (because an occasional company had a third lieutenant), the number of foreign-born lieutenants should be rather more than twice the number of foreign-born captains. This may have been the correct proportion, but evidence is lacking, for there were many disappointing blanks in the Descriptive Books where the nativity of the lieutenants should have been recorded. It was necessary, therefore, to depend on such information as is available in chance references in memoirs or in compilations of officers made for particular nationality groups, and on Heitman's compilations. Comments on nativity in these occur less frequently for captains than for colonels, and far less frequently for lieutenants than for captains, as is to be expected from their relatively lesser importance. Representatives of almost every nationality were, naturally, to be found. Lieutenants as well as higher officers had had experience on European battlefields. Space will be allotted to individuals only where relative importance or intrinsic interest seems to justify such detail. The Germans, oddly enough, do not stand out in such overwhelming numbers as they have exhibited in other categories.

The career of Louis Dallarmi typifies the handicaps under which the foreigner fights in a new land. After eighteen years experience in the Bavarian army, including some months of combat in the Schleswig-Holstein campaign, he came to northern New York, where he was engaged in business in 1861. He helped to recruit a company of Germans, which entered the Ninety-seventh New York Infantry. His superior military attainments would have given him a higher rank if he had but known English better. He was regarded as the best-trained line officer of his regiment. On the eve of the Battle of Antietam, he—although only a second lieutenant—was placed by Colonel Duryée in temporary command of two or three companies consolidated for this conflict; however, while marching into battle at the head of his company, he was killed.[48]

The tribute of General Meagher sent to Colonel Nugent on the death of "our gentle, gallant, noble young friend and comrade," Lieutenant Temple Emmett of the Eighty-eighth New York, is transparently sincere:

> I am grieved to the heart to hear this; for I esteemed, trusted, loved him as a favorite brother. His spotless integrity, the sweetness of his

[48] Hough, *History of Duryée's Brigade during the Campaign in Virginia under Gen. Pope*, 181. Dallarmi was in command because his captain was absent and the first lieutenant had just been suspended.

manner, the innate refinement, and the delicacy he betrayed in every word and look; the high proud character of his mind, his perfect self-possession, such utter fearlessness in battle, made us all admire and love him. Beautifully and bravely has he, in his short career as a soldier upheld the historic honor of his family, discharging at the peril of his life, the grateful duty to the country in which no name is more revered than that of Thomas Addis Emmett. In him I lose a companion [he was on Meagher's staff] affectionate and devoted, whose society brightened whilst it softened many of those ruder associations which all of us have to submit to in active military life.[49]

Emmett clearly did not belong to the group condemned by a reporter of the *Irish-American* with the following sharp words: "We have a few lieutenants of Irish-English pseudo gallantry. I feel as much ashamed of them as they do of my native land." [50]

One is impressed again by the presence of Irish officers in an Irish regiment, as Lieutenant John Mallory in Company D and Lieutenant D. C. Fannery in Company A, both in the Irish Tenth Ohio, and by the presence of foreigners in colored regiments, as John M. Hamilton, Canadian-born first lieutenant in the Nineteenth United States colored troops.

That influential pressure was brought to bear even on those responsible for appointments to this relatively minor rank was clearly betrayed by Seward's request to the French legation that report of the appointment of Oliver Bixee as first lieutenant in the Twenty-fourth New York Cavalry be conveyed to Prince Napoleon. Lesser nationalities were represented, as, the Welsh in the person of Pryce W. Bailey, first lieutenant in the Thirty-third New York, and the Scotch in the person of George Duff, a second lieutenant.[51]

Among the dozen or so Swedes who served as lieutenants three might receive special attention. The first, Lieutenant Thomas J. B. Nordenstrohl of the Ninety-ninth New York, was appointed topographical engineer for the Third Division of the Eighteenth Army Corps by General Butler; although discharged in July, 1864, he remained connected with the army

[49] New York *Irish-American*, August 15, 1862. He was not killed, but died of disease which was probably caused by war conditions. He was a grandson of the Irish-American patriot of the same name. See Thomas A. Emmett, *The Emmett Family* (New York, 1898), 322–23.

[50] New York *Irish-American*, May 31, 1862.

[51] For the officers of the Tenth Ohio, see Company Descriptive Books; for Hamilton, see Henry (comp.), *Military Record of Civilian Appointments*, II, 282; for Bixee, see Notes to the French Legation, VIII, No. 5, Division of State Department Archives, The National Archives; for Bailey, see Judd, *The Story of the Thirty-third N.Y.S. Vols.*, Appendix, 11.

at least until 1874. The second, John Adam Gustaf Mikael Schurer von Walheim, obviously of the nobility, who had formerly been a lieutenant in Västmanlands Regiment, became a second lieutenant in the Third New Jersey Artillery in 1865.[52] Finally, note may be taken of Lieutenant Joseph E. Osborn (who had Anglicized his name), son of the Reverend Mr. Esbjörn, a well-known figure among Swedish circles in the West. From Columbia, Kentucky, on March 16, 1864, Osborn wrote a letter to his father which breathes a deep sincerity and sense of responsibility. He stated that he wished to be "an honor to his family, relatives, and friends, as well as to the land which he served and the uniform he wore." He recurred repeatedly to comments on the cruel treatment accorded by Confederates to negro soldiers and their commanders.[53] Since he was then commander of an ordnance depot, he naturally reflected his interest in the muskets and ammunition on hand.

In the fairly long list of lieutenants serving in colored regiments were several Hungarians: the brothers Emil and Sigismund Zsulavszky, who functioned under their brother, Ladislaus, colonel of the Eighty-second Colored Regiment; and A. P. Zimandy, a lieutenant in the Fourth United States Colored Infantry. Likewise, Louis Tenner and Charles Utassy were lieutenants in the Garibaldi Guard; and Alexander Jekelfalussy, a former officer of the Honvéd army, served as lieutenant under Colonel Mihalotzy in the Twenty-fourth Illinois.[54] Edward Zerdahelyi represents a different type from the Hungarians hitherto encountered in this study. He was a pianist of some note, a friend and pupil of Franz Liszt. As many of the Hungarian exiles were of high birth or station, it is not strange that he came from a noble family. As an officer in the Honvéd army he was entrusted by the revolutionary Hungarian government with a large sum of money for a confidential mission to Germany, but he was captured at the border by the Austrian police and kept in a dungeon at Olmütz in heavy irons for about two years. By his refined manners and musical talents he

[52] See Hokanson, Swedish Immigrants, 101, for Nordenstrohl; for Von Walheim, ibid., 103.

[53] Osborn was evidently repeating a rumor when he reported the treatment of a sutler whom he knew personally: "Although he begged for mercy on his knees, he was chopped to pieces until there remained no piece larger than his head." This letter is preserved in the Esbjörn Collection.

[54] For Emil and Sigismund Zsulavszky, see Vasvary, Lincoln's Hungarian Heroes, 88, 89; for bare mention of Zimandy, ibid., 88; for Tenner and Utassy, ibid., 84. Jekelfalussy became conspicuous for his attitude toward an order to give up fugitive slaves caught in Union camps. He wrote Mihalotzy on June 22, 1862, that he could not obey such an order and resigned his commission, but the resignation could hardly have been acted upon, as he is known to have served two more years. Ibid., 57.

made many friends among cultivated Americans and supported himself here by his music. It is perhaps not strange that a musician reached no higher rank in the Garibaldi Guards than that of lieutenant.[55]

Of the Poles who held the rank of lieutenant, Edmund L. G. Zalinski seems of greatest intrinsic interest. In February, 1863, as a sixteen-year-old high-school lad, Zalinski ran away from his home in Syracuse to enlist in the Second New York Cavalry. Attracted to the daring young fellow, General Miles soon made him an aide-de-camp on his staff; and for his bravery in the Battle of Hatcher's Run the youth received the rank of second lieutenant, with which he emerged from the war.[56]

Data concerning the noncommissioned officers—the corporals and the sergeants—are more abundant; for the Descriptive Books frequently contain records of nationality for these petty officers when they are wanting for commissioned officers.

But the enormous numbers become so baffling that nothing more than a generalization can be attempted here. Whatever reluctance to accord commissions for high-ranking offices to foreign-born citizens may have existed on the part of Union leaders, that reluctance was not strongly apparent when it came to the offices which carried little honor but much drudgery. Without any attempt to give figures, the relative liberality with which these posts were distributed among the various nationality groups may safely be noted. In contrast with the Confederate army, where the Irish held these low posts in the greatest numbers, in the Union army the Germans outnumbered the other groups; next came the Irish, second but by no means crowding the Germans; then came the Anglo-Saxon cousins —British, Scotch, Welsh, and Canadian; trailing far behind and relatively insignificant in numbers were the Scandinavians, Hungarians, Swiss, French, and Poles. Widely scattered and utterly insignificant in numbers were the Austrians and Italians, while the representation of Russians, Dutch, and Belgians was small but by no means nonexistent.

Naturally the noncommissioned officers came from the same humble ranks from which the privates were generally drawn. In the regiments already shown to have been composed of foreign-born or to have had a large element of foreign-born, the proportion of foreigners among the

---

[55] He was personally acquainted with the most famous men of Europe of the time—Garibaldi, Mazzini, Gladstone, and Macaulay. *Ibid.*, 88; Piványi, *Hungarians in the American Civil War*, 43–44.

[56] It is interesting that Zalinski later rose to be professor of military science at the Massachusetts Institute of Technology; he also invented numerous military devices. Haiman, *Polish Past in America*, 98, 113; Heitman (comp.), *Historical Register and Dictionary*, I, 1068.

sergeants and corporals ran high. Frequently, in German or Irish companies all the noncommissioned officers were of the nationality represented
by the group. In some of the Swedish companies (as in the almost solidly
Swedish company which went out from Galesburg into the Forty-third
Illinois) all the sergeants and corporals had been born in Sweden. Almost
all the low-ranking posts in the companies of the Fifteenth Wisconsin were
held by Scandinavians.

In the average unit of the Union army, frequently three of every four
sergeants and six or seven of every eight corporals were of the same nationality as that characterizing the unit as a whole. It is a striking fact that
the other sergeant and the other two corporals were usually also foreign-
born, but of some other nationality. For instance, in a given German company, the fourth sergeant was possibly an Alsatian or a Swiss; the odd
sergeant in a Swedish company was a German; or the complement of
eight corporals in a German company was perhaps made up of five Germans, two Frenchmen, and a Scotchman. Very often, the odd one or two
"noncoms" were recorded as having been born in some state of the Union,
but even these native-born officers frequently had German or Norwegian-
sounding names which suggest that the men were of the same blood as
that predominating in the company. Where the regiments were composed
of several nationalities, as was the case with the Garibaldi Guards and the
Polish Legion, the noncommissioned officers were likely to represent several different nationalities. Occasionally, rather anomalous situations arose,
as in the One Hundred and Seventy-fifth New York, a part of the Corcoran Legion, where instead of Irishmen there were, in one of the companies, five German sergeants and seven German corporals plus one French
corporal. Even in companies constituted almost exclusively of native
Americans there were often one or more foreign-born sergeants or corporals—presumably to help whip the recruits into shape.[57]

Just as among native-born officers, both men of integrity and men of
evil propensities were present. Unlike the Americans, however, they frequently possessed a background of valuable training and military experience. Frederick Fuger, whose name properly indicates his German
nationality, was representative of the better element. Serving as a sergeant
in Battalion A of the Fourth New York Artillery, he found himself in
command after all the officers had been killed or wounded and after five
cannon had been put out of order by Pickett's attack on Cemetery Ridge

[57] These generalizations are based on the Descriptive Books for literally thousands of companies scrutinized for these data.

at Gettysburg. With the greatest courage Fuger fought on with the one cannon which could still be fired, until the battery was ordered back. For this deed he received the gold medal.[58] On the other hand, the most numerous cases of desertion by officers occurred among the noncommissioned foreign-born officers. Many of the foreign-born officers so discharged their duties as to win promotion; some were reduced in rank, and some were dismissed from the service.

[58] Kaufmann, *Die Deutschen im Bürgerkriege,* 501.

CHAPTER ELEVEN

Knights-Errant and Soldiers of Fortune*

PROBABLY no war has ever been fought in modern times, certainly not one in which a moral principle was involved, to which have not been drawn men in whom the love of justice burns brightly—knights-errant; and no war has ever been fought to which have not gravitated men to whom fighting was as the breath of life—soldiers of fortune. Certainly, there was no dearth of either in the American Civil War, on either the Northern or the Southern side; the Federal armies seemed to draw rather more than their due quota. Europe poured into the Union army hundreds of her best artillery, cavalry, and infantry officers. Some were motivated by zeal for liberty for all men, which they conceived as the actual cause for which the North was fighting; others were eager for a chance to prove their valor and military skill; still others were ambitious for the actual experience which they hoped would win them promotion in the army of the homeland.

Perhaps no better picture of the situation in regard to these adventurers is to be found than the one presented by the English journalist William Howard Russell. Writing on August 4, 1861, he said, "There are daily arrivals at Washington of military adventurers from all parts of the world, some of them with many extraordinary certificates and qualifications; but, as Mr. Seward says, it is best to detain them with the hope of employment on the Northern side, lest some legally good men should get among the rebels. Garibaldians, Hungarians, Poles, officers of Turkish and other contingents, the executory devises and reminders of European revolutions and wars, surround the State Department, and infest unsuspecting politicians with illegible testimonials in unknown tongues." [1]

There can be no question but that Seward approved and sought the enrollment of trained European officers in the undisciplined and raw American army. Then, as always, the great, crying need of a new army

---

* Some repetition in this chapter of officers treated in Chapters IX and X seems unavoidable for completeness of the record.

[1] Russell, *My Diary North and South*, 483.

scrambled together from civilians was trained officers. Through the American consuls abroad and through agents expressly sent to Europe, Seward encouraged the war-eager officers of the Old World to cross the sea to find the fighting for which their souls thirsted. McClellan, upon whose writings the above statement is based, does not explicitly say that Seward made promises to these foreign officers, but it is difficult to believe that agents sent to attract military men here could abstain from such promises. McClellan received from General George Klapka, who had distinguished himself in the Hungarian revolutionary army of 1849, a communication in which that Hungarian leader revealed that he had been invited by one of Seward's agents to enter the Union army. Klapka was indeed ready to come, but shamelessly stipulated such conditions that his letter sent McClellan storming to President Lincoln, furiously demanding prohibition of such dabbling with military affairs by the Secretary of State. As a matter of wonder and interest it should be recorded that Klapka demanded merely the advance payment of a bonus of $100,000, a later salary of $25,000 a year, for a short period the position of chief of general staff, and later, after he had acquired a greater facility with the English language, appointment to McClellan's place as general in chief of all armies! [2] How many German and Austrian officers were sought out through Seward's agents cannot be established. Seward felt that volunteers should not be refused because they did not speak English.

Another European officer of great prominence who was approached in these early days was General Giuseppe Garibaldi; he was tendered a command in the American armies by the President's direct authority with the consent of the King of Italy. There was much approval of this suggestion by the American press, as it was thought that because of his long residence in the United States, Garibaldi, as an act of "gratitude and from interest in humanity," might be willing to serve the Union cause.[3] Rumors

[2] McClellan, McClellan's Own Story, 143. McClellan reports that the president became very angry and told him that he should not be troubled in this way again. General Klapka was regarded as a brilliant soldier, evidence of which may be found in the fact that he was only twenty-nine years old when entrusted with the defense of Komárom. Vasvary, Lincoln's Hungarian Heroes, 28. McClellan said that Seward's policy was "drumming up officers from all parts of the world."

[3] The New York Evening Post, August 8, 1861, wrote of Garibaldi: "Just now, when our new regiments need experienced officers, his presence would be a great gain. As general of a division of our adopted sons, which form so large a part of our army, he would be of very special value. His name alone would be a power for every army." It will be recalled that Garibaldi lived in the United States for several years, engaging in candle-making and running an American trading vessel.

of Garibaldi's entry into the Union army persisted through the European press throughout 1862 and greatly disturbed the Confederate representative abroad, A. D. Mann.[4] By August, however, the United States ambassador to Prussia disavowed the statement of the *New Yorker Staats-Zeitung* about acceptance of foreign officers and declared that he was to refuse all such offers.

Apparently, foreign governments were not resentful about commissions offered to their subjects as prospective officers of the Union army nor about encouragement given them at the American embassies during at least the early period of the war. There is not the slightest hint of a sense of impropriety on the part of the United States in Seward's Circular to Consuls No. 11, under date of May 8, 1862, for this says blandly,

> The Department considers it to be its duty to inform you that, since the outbreak of the rebellion in this country, many military officers who have served with distinction in the armies of Europe have arrived for the purpose of offering their services to the Government. . . . As, however, it is not now in contemplation to increase the number either of officers or soldiers already in the field, you will inform all such foreign officers as apply to you for service in the Army of the United States, that the Government, while grateful for such offers, must, for the future, decline accepting them, as the list of officers is complete, and recruiting for the rank and file has been ordered to cease.[5]

[4] This statement appeared in the *Kölnische Zeitung* and was copied by the Chicago *Illinois Staats-Zeitung* in its issue of August 7, 1861.

It is interesting that about a year later, in September, 1862, the consul at Vienna approached Garibaldi directly, for which action his commission as consul was withdrawn. It was only when the King of Italy requested that the indiscretion be overlooked that he was directed to resume his consular duties. Instructions to Consuls, XXXI, 567–68 (Division of State Department Archives, The National Archives).

Dudley A. Mann reported to Secretary of State Judah P. Benjamin under date of September 26, 1862, the correspondence of the consul at Vienna with Garibaldi, and repeated the rumor that Garibaldi had, on November 1, 1862, requested permission of King Victor Emmanuel to carry out the design. An item was telegraphed from Turin to a Brussels paper to the effect that Colonel Giovanni Cattabeni, one of Garibaldi's lieutenants, was to proceed to the United States with two thousand volunteers. *Official Records of the Union and Confederate Navies in the War of the Rebellion* (Washington, 1894–1927), Ser. 2, III, pp. 534–88. This work is hereinafter cited as *Naval Records*.

[5] Instructions to Consuls, XXXII, 369–70. It might be desirable at this point to explain briefly the character of the material from the State Department Archives which will be frequently cited in this and Chapters XIV and XV. Communications from consuls to the department were known as "Consular Dispatches"; those going out to the consuls were labeled "Instructions to Consuls." Communications from ministers resident abroad were designated

In other words, no longer were American agents to solicit foreign military officers, though earlier, when the latter had presented themselves at the offices of our ministers abroad, they had been frequently furnished with testimonials to the War Department. Now no more of them were needed.[6] In another instance, which occurred just about this same time, in response to the offer of a General (Girolamo?) Ulloa, F. W. Seward, an assistant to his father in the State Department, stated that "officers of volunteer regiments are appointed by the Governors of States and there is no vacancy in the regular army of the United States at the disposal of the Secretary of War, of suitable rank to confer on General Ulloa." [7]

By October of that same year, however, there was a suggestion of a shift to encouraging immigration as distinct from encouraging recruitment for our armies:

> The War Department has been consulted heretofore concerning the offer of inducements to foreign officers and soldiers to migrate and join our armies. But it has thus far found no such necessity for a measure of this kind as would overbalance the inconveniences and annoyances which might result from it. The country presents inducements to emigrate as well in military as in civil life, but it is in no such straits as to require extraordinary efforts or sacrifices to promote such an immigration. All that seems necessary for our representatives abroad to do is to direct attention to such social facts which are or ought to be universally known.[8]

By the early months of 1863 our policy in regard to foreign enlistments had crystallized, probably under pressure from foreign governments opposed to open recruitment in their countries. Seward wrote to B. F. Tefft, American consul at Stockholm, in a letter which was typical of those sent to all United States consuls in Europe: "In regard to the application of individuals in Sweden for enlistment in our armies, you are informed that

---

"Diplomatic Dispatches." Communications passing back and forth between the State Department and the various embassies, which might be written by the foreign minister or by a secretary of a legation in behalf of the foreign government, and by the secretary of state or an assistant on behalf of the United States, were of four types: Notes from a given legation; Notes to a given legation; Memorandum from a given legation; and Memorandum to a given legation. Memoranda are bound with the Notes. Since all of this material is located in the National Archives, no further reference will be made to the location of this class of material. Designation in the case of Consular Dispatches will be made by citing the city from which the dispatch was sent, together with volume.

[6] One paragraph of the above circular stated, "Some of those who brought testimonials from United States ministers abroad have been furnished with commissions." *Ibid.*, XXXII, 11.

[7] *Ibid.*, XXXII, 317.   [8] *Ibid.*, XXXI, 544.

such persons will have no difficulty in so doing on their arrival in the United States. No other answer can be given if we wish to avoid giving offense to foreign governments." The letter pointed out that this country had never permitted foreign enlistments within its boundaries and must, therefore, respect the same attitude on the part of foreign countries.[9] From this time on, officers were informed that no encouragement could be extended to foreign officers to desert or change their allegiance, nor could the government sanction recruiting within the limits of any foreign territorial jurisdiction. The same answer was returned when a tender of services was made in May, 1863, through the Swedish minister resident in Washington.[10]

The method by which knights-errant and soldiers of fortune made their approach for commissions is well illustrated by those who came from Sweden. Some approached Mr. Jacob S. Haldeman, the American minister in Stockholm, for letters of introduction to President Lincoln or Secretary Seward or Secretary Stanton or even General McClellan. Arrived in Washington, they sought an interview with Lincoln or Seward, to whom they were usually presented through Count Charles Edward Piper, the Swedish minister to the United States in the first years of the war, or through Admiral John A. B. Dahlgren, whose good offices they sought on the ground of his Swedish parentage. Others, even officers of the Swedish army, enlisted as privates and rose from the ranks. Occasionally promotions were won by the most arrant lobbying. Count Piper earnestly and persistently sought appointment and promotion for his protégés. Princess Agnes Salm-Salm, as she has frankly revealed in her book, used every influential person whom she was able to meet and charm to advance her husband's interests—among others, Senator Ira Harris of New York, Governor Edwin D. Morgan of the same state, Governor Richard Yates of Illinois, Provost Marshal–General James B. Fry, and Governor Joseph A. Gilmore of New Hampshire. Germans, Hungarians, and French came, likewise armed with letters of introduction to influential persons.

Meanwhile many foreign officers, some of them men of great distinction in their respective countries, were finding their way to positions in the Union armies. Seldom in the history of wars have princes of blood

---

[9] This letter is dated February 5, 1863. *Ibid.*, XXXVII, 36–37. The volume is labeled "Spain, Portugal, Belgium, Denmark, Germany, Italian States, Turkey, Great Britain, and China."

[10] See letter to C. J. Ogden, consul at Quebec, January 5, 1864, *ibid.*, XXXVI, No. 82, p. 80; letter to W. Marsh, consul at Altona, April 7, 1864, *ibid.*, XXXVII, No. 70, December 30, 1863–January 19, 1865. For the refusal to the Swedish minister, May 7, 1863, see *Official War Records*, Ser. 3, III, pp. 195–96.

royal graced the ranks of knights-errant in a democracy. It is probably suitable to begin with the Bourbon princes, the Comte de Paris and Duc de Chartres. It does not alter their status as knights-errant that these young men embraced their first opportunity to study warfare in the field, doubtless because they expected at no distant date to head a war of their own to recover the lost Bourbon throne of France. Furthermore, it should be recognized that they were debarred from any military career in their own country and that, unless they could find temporary service in a foreign country, the door to military education derived from experience was closed to them. Contrary to common opinion, they did not come to America with the object of entering the war. The Prince de Joinville, who will be recalled as their uncle and the son of King Louis Philippe, had come to place his son, the Duc de Penthièvre, then only sixteen years old, in the Naval School at Newport. The group were traveling here when the war broke out and decided to take advantage of the opportunity to gain the experience of a campaign. The princes laid down the condition that they were to receive no pay but should, on the other hand, be free to resign whenever they desired.[11]

The three noblemen arrived in Washington very promptly, in September, 1861. Without, perhaps, sufficiently considering the effect likely to be produced on the sentiments of Emperor Napoleon, President Lincoln welcomed them personally, bestowed upon each of them the honorary rank of captain, and assigned them to the staff of General McClellan, the general in chief of the Army of the Potomac. Officially merely guests at headquarters, they acted as aides-de-camp to McClellan, bearing dispatches, making reconnaissances, and coming frequently under fire. They remained in the service until the close of the Peninsular campaign in July, 1862, and acquitted themselves well, being a part of McClellan's military family from September 20, 1861, to the close of the Seven Days' Battles. They were enrolled quite simply as Captains L. P. d'Orleans and R. d'Orleans, serving precisely as did the other aides, and taking their full share of all duty, whether agreeable or disagreeable, dangerous or the reverse. The Duc de Chartres had received a military education at the military school at Turin; the Comte de Paris, military instruction only from his tutors. Their uncle, who accompanied them as a mentor throughout the campaign, held no official position, but frequently rendered im-

---

[11] Henry Charles Fletcher, *History of the American Civil War* (London, 1865–1866), I, 174–76; Benson J. Lossing, *Pictorial History of the Civil War in the United States of America* (Hartford, 1866–1868), II, 131; Baltimore *Der Deutsche Correspondent*, September 16, 1861. The naval academy was transferred to Newport for the period of the war.

portant service. McClellan's verdict on them was "that there could be no doubt as to their courage, energy, and military spirit," and he pronounced the Prince de Joinville "a man of far more than ordinary ability and of excellent judgment." He declared himself warmly attached to them, a feeling evidently reciprocated, for the Comte de Paris was partial to Mc-Clellan in his book.[12]

Probably no fairer appraisal of either of them has been made than that by the Irishman "Gallowglass," a correspondent of the *Irish-American:*

> That young man with the fair complexion and altogether fine appearance (for blood will tell), is one of the most active aids [*sic*] on the staff of the Commander-in-chief: that is the Duc de Chartres. He is met at all hours; he is always on the road, ever busy. *Mon Dieu,* is it not very strange? He was born in a palace; he was reared in luxury; he is a Prince of the House of Orleans; he is a representative of the best blood of Europe; and here you will see him riding like a dragoon daily and nightly, taking like a man whatever hardship, whatever discomforts, whatever dangers this kind of campaigning affords. If he has not his princely honors now—who knows what he may have in the future—at least he has won his citizenship in the service of the Republic, and the gratitude of the people.

The Comte de Paris was described as tall, lean, youthful-looking, but not a graceful rider when compared with "Little Mac" mounted on his "Dan Webster." The two princes evoked, naturally, much interest and could be termed favorites with the men.[13]

The research revealed a bewildering number of foreign officers who, lured by the prospect of actual combat, secured leave of absence to enter the Union army. Among the early arrivals were two old Garibaldi officers —Colonel Luigi Navone and Achille di Vecchi—who, arriving in New York in early July, proceeded at once to Washington to offer their services; they attracted attention everywhere by their dress and Herculean figures. Navone had fought for seventeen years, in the course of which he had acquired fourteen scars on his muscular body; Di Vecchi, on the other

---

[12] The Prince de Joinville made a painting of the engagement at Gaines's Mill, which was widely published. For McClellan's opinion, see McClellan, *McClellan's Own Story*, 123, 144–45; for the opinion of the Comte de Paris on McClellan, see De Paris, *History of the American Civil War*, I, 259–60, 580, 612.

[13] "Gallowglass" was Captain James Turner, who, though aide to Meagher, continued to send in articles occasionally to the paper (issue of July 5, 1862); for the description of the Comte de Paris, see Evan R. Jones, *Four Years in the Army of the Potomac. A Soldier's Recollections* (London, 1881), 64.

hand, only twenty-four years old, had served but four years under Garibaldi. Towering six feet and two inches in height, he affected long flowing hair, parted in the middle.[14] Lieutenant Luigi Vizia, an Italian officer who had had many years experience in the engineer department and had served with credit in the campaign of Italian liberation, also hastened to America to offer his sword to the American government.[15]

Not all French officers secured leave of absence easily. Several officers, superior and subaltern, negotiated with the French government with a view to service in the Federal army. Some proposed offering an indemnity to the government for their temporary displacement—at the same time expecting from the United States a salary of twenty thousand francs ($5,000) a year, to be guaranteed for several years. At first the French government seemed reluctant to refuse its consent, but on September 28, 1861, on the Emperor's formal order, the Minister of War declared that he did not wish to give any authorization. This action was interpreted by many Northerners as sympathy for the Confederacy but was represented by the French government as a desire to avoid all appearance of intervention. The order did not prohibit departures, but no leave was granted with preservation of rank in the French army. This meant, in effect, that an officer could resign, with abdication of his nationality, to serve where he wished.[16]

Sometimes it seems difficult to distinguish between the Irishmen who entered the Union forces from warm sympathy for the cause and those who volunteered from sheer love of fighting—between the knights-errant and the soldiers of fortune. Captain B. S. O'Neill of the Sixty-ninth New York, a handsome Irishman, popular with the entire brigade, evidently belonged to the former class, for he left Ireland at the outbreak of the American war for the sole purpose of joining the Irish Brigade. He gave his life for the cause which he espoused, as he fell at the assault on the lines before Petersburg in June, 1864.[17] Difficult also to classify was Captain John D. Hearn. A leading revolutionist in 1849 in his native district of Ireland, he was arrested on suspicion and discharged after some months

[14] Chicago *Illinois Staats-Zeitung*, July 11, 1861, for Navone and Di Vecchi.

[15] Moore (ed.), *Rebellion Record*, II, Pt. 1, p. 40, for Vizia. It was reported that on his way to America, Vizia fell in with an agent of the Confederate government who tried to persuade him to take service with that government, offering to pay his passage. New York *Evening Post*, July 26, 1861. None of these Italians appear in *Official War Records*, but if they had been aides, they would have made no reports to be published in *Official War Records*.

[16] New York *Courrier des États-Unis*, October 4, 1861.

[17] Mulholland, *The Story of the 116th Regiment Pennsylvania Infantry*, 237.

without trial. In 1850 he betook himself to the United States, where he joined the Fenian Brotherhood and became a founder of the Mitchell Light Guards in New York. He returned with John O'Mahony to Ireland in 1860 on a perilous mission; but when he learned of the formation of Meagher's brigade, he resigned a good mercantile position there and returned to America to help the Union, first on General Meagher's staff and later with the Irish Legion as captain in Corcoran's Zouaves. He paid a price for his knight-errantry; he was taken prisoner at Reams Station in August, 1864.[18]

Volunteer officers came in goodly number from Germany. Count Hermann von Haake, connected with the Prussian army, obtained a furlough to come to the United States, where he procured a commission as first lieutenant in the Steuben Rifles, the Seventh New York Volunteers. Upon expiration of his term of service he secured a similar commission in the Fifty-second New York, largely a German regiment, and fell at Spotsylvania at the head of his company in Grant's Virginia campaign of 1864.[19] Otto, Baron von Steuben, was another Prussian officer who joined this same regiment; he fought and fell also in the terrible struggle at the Bloody Angle at Spotsylvania beside his friend, Count von Haake.[20]

As early as July, 1861, several staff officers of that same country were reported in the American press as present in New York on furlough from their commands. August Becker said of them in the New York *Democrat:* "They have come across from the same motives which brought Von Kalb and Steuben in the first revolution, an opportunity to find distinction and to serve the cause of the United States which they regard as the right cause." [21] A few days later the *Illinois Staats-Zeitung* stated that at that moment there were no less than thirteen Austrian and Prussian officers ready in New York to serve in the Schwarze Jäger Regiment (the Fifty-fourth New York). They were not, it frankly declared, of the character to make "gaiter" service "at home" in America—meaning, doubtless,

---

[18] Cavanagh, *Memoirs of Gen. Meagher,* Appendix, 17–18.

[19] Tenny, *The Military and Naval History of the Rebellion in the United States,* 778.

[20] *Ibid.,* 779. See also Johnson and others (eds.), *Campfire and Battlefield,* 479. Both were fighting as line officers. Von Steuben's first name was established from *Official War Records,* Ser. 1, X, Pt. 1, p. 151.

[21] Quoted from the *Democrat* by the Chicago *Illinois Staats-Zeitung,* July 11, 1861. This issue mentions, among others, a Herr von Hardenberg, but as there is no trace of a Von Hardenberg in any of the official records, the author is forced to regard him as a myth who somehow crept into the papers, or at least as someone who never entered the army. No copy of the *Democrat* of around this date is extant.

that they had foreign manners and affectations—but their technical military education would be able to raise the regiment to an efficiency attained as yet by none of the German-American regiments.[22]

Among the cavalrymen seeking service here was a Colonel George W. von Schack, who secured a three years leave of absence from his post as captain of cavalry in the Prussian army. Accepting the rank of major in the Seventh New York Infantry, he became its commander with the rank of colonel in February, 1862. He seems to have been as brave as he was handsome, distinguishing himself in the Seven Days' Battles of the Peninsular campaign and thereby winning a brevet brigadiership. After his heavy losses at Antietam and Fredericksburg, he reorganized the regiment and fought with Grant through to the surrender. It is of passing interest that he then resigned his commission in the Prussian service and took out papers to become a United States citizen. In his regiment had served another Prussian officer from the Garde du Corps, Captain von Buggenhagen, who died in Washington on New Year's night, 1863, as a result of severe wounds inflicted at Fredericksburg.[23]

Several other Germans qualify in this category. Hubert Dilger was an artillery officer of the army of Baden, Germany. He came to offer his sword to the Union. He led Company I of the First Ohio Artillery as battery chief and belonged to Blenker's German division, first encountering the enemy at Cross Keys in the Shenandoah Valley. He rendered brilliant service at Second Bull Run, Chancellorsville, and Gettysburg. At Chancellorsville he conducted the only shooting which could be done in Buschbeck's brigade, miraculously escaping capture by the foe. In late summer he moved with the Eleventh Corps to Chattanooga and shared honorably in the great battles fought there. He moved with Sherman through Georgia and the Carolinas until the Union forces were close to Richmond. He was known throughout the entire Northern army and counted as one of its brilliant officers. It was said that "the infantry always went into a battle with better spirit when it knew that Dilger's Battery was with them." Dozens of officers held that Dilger was the best artillerist of the entire Union army. It is rather difficult to understand why so obviously able a man remained only a captain despite his many acknowledged deeds.[24]

[22] Chicago *Illinois Staats-Zeitung*, July 16, 1861.

[23] Mulholland, *The American Volunteer, the Most Heroic Soldier the World Has Ever Known* (Philadelphia, 1909), 17; Kaufmann, *Die Deutschen im Bürgerkriege*, 547. For Von Buggenhagen, see Princess Agnes Salm-Salm, *Ten Years of My Life* (London, 1875), 49–50. See p. 265 of text.

[24] Kaufmann, *Die Deutschen im Bürgerkriege*, 402–403.

The prince of all the German knights-errant for character and idealism was probably Otto von Fritsch, who came from a cultivated home, had had a military training, and was an officer in the Saxon Cavalry Guard. On honorable leave to go to Mexico in order to fight for Emperor Maximilian, he became involved with the Mexican revolutionists and consequently was required by the French officers to leave Mexico. He then determined to wield his sword in the cause of freedom in the United States. Here he promptly became adjutant to General von Schimmelfennig, made an excellent record, and was severely wounded at Chancellorsville. Of all the memoirs left by foreign participants, none is more fascinating, or more valuable for revealing the inner motivation of the foreigners in the Northern army, than the record of Von Fritsch's adventures, *A Gallant Captain of the Civil War.* Though Von Fritsch fought in two wars, one after the other, he was no soldier of fortune in any sense of the word but seems to have been actuated by pure knight-errantry.

About 1863, however, the Prussian government refused furloughs to active officers who were seeking them for the purpose of sharing in the campaigns in the United States, because it expected fairly soon to take the field against Austria and, therefore, to need its officers itself; on the other hand, inactive Prussian officers, some of whom were already preparing to depart for New York in order to join the American army, would be allowed leaves of absence.

Several Englishmen appear in the list and deserve attention. John Fitzroy de Courcy, a major in the English army, served on McClellan's staff and attained the rank of colonel of the Sixteenth Ohio. Though he commanded a Turkish regiment in the Crimean War, his classification as a soldier of fortune is hardly in order, when we recall that England and Turkey were allies in that war. He was several times entrusted by Union generals with the command of a brigade of three or four regiments.[25] The name of a less well-known officer of the English army, a Captain Lambert, appears as acting inspector general on the staff of one of our less distinguished commanders, General David Hunter. Nothing, it was declared, escaped his attention, not even a bottle of something (which he designated as "B") that stood in the tent of the regimental commander.[26] Another

---

[25] Oddly enough, the author is indebted for this item on an English officer to the Chicago *Hemlandet*, October 16, 1861. For his command, see *Official War Records*, Ser. 1, III, Pt. 1, p. 236.

[26] W. W. H. Davis, *History of the 104th Pennsylvania Regiment, from August 22nd, 1861, to September 30th, 1864* (Philadelphia, 1866), 189. The bottle probably contained bourbon. It proved impossible to learn his first name and thus to identify him in *Official War Records*.

Englishman, Robert Johnstone, served as lieutenant colonel of the Fifth New York Cavalry. He told a hostess in the Shenandoah Valley that all his life he had delighted in anything big, and that he could not remain idle while so big a nation was being split asunder.[27]

So eager was a Russian for a commission in the Union service that he left Russia without a passport—in violation, of course, of Russian law. He had sent in his resignation from his position as lieutenant in the Imperial Guard but had not received notice of its acceptance. He presented himself in the American consul's office at Stockholm about July 15, 1862, despite a previous discouraging reply from Consul Charles A. Leas to his letter from Helsingfors, which had declared his warm sympathy with the Union and his desire to aid her in the conflict. His request for a recommendation from the consul was refused in view of Secretary Seward's Circular No. 11. There is no evidence that a commission was given to this Lieutenant Waldemar Becker.[28]

Considering the size of Sweden and the relative paucity of officers in the Swedish army, the number of officers from that country who secured leave of absence and the number of Swedish volunteers who actually served in the Union army are truly astonishing. It is possible to count, from Baron Ernst von Vegesack to the brothers Herman and Frederick Banforth (who came over against the wishes of their parents in 1864 and joined the Fifty-sixth Massachusetts as privates), about thirty-five Swedes who came over as knights-errant, in addition to several soldiers of fortune of that nationality. Shortly after the beginning of hostilities there were a number of Swedes in Washington eagerly seeking posts, among others Axel Grundström, August H. Edgren, and one Hollertz. It is no less astonishing to find the Swedish government, presumably neutral, financing the expenses of some of the officers in order that Swedish subjects might aid one of the belligerents. Foreign Minister Christophe Rutger Louis Manderström made this abundantly clear in a letter of March 19, 1863, concerning Lieutenant Carl Constantine Weinberg: "His Majesty, the King, who has vouchsafed to relieve the economical difficulties united with his voyage. . . ."[29]

[27] Cornelia McDonald, *A Diary with Reminiscences of the War and Refugee Life in the Shenandoah Valley, 1860–1865* (Nashville, 1934), 62. He was serving by May 24, 1862, but he does not appear in the records after August 20, 1863. *Official War Records*, Ser. 1, XII, Pt. 1, p. 587, and XXIX, Pt. 2, p. 76.

[28] Consul Leas to Seward, July 17, 1862, Consular Dispatches, Stockholm, IV, No. 27.

[29] Chicago *Hemlandet*, December 4, 1861. The name of Nils Rosenstjerna occurs in the *Hemlandet*'s list of Swedish officers, and is classified by Hokanson with the officers enlisting

The pressure on the American minister and consuls by the officers in the royal army of Sweden and Norway does not seem to have been strongly manifest until the very beginning of 1863. By that date, however, they were besieging Consul B. F. Tefft at Stockholm to know what encouragement the United States would offer for their services. On January 23 he wrote that he was receiving a "number of applications from gentlemen of this country who have been officers in the royal army of Sweden and Norway by letter and in person," anxious to know what encouragement the United States was likely to hold out to them.[30]

Among the Swedish officers who came over as early as 1861 to seek service under the United States flag was Axel Silfversparre, who filled a lieutenancy in the Swedish army. To those familiar with the welcome which General Frémont accorded foreign officers it will be no surprise to learn that this Swedish knight-errant served first for a time under Frémont at Cape Girardeau, Missouri. In December he secured a leave of absence in order to organize a battery of light artillery manned by Swedish residents. He visited the Swedish settlements in Illinois and succeeded in winning seventy-five recruits, who by February 20, 1862, were ready to be mustered in as Battery H, First Illinois Light Artillery, under Silfversparre as captain. He arrived at Pittsburg Landing with his battery just in time to share the next day in the Battle of Shiloh and to display at once his unusual skill. After this battle, he was transferred with his battery to Sherman's division. He served under Sherman to the end of his period of service and won his commander's regard.[31]

Major Adolph Carlsson Warberg, a lieutenant colonel in the Royal

---

as privates. *Swedish Immigrants,* 89. This count is based on the individuals named in Hokanson's book, Chapters VIII–X, and on a list published in Chicago *Hemlandet,* December 4, 1861. It is not possible to verify all of them through our various official and semiofficial records (*Official War Records;* Heitman [comp.], *Historical Register and Dictionary;* Henry [comp.], *Military Record of Civilian Appointments;* and the Department of State Archives), but Mr. Hokanson has had access to the Swedish records in Stockholm. Hollertz is not mentioned by that author but appears in a list in the *Hemlandet.* Of those here mentioned Axel Grundström enlisted in the Eighteenth New York Infantry in July, 1861, and won his way to a commission. Hokanson, *Swedish Immigrants,* 89. He does not appear in *Official War Records.* August H. Edgren enlisted in the Ninety-ninth New York and was commissioned. Hokanson, *Swedish Immigrants,* 88–89. For the financial aid, see Hokanson, *Swedish Immigrants,* 82. For the full list of Swedish knights-errant, see Appendix, Section F.

[30] B. F. Tefft to Seward, Consular Dispatches, Stockholm, 1863, IV, No. 3.

[31] Hokanson, *Swedish Immigrants,* 72, 113–14. Silfversparre's name occurs a number of times in *Official War Records,* always as captain in the First Illinois Light Artillery. Ser. 1, XVII, Pt. 2, p. 146; Ser. 1, LII, Pt. 1, p. 20. He had resigned by March 3, 1863. See *Official War Records,* Ser. 1, XXIV, Pt. 3, p. 82. See pp. 135–36 of text.

Alfsborgs Regiment when he secured leave to seek active service in the American theater, entered the Union army in April, 1862, as additional aide-de-camp to General Frémont with the rank of major, and, when the latter resigned, served on the staff of General Banks. He came armed with testimonials from the American minister in Stockholm, the Swedish Minister of Foreign Affairs, the Minister of War, and his own immediate superior, and consequently he received appointment on recommendation of President Lincoln. From this service he was honorably discharged on March 31, 1863, but toward the close of 1864 he received a fresh appointment as lieutenant colonel of the First United States Colored Cavalry. He seems to have rendered valuable service and displayed marked bravery in leading a reconnaissance party into the suburbs of Richmond, thereby gaining most valuable topographical and military information.[32]

Another Swedish officer on leave was Axel Leatz, a quartermaster sergeant in the Södermanland Regiment in 1859 at the age of twenty-one. He seems to have enlisted in 1863 as a private in the Fifth New York, but he first appears in the *Official War Records* as a lieutenant recommended for a brevet captaincy for service at Bethesda Church on August 1, 1864. A letter written home from a hospital in Annapolis and printed in an American-Swedish paper tells the last chapter of his story. In storming the enemy's breastworks in the vicinity of Richmond on June 2, 1864, at the Battle of Cold Harbor, he received a bad wound in his shoulder and was left unconscious on the battlefield when the Federals were pushed back. He seems to have been operated on by a Confederate surgeon the next day in the open air and carried off to Libby Prison. Here he lay, suffering "unbelievably," as he reported, until August 20, when, in an exchange of prisoners, he was sent with six negro officers and four thousand men under guard to Annapolis. Here in the Officers' General Hospital he received all possible care and made the transition from despair to hope. Although he feared that his arm could never be fully restored, he looked forward to rejoining his regiment—which, as a matter of fact, he did. In February, 1865, he was still in service as aide-de-camp and still holding the rank of lieutenant, on the staff of (Brevet) Brigadier General Frederick Winthrop.

[32] Chicago *Hemlandet*, December 7, 1864. Interestingly enough, this information on Warberg came to the editor of the *Hemlandet* through Swedish newspapers which were publishing items about their officers on leave. See also Notes from the Swedish Legation, November 1, 1862, May 19, 1863, IV, and *Official War Records*, Ser. 1, XII, Pt. 1, p. 35, for Warberg's service on Frémont's staff in June, 1862.

From this same letter we also learn that Lieutenant Carl Constantine Weinberg, mentioned previously, had been serving in the same regiment with Leatz and had been killed at Cold Harbor; and that a Lieutenant Pehr Gustaf Bergquist, on leave from the Wermland Jäger Regiment, had lost a limb in June and died of the wound.[33]

No other Swedish knight-errant equaled the Baron von Vegesack in importance or in recognition which he received. Ernest Mattais Peter von Vegesack of His Majesty's Dalarne Regiment, in which he held a commission as captain, proceeded to Washington in August, 1861, on a furlough especially granted him by his commander, the Duke of Dalecarlia, armed with a recommendation from Duke August, brother of the king. He had served the sister state of Denmark in the Schleswig-Holstein War, thereby adding to his asset of military training, actual experience in the field. After several periods of service with General John E. Wool at Fortress Monroe as aide-de-camp with the rank of major, he resigned to enlist as a private, serving thus in the battles of Yorktown and Williamsburg. After the battle of Hanover Courthouse, he served on McClellan's staff; and after he had proved his mettle at Gaines's Mill by covering Fitz-John Porter's retreat, he received what he sought, command of a regiment—the Twentieth New York. He soon made these German Turners the soldiers they were intended to be. He commanded a brigade at Second Bull Run, but his greatest contribution was earlier, at Antietam, where he personally led the charge when his gunners stormed the center of that battlefield after it had twice been taken and twice lost. It is unquestionable that his calm courage gave the Twentieth New York the steadiness which it had lacked before. He took part in the great battles of the East, Fredericksburg, Chancellorsville, and Gettysburg, and then in August, 1863, resigned to return to Sweden.

The encomium bestowed upon him by Thomas W. Hyde seems to have been deserved: "Of all the foreign officers I knew, and there were scores of them with us, he was the best. None of the old captains of Gustavus Adolphus did more honor to the fatherland. He is now a major-general in well-earned retirement in his native Sweden, but he deserves thanks from

---

[33] Axel Leatz's letter, dated September 14, 1864, appears in the December 7, 1864, issue of the Chicago *Hemlandet*. For proof of his return to his regiment, see *Official War Records*, Ser. 1, XLVI, Pt. 1, p. 280.

Wermland, like Skåne, is a province of Sweden. See Count Piper's statement (undated) about Weinberg to Seward, Notes from the Swedish Legation, IV. Weinberg's death is recorded in *Official War Records*, Ser. 1, XXVI, Pt. 1, p. 182. He appears here merely as Constantine Weinberg.

the Republic in no less degree than Lafayette, only that our needs were less. I have no doubt that all the honors he has received at home will fade as he remembers our plaudits when he breasted the storm of bullets at Antietam and redeemed the honor of the Twentieth New York Volunteers." He did not receive the brigadiership he coveted except by brevet; but in 1893, for having, as aide-de-camp, successfully changed the position of troops under fire at the Battle of Gaines's Mill, he was given the Congressional Medal of Honor, which the Swedish king graciously allowed him to wear.[34]

Jacob, Baron von Cedarström, was presented to Secretary Edwin M. Stanton in March, 1862, and won a place, along with Lieutenant Adolph C. Warberg, as aide-de-camp with the rank of captain on the staff of General Frémont, making with him the campaign of the Shenandoah; but with that general's withdrawal from the command, Von Cedarström was removed from active service. He then was placed on the staff of General Bohlen, where he served until General Pope dismissed Frémont's staff. Finally the baron was ordered to accompany McClellan, and thus he saw service at Antietam. He again went on the inactive list when McClellan was relieved, though in May, 1863, he once more became an additional aide-de-camp. He resigned only in January, 1864.[35]

Corfitz Ludvig Joakin Stael, Baron von Holstein, is interesting from the fact that, though little more than a cadet in the Karlberg Royal Military Academy, he came over to enlist under the name of Charles Holstein and had the ability to rise to the rank of major of the Fifty-second Colored Regiment. Likewise, Lieutenant Colonel Carl Gustaf von Knorring, a baron, is of interest because, after rising from private to captain in the Third Rhode Island Artillery, he was promoted to the rank of lieutenant colonel on the staff of the general in chief. If for no better reason than to distinguish him in the mind of the reader from Major General W. S. Rosecrans, and to recognize the ability that brought him to the rank of lieutenant colonel, Frederick Anton Ulrik Rosencrantz should be briefly noted. A captain in the Royal Life Guards, he enlisted in the German Turner Regiment in 1861 and rose to captain and brevet major by August,

---

[34] Hyde, *Following the Greek Cross*, 89. For letter of introduction from the Swedish consul general of August 30, 1861, see Piper to Seward, February 11, 1862, Notes from the Swedish Legation, VI, 114–15; in regard to the king's consent for him to wear the decoration, see Notes from the Swedish Legation, IV, 124. See also Hokanson, *Swedish Immigrants*, 83–84.

[35] For Baron Cedarström's interview with Secretary Edwin M. Stanton, see Seward to Piper, March 6, 1862, Notes to the Swedish Legation, VI, 97; for his experience as aide-de-camp, see Piper to Seward, May 19, 1863, Notes from the Swedish Legation, IV. See also Hokanson, *Swedish Immigrants*, 91.

1864. The higher rank of brevet lieutenant colonel was accorded him on April 9, 1865, for his service in operations resulting in the fall of Richmond and the surrender of General Lee.[36]

Three other Swedes and one Dane merit passing attention, although their names do not occur in the official records. Charles Hamberg, a lieutenant in the Gothland Reserve, came over in 1863, under a promise from Minister Haldeman of immediate employment. He came armed with a certificate from the general in chief of the Topographical Corps in Sweden testifying to two years service in the corps and giving assurance that he understood English. He received a lieutenant's commission in the Twenty-third Colored Regiment and a captaincy by brevet. A Dane, one Theodor von Rosenörn, who had served as a lieutenant in the Sixth Regiment of Dragoons of Denmark but had left the service, received the good services of Count Piper in being brought to the attention of Seward. The second Swede, Major Adam Hoffkill, was alluded to by Seward, in a certificate to Count Piper, as "late in the military service of the United States." He died shortly before February 10, 1864. One could dismiss Von Rosenörn and Hoffkill with the assumption that they failed of an appointment despite the good offices of the embassies, were it not that Seward's definite remark about the latter cannot be dismissed. One is driven to the conclusion that he filled the post of a non-commissioned officer or served as a private and thus did not enter the records. This may, of course, also be true of the Dane.

To a more important position the third Swede must be assigned. Lieutenant Carl Augustus Rossander, who had been serving in Swedish artillery regiments since 1855, came to the United States in January, 1862, and secured a post as first lieutenant in the Third Rhode Island Artillery, serving only about a year before he resigned. The governor and state legislature of Rhode Island honored him with special resolutions.[37]

It seems rather strange that although contemporaries tell us that there

[36] For Baron von Holstein and Baron von Knorring, see Hokanson, *Swedish Immigrants*, 86; for Frederick Anton Ulrik Rosencrantz (to distinguish him from his fellow countryman, Palle Rosencrantz), see *ibid.*, 85–86; Heitman (comp.), *Historical Register and Dictionary*, 846. Heitman gave Von Holstein only the rank of major, while Hokanson gave him the rank of lieutenant colonel. Heitman (comp.), *Historical Register and Dictionary*, II, 112.

[37] Notes from the Swedish Legation, IV, for Hamberg and for Von Rosenörn; for Secretary Seward's certificate to Count Piper, February 10, 1864, see Notes to the Swedish Legation, VI, 131. Hamberg received rank as lieutenant in the Twenty-third United States Colored Infantry and became captain by brevet in June, 1865, probably for his topographical services. See *Official War Records*, Ser. 1, XLVI, Pt. 1, pp. 1164, 1165. Hamberg, it might be added, was one of those who came with the "permission and recommendation" of his government. Hokanson had some errors on Rossander.

were many Austrian officers fighting on the Union side, the research revealed actual records of so few. One of these, Lieutenant H. Danscha, was actually only a former officer; for the recommendation of William Marsh, American consul at Altona, Germany, stated that he had "served in the Imperial Army of Austria" and had been "honorably discharged," and added that he had seen service and distinguished himself on the battlefield. No reflections should be cast upon his record, for his discharge was signed by Archduke William. Likewise, the consul at Bremen in September, 1862, warmly recommended Karl von Bukowics, a student of the Military Academy at Vienna who had gained experience in the Austrian army, for a majorship in the cavalry or infantry, expressing the opinion that Bukowics' talents were such that he would soon reach a brigadiership. The most distinguished person encountered in this group was a Count Gustavus Saint Alb, who had been an officer in the Austrian army; upon coming to the United States to find active service, he was placed on General MacDowell's staff with the rank of captain. He was pronounced clever and amusing; and, in contrast with many of the foreign officers, he spoke English fluently. He arrived at MacDowell's headquarters in northern Virginia on May 13, 1862. It should also be added that it is possible that Danscha and Von Bukowics were Germans who had taken service in the Austrian army; that might explain their application to American consuls in German cities.[38]

Alberto C. Maggi was one of the few Italian adventurers who found his way into the Union army, serving successively as lieutenant colonel of the Twenty-first Massachusetts and as colonel of the Thirty-third. His appointment to the latter post came in June, 1862, from Governor Andrew, who pronounced the Italian "a remarkable soldier." Evidently Maggi felt that he would be more at home in a contingent consisting of foreigners, for in August the governor (in reporting the departure of the regiment for Washington) forwarded Maggi's request that if his regiment were sent immediately into the field it should be assigned to Sigel's division. The records afford evidence that he commanded a regiment at Roanoke Island.[39]

[38] For Bukowics, see Consul Börnstein to Seward, September 15, 1862, Consular Dispatches, Bremen, XII, No. 67; for Count Alb, see Townsend, *Campaigns of a Non-Combatant*, 237. The date of Count Alb's arrival at General McDowell's headquarters can fortunately be fixed, as it is noted in a communication by that officer in *Official War Records*, Ser. 1, LI, Pt. 1, p. 74. The other two cannot be found in the official records.

[39] *Official War Records*, Ser. 3, II, pp. 114–15, 391; for Maggi's report on the engagement at Roanoke Island, see *ibid.*, Ser. 1, IX, p. 100.

A Major F. Lecomte of the Swiss army, who served as a volunteer aide-de-camp to McClellan, was the only Swiss knight-errant whose presence in the Union army was established by this study. He left the army during the siege of Yorktown and was obviously merely seeking an opportunity to study military science at close range. Unfortunately, there is extant only one brief reference to him by McClellan and one reference in Rudolf Aschmann's *Drei Jahre in der Potomac Armee,* as the result of his visit to the Swiss company of the Sharpshooters; his own book yields no personal data. He was mentioned in the *Official War Records* only once—as volunteer aide on McClellan's staff when the latter embarked for his Peninsular campaign.[40]

Usually able men, sometimes scamps, but always courageous—often to the point of foolhardiness—the soldiers of fortune proved to be the most colorful, romantic, and fascinating group in this, as in any, army. Knowing no real country as their fatherland, they were confined to no one country but came from all nations. Also in the Union army, along with the true knights-errant who could espouse the cause of a foreign country to the point of being willing to die for it and the genuine soldiers of fortune who were attracted to a war as by a magnet and made good fighters, were mingled adventurers and swindlers. It is astonishing how many German noblemen found it necessary to get away from European difficulties and seek a refuge in the United States. The Prussian army furnished a considerable contingent of officers who had run away from their creditors when their careers met with shipwreck, or who wished to escape the consequences of some duel or breach of discipline, if not of some less pardonable sin. Some represented themselves as officers without ever having been officers. Some bluffed their way to a colonel's position only to fail to meet the obligations of the post; these tended soon to disappear. Military adventurers of all sorts from all parts of the world flocked to Washington.

Some of these adventurers were known throughout the army and even throughout the country. Prince of the soldiers of fortune, perhaps, was Prince zu Salm-Salm, with whom must be coupled his adventuress-wife. Prince Felix Salm-Salm belonged to one of the oldest of the German princely families, whose principality was situated in Westphalia, belong-

---

[40] McClellan, *McClellan's Own Story,* 123; George B. McClellan, *Report on the Organization and Campaigns of the Army of the Potomac, to which is added an Account of the Campaign in West Virginia . . .* (New York, 1864), 61; Aschmann, *Drei Jahre in der Potomac Armee,* 18; *Official War Records,* Ser. 1, V, p. 23.

ing to Prussia. Indulged by his father, Prince Felix became extravagant and reckless. When very young, he was made an officer in the Prussian cavalry, distinguishing himself by his bravery in the Holstein War, in which he was once left on a battlefield with seven wounds and taken prisoner by the Danes. For his exploits in that war, the King of Prussia sent him a sword of honor. Like other Catholic families, his family followed the practice of sending their sons to the Austrian and the Prussian armies. Accordingly, Prince Felix resigned his post in the Prussian army to enter the army of Austria. In Vienna his extravagance soon threw him into the hands of the moneylenders, so that it became advisable for him to leave Vienna.

With testimonials from the Crown Prince of Prussia to the Prussian minister resident in Washington, he came to the United States, where he arrived sometime after the outbreak of war. As he knew no English, he wanted to serve with a German regiment, and Blenker proved willing to accept him as his chief of staff. At this time he was about thirty years of age and of middle height, possessed a handsome face and a good figure, and wore a monocle with the traditional skill of a Prussian officer of the guard. Through the good offices of the Prussian minister he secured an audience with President Lincoln. When told that his guest was a prince, Lincoln clapped him on the shoulder. "That won't hurt you with us," he said. The prince succeeded in getting on Blenker's staff, which was famous as the "waiting-room" for German officers. Somewhat later his wife secured for him the post of regimental chief in the old Blenker regiment, the Eighth New York, and then in the Sixty-eighth New York; finally, by powerful influence she won for him a general's title. Princess Salm-Salm was almost more distinguished than her husband, whom she even accompanied to the field; but her record belongs with those of the other foreign-born women of the Union services, and so it must await a later chapter.

A brave but cautious officer, Salm-Salm found little opportunity to distinguish himself in his first campaign. Always conspicuous yet self-controlled, he was now foremost and now unhorsed in the hurdle races with which some of the generals beguiled the tedium of the first winter. Together with his regiment, he was mustered out of the service in the spring of 1863 at the expiration of his two years enlistment. The accommodating governor, under the manipulation of the princess, appointed him colonel of the Sixty-eighth New York, which proved practically a recruiting job, as the regiment mustered hardly enough men for a company. Again his wife used her wiles to induce various important persons to assign men to the regiment until it mustered a thousand men. In the course of her efforts she herself received a captain's commission. Prince Salm-Salm saw battle service in the West in 1864 under General James Blair Steedman, but most of his actual fighting took the form of raids against Confederate guerrillas. Before the close of the war, however, the princess wangled a brevet brigadiership for him from the authorities at Washington.

Prince Salm-Salm is even better known for his excursion to Mexico, where he espoused the cause of Maximilian and became the dashing chief of the Foreign Legion. The volunteer leader of every bloody midnight sortie, he was foremost in defying the desperation which settled on the beleaguered imperial court. After the inevitable downfall of the empire, Seward unbarred for him the prison doors in Mexico, thus enabling him to return to Germany. In the conflict of Germany with France, he fell at Gravelotte, fighting bravely at the head of a battalion for his own fatherland. He has been pronounced the very ideal of a soldier—of a soldier of fortune.[41]

A popular ballot would probably rate Colonel Sir Percy Wyndham second among the soldiers of fortune in the Union army. Of a noble English family, son of Captain Charles Wyndham of the Fifth Light Cavalry of the English army, he was born aboard the ship *Arab* in the year 1832. He entered the Students' Corps in Paris and shared in the February revolution of 1848. In July he secured transfer to the French navy with the rank of ensign of marines. He resigned this commission in April, 1850, and the following year entered the artillery branch of the English army. Though he resigned again in October, 1852, he promptly received a commission as second lieutenant in the Austrian Lancers, where he served for two years. In May, 1860, he resigned from the Austrian service to enter the Italian army, where he served as captain, greatly distinguishing himself by his gallantry at the battles of Palermo, Rager, and Capua. By July he had been promoted to the rank of major and placed in command of his regiment; by October he had been promoted on the field before Capua to a lieutenant-colonelcy, and given command of a brigade by Garibaldi in person. Knighthood received on the field from King Victor Emmanuel and ap-

[41] The fullest account of Prince Salm-Salm is to be found in the book by his wife, Princess Agnes Salm-Salm, *Ten Years of My Life*. See also *The National Cyclopaedia of American Biography*; Wilson and Fiske (eds.), *Appletons' Cyclopaedia of American Biography*, V, 378; Kaufmann, *Die Deutschen im Bürgerkriege*, 546–47; Rice, "Afield with the Eleventh Army Corps at Chancellorsville," in Hunter (ed.), *Sketches of War History*, I, 36–61.

pointment as a Chevalier of the Military Order of Savoy completed his honors in Italy.

By October, 1861, however, the lure of active combat in America was so strong that he obtained leave of absence for twelve months and came to the United States to offer his service to the Union cause. Early in February, 1862, on recommendation of McClellan, the governor of New Jersey appointed him colonel of the First Cavalry of that state. Under the joint influence of Colonel Wyndham and Lieutenant Colonel Karge, the regiment by mid-May was performing good service. A few weeks later it drove the enemy through Harrisonburg, Virginia, but fell into an ambuscade in the woods. Wyndham was captured, but by luck and wit he soon escaped, so that by the close of October he was again in the fight. The regiment was almost constantly on duty from the day Colonel Wyndham took command, and its impetuous colonel was frequently placed in command of a brigade when services of an extraordinary character were about to be undertaken. His services for the American flag terminated when he was severely wounded at Brandy Station in June, 1863, and mustered out of service about a month later. His restless spirit demanded action, and when war broke out again in Europe in 1866–1867, he was soon serving on Garibaldi's staff.[42]

From France hailed the third outstanding adventurer in search of war, Colonel Gustave Paul Cluseret, an officer of education and experience; brought up in the French army, he had distinguished himself on the Crimea and in Algeria and afterwards in the Italian war for independence. In 1860 he resigned his commission in the French army to join Garibaldi, under whom he assumed command of the French Legion. In this post he was brevetted colonel for gallantry and was wounded at the siege of Capua. Attracted by the struggle in the United States, he offered his services to the Union government. On his arrival in Washington early in 1862, he secured an appointment as aide-de-camp with the high rank of colonel on the staff of General McClellan, but he was soon thereafter assigned to

---

[42] Miller (ed.), *The Photographic History of the Civil War*, IV, 102; Heitman (comp.), *Historical Register and Dictionary*, II, 164. Wyndham finally started a comic paper in Calcutta and married a wealthy widow. His colorful career was terminated by a tragic death resulting from a balloon ascension at Mandalay, Burma. For more details, see Toombs, *New Jersey Troops in the Gettysburg Campaign*, 402–406.

A Confederate record of Wyndham's capture represents him as cursing his command for cowardice at the Battle of Brandy Station, for, although he had been urging them forward the whole day and leading them personally, he could do nothing with them. T.E.C., *Battlefields of the South*, II, 73.

the command of General Frémont. Within little more than six months he was appointed to the rank of brigadier general, probably for conspicuous gallantry at the Battle of Cross Keys. He saw service in the Shenandoah Valley before he terminated his service with the Union army in early March, 1863, after scarcely a year in the field. The comment of the Cincinnati *Commercial* that Colonel Cluseret led the advance at Cross Keys "as usual" is significant.[43]

It seems, in the light of a resuscitated Poland, suitable to speak of Konstantine Blandowsky as a Polish rather than a German soldier of fortune. Born in 1832 on an estate in Upper Silesia, he just escaped being a Russian Pole. As a result of the Polish Revolt of 1830, after which his family was forced to leave Poland, he received an officer's training at Dresden. He fought in the French Foreign Legion in Algiers, took part in various unsuccessful Polish revolutions, gravitated to Italy to fight in the Polish Legion against Austria, and then betook himself to Hungary to serve as an officer in the Hungarian movement for independence. Escaping the traitorous surrender of the Hungarian army by his timely departure to Turkey, he made his way to America. Although he had lived quietly in St. Louis for a decade prior to the Civil War, his instant response to the call to arms in the United States was in keeping with his character. He became a captain in Sigel's Third Missouri Volunteers. Mortally wounded at the capture of Camp Jackson, he died on May 25, 1861, too early to have any important share in the American struggle.[44] As a military instructor of the St. Louis *Turnverein* he had, however, rendered an important service to the Union cause during the critical period.

A number of Germans clearly fall in the class of soldiers of fortune, some of them well known and recognized as such by many American soldiers in the Union army. Major Valentine Bausenwein was a German who had served as adjutant with Garibaldi and had won flattering recommendations from that hard fighter. Arrived in America, he received a majorship in a German regiment, the Fifty-eighth Ohio, and soon rose to its command.[45] Henry Bohlen's name deserves to be better known by the

[43] Duyckinck, *National History of the War for the Union*, II, 470; *The National Cyclopaedia of American Biography*, V, 255. Frémont praised the cool and effective handling of his troops at Cross Keys; see *Official War Records*, Ser. 1, XII, Pt. 1, p. 658.

[44] Schnake, "Der Ausbruch des Bürgerkrieges," in *Der Deutsche Pionier*, XI (1879–1880), 241–43, and note; Chicago *Illinois Staats-Zeitung*, May 30, 1861; Robert Rombauer, *The Union Cause in St. Louis*, 234; Rosengarten, *The German Soldier in the Wars of the United States*, 138–39; Kaufmann, *Die Deutschen im Bürgerkriege*, 438.

[45] For Bausenwein, see the Madison *Emigranten*, Extra Sheet, Nos. 40–41.

present generation of Americans. So far as the American Civil War is concerned, he came to take part in it like a son hastening home to the defense of his country. Early in 1831, when the revolutionary wave which had begun in 1830 was sweeping Europe, Bohlen, then only twenty, was appointed on the recommendation of the aged Lafayette to the staff of Marshal Étienne-Maurice Gérard, and in this capacity he served during the siege of Antwerp. In the war with Mexico he served on the staff of General W. J. Worth and fought in many conflicts. The Crimean War found him in the French army as an observer. In 1861 he was living in Europe in great splendor, enjoying a brilliant social position from the large fortune which he had amassed in the liquor business in Philadelphia; but he threw aside these inducements to ease, returned to Philadelphia, and raised the Seventy-fifth Pennsylvania Volunteers among Germans, largely at his own expense. He led his regiment with such gallantry as to be warmly commended by both Generals Frémont and Sigel, and to be promoted before long to the rank of brigadier general. He died in action in August, 1862, at Freeman's Ford on the Rappahannock.[46]

The lesser soldiers of fortune of many nationalities played their separate roles on the American stage and sooner or later went the way of all flesh, some of them falling on the battlefields of the New World. Many of their names have sunk into oblivion, but some still merit attention here. The number hailing from Germany was certainly generous. Ernest F. Hoffmann, after graduating from the Royal Academy of Engineers at Berlin, served during the twelve years between 1844 and 1856 in the Royal Engineers. Then the spirit of the adventurer took possession of him, for after the Schleswig-Holstein war he entered the English service to fight in the Crimean War. After serving in this, he took part in the Italian Wars, serving on the staff of Garibaldi as captain and then as major of the Royal Italian Engineers. In the course of this early service, he received two decorations from Prussia and one from Italy in recognition of his distinguished conduct in battle.

When news of the conflict in America reached him, he hastened here to enter the Union service as a major and aide-de-camp in May, 1862. He was soon on the staff of General Schurz and assistant adjutant general in the Eleventh Corps, and by June, 1863, he was chief engineer of that corps. He founded the topographical bureau not only for the Eleventh Corps

[46] Kaufmann, *Die Deutschen im Bürgerkriege*, 484–85; Rosengarten, *The German Soldier in the Wars of the United States*, 110; Wilson and Fiske (eds.), *Appletons' Cyclopaedia of American Biography*, I, 302.

but also in General Thomas' army. Then followed service as chief engineer with General Pope and with Sherman. His duties for Sherman consisted chiefly in compiling maps of battles and marches. It is interesting that until October, 1867, he stayed on in the Thirty-fifth United States Infantry, rendering good service in the coast survey. Probably his best war service was his restoration—in one single dark night—of the bridge over the Hiawassee River in Tennessee after its destruction by the enemy. According to Kaufmann, General James Harrison Wilson praised Hoffmann highly: "His modesty was equal to that of a girl, his courage to that of a paladin. He was ready for every duty, no matter when and how it came, he was prompt and practical to a degree that no American could surpass." [47]

Another German engineer officer was William Hölcke. An engineer officer in his homeland from 1849 to 1851, he served as an officer in the British German Legion during the Crimean War. He then turned up on this side of the ocean as first lieutenant in the Missouri Volunteer Engineers as early as August, 1861, serving later on Frémont's staff as captain in the Department of the West. Clearly the chief engineer in the Army of the Southwest, he was engaged in engineering duty on fortifications in Missouri, Kansas, and Arkansas. He closed his record during the war as chief engineer in the Department of Missouri with the rank of lieutenant colonel. [48]

Edward Siber, who wielded one of the best swords which Germany gave America, was openly pronounced by General Sherman as the best-trained officer of his army. In 1847, he left his post as captain and general staff officer in the Prussian army to enter the Schleswig-Holstein patriot army, in which he served with distinction; after the Danish war he went to Brazil at the call of Emperor Dom Pedro to serve as teacher in the army. At the outbreak of the American war he came to the United States and immediately became colonel of the German Thirty-seventh Ohio, to which he gave a model training—to officers as well as men. His aging

[47] Kaufmann, *Die Deutschen im Bürgerkriege*, 513–14; Henry (comp.), *Military Record of Civilian Appointments*, I, 339–40. General Wilson employed him after the war as first engineer on the embankment work on the Mississippi River.

[48] Wilson and Fiske (eds.), *Appletons' Cyclopaedia of American Biography*, I, 339; *Official War Records*, Ser. 1, XLVIII, Pt. 1, p. 474. He may have been living here in 1861, but the evidence seems against this possibility, as he was being sent to General Frémont, to whom the less distinguished foreign volunteers were pretty regularly sent. See letter of Frémont to Grant, August 13, 1861, which shows that the former had had advance notice of Hölcke's impending arrival. *Official War Records*, Ser. 1, III, p. 438.

body stood the strain for two years, but after the siege of Vicksburg he had to leave the service.[49]

As early as July 11, 1861, several former staff officers from German armies had already come to New York to enter the Northern army. Conspicuous among these was Herr Paul von Radowitz, a former officer of the Prussian Garde du Corps and the son of a war minister; by September, 1861, he had joined McClellan's staff, where he served throughout the war and repeatedly distinguished himself, especially at Antietam.[50] Even more brilliant was his friend, Herbert von Hammerstein, who for several years had been an officer in the Austrian army, and who came to the Union army for adventure. Like most of the others of his class, he was assigned in September, 1861, to McClellan's staff with the rank of major. The commander seems to have esteemed the Austrian highly; whenever there was a difficult or important service for an adjutant, Von Hammerstein or Von Radowitz was called upon to perform it. Later, in 1863, Von Hammerstein became first lieutenant colonel and then colonel of the Seventy-eighth New York Regiment and finally was transferred in June, 1864, to the command of the One Hundred and Second New York. He did not leave the service until January of the closing year of the war, and even then he returned to the Regular Army in July for a period of service.[51]

In sharp contrast with these members of the European aristocracy, but imbued with the same spirit of the fight, was a humbly placed fellow countryman of Von Radowitz, John Arnold, who had as a bricklayer wandered over a great part of Europe and Asia. After the outbreak of the Crimean War he took part in the campaign against the Russians under the British flag. Shortly thereafter he made his way to America, where the agent of the filibuster General William Walker induced this inoffensive

[49] Kaufmann, *Die Deutschen im Bürgerkriege*, 553. Siber appears repeatedly in *Official War Records*.

[50] Kaufmann, *Die Deutschen im Bürgerkriege*, 540. McClellan related that since he happened to be in Germany when the Austro-Prussian War broke out, he called upon the Prussian Minister of War to urge him to recall Von Radowitz because he was an excellent soldier, but that his suggestion was not heeded. Von Radowitz was last heard of as a croupier in a gambling den. McClellan, *McClellan's Own Story*, 144.

[51] Kaufmann, *Die Deutschen im Bürgerkriege*, 507; Heitman (comp.), *Historical Register and Dictionary*, I, 989. Von Hammerstein suffered a frightful fate. Failing to find employment after the war, he entered the regular Federal army as a private, hoping for rapid promotion, "but his habits were against him," according to McClellan. In the army he was used to carry the mail from one post to another in the West. He was caught in a snowstorm on one occasion, and both legs were so badly frozen that they had to be amputated. His relatives in Austria heard of the misfortune and had him brought home. See Kaufmann, *Die Deutschen im Bürgerkriege*, 507, for Von Hammerstein, and p. 540, for Von Radowitz.

stranger, unfamiliar with American politics, to engage in the Nicaraguan campaign. Safely back in the United States from his dangerous adventure, he devoted himself to his trade—but only for a few years, as Lincoln's first call brought him to the flag as sergeant in Captain Mihalotzy's company. Because of his protest to General Benjamin M. Prentiss—in behalf of his comrades against the bad care accorded the soldiers—he was removed from office, but he recovered his post when the reorganized company joined Hecker's regiment and was moved to Missouri. When he heard of the dangerous position of his company at Iron Mountain, he rose from his sickbed in St. Charles to make the trip to Pilot Knob. However, he died en route on August 1, 1861, an early sacrifice to the cause.[52]

Ireland could not fail to furnish, for this war as for other wars, her quota of adventurers. Prominent among them was a former member of the Pope's Irish Brigade who had distinguished himself in the army of the pontiff during the difficulties in Italy. John H. Gleason was a tall Irishman, every inch of his six feet and five inches bearing the stamp of the soldier. He was presented with a gold medal on October 5, 1860, for his brave services at the Battle of Ancona and was promoted from the rank of sergeant to that of lieutenant in recognition of his having taken Monte Moratta while in charge merely of a company of skirmishers. He came over to join the Sixty-third New York Regiment of Irishmen, entering Company H as a lieutenant and rising to be captain of Company B and eventually to be lieutenant colonel.[53]

Well known in the First Cavalry Division was Colonel Tim Hanley of the Ninth New Jersey Cavalry Regiment, for he had seen service in both the British and Austrian armies and wore three medals on his breast. He passed from the captaincy of Company K, Seventeenth Pennsylvania Cavalry, to the New Jersey service. A Galway man, Captain John Gosson was a born soldier, but he had no predilection for the British army, especially after his activity in the organization of 1849 had led to his arrest on suspicion although he had been discharged without trial after some months. He entered the Austrian service as a lieutenant and served under an old Catholic Austro-Irishman, General Count Nugent, in Syria. This service was followed by a commission in the Seventh Hussars of Austria, a Hungarian regiment headed by Prince Frederick of Leichtenstein.

[52] Moore (ed.), *Rebellion Record*, I, Pt. 3, p. 131; Cavanagh, *Memoirs of Gen. Meagher*, 460, 462.

[53] The battle of Ancona occurred in the marshes when the Papal States were annexed by the King of Sardinia in 1860.

He returned to Ireland after some years as a dashing soldier and won the hand of the daughter of an English baronet. Arriving in the United States in 1861, he gravitated, as naturally as the flower turns to the sun, to Meagher's side in the Irish Brigade; and there he kept his place throughout the war.

John J. Coppinger had wandered from the land of his nativity, the Emerald Isle, to become a captain in the Roman army. While serving in that capacity he was made a chevalier for the defense of the La Rocca gateway during the struggle for the Papal States in September, 1860. One year later he was serving as captain of the Fourteenth United States Infantry, and shortly thereafter he was in the Army of the Potomac. He participated in many battles and was wounded at Second Bull Run and Appomattox Courthouse. For gallantry at Trevilian Station he was brevetted major, and he closed his war career as colonel of the Fifteenth New York Cavalry. Captain Daniel J. Kelly, who was serving in the Papal Brigade shortly before our Civil War, became chief of staff for General Shields (an Irishman thus being properly assigned to an Irishman) and greatly distinguished himself at the Battle of Port Republic. Occasionally, one reads interesting bits of information about Irishmen whose names are not known. There was, for instance, the Irish sergeant of the First Louisiana United States Regiment, who, while going up by boat to Baton Rouge, in December, 1862, entertained his comrades with tales of his service in India—tales about the skill of the Sikhs at Sobraon and Chilianwalla.[54]

If one were to judge from this research, England did not furnish to the Northern army her usual quota of soldiers of fortune, possibly because her class of wanderer found himself less sympathetic toward the stronger combatant in the struggle. The records do show one Thomas Blair, a Scotchman, who had been in India three years in the service of the East India Company and had been a participant in the Sepoy Mutiny; he then enlisted in the United States Engineers' Battalion in 1865 as the war was about to close. A second man in search of adventure was a Major Warrington, an imposing man of middle age who presented himself in the fall of 1861 at the headquarters of the Irish Brigade to place his sword and

[54] For Hanley, see James Albert Clark, *The Making of a Volunteer Cavalryman* (*Military Order of the Loyal Legion of the United States,* Commandery of the District of Columbia, *War Papers,* No. 70), 16, 18; for Gosson, see Cavanagh, *Memoirs of Gen. Meagher,* Appendix, 15–16; for Coppinger, see Henry (comp.), *Military Record of Civilian Appointments,* I, 282; for Kelly, see New York *Irish-American,* June 12, 1862. A record appears in *Official War Records,* Ser. 1, LI, Pt. 1, p. 1281, for Kelly as sergeant. For the unnamed Irishman, see Hosmer, *The Color Guard,* 46.

experience at the disposal of the United States. He was a fine figure of a man, with a haughty profile, a complexion slightly too ruddy (probably from too much port), and hair and mustache beautifully silvered; the courtly, even arrogant, manners attributed to him are in keeping with the rumor that he was an illegitimate son of George IV. This aristocratic-looking Englishman soon became a conspicuous figure at headquarters on Broadway, making himself useful in routine clerical work and recounting tales of his life which his auditors took with the proverbial grain of salt. Though he was left behind in New York to superintend the forwarding of recruits when the brigade went to the front, he reported at Camp California for duty and was assigned a place as volunteer on the staff. Strangely enough, however, while the brigade was in the trenches at Fair Oaks, he disappeared after failing to deliver an order from General Meagher to Major Cavanagh—presumably as a result of finding the bullets too numerous for his taste.[55]

Palle Rosencrantz, a Swedish colonel, barely escapes classification as a knight-errant; however, when a man has served in the wars of four countries other than his native land, his love of fighting for the sake of the fight has been pretty well demonstrated. He was serving in the Skåne cavalry, but in 1848 he went over to the Danish service, returning to the Swedish army three years later. In 1853 he could be found in the French service. When the Crimean War developed, he entered the German Legion, which was organized by the British in Helgoland; unfortunately (at least, to his thinking), the abrupt termination of that war prevented him from taking an active part or winning any glory. With the outbreak of the American Civil War he turned his face to America as a new field of opportunity; he commanded a corps in West Virginia, and for two years he acted as major in the Fourth New York Cavalry.[56]

By the test of service under several flags a second Swede, Elof Oscar Hultman, also qualifies as a soldier of fortune. He had served his own country as lieutenant in several regiments; had served in the Foreign Legion of the French army in Algeria in 1861; had secured a captaincy in the Fifty-eighth New York; and had received, later that same year, a majorship on the staff of General Blenker, under whom he participated in a number of battles. By 1862, however, he had left the American service

---

[55] See Henry (comp.), *Military Record of Civilian Appointments*, II, 47, for Blair; for Warrington, see Cavanagh, *Memoirs of Gen. Meagher*, Appendix, 19–20. Warrington fails to appear in the official records, possibly because he was with the brigade so short a time.

[56] Hokanson, *Swedish Immigrants*, 94; Chicago *Hemlandet*, November 27, 1861.

to serve for a short period with the French and Mexican armies before returning to his old regiment in Sweden.[57]

A third soldier of fortune of this nationality was Captain Christian Peterson. After six years as an underofficer in the Swedish-Norwegian army, he rendered thirteen months service as sergeant in the Danish-German War. In the summer of 1861 he volunteered for the Thirty-third Illinois Regiment and served in Missouri until the close of the year. On one occasion during 1861, he functioned as commandant at Camp Butler near Springfield, Illinois, where were stationed two companies of infantry.[58]

Peculiar interest attaches, because of his more-famous aviator relative, to Måns Olsson Lindbergh, who was an underofficer in the Southern Skånian Infantry of the Swedish army. His father, Ole Månsson, was a well-known leader of the agricultural estate in the Swedish *Riksdag,* or parliament, in the decade of the fifties, who migrated to Minnesota in 1859, just as the superior court of Sweden was convicting him of embezzlement in his capacity of a director of the loan office of the Bank of Sweden at Malmö. It is likely that his foes—and they were many because of his liberal ideas—distorted facts so as to "frame" him and that he was guilty only in a technical sense.

The son, Måns Olsson, while a student at the University of Lund, took the name of Lindbergh, probably simply for the purpose of being easily distinguished from the countless other Olssons; but this name later also served partly to disassociate him from the scandal connected with his father's name. In 1855 he enlisted as a volunteer in the British army and served in Britain's Swiss Legion, partly in England and partly in Asiatic Turkey, for a year during the Crimean War. For five years, from April 1857, to April 1862, he served his native land in the Royal South Skånian Infantry Regiment. In 1862 he and a younger brother came to this country, separating in Chicago, the latter joining the father and a still younger brother, Charles (grandfather of the present-day aviator), in Minnesota, while Måns enlisted in the Eighty-second Illinois Regiment. The military experience of the latter in Europe accounts for his rapid promotion through the noncommissioned posts to the rank of captain by the close of the war. He served throughout the war, participating in many battles—among

---

[57] Chicago *Hemlandet,* October 6, 1861; Madison *Emigranten,* Extra Sheet, Nos. 40–41; Hokanson, *Swedish Immigrants,* 93.

[58] Madison *Emigranten,* November 11, 1861. These Swedish officers are not listed in *Official War Records.*

others, Chancellorsville, Gettysburg, Chattanooga, and Lookout Mountain—and many minor skirmishes. He was cited by Lincoln as brevet captain in the United States Army, an honor which he did not accept because of his impending departure for his native land. The feat for which he was brevetted was probably the taking of a mountain pass in Tennessee on October 30, 1863, with only thirty men.[59]

Some other soldiers of fortune came to the Union army from Austria and Hungary. Occasionally a soldier revealed his claim to membership in this fraternity by virtue of his career subsequent to his American experience. Adolf von Lüttwitz is a case in point. A former officer of the Austrian army, he found a post in the Northern army first as captain in the Fifty-fourth New York and then on Schurz's staff; later he assumed command of the pioneers of Schurz's division. Long after the Civil War was ended he entered the service of the British army and fought in the Boer War. A true adventurer was Gotthilf Bourray d'Ivernois, who gravitated from the Austrian service to the Papal army and then to the Union army, where he commanded the Sixty-eighth New York. He fought well in the latter post but was discharged for drunkenness.[60]

Among the Hungarian heroes were some who had fought in two, three, or even four wars; some had begun their military careers by participating in the Polish War and had continued them in the Hungarian Revolution; and some had fought in the Crimean War or in Italy with Garibaldi. Without going into detail we may mention Philip Figyelmessy; Alexander Gaal, who fought in the Hungarian Legion in Italy and enlisted here im-

[59] Skåne is an old province in southwestern Sweden, now merged into a larger province. Lindbergh's subsequent career in promoting a Swedish colony in Minnesota does not concern us here. It might merely be stated, however, that in 1866 he returned to Sweden, where he re-entered the Royal South Skånian Infantry, with which unit he remained until April, 1868. King Charles XV bestowed upon him after his return the royal silver medal for "bravery in action." He died of tuberculosis at the age of thirty-five in 1870.

There are in the Minnesota Historical Society some valuable photostats of the Swedish paper *Cimbrishammbladet* for June 17, 1867, and November 18, 1867; the originals are preserved in the Royal Library in Stockholm. The *Cimbrishammbladet* reproduced an article entitled "Svensk Krigare i Utlandet (Swedish Soldiers Abroad)," and this article, together with one in the issue of November 18, 1867, recorded exactly Lindbergh's promotions in the United States army: sergeant in 1862; color-bearer in March, 1863; second lieutenant on June 23, 1863; first lieutenant on October 7, 1863; company commander, 1864; and captain, 1865. When he was personally attacked in Sweden because of his plan to lead a Swedish colony to Minnesota, he published a testimonial by A. Thott, chief of the Skånian Regiment, in the *Nyeste Oresundsposten*, November 13, 1868. A copy of this is preserved in the Royal Library. (Photostat in the Minnesota Historical Society.)

[60] Kaufmann, *Die Deutschen im Bürgerkriege*, 529, 485–86; Hokanson, *Swedish Immigrants*, 529.

mediately after his arrival in 1864; Charles Semsey; Emery Szabad; Ladislaus Zsulavszky (a nephew of Louis Kossuth, as the reader will recall), who organized and became colonel of the Eighty-second Colored Regiment; and Peter Paul Dobozy. Semsey and Zsulavszky both fought in the Crimean War after the failure of the Hungarian revolt, and Dobozy took part in the Italian War.

Outstanding in the group is Figyelmessy, who had attained the rank of major in the Hungarian revolt and had received a medal for bravery. When he was declared an outlaw for helping political prisoners to escape, he fled to Constantinople with his wife and joined Kossuth in Asia Minor. Though there was a price on his head, he traveled in disguise in Hungary for some time, distributing far and wide copies of Kossuth's revolutionary proclamation. In 1859 he organized in Italy a Hungarian hussar regiment and fought there for two years. Garibaldi addressed him as a "hero of heroes," and King Victor Emmanuel appointed him a colonel, even offering him a post in the Italian army, which he declined. He arrived in America in the fall of 1861, where Secretary Seward, who had probably encouraged his coming, offered him a colonelcy in one of the volunteer regiments. Figyelmessy, however, declined this, evidently preferring service on General Frémont's staff, where he became inspector general at Wheeling. He had little opportunity for distinguishing himself in the war in America.[61]

After the overthrow in 1849 of the revolutionary government in Hungary, Lieutenant Colonel Emery Szabad served in the Hungarian Legion in Italy under Figyelmessy, conducting himself honorably in the Neapolitan campaign. About a year after the outbreak of the war in America, he sought the new field of action, serving under General Daniel E. Sickles, with whom he had become acquainted in London. After being captured for the first time in his life by the Confederates and incarcerated for several months in Libby Prison, where he kept a diary, parts of which were later published, he returned to service as adjutant on the staff of General L. B. Ayres in March, 1865. Two weeks later he was promoted to the rank of colonel as a reward for gallantry at Petersburg.[62]

A last Hungarian-Rumanian remains to be noted, Captain Nicholas Dunka, born in Walachia but of Hungarian parents, who identified himself with the Hungarian war for independence. He served as a lieutenant

[61] Vasvary, *Lincoln's Hungarian Heroes*, 52–53.

[62] Parts of his diary were published in *Every Saturday*, and will be referred to in a later chapter. The above account is based on a note at the heading of the excerpts in *Every Saturday*, and on Vasvary, *Lincoln's Hungarian Heroes*, 83.

beside Figyelmessy under Garibaldi in his Sicilian and Neapolitan campaigns. Drawn with his countrymen into the American conflict, he became an officer in Blenker's division, and was ordered to serve on General Stahel's staff and later on Frémont's staff as adjutant with the rank of captain. The young soldier fell at Cross Keys; his loss was reported by Frémont in the words, "On my staff, I lost a good officer killed, Captain Nicholas Dunka." [63]

Although a soldier of fortune named Von Traubenfass joined the United States Regular Army shortly before the outbreak of war, he was nonetheless an adventurer and should be noted here for the intrinsic interest of his story. His name suggests a German origin, but the chronicler who rescued him from oblivion did not reveal his nativity. He had served in the Spanish Legion, in the war on the Rio Grande (the Mexican War, presumably), in the Schleswig-Holstein campaign, and in the pay of a half-dozen Indian princes; and he displayed a galaxy of orders bestowed on him by deposed potentates. His last post, before he received a commission in the United States Regular Army as instructor of cavalry or inspector of horses, had been in the Garibaldian army. [64]

Another example of the loose adventurer bound to turn up in every army is afforded in Lieutenant Colonel Louis Kazinski, who attained his rank in a German regiment that he had helped to organize. When the regiment started for the field, he resigned his post under the pretext that the agents of the government had interfered in his affairs. This proved to be a prudent move, for about the same time the colonel of the regiment, with whom Kazinski had shared the cares and profits of the organization, was arrested for embezzlement. Fortunately for Count Kazinski, he had been better advised and had taken the precaution to disappear. This "count" seems to have been no novice in matters of this kind, for some years before, in the Crimean War, he had been involved in a somewhat similar proceeding. He had, however, not hesitated to use his British experience to secure the position of lieutenant colonel in the Union army. [65]

A fact which cannot have escaped the reader is the remarkable number of men in the Union army, privates as well as officers, who bore titles of social rank. He will instantly recall General von Steinwehr, General von

[63] For Frémont's praise, see *Official War Records*, Ser. 1, XII, Pt. 1, p. 655. See also Vasvary, *Lincoln's Hungarian Heroes*, 50–51.

[64] The statements about Von Traubenfass are from Edward Dicey, *Six Months in the Federal States* (London, 1863), II, 48. Though Dicey makes light of Von Traubenfass, he is obviously a real character and a soldier of fortune.

[65] New York *Courrier des États-Unis*, January 7, 1863.

Schimmelfennig, Baron von Steuben, Colonel von Gilsa, and Lieutenant Colonel von Radowitz; the Swedish noblemen, Baron von Vegesack, Colonel von Knorring, and Baron Cedarström; the English gentlemen of title, Wyndham and De Courcey; the Italian, Count di Cesnola; the Austrian, Von Bukowics; and the Dane, Von Rosenörn. A Dutchman not previously mentioned, Captain George van Ess, was also of high birth. These are but a few of the many men of high social rank who move through these pages. In the biographical section of Wilhelm Kaufmann's book *Die Deutschen im amerikanischen Bürgerkriege,* the writer counted no less than fifty-seven Germans with titles who served in the Union army. But it is only in the Descriptive Books, where titles appear even after the names of non-commissioned officers and men in the ranks, that the list of titled foreigners seems really impressive.

A few selections, though the number could be greatly increased, are sufficient to substantiate the statement that many men of title accepted offices of low rank. The first lieutenant of Company B, Fifty-second New York Infantry, was Eugene von Schoning, who fell near Fair Oaks; and a second son of the same noble family was serving at the same time as first lieutenant in the Second Missouri. Otto, Baron von Fritsch, was captain of Company A, Sixty-eighth New York Infantry. In that same regiment Fritz von Werth was serving as captain of Company K. Stephen von Unrah consented to enter Company B as a common soldier, while a Frenchman, Julius Maffré de Verdts, marched and fought as a private in Company C of the so-called "Polish Legion" until he was promoted to first sergeant. In the records his name appears as captain of Company K in the same regiment only a short while later, indicating that education and zeal brought here, as elsewhere, their due reward. Otto von Barries was captain in Company E and Louis von Waldeck second lieutenant in Company K of the One Hundred and Nineteenth New York, the latter having risen to a commissioned position from first sergeant.

Although George van Ess was of the comparatively advanced age of thirty-six, he did not disdain to enter Company K, One Hundred and Nineteenth New York, as a common soldier. Ludwig von Blessing and Carl von Heintze were lieutenant colonel and captain respectively in the Thirty-seventh Ohio. In the Seventy-fifth Pennsylvania, not recognized as a German regiment, the lieutenant colonel and the quartermaster both bore the title of "von." Herman von Rothburg, first corporal of Company B, Fifth New York, derived his title from Austria.

These men, presumably gently reared, did not escape financial difficulties in America; in fact, such difficulties were probably an old story with many of them. Lauritz von Barentzen became major of the One Hundred and Sixth Ohio but found himself in financial difficulties after he had been in the service two months. He had been directed in Washington to pay his own expenses and assured that when he reached Columbus, Ohio, the governor would reimburse him at the rate of ten cents a mile.[66] A title did not keep August de Tapper of Company B, One Hundred and Nineteenth New York, from deserting early in the war—on June 19, 1862, as recorded in the Descriptive Book.[67]

This chapter must not close without a word about two young adventurers whose names arrest attention. In the popular mind, both have been associated with Africa, and it may be a surprise to learn that they were associated with the American Civil War. The writer in a previous study has had occasion to call attention to the Civil War record of Henry M. Stanley, known in his native Wales as John Rowlands. Strangely enough, he had a war record with both the Confederate and the Union armies. After enlisting in a Confederate company in Arkansas and making a good record on the Southern side, he was captured at Shiloh and ended his imprisonment by enlisting in the Union army. His physical condition was not good, and for that reason he was discharged a month later. As if to miss no possible experience, he returned from a short visit home to join the Federal navy, serving on the *North Carolina* and the *Minnesota* until February, 1866, when he closed his remarkable career in the United States by deserting at Portsmouth, New Hampshire.[68]

To make the story complete, the name of David Livingstone himself should appear on the Union muster rolls; it does not; but the family was represented, as is evidenced by the name there of his son. Of a restless, roving temperament, the young man had come out to America and landed in Boston. There he promptly enlisted in a Massachusetts regiment and,

[66] Company Descriptive Books; letter (asking reimbursement) of Von Barentzen to Governor Dennison of Ohio, Camp Chase, December 2, 1861, Executive Correspondence of the Governors of Ohio, December 1–15, 1861. Of the group named, the following are identified in *Official War Records*: Von Schoning, Von Waldeck, Von Blessing (also spelled "Blessingh" and so spelled in *Official War Records*), Von Heintze, and Von Barentzen.

[67] The nearest approach to this name found in *Official War Records* is that of Augustus Tappin, but he does not seem to be the person designated.

[68] "Stanley, H. M.," in *Confederate Veteran*, II (1894), 332; Lonn, *Foreigners in the Confederacy*, 198–99; Dorothy Stanley (ed.), *The Autobiography of Sir Henry Morton Stanley* (Boston and New York, 1909), 167 ff.

while a mere lad of eighteen, fell at Gettysburg. The comment of his father in a letter to a friend is touching: "My son is in the Federal army in America, and no comfort." [69] Knight-errant or soldier of fortune? It is difficult to classify these two youths, but that both were actuated by a spirit of adventure is clear.

[69] William Garden Blaikee, *The Personal Life of David Livingstone* (New York, 1887), 339–40.

CHAPTER TWELVE

Special Services in the Army

IN THE field of special services, including those performed by chaplains, physicians, engineers, quartermasters, and hospital attendants, the personnel no more could be restricted to the native-born than it could be in the fighting troops. Just as many foreigners, because of their enforced military training, were able to render a peculiar service as officers in the field, so some of them had a special fitness for other fields of service. It was inevitable that many of the musicians should be drawn from the German element of our population; that the superior training of physicians from Heidelberg, Vienna, Edinburgh, or London should be welcome for the wounded; and that the engineer department should profit from the technical skill and training of certain men born abroad. Most of all, it was inevitable that foreign-born soldiers would turn for spiritual comfort to men of their own nationality who could speak the words of solace in a tongue which they readily understood.

CHAPLAINS

A few words of explanation as to the status of the chaplains—their rank and pay—and as to their classification as hospital chaplains or chaplains in the field with the volunteer regiments will not be out of place. During the first three months service of the state militia, arrangements for chaplains were quite irregular. Some of the state organizations had chaplains, but others had made no provision for such officials, in which case the governor might exercise his right of appointment. At the termination of this brief service, these chaplains were all mustered out with their respective units.

Under a law of Congress of August, 1861, empowering the President to provide for the appointment of chaplains for all regiments, each of whom must be a regularly ordained minister of some Christian denomination,[1] President Lincoln gave each colonel the right to choose a chaplain for whom a majority of the field and company officers of his regiment had voted.[2] A candidate so chosen must be reported to the War Department and (if the unit was composed of state volunteers) to the governor; if acceptable to both, the individual received official appointment from the War Department. Thereupon the chaplain's name was placed upon the field and staff roll of the regiment. The War Department as early as May 4, 1861, had issued a general order that chaplains were to receive the same pay and allowances as captains of cavalry; an amendment of July 17, 1862, decreed that chaplains should be borne on the staff rolls immediately after surgeons and be entitled to full pay when on leave, even if prisoners of war.[3] The salary was, therefore, $100 a month, and when on duty each chaplain was entitled to draw two rations a day. Because of the looseness of the colonels in appointing to office men unsuited to the duties, as we shall see, Congress soon stipulated that every candidate must present recommendations from proper ecclesiastical authorities.[4]

During the war, the post of hospital chaplain corresponded to that of chaplain of the Regular Army in peacetime. The hospital chaplain was appointed by the President by virtue of the discretionary powers vested in him under the Constitution, which he usually availed himself of only in the time of emergency. Such appointments were tardily legalized by Congress on May 20, 1862.[5] The other group, by far the larger, consisted of the chaplains attached to the volunteer units in the Union army—one for each volunteer regiment.

With the large number of Irish troops in the Union army, it was natural that there should have been a considerable number of Catholic priests. These were by no means all Irish though there were certainly many Irishmen serving in that capacity, for there were also Austrian, Italian,

---

[1] *The Statutes at Large of the United States of America*, XII (Boston, 1863), Chap. IX, Sect. 9. This work is hereinafter cited as *United States Statutes at Large*.

[2] General Orders, No. 15, *Official War Records*, Ser. 3, I, pp. 154, 157.

[3] General Orders, No. 158, *ibid.*, IV, 227–28; *United States Statutes at Large*, XII, Chap. CC, Sect. 9.

[4] This was largely owing to a protest by the paymaster general sent to Senator Henry Wilson: "I regret to say that very many holding this position [of chaplain] are utterly unworthy. . . . It is said one regiment employs a French cook and musters him as chaplain to meet the expense. I cannot vouch for the truth of this rumor, but I do know that some are utterly unworthy of their position." *Official War Records*, Ser. 3, I, p. 728. This letter is dated December 5, 1861.

[5] See General Orders, No. 55, May 24, 1862, in which the statute is quoted. *Ibid.*, Ser. 3, II, p. 222.

German, and French priests. Indeed, owing to the catholicity characteristic of that church, it was possible to find a French-Canadian serving as
a chaplain in the Irish Brigade, to the satisfaction of all, and a German
priest officiating in the so-called "Polish Legion." No effort will be made
to enumerate all the Roman Catholic priests in the service; such a procedure would degenerate into a catalog and would be dull and unrewarding, but enough will be introduced to afford a picture of what the foreign-
born priests contributed in quantity and quality to ease by spiritual means
the disagreeable and often agonizing path of the soldier.

A proper starting point is, perhaps, the Irish Brigade. To emphasize
the point just made of the catholicity of the Roman Church, the name
first mentioned might well be that of Father Thomas Willet, who reported at Fort Schuyler on November 10, 1861, and served for a time as
the French-Canadian father-confessor of the Irish Sixty-ninth New York.
His surname had originally been Ouellett, which sufficiently attests its
French origin and the changes in spelling sustained at the hands of Irish
scribes. After seeing service with the regiment in the Peninsular campaign,
at Antietam and Fredericksburg, he sought and obtained a discharge
(because of the reduction of numbers in the regiment to the point where
his services were no longer needed) in order to enter hospital service in the
Department of North Carolina. Here he served from shortly after his
acceptance on May 30, 1863, to January 9, 1864, when he was recalled
by his superior in New York. He then found his old regiment in process
of reorganization, and, upon his unanimous re-election, rejoined it about
the first of May, serving through to the end of the war. He was described
as a martinet toward the men in regard to their religious obligations, but
as an eloquent, forcible preacher, acceptable to the Irishmen not only for
himself but for the many past associations of Irish knight-errantry with
France.[6]

Father William Corby, the American-born son of an Irish pioneer
who settled in Michigan, was known throughout the Brigade as the
chaplain of the Eighty-eighth New York Regiment. Like Colonel Mulligan of the Twenty-third Illinois, he was such an outstanding "Irishman"
that it seems scarcely possible to omit mention of him. He was one of
several members of the faculty of the University of Notre Dame in South
Bend, Indiana, who went to the front. The story of his solicitude for a
private in Company B who died of sunstroke on the march has often been

[6] Dom Aidan Henry Germain (comp.), *Catholic Military and Naval Chaplains 1776–1917*
(Washington, 1929), 58, 104–107.

told. He served through three years of the fiercest fighting of the war, resigning only at the close of 1864 to return to the University at the request of its president. His name is inseparably associated with the general absolution which he gave to the Irish Brigade on the battlefield of Gettysburg, which episode will be related at the proper place. The third of the New York regiments of the Brigade, the Sixty-third, had for its chaplain the Irish-born Father James Dillon, also from the University of Notre Dame, who shared the vicissitudes of the Peninsular campaign but resigned, probably because of his health, in the following October. He also conducted Mass for the Tammany Regiment, which consisted largely of Irishmen. Father Lawrence McMahon, who served just short of a year (from June, 1862, to the last of May, 1863), was the Canadian-born chaplain of the Twenty-eighth Massachusetts. Father Edward McKee, who ministered to the One Hundred and Sixteenth Pennsylvania only through the Fredericksburg campaign, was succeeded much later (in 1864) by Father Bernard McCollum.[7]

Only one chaplain connected with Corcoran's Irish Legion has been identified, but Father Paul Gillen, a North of Ireland man, was in himself the equivalent of a host of men. During the first year of the war he was a free lance, moving from one part of the army to another in order to seek out, and minister to, Catholic soldiers. He traveled in an old-fashioned, flat-bottomed vehicle, which carried a few army blankets—for his "rockaway" was his bed at night—some provisions, a chapel tent of his own architecture, and a folding altar. General Grant ordered his arrest and expulsion under a general order forbidding "citizens" within army limits. Father Gillen then accepted a commission as chaplain in the One Hundred and Seventieth New York, where he labored until the end of the war.[8]

[7] For Corby, see *ibid.*, 64–65; for Father Dillon, see *ibid.*, 66–67; for Fathers McMahon, McKee, and McCollum, see *ibid.*, 84, 83–84, 82–83. The best source for Father Corby is, of course, his own book: William Corby, *Memoirs of Chaplain Life* (Notre Dame, Ind., 1894). For Father Dillon, see also Charles G. Herbermann and others (eds.), *The Catholic Encyclopedia* (New York, 1907–1922), VIII, 140. It might be added that the chaplain who went out with the Sixty-ninth Militia for the three months service was Father Thomas H. Mooney, who was Irish, as his name indicates. Germain (comp.), *Catholic Chaplains*, 85–86.

To determine the nativity of many of these Catholic chaplains has been one of the most trying bits of work connected with the research, involving the writing of endless letters. Very few appear in the *Catholic Encyclopedia*, with the result that the writer has had to trouble Catholic chancellors and officials all over the country, who have kindly consulted their records. In view of that fact, it is impracticable to give in every case the source which proves the land of origin.

[8] Corby, *Memoirs of Chaplain Life*, 207–10, has something about Father Gillen, but the best source is a manuscript by David Powers Conyngham, "Heroism of the Cross or Nuns and

Other Irish regiments likewise had Irish chaplains: Father Thomas M. Brady served with the Fifteenth Michigan; Father William O'Higgins served with the Ohio Tenth; and Father Thomas Scully, who suffered three weeks imprisonment at Richmond, was one of the several chaplains of the Ninth Massachusetts. Father Scully was succeeded by Father Costney Egan, who served from September, 1863, until the regiment was mustered out. He will be more fully discussed later. An Italian from Savoy, Father Peter Tissot, served the Irishmen of the Thirty-seventh New York to their satisfaction; but an Irishman, Father Daniel Mullen, looked after the spiritual welfare of the Irish Ninth Connecticut from November, 1861, to the end of August, 1863. Father Francis Fusseder, an Austrian, was, of course, equipped to serve the Germans of the Twenty-fourth Wisconsin acceptably.[9]

Probably no priest in the service was better known than Father J. F. Trecy, also an Irishman, who officiated so unostentatiously at General Rosecrans' headquarters, and whose devotion to his chief was second only to his devotion to his faith. Born in Ireland, he came with his family to this country in 1836 as a lad of ten. After a period of strenuous service as a priest in the frontier country of Iowa and Nebraska, he was, at his own request, sent to the South to recuperate his health. He joined the diocese of Mobile, where he labored till the outbreak of the war. Always a Union man, he met little difficulty with his congregation at Huntsville, which, except for three families, was Unionist. Before long, however, the good father had to flee for his life to General Rosecrans, with whom, after a dangerous and futile return to Huntsville for his personal possessions, he remained as constant friend and spiritual adviser. He was esteemed for his worth by his command and the staff alike. He usually slipped into headquarters in his quiet way about ten o'clock at night, entertained the circle with his collection of "grapevines," which he had a faculty for picking up in the streets, and then as quietly slipped out again to bed. He enjoyed merriment with the gayest and was erudite with the learned.[10]

Religious devotion was a marked feature at the headquarters of the

---

Priests of the Battlefield," Chap. XIV. The manuscript is preserved in the archives of the University of Notre Dame. See also Germain (comp.), *Catholic Chaplains*, 69–70.

[9] *Ibid.*, 59–60, 68, 68–69, 86, 92, 94–95, 102–104. For treatment of Scully (at some length) and of Father Tissot, see Conyngham, "Heroism of the Cross," Chap. IX and Chap. XI, respectively. This regiment was not wholly German.

[10] W. D. B[ickham], *Rosecrans' Campaign with the Fourteenth Army Corps . . .* (Cincinnati, 1863), 136, 140–41. There are three chapters (I–III) devoted to Father Trecy in Conyngham, "Heroism of the Cross."

Catholic general Rosecrans. On the night before the Battle of Stone's River at the close of 1862, High Mass was celebrated in a little tent opposite the general's marquee. The Reverend Father Peter Cooney, the zealous Irish-born chaplain of the Thirty-fifth regiment of Indiana Volunteers, officiated, assisted by Father Trecy. General Rosecrans knelt humbly in the corner of his tent; his chief of staff, Julius P. Garesché, no less devout, at his side; a trio of humble soldiers, meekly in front of the tent. Father Trecy was later commissioned chaplain of the Fourth United States Cavalry, but he was allowed great latitude in visiting Catholics in other commands. He was distinguished from other Catholic chaplains in that he wore top boots, spurs, and a soldier's coat and hat. The service for which Father Cooney was most beloved was the trip he made after each payday to take back to Indiana the money drawn by the men of his regiment, in order to distribute it to their families or to deposit it to their credit if they were without dependents.[11] He was another of the Catholic prelates drawn from the University of Notre Dame.

The Reverend Thomas Kelly of the Ninetieth Illinois (readily recalled by the reader as a regiment of Irishmen) was little known to the men of his regiment before the war except at the altar. But when he was obliged on account of the state of his health to resign in July, 1863, after less than a year with the regiment, his departure called forth from the officers of the regiment resolutions which to a remarkable degree set the man before us: "A staunch and unwearying patriot, he enunciated, in the simplest eloquence, the maxim that, after our Creator, our next duty we owe our Country." He evidently possessed the usual strain of Irish humor, for it was said that at the social board his wit made him many friends both within and without the regiment. With the abundance of compliments usual on such occasions, the resolutions declared, "Such a combination of virtue could not fail to call forth our heart-felt admiration and link between him and us the triple tie of friend, companion, and priest." [12]

The Eightieth Ohio Volunteers had as chaplain George W. Peeper, who was apparently a Protestant though Irish-born. After seeing action as captain of one of the companies in this regiment and resigning because of

---

[11] The Reverend Thomas McAvoy has published "The War Letters of Father Peter Paul Cooney of the Congregation of the Holy Cross," in *Records of the American Catholic Historical Society*, Philadelphia, XLIV (1933), Nos. 1, 2, and 3. The series includes a brief biographical sketch of Father Cooney. See also B[ickham], *Rosecrans' Campaign*, 205–206; Germain (comp.), *Catholic Chaplains*, 63–64.

[12] New York *Irish-American*, September 19, 1863; Germain (comp.), *Catholic Chaplains*, 72–73.

ill-health, he returned as chaplain, continuing to engage in many battles as aide-de-camp. In his insistence on active participation in conflict he was only running true to form; for he had served in Ireland as secretary of the United Kingdom Alliance and had engaged actively in the Irish Revolution, so that his departure for the United States in 1859 was obviously for his self-preservation.[13]

The senior chaplain of the First Division of the Fifth Corps, Father Costney L. Egan, of the Ninth Massachusetts, who was asked to give the memorial address to this division on the day of Lincoln's funeral, was an eloquent Irishman, who played on the emotions of his auditors as on the strings of an instrument. The record of his address on that memorable occasion gives some hint of how much chaplains like him, of whatever creed, could contribute to the morale of the army. The entire scene must have been moving. The division was formed in a hollow square, facing inward. The old, battle-torn, smoke-stained flags, draped in crepe, were brought to the front of the regiments; behind these "the men stacked arms, and stood, tense and motionless, as a hushed sea. . . . On the open face of the square, on a little mound, we planted the red Maltese cross of the division,—itself emblem and memorial of great things suffered and done for men. Around it gathered the generals and staff. . . . With countenance precluding speech, in measured articulation made more impressive by its slightly foreign cast, he launches forth his thrilling text, 'Give me here the head of John Baptist in a charger. . . .' "

"And will you endure this sacrilege?" he cried. "Can heavenly charity tolerate such crime under the flag of this delivered country? Will you not rather sweep such a spirit out of the land forever, and cast it, root and branch, into everlasting burning!" When General Chamberlain told him he must not stop, but must turn the excitement to some good, he whispered, "I will." "Thus admonished of the passion he was arousing, he passed to an exhortation that rose into a prayer, then to a paean of victory, and with an oath of new consecration to the undying cause of freedom and right," he left the audience better soldiers and better men. One can gather from the comment of the general the quality of Egan's eloquence: "Who that heard those burning words can ever forget them." [14]

[13] Augustus Woodbury, The Second Rhode Island Regiment. A Narrative of Military Operations . . . from the Beginning to the End of the War . . . (Providence, 1875), 27; Henry (comp.), Military Record of Civilian Appointments, I, 37.

Father Thomas Quinn had gone out with the First Rhode Island Militia for the three months service.

[14] Joshua Lawrence Chamberlain, The Passing of the Armies (New York, 1915), 283–86.

The Reverend Francis MacAtee, a Jesuit father who was attached to the Thirty-first New York Infantry from October, 1861, to June, 1863, rode through rain and sleet, snow and slush, always ready to hear confessions, to give advice, to visit the sick, and to comfort the troubled soul. Gentle and tender, yet friendly, he seemed to some of his charges the ideal priest. In Captain Hogg's company of the Second New York Artillery were some thirty Catholics, to which he added those from other companies until he often marched sixty men down to the camp of the Thirty-first, where stood the little chapel of the Jesuit priest.[15] The Reverend Fred Herzberg and Father Anthony Zyla, who died in the hospital April 5, 1865, were chaplains of the Polish Legion, according to the Regimental Descriptive Book. The latter name, at least, suggests Polish nativity.

Even within the functions of the Catholic Church, language could prove a barrier, as was evidenced in the case of the German-born priest, the Reverend Gustavus Miettinger. He was mustered into service as chaplain of the Second New York Infantry on July 14, 1861, but after six months service he found his situation unsatisfactory, as the soldiers of this regiment were chiefly Irish or Protestant. He spoke sufficient English for the confessional but not for the preaching of sermons or the general duties of a chaplain; indeed, he wrote his letters to headquarters in his native tongue. Hence, as there was no German Catholic regiment available, he was discharged from the service in March, 1862.[16] Another German priest, the Reverend Joseph A. Stephan, served for a few months in 1863 as hospital chaplain at Nashville. To the hospital at Washington a Swiss-born priest, Father Bernardin Wiget, was assigned in October, 1862.[17] Of the comparatively small group of thirteen Catholic hospital chaplains, five were recorded as Irish, one as German, one as Canadian-French, and one as Swiss.

Father Egan served from November 25, 1863, to June 21, 1864. See Germain, (comp.), *Catholic Chaplains*, 68, and Conyngham, "Heroism of the Cross." He entered the service as a result of being asked to visit two Catholic Italians who had been condemned to be executed. He was then asked to visit the Ninth Massachusetts Regiment, which had been without a chaplain since the departure of Father Scully. He thereupon offered his services to that regiment.

[15] Letter of George Hogg on "2 New York Artillery," in New York *Irish-American*, February 13, 1862; Germain (comp.), *Catholic Chaplains*, 81–82.

[16] Germain (comp.), *Catholic Chaplains*, 84–85. In Jacket for Gustavus Miettinger, The National Archives, there is a long letter by him in German script to departmental headquarters detailing the facts given in the text.

[17] Germain (comp.), *Catholic Chaplains*, 57–58. The possibly disproportionate amount of space given to the Catholic chaplains was because more data was available than for foreign-born Protestant chaplains.

Foreign-born Protestant chaplains, except German and Scandinavian pastors, encountered in the course of the research are comparatively few. The Reverend Alexander McLeod was born in Canada and was appointed from Delaware. He was chaplain of the Eighty-fourth Pennsylvania Volunteers, was in the field with the regiment for one year, and then became a hospital chaplain. His training had been varied, for he had studied for two professions; first for medicine, at the University of Philadelphia from 1817 to 1820, in pursuit of which calling he had served aboard an East Indian ship; and then for the ministry from 1842 to 1844. After his theological training he had been in charge of parishes in Ohio and Pennsylvania until the coming of war.[18]

Though there were, as has been indicated, German Catholic priests, the larger number of German clergy in the country were of the Lutheran persuasion. While an application for a chaplaincy is not tantamount to filling such a post, the applications do show the disposition of the Lutheran clergy and merit a moment's attention. Several of these applications were made to the governor of Ohio. One ordained pastor, who was a graduate of Wittenberg College at Springfield, had belonged to the Miami Lutheran synod since 1858 and felt that his going into the military service would influence others; another, pastor of the Lutheran Church at Lithopolis, Ohio, stressed his familiarity with both German and English and won the recommendation of the Military Commission of Ohio; a third was cast out from the church, apparently at Van Wert, Ohio, believing in "peace upon any terms," because he approved of putting down the rebellion by the bayonet.[19]

There seems to have been much latitude in the appointment of chaplains in some of the German regiments—certainly in Blenker's division. Dr. John A. Forsch was appointed chaplain for the Steuben Regiment just before the First Battle of Bull Run; August Becker, a significant journalist and poet and a Forty-eighter, was appointed to look after the spiritual needs of the same regiment a little later. Wilhelm Stengel, who accepted the chaplaincy of McCook's Ninth Ohio, a regiment of Germans, informed the men of the regiment in his opening sermon that they need expect no Bible lectures and no church ceremonies—that he would point the soldiers only to their duties as men and soldiers and would select his

[18] Henry (comp.), *Military Record of Civilian Appointments*, I, 34.

[19] The first clergyman was J. C. Brodfuhrer, whose application was dated August 8, 1862; the second, the Reverend Mr. Erich, whose application was dated August 4, 1862; the third, the Reverend George A. Exline, mentioned in the letter of C. P. Exson to Governor John Brough, May 3, 1864. Executive Correspondence of the Governors of Ohio.

illustrations from history. He was in the regiment as a man not of words but of action, and had brought with him a good revolver; therefore, when the regiment was in battle, the men would see him, not on his knees but in the foremost ranks with the fighters, ready to let his good weapon speak to the enemy. He closed his "sermon" with the following words: "Freedom—a road—Death to the traitors." His sermon seemed to find general approval, though many approved with smiling mien. His successor, Joseph A. Fuchshuber, was a man of much the same stripe. His sermons could be called free-minded lectures, but he gave good advice to the soldiers, wrote letters for them, and made himself useful in the hospital.[20] Albert Kraus, who functioned for the men of the Twelfth Missouri under Osterhaus, was known as a Forty-eighter and a liberal in religion; but in order to comply with the law which stipulated that chaplains could be appointed only from the ranks of ordained ministers, his friends founded a free community so that he could bear the title of "Reverend" before his name. Thus, it came about that a German lord of the manor became a chaplain in the American army and that a German "clergyman" went constantly into the firing line and lent aid to the wounded.[21]

The chaplains—so called—in Blenker's division were a good deal of a farce and a sight for visitors. Every regiment had its official to look after the spiritual needs of the men, appropriately termed by the Germans *Seelensorger,* "although the religious needs of Blenker's soldiers could scarcely have been greater than those of Wallenstein's mercenaries" of the Thirty Years' War. By 1860 it had become the fashion with members of a considerable part of the German-American world to appear scoffers at religion—"freethinkers" they loved to call themselves. This was almost entirely a result of the great influence of the Forty-eighters. Since the post of chaplain had been established and provision made in the budget for chaplains, Blenker arranged for one for each of his regiments. However, as one writer noted, "he took the qualifications of his spiritual aides lightly; the chief requirement seemed to be that the men so appointed should know how to adorn the tipple table. Accordingly, one of these Christian chaplains was a Jew; another had never been known to be sober; . . . and the

---

[20] See Chicago *Illinois Staats-Zeitung,* July 20, 1861, for Forsch and Becker; for Stengel, the first chaplain of the Ninth Ohio, see *ibid.,* August 10, 1861; for the Reverend Mr. Fuchshuber, see Kaufmann, *Die Deutschen im Bürgerkriege,* 501.

[21] For Kraus, see Kaufmann, *Die Deutschen im Bürgerkriege,* 521. A plan was formulated to have Louis Wittig, editor a few years earlier of several German papers, for chaplain of Schimmelfennig's Pennsylvania regiment, but the law precluded his appointment. Chicago *Illinois Staats-Zeitung,* August 6, 1861.

others were mostly German journalists, who sought the comfortable shelter in order to work for their newspapers and then contributed eulogies out of gratitude so that Blenker's fame should not fade." [22]

The only outstanding nationality group of the Lutheran confession besides the German was the Scandinavian, and the only military organization in which the Scandinavians were numerous enough to affect the selection of the chaplain was the Fifteenth Wisconsin. Oddly enough, here Colonel Heg secured the appointment, not of a Norwegian, as might have been expected, but of a Dane, the Reverend Claus Lauritz Clausen. He, oddly enough, had resolved, along with the Norwegian pastors of the Wisconsin synod, that "slavery in and for itself is not a sin." It should perhaps be added that he later saw the absurdity of the position taken by the synod and through the agency of the *Emigranten* recalled the declaration to which he had assented with the Norwegian pastors. He had, since his arrival in Wisconsin in 1843, filled several pastorates and made himself one of the outstanding clergymen among the Scandinavian Lutherans. His friendly personality won him friends everywhere he went, undoubtedly constituting one of the reasons why Colonel Heg invited him to assume the chaplaincy of the regiment and why he filled the post with success. After he resigned, the officers selected a sergeant of Company G, one J. H. Johnson, who had manifested interest in the soldiers' spiritual welfare, for the duties of chaplain to a group of Lutherans, though it was in the Swedish Methodist Church that he had worked as a lay preacher.[23]

It should not be forgotten that Scandinavian ministers, especially the Swedish ones, sometimes made special trips to camp to conduct Lutheran services for Scandinavians. The reader may also recall that these clergymen served as unpaid messengers to carry food and clothing to the soldiers and to return with money from the soldiers for their families—especially if their visits coincided with payday. It goes without saying that the Regular Army chaplain performed the service gladly for his countrymen and for the men under his charge. The Reverend E. Anderson, chaplain of the Thirty-seventh Illinois, affords an illustration of this generalization. A Chicago paper carried a notice of his expected arrival in the city on October 8, 1861, and of his willingness to take back to the soldiers any small packages or letters which friends wished to send.[24]

[22] Kaufmann, *Die Deutschen im Bürgerkriege*, 178 n.

[23] Chicago *Hemlandet*, January 29, 1862; Luther M. Kuhns, "An Army Surgeon's Letters to his Wife," in *Proceedings of the Mississippi Valley Historical Association*, VII (1913–1914), 306 n.; J. A. Johnson, *Det Skandinaviske Regiments Historie*, 113–16.

[24] Hokanson, *Swedish Immigrants*, 73–74; Chicago *Tribune*, October 9, 1861.

Records of two chaplains of the Episcopal Church who were born outside the limits of the United States were turned up by the research. The first, the Reverend William Vaux, was an Englishman by birth and was appointed to a post with the Regular Army in 1849, in which position he served continuously from that date through and beyond the Civil War. During the war years he served as chaplain at hospitals and at Arlington Cemetery. Eglington D. Barr, born in Scotland, had a history as chaplain to a military unit which antedated the war, for he was serving the Fifty-first New York Militia in that capacity in 1858. The outbreak of war found him in New Orleans, acting as rector of St. Paul's Church in that city, where he lost all his property, was made a prisoner by the Confederates, and had his life threatened for refusing to follow the example of supporting the Confederacy set by his bishop, Leonidas Polk. He managed after much hardship to reach the Union lines, though he was utterly destitute when he arrived. Here he was made chaplain of the Eighty-first United States Colored Infantry.[25]

An occasional stray Methodist chaplain of alien birth was encountered during the research. The Reverend W. J. O'Neill (brother of Lieutenant Colonel Henry O'Neill), of the Corn Exchange Regiment and, like his elder brother, born in Ireland, was appointed chaplain of the same regiment by Governor Andrew Gregg Curtin from the Wilmington Conference.[26]

These clergymen, Catholic and Protestant alike, contributed to scenes on every battlefield, which, though unrecorded in the *Official War Records,* were as heroic as the charges of the fighting soldiers in the ranks. In the midst of the din and tumult of battle, when terror and death were all about them, they were out on the field, divested of fear by their faith, constant in their duty, and loyal to the United States flag. When darkness settled over the field, over victor and vanquished alike, they could be seen, lantern in hand, seeking out the wounded, kneeling beside them on the ground, consoling them in their agonizing pain, and, in the case of the Catholic clergy, shriving the dying. They were made the custodians of the last messages of dying soldiers to their beloved at home. It mattered not to a Catholic priest that he might be tending a Protestant; to a Protestant clergyman, it was immaterial whether he was whispering words of consolation to a Protestant, a Jew, or a Catholic.

[25] For Vaux, see Henry (comp.), *Military Record of Civilian Appointments,* I, 45; for Barr, see *ibid.,* II, 41.

[26] *History of the Corn Exchange Regiment, 118th Pennsylvania Volunteers,* 652.

SURGEONS

As Americans were practically without experience in caring for the illnesses and wounds of soldiers in the field (for the only war within the experience of active men had been child's play compared with what the country was then facing), it was perhaps not unnatural that some state officials turned to foreigners for initial direction in the medical service. To organize the medical staff of each regiment, inspect and vaccinate recruits, attend to the sick, and instruct the surgeons, assistants, and stewards, the authorities selected Dr. Thomas Ellis, an Englishman by birth, for post surgeon at New York City. They were influenced by the fact that he had been a staff surgeon in the British army and had served at the Cape of Good Hope, where he had performed similar duties during the Kaffir War. His work there had won the commendation of the heads of the British army. For wounds received on the battlefield he was allowed by British authorities to retire with an honorable discharge and a pension. His service while he was stationed in New York was characterized by remarkable success. During this period not a single death occurred in any of the camps under his care, despite the fact that the average number of troops in and around New York was over three thousand. Because of this valuable experience he was later made post surgeon and medical director in Virginia for the care of the wounded there.[27]

A noteworthy number of surgeons had been born in England and later served with the Union armies. George H. Humphreys, for instance, who while yet a medical student had served with the British army during the Crimean War, had later had experience with the French army in the war against Austria.[28] James H. Pooley, another Englishman, who served with the Union army from August, 1861, to the spring of 1863, saw hospital duty near Washington, was with the cavalry in the Army of the Potomac, and finally served with a light battery in the Ninth Army Corps. Another, Henry J. Phillips, brought to his service with the American army experience as assistant surgeon with British troops in the Crimean War; and after being with the One Hundred and Second New York Regiment in Virginia and about Washington, he was stationed in Alabama. Joseph

[27] Thomas T. Ellis, *Leaves from the Diary of an Army Surgeon* (New York, 1863), Introduction, 5–6, 18.

[28] Graham, *The Ninth Regiment New York Volunteers*, 40.

H. T. King served on the hospital transport *Monitor*, carrying sick and wounded from the armies of the James and Potomac to Fortress Monroe; he was later in charge of the medical service of an artillery brigade in Richmond. Among the other surgeons of English birth worthy of special mention is Dr. N. S. Townsend, one of the most distinguished in the group, who was a medical inspector in the western armies from early in 1863 to the end of the war; he won the rank of lieutenant colonel.[29]

Also to be classified as British, though not English, were several Scotchmen: Dr. D. M. McLaurie, who also won a lieutenant-colonelcy; James Wilson, surgeon to the Eleventh Indiana; William S. Cooper, whose service as surgeon of the One Hundred and Twenty-fifth New York was only an episode in an adventurous career; Charles Smart, who after serving the Irishmen of the Sixty-third New York became a medical inspector in the Army of the Potomac; and Alexander Ingram, who after duty with General McDowell was on general hospital duty in Washington until 1864.[30]

Before the group of colorful Irish surgeons is discussed, a few Britishers born outside the British Isles should be noted. Surgeons born in Canada though living in the United States at the time of appointment were George Rose, who was brevetted major for his services; Neil T. Graham, who after a tour of duty at the Marine Hospital at Cleveland served with the Twelfth Ohio through its entire term of enlistment and then returned to take charge of the General Field Hospital at Sandy Hook, Maryland, until the end of the war; and William S. Termaine, who served as surgeon of a colored regiment.[31] Born in the island of St. Thomas in the West Indies of the English branch of a Spanish-Portugese family, Dr. Jacob M. Da Costa is hard to classify, but he may probably most safely be called British. He was educated for his profession partly in Europe and partly in America, for, though he graduated from Jefferson Medical College, he had studied at Dresden and had spent one year at Vienna and another at Paris in graduate work. During the war, he was actively connected with military hospitals, chiefly near Philadelphia.[32]

---

[29] Henry (comp.), *Military Record of Civilian Appointments*, I, 105, 87, 82–83, 73–74, 122–23.

[30] See *ibid.*, 96, for McLaurie; see Regimental Descriptive Book, Eleventh Indiana Regiment, for Wilson; Simons, *A Regimental History. The One Hundred and Twenty-fifth New York State Volunteers*, 291–93, for Cooper; Henry (comp.), *Military Record of Civilian Appointments*, I, 113, 96, 83–84, for Smart and Ingram.

[31] Henry (comp.), *Military Record of Civilian Appointments*, 108, 120; *The National Cyclopaedia of American Biography*, XXIV, 357.

[32] *The National Cyclopaedia of American Biography*, IX, 342.

The Irish mustered a goodly number of surgeons in the Union service, many of whom manifested the same quality of physical courage that characterized their countrymen in the ranks. First and foremost were those of the Irish Brigade, where one would have expected to find Irish physicians ministering to the wounds of Irishmen. The first surgeon of Meagher's staff, appointed by Governor Edwin D. Morgan, was Philip O'Hanlon, who had been surgeon to the Metropolitan Guard.[33] Dr. Lawrence Reynolds and a Dr. Taylor were surgeons in the Sixty-third Regiment, while Dr. Richard Powell served the men of the Eighty-eighth. Patrick O'Connell was a very young surgeon who enlisted for three years in October, 1861, with the Twenty-eighth Massachusetts, but was mustered out in June, 1863. Associated with him as assistant surgeons were Peter Habon, George Snow, a native of Massachusetts, and James Rood, all young men ranging from twenty-two to thirty-one years of age, and John Barringer, who might still be termed young, though he was in his late thirties. A Londoner, Dr. W. C. Todd, surgeon of the last regiment of the Brigade, the One Hundred and Sixteenth Pennsylvania, was highly respected for his professional abilities and military bearing. Doctors Pascal Smith and James A. Reed and a Doctor Francis were all attached at one time or another to the Brigade.[34]

Dr. Lawrence Reynolds, one of the most distinguished of the group, was a graduate of the College of Surgeons of Dublin, a gentleman of culture and varied accomplishments, a man of the world, with a mind generously endowed with Irish wit. In his professional capacity he had to acknowledge few superiors. To training at one of the best medical schools of the day he had added a wide experience in one of the most trying and terrible campaigns of the time. He was with the allies through the Crimean War and the siege of Sebastopol. Thus, he entered the Irish Brigade equipped with experience gained from travel and with *savoir-faire* in the art of living, the best of stocks in trade for the strain of war. He had the capacity to make something out of nothing, to adapt himself philosophically to circumstances, however disagreeable and adverse, and to seize on the pleasant side of every occurrence. The doctor was an inimitable storyteller and a master in repartee. His philosophy might be said to have been derived from the eclectic school, and he put it into practice in a

[33] New York *Irish-American*, August 23, 1862.

[34] Regimental Descriptive Books, Sixty-third, Sixty-ninth, and Eighty-eighth New York Regiments, Twenty-eighth Massachusetts, and One Hundred and Sixteenth Pennsylvania. For Dr. Todd, see New York *Irish-American*, May 31, 1861. The last three assistant surgeons of the Massachusetts regiment were probably, but not necessarily, Irish.

myriad of ways. Marooned in a dilapidated hut on one occasion, while some men were out on picket, he regaled his fellow comrades with tales of his experiences at Scutari, Turkey, and with a dish called "kaybirds" (cabobs?), bits of meat an inch square grilled before a log fire. To all his other talents was added the gift of the poet, so that he became the chief bard of the Irish Brigade.[35]

Dr. Reynolds faced health conditions squarely and declared that it would be utterly impossible to keep scurvy out of his hospital without plenty of onions, potatoes, and whiskey. He had no hesitation in pronouncing the Federal soldier the best fed and best clothed in the world, and he denied that the Irish Brigade was overworked. It did no more marching than other brigades with which it was often associated, but, he declared, it did more fighting.[36]

A few Irishmen of the medical fraternity reached really distinguished positions in the army. Dr. James Moore, as chief medical director of Sherman's army, proved himself not only a skillful practitioner but also an executive of fine organizing ability. The dispatch with which hospitals were established and the competent manner in which the wounded were cared for during the march through Georgia and the Carolinas reflected great credit on him.[37] Dr. Bernard J. D. Irwin of the Regular Army was appointed medical inspector of the Army of the Ohio in 1861 and was present at many battles. In September, 1862, he was given full rank as surgeon in the United States Army, and served the last two years of the war as superintendent of hospitals at Memphis, Tennessee. For his services he attained the brevet rank of colonel.[38]

As a mere lad, Dr. George Curran came with his parents from Ireland to Seneca Falls, New York. After graduation from the Medical Department of Harvard, he enlisted as a private in the Thirty-third New York Volunteers, was appointed hospital steward when the regiment reached Washington, and was promoted in 1862 to the post of assistant surgeon. After Antietam, General Smith in a special order complimented him for having advanced with his regiment into the thick of the fight. Dr. Robert B. Cruice was appointed assistant surgeon to the Twelfth Pennsylvania

[35] Cavanagh, *Memoirs of Gen. Meagher*, Appendix, 20–21.

[36] New York *Irish-American*, August 2, 1862.

[37] David Powers Conyngham, *Sherman's March through the South with Sketches and Incidents of the Campaign* (New York, 1865), 382. Moore led a charge before Raleigh, when Lieutenant Colonel Kimmel was wounded, only to be wounded himself. Joel and Stegman (authors and comps.), *Rifle Shots and Bugle Notes*, 236.

[38] Henry (comp.), *Military Record of Civilian Appointments*, I, 84.

Cavalry in January, 1862; he was with General Hancock's division until his resignation in August, 1863.[39] Doctors William F. Smith, assistant surgeon to the Second Rhode Island Volunteers, and Samuel S. Jessup, assistant surgeon to the United States Volunteers, were both Irishmen and were appointed late in the war—in 1864.[40]

The reader will suppose that a large number of surgeons were appointed from the German element of the population, not only because of the large number of German soldiers who would wish to be attended by their own countrymen, but also because many of the German professional men were as eager to serve their adopted country as were others of their compatriots who were serving in the military. Kaufmann in his work has listed thirty-seven surgeons of German birth in the Union armies, to which others must be added, some of them being the most eminent surgeons in the United States and possessing international reputations.

Dr. Ferdinand H. Gross became medical director of the Fourteenth Army Corps after service on the staff of General James Scott Negley. He was brought to America when his physician father emigrated to Pennsylvania in 1833 and established himself in Pittsburgh. Young Gross, a graduate of Jefferson Medical College at Philadelphia, was practicing medicine with his father in Pittsburgh when the war broke out. When Colonel Negley raised his regiment in Pittsburgh, he accepted the proffer of this young physician's services and appointed him brigade surgeon. Since no provision had been made for this post in the President's call, Dr. Gross enlisted as a private in the thirteenth Pennsylvania Volunteers, but he was immediately detached from the regiment and commissioned by Governor Curtin as aide-de-camp with rank of captain on General Negley's staff. In this capacity he made the three months campaign. Eager, however, to enter that branch for which he was best fitted, Captain Gross appeared before the examining board of Pennsylvania and was commissioned as surgeon. He acted as medical officer to the One Hundredth Pennsylvania Regiment; but in October, 1861, he was named by the President as brigade surgeon and again ordered to General Negley's command, then operating in Kentucky. When the Eighth Army Division was organized, Dr. Gross was chosen medical director of the division; and in this capacity he shared in the bloody battle of Stone's River, where he per-

---

[39] Dr. George Curran was born in county Clare in 1848, and came to the United States at the age of twelve. Judd, *The Story of the Thirty-third N.Y.S. Vols.*, Appendix, 10; for Dr. Robert B. Cruice, see Henry (comp.), *Military Record of Civilian Appointments*, I, 68.

[40] Henry (comp.), *Military Record of Civilian Appointments*, I, 114, 85.

sonally saved the ambulance train, and co-operated with General Rose-crans' medical director in re-establishing hospitals and providing shelter for the wounded. Not long after this battle, he was, by order of General Rosecrans, made medical director of the Fourteenth Army Corps and assigned to the staff of General Thomas.[41]

A second German who stood at the top of his profession in America and was respected in the medical circles of Germany bore the name of Dr. Adam Hammer. When he was at the midway point in his university career at Heidelberg, his father migrated to America; he, however, remained in Europe, devoting himself to medicine. After his graduation, he entered the military service of Baden as assistant surgeon, in which post he remained till 1845. He participated in the revolutionary movement of 1848 in Baden, with the result that he had to flee with his intimate friend, Friedrich Hecker; he came to St. Louis, where he founded a practice. After his return in 1853 from a period of pathological study in Europe, in order to help fill the need for medical schools, he founded the first German medical college in St. Louis, which opened its doors September 1, 1859, as *Das Humboldt-Institute*. At the outbreak of war he could not look on idly; he shut the institute and entered the war as lieutenant colonel of the Fourth Missouri Infantry. From the termination of his three months service until the very close of hostilities, he undertook the direction of various military hospitals with the greatest zeal and ability.[42]

One of the most famous German surgeons in the United States, Dr. Gustav C. A. Weber, became the general medical director of the Ohio troops. Trained in medicine at the University of Bonn, he had made a distinct place for himself as a physician and professor of medicine in Cleveland. He had much to do with the organization of medical care for the soldiers in the war and especially with the appointment of able surgeons. He was outstanding for his service and devotion at the battlefield of Shiloh.[43] Dr. Ernst Schmidt, a professor at Humboldt Institute, followed his leader, Dr. Hammer, to the field to become a regimental physician in the Missouri Volunteers and later the general medical director of the

---

[41] Fitch (comp.), *Annals of the Army of the Cumberland*, 114–16. For a list of the German surgeons, see Appendix, Section G. Kaufmann failed to record Dr. Gross.

[42] "Dr. Adam Hammer," in *Der Deutsche Pionier*, X (1878–1879), 242–43. As early as March, 1861, he had armed his students and kept them concealed at night in a brewery in order to fall upon any one who might attack the arsenal. Kaufmann, *Die Deutschen im Bürgerkriege*, 507.

[43] Kaufmann, *Die Deutschen im Bürgerkriege*, 562.

Sixteenth Army Corps. His radical views and red beard brought him the nickname of the "Red doctor."

Dr. Rudolph Welker, assisted by Dr. George Stemmer (head nurse), and a Dr. Balsch, completed a field apothecary service for Blenker's regiment as early as May, 1861. Welker secured two great ambulances which contained well-arranged chests with numerous compartments for medicaments. There were stores of linen and bandages, slings, and instruments for amputations. These offered almost the completeness of a hospital. At this early date there were already three German doctors in attendance on Illinois regiments at Camp Yates—Dr. William Wagner, a Dr. Ballade, and a Dr. Steele. Before long the organization of Colonel Hecker's Eighty-second Illinois brought two more German surgeons into the service.[44]

Dr. Karl Hartman of Cleveland became the staff physician of a German regiment, the One Hundred and Seventh Ohio. He was a Forty-eighter, and while he was with the Eleventh Corps at Chancellorsville, he drew his sword to help get the regiment into a better position. Unfortunately, he fell in the battle. Dr. Theodor Häring was the regular staff physician for the Ninth Wisconsin; Dr. Franz Hübschmann, for the German Twenty-sixth Wisconsin; and a Dr. Horck, for the Forty-sixth New York. Dr. Hübschmann was one of the ablest doctors in the Union armies and rose to be the medical director of a division. At Gettysburg he worked with nine assistants for three long days over five hundred wounded who were in the hands of the Confederates. Dr. Abraham Jacobi, a Jew, as his name indicates, was a Forty-eighter and, at the time of the war, one of America's most distinguished physicians. Kaufmann seems to have claimed a war record for him also, but since he was lecturing in New York medical schools during the war, this claim seems hardly credible. Edmund Märklin served as apothecary with the half-German Thirty-fourth Wisconsin.

---

[44] For Dr. Schmidt, see Chicago *Illinois Staats-Zeitung*, August 9, 1861; for Dr. Welker, see *ibid.*, May 20, 1861. Since the names of Dr. Welker as surgeon, of Dr. Balsch as assistant surgeon, and of George Stemmer as head nurse are to be found in official records, it is believed that the names as given in the *Illinois Staats-Zeitung* were distorted into "Welcher" and "Basch."

For the three doctors at Camp Yates by May 20, see *ibid.*; for the surgeons of the Eighty-second Illinois Regiment, see Regimental Descriptive Book.

Dr. Schmidt described for the readers of the *Illinois Staats-Zeitung* the conditions and provisions for the care of soldiers in the three months service. *Ibid.*, August 21, 22, 23, 1861. Drs. George Schötzer and Charles Börner were the two German surgeons with the Eighty-second Illinois. Regimental Descriptive Book.

Dr. Louis Meyer of Cleveland rose from staff physician in the Twenty-fifth Ohio to be the chief physician of the Eleventh Corps, allowing himself to be captured at Chancellorsville in order to help the Union men who had been wounded in that battle. Dr. Rudolf Neuhaus, who had been a regimental physician of the *Freischärler* (insurgents) in the Baden revolt of 1849, was a physician in Sigel's corps and was himself often wounded in serving the injured. On the Rappahannock in August, 1862, he was struck by three bullets, and after the Second Battle of Bull Run he became incapacitated and had to leave the service. Dr. Konrad Schenck and Dr. Julius C. Schenck, father and son from Cleveland, served as regular doctors in the Thirty-seventh Ohio. Dr. Joseph Spiegelhalter and Dr. H. M. Starkloff were both distinguished German surgeons who served in the Twelfth Missouri. Dr. Edward Borck was a physician who, though he went before the Army Board immediately upon graduation from a Baltimore medical school, had already acquired some experience as a volunteer medical cadet in the Schleswig-Holstein war; he acted in the capacity of a surgeon with the Tenth Maryland Infantry and the Third Maryland Cavalry and even had charge of the medical affairs for a brigade on Banks's Red River expedition.[45]

The Polish element of the country contributed to the armed forces, in addition to the officers and men already discussed, several prominent physicians. Dr. Samuel Brilliantowski and Dr. Robert Thormain (who won some notice as a poet) were both of New York. Another Polish surgeon of a titled family bore the name of Dr. Franz A. von Moschzisker, had been a staff physician in the Austrian army, and had shared—not unnaturally for a Pole in the Austrian-annexed area of Poland—in the uprising of 1848 in Hungary. He served in the great hospitals near Washington during our Civil War. The lone Austrian encountered in the search was Dr. Anthony Heger, who had been appointed surgeon in the old army in 1851; he had charge of the hospital at Point Lookout, Maryland, for the greater portion of the war. For meritorious service he was accorded a fairly high military rank, that of brevet lieutenant colonel.[46]

The Frenchmen serving in the medical service of the Union were rela-

[45] For all these men, see Kaufmann, *Die Deutschen im Bürgerkriege*, 508, 514, 515, 519, 531, 532, 535–36, 548, 553–54. This may be the H. M. Starkloff of Galesburg. See p. 133.

[46] For Dr. von Moschzisker, see *ibid.*, 534; for Dr. Heger, see Henry (comp.), *Military Record of Civilian Appointments*, I, 80. For the three Poles, see Haiman, *Polish Past in America*, 94, 104–105.

tively few, but they seemed to make up in quality for what they lacked in numbers. John J. Milhau, though born in France, joined the Regular Army for medical service in 1851. With the coming of war he was made an inspector of hospitals, medical director of the Fifth Corps of the Army of the Potomac, and, after April, 1863, regular surgeon. In his services on the field he must have displayed unusual courage, for he was accorded the high rank of brevet brigadier of the United States Army. Dr. D. M. P. Vaudrey, a French physician who had been living in Watertown, New York, only a short time and therefore spoke English imperfectly, early tendered his services in the hope of being able to find a post in a French regiment. Because he was an old practitioner with military as well as civil experience, he was accepted by the Medical Commission of the army. Dr. Henri Auguste Thepault was serving as surgeon in the Chasseur Regiment, Eighty-fourth New York, in the latter part of 1862. His countryman, Dr. Eugene H. Abadie, entered upon the Civil War with a long background of medical service with the regular American forces, for he had been appointed assistant surgeon in the Regular Army as early as 1836 and promoted to surgeon in 1853. Caught in Texas by the war, he was paroled as a prisoner of war and was stationed for service in Washington and at West Point until 1864. As a member of the medical board at Philadelphia and Chief Medical Officer of the Division of West Mississippi, he was still able to render service to the Union in his own field. He also was recognized for his services during the war by a brevet colonelcy.[47]

The Scandinavian doctor naturally to be expected in the Fifteenth Wisconsin was Dr. Stephen Oliver Himoe, who was, like Colonel Heg, a Norwegian. Brought to Wisconsin at the early age of thirteen, he had received his formal education in American schools and his medical training at St. Louis Medical College. As he was located in Kansas in 1861, he first took service as surgeon on the staff of the Fifth Kansas Cavalry. However, he transferred to the Fifteenth Wisconsin when it was organized, partly because of his nationality but also, undoubtedly, for sentimental reasons, since he was married to Colonel Heg's sister. He was on the battlefields of Perryville and Stone's River; after the latter battle he had charge of the hospitals at Murfreesboro, and during the carnage at Chickamauga he was in command of some of the field hospitals. For personal

[47] See Henry (comp.), *Military Record of Civilian Appointments*, I, 51, for Dr. Abadie, and I, 97–98, for Dr. Milhau; New York *Courrier des États-Unis*, May 11, 1861, for Dr. Vaudrey; Notes to the French Legation, VIII, No. 49, for Dr. Thepault.

reasons he felt obliged to resign in November, 1863, after two years of efficient service.[48]

There were a number of other Scandinavians, notably Swedes, in the medical service. From Jamestown, New York, went a Dr. Finke, in August, 1861, possibly inspired to offer his services by the company of Swedes who went from that state. Dr. G. W. Barck of Galesburg, Illinois; Dr. Charles J. Nordquist of New York, serving the Eighty-third New York; and Dr. John A. Ouchterlonly of Louisville were classified as army surgeons. Dr. J. W. Florine of Andover, Illinois, served as pharmacist and physician.[49]

If surprise is felt at the large number of officers produced by so small a group as were the Hungarians in the United States in 1861, much greater must be the amazement that such a group of fighting men as the exiles essentially were, could contribute about a half-dozen medical men to the army. Dr. Ignatius Langer, a staff surgeon in the Hungarian war for independence, tried farming near Davenport after his arrival in the United States in 1850. His services as a surgeon in the Army of the Potomac during the Civil War were highly valued. The names of Dr. Bernard Simig and Dr. Rudolf Tauszky have come down as surgeons in the Union army during the war. Dr. Alexander Fekete was a soldier who escaped from an Austrian prison to America, where he took a degree in medicine and was thus equipped to serve as a surgeon with the Thirteenth Missouri Regiment of Cavalry.[50] Most interesting in the group, though not associated with the Hungarian Revolution, was Dr. Bernard Bettelheim, a sort of soldier of fortune in medicine. Though he received his preparatory education in Hungary, he took his medical degree at the University of Padua. Wandering to London, he became acquainted in a missionary school with David Livingstone; but when the latter started for Africa on his mission-

[48] For Dr. Himoe, see Kuhns, "An Army Surgeon's Letters to his Wife," in *Proceedings of the Mississippi Valley Historical Association,* VII (1913–1914), 306–20; Ager (ed.), *Oberst Heg og hans Gutter,* 150 n.; Blegen (ed.), *Civil War Letters of Colonel Heg,* 49 n. After Dr. Himoe became brigade surgeon, a Swede, Dr. St. Sure Lindsfeldt, succeeded him as regimental surgeon. J. A. Johnson, *Det Skandinaviske Regiments Historie,* 86.

[49] Hokanson, *Swedish Immigrants,* 74, states that Dr. Finke, of Jamestown, New York, acted as hospital steward; but the Chicago *Hemlandet,* August 7, 1861, says that he went as a doctor. For the other army surgeons and doctors, see Hokanson, *Swedish Immigrants,* 74. Every effort has been made to check these minor figures of the medical service; Doctors Lindsfeldt, Nordquist, Spiegelhalter, Thormain, and Brilliantowski appear in the *Volunteer Army Register.*

[50] Vasvary, *Lincoln's Hungarian Heroes,* 65, 80, 84, 51. Tauszky is in *Volunteer Army Register.*

ary enterprise, Bettelheim sailed for Japan, where he practiced his profession and translated the Bible into the native language. In 1854 he betook himself to the United States on one of Admiral Perry's ships and settled in a Missouri town. He responded to the call of President Lincoln in 1861 by offering his services as a surgeon, and his offer was accepted.[51]

MUSICIANS

One of the distinguishing characteristics of the Union army was its numerous bands of musicians; the Confederates, certainly at first, had very few of these. About one half of the Northern regiments had fine bands. The soldiers in gray, however, were as fond of music as their adversaries in blue; for they would often gather at the bank on their side of the river to catch the strains floating up from the Federal bands. The period of something over a year between the spring of 1861 and midsummer of 1862 was the time when music was at its best in the Union army. The militia regiments from the different states hastened first to Washington and then to other points to face a three months tour of duty, and practically every other regiment carried with it its regimental band, consisting as a rule of the best professional musicians residing in the locality from which the regiment had departed. At the end of the three months, the short-term troops were replaced by those of longer terms. Since the musicians who had served with the three months troops had gained familiarity with the military field movements, they were engaged to go with the regiments then being formed for three years or the duration of the war. One inducement held out for re-enlistment was the announcement that a famous band would be attached to some particular regiment. In addition to the government pay of the musicians, usually larger than that of the private, the bands frequently received extra pay from a regimental fund, collected by assessment of the officers or by contributions from friends of the men of the regiment. During the first year and a half of the war, the Union armies included among the numerous regiments many bands from the Northern, Midwestern, and Western states which enjoyed national reputations, such as Gilmore's Band of Boston, which had gone to the field with the Twenty-fourth Massachusetts, and Dodsworth's Band of New York. A little later, in the fall of 1862, Flagg's Brass Band went to camp with the

[51] Vasvary, *Lincoln's Hungarian Heroes*, 48. More than fifty years after his death a memorial was erected to him on the Japanese island which had been the scene of his labors.

Forty-fourth Massachusetts, receiving $3,000 for its services; it did not, however, go to the front. Undoubtedly, many of the musicians in these bands were foreigners.[52]

At this early period each band consisted of twenty-two pieces [53]— two principal musicians from each company and two from each complete regiment—naturally under a conductor. So great was the demand for musicians that it was somewhat difficult to obtain a good band, according to Colonel W. W. H. Davis, but in Lehigh County he engaged one composed of young Germans. There were two principal musicians and a leader, one John Jobst, who as conductor drew the pay of second lieutenant. In addition there was a drum corps of ten boys—one from each company.[54]

All through the Peninsular campaign there was an abundance of good music, especially on pleasant evenings, when every band in the army would play. The members of the bands were, no doubt, already excellent players when they enlisted, but competition with distinguished musicians from all parts of the North gave them a delicacy of touch and enabled them to draw from their instruments a sweetness of tone which made their music irresistible. Fifty bands were playing at the same time on a certain Sunday evening at White House, which was located on Pamunkey River in Virginia; from a safe distance, the effect produced must have been a stream of rich melody.[55] As the army approached Richmond, the playing of the bands was prohibited lest it reveal to the foe the Federal strength and positions. There arose, however, in the War Department, complaints over the heavy expenditures for these bands. Critics in the department pointed out that not less than $4,000,000 a year was being spent for this purpose alone. The members of the bands were enlisted as musicians and not as soldiers subject to active duty in the field. It was roughly computed in July, 1862, that there existed 618 bands, with nearly 15,000 men serving strictly as bandsmen, or that there was one bandsman for every 41 fighting

[52] Gates, The "Ulster Guard" and the War of the Rebellion, 213–14; Albert W. Mann (comp.), History of the Forty-fifth Regiment, Massachusetts Volunteer Militia, "The Cadet Regiment" (Jamaica Plains, N.Y., 1908), 195–96.

[53] Mann (comp.), History of the Forty-fifth Regiment, 194, says twenty-four pieces; W. W. H. Davis, History of the 104th Pennsylvania Regiment, 13, says twenty-one; Joel Cook, The Siege of Richmond. A Narrative of the Military Operation of Maj. Gen. G. B. McClellan (Philadelphia, 1862), 66, says there were twenty musicians with one principal musician with the rank of first lieutenant. Possibly the number varied at different times. The Scandinavian Regiment went to the front with only seven musicians.

[54] W. W. H. Davis, History of the 104th Pennsylvania Regiment, 14. A little later each regiment was allowed twenty drummers.

[55] J. Cook, The Siege of Richmond, 66, 100.

men! This enormous expense was deemed unwarranted, considering that such service was of the ornamental kind rather than of the serious kind suitable for war. Rumors began to float about that a new dispensation would allow only one band for each brigade. This proved to be the case, for by a law of July 17, 1862, all regimental bands were ordered to be discontinued. Each brigade in volunteer service was allowed to have sixteen musicians in a band. The pay, duties, and term were those of a regular soldier; hence, within thirty days nearly all the bands were out of service, as few men of superior musical ability were willing to serve on those terms.

After that, if a regiment had a band, it was formed of enlisted men or company musicians detailed for that purpose with the same pay and rations as the private. The Forty-fifth Massachusetts Regiment offers an illustration of how a regimental band could still exist. Its colonel was determined that his regiment should have a band. He instituted a search among the men of the different companies for those of musical inclination with some knowledge of the instruments used in a band. It was understood that these men would renounce their guns to serve as musicians unless because of losses they were needed as fighting men, in which case every man must return to his company. It was their duty to furnish music in camp at guard mount and dress parade, to give evening concerts, or to provide music whenever it seemed desirable for the good of officers and men. Instruments were provided by officers and friends, as had been done earlier. At the expiration of the term of service, every member of the band was presented with the instrument which he had used. Many other regiments followed this example after they reached the front. Excellent corps of musicians for marching purposes were also formed out of the martial music corps, the flute and fife players, though their music was too monotonous for concert purposes.[56] The men composing these bands in many cases were musicians only while in camp or on parade, for on the march and in action they bore rifles. Bands which enlisted after 1862 were eventually organized into drilled ambulance corps and, as a matter of fact, served in several engagements in greatly exposed positions. Some of them were killed on such duty. The service in this capacity of the band of the Fifty-sixth Massachusetts at the Battle of North Anna River merits recapitulation. The surgeon was confronted with the problem of transporting the wounded over the greatly swollen river. As there were

[56] Baltimore *Der Deutsche Correspondent*, October 4, 1861; Fox (author and comp.), *Regimental Losses in the American Civil War*, 123; Mann (comp.), *History of the Forty-fifth Regiment*, 185, 195; *United States Statutes at Large*, XII, Chap. CC, Sect. 594.

no hospital attendants to call upon, he turned to the bandsmen, who had been ordered back to report to the surgeon at the beginning of the battle. They first offered to get the wounded across the river by carrying them on their backs, but that plan had to be abandoned because the wounded would have become too exhausted and chilled. They then made rafts large enough to carry three men at a time, stripped off their clothes, and pushed the raft across by swimming and wading. It required the hardest kind of work the whole night through thus to transport the fifty wounded.[57] The bandsmen of the Forty-fifth Massachusetts had been well trained by the surgeon to give first aid and to use stretchers, bandages, and tourniquets. They rescued the wounded and carried them to the field hospital. They were also sent as messengers on dangerous errands often requiring them to cross the line of fire.[58]

Everywhere throughout the Union forces the Germans were recognized for contributing music to the army. The German bands were the best. The adjectives "excellent," "soul-stirring," and "deeply emotional" were constantly applied to them by American commanders. It would be impossible to follow the Regimental Descriptive Books without noting how often the nationality following the name of a man entered on the roll as musician was "German." This was often true even when a regiment was not recognized as a German organization. One of the most famous bands was the Silver Cornet Band, so named because the thirteen members all had silver instruments. In 1861, it had already been organized for eight years as a band, and in addition most of the members were performers of many years experience. During the stay of the Nineteenth Ohio in Cleveland, it secured the services of this band to accompany it through its three months campaign.[59] The Ninth Wisconsin Regiment of Germans had perhaps the best band in Blenker's division. General J. L. Chamberlain had a German band in his brigade and referred to it as follows when he had established headquarters in an old Virginia mansion: "Here at about four o'clock the fine German band of my First Brigade came over to re-

---

[57] For the testimony of Army Surgeon Edward P. Roche, see Mann (comp.), *History of the Forty-fifth Regiment,* 197, 190.

[58] *Ibid.*

[59] "History of the Nineteenth Regiment, Ohio Volunteer Infantry," 2 (MS in Ohio Historical Society). It would seem that this band offered its services as a regimental band instantly, for the writer found in the archives of the Ohio Historical Society a letter to that effect dated April 19, 1861. It was, however, written from Eaton, Ohio. (If it is the same band, the leader, Captain Jack Leland, did not make the offer.) Executive Correspondence of the Governors of Ohio, April 16–24, 1861.

ciprocate the smiles of heaven by choice music, ministering also to our spiritual upgoings." [60]

Occasionally, merely having members of a famous band did prove an advantage in gaining recruits. C. E. Davis stated that Company E of the Thirteenth Massachusetts had four musicians from the Germania Band, who furnished music at guard mount and also at dress parade. One of the airs which the little group played at sunset while the flag on the fort was being lowered was from the opera *Grenada*. To this air the boys fitted the following words: "Corporal of the guard, corporal of the guard, corporal of the guard, post eight." This version never lost its popularity; it was carried into the service from the drill at the fort by the regimental band, was frequently played by it, and was heard again after the arrival home.[61] The Frémont Hussars, or Fourth Missouri Cavalry, boasted a band, in which all but three members were German-born. Six musicians in the First Missouri Infantry—two from each of three companies—were Germans, according to the Regimental Descriptive Book.[62]

It would be a serious mistake to think that only Germans provided music for the Union army. That they were numerous is true, but, as with every other kind of service in that army, men of every nationality were to be found serving as musicians. An Englishman named James J. Wilson, the principal musician of the Ninety-seventh Pennsylvania, had been performing in Guss Fensible's Cornet Band; but after the passage of the law of July, 1862, he was transferred to the ranks—though by 1864, it might be noted, he was on the noncommissioned staff. Shortly after the discharge of the regimental bands, twenty-three bandsmen, all bearing Irish names, were discharged at Harrison's Landing, Virginia. We have, however, more direct evidence of Englishmen performing with the horn; there was one in Company D of the One Hundred and Eighty-second New York Regiment (an Englishman in Corcoran's Irish Legion), and one in the Fifth New York Infantry.[63] The research has revealed that there was one Swiss musician in Company I of the One Hundred and Sixth Ohio (his presence in a German regiment was not strange); a Norwegian in the Second Wisconsin; and an Italian as a leader of the military music

---

[60] Chamberlain, *The Passing of the Armies*, 276.

[61] C. E. Davis, *Three Years in the Army*, xxi.

[62] Company Descriptive Book, Fourth Missouri Cavalry; Regimental Descriptive Book, First Missouri Infantry.

[63] Company Descriptive Book, One Hundred and Eighty-second New York Infantry; Regimental Descriptive and Letter Book, Fifth New York Regiment.

at Hart's Island.[64] The membership of a band could be made up of mixed nationalities, as in the band of the Fifth New York, where there were three Irishmen, two Germans, two Englishmen, and ten natives. Likewise, the list of the musicians of another New York regiment showed six nationalities and included eleven Germans, one Sicilian, one Englishman, one Irishman, one Swede, and one American.[65] A Welshman who came to the United States in 1845 deserves special mention for his participation in two wars. Though a blacksmith when he enlisted at Watervliet Arsenal at West Troy, New York, Edward P. Jones manifested musical ability and as a result was appointed leader of a band which served during the Mexican War. After his discharge from the service, he settled at Troy, where he formed a band, consisting chiefly of the members of the arsenal band, soon celebrated as the Troy Cornet Band. When the Civil War broke out, this band as a body joined the Second New York Volunteers, though their leader became a captain by virtue of recruiting a company for the One Hundred and Twenty-fifth New York Regiment.[66]

Drum majors of regimental and brigade bands were the same resplendent figures that they were in civilian bands. The Forty-fifth Massachusetts was unusually fortunate in having an Italian drum major, formerly of Gilmore's Band, to lead them at their first appearance at dress parade. "He [Marianni] was very tall and commanding in appearance, always proud, and at the same time jolly. When he marched before us, dressed in his gorgeous uniform, with his long gold-headed baton and his bearskin hat, with pompom topping all, he was inspiring. I used to think of him, as a 'moving shield' to cover the defects of our inexperienced work." [67]

On one occasion the drum major of a German regimental band furnished considerable amusement. He was a tall, stout German and was dressed fantastically, according to custom. Medals and ornaments covered his brightly colored clothes, and an enormous bearskin shako added to

[64] The Swiss was John Fehnder, who enlisted at Cincinnati, October 4, 1864, for one year. See Peter Weidner Papers, W 422, Ohio State Historical Society (Furloughs); the Norwegian was Christian Rasmussen, mentioned by one Jacobsen writing to the Madison *Emigranten*, August 10, 1861, of actions of the regiment; Polemie, the Italian leader at Hart's Island, is mentioned in the Italian correspondence to Seward in a note dated October 26, 1864, Diplomatic Dispatches, Italy, III.

[65] Regimental Descriptive and Letter Book, Fifth New York Regiment; Chicago *Illinois Staats-Zeitung*, May 11, 1861, quoting correspondence from Washington of May 9, 1861.

[66] Simons, *A Regimental History. The One Hundred and Twenty-fifth New York Volunteers*, 209–10.

[67] Mann (comp.), *History of the Forty-fifth Regiment*, 186.

his already great height. Marching backward until the band had caught the exact measure of his motions, he turned then to march up the road, just at the point where the next backward step would have placed him astride a broken beehive, which was surrounded by an immense swarm of infuriated bees. "Dunder and Blitzen, vat is dis?" yelled the astounded drum major, leaping frantically in the air and throwing away his baton in order to use both his large hands as the arms of a windmill to beat the bees from his head.[68]

In the Twenty-eighth Massachusetts the drum major was, appropriately, an Irishman who deserted, and the Irish band leader was discharged after perhaps six months for disability. The band boasted twenty-three members, but unfortunately, their nativity was not recorded.[69]

Occasionally we encounter in a mere bugler a musician of rare talent. Such a one was Karl Bergmann, the well-known and able director of the former Germania Band and in later years the director of the excellent German Philharmonic Society in New York; another was Joseph Noll, a beloved violin virtuoso and leader of the huge National Guard Band. Both of these men were buglers in the Union army in August, 1861. Most of the buglers in the Frémont Hussars (the Fourth Missouri Cavalry) were Germans, though there were one Swiss, one Welshman, and three natives among the number. A bugler in Company A of the One Hundred and Seventy-fifth New York Volunteers recorded himself as being from Poland, but whether he was from the portion under Prussian or that under Russian domination does not appear.[70]

Three buglers merit special attention. The trumpeter of the City Guards of Worcester, a Massachusetts Home Guard company, was one of the famous six hundred who made the charge at Balaklava. The French bugler in Zagonyi's Guards provided excitement at the battle at Springfield, Missouri. He had not paid any attention to Zagonyi's order to sound a signal but had darted off with Lieutenant Mathenyi. In Zagonyi's own

[68] Gerrish and Hutchinson (authors and comps.), *The Blue and the Gray,* 578. The entire regiment fared as ill as did the drum major under the attack of the bees.

[69] Regimental Descriptive Book, Twenty-eighth Massachusetts Regiment. Another German offered his services to the governor of Ohio: "With the experience of nearly ten months as Drum Major I feel competent to drill and prepare martial bands for the field in the shortest possible time or to fill any company office to which your Excellency might appoint me." Frederick Meisner to the Governor, August 13, 1862, Executive Correspondence of the Governors of Ohio, August, 1862.

[70] For Karl Bergmann, see Chicago *Illinois Staats-Zeitung,* August 13, 1861; for the buglers in the Frémont Hussars and the Polish bugler, see Regimental Descriptive Books for the regiments concerned.

picturesque words, "The bugler (Frenchman) I ordered him two three time to put his sword away and take the bugle in his hand, that I shall be able to see him. Hardly I took my eyes down, next minute I seen him, sword in the hand, all bloody; and this he done two or three times. Finally, the mouth of the bugle being shot away, the bugler had excuse for gratifying himself in use of the sword." When this bugler was rebuked and dismissed from the Guard as "unworthy," he said, displaying his mutilated bugle, "I could not bugle viz mon bugle, and so I bugle viz mon pistol and sabre!" The third was the Swiss bugler of the Frémont Hussars. The commander of that cavalry unit recorded that "his note in the wild Ozark Hills would mark the headquarters of the 'Vierte Missouri' for miles around. From a hill-top, half a mile in advance of the marching command, I have turned the regiment into its camping ground and dismounted it in perfect order by the melodious telegraphy of Wettstein's brazen lips alone." [71]

Just a word must be vouchsafed to the contingent of drummers. We have already learned that there were ten drummers in a regiment; these were sometimes full-grown men but often mere boys. Sometimes they were promoted from the drum to a commissioned office; sometimes they displayed gallantry on the field worthy of a medal. Henry S. Cohn is an illustration of such rise to office: he entered the Fifth Kentucky as a drummer but returned from the field with a captain's commission. Johnny Klemm, a drummer boy from Michigan only sixteen years old, is an exemplification of the gallantry sometimes displayed. At Chickamauga he threw away his drum and fought in the ranks, shooting a high-ranking Confederate officer who tried to capture the cocky little Yankee.[72] One of the brave drummers was J. C. Julius Langbein. He was brought to this country from Germany when he was only two years old. His enlistment came early, for two weeks after the first gun was fired on Fort Sumter, he entered the Ninth New York as a drummer. He was so childish in appearance that his comrades nicknamed him "Jennie," a name which he was unable to lose during his entire term of service. He was only a small boy when he won the Congressional Medal at the Battle of Cam-

---

[71] For the English bugler who had been at Balaklava, see Marvin, *History of Worcester in the War of the Rebellion,* 47; for the Frenchman in Frémont's Guard, see Jessie Benton Frémont, *Story of the Guard,* 144–45; for the Swiss, see G. E. Waring, *Whip and Spur* (Boston, 1875), 70.

[72] For Cohn, see Kaufmann, *Die Deutschen im Bürgerkriege,* 489. Rosecrans secured for Klemm after the war an appointment to West Point so that he became an officer in the regular army. *Ibid.,* 519.

den, North Carolina, on April 15, 1862. Under heavy fire he voluntarily went to the aid of a wounded officer, sought medical assistance for him, and then helped to carry him to safety.[73] Another tale of a drummer boy came from the Eighty-eighth New York. War had made something of a stoic of Edward Welch, an Irish lad who was the pet of the regiment, for he had lost his father in one battle, and his captain in the next. When several soldiers, coming in for a last look at their captain, sobbed aloud, the little lad, holding down the eyelids of the dead captain, said, "Don't cry, Dan; it's no use crying"—a philosopher in mind, a boy in years.[74]

The services of the bands in the camp, on the march, and on the battlefield were significant in giving pleasure, in relieving the exhaustion of the men, in lifting their flagging spirits, and in caring for the wounded and the dying. The serenades of the various bands and their part in breaking the tedium of camp life have already been described. The news of the surrender of Fort Donelson brought out all the bands in the Army of the Potomac to celebrate the victory. The presence of lady visitors was usually seized upon as an excuse for a serenade. The band of the Twelfth Massachusetts Volunteers gave a concert in Frederick, Maryland, which was a success financially and artistically. The audience was large and brilliant, graced as it was with the presence of no less than six generals, as well as many persons distinguished in civil and military life. One of the outstanding features was a drum solo by Guillaume Du Bois, who scarcely needs to be introduced to the reader as a Frenchman; but it is in point to add that he had been for thirty years a drummer in the French army. When the regiment, with colors flying, marched up Bolivar Heights through Charlestown past the spot where John Brown had been hung, the band burst into music, and it takes little imagination to guess what the air was. We can readily feel how much the bands added to the religious services when they throbbed out "Old Hundred." Naturally, when most of the bands were mustered out in the summer of 1862, there was sincere regret on the part of the men.[75]

The scenes presented by men on the march were impressive and vivid. At the evacuation of Yorktown on the Peninsula, the musicians in General John Sedgwick's division sprang to their long-silent instruments and struck up "Dixie" and other favorite airs—to the great amusement of

[73] His character after the war is in accord with that displayed here: he became an assemblyman and judge at Albany, New York. Mulholland, *The American Volunteer,* 47–48.

[74] New York *Irish-American,* July 12, 1862.

[75] Benjamin F. Cook, *History of the Twelfth Massachusetts Volunteers (Webster Regiment)* (Boston, 1882), 35–36, 39, 26, 50.

the men marching to their camps in brigades with flying colors. Add to the picture the Tammany Regiment, marching with fixed bayonets to emphasize the feelings of the Irishmen in that unit.

ENGINEERS

Certain individuals have already been mentioned in the discussion of the rank won by various foreigners or foreign-born, but in order to comprehend how great was their contribution to the winning of the war, it is necessary here in some instances to repeat their names—at the risk of wearying the reader—in connection with some of the highly specialized fields of service.

The Engineer Department was, even at the time under consideration, a highly specialized branch of the military service. There was room for the skill and training of the German engineer, and the Union army profited from engineers who had been driven from Europe after the revolt of 1848. One of the most distinguished of this group was Hermann Ulffers, a Westphalian who had a singularly dramatic career. After sharing in the revolt of 1848, he fled to America, where he worked as an engineer on a railroad and then for five years with the geological survey in Illinois and Missouri. When Governor Claiborne F. Jackson demanded of the state servants of Missouri a declaration of allegiance to the South, Ulffers renounced his position and entered the Union army as an engineer, taking part in several battles in the West. He was then called to Sherman's staff as adjutant and shared in that general's campaign against Atlanta until he was captured. After a long imprisonment, he managed to escape from Andersonville Prison and, after tremendous hardships, to reach the Union lines in December, 1864. Though wrapped in rags and wasted to a skeleton, so that his comrades did not recognize him, he recovered sufficiently to enter the service again and to continue to serve until the end of the war.[76]

A second German engineer who had been driven out of Germany was Johann Albert Neustädter. Since he had served in the artillery branch of the Prussian army for six years, he entered the revolutionary army of Baden as an artillery officer at the Fortress of Rastatt. After the surrender of that fort, he fled with Carl Schurz through a trench out of the city and

[76] Kaufmann, *Die Deutschen im Bürgerkriege,* 558; "Hermann Ulffers," in *Der Deutsche Pionier,* XI (1879–1880), 395–96.

escaped to France and Switzerland, finally settling in America in 1850. During the Civil War here he became an artillery officer, planning, among other engineering works, the fortress of Lexington, Missouri. Like Ulffers, he found a place on the staffs of Generals Frémont, Smith and—finally— Sherman.[77] Another German engineer, Henry T. Flad, had commanded an engineer company of German revolutionists in 1848. He entered the American war as a private in the Third Regiment of the Missouri Reserve Corps; still only thirty-seven years old, he rose to the rank of colonel of engineers. He was one of the important engineers of America and distinguished himself in the war as a bridge builder. His stature is indicated when it is stated that he was later one of James B. Eads's chief assistants in the construction of the bridge over the Mississippi at St. Louis.[78]

F. A. von Blücher, a relative of the great field marshal who helped Wellington defeat Napoleon at Waterloo, served as a major in the Engineer Corps of the Department of the Rio Grande for the United States. To his credit must be placed the defenses of Corpus Christi in Texas. One of the captains of engineers in the Confederate army in Texas was a German whose heart was not in the cause he was serving. Pressed into the Southern service, Henry F. Dietz drew all the plans for the defense of Galveston and its neighborhood. Early in March, 1864, he found an opportunity to desert and to serve under the symbol of the cause with which he sympathized. He fell as a Union officer in the battles around Petersburg.[79] Joseph von Egolf, another German engineer officer, was a captain on General Joseph B. Carr's staff and fell at the Second Battle of Bull Run. Wilhelm Heine, a Forty-eighter, has already been mentioned as attaining the rank of brigadier. After a short period of service with the fleet, he entered the Army of the Potomac to work with the Engineer Corps. At a late period he led a German regiment, the One Hundred and Third New York. Hermann Haupt, who came to Pennsylvania as a child, belongs here only because he was born in Germany. Although General Pope dismissed him as chief of transport in the Army of the Potomac, he was obliged to recall him when the transport service broke down com-

[77] Schnake, "Der Ausbruck des Bürgerkrieges," in *Der Deutsche Pionier*, XI (1879–1880), 385 n.; Kaufmann, *Die Deutschen im Bürgerkriege*, 536; *Official War Records*, Ser. 1, VII, p. 449.

[78] Kaufmann, *Die Deutschen im Bürgerkriege*, 497; Robert Rombauer, *The Union Cause in St. Louis*, xii; *Official War Records*, Ser. 1, XXXIX, Pt. 2, pp. 63, 478.

[79] Kaufmann, *Die Deutschen im Bürgerkriege*, 484, 492. This Dietz cannot be identified in the *Official War Records* as can Von Blücher. His desertion is noted by the Confederates, *Official War Records*, Ser. 1, XXXIV, Pt. 2, p. 522.

pletely. He was acknowledged as an excellent engineer, and he especially distinguished himself in the building of bridges. Captain Joseph Pietzuch, who fled to the United States after the short-lived revolt in Vienna, brought with him to the service training in architecture and experience in the pioneer corps of the Prussian Guards at Berlin. It is, therefore, not strange that when he entered the Thirty-second Indiana Regiment, he was put in command of pontoniers to rebuild destroyed bridges and repair railroads and roads—or that he built the first pontoon bridge over Green River at Murfreesboro in December, 1861.[80]

At the outbreak of the war the United States possessed practically no staff maps. To this lack of maps many serious errors of the military leaders can be attributed. Bit by bit this was remedied. For the map makers, the Union officers drew heavily on the German topographical engineers in the service. One Hugo Gollmer was a significant contributor in this field; even before Lincoln's inauguration he had taken a hand in military preparations by organizing a Turner company in St. Louis. Later he was an officer in the Seventeenth Missouri Regiment, from which he was transferred to the topographical service. Here he produced the first war maps for the Missouri campaign.[81] Above him ranked the Hungarian John A. Fiala (already noted among the colonels), as chief of the topographical section of Frémont's staff. Behind him lay experience as a railroad engineer, a fact which partly explained General Sigel's praise of him as "an unusually able officer." It was he who suggested and planned the fortifications for St. Louis.[82] Another German topographical engineer who shared in Frémont's pathfinder expedition and attained in the course of the war the rank of major on General Silas Casey's staff was Von Engel. Louis E. Korth, a seventeen-year-old German lad when he entered the Army of the Potomac, soon found himself on Blenker's staff and worked later in the topographical division. A varied career in the Union service was experienced by Adolph G. Metzner, an engineer officer who came from Grand Baden to America in 1856. He entered the Union army in August, 1861, at Indianapolis as second lieutenant of Company A of Willich's Thirty-second Indiana Volunteers and served with it as lieutenant and captain until detailed in

[80] For Von Egolf, Heine, and Haupt, see Kaufmann, *Die Deutschen im Bürgerkriege*, 494, 510, and 509, respectively; for Pietzuch, see William H. Powell (comp.), *Officers of the Army and Navy (Volunteer) Who Served in the Civil War* (New York, 1893), 261. All can be identified in *Official War Records*.

[81] Kaufmann, *Die Deutschen im Bürgerkriege*, 504.

[82] *Ibid.*, 497. See Chapter IX of text. He appears in *Official War Records*, Ser. 1, XII, p. 35.

March, 1863, as topographical engineer of the Second Division of the Twentieth Army Corps, a responsible position for a man scarcely thirty years old.[83] Ladislas A. Wrotnowski, whose name properly suggests that he was Polish by birth, was the topographical engineer on General Godfrey Weitzel's staff. Captain William Le Baron Jenny was a French officer in this field of the service. He was a graduate of the School of Topographical Engineers in Paris, was commissioned in the Northern army as an engineer, and rendered immense service by his knowledge of roads and their construction and by his handling of pontoon trains. The maps made by two Poles are preserved in the Atlas of the *Official War Records*.[84]

The topographical section of the army has been termed "the nervous department." The map maker naturally touched sensitive points and brought forth searching criticism from a commander who insisted on knowing exact location, range, direction, sinuosities, elevations, meanderings of streams, depressions, and the proportions of every rivulet, road, ridge, and ravine within the scope of the field of operations. Any engineer in this section was likely to feel, after wrapping himself in his blankets at night, that his bureau was the most thankless branch of the service.

THE SIGNAL SERVICE

Poles were pioneers in the signal service of the United States, which was first organized during the Civil War. Captain Joseph Gloskowski certainly ranked among the important men in this field, and official reports of the Peninsular campaign praised his efforts in many battles. At Antietam he sent important messages, one of which in all likelihood saved General Burnside from being cut off from his forces; for three days at Fredericksburg he constantly transmitted messages by flags, though they "were the special mark [target] of the enemy's artillery." At Chancellorsville his signals proved the only means whereby communication could be maintained between Hooker's staff and parts of his army. Another pioneer

[83] For Major von Engel, see Kaufmann, *Die Deutschen im Bürgerkriege*, 495; for Korth, see *ibid.*, 520; for Metzner, see Fitch (comp.), *Annals of the Army of the Cumberland*, 157; *Official War Records*, Ser. 1, XXX, Pt. 1, p. 537.

[84] For Wrotnowski, see Haiman, *Polish Past in America*, 102; *Official War Records*, Ser. 1, XV, p. 235; Ser. 1, XXVI, Pt. 1, p. 17; for Jenny, see John H. Brinton, *Personal Memoirs of John H. Brinton* (New York, 1914), 331. The Polish map makers were C. A. Czartoryski and Joseph Gorlinski.

of the Signal Corps, also a Pole, was Lieutenant Julius C. Krzywoszynski, who was attached to Grant's army.[85]

MISCELLANEOUS SERVICES

Foreign-born were found in all the various branches of the service. It was a German, Otho E. Michaelis, who filled the post of chief of the ordnance, Department of the Cumberland, in August, 1864, and provided the munitions for the siege of Atlanta and the march through Georgia. An Englishman, Captain Dendy Sharwood, was detailed for some time as acting brigade commissary, rendering efficient service in that post. He came to the service from a business career in Philadelphia and brought to his new profession education, intelligence, extensive knowledge of the world, and courage. The highest tribute paid him was that of a member of his regiment, who said, "He was respected throughout the entire regiment. It was men like him who gave tone to the regiment. . . ." A German named Adolf Krebs was assigned shortly after the outbreak of the war to a place in the Commissary Department of the Army of the Potomac.[86] In the Quartermaster's Department one finds a German and an Irishman who was later in the Commissary Department. An inspector general of the Department of the Cumberland with the rank of lieutenant colonel was a native of Dublin. He pursued civil engineering through the Northwest, so that at the outbreak of war it was natural for him to raise an engineer corps; when it was rejected, he enlisted as a private in the Twelfth Illinois and rose to the rank of lieutenant colonel of his regiment. He was assigned to General Rosecrans as chief of staff and then became his inspector general. A Canadian, Charles L. Hudson, acted as assistant adjutant general in the subdistrict of Meridian.[87]

[85] For Gloskowski, see Haiman, *Polish Past in America*, 134–35; for Krzywoszynski, see *ibid.*, 135. He later commanded a company of the Twenty-second Colored Infantry. Both appear in *Official War Records*, Ser. 1, XXXVI, Pt. 2, p. 353; Ser. 1, XLII, Pt. 1, p. 655.

[86] For Michaelis, see Henry (comp.), *Military Record of Civilian Appointments*, I, 34; for Sharwood, see *History of the Corn Exchange Regiment, 118th Pennsylvania Volunteers*, 653. This Englishman had real military ability, for at the battle at Rappahannock Station, in the absence of field officers, he commanded the regiment. He died as a result of exposure. For Krebs, see "Adolf Krebs," in *Der Deutsche Pionier*, XVI (1884–1885), 513–14. By trade Krebs was a lithographer before and after the war. He was in Confederate prisons at Andersonville and Florence for eight months until he was exchanged. Michaelis and Krebs appear in *Official War Records*, Ser. 1, XXXIX, Pt. 3, p. 163; and Ser. 1, XXIV, Pt. 3, p. 255.

[87] The German noted in the quartermaster's department was Theodor Gülich, recorded in Kaufmann, *Die Deutschen im Bürgerkriege*, 506; for the Irishman, William P. Martin, see

One field of special service, not, indeed, unique but new enough to attract wide attention, was confined to a handful of men; but because of its subsequent development, it should not be omitted. This was the balloon observation service.[88] It is characteristic of the entire Union army that even in the very small number of trained aeronauts attached to the Balloon Department during the Civil War (nine all told, according to the most exhaustive study made of this subject) one of the most colorful of the personnel should have been a foreigner. John H. Steiner, German-born though resident in Philadelphia for some few years before the war, had already gained a wide reputation in the field of aeronautics, more especially in the central West. He made an ascension from Erie, Pennsylvania, in 1857 which nearly terminated his career, as he escaped drowning in Lake Erie by a narrow margin. In 1858 he attracted considerable attention by competing in a free-balloon race with the Frenchman Eugene Godard, who later became balloonist in Emperor Napoleon's Italian campaign. Like so many of his fellow aeronauts, Steiner yearned to try to make the trans-Atlantic crossing by air and announced his intention to do so in the summer of 1858. In August, 1859, he made the first balloon ascension ever made in Toronto, Canada.

This German entered the balloon corps at the close of 1861 and found himself assigned to Brigadier General Charles F. Stone's Corps of Observation on the Upper Potomac. By February, 1862, however, he was selected to take charge of a balloon which was to be sent to Cairo and Island No. 10 for service in the Department of the West. He was relieved of duty with this department in July, 1862, whereupon he rejoined the organization under T. S. C. Lowe with the Army of the Potomac, and served there until his resignation in December, 1862.[89] It is perhaps necessary to state that neither he nor any of the other aeronauts, including Colonel Lowe, who headed the corps, held any military rank, but all were rated as civilian employees. Although Lowe had responsibility for the functioning of the

---

Henry (comp.), *Military Record of Civilian Appointments*, I, 32. The Irish inspector general on Rosecrans' staff was Arthur Charles Ducat. See Fitch (comp.), *Annals of the Army of the Cumberland*, 48–49; for Hudson, see Henry (comp.), *Military Record of Civilian Appointments*, I, 345. All except Gülich are to be found in *Official War Records*, Ser. 1, LIII, p. 80, for Martin; Ser. 1, LII, Pt. 1, p. 424, for Hudson. Ducat appears repeatedly in *Official War Records*.

[88] The fullest work on this subject is F. Stansbury Haydon, *Aeronautics in the Union and Confederate Armies* (Baltimore, 1941).

[89] For Steiner, see *ibid.*, 262–63; *Harper's Weekly*, July 4, 1867; July 10, October 23, 1858; Cincinnati *Gazette*, October 20, 1858; Toronto *Globe*, August 4, 1859.

organization, the title of colonel, by which he was called on occasion, was his only by courtesy. Steiner enjoyed a similar courtesy title of captain.[90] The fact remains that here was another foreigner functioning in a highly specialized field of service connected with the army.

[90] Hayden, *Aeronautics in the Union and Confederate Armies*, 669–70.

CHAPTER THIRTEEN

Life in Camp and Field

LIFE in camp for the soldiers of the Union armies, whether they were in the Steuben Regiment, the Gardes Lafayette, the Scandinavian Regiment, the Scotch Highland Guard, or the Irish Brigade, presented the features common to every camp whether occupied by native-American or foreign-born soldiers. All alike enjoyed the same discomforts; all sought relief from the horrors of war by various diversions; and all panted for news from the newspapers and yearned for the letter from home, however scanty and ill-written.

Pictures of the miseries of army life recurred constantly in the letters of the foreign-born, touched sometimes by a note of stoicism—owing to their previous hard life—or of appreciation, which was not always present in the letters of those native-born who had come from homes little conditioned to hardships. Knute Nelson, for instance, in describing his trip aboard ship from Baltimore to Fortress Monroe, told of the overcrowding on the decks of the *Adelaide* and of the incessant rain, but counted himself lucky in getting such a berth as a chair on the main deck in which he could wrap himself in a blanket. At Fortress Monroe the soldiers camped in the sand, he said; one half of each company slept in tents, the remainder in holes dug in the sand. The second night all had tents but slept on the wet ground. He related that after leaving Baltimore they had had nothing to eat except bread and water until the night before he wrote, when the Ellsworth Zouaves had generously brought them some hot coffee. "Hot coffee with bread is a luxury to us soldiers on a tramp," he stated. "Notwithstanding all this we are all hale, hearty, and happy." It should be added that this spirit in a lad of seventeen was not always to be found in men twice his age. An old Swiss soldier pointed out that in his native land his regiment for three years never once slept under a roof, but had to do with tents as a shelter, while the ground was frozen or covered with mud and water.[1]

---

[1] Knute Nelson to his parents, Virginia, July 22, 1862, Knute Nelson Papers. For the opinion of the Swiss soldier, see Aschmann, *Drei Jahre in der Potomac Armee,* iv.

An over-all picture could be drawn of the evening scene at practically every one of the camps scattered through America. Some men, wearied by a long march or the day's strenuous drills, stretched their weary limbs on the straw. Some told stories around the campfires or sang patriotic or popular songs. Some sat in their tents and read the newspapers or a book, with a bayonet stuck in the ground for a candlestick. Some played cards; indeed, it was a rare company in which a game was not in progress. Some, reared in a Sabbath-school atmosphere, pored over the Bible; sometimes they held a prayer meeting. However, at the tap of the drum at nine o'clock the laughter, song, storytelling, reading, and prayer meeting ended; lights went out; and silence reigned through the camp except for the steady tread of the sentinel.

Often some Don Quixote entertained a group of his fellows with an account of his adventures. The tales of a soldier of fortune were invariably interesting; but the record of a mere wanderer over the face of the globe, as pieced together by the members of his company, makes interesting reading too. Aschmann describes one such Swiss, who joined the Swiss sharpshooters in Washington and was recognized by many of the company: "One had known him in Switzerland as a barber, who on account of a love affair had betaken himself to America; a second had seen him as a waiter in a basement restaurant in New York; a third had encountered him as a physician in Charleston; a fourth had seen him in Charleston in the garb of a Catholic priest, where he had done well 'in a worldly way'; and according to a fifth, he had been a servant in the Turkish consulate in New York. His explanation of these metamorphoses, which must have been entertaining to his listeners, was this: As a Catholic, he had served as a choir boy; he spoke French and had therefore secured a position with some monks in Charleston but was not spiritual enough to be acceptable to the 'brothers'; after his dismissal he betook himself back to New York, where he let himself be led astray and was consequently obliged to turn servant; now he was a soldier, but after the first hostile fire, he played his last role—that of deserter." [2]

It was not unusual for a company, in order to pass the long, winter evenings, to form, as did this Swiss company, a "Jasser" and Story Club. Each member was obliged, when his turn rolled around, to do his best for one evening to entertain by stories, fairy tales, or jokes. The men especially made merry over the stories of one Zürchers, who loved to tell tales

---

[2] Aschmann, *Drei Jahre in der Potomac Armee*, 25, 26.

but could seldom find the right words. One evening, when his theme dealt with the fat cow, he asserted, "In St. Gall I saw in the theatre an eleven hundred pound sow." This was truly a new kind of "prima donna." Once he called a cuckoo a nightingale. Naturally, this afforded occasion for laughter. In the front row someone asked, "How does the nightingale call?" Instantly a dozen of the rear men answered, to the great anger of the relater, "Kuku, kuku." [3]

Sometimes there was in the company a man who could entertain by the products of his pencil, usually caricatures of his colleagues or of their superior officers. The sergeant major of this same Swiss company delighted his comrades with a caricature of Colonel Hiram Berdan, who was highly unpopular with the Swiss in his regiment. The artist displayed the result of his evening's work on the parade ground the next morning. Before an oven stood the universally beloved lieutenant colonel, Frederick Mears, in apron and baker's clothes; beside him appeared Captain Trepp of the Swiss company as journeyman. The baker was busy removing from the oven a pan on which appeared Colonel Berdan in full uniform, while in a basket near by were two recently baked little officers, whose physiognomies were readily recognizable by all the soldiers. The whole was pointed by the words below, "Newly baked officers to be had." [4]

The mere cross section of life which the various members of these foreign companies almost invariably represented must have afforded interesting conversation. One soldier had crossed the northern seas as a whale fisher; one had plied the length of the Mississippi and told of alligators and deeds of southern desperadoes; one had dwelt in Australia, Peru, and Chile; one had been a gold digger in California a decade before but had brought away little of the precious metal; one had lived with Indians in the far West and had hewed a home in the primeval forest.

Underneath this generalized picture were to be seen marked differences as one passed from the camp of an American regiment to that of a German regiment, from a German to an Irish regiment, and from an Irish to a Swedish group. Citizens of foreign birth—whatever their nationality—adhered to their mother tongue and fostered in their special regiments the

---

[3] *Ibid.*, 115–16. Jass was a card game greatly in vogue in Switzerland and South Germany at the time of the Civil War. Hence, the club was formed to tell stories and to play this particular game.

[4] Naturally, Colonel Berdan was furious, but no one would betray the artist. The men regarded Berdan as a political appointee without military knowledge, while Lieutenant Colonel Mears was held an excellent soldier. *Ibid.*, 15–16.

traditions and usages which life in the New World had never caused them to forget. It is the purpose of this chapter to emphasize these differences and the ways of life peculiar to each nationality group.

The very way in which certain camps were laid out created a foreign atmosphere. Let us approach first the camp of the Irish Brigade at Camp Winfield Scott, near Yorktown, in May, 1862. The Sixty-third and Sixty-ninth regiments were arranged in line with a considerable space between them; to the rear and between them the Eighty-eighth lay encamped. Between the companies ran a broad avenue or company ground, bordered on each side by the tents of the men. Close to the tents and all around them stood diminutive cedars, beautifully shaped and as green as emeralds. Between many of the tents were to be seen devices of various kinds—harps and shamrocks preponderating—and several of the tents had emblazoned on them the words "Hail, Columbia." The pride of the companies which erected them was, however, the arches at the ends of the company street, the chief adornment of the entire camp. The quarters of each colonel were nicely decorated, and the priests saw to the erection of tasteful chapels. That of the Sixty-ninth, surrounded by two rows of cedars, well arranged and neatly set in place, was regarded as a "gem"; a larger chapel was used jointly by the other two Irish regiments. At a little distance to the rear, across the fields under the shade of some tall trees, stood the headquarters of General Meagher—one large tent for the general and four smaller ones for the members of his staff, all surrounded by cedars.[5] Another source provides some additional details concerning Meagher's headquarters, which he termed "strictly Hibernian." The emerald-green standard was entwined with the red, white, and blue, but the gilt eagles on the flag poles held the shamrock sprig in their beaks. The soldiers on guard had "69" or "88" stamped on their green hatbands, while the brogue of every "county from Down to Wexford fell upon the ear." [6]

The Swiss company of Berdan's Sharpshooters contrived to give their camp a flavor of the homeland by adorning the snow-white tents with foliage and fir boughs, and, most of all, by christening the company streets with names famous in Swiss history—Tell Strasse and Winkelried-gasse. First and foremost there must be cleanliness, for the members of this

---

[5] We owe this detailed description to "Gallowglass," who had been a reporter of the New York *Irish-American*, before he joined the Irish Brigade, and who continued to send articles to his paper. For this account, see issue of May 17, 1862. "Gallowglass" was Captain James Turner, as the reader will probably remember.

[6] Townsend, *Campaigns of a Non-Combatant*, 130.

company had been greatly revolted by the filth and vermin they had found in an Irish camp while on the advance into Virginia.[7]

Most colorful of the German headquarters was Blenker's camp. German fashion, the tents stood in rows, each regiment separated from the others. The lanes between them were ornamented, like Meagher's, with recently planted fir or cedar trees; the whole left a friendly, even imposing, impression. Most of the soldiers, using the canvas as a roof, had improved their tents by means of boards and doors, oftentimes even managing a window and stoves and some pieces of hand-hewn furniture. Headquarters for the staff commanded wooden floors and roaring fires.

Princess Salm-Salm described the charming surprise prepared for her husband and herself, after he took command of the Eighth New York Regiment, on their birthdays, which happened to fall on the same day. A band was sent to serenade them one morning as the graceful preliminary to the displaying of the little garden which had been laid out for them in the old Italian style. The individual beds into which it had been divided were surrounded with stones and formed into figures. Little trees and shrubs were planted here and there, and on one bed, the soldiers in their fantasy had planted an enormous birthday cake. A real cake being clearly impossible, this had been made of mud and ornamented—according to the confectioners' mode—with green leaves, colored sand, and stones representing fruit.[8]

At Aquia Creek, Virginia, where Prince Felix Salm-Salm expected to be stationed during the winter of 1862–1863, he established elaborate headquarters. He procured a large hospital tent, which he was able to have decorated tastefully, even gorgeously, as he was fortunate enough to have among his soldiers workmen of all trades—carpenters, upholsterers, and masons, among others. The canvas was rendered less transparent by being doubled and decorated with white and red woolen damask arranged in festoons, flags being fastened between the festoons. The board floor boasted a carpet, and the *salon,* as the Princess insisted on calling the interior, was furnished with a sofa which the soldiers had skillfully made. Though the cushions were filled with straw, they were neatly made and covered with damask. The chef-d'oeuvre, however, was a large mirror which the Prince had secured from a neighboring village. For the bedroom the soldiers had managed to construct of boards a large bedstead, which they had provided with a straw mattress; over this was spread a buffalo skin, while a second

[7] Aschmann, *Drei Jahre in der Potomac Armee,* 9–10, 30–31.
[8] Salm-Salm, *Ten Years of my Life,* I, 35.

skin served as coverlet. Overhead the bed was almost regal, for it had a canopy decorated with white and red damask. Behind the canvas palace stood a smaller tent which served as kitchen and bedroom for the negro servant girl whom the Princess had brought with her from Washington. A tea service for six persons and a half-dozen knives and forks completed the equipment.[9]

The ménage of the Bourbon princes during the Peninsular campaign was a separate establishment and so merits special mention; for, in addition to their uncle, the two princes were accompanied by a physician and a captain of *chasseurs à pied*. Their little establishment was pronounced the jolliest one in camp by General McClellan, who often found it a great relief to listen to the laughter and gaiety resounding from their tents.[10]

A very different type of headquarters was Colonel Heg's while he was stationed near Island No. 10 in the Mississippi in April, 1862. His tent was pitched on shore, but, together with most of the officers, he slept on board the steamboat *G. W. Graham,* one of the largest boats on the river. He had a fine stateroom and ate in the cabin with the captain and the other officers of the vessel. In August this same Norwegian officer, in camp near Iuka, Mississippi, wrote his wife that when night came he hung his hammock between the trees and rolled himself up in his blankets—and there was his tent.[11] Of course, the writer does not intend to imply that there was any special Norwegian flavor about Colonel Heg's headquarters, as here pictured.

Camp routine was basically the same in all the camps of the various nationalities, but despite the similarity there were, of course, certain individual differences. The long days of the summer of 1861 were devoted to drill and a part of the night to theoretical study—for the officers, apparently—in the French Fifty-fifth New York, its colonel, De Trobriand, tells us. Blenker's German Chasseurs began its daily drill in Tompkins Square before it ever moved to a real camp, and Schwarzwalder's Fifth New York drilled at the Battery. A Swedish Minnesota company began

[9] *Ibid.,* 37–38. On an island in the Tennessee River near Bridgeport, the Prince constructed an elaborate building thirty feet long, placing it on poles above the ground. Since this was virtually a house, no description is held necessary. See *ibid.,* 112–13.

[10] McClellan, *McClellan's Own Story,* 144–45.

[11] Blegen (ed.), *Civil War Letters of Colonel Heg,* 75, 125. On another occasion, May 12, 1863, he wrote his wife, Guinild, that he had a tent about twelve feet square, with a good floor, and that on one side was his bed and on the other side, his "parlor," furnished with a table and a couple of chairs. *Ibid.,* 210.

its camp life at Fort Snelling with two hours of drill a day, soon increased to seven hours. The men were subjected to severe training at once, as the intention was to create of them a Jäger company—able to stand, lie on their backs, load, and spring to their feet in response to signals by a trumpet. Meals followed the usual routine: breakfast at seven, dinner at twelve, supper at six.[12] The Scandinavian Fifteenth Wisconsin was grounded in the elements of the drill at Camp Randall before its departure from Madison. A glimpse of the routine from the officer's point of view can be gleaned from Colonel Heg's report to his wife that he met his captains and lieutenants twice a day, for an hour each time, to give them instruction. He also kept his companies drilling one hour a day—and this was in late July near Jacinto when the regiment was in the field. We learn the kind of soldiers that Heg was drilling when we read that his soldiers thought him strict but were "glad of it." [13]

A German officer in Hecker's regiment feared the tedious monotony of American camp routine, which sustained, in his opinion, not the least comparison to the camp life of a German soldier. He was, however, agreeably surprised to find himself mistaken, for all hardships were cheerfully met. This officer did not suffer from the delusion that playing soldier and being soldier were one and the same thing. This regiment enjoyed the advantage of having Captain August Mauff as instructor for the under-officers; he was an able man of practical experience and quiet temperament, who knew how to win underlings.[14] Irish regiments could give flavor even to such a dull and burdensome thing as military drill. At initiation into the first position of a soldier, which usually made the joints creak, Celtic soldiers often burst into such informal ejaculations as, "Ah! but it's the divil's own way to stand!" They took their drill seriously, and assumed a solemn expression during its execution.[15]

The first reaction of a foreign-born recruit to the life of a soldier may be gleaned from a letter written to a friend on June 24, 1861, by Knute Nelson, who had enlisted in the Fourth Wisconsin, from Camp Utley,

---

[12] De Trobriand, *Quatre Ans de Campagnes*, I, 76; Chicago *Hemlandet*, September 18, 1861. For the Fifth New York Regiment, the soldiers of which lived in tents like those furnished the Hudson Bay Indians, see Moore (ed.), *Rebellion Record*, I, Pt. 2, p. 49.

[13] Madison *Emigranten*, February 17, 1862; Ager (ed.), *Oberst Heg og hans Gutter*, 8; Blegen (ed.), *Civil War Letters of Colonel Heg*, 65, 115.

[14] Chicago *Illinois Staats-Zeitung*, July 9, 1861.

[15] MacNamara, *The Irish Brigade in Bivouac and Battle*, 17, 18. In February, 1862, the Fourth New York Regiment had four hours of battalion drill, two hours in the morning and two hours in the afternoon. New York *Irish-American*, February 1, 1862.

Racine. Running through his comments is the interest of a country lad in a wider world than had yet been his portion. He did not believe that a more secret place could be found in the entire state than Camp Utley with its mass of pines and its pretty shade trees scattered here and there. To him the board was very good—"the same as is found in American hotels except cake and pie"; to him it was a pretty sight to see so many men at drill. Rising at four-thirty and drilling from five to six did not daunt him, nor did the fact that he was kept at drill for seven hours a day. He found standing guard at night the worst task, though it was mitigated by the fact that men who stood guard at night were free the next day and that he had become accustomed to it. Already he found himself physically stronger, he declared.[16]

The various regiments of foreign-born held reviews and parades and flag presentations in their home camps before they ever went to the capital or to the front, just as did the native regiments. Usually, at their departure they were escorted to the pier or station by a band and by a throng of their fellow countrymen. On May 2, 1861, when a regiment containing a German company left Erie, Pennsylvania, it was escorted to the railroad station by the ringing music of Mehl's German band.[17] How close to the hearts of the German population of New York, and especially of Turners, was the regiment of United Turner Rifles was shown by the interest with which all its movements were followed and by the tension on the day of its departure. Early on the morning of June 14, a greater excitement prevailed among the German population than at the leaving of any other German regiment. The various societies gathered, according to the published program, in their localities; it would have been easier to name the societies absent from, than those present in, the procession. At two in the afternoon the "Social Reformers" escorted the Turner members from their hall to the *Harmonie Halle,* where the *Schützengilde* joined them. The procession moved up the Bowery to Union Square, where other societies were awaiting the arrival of the regiment; it, meanwhile, was being escorted from its camp in Turtle Bay by a delegation of various *Turn* societies. During the morning a mass of humanity had thronged through the camp while thousands of spectators occupied the surrounding hills. Accompanied by the De Kalb Zouaves and the Turners, the procession

16 Knute Nelson to G. Thompson, June 24, 1861, Knute Nelson Papers.

17 This regiment must have been a mixed one, for, besides the Jäger company, there were Yankee companies, Irishmen, and a company of Grenadiers. Chicago *Illinois Staats-Zeitung,* May 7, 1861.

moved up Broadway to City Hall. All the side streets were densely packed; onlookers waved greetings from all the doors and windows and threw flowers. It was nearly five o'clock before the regiment, over eight hundred strong with its music corps and drummers, reached City Hall, where for several hours thousands had been waiting. Here the usual presentation of a costly Union flag and a German flag was made with appropriate speeches. The elaborate ceremonies concluded with the regiment's being escorted by the *Turn* societies to its ship.[18]

Thielmann's German Dragoons in Chicago marched on a day early in August to the office of the *Illinois Staats-Zeitung,* appearing for the first time in their new uniforms in order to afford the editor of that paper an opportunity to inspect them and to express to him their appreciation for the warm interest he had taken in their organization. On this occasion a German who had been driven out of Louisiana, the subsequently famous journalist Wilhelm Rapp, gave a short patriotic speech, which was received with thundering hurrahs. This company, after receiving a cavalry flag, rode through the companies of Colonel Charles Knobelsdorff's regiment to the St. Louis Railroad Station.[19] The Scandinavians of the Fifteenth Wisconsin had sufficient numbers by February 13, 1862, to be mustered in. Following the ceremony of taking the oath, they paraded through Madison, drawing up in a long, single rank before the capitol, where they went through a drill with their weapons before re-forming in companies to return to camp. A few days later, on Washington's Birthday, the regiment drew up in a square before the capitol for the presentation of flags by Governor Louis P. Harvey.[20]

The Swedes of New York seem to have broken loose from the puritanical attitude of many of their countrymen, for five days before the departure of their company they staged an officers' ball in the city, on which occasion Swedish women proffered the company a silk American flag, which the members of the company swore to defend with their blood. A short time before, a lawyer named Stallknecht had given them a bass

---

[18] *Ibid.,* June 18, 1861. A partial list of the societies represented shows how great was the interest in this Turner regiment: New York Song Society, Mozart Male Chorus, Dramatic Club, Arion Society, Helvetia Male Chorus, New York Schützengild, Bloomingdale *Turn* Society, Brooklyn *Turn* Society, Hoboken *Turn* Society, and Jersey City *Turn* Society.

These are from a printed program located in Peabody Library, Baltimore. *Proceedings at the Mass Meeting of Loyal Citizens in Union Square, New York, on the 15th Day of July, 1862* (New York, 1862).

[19] Chicago *Illinois Staats-Zeitung,* August 6, 22, 1861.

[20] Madison *Emigranten,* February 17, 24, 1862.

drum, upon which they had vowed to write his name in the enemy's blood after their first battle; from the same person they had received a package of books—romances and novels. Two days before their departure, the entire regiment went to New York, where at a review the women of that city presented them with a regimental flag and the women of Brooklyn, with guidons. On May 25, in front of the Astor House, a full review of the regiment was held, after which it embarked for Fortress Monroe.[21]

As long as regiments were within reach of the home folk, visits were the order of the day; and seldom indeed did visitors go empty-handed. While the friends and relatives of foreign-born soldiers did not constitute a constant stream to the camps, many of them did find their way to the places where their menfolk were stationed, especially if their relatives were in a so-called "foreign" regiment or company. The German regiments simply had to have their beer, and it sometimes flowed in too abundantly. "At Camp Ellsworth in Keokuk, Iowa," not only did the local dealers cater to the demand for beer, "but donations in the form of kegs of whiskey, bottles of brandy, and barrels of beer kept pouring" in so steadily that an appeal had to be made to the "home folks to send pipes, tobacco, and books" instead, if the men were not to be utterly "incapacitated for coming campaigns." In some companies it was customary to have from two to a dozen barrels of lager beer on tap.[22] The absolute prohibition of fermented liquors in camp became a necessity, but it was strongly resisted by the Europeans, especially the Germans and Irish. The First Minnesota, including Germans and Scandinavians among their number, lived well at Fort Snelling. The people in the near-by towns visited them often and always brought some baked articles for the "boys." "And when they marched to St. Paul or St. Anthony, they were always well received." [23]

Advertisements in the *Courrier des États-Unis* of the departure of boats

---

[21] *Ibid.*, August 10, 1861. The Zouaves of Von Gilsa's German regiment, while stationed at Central Park, also organized a military ball. New York *Courrier des États-Unis*, May 13, 1861. See above, p. 132.

[22] Shannon, *The Organization and Administration of the Union Army*, I, 219. The tales of how the soldiers got the better of the sutlers are so numerous that it is sufficient here to allude to only one: A long train of army wagons loaded with lager passed a camp on its way to Blenker's divison. As it was ascending a hill, someone crept up to one of the wagons and cut the straps that held the tail gate and the ropes holding the canvas cover over the end of the wagon, so that barrel after barrel rolled out. In a moment thousands of men were running to the train with tin cups and pails. It finally proved necessary to charge the marauders with a regiment of cavalry to drive them off and protect the train to its destination. C. B. Fairchild (comp.), *History of the 27th Regiment N.Y. Vols.* (Binghamton, N.Y., 1888), 29.

[23] See a letter to Chicago *Hemlandet*, January 25, 1862. Much the same statement appears in Madison *Emigranten* in the issue of June 1, 1861.

and trains from New York for Camp Lafayette on Staten Island are illuminating as to the way in which French citizens were visiting the Gardes Lafayette. Since the paper stresses the numerous departures on Sunday, the inference is clear that that was the special visiting day.[24] Frequent inspections took place. For instance the Garde de Garibaldi was inspected at its headquarters on Broadway by several officers of the staff and by two citizens who had been active in its organization. Likewise, the First Wisconsin was formally reviewed by Governor Randall about May 10, 1861.[25]

The ceremonial of presentation of flags went on constantly. However, it will be necessary to detail but a few here. Because of certain individual features, the presentation of a flag at Camp Dennison by the German women of Cincinnati to the First Cincinnati German Regiment, under command of General McCook, constitutes a good example. The flag differed from those described earlier in that it had two streamers from the top; on the one were the words *Deutsches Regiment von Cincinnati,* and on the other, *Kämpft tapfer für Freiheit und Recht.* In the usual setting of an open square with a provisional stage, surrounded by the deputation of women, the formal presentation was made; the flag was accepted by Colonel McCook, who regretted his inability to express his thanks in German. Lieutenant Colonel von Willich contributed the unique feature: already the band had played "Hail Columbia" when the flag was unfurled, but, baring his head, Von Willich asked for the "Marseillaise," explaining that he was asking "for this most beautiful of songs of freedom of humanity, and of right"—a beautiful tribute to France by a German. As protectors of freedom and of the hearth, the regiment must inspire confidence and defend the flag to the last man. Then came the playing of the "Star-Spangled Banner"; the grouping of the soldiers about the women while one of the deputation made a brief speech; the expression of thanks by each captain for his company; the presentation to Von Willich of a sword for his zeal in drilling the regiment; and the playing of "Frisch Kameraden auf's Pferd." Von Willich's expression of his appreciation for the gift of the sword closed the ceremony.[26]

The scenes just described were duplicated when the various regiments moved to camps nearer the front. Any citizen leaving for the camp where soldiers of his community were quartered carried with him gifts of money,

[24] New York *Courrier des États-Unis,* August 10, 1861.

[25] *Ibid.,* May 4, 1861; Chicago *Illinois Staats-Zeitung,* May 11, 1861.

[26] Chicago *Illinois Staats-Zeitung,* June 3, 1861.

and barrels and boxes of stores. These visitors, it is safe to say, could have been counted by the hundreds and thousands during the war. Soldiers and officers returning from a furlough home came back laden with presents for the soldiers of their companies or regiments. Colonel Heg serves as a good case in point. He had been rather severely injured by a fall from his horse at Perryville and as a result had been granted thirty days leave to recover. When he returned from Wisconsin to Nashville early in December, 1862, he came laden with a mass of gifts for Company C— shoes, overshoes, and socks chiefly. Barrels of beer and cigars went to Camp Yates for Captain Lothar Lippert's company and the German Union Rifles.[27] Regiments which had been overlooked earlier received flags at more advanced camps, as was the case with a Chicago Turner company, which was given a flag from friends while at Camp Cairo. The ceremony here was varied by a preliminary religious service, for which all the companies and many civilians assembled.[28]

The celebration accompanying the presentation of two flags—one American and one French—to the Gardes Lafayette became the occasion for a visit by President Lincoln to that regiment. The day chosen was January 8, 1862, the anniversary of the Battle of New Orleans. The effect of the red trousers and blue cloaks of the French soldiers against the white of the snow-covered ground added to the picturesqueness of the scene. Although flag presentations were an old story by 1862, the number of carriages and of men and women on horseback was considerable for the season of the year. The President arrived in an open barouche with Mrs. Lincoln, General Shields, and N. P. Welles, a distinguished writer. A member of Congress, F. A. Conklin, made the presentation speech, to which Colonel de Trobriand responded. The drums rolled, the trumpets sounded, the color guard returned to the ranks, and a review of the troops ended the military ceremony. The program included a collation in the dining hall, the walls of which were ornamented with garlands and military trophies and draped with flags for the occasion. The regiment took pride in serving only dishes which its French cooks had prepared. The triumph of those culinary artists was complete—indeed, they displayed too much talent and so administered to their colonel a defeat, for the generals promptly had the cooks detached and removed to their own quarters.

[27] See Blegen (ed.), *Civil War Letters of Colonel Heg*, 153 n., for the gifts carried by Heg to his soldiers; Chicago *Illinois Staats-Zeitung*, May 9, 1861, for the gifts to the German companies.

[28] Chicago *Illinois Staats-Zeitung*, May 5, 1861.

Thus, as Colonel de Trobriand dryly remarked, a half dozen of his fighters were saved "by the heat of the kitchen from the fire of the foe." The President in his reply to the toast drunk in his honor declared that "he had not eaten so well since entering the White House" and that if the Fifty-fifth New York fought as well as it "treated its guests, victory [was] assured." [29]

In addition to flag presentations there were frequent inspections of foreign, as of native-born, regiments. When the Gardes Lafayette was located before Yorktown, McClellan expressed his intention to examine its position for himself. When the proposed visit was announced by a member of the general's staff, De Trobriand put his companies under arms to receive the commander, who soon arrived, accompanied by Generals E. D. Keyes and John J. Peck and a numerous staff. The enemy, who always kept an eye upon the movements of the regiment, easily detected a group of superior officers. They trained their guns with particular care and fired. Two shots came, one after the other, with their well-known whistling sound and burst with a remarkable precision just beyond the visitors—who returned into the wood without going farther, postponing their visit to another day, which never came. [30] In May, 1863, inspection was made of the brigade of which the Scandinavian Regiment was a part. The report, which was sent by Rosecrans to Colonel Heg and was read to the men at dress parade, was to the effect that the inspector found the brigade well instructed in its duties and the men and officers vigilant. Naturally, such a report pleased and inspirited the men. [31]

A visit of inspection by General Butler to the Turner Regiment of New York in July, 1861, produced great festivities in that German camp. The veranda at headquarters was decorated with flowers and twigs; at both ends waved United States flags, and between them floated the two German tricolors beside the Turner flag. Before the house a stage had been improvised and the surrounding space assigned for spectators. At six o'clock in the afternoon, General Butler appeared on horseback, accompanied by his wife and daughter, many other women, his staff, and the four colonels

---

[29] De Trobriand, *Quatre Ans de Campagnes*, I, 131–32. It is perhaps suitable to record the fate of these two flags. The French tricolor left Tennallytown to return to New York, where it was from time to time taken from its case to honor the departure of new contingents to the Fifty-fifth Regiment, which replaced the French militia regiment. The American flag received its baptism of fire at Williamsburg, but, rent by shot and shell, it left its scraps at Fairfax and Malvern Hill, and finished its honorable career at Fredericksburg with scarcely more than the staff and a morsel of fringe. *Ibid.*, I, 133.

[30] *Ibid.*, I, 182–83.

[31] Blegen (ed.), *Civil War Letters of Colonel Heg*, letter to his wife of May 7, 1863, p. 209.

of the regiments stationed at that point. Colonel Max von Weber, commander of the regiment about to be inspected, and his officers received the guests and escorted them to the veranda for refreshments before the program began. The Turner exercises, especially the building of the pyramid, brought forth stormy applause from the guests, and warm approval from Butler of the poise and control of the men. At twilight the melting tones of the zither rang through the air, and in the course of the evening a concert of German music entertained the guests.[32]

The grand review of the army in the latter part of April, 1862, was a gala occasion and passed off with éclat. It must have made a great impression of the might of the Federal army on the foreign soldiers who participated. It took place on the plains back of Spofford Mountains and occupied two whole days. Corps after corps filed past—infantry, cavalry, and artillery companies, to the number of 120,000 men. The dramatic climax of the review came when, on the afternoon of the second day, Lincoln halted his horse in front of a Pennsylvania regiment, dropped the reins, and reaching out his arms toward the men cried, "My God, men, if I could save this country by giving up my own life, how gladly I would do it." [33]

A ceremony which must strike the reader of today as a bit odd was the baptism of one of the big guns belonging to the Sixty-ninth New York and mounted at Fort Corcoran. The colonel of the regiment chose the name of Colonel David Hunter, commander of the brigade, for the gun, and Father Mooney, chaplain of the Sixty-ninth, performed the ceremony of baptism and spoke briefly, closing with these words, ". . . and thus may he [the gun, now formally christened the Hunter Gun] soon speak to the glory of the Stars and Stripes, honor to the name that he bears, and lasting credit to the Sixty-ninth." [34]

In the winter of 1864 a new note in entertainment was injected into the Army of the Potomac. In honor of the many women who had been given permission to visit their relatives and friends in the army, some balls were held in festival huts expressly arranged by the soldiers. General David B. Birney, who was in command of a division and was using a beautiful, roomy, country house for his headquarters, held every Wednesday evening a sort of soiree, to which all officers of the division were invited. Two good music corps entertained the guests in agreeable fashion, while material refreshment took the form of cold food and good drinks.[35]

[32] Chicago *Illinois Staats-Zeitung*, July 1, 1861.
[33] Mulholland, *The Story of the 116th Regiment Pennsylvania Infantry*, 96–97.
[34] Moore (ed.), *Rebellion Record*, II, Pt. 3, pp. 42–43.
[35] Aschmann, *Drei Jahre in der Potomac Armee*, 163.

Nowhere do differences between nationalities appear more quickly than in their tables. In general the soldiers who came from foreign homes ate the food provided by Uncle Sam, which meant that they received the typical American fare. The old tradition that the Civil War hero in the Union army subsisted on a steady diet of hardtack and salt pork is quite incorrect. In times of stress, during a prolonged battle or march, or when being transported long distances by boat, he might have lived on that or less. But the description of a Dane stationed at a camp south of Mason and Dixon's line is probably a more accurate picture of the soldier's fare and the way it struck the foreign-born soldier: "Our fare is especially good and rich but we do not get so much soft bread as we could wish; coffee we get twice a day, meat three times and as a rule soup or beans at dinner. The meat and cold meat we get is fair; likewise we receive especially good fresh meat each other day. . . ."[36] Potatoes were often mentioned as a regular item. When one recalls the kind of diet to which a soldier reared on a foreign fare—for many foreigners continued the customs of the homeland as to diet—was accustomed, he readily understands why there was discontent. A German, for instance, accustomed to a meal of rye bread, wieners, pumpernickel, potato salad, cottage cheese, caraway-seed bread, sauerkraut, and sausage of many kinds, doubtless found the usual American fare flavorless and flat.

However, the foreign-born soldier could complain just as bitterly as any native when the food was scarce or inferior in quality. Witness the letter by a Swedish soldier from Bishop Hill in Company D, Fifty-seventh Illinois Regiment, written probably in July, 1862: "Our provisions have been rather scanty for a time back, so we have, for example, for a long period not had other than rather spoiled and poor bacon, a kind of smoked sides of meat; and we have been compelled in this great heat to eat and cook spoiled meat with poor crackers with it, till now at last we have received recently a young and somewhat able person in the bake-shop who supplies us with bread so that at least we do not have to starve to death." A Nor-

---

[36] Madison *Emigranten,* August 12, 1861. Written originally by a correspondent to *Dagbladet,* another Norwegian magazine. One Norwegian private wrote cheerfully of his first taste of army fare as he was transported up the Mississippi from New Orleans: "The government furnishes us good coffee, hard tack, and bacon, and a man can live nicely on these, world without end." L.L. Caldwell to his wife, Morganza, Louisiana, June 30, 1864. Manuscript Collection of Civil War Letters, Luther College Library, Decorah, Iowa.

Another Norwegian complained of the brackish water on board *Star of the South,* the vessel from Fortress Monroe to New Orleans, but he stated that when they made coffee, he always filled his canteen and drank cold coffee exclusively—and kept well. Luman to his wife, February 16, 1864, Manuscript Collection of Civil War Letters, Luther College Library.

wegian complained about the same time, "Sometimes we get a little coffee and sometimes not, and it is pretty hard to stand it with such food and such marching." He was both interested and angered by the sutler's prices when he found butter offered at seventy-five cents a pound.[37] Added to quality was the question of quantity. It was reported that the men in the Steuben Regiment were more satisfied with their food than with their equipment, but the portions were apparently not generous, as Colonel Bendix was forced to supplement them with bread and cheese.[38]

It was not long before Blenker informed the authorities that his troops were not accustomed to white bread and that they must have dark bread. Hence, money was granted to him to buy rye and erect a bakery for black bread. Likewise, beer was not a luxury but a necessity to the Germans— at least, it was so regarded by them. Therefore, Blenker received the right to allow beer to be sold at Hunter's Chapel. This concession, however, carried other problems in its train, for Hunter's Chapel became soon the object of pilgrimage of the soldiers of all the other divisions, and the consumption of beer in the German camp equalled that at a festival. William Russell, correspondent of the London *Times,* stated that Blenker received monthly $6,000 to $8,000 for issuing licenses to sell this beverage. The reproach should probably be levied at Blenker's quartermaster rather than at him, for he had ordered a certain profit on the sale for the benefit of the regimental treasury. While the quartermaster received the money, the treasury remained empty.[39]

The sutler of a German regiment was expected to achieve the impossible in order to supply lager, Rhine wine, and bologna. Whenever he appeared with a fresh stock of these goods, the crowd around his tent gathered in numbers greater than those at a parade of that regiment. Naturally, the other regiments regarded the presence of a German regiment in the brigade as highly desirable.[40]

Germans were far from the only foreigners who craved their own type of food. Furthermore, an almost childish yearning for favorite foods manifested itself among officers as well as privates. Colonel Heg wrote repeatedly about articles of food which he wished his wife to send him. As early

---

[37] Written to the Chicago *Hemlandet* by C. Valentine of the Illinois Company and dated August 6, 1862; for the Norwegian, Lars O. Dokken, who was in the Fifteenth Wisconsin, see Ager (ed.), *Oberst Heg og hans Gutter,* 111. One Swedish soldier denied that he had ever seen any spoiled meat. Chicago *Hemlandet,* January 2, 1862.

[38] New York *Courrier des États-Unis,* May 4, 1861.

[39] Kaufmann, *Die Deutschen im Bürgerkriege,* 179–80.

[40] Rossiter Johnson and others (eds.), *Campfire and Battlefield,* 501.

as August 9, 1862, after only about six months of camp fare, he suggested that if she found an opportunity to send anything safely, she might send "10 or 20 pounds of good white lump sugar—a keg of nice Butter—a jar or two of preserves—and have them buy me a box of *Catawaha* [?] *Wine* on their way at Chicago—a good nice cheese would be all right." He added that he did not expect the entire list but all would be acceptable. He admitted that he could buy all the items in Mississippi except butter, but that they cost "like Sixty." His letter of August 31 revealed that she had sent some of the things he had mentioned. "Your jelly came just in time for this march. Your stuff that you sent me has made our mess good-natured several times, and I have still some of it left. After I get into camp at night I have one of the bottles of jelly, some crackers, a cup of coffee and a little white sugar with it, and I tell you it has tasted good." In his letter of April 23, 1863, he asked her to send some maple syrup to go with the buckwheat cakes he had regularly for breakfast. A month later he explained that he could get "dry" peaches and apples, salt fish, and smoked salmon shipped down by the government to be sold at cost to officers—which items are some indication as to his Norwegian taste. When the soldiers of the Union army were consuming the food found in Tennessee, he complained that the only thing they had had was cornbread baked out of "Water and Meal without anything else in it." But later he was "lucky enough to get hold of a lot of Honey" and to find a few pigs that had "not starved." They had plenty of coffee but no sugar.[41]

Of course, all regiments resorted to foraging. It began early, for a Danish captain of the Scandinavian Regiment stated in August of the first year of the war that his men could have a good chicken dinner—at least until their officers detected them, "since there is left behind a vast mass of feather." On one occasion this same regiment arrived at a camp to find that some "jayhawkers," meaning, apparently, some guerrilla regiment, had placed a guard over some beehives, intending to remove the honey that night. A conscientious officer told the sergeant of the guard to send for additional guards or his "boys" would "jayhawk" the hives. He knew his Scandinavians, for before reinforcements arrived every hive was gone. He added rather naïvely that their general would pay for all that his soldiers plundered—"and so we jayhawk all we can." [42] The account of a member

---

[41] These items about food which Colonel Heg desired his wife to send him all occur in Blegen (ed.), *Civil War Letters of Colonel Heg*, 121, 130–31, 205, 214, 229.

[42] Kuhns, "An Army Surgeon's Letters to his Wife," in *Proceedings of the Mississippi Valley Historical Society*, VII (1913–1914), 311.

of the New York Turners sounds as if the Germans, too, could depart widely from their customary army diet: "I succeeded on a brief reconnaisance in buying in a negro hut, which reminded me of the Witches kitchen in *Faust,* a couple of eggs and a handful of coffee; others were so lucky as to get corn-bread, milk and similar delicacies. The musicians had procured an old kettle, in which they prepared a soup of crabs, clams, and oysters, which they had fished in the near-by creek." [43]

A letter from the Scandinavian Regiment, dated June 29, 1862, indicated that in the case of the plantation of the Reverend Mr. Harris, Colonel Heg had relaxed his order forbidding foraging because Harris was the nephew of the "rebel" governor of Tennessee. The result was the expected one: "Officers and soldiers rushed with like bloodthirstiness [! !] over the poor hens and geese, while outright battles arose between some bold turkeys and attackers. As we a few hours later arrived at Trenton, we lived like princes." [44] Relaxation of the rule may have had no relation to Heg's complaint a few days later that many of his troops were behaving badly, stealing and robbing at night.[45] In any case, Scandinavian soldiers also succumbed to temptation, but their colonel seemed equal to the situation, for he added that he had arrested a few of them. There is a touch of Scandinavian humor in the report which came from a camp at Nashville toward the close of the year of good living on turkeys, geese, and chickens "without its costing our dear provider, Onkle [*sic*] Sam one cent." [46]

The Scandinavians complained mostly of the absence of brandy—of receiving it "almost never"—but they admitted that they were constantly provided with smoking and chewing tobacco. Their chief officer, however, rejoiced over the prohibition of brandy. Colonel Heg wrote March 29, 1862, at the beginning of his campaign, "They [the officers] are all different from what they used to be, as they get no liquor." [47]

As usual, the French soldiers, at least the officers, craved good food—and had it. The cuisine of the Gardes Lafayette enjoyed such a reputation that some visitors voluntarily took potluck at its table and ate utterly unexpected dishes. They had bullfrog legs, with thighs, as De Trobriand

[43] Madison *Emigranten,* August 12, 1861; Chicago *Illinois Staats-Zeitung,* June 23, 1861.
[44] Madison *Emigranten,* July 7, 1862.
[45] Blegen (ed.), *Civil War Letters of Colonel Heg,* 99.
[46] Madison *Emigranten,* December 8, 1862.
[47] This complaint about brandy came from a member of the New York Scandinavian Company copied from the *Dagbladet* by the Madison *Emigranten* in its issue of August 10, 1861. For Heg's comment on the improvement in the officers, see Blegen (ed.), *Civil War Letters of Colonel Heg,* 69.

boasted, the size of chicken legs; but they had rarer delicacies, a fact which he felt sure would be attested by "Count de V.," a French officer attached to General Erasmus D. Keyes's staff. He had enjoyed vastly a particular salad, and, intrigued by its flavor, had demanded to know the recipe in order to take it back to France; there, he declared, it would rank above the potato salad of Parmentier and beside wild turkey Brillat-Savarin. When the secret was revealed and the "delicious" salad turned out to be black snake, the nutritive qualities of which had been discovered by the Zouaves of the regiment, the "secret" destroyed the count's appetite and his taste for the cuisine of the French Fifty-fifth. He never returned nor did he introduce the dish in France.[48]

The Swiss, naturally, had their own tricks to secure the food and drink most to their taste. Captain Aschmann has accommodated us with the secret of sausage à la Suisse, as it was served at the American-Swiss company table. His servant secured beef and skin at the place where the army cattle were slaughtered; he bought bacon, salt, and pepper at the commissary and with these ingredients turned out St. Galler or Lyon sausage at will to his financial advantage.[49] When it came to securing spiritous liquors, the Swiss were more resourceful than the Germans. Comrades, returning from furlough, smuggled the liquid into camp with them, or milk cans yielded something quite different from milk. One Swiss from Unterwalden had reduced his traffic in whiskey to a science, so that he maintained the chief depot for it in the company. Inside his tent a hole well covered with boards and earth constituted his wine cellar. Although he was punished many times, the authorities never traced the source of his supply. The Swiss could not, like the Americans, "see a sin in taking a drop on the teeth." [50]

Of course, foreign-born soldiers whiled away the leisure hours in camp with conversation, jests, and witticisms, and one may be sure that nowhere was the conversation brighter and wittier than in the French and Irish camps. Since the Prince de Joinville sketched admirably and also possessed a keen sense of the ridiculous, his sketchbook proved to be an inexhaustible source of amusement. His deafness was a disadvantage to him, but it probably explains why the fun in the camp of the Bourbon princes was sometimes so rollicking. In the tents of the Massachusetts Ninth Regiment the officers would often assemble and, with the Irish zest, vent their witti-

[48] De Trobriand, *Quatre Ans de Campagnes*, I, 185–86. This was probably Villiers.
[49] Aschmann, *Drei Jahre in der Potomac Armee*, 165–66.
[50] *Ibid.*, 22.

cisms, perpetrate their jokes, and tell everlasting tales, which were sometimes without point, perhaps, but certain to be full of genuine humor.
These impromptu parties took place all over the camp and planted the
seeds of many warm friendships which lasted through life. Many a ludicrous incident occurred, especially during the early period of camp life,
when the Massachusetts Ninth was stationed on Long Island. Likewise, at
Camp California near Washington, the Irish Brigade whiled away leisure
moments with gaiety. Among the officers of the Eighty-eighth the tent
of a certain captain became the favorite resort of all who were passionately
Irish; they spent many hours there, chatting sociably or speculating on
the chances and glories of the dark struggle in which they were engaged.
Theirs was the temperament to cast off the dark shadow of war and death
by bright, cheerful hours about the campfire. An auditor was likely to
hear, according to the reporter, an expression of the wish "Would it were
up on the mountains or the plains of Ireland we were marching, and the
English watch-fires younder." [51]

There existed an absolute hunger for reading matter, especially newspapers, among many of the foreign-born soldiers. One would suppose that
the officers had received enough education for them to want books in their
hands when they had leisure for reading. Colonel Heg in his letters to his
wife first expressed interest in the newspapers. On July 11, 1862, he complained that the papers were generally about two days old; but on August
5 he reported that the Madison papers were arriving with each mail. He
manifested the interest of the person reared on a farm in the crops and
the harvest. A week later he was studying military tactics. The colonel of
the brigade, a man of about Heg's age and a captain in the Regular Army,
was conducting a military school every day, and in this school Heg read
and studied military science. He rejoiced in the association with this
officer, as it was most valuable to him. [52] Hans Mattson, likewise, reported
from Little Rock late in 1863 that he was studying a book on bayonet
exercises late at night. About eight months later Mattson and Lieutenant
Colonel Everett W. Foster were reading aloud to each other every evening,
mostly from the Bible. "We read much from the Book of Job—also from
Matthew and John—indeed I never knew before what excellent senti-

---

[51] McClellan, *McClellan's Own Story*, 145; MacNamara, *The Irish Brigade in Bivouac and Battle*, 31–32; New York *Irish-American*, March 22, July 26, 1862.

[52] Blegen (ed.), *Civil War Letters of Colonel Heg*, 116, 118, 122. On July 15, 1863, he reported that he was borrowing books from "some of my citizen neighbors and have plenty to read." *Ibid.*, 231.

ments and teachings there were in the Bible—we also read much from Tupper proverbial philosophy (you have that book in my library) I read yesterday a fine chapter on education—I wish you to read it—study it." [53]

The private also wanted reading materials. While C. F. Johnson was under arrest at Fort Rip Raps for having signed a paper of protest, he had the run of the library; accordingly, he availed himself of the opportunity to "read something of Fredrika Bremer's." The lad Knute Nelson, in a letter to his father, asked for a copy of *Frithjof's Saga* and later passed this mature judgment: "The honest plain rough words of Frithjofs I like and admire." He had loaned the last copy, he wrote his brother in February, 1864, to a Dane in a New York regiment who had no books he could understand. The Dane had seen the book in Knute's hands, and Knute could not refuse to lend it to him; but very soon the Dane's regiment had been separated from Nelson's brigade, and thus the boy had lost sight of both the man and the book. [54]

The chaplain of the Fifteenth Wisconsin, the Reverend C. L. Clausen, did his utmost to satisfy this desire for reading matter. Before the regiment was fully organized, he had inserted in *Emigranten* a notice soliciting books for a regimental library. His few days as chaplain had convinced him of the necessity of a little library, consisting partly of religious writings, especially devotional books and sermons, and partly of general and amusing books, such as history, biography, and anecdotes. [55] From the pious Danish clergyman the following statement is not unexpected: "One of the most beneficial ways in which one can help them [the soldiers] to use this free time is to provide them with a good store of useful reading. Otherwise the great temptation of cards and all the sins usually associated therewith will greatly increase. . . ." If the soldiers could read good books, however, "their souls [would] be more approachable for the preaching of god's holy word." [56] The religious-minded Scandinavians did not fail to try to provide their soldiers with devotional books. One H. A. Preuss advertised in the *Emigranten* for sufficient contributions or purchases of

---

[53] Hans Mattson to his wife, Pine Bluff, Arkansas, August 3, 1864. Mattson Papers. Martin Farquhar Tupper was the author of *Proverbial Philosophy*.

[54] C. F. Johnson, *The Long Roll*, 37; for Knute Nelson's letter to his brother in February, 1864 (exact date not given), see Knute Nelson Papers. Esias Tegner is one of Sweden's most famous poets. *Frithjof's Saga* is a romantic paraphrase of an old saga, which has been translated into almost every European language.

[55] Madison *Emigranten*, January 13, 1862. The editor supported the effort in a separate article in this same issue.

[56] *Ibid.*, January 13, 1862.

a devotional compilation at fifteen cents a copy to enable him to distribute them gratis to the soldiers of the Fifteenth Wisconsin.[57] The Reverend Sewall Brown wrote of encountering at Maryland Heights in March, 1865, John Sangden, a Swede who wanted something in Swedish to read. The only thing available was Baxter's *Saints' Everlasting Rest* in Danish. Unable to express his thanks in English he shook the clergyman's hands repeatedly. Another clergyman told of seeing an Irish woman, who had arrived at a hospital too late to see her dying brother, pore over a textbook on physical geography, because her brother, "a great 'scholard,' used to read it." [58]

Nothing, however, could take the place of the newspaper—especially a newspaper in their own tongue—to inform the soldiers, not only on things at home, but also on the progress of the war. The absence of news, especially of news of battles on other fronts, fretted them. Heg reported once, while stationed near Franklin, Tennessee, that he had not seen a paper from the North for over a week; and a few days later he wrote, "There is no [news] to be had here, so we are entirely ignorant [of what] is going on—and but very little [info]rmation do we get of what is transpiring [aroun]d here—always all kinds of rumors—nothing reliable. I do of course get some information from Gen. Mitchell [General Robert B. Mitchell, the division commander] and what he gets is also limited I should judge." [59] Privates felt the same way, for Lars O. Dokken, writing from Camp Lyon in the spring of 1862, felt that the folks at home knew much more about the war in general than he—"for you get *Emigranten* before we do." [60] Subscriptions came in to the foreign-language papers. A soldier of the Fourth Minnesota sent the editor of the Norwegian *Emigranten* a dollar for an eight months subscription. He could buy American papers at his camp near Corinth, he wrote, but "I cannot find myself at home to be without our *Emigranten*." Knute Nelson wrote repeatedly about the same paper and asked his brother to send it every week after the family had read it. William Wildson sent in thirty-five subscrip-

[57] *Ibid.*, February 3, 1862.

[58] E. P. Smith (author and comp.), *Incidents among Shot and Shell*, 273, 384–85.

[59] Blegen (ed.), *Civil War Letters of Colonel Heg*, 131, 132. C. F. Johnson complained of lack of accurate news concerning the First Battle of Bull Run. It was not until July 26 that the men were certain of a Union defeat. Then he added a sentence which gives an insight into the caliber of the soldier of some of the foreign regiments: "It has made us all feel badly but I cannot but think that the people at home must feel worse about it than we do." Johnson, *The Long Roll*, 33–34.

[60] Ager (ed.), *Oberst Heg og hans Gutter*, 104–105.

tions to the new Norwegian organ, *Faedrelandet* (Fatherland). "As soon as the Emigranten comes," he wrote, "there are many hands about them, all wish to see it, and some wish to see them first, but the conditions are that one shall read aloud for his comrades in the same tent so that they all can have it cleverly at the same time as far as possible." [61] The Minnesota Conference of the Lutheran Church voted to send *Emigranten* to the soldiers at Fort Snelling.

The Swedes felt the same way about *Hemlandet*, and an order early went forward for twenty copies for a Minnesota regiment. A private in Hans Mattson's company wrote on January 14, 1862, that the soldiers read *Hemlandet* "once a week which is always interesting and the sheet is almost worn out before all have read it through." In vain had they looked for letters from correspondents from other Swedish companies from Illinois: "We think of and talk much of them and could wish that we were in one regiment." Since, however, that was impossible, this subscriber proposed that the different groups send letters occasionally to *Hemlandet*. Another soldier wrote with less enthusiasm that he had just received a copy of the paper and that it was "fairly interesting"—chiefly, it would appear, because it presented the facts without the evasions to which he felt the American papers resorted.

The Irish sent in their subscriptions to their papers, the New York *Irish-American* and the Boston *Pilot*. Perhaps not every Irishman felt as did "Gallowglass," but he probably expressed the feeling of many soldiers when he wrote, "I open the New York papers with an eager curiosity. Metropolitan gossip and news are to me almost the breath of life; and many are the blessings I entreat on the heads of those who send the newspapers containing the same." One subscriber to the *Irish-American* complained that it had failed to reach the soldiers lately; its absence was a loss for which there was no substitute. Lieutenant W. F. Mechan forwarded to the *Irish-American* fifty-one subscriptions from Company H of the Sixty-third New York handed him by the captain of that company.[62]

Letters meant to the "boys in blue" just what they meant nearly a century later to the boys in khaki in World War II—almost the breath of life and the maintenance of morale. Officers and soldiers waited eagerly

[61] Madison *Emigranten*, September 15, 1862; Knute Nelson to his brother William, March 25, 1864, Knute Nelson Papers; see La Crosse *Faedrelandet*, January 14, 1864, for Wildson's transmission of thirty-five subscriptions to that paper.

[62] Chicago *Hemlandet*, January 14, 1862; New York *Irish-American*, July 5, June 18, August 2, 1862. It is striking that about twenty copies of *Slavie*, the Czech paper, were going to soldiers in the field. Capěk, *The Czechs in America*, 157.

for the mail trains or mail boats and complained if they felt that they had been neglected by their families. The foreign-born soldiers mourned the lack of mail even as did their American brothers. On July 17, 1861, C. F. Johnson recorded that he had "just gotten two letters with more than ordinary pleasure: one from my Father in Minnesota and the other from my Sister in Hudson City," the first from either since he had left New York with the Hawkins Zouaves on June 5.[63] Lieutenant Widwey wrote to an unnamed friend, from the camp at Dranestown, Maryland, on September 8, 1861, acknowledging a letter which he had just received: "This was unexpected, as I in many weeks, I may say months, have continued to write to many, but have not received reply, and I had just decided to cease wasting paper in this way, when I received several letters besides yours at one time. . . ." A certain Johannes Johannesjön lamented on November 4, 1862, that his last letter had been written home the first of October and that he had not heard anything since, not even whether they had received the money he had sent or not. He begged his "dear Parents" to write as soon as they received that letter and made a bid for sympathy by saying that he was ill in the hospital.[64]

Hans Mattson made grudging admission to his wife of the receipt on November 20, 1863, of "one little short but still very dear letter" written the first of November, which means that the letter took about three weeks for transmission from Minnesota to Little Rock. Colonel Heg often begged his wife "to write—and long letters"; he complained of the silence of his brother, who, however, had written to another man in the regiment. George M. Anderson wrote his father on September 26, 1863, that he had received only three letters since August 16, though he had written each week; but he then conceded the uncertainty of the mails. He closed with the plea that his father write as often as he could.[65] One Scandinavian

[63] Johnson, The Long Roll, 30.

[64] It is impossible to be sure of the spelling of this name. It looked as if it should be spelled as it is given here. It is possible that what appeared to be a "j" is the long "s." It is not unusual for the "s" to be doubled in names where the given name with which it is combined ends in "s," as is the case here; here the name may well be "Johannessen." This letter is in the Manuscript Collection of Civil War Letters, Luther College Library.

[65] Mattson was writing to his wife from Little Rock, Arkansas, when he acknowledged this letter. Mattson Papers. For Heg's letter begging his wife to write, see Blegen (ed.), Civil War Letters of Colonel Heg, 113; George Anderson's letter is in the Manuscript Collection of Civil War Letters, Luther College Library. The filial regard in this letter is touching: "I see dear father from your letter that you have bought me a pair of colts. Hope that I can soon see the time that I can repay you dear father for all the goodness that you have shown me— You have this summer had much trouble that I know for I know that we both last summer had enough to handle. Next summer I hope that I can be with you."

declared rather bitterly from Island No. 10 that "everybody in the company gets letters except myself." Even that boy-philosopher Knute Nelson complained in July, 1862, that for a whole month he had had no letter from home. He was fine enough to write to his mother in connection with his stepfather's health that it would be "only half a home to come to if you or father were gone from it." Lars O. Dokken resented the capture by the Confederates of a red notebook in which he had carefully preserved all the letters he had received from his relatives.[66] Letters came directly from Norway; they revealed that there was knowledge of the Fifteenth Wisconsin in Norway, gained either from Consul Olaf C. Dreutzer, United States consul at Bergen, or from Norwegian officers on leave who were serving in the Federal army.[67]

A series of fifteen manuscript letters in German script, preserved in the files of the Ohio Historical Society, contain little of importance; but they reveal that some German or Swiss soldiers, not long in America, were keeping in touch with the homeland and receiving news of parents, grandparents, and old friends in Germany. Sometime in April, Corporal Joseph Fürer of Company D, Nineteenth Ohio, was advised that his brother Carl meant to send him his photograph and hoped for one of Joseph in his uniform. These chatty letters from his homeland probably helped the morale of one soldier in the Union army.[68]

If the Civil War soldier begged for letters, he was also willing to pay the price of writing them and often wrote them under difficulties. One letter Mattson wrote to his wife while he was lying on the ground and using a spade for a writing table; another he wrote to the sound of a band serenading his colonel. Colonel Heg told his wife that he was writing his letter of July 14, 1862, "as usual" with his tent full of people and while being constantly interrupted by questions and the necessity of signing papers.[69] In repeated instances, a soldier's letter stated that he was replying

[66] The man who complained of never getting any letters was John Thoe. See Ager (ed.), *Oberst Heg og hans Gutter*, 127; Knute Nelson to his parents, Vicksburg, July 8, 1862, Knute Nelson Papers. The loving letter to his mother about his stepfather is undated. Lars Dokken's letter about the loss of his notebook is given in Ager (ed.), *Oberst Heg og hans Gutter*, 117.

[67] Colonel Heg received several letters from Norway, one from O. E. Dreutzer, the American consul at Bergen during the Civil War, after 1862. See Blegen (ed.), *Civil War Letters of Colonel Heg*, 203.

[68] Executive Correspondence of the Governors of Ohio, 1864. The letter concerning the subject of photographs was dated St. Gallen, April 1, 1864. The letters run from April 5, 1864, which suggests that this soldier was possibly a late arrival from Europe.

[69] Mattson's first letter cited above was dated September 27, 1862, and the second was dated May 5, 1862; both are in Mattson Papers; Heg's statement was found in Blegen (ed.), *Civil War Letters of Colonel Heg*, 109.

to a letter just received.[70] Usually the letters were devoted to personal affairs, but occasionally they described military movements. Descriptions of military actions were more likely to occur in letters to the editors of the various foreign-language papers, however, and to be intended for publication, as when Hans Mattson wrote to *Hemlandet*. However, Major Ole C. Johnson's account of the Battle of Murfreesboro, written to his brother John, was published in the issue of *Emigranten* of January 17, 1863. Probably the most dramatic scenes in connection with letter writing came on the eve of a battle, and occurred among such emotional groups as the Irish. On July 12, 1861, on the evening after orders to march toward what was to become the battlefield of Bull Run had been issued, men were seen in every tent of the Sixty-ninth New York—"some seated on kegs, others on their knapsacks, others again on rude blocks, and two or three on drums—writing their last letters home." [71]

The soldiers of foreign origin did not hesitate to invest in fancy stationery—or possibly that was the only kind available. Knute Nelson, as an illustration, wrote several letters home on stationery especially printed for the Fourth Wisconsin Cavalry. It was of the conventional correspondence-letter size of that time and bore a portrait of Colonel Paine at the top and below it his name and that of the regiment. Above his portrait appeared the words,

> We swear to stand around the flag,
> In the Battle's Wildest Storm.

The second example of regimental stationery encountered by the writer was printed for the Second Minnesota Cavalry Volunteers. It was headed by a list of the battles participated in by that regiment.[72] A third piece of stationery carried the picture of a sailor and the flag and eagle, and the legend "Our Brave Gun-Boat Boys." The most elaborate stationery found was that on which Chaplain Gustavus Miettinger of the Second New

[70] Johannesjön opened his letter of November 4, 1862, with the statement, "Your letter dated the first I received the 4 November," showing that he was writing instantly in reply. Hans Mattson often replied to his wife's letters the same day on which they arrived. On one occasion he was sitting up late at night reading when the mail arrived with a letter from her to him; he wrote her instantly. See letter of November 20, 1863, Mattson Papers.

[71] Thomas Francis Meagher, *The Last Days of the 69th in Virginia. A Narrative in Three Parts* (New York, 1861), 3.

[72] The stationery for the Second Minnesota Cavalry was arranged as follows:

> Battles
> Participated in by the
> Second Minnesota Cavalry Vols.
> Takkahokuta, July 28, 1864
> Teeton Mountains, Aug. 8, '64

York Infantry wrote his resignation. A camp scene in black and white, which resembled a steel engraving, covered the upper third of the page.

It has been frequently noted that the army of World War II was not a "singing army." The army of the Civil War, on the other hand, definitely was a singing army. The soldiers sang around the campfires, in their tents, at religious services, and on the march; they sang from sheer joy of life, and they sang to keep up their spirits. They sang ballads, popular airs, and all the war songs which the period brought forth; but, above all, they sang what may properly be termed national airs. "The Star-Spangled Banner," good old "America," "Columbia, the Gem of the Ocean," and "God Save America" could constantly be heard, swelling up from the various company quarters. Soldiers on the march forgot their weary, aching feet by striking up songs. On the night of May 13, 1861, the Sixth Massachusetts was moved to Federal Hill in Baltimore; there, close to the campfires, the infantry passed the night in the rain, singing every song they had ever known and cheering lustily when Union friends came into camp.[73]

Sometimes a perfect medley arose. An eyewitness has reproduced a scene of the Union army marching into Culpeper, "exciting and martial," as he claims:

> Regiments were pouring by all the roads and lanes into the main street, and the spectacle of thousands of bayonets, extending as far as the eye could reach, was enhanced by the music of a score of bands throbbing all at the same moment with wild music. The orders of officers rang out fitfully in the din, and when the steel shifted from shoulder to shoulder, it was like looking down a long, sparkling wave. Above the confusion of the time, the various nativities of volunteers roared their national ballads, "St. Patrick's Day," intermingled with the weird refrain of "Bonnie Dundee," and snatches of German sword-songs were drowned by the thrilling chorus of the "Star-Spangled Banner." Then some stentor would strike a stave of "John Brown's body lies a mouldering in the grave," and the wild, mournful music would be caught up by all,—Germans, Celts, Saxons, till the little town rang with the thunder of voices, all uttering the name of the

Then below (apparently to be filled in) was

C——, 2 Minnesota Cavalry Vols.

See Knute Nelson Papers; Allotment Papers, Minnesota Historical Society; and Jacket for Father Miettinger, War Records Office. The colonel of the Fourth Wisconsin Cavalry was Halbert E. Paine.

[73] Marvin, *History of Worcester in the War of the Rebellion,* 55–56.

grim old Moloch, whom—more than any one save Hunter—Virginia hates. Suddenly, as if by rehearsal, all hats would go up, all bayonets toss and glisten, and huzzas would deafen the winds, while the horses reared upon their haunches and the sabres rose and fell.[74]

The German regiments gave evidence from the very beginning that they would express themselves in music. When the Twenty-ninth New York first came to Washington, its members were stationed in the Capitol. Their knapsacks were piled on the Senate tables or desks; their weapons were hung on the wall and candelabra. German songs resounded through the well of the Senate and that of the House. On one occasion as much of the entire military as could pack into the House building gave a beautiful concert under the direction of a Captain Bauer. In the evening in camp the German-born soldiers sang songs reminiscent of German heroes and German fame and loyalty—songs sometimes gay, sometimes sad. Once a detail of three hundred Germans returning over the snow to camp from picket duty as the sun was rising struck up a German war song, "Morgen Roth." [75] A member of the Hecker regiment suggested that someone compile a collection of the favorite German folk songs to be sent promptly to the regiment. That the Choral Society of Chicago might do this was clearly the implication of this soldier's suggestion, for he was careful to assure the Choral Society both that it had many friends in the regiment and that songs of German courage resounded widely in the forests and meadows of Missouri and Kentucky.

One German company, in early May, 1861, arrived late at their camping site with no food and no beds, and with only green officers. Some of them lit a fire and began to sing the "Lorelei." Soon this and other German folk songs worked a charm on all, so that in less than half an hour all were up from the ground and about the fire. Good and bad wit as well as droll anecdotes charmed away the hours until the longed-for daylight came. The arrival of the Great Western Band on the evening of July 16, at the camp of the Hecker regiment at Alton was a joyous occasion. The band was received by three companies of the regiment at the station, whence all marched to stirring music the two miles to the camp. There the band was welcomed with loud cheers and escorted to headquarters, where it was greeted by Colonel Hecker with a ringing speech. The writer did not find evidence of the organization of a singing society among the

---

[74] Townsend, *Campaigns of a Non-Combatant*, 248–49.

[75] Chicago *Illinois Staats-Zeitung*, July 21, 1861. For the episode of the singing on the return from picket duty, see Hyde, *Following the Greek Cross*, 31.

German soldiers until the close of 1863; then one called the "Theodor Körner Liedertafel," after Germany's soldier poet, did appear in the Black Jäger Regiment of New York.[76]

We may be very sure that the "Marseillaise" was sung by many besides the Germans on the occasions when Von Willich requested it; it was also sung by the French—above all—and American soldiers in the Union army. De Trobriand has recorded only one such occasion, that on which he was leading his brigade of about four thousand men to Tenallytown, but his description of that is well worth repeating in his words: "The route was smooth and agreeable. It followed the meanderings of Rock Creek, in the shade of the willows and poplars, penetrating into the forest in order to arrive at the Swartz Farm, where we were to pitch our new camp. The men kept step to the singing of the *Marseillaise* or the song of the Girondins, hymn[s] unknown to the echoes of this region which repeated them for the first time—probably also for the last time." [77]

The Irish were little given to bands—as someone has aptly said, they were more given to making music with the musket than with horn or trumpet—but they could and did sing. Snatches of song were often heard from their camps—chiefly the songs written expressly for the Irish Sixty-ninth. The melting, liquid tones of an Irish tenor or baritone charmed many in addition to the Irish listeners.[78]

To learn of the singing propensities of the Scandinavians it has been necessary to turn to the records left by the Swedish and Norwegian participants themselves. The day that Mattson's men marched into the Kentucky town of Shepherdsville, New Year's Day, 1862, the whole company took up the march in the morning with song and kept up their singing all the way. Again, after the Battle of Murfreesboro, in January, 1863, as the Third Minnesota was marching back to camp, Mattson with his company rode ahead of the regiment through a lovely night. The men of his company sang Swedish songs and marches all the way until his horse fairly danced to the music and Mattson rode along thinking, "Who would not be a soldier?" Colonel Heg has recorded for us, also, how his Scandinavian Regiment in late September, 1862, marched through Louisville

[76] Chicago *Illinois Staats-Zeitung*, May 7, July 9, 23, 1861. It is possibly worthy of note that the "Liedertafel" existed after the war and accompanied the Veterans' Association to Gettysburg three times: to assist at the laying of the cornerstone, at the dedication of a monument to this regiment, and at the reunion of the Blue and the Gray in 1893. Werneck, "Historical Sketch," in Fox (comp.), *New York at Gettysburg*, I, 404–405.

[77] De Trobriand, *Quatre Ans de Campagnes*, I, 99.

[78] Meagher, *The Last Days of the 69th in Virginia*, 3–4.

singing Norwegian songs and attracted more attention than any other of the regiments. The letter written by Private Luman, whom we have already encountered, to his wife tells us that there were several good singers in his Company B (of some Iowa regiment) and that while they were aboard ship on the Gulf, they sang every evening the popular war songs. It sounded "nice," he felt, over the water, so that the sailors not on duty gathered around to listen.[79] It was, however, perhaps at religious services that the Scandinavians sang with the deepest emotion.[80] Mattson loved to go to hear the men at evening prayer; there in the snow they stood, in two ranks with bared heads, perfectly still, while the Lord's Prayer and the blessing were read. Then they sang as with one voice "In Thee, O Lord, My Trust I Place."

The foreign-nationality regiments were both honored and exploited by composers. Thomas D. Sullivan composed a set of rollicking quadrilles which he dedicated to the Irish Brigade and which were popular with that group. A book of war songs for the German troops, some old, some new, some revised, and some in English, was put out and offered for sale through the columns of the *Illinois Staats-Zeitung* at ten cents per copy. A poem composed by Edmund Märklin in honor of General Sigel, obviously in imitation of Schiller, had a vogue in German regiments. Two songs which were partly revisions of Danish songs were sent in to *Emigranten* from the Scandinavian Regiment while it was stationed at Camp Randall near Madison.[81]

[79] Mattson to his wife, June 20, 1862, Mattson Papers; Blegen (ed.), *Civil War Letters of Colonel Heg*, 140; for Luman's letter to his wife, February 16, 1864, see Manuscript Collection of Civil War Letters, Luther College Library.

[80] Mattson to his wife, Camp Dana, January 14, 1862, Mattson Papers.

[81] New York *Irish-American*, February 8, 1862; Chicago *Illinois Staats-Zeitung*, May 15, 1861; Madison *Emigranten*, February 10, 1862. The poem by Märklin went as follows:

> Der Reitersmann und sein feurig Ross
> Vor Kampflust brennen sie beide,
> Nach dem Strause sehnt sich der brave Genoss
> Und der Säbel heraus der Scheide.
> Ein Wenig Geduld, und der wackere Franz
> Der Sigel führt uns zum lustigen Tanz!
> Schon stimmt man in Lager die Geigen,
> Dem Feinde den Kehraus zu zeigen.

Oddly enough, the poem made the rounds of the camps in German translation, though written originally in English. Hense-Jensen, *Wisconsin's Deutsch-Amerikaner*, 188 (English), and 189 (German). See Ager (ed.), *Oberst Heg og hans Gutter*, 5, for a poem to the Fifteenth Wisconsin by Hans Reynolds. George Bleyer of Company A, Twenty-fourth Wisconsin Regiment, who died of wounds on January 24, 1863, had sent home a poem of considerable merit entitled "On Picket."

Entertainment must be, of course, provided for soldiers in camp. In World War II the American government made it possible for Hollywood stars to visit and entertain its soldiers in the most remote spots of the globe; but in the Civil War soldiers had largely to provide their own entertainment, and this they did. Serenading the officers was popular with the men and flattered the officers. On February 14, 1862, a number of officers from other regiments visited the camp of the Irish Sixty-ninth Pennsylvania with the excellent band of the Fire Zouaves and serenaded Colonel Joshua T. Owen, who, after a number of patriotic airs had been rendered, appeared and thanked them in a brief speech. During the march of McClellan's army into Virginia on his Peninsular campaign in April, 1862, the bands of the regiment played from seven-thirty to eight o'clock each evening. The best feeling existed between neighboring regiments and brigades. The bands played marches and inspiring airs, which the men applauded lustily until the forest rang with the echoes of the music. The musicians on one such occasion, in acknowledgment of the applause from an Irish regiment, struck up "St. Patrick's Day" and other Irish airs, evoking further vociferous applause.[82]

Colonel Heg disclosed interesting relations between his Scandinavians and the "Jayhawkers," by whom he probably meant the Seventh Kansas Cavalry, nicknamed because of the recent pillage and conflict in the settlement of Kansas. The two regiments occupied camps side by side, and the Jayhawkers serenaded Colonel Heg one night in June, 1862, singing "Dixie" and "John Brown" until he came out and addressed them. The Jayhawkers proposed partnership with the Scandinavians, who could, they declared, beat them at stealing honey! When Colonel Heg was left in command of the brigade for a month during the absence of Colonel William P. Carlin in February, 1863, he was serenaded by the band of Carlin's regiment, the Twenty-first Illinois. By August of the same year he was writing of two brass bands in his brigade, which called often at his tent to serenade him and to "have a glass of beer or something of that kind." On August 6, which Lincoln had set aside as a day of national thanksgiving for the victory at Gettysburg, all the bands were out playing and serenading the officers.[83]

[82] For the serenade of Colonel Owen, see New York *Irish-American*, March 1, 1862; for the playing of the bands on the Peninsular campaign, see *ibid.*, April 19, 1862.

[83] For the serenade of Colonel Heg by the Kansas Jayhawkers, see Blegen (ed.), *Civil War Letters of Colonel Heg*, 94. Heg sent his wife a copy of the song "Jayhawkers' Dixie"; for serenade of Heg by the band of the Twenty-first Illinois, see *ibid.*, 193, 234, 238.

Special musical entertainment might take the form of solos or concerts. At Fort Corcoran in July, 1861, the men of the Sixty-ninth New York ranged themselves in a circle around the flagstaff to hear the song "The Starry Banner" sung by its author, John Savage. A friend of the quartermaster of the Fourth New York Regiment, a real singer and a poet of beautiful fancy, recited in a rich and flexible voice a new poem "from the bright pictures of his mind." [84]

Constant visits from one company to another and from regiment to regiment, not to mention the visits of outsiders, relieved the ennui of camp life. The editor of the *Irish-American,* accompanied by two officers and Colonel Henry M. Baker of the Eighty-eighth New York, visited the camp of Colonel Cass and the Ninth Massachusetts. In June of 1862 a Colonel Botch, a member of Governor Morgan's staff, made a tour of inspection under orders from the governor to look after the status and efficiency of the New York troops in the field. Among others, he visited the regiments of the Irish Brigade, accompanied by General Meagher, at their encampment near Fair Oaks, Virginia. Perhaps no other visit had more far-reaching consequence on a certain detail of dress than did that of some women, termed affectionately the "cake and pie brigade," to the Nineteenth Illinois, which contained a number of foreigners and was stationed at Camp Douglas. The women arrived just when the fad of wearing havelocks was at its height, so that they were received by the men not under drill *en havelock.* As the sturdy-looking men emerged from their tents, wearing the ugly headdresses (irreverently dubbed "nightcaps"), a shout went up from officers, privates, and the women: The havelocks were worn in every imaginable fashion—as nightcaps, turbans, sunbonnets, bandages, and sunshades. Therewith the fate of the havelock was sealed, and it soon disappeared.[85]

The foreign-born, naturally, enjoyed visiting their compatriots in other regiments. A soldier of Company A of the Scandinavian Regiment (Fifteenth Wisconsin) related in a letter to *Emigranten* that many Norwegians in the Twelfth Wisconsin, encamped near by, had come over to

---

[84] See John Lynch of Company H, Fourth New York Regiment, to P. J. Ryan, in the New York *Irish-American*, February 1, 1862; see *ibid.*, August 2, 1862, for the recitation.

[85] See *ibid.*, July 5, 1862, for the inspector's visit; for the episode of the havelock, see Mary Livermore, *My Story of the War,* 113. General Henry Havelock had devised for the British troops in India a white linen headdress, named in his honor the "havelock," to be worn over the uniform cap to protect the men from sunstroke. As Union men were going "South," inexperienced women began in a perfect frenzy to make havelocks, turning them out by the thousands in all patterns and materials. *Ibid.*, 112–13.

visit the men of his regiment. Luman, while at Morganza, Louisiana, wrote that his prospective brother-in-law had been over to see him twice. Aschmann of the Sharpshooters recorded that he had the satisfaction of finding in General Burnside's corps, when it joined his corps at Fredericksburg, several earlier acquaintances, with whom he spent some happy hours. Colonel Heg embarked on a round of festivities while he lay in camp near Corinth, Mississippi, which lasted through July and August of 1862, and was resumed in the summer of 1863. On July 6, 1862, he wrote his wife of visiting Colonel Robert C. Murphy from St. Croix Falls, Wisconsin, commander of the Eighth Wisconsin, and of drinking beer and wine with him until nearly night. On July 25 he took dinner with the officers of Company A, and in his next letter to his wife he enumerated the items of the excellent menu on that occasion. Shortly before August 3, he had met General Grant and had had a long talk with him about going home to raise another regiment; on July 7, 1863, he had been invited to the headquarters of General Jefferson C. Davis, where, after being entertained with music and whiskey, he had been rudely recalled to duty by an order to make a reconnaissance with two of his regiments.[86]

Princess Salm-Salm gave a clear picture of festivities and visits in her husband's various camps. Of her life with the Eighth New York near Chantilly, she wrote, "As we had to do nothing but amuse ourselves, and kill the time agreeably, scarcely a day passed without some excursion, pleasure party, dinner, or ball; and for the entertainment of the soldiers care was taken likewise." The most sumptuous festival she recalled was one given by General Daniel E. Sickles in a hall created by uniting a dozen or more hospital tents. "This immense tent was decorated inside and outside with flags, garlands, flowers, and Chinese lamps in great profusion, and offered a fairy-like aspect. The supper laid under the tent for about two hundred persons, ladies and gentlemen, could not have been better in Paris, for the famous Delmonico from New York had come himself to superintend the repast, and brought with him his kitchen aides and batteries, and immense quantities of the choicest provisions and delicacies, together with plate and silver, and whatever is required to make one forget that it was a camp supper." Of their own entertainments she says: "And every evening we had receptions in our tent. We played a rubber of whist,

---

[86] Related by Torston C. Nyhuus and published in Madison *Emigranten*, July 7, 1862; Aschmann, *Drei Jahre in der Potomac Armee*, 83–84; for Colonel Heg's visit, see Blegen (ed.), *Civil War Letters of Colonel Heg*, 102, 114, 115, 229. Of course, he celebrated the Fourth of July with General McCook, but that belongs to another portion of this chapter.

whilst Groeben [Alfred I. Groeben, a factotum] was brewing punch or eggnog for our guests, who retired always at midnight." Great preparations were made when a visit of the President and Mrs. Lincoln to the Army of the Potomac was announced. It was arranged that the Lincolns should stay at General Hooker's headquarters, but the real master of ceremonies was General Sickles, who knew something of form from a visit to Europe.

While Prince Salm-Salm was encamped on an island in the Tennessee River near Bridgeport with the Sixty-eighth New York, his wife made many excursions on horseback and by carriage. She received visits from the generals stationed at Stevenson or Chattanooga, and in return she paid General James Blair Steedman a week-end visit in Chattanooga. One of the features of that visit was an excursion on horseback to Lookout Mountain on October 26, 1864; the trip up was followed by an excellent breakfast, which General Steedman had sent up in advance. Because General Gordon Granger, whom she visited in Stevenson, entertained his guests with fine music and lavish dinners, Princess Salm-Salm pronounced him a *bon vivant*.[87]

Nowhere else in the army was there such general ostentation and display as at Blenker's headquarters. McClellan, who liked the military chic of Blenker and the discipline in his division, was a frequent visitor, a fact which aroused the jealousy of the American generals. General W. B. Franklin termed a visit to Blenker's division as good as a circus or an opera. We can do no better than present the picture in General McClellan's own words:

> As soon as we were sighted, Blenker would have the "Officer's call" blown to assemble his polyglot collection, with their uniform as varied and brilliant as the colors of the rainbow. Wrapped in his scarlet-lined coat, his group of officers ranged around him, he would receive us with the most formal and polished courtesy. Being a very handsome and soldierly-looking man himself, and there being many equally so among his surroundings, the tableau was always very effective, and presented a striking contrast to the matter-of-fact way in which things were managed in the other divisions.
>
> In a few minutes he would shout, "Ordinanz numero eins!" whereupon champagne would be brought in great profusion, the bands would play, sometimes songs be sung.

[87] Salm-Salm, *Ten Years of My Life*, I, 39–40, 119, 122–25, 128–29.

General Blenker made unnecessary and costly expeditures which had nothing to do with war. One example, perhaps the most striking, was a torch parade arranged in honor of General McClellan, in November, 1861; this exceeded in pomp and expense everything that anyone had ever before seen in Washington. Two thousand of Blenker's soldiers marched as torchbearers, and as many more moved in the procession. Blenker himself, followed by fifty-six of his staff officers, rode at the head of the procession. All the participants were splendidly mounted and appeared in the brilliant uniforms characteristic of European armies. A dozen bands followed the procession. The whole affair concluded with a display of fireworks which must have cost many thousands of dollars. All Washington was astonished and attributed the pompous occasion to an effort on Blenker's part to win for himself one of the four corps generalships, the establishment of which had been announced.[88]

It goes without saying that civil amenities were exchanged between the contending forces. When news of a victory arrived at the camp before Yorktown, chance had brought the French Fifty-fifth New York opposite the Confederate Louisiana Tigers; consequently, the French batteries, Union and Confederate, replied to each other, and each evening at the same hour the tatoo which Parisians heard upon the Place Vendôme was heard also on the banks of the Warwick in both hostile camps. Also, some nocturnal colloquies were exchanged in French. Both sides had already been calling out to each other their respective victories: to the "Bull Run" and "Ball's Bluff" of the Confederates, the Federals had replied with "Laurel Hill," "Donelson," "Roanoke," and "New Bern." [89] However, the capture of New Orleans and Baton Rouge extinguished the spirit of the Tigers, who no longer responded to the "blows of language except by the shots of the musket."

More striking was the relationship of two opposing German regiments outside Arlington. A German picket guard heard his own tongue spoken by a Confederate scout opposite. The exchange of a few words revealed that they were fellow countrymen; hence, they proceeded to meet each other in perfect confidence. So "sympathisch" did they find themselves that after posting a sufficient number of guards along the prescribed lines, the majority returned to the neutral ground, built a fire, and passed the

[88] See McClellan, *McClellan's Own Story*, 141–42, for his visit; see Kaufmann, *Die Deutschen im Bürgerkreige*, 178–79, for the torchlight parade.

[89] De Trobriand, *Quatre Ans de Compagnes*, I, 179.

greater part of the night together on the most informal, amicable terms.[90]

The horse racing, the Olympic games, and the theatricals in the Irish Brigade on the Peninsula became known throughout the Army of the Potomac. Many fine races were run, the horses of General Charles Griffin, the brigade commander, as well as the white Arabian of Colonel Patrick R. Guiney, and the splendid animal "Dick," owned by Lieutenant Colonel Patrick T. Hanley, participating in these. Races were also arranged between horses which were owned by officers of the Irish Brigade. Those were exciting times for the Irishmen, and the brigade would turn out en masse to watch the racing carnivals.[91] These were terminated only by the order to the brigade to advance on the Peninsula.[92]

The theatricals of the Irish Brigade—though, unfortunately, rain fell on the opening night—had had several rehearsals, with the result that they came off satisfactorily. They were given in a delightful little dell in a wood at the rear of brigade headquarters. The stage was erected on a high, semicircular spot, from which the ground sloped gently upward to the entrance, so that the seating place enclosed between wickerwork walls gave the semblance of parquet, pit, and footlights. *Paddy Miles: or the Limerick Boy* was the play given; the costume of Paddy was furnished by a boy from the sutler's tent, while the role of Paddy was taken by a droll genius from Company K, Sixty-ninth Regiment. "Dear Jane" was played by a handsome lad who had been in the Papal Brigade; according to the *Irish-American,* his attractiveness was to have been rewarded on the opening night by a bucket of flowers from General Meagher's "private box." [93] The idea of a theatrical performance was not a distinctively Irish idea; for, as the reader may recall from his general reading, a theater built for John Sedgwick's brigade under control of the Sedgwick Brigade Lyceum Association opened February 22, 1862, and a burlesque was given by the dramatic club of Hawkins Zouaves on June 30, 1862.

The great national holidays were usually observed in camp; however,

[90] New York *Tribune,* September 25, 1861.

[91] MacNamara, *The Irish Brigade in Bivouac and Battle,* 178.

[92] A full account is given in the New York *Irish-American,* June 21, 1862. This paper, knowing the interest of its readers in races and in the owners of the horses, printed the list of eleven entries, the names of the horses, their owners, and the place taken by each horse. Details are here omitted to avoid repetition, as an account is given of the races and celebration held on St. Patrick's Day, 1863. See below in this chapter.

[93] *Ibid.* This grand gala day was May 30 or 31, for the report sent to the New York *Irish-American* was dated May 31 at the camp of the Irish Brigade beyond White House, Virginia.

they were by no means always celebrated, for there was the precedent established during the American Revolution of violating Christmas in order to execute military maneuvers. Although, as everyone knows, the great French holiday is the *Jour d'An* (New Year's Day), Christmas Day was also observed by the French troops. The commander of the Gardes Lafayette could recall, when he was recording his experiences in the American war, the traditional midnight revelry of Christmas and the serenades —varied by polyglot choruses in English, French, and German—which were exchanged between the regiments of his brigade. Hans Mattson revealed that his company managed to preserve some of the Swedish customs in their camp the first Christmas afield. He had bought twelve geese to roast or boil; he also had a half barrel of corn meal, from which he planned to cook *Julgrät* (Christmas porridge) for his entire company. He felt assured of a festival and hence of a happy day. Since a Captain Rice of the same regiment had some excellent egg toddy, they seemed confident between them of a real Christmas celebration. The holiday spirit seems to have taken hold of his "boys" ahead of time, for though he was writing of his plans on December 23, he described an improvised band with rails for flutes, pork barrels, camp kettles, and cheese boxes for drums as producing much laughter, if not music. Mattson did not forget to record that Christmas promised to be a beautiful day, "just like a June morning—the birds are singing in the woods." [94]

The nationality group which managed the happiest and most colorful Christmas was, as the reader may surmise, the Irish Brigade. Tasteful decorations of cedar, woven into fairy shapes, festoons, and flowers, decorated the camp on December 25, 1861. The men of the three New York regiments were up with the dawn, polishing their shoes, brushing their clothes, and preparing for early Mass, which was celebrated in the camp of the Sixty-ninth at eight o'clock by the chaplain, the Reverend Father Willett. Christmas morning was made notable to these ardent Catholics by the baptism of two men, one each from the Eighty-eighth and Sixty-third regiments, who were then "received into the bosom of the Church" by Father Dillon, chaplain of the latter regiment. [95]

Colonel Heg, as a high-ranking officer, shared in the festivities of

[94] De Trobriand, *Quatre Ans de Campagnes*, I, 131, for French festivities; for the Swedish Christmas, see letter of Mattson to his wife from Camp Anderson, December 23, 1861, Mattson Papers.

[95] New York *Irish-American*, February 1, 1862. As explained in Chapter XII, Willett was not Irish but French-Canadian.

the American officers in the encampment near Nashville on his first Christmas in the field, 1862. He was invited by a Mr. Heyer to Christmas Eve supper at his boardinghouse in a schoolhouse close by the camp. Heg and the physician of his regiment, Dr. Himoe, contributed the most rollicking fun by each escorting into the house a "lady"—actually, of course, a boy dressed in woman's clothes. Heg and his regiment celebrated Christmas Day in a less jolly way by obeying orders to go out with a wagon train for forage, starting at seven in the morning and, in his own words, "spending Xmas among Secesh." [96]

Princess Salm-Salm pictured a gay holiday, the last wartime Christmas, which she spent with the half-foreign Sixty-eighth New York at Bridgeport, Tennessee. To celebrate the victories over General J. B. Hood, the Princess dressed the house and the veranda with holly and with mistletoe, found in the woods near by in great abundance. The group had Christmas Eve supper at the home of a Reverend Mr. Gilford in Bridgeport and consumed several gallons of whiskey punch while they passed the hours with singing, dancing, and playing games of every kind. Christmas Day was largely a repetition of these festivities at the quarters of Prince Salm-Salm.[97] Meanwhile, foreign soldiers scattered in American or mixed regiments had no opportunity for their own kind, or sometimes for any kind, of Christmas celebration. A Dane in the Eleventh Wisconsin wrote from Big River Bridge, Missouri, that his company had spent Christmas Day on picket duty on the alert against a threatened attack by the enemy. A Swedish soldier in the Twelfth Illinois, stationed at Smithfield, Kentucky, spent a rather "dull Christmas as well as New Year. It was just as usual. The only difference I could see was that whiskey was plenty here so that the large majority in the camp were drunk and the guard house was almost full." [98]

Knute Nelson recorded in 1863 how he spent each of preceding wartime Christmases in the Fourth Wisconsin: of the Christmas season of 1861, which had found him at Patterson Park, Baltimore, he could relate briefly that "those days had no observance whether in food or freedom from the other days. If it had not been for the circumstance that a Unionist invited my company to a Christmas dinner and we were splendidly pro-

[96] Blegen (ed.), *Civil War Letters of Colonel Heg*, 158.

[97] Salm-Salm, *Ten Years of My Life*, I, 132–33. The punch was brewed by a friend of the Prince, the famous Otto von Corwin, who was at the front as a correspondent of the London *Times* and the *Augsburger Allgemeine Zeitung*.

[98] This sounds as if drunkenness was common with the Swedes. It was not.

vided with food and drink of the best quality for about three hours, followed by songs by the daughters of the household, Christmas Day would have been uncelebrated by me or my comrades." The next Christmas found him at Baton Rouge. "This," Nelson observed, "was a dull druging home-sickish day only relieved by a scanty dinner of Geese cooked abominably as only a soldier can cook: and to make it still more discouraging I had been on Picket the night before which left me rather with my eyes down and a grinding headache. Strong coffee and the Geese however set me right after dinner." The third Christmas, also spent at Baton Rouge, he pronounced not inferior to the other two except for the lack of "the sweet heavenly strains of female loveliness"—a reference to the singing which had followed his dinner in Baltimore. The meals on his third Christmas in camp were a little superior to the ordinary fare. Dinner at eleven with the quartermaster afforded the typical American menu of baked goose and turkey, potatoes, cookies, the best of "sugar-loaf cake" with tea and coffee that he pronounced "superb." "A dinner for an epicure and what was it not for a soldier" was his verdict. He did not "conspire" with a "drop of Liquor or even a mild Cigar, and the better was I for it sure." He occupied himself in the morning with Macaulay's *Sketch of Warren Hastings,* a literary feast well worthy of the day. During the afternoon he chatted with some schoolmates, not about home, but about camp incidents. After supper he visited a colored family, to whom he read aloud from an illustrated paper "agreeable to request." The philosophy of this unusual lad comes out in his comment on his wartime Christmases: "They have been strange Holidays to me; not indeed like those of home and yet not unhappy either and most sober and instructive to a wild wayward boy." [99]

A correspondent to *Faedrelandet* lamented the drab Christmas he spent. For rations, the men were receiving only three biscuits (hardtack) a day—this fare being meted out to them on Christmas Eve and Christmas Day also—while they had to work with all their strength. Fate seemed even harsher to a group of Swedes, members of the Forty-third Illinois, who were sent on an expedition against guerrillas under Colonel Engelman

[99] This account of Nelson's Christmases is based on a description which he wrote on his third Christmas at the front, headed "Thoughts and Observations," to be found in the Knute Nelson Papers, Box 3. The Baltimorean who was kind to Nelson's company was a Mr. Leach. On leaving Baltimore the company presented him with a large album and a copy of Burns's complete works, "valued at $10," Nelson tells us. The men intended to inscribe their names in the album with "suitable effusions [Nelson's expression]," but were ordered off suddenly and so left the album blank.

and made the trek from Bolivar, Tennessee, to Jackson, Mississippi. Aschmann, the Swiss sharpshooter, drew advance-guard duty more than six miles from camp as his portion for Christmas Day, 1863, so that a tour of duty meant four days out and back without any shelter; in addition to this hard luck he drew two days of dreadful storms on December 26 and 27 and "such darkness that one could hardly see a pace before him." [100]

The manner in which New Year's was observed in the army constituted, in the main, a repetition of the observance of Christmas—sometimes special fare and festivities. An observer from the Washington side of the Potomac River gave his impressions of the regiments on the Virginia side: "Many of the regiments across the river had a gay and happy time. . . . The German regiments were the merriest. Their camps were handsomely decked in evergreens, and lager flowed in inviting streams. On the Washington side there was more quietness." With the French Fifty-fifth on New Year's Eve, 1861–1862, serenades were again the order of the day.[101]

Knute Nelson spent New Year's Day of 1862, as he had his first Christmas, in Baltimore in an old, leaky, ragged tent, sleeping on the frozen ground with some musty straw underneath and—far from feasting—having only the everyday fare of the camp. The next New Year's Day he was camping at Baton Rouge, on the battlefield, he recalled, where three companies of the Sixth Michigan had routed an entire Southern brigade. This day, he recorded, seemed no more than "Bleak windy January 1st, 1863." New Year's Day one year later found him still near Baton Rouge, but chance had put him on duty with two men of his own company on the opposite side of the river, where he was halted on his return from carrying dispatches to Plaquemine by the difficulty of bringing the flatboat over to take the horses across. New Year's Eve he had spent at the home of an Englishman, who, after ordering a negro to groom and feed the horses, had entertained his guests hospitably with a plain, substantial meal— "superb" as compared with army rations. Before a blazing fire in the parlor the party were entertained until midnight by the jokes and puns of a third guest, a north "Alabamean" who had served for some years as an overseer in Louisiana; his jokes were doubly amusing because they were told "in his dry nasal North Alabama Provincialism." The overseer's house, minus the overseer, served as a bedroom for the guests.[102]

[100] La Crosse *Faedrelandet*, January 14, 1864; Chicago *Hemlandet*, January 14, 1863; Aschmann, *Drei Jahre in der Potomac Armee*, 159.

[101] De Trobriand, *Quatre Ans de Campagnes*, II, 50.

[102] We get a good insight into the character of this youth when we read that he crossed the

The Swedes of Company D of the Third Minnesota drew sad portions for their first holiday season: on Christmas Day they marched from Lebanon Junction to headquarters at Camp Dana; on New Year's Day they had to march to Shepherdsville to guard a railroad bridge over Salt River, and here our informant saw something he had never seen before— the auction, for ten dollars, of the labor of a little negro boy for a year. The quick sympathy of the Swede set him to thinking about buying the lad to set him free, for he did not understand the selling of the labor of a slave for a limited period.[103]

The celebration of anniversaries was a must for groups regarding annual events with the enthusiasm of Germans and Irishmen. First and foremost in Irish regiments was the celebration of St. Patrick's Day. The Eighty-eighth New York started its functions, as usual, by celebrating High Mass with all the solemnity and imposing ceremonies possible in a camp. A new and elegant vestment had been purchased by the men for their chaplain, the Reverend Father Corby. A spacious chapel had been created of canvas appropriately ornamented with evergreen wreaths, festoons, and bouquets. Here at eight o'clock the exercises of the day began with High Mass accompanied by martial music. General Meagher and his staff and hundreds of invited guests were present. Father Joseph G. O'Hagan, chaplain of the Excelsior Brigade, gave the sermon. The day continued with unique festivities, which attracted the whole Army of the Potomac, generals as well as privates, to Falmouth on March 17, 1863.

As a further celebration of the day, the Irish Brigade held a grand steeplechase in the good old Irish fashion. It was observed with all the exhaustless spirit and enthusiasm of the Irish nature. For days before the event, vast preparations were made: a race course was marked out, and announcements of the race in bold characters were posted on every side: "Grand Irish Steeple Chase to come off 17 of March, rain or shine, by horses, the property of, and to be ridden by, commissioned officers of that brigade." The prize was announced as a purse of five hundred dollars. The quartermaster sent to Washington for liquors and meats and ordered vast supplies for the banquet to follow the race: thirty-five hams, the side of a roasted ox, a pig stuffed with boiled turkeys, an unlimited number

river in a small skiff and procured from the harbor master a crew of negroes to bring the flatboat over, if he could. He added tersely, "And I could." Found in the paper headed "Thoughts and Observations on New Years in the Army." Knute Nelson Papers, Box 3.

[103] See a letter from Camp Dana, January 15, 1861, in Chicago *Hemlandet*, January 29, 1862.

of chickens, ducks, and small game, eight buckets of champagne, ten gallons of rum, and twenty-two gallons of whiskey. A bower capable of seating some hundreds was erected, for a general invitation had been extended to all the officers of the Army of the Potomac. On the evening before the races, a serious consultation was held as to the person best qualified to mix the punch, a task which had been assigned to General Meagher and his staff.

By eleven o'clock on the morning of March 17 the grandstand was crowded with distinguished guests, officers, and about a dozen ladies in colorful costumes. At least thirty thousand officers and privates assembled for the fun. Large crowds of soldiers gathered near the hurdles which were four and a half feet high and near the ditches where the leaps would be highest and widest. The course ran over a gently rolling stretch and included eight leaps, about equally distant from each other. A blue sky smiled upon the gayly dressed and excited crowd. Shortly before eleven o'clock General Hooker, then commander of the Army of the Potomac, arrived, accompanied by members of his staff and by the lieutenant colonel and Captain J. O. Lynch of the Sixty-third; as he took his place on the grandstand, he was greeted by cheers. The consolidated band (the sum total of many regimental bands) poured forth "a Niagara of sound." At the first suitable opportunity, Hooker proposed three cheers for General Meagher and his Irish Brigade, to which he added, "God bless them."

General Meagher, in the costume of a fine old Irish gentleman, officiated as clerk of the course; at exactly eleven o'clock he waved his whip, a bugle sounded, and the six entrants in the race, including Meagher's gray horse, Colonel Mulholland's chestnut, and Quartermaster McCormick's bay, were off. The victory of Meagher's horse in two heats was popular with the men and was greeted with a wild, enthusiastic cheer from the throng. The sweepstakes, open to all, followed, with all the incidents of the old-fashioned course. After a collation of sandwiches and wines at headquarters came the other events: a foot race open to noncommissioned officers and privates; the casting of weights; a race for a greased pig, the prize to be the pig itself; a wheelbarrow race by blindfolded contestants; a hurdle race; a sack race; and a contest in which Irish reels, jigs, and hornpipes were danced. Meanwhile, French, German, English, and the Irish brogue were flying about indiscriminately emphasizing the polyglot character of the crowd.

The final entertainment at night, consisting of theatricals and recitations, was the grand climax. Dr. Lawrence Reynolds, as poet laureate of the brigade, read a poem which recounted the history of the brigade. Healths were drunk, and songs and toasts were offered freely. Soldiers and drummer boys gathered near the huge barrel of punch.[104]

Just as March 17 is an Irish day, so May 17 is a Norwegian fete day, celebrated as Norway's Independence Day. During the war the celebration of this holiday was especially outstanding at Island No. 10, where the Scandinavian Regiment had some companies stationed in 1862. For these companies, Captain Torkildsen sent to Cairo for several casks of ale. All who wished to share in the festival had to help share the expense, officers paying two dollars and privates twenty-five cents. The first hint of an unusual occasion came as the sun rose, when a salute of thirteen cannon shots was fired. Later in the morning a parade was staged. In an effort to prevent disorder, the men had been ordered not to imbibe of the ale at will but to wait until the name of each was called, in order, by some official at the ale cask; nevertheless, some disorder occurred. At sunset, there was to be another salute of cannon shots; this did not, however, redound to the honor of Norway, for a part of the company had become drunk and some disorder arose at the battery, with the result that one of the men was placed in the guardhouse. Some of his comrades, who felt that injustice had been done him, broke into the guardhouse to free him but were prevented from doing so by the officer of the day. One of the disorderly men struck this officer several times. Major Reese arrived upon the scene, called out five companies to surround the men of Company A, among whom the disorder was centered, took away their weapons, and put six or eight of them in the guardhouse with an entire company stationed there to guard them. Six of Company A were later held for court-martial. This unfortunate outcome did not prevent the Norwegians from celebrating the day again in 1864.[105]

There were echoes of the celebration of other holidays. A Norwegian soldier from Iowa at Camp Benton in 1863 told of the recognition of Washington's Birthday by a parade through the chief streets of Davenport, evidently before several brigadiers whose names were unknown to that

[104] For a full account of this celebration, see Mulholland, *The Story of the 116th Regiment Pennsylvania Infantry*, 191–96; see also Rossiter Johnson and others (eds.), *Campfire and Battlefield*, 502; Cavanagh, *Memoirs of Gen. Meagher*, 478–80.

[105] Ager (ed.), *Oberst Heg og hans Gutter*, 78; Madison *Emigranten*, June 9, 1862, July 18, 1864. The date May 17 marks the founding of the Norwegian constitution in 1814.

soldier.[106] The Fourth of July did not, of course, pass unnoticed in the camps. On that day in 1862, in the camp of the Army of the Potomac, salutes were fired, bands played patriotic airs, and Generals McClellan, Sumner, and Sedgwick, with a numerous staff, reviewed the troops. In the west at Humboldt, Tennessee, the day was observed by Colonel Heg's Fifteenth Wisconsin. The regiment, with three companies of a Minnesota Cavalry Regiment, was drawn up in a suitable spot in a grove. The Declaration of Independence was read, Governor Alexander Ramsey of Minnesota delivered an address, and the band played—all in the presence of a number of citizens. Knute Nelson's first Fourth of July in the army, that of 1861, passed (in contrast to his Christmas season) with great festivities. There was racing, followed by a dinner "such as he had never seen or tasted." From only one quarter in the Army of the Potomac—from any army, the writer might add—has any evidence been forthcoming of the celebration of Halloween, and that was in the Irish Brigade, probably in the Connaught Rangers. Strains of song issued from the tent of a certain jolly quartermaster until the early hours of the morning, while jest, joke, and laughter filled the watches of the night. An aromatic beverage was brewed with gusto by a man from Galway; and the party regretted the absence of nuts, apples, candles, lead, and fiddles to make this Halloween at the base of the Blue Ridge Mountains in Virginia seem really Irish.[107]

In contrast to the elaborate steeplechase races of the Irish, the contests in rifle shooting arranged by the Swiss sharpshooters sound tame indeed. However, now and then, as the exigencies of war permitted, the Swiss held rifle practice, at which little prizes were awarded to the best contestants. In October, 1861, there was arranged for the entire regiment a grand target-shooting contest, which was honored by the presence of President Lincoln, some cabinet members, and many high officers. The time of the chief executive seems to have been well expended in these visits to the camps, for Aschmann has written, "Such high visits made us proud and awakened in us the desire soon to justify in battle the expectations which

---

[106] It would appear from the context of the letter that this soldier belonged to the Eighth, Twelfth, or Fourteenth Iowa. Letter of G. O. Hanson to his uncle, March 4, 1863, Manuscript Collection of Civil War Letters, Luther College Library.

[107] For the Fourth of July in McClellan's army, see New York *Irish-American*, August 2, 1862; for the celebration in Heg's command, see Blegen (ed.), *The Civil War Letters of Colonel Heg*, 99; "Impressions," in Knute Nelson Papers; for Halloween in the Irish Brigade, see New York *Irish-American*, November 22, 1862. Of course, Independence Day was observed in all the camps. C. F. Johnson described how it was observed in the Hawkins Zouaves with a burlesque on dress parade. *The Long Roll*, 151–52.

were cherished from us." Nearly all the generals in Washington, as well as other highly placed persons, visited the sharpshooters. As was to be expected, the Swiss consul general, his sons, and other distinguished Swiss came often to this camp. Especially did the visits of Colonel Ferdinand Lecomte, who joined McClellan's staff, and Colonel Augusto Fogliardy, both of the Swiss army, flatter the Swiss company of Berdan's regiments.[108]

Banquets which were a part of great, gala occasions, have already been discussed. It remains to note those feasts which were events in themselves. An early example was the farewell banquet given Hecker in St. Louis on the occasion when he severed his connection with the Third Missouri (the reader will recall that he had modestly entered the war as a private) to accept the colonelcy of an Illinois regiment. That portion of Concordia Park where the ceremony was held was illuminated. The ceremony opened with a serenade by the regimental band. Colonel Sigel, to honor an old friend, left his duties to attend for a brief period. In response to a toast, Hecker spoke with the revolutionary fire which always distinguished him. After a toast to Sigel was offered, that officer said that it was his pride that men like Hecker had served with him and that he had seen the present exaltation of the Germans. The regimental physician, Dr. Ferdinand Häusler, delivered one of his extempore poems, which was interrupted by witty interpolations by Hecker. Toasts to General Lyon, President Lincoln, the Union, and Victory were offered.[109]

The other outstanding celebration of this sort was the welcoming banquet tendered by the officers of the Irish Brigade to General Meagher when he took command of that unit. The men had already had a frenzy of excitement and enthusiasm when word spread through the camps of the three regiments that the Senate had confirmed Meagher's appointment as brigadier general. The officers interrupted the drill to let the enthusiasm of the men vent itself. As the general passed through the grounds of the encampment, he had to approach the area of each company to receive the wild welcome of cheers. The officers waited upon him in a body to congratulate him and express their satisfaction. The delight of the rank and file was overpowering. Meagher took command formally on February 5, 1862, at a full-dress parade in the presence of friends from Washington and near-by camps, even General Shields honoring the occasion with his

---

[108] Aschmann, *Drei Jahre in der Potomac Armee*, 17–18, 117–18.

[109] Chicago *Illinois Staats-Zeitung*, February 22, 1862. The occasion loomed so large in the eyes of the editor that he accorded space for a lengthy report and an editorial on the subject.

presence. An informal evening dinner in Colonel Henry M. Baker's quarters ended with what was called an "Irish wold dog." To conclude a big day, the privates piled barrels in front of Colonel Baker's tent and kept the fire going for hours.

The grand event was the banquet tendered General Meagher by the officers of the brigade, and it was, indeed, considering the difficulties of camp life, a grand affair. The invited guests included General Samuel P. Heintzelman, commander of the division; practically all the Irish notables of the army, General Shields, Colonel Cass, and Colonel Henry D. Terry of the Fifth Michigan among others; and some civilians, such as P. J. Meehan, editor of the *Irish-American*. The tables were laid out in a spacious marquee, fitted out and decorated for the occasion with rich and varied drapery, the national flag, and cedar boughs, and with Loudon, Fontenoy, and other names glorious in Irish history emblazoned on the walls. The tables "groaned," to use the language of the Irish reporter, with tempting viands—ham, fowl, joints—and an abundance of wine. The band of the Second New Jersey Regiment played national airs. The air vibrated with music, wit, mirth, and eloquence. A congratulatory address was read and presented to Meagher, to which he responded with a long address concluding with a military order banning oratory for the duration of the war. The festivity had been fixed for two-thirty in order to comply with camp regulations, but, since the cook did not arrive until after that hour, it is easy to imagine the illegal hour which terminated the unusual celebration.[110]

Most fantastic of all the war banquets, however, was that which was held on the bloody Saturday when the Irish Brigade was being mowed down by the hundreds on the slope behind Fredericksburg, and which came to be known as "The Death Feast." Elaborate preparations had been made for the reception of some new colors; when their arrival was reported to Meagher, he determined to carry out the original program without delay, although ceremonies had to be transferred from the large hall which

[110] From the fall of the Stuart dynasty in England to the French Revolution, Irish soldiers were to be found in the various armies of the continent, but by far the largest numbers were in the French army. This exodus was owing partly to the hope of a Stuart or Catholic restoration and partly to discriminatory legislation. So numerous were the Irish soldiers fighting for the lilies of France that they constituted whole Irish brigades. The most famous battles in which they participated were Fontenoy (fought May 11, 1745 [New Style], and always regarded as a French victory, since the Allies had to withdraw from the field) and Loudon or Nerwinden. See John Cornelius O'Callighan, *History of the Irish Brigade in the Service of France, from the Revolution in Great Britain and Ireland under James II to the Revolution in France under Louis XVI* (Glasgow, 1870), *passim*.

had been especially constructed in the camp on the northern side of the river to the little theater in the town. Accordingly, on December 15, twenty-two generals assembled with their host. Ranged around the walls in the main body sat the officers of the brigade and their guests, while in the center stood two rows of tables weighted with the dishes of an elaborate banquet, which had been cooked in neighboring houses. A corps of military waiters calmly served the courses, indifferent to the thunder of the batteries and the bursting of shells close to the building.

The new colors were first presented to those commanding officers of the separate regiments of the brigade who were able to be present. Then Meagher, as chairman, began, according to the custom of the time, to call the toasts of the evening. He did not hesitate to indulge his bitter indignation by denouncing the political partisanship and the criminal incapability which were drenching the fields about them with the blood of their own brave countrymen. In proposing a toast to General Alfred Sully, a son of Irish parents and a West Point graduate, Meagher said, "*He* is not one of your Political Generals, but a brave and accomplished soldier—who attracted his 'star' from the firmament of glory—by the electricity of his sword!" This extraordinary banquet closed with a singularly dramatic ending. As Meagher was paying tribute to the still-unburied dead, accompanied by the continuous boom of the guns, one of the waiters marched in, bearing, as if for dessert, a cannon ball which had just demolished a stone house a few yards from where the men were seated. That was hint enough, and the assemblage abruptly broke up, each to betake himself again to his post.[111]

A religious service was a distinct event to break the military routine, and some kind had been held from the very beginning—even before the regiments had left their home camps. This was true of regiments of all nationalities. The members of one of the companies of the Thirteenth Massachusetts Volunteers appeared for the first time in their uniforms at divine service held at the Dudley Street Baptist Church in Roxbury. The Irish Brigade of Chicago likewise displayed their uniforms at the first opportune religious service; they had received them on Saturday, June 22, and accordingly they held a church parade the next day, attending High Mass in Holy Name Cathedral. The last Sunday in April, Captain Stohlbrand's artillery company of Scandinavians attended a service conducted in their drill hall in Chicago by the Reverend L. P. Esbjörn from the Swedish theological school at Rock Island, Illinois. The Reverend Mr.

[111] Cavanagh, *Memoirs of Gen. Meagher*, 71–73.

Esbjörn closed his service with the singing of King Gustavus Adolphus' stirring battle hymn, "Förfäres ej den lille hop (In Vain the Little Hope)." Mattson's Scandinavian Guards from Red Wing, Minnesota, were stationed at Fort Snelling by October 4, 1861. Swedish pastors of the Minnesota Conference visited the company each week; and, in addition, the company held in their quarters morning and evening prayer service in Swedish. The Conference had decided to send pastors to conduct service in the afternoon after drill and to administer Communion at intervals.[112]

After the soldier moved nearer the front, daily religious services formed some part of every day. With the Irish the mingling of ardent devotions with more mundane affairs seemed inevitable. According to Colonel Mulligan's account of his Illinois Irishmen at Lexington, Missouri, some part of each Sunday they spent in singing and praying, and, later, in casting shot and stealing provisions. The reader will readily recall the High Mass held in the Irish Brigade on St. Patrick's Day on the Peninsula. He will also meet with a smile the implied criticism of too-great religious fervor contained in Colonel Heg's statement that Company K never did anything "except read their Norwegian prayer books and hang out a long face." To lead the services in the Scandinavian camps, ministers from home communities sometimes made special trips. The ritual, usually conducted in the open air with the men in military formation, brought warm commendation from American commanders. The singing of Gustavus Adolphus' battle hymn by the strong men's voices made a deep impression upon all spectators.

Services were, of course, conducted in the hospitals. Contributions were made by various nationalities in different ways. On one occasion when a member of the Christian Commission expressed the desire to conduct some singing in the hospital if someone able to play the piano could be found, an Englishman who had been detailed as hospital steward volunteered. He must have been a picturesque figure as he sat before the piano on a cracker box, in a red-flannel shirt with sleeves rolled up above his elbows, but he functioned ably in the capacity of organist and leader in the singing of our national anthem and of hymns.[113]

There was constant expression of deep religious faith on the part of

[112] For the service in the Baptist Church, see C. E. Davis, *Three Years In the Army*, xviii; for the Swedish service, see Chicago *Hemlandet*, May 1, 1861; for the service for the Scandinavian Guards at Fort Snelling, see Chicago *Hemlandet*, October 23, 1861; for the Irish Brigade of Chicago, see Chicago *Illinois Staats-Zeitung*, June 24, 1861.

[113] E. P. Smith (author and comp.), *Incidents Among Shot and Shell*, 432; Blegen (ed.), *Civil War Letters of Colonel Heg*, 115; Hokanson, *Swedish Immigrants*, 73-74.

the Scandinavians, even by mere youths like Knute Nelson. J. Johannessen, urging his mother not to worry about him, said, "If God helps me, then I will surely come back. But if such happens to me that I die, then I pray from my heart that I can meet with you in the eternal life—Amen." John Throe, after he escaped unharmed from his third battle, Chickamauga, wrote: "God be praised and thanked! He held his hand over me, as He always has done, so that I came unharmed out of this." [114]

Perhaps it is only necessary to recall some of the many stories of religious faith in World War II to know that no war fails to bring men face to face with the eternal verities. A young man in 1944, whose father was troubled over the state of his son's soul, wrote to his mother, "Tell Dad he needn't worry about me. There are no atheists in the fox-holes." In the Civil War as in the war nearly a century later, a mass of religious tracts and writings were distributed gratis to the soldiers.

Like their native brothers-in-arms, the soldiers of foreign origin had to seek diversion in order to find relief from boredom. Cards were for some of them a first refuge. An American has recorded the tale of a Belgian who lay near him in a hospital in Libby Prison. This Belgian did not lack for friends and countrymen, who helped him while away many weary hours with his national card game, "Sixty-six." However, he replied to the American's appeal to be taught the lively game with an emphatic refusal: "I show you how to play, and you play awhile for fun, then you play for a little money, you win, then you play for a pile, and you win, then you play for a big pile, and then you lose him all, then you say, 'Tam that Tutchman, I wish the tevil had him before he show me how to play cards.'" But the American persisted until he, too, could play "Sixty-six."

Some entertained themselves by sketching, as did the Prince de Joinville of the higher social scale and Charles Frederick Johnson of the lower social scale. Others entertained themselves by putting down their thoughts and observations on paper. Johnson kept a diary of his experiences in the Hawkins Zouaves. As paper and pencils were scarce, he saved any paper he could find for his journal and bound it into ten manuscript books with newspapers for covers, the quality of his binding attesting to his training as a bookbinder in St. Paul before the war. He accompanied his journal with pencil sketches of various scenes and incidents, inset into the body of

[114] For Johannessen, see letter by him (undated), Manuscript Collection of Civil War Letters, Luther College Library; for John Throe, see Ager (ed.), *Oberst Heg og hans Gutter*, 133. This last-named soldier fell at New Hope Church in May, 1864.

the page, top, bottom, or middle, as fancy dictated; these illustrations are lively, if at times somewhat crude.[115]

One sergeant entertained himself late at night by writing comments concerning one of the men, on the line reserved for "Comments" in the Descriptive Book of the Pontoon Battalion. His remarks were such drivel that we shall not detain the reader with excerpts. In another comment, obviously from the same pen, boredom was openly confessed: "I take the present opportunity of pening you a few lines which I take pleasure in so doing as I am rather lonesome and can't imploy my time to any better advantage all though my mind is offly tangled and hardly know where to commence my argument. . . ." Then he indulges in a bit of philosophy, natural to a soldier. ". . . I should like to chang the mood of living to one that would be more benefitial more plesant more happier more useful . . . there is no doubt in my mind but the energie of man is never at an end till deth over take him or her." Once he indulged in some very poor poetry.[116] Many, both officers and privates, confessed to boredom. Colonel Heg declared that a quiet camp life "soon becomes tedious" and men long for the "excitements incident to active operations." Frank Forsten, writing from a Minnesota regiment to *Hemlandet*, said that the Swedes found army life monotonous. Another showed his boredom by an odd slang expression: "Tywärr! [Too bad!] The dearly bought honor of war remains almost always eclipsed by the long periods of quiet." [117]

Payday, a red-letter day with the soldiers, was slow in rolling around

[115] Johnson was stationed at various times at Camp Riker, Roanoke, Hatteras, and Newport News, and shared in the Battles of South Mountain and Antietam. Unlike some amateurs, Johnson was glad to profit from the aid of professionals. A Corporal Davis, who accompanied an expedition as official artist, looked over some of Johnson's sketches and offered suggestions: "I needed to show more decisive shading in my pencilings, make my objects stronger and in sharper relief." He constantly had an eye out for possible subjects for sketches. "These wind-mills, by the way, are almost the only things picturesque on the Island, and as objects of study for an amateur artist they are admirable." Johnson, *The Long Roll,* 76.

On October 19, 1865, in a fit of disgust at its "miserableness," he burned a part of the journal, No. 13, which he had kept so religiously. Repenting of his hasty act too late, he wrote a synopsis for the period covered—October 12, 1863, to January 1, 1865—from an incomplete diary and memory. See preface to his manuscript biography.

[116] A sample of his poetry runs as follows:

> There is nothing grate there is nothing wise
> Which Idle hands and minds supply
> Those who all thought of toil despise
> Where nothing lives and nothing dies.

Company Descriptive Book, Company A, Pontoon Battalion, Third Pennsylvania Brigade.

[117] Blegen (ed.), *Civil War Letters of Colonel Heg,* 180; Chicago *Hemlandet,* September 18, 1861, January 22, 1862.

for the first time and recurred at irregular intervals. Relatively little of the money which Uncle Sam paid his soldiers remained in their pockets; for some had debts to discharge, many had wives and families to look after, and the unmarried among the foreign-born often had parents toward whom they felt financial responsibilities. The amount of money sent home from the various groups, whether German, Irish, Scandinavian, or of some other nationality is astonishing. The Steuben Regiment after one payday sent over $2,000 by Adams Express and another $1,500 by a man who was going to New York in a few days, or $3,500 in all. Upwards of $20,000 was remitted to the families of the men in the three New York regiments of the Irish Brigade immediately after their payday in late January, 1862. As this was the first pay since their enlistment the preceding September, the remittances were doubtless sorely needed by most of the families. No one realized this better than the officers, and so we find Colonel Baker of the Eighty-eighth Regiment standing by the paymaster, inquiring of each soldier, as he was paid off, if he had a wife or family and advising him to send the balance after settling with the sutler to his family or friends. It is interesting to note that, contrary to the usual concept of the Irish as spendthrifts, the bills of the sutler were very moderate in this regiment, not averaging more than two dollars per man. In May following, in addition to the sums sent by the men just after payday, the captain of one of the battery companies of the brigade sent $3,800 by Adams Express to the families of his men. A little later, in early July, the paymaster visited the Fifteenth Wisconsin; and Colonel Heg wrote that $8,000 was being sent home to Scandinavian families. The soldiers often got a considerable return in the form of packages of food and clothing from home.[118]

The methods of sending the money were various. The members of the Irish Brigade entrusted their first pay to Quartermaster P. M. Haverly for conveyance to New York, but at Washington he had to transfer most of it to the Adams Express and to a gentleman connected with the *Irish-American;* the men connected with that paper had the satisfaction of distributing the portion entrusted to them two days sooner than the amount handled by the express company was distributed. The Swedish soldiers, at least those of the West, seemed inclined to send the money

[118] The example of the Steuben Regiment was warmly commended to the Germans of western regiments by the Chicago *Illinois Staats-Zeitung*, August 6, 1861; for the Irish Brigade, see New York *Irish-American*, February 1, 1862; for the Scandinavians, see Blegen (ed.), *Civil War Letters of Colonel Heg*, 106.

through their captain, someone they knew and trusted. Hans Mattson, for instance, transmitted $465 to his wife, who was to turn various portions of that sum over to the wives, parents, or other persons designated according to the list Mattson had prepared. Though the individual sums sent were small, $20 to $70, the total came to a neat sum. The money was apparently transmitted to Mattson's wife by a man named Aaker. Mattson sent $160 as his own, but informed his wife that $60 of it belonged to one of his men, who wished her "to hide it." [119]

By June 8, 1862, another payday had rolled around, for Captain Mattson sent to his wife by express $345 to be paid out according to an enclosed list; this time, however, he warned her to take a receipt from those she did not know. The sums ranged from $15 to $40, and the total included another sum of $40 from the same man who wished her to "hide" his money for him. Then followed instructions as to how she could reach the recipients who lived at some distance from her home in Red Wing. One man's wife, who lived near Geneva, would come for or send for the money. One man was sending his money to Boston to pay a debt; another wanted Mrs. Mattson to keep his $50 until his return, when he would send it to his wife in Sweden. In somewhat similar fashion, Colonel Heg received from some of his soldiers $300, which he handled with less trouble to his wife: he sent it to her, advising her that she was to deposit it in the bank for her use, and he would pay the soldiers the next payday—a sort of forced loan, although he had doubtless made proper arrangements with his men.[120] Fortunately, the letters of Knute Nelson make it possible to follow the individual transactions of a private soldier in the disposition of his pay. On February 6, 1862, Knute sent to his parents $45 by express from Baltimore to Fort Atkinson, Wisconsin, and urged them to collect it in all haste. On September 8, 1861, while he was still stationed at Camp Randall, he sent home in a letter to one Ole Wigdoll a ten-dollar bill from his first pay; this he felt a safer and swifter method of sending the money. Again on July 29, 1862, and March 4, 1863, he sent money to Fort Atkin-

[119] On transmission by the Irish Brigade, see New York *Irish-American*, February 1, 1862. Mattson's list is interesting. A sample follows:

From	To	Residence	Sum
Gustaf Anderson	his wife	Vasa (Minn.)	$25
P. M. Sanborg	his wife	Red Wing	20
Nils Abrahamson	his father	Vasa	70

Undated letter of Hans Mattson to his wife (but before June 8, 1862), Mattson Papers.

[120] *Id.* to *id.*, Murfreesboro, June 2, 1862, *ibid*; Blegen (ed.), *Civil War Letters of Colonel Heg*, 203.

son by express and directed his parents to call at the express office for it immediately after receiving his letter. Altogether he sent home probably $240.[121]

A system of allotments appeared as early as April, 1862. By arrangement with the paymaster, soldiers could allot certain portions of their pay to given persons. From near Yorktown, Virginia, one George Arndt allotted $5.00 of his pay each month to a Charles Schaffer, which the latter was to save for him until his return to Stillwater, Minnesota; in the event of Arndt's death, it was to be turned over to his mother or, if she were not then in Stillwater, to F. H. Brauer. John P. Kuss of Minnesota allotted $11 of his pay monthly as long as he was in the service. G. André had to provide for the transfer of his allotment money for the future from New Ulm, Minnesota, to Cincinnati, as his family had moved thither to be with his wife's mother. The system brought many complaints to officers from the soldiers; because their families were not receiving the money, the soldiers clamored to have the system of allotments abolished so that they might send the money by express. There were ugly rumors to the effect that the paymaster speculated with the money. At the request of all the men, the captain of Company G, Fourth Minnesota Volunteers, asked to have his company stricken from the allotment rolls. Men who had had their allotments withdrawn each time they were paid and then found, as did Corporal John Keim of Company I, Fourth Minnesota, that their wives had received no money were naturally angry and dissatisfied with the system.[122] As the names indicate, these men—and most of the men in Company G—were German-born.

The devotion of the men to their religious faith was demonstrated by the soldiers of Mattson's company, who sent money—although the sum

[121] Knute Nelson to his parents, September 8, 1861; February 6, July 29, 1862; March 4, 1863; Knute Nelson Papers. The first letter reveals, incidentally, that he received no pay for the first six weeks of his service because when he and several companions learned that Captain Lohmiller and his officers were given to drink and were not alert to their work, they transferred from the captain's company. The same letter, however, stated, "But we did not mind that if we could only get into a well-behaved company. We are well satisfied." It is clear that he sent $200 at this time; it is not clear what amount he sent in his letter of July 29, 1862, but it is likely to have been $40 or $45, as those were the sums sent just before and afterward.

[122] For Arndt's allotment, see G. Arndt to Charles Schaffer, April 10, 1863; for the striking of Company G, Fourth Minnesota, from the Allotment Rolls, see request of Captain Charles Luey, February 24, 1863; for Corporal Keim, see Captain Henry Platt to Charles Schaffer, April 2, 1863. Allotments, Minnesota State Treasurer's Archives, Minnesota Historical Society.

was small—to the Swedish Lutheran Church at Chisago Lake, Minnesota, for the purchase of an organ.[123]

Being human, the foreign-born in the Union army suffered their days of war-weariness, discouragement, and homesickness. Despite the bolder face which the officers presented to their men, their private letters reveal that they, too, had their hours of weakness and pangs of doubt. The tone of Colonel Mattson's letters to his wife revealed clearly that he was suffering from acute attacks of homesickness and was yearning to see her. In August, 1863, he wrote, "Although I know it is bad and foolish for me to leave the Army—yet I cannot help it. . . . I am impatient to see you— I care not for the consequence—I shall resign as quick as the object of this expedition is fulfilled—we are to drive the rebel out of Little Rock and hold that place." On November 20, 1863, he stated that there was no hope for his resignation, as the generals would not approve resignations except for illness. "What a fool I was ever to dream of resigning—but the days are passing now and we must be patient." He would not make any more promises about coming home which might only disappoint her. In May, 1864, while he was stationed at Pine Bluff, Arkansas, he was again in the grip of despondency, after the campaign of General Banks had proved a failure: "Oh I pray to God that the war will soon be over. I long for home so much." This, however, was his last outburst, for he had a furlough home in 1864, and the next winter he had his family with him in Arkansas.[124]

Although Colonel Heg was somewhat older than Mattson and possessed a strong sense of duty, he still suffered discouragement at times. In May, 1862, when he was thinking fondly of a furlough, he wrote his wife, "I do not wish to go away from here until I am certain that we are perfectly safe. It would be wrong for me to be away should there be any fight here." In July he became critical and declared that the war would have been ended before then if politicians had not had the running of it. "We have been fighting for *Slavery* so far, long enough," he declared. By September, when he was ten miles from Nashville, he expressed himself on the military situation as follows: "It has looked black for some time and how soon this war will end, it is hard to tell but it cannot last very long." However, he hastened to add, "Do not think however that I am either homesick or discouraged. . . . I am going to see the end of this struggle if possible." On September 5, he admitted that the accounts "look blue—but I never

[123] Chicago *Hemlandet*, March 26, 1862.

[124] Letters of Mattson to his wife, August 20, November 20, 1863; May 6, 1864. Mattson Papers.

lose courage—it will soon brighten up again. Our cause is bound to suc-ceed—but we have a great many bad generals, and poor officers, and it will have to be a good many changes made before we succeed." A few days later he wrote bluntly, "Let me tell you, I am getting tired of the loose discipline that is carried on by the American officers." In January his discouragement was sufficient to make him declare that he would leave the service the next fall, whether the war were ended or not. But by Febru-ary his spirits were up with anger against the Copperheads: "The only dis-couraging thing we get down here are the reports of the *Northern Rebels.*" [125]

Despite the well-kown Irish propensity for fighting, it is possible to find an Irishman writing from his prison in Richmond in 1861: ". . . Old Abe would not let the regiment go home. Well, it served us right, when we were fools eough to fight in such a cause; but I hope the time will come when Irishmen will mind their own business." [126] A German cavalryman, in contrast with many of McClellan's American followers, was frankly critical of the general: "One did not know what one should make of Mc-Clellan. His movement, his arrangements at the battle of Malvern Hill and his retreat to the south side from there were master strokes, but his indecisiveness no one could explain." The German came to the conclusion that politics had beclouded McClellan's vision and that vacillation had caused his failures. [127]

If officers became discouraged and dissatisfied, the common soldiers under less comfortable conditions were certain to grumble and lose hope. A Swedish private, writing from a camp near Bolivar, Tennessee, in the fall of 1862, burst out: "What can a soldier do in this war to crush the rebellion when his hands and feet are tied? Answer: very little or better nothing. Here arises a question. Who ties the soldiers hand and foot? Answer: our friendly lord generals and dept. chiefs to whom the highest

[125] Heg to his wife (Guinild), May 5, July 15, September 5, 11, 1862; January 21, Feb-ruary 16, 1863, in Blegen (ed.), *Civil War Letters of Colonel Heg,* 82, 109, 134, 137, 178, 189. Colonel Heg had to meet a deep pessimism in his wife, who insisted from the first that the war would leave her a widow. In his replies he tried to bolster her spirits. Note how he wrote on September 5, 1862, "I know you are courageous enough to get along in my absence —let me see and hear that you are no coward. I am not a coward and I know you are not either, when it comes to scratch." But her premonitions were correct. See above, p. 239 n.

[126] New York *Times,* September 8, 1861, copied from the Augusta (Ga.) *Constitutionalist.* Obviously the Confederate paper had printed with pleasure this evidence of disaffection on the part of an Irish soldier of the Northern army.

[127] F. A. Harter, *Erinnerungen aus dem amerikanischen Bürgerkriege* (Chicago, 1895), 79–80.

command is entrusted. Officers of different rank even down to the private are merely his tools, directly bound to obey orders." This Swede did not cavil to attack Grant: "But again a question: give an example when a commander tied his army hand and foot. Answer: It was Pittsburg Landing. For the enemy falling upon us Sunday morning, April 6, who was to blame except Gen. Grant who had not placed pickets for a longer distance than merely ¾ mile distance from the camp, so that Beauregard with his army could on Saturday evening come so near to our army that he heard the drums and music in our camp both at dress parade and manoeuvers." [128]

False rumors were followed by disillusionment. We can readily understand how great was Knute Nelson's joy, later to be dashed, when he wrote from near Vicksburg on July 8, 1862: "We have received the joyful news of the capture of Richmond and 350,000 Rebells. This looks like the beginning of the end. I expect to be home next Christmas. . . ." We can imagine his disappointment when he learned the truth of the complete failure of McClellan's campaign. It is striking how these foreign-born men, often modest in education as well as means, cleaved to the heart of the issue.[129] If the news of the failure of the Peninsular campaign discouraged the western soldiers, it is easy to comprehend the reaction and bitterness of those who had endured its miseries. A single excerpt, from the pen of the Swiss sharpshooter whom we have cited before, will suffice to illustrate this: "In vain were all our strenuous marches, our hot battles, our hunger, our deprivations. Thousands of wounded and dead had spilled their blood in vain. . . . Did not our campaign resemble a complete defeat? Doubt of the result of our further action arose indeed. On whom lay the blame of the failure? Some ascribed it to the generals, while others sought for it in Washington." [130]

A young Swede, writing to the Reverend T. N. Hasselquist, editor of *Hemlandet,* in March, 1863, could say: "And we only wish that the war might soon come to an end. But only a good and complete victory, the extermination of slavery, and the subjection of the pride of the big Southern aristocracy." With equal discernment the lowest soldier saw how the sharpers cheated the government. Luman wrote his wife in February,

[128] Chicago *Hemlandet,* November 12, 1862. In the same trenchant style he analyzes the entire battle.

[129] The first touch of childishness in this mature youth came out at the end of this letter when he wrote, "Have a good supper ready and good beer on the table." Knute Nelson to his brother William, July 8, 1862. Knute Nelson Papers.

[130] Aschmann, *Drei Jahre in der Potomac Armee,* 81–82,

1863, "Every one tries to take advantage of the government. For instance, our cavalry horses, for which a good price is paid, are a poor lot, vicious, windbroke spavined and balky." [131] Of course, many saw and deplored the demoralization of war. Lieutenant Osborn, writing to his clergyman father concerning the ugly mutilation of a commander of negro troops on November 15, 1864, lamented that the most dreadful barbarity was perpetrated by men who lived in the nineteenth century and had pretensions to being civilized. That, he thought, was merely evidence of man's natural bestial character and but one of the many demoralizing aspects of the war. [132]

One last camp experience remains to be described—the last event in very truth for many—the funerals. At first, before death had become so frequent and common an event as to blunt its sharp edge, camp funerals were surrounded with much solemnity and pomp. Let us take for an example the funeral of a German soldier at Camp Yates near Springfield before the war had much more than begun. Around six in the afternoon the companies still stationed in the camp gathered before the hospital. Eight comrades carried the coffin out; then twelve dragoons, expert singers, sang in German a funeral song; a clergyman made a brief address; and, finally, the singers closed the ceremony with a choral song. Then the procession moved slowly to the station, for in the early days the body was sent home for burial at the hands of the family. [133] More dramatic was the funeral ceremony for a soldier fallen and buried near the battlefield of Little Bethel. On the evening of June 30, 1861, the members of his company formed between their tents and marched, with torches in their hands and the rolling of the drum as accompaniment, to the quarters of Colonel John E. Bendix, where almost the entire Steuben Regiment was present in attendance on the ceremony. After a funeral march, Chaplain Forsch gave a short discourse, in which he eulogized the life and character of the fallen comrade, offered a few words of comfort to the widow, and read a resolution pledging the group to support the widow and children of the de-

---

[131] The first letter is from J. R. Andberg, a lieutenant in Company C, Forty-third Illinois Regiment, and is in the Hasselquist Collection, Augustana College Library. It has been published with translation by the Augustana Book Concern. The second letter of Luman to his wife, February 14, 1864, is in the Manuscript Collection of Civil War Letters, Luther College Library.

[132] Manuscript letter by Joseph E. Osborn to his father, the Reverend Lars Paul Esbjörn, in the Esbjörn Collection of Letters, Augustana College Library.

[133] This dead soldier's name was George Mathei. Chicago Illinois Staats-Zeitung, May 15, 1861.

ceased man. The resolution was adopted, each man of the regiment dedicating one day's pay as a beginning.[134]

More ostentatious was the funeral in St. Louis, in late May of the same year, of a Polish captain of a Turner company, Captain Blandowski of the Third Missouri Regiment. At eight o'clock in the morning, Companies A, B, and C, Turner companies of Blair's regiment, moved from the arsenal to the Hospital of the Samaritan to act as escort. To these three companies were added the company of Zouaves, a deputation from the Turner society of the city wearing their original dress and bearing the society flag, and a company of Home Guards, the whole forming an imposing line for four squares. Drums rolled and arms were presented as the funeral parade passed. Lieutenant Colonel Hassendeubel with his suite headed the procession; a battalion of the regiment followed; and then came the hearse, with the dead officer's sword, hat, and gloves lying on the casket. The company which Captain Blandowski had commanded marched just behind the hearse without side arms. Then followed the family of the deceased, General Sigel with his adjutant, and various officers of the St. Louis regiments. At the grave a biography of Captain Blandowski was read, followed by a speech. Three salvos over the grave, and all was over.[135]

When a member of Hans Mattson's Scandinavian Guards died in March, 1862, the company buried him with military honors in a wood near the camp, fired a salute of twenty guns, and raised a little memorial over the grave. The death of Lieutenant N. P. McCool of Company C of the Forty-third Illinois occurred during the early period of the war, and so the officers of that regiment had time to draw up resolutions to be published in *Hemlandet* and the Galesburg *Democrat;* their choice of these papers would seem to indicate that McCool was a Swede from Galesburg. The officers also agreed to wear mourning for thirty days.[136] When Captain John Kavanaugh of the Sixty-third was killed in battle in the fall of 1862, his remains were sent to New York in charge of his brother-in-law. Though the fallen man had belonged to the Irish Brigade,

---

[134] A more elaborate ceremony was accorded his funeral in Chicago, but that scarcely belongs to this story.

[135] *Ibid.,* May 30, 1861.

[136] John Grillon was the name of the soldier of Mattson's company who died in March, 1862. Mattson wrote an article to the Chicago *Hemlandet,* praising his soldierly qualities; the article appeared in the issue of March 12, 1862. The resolutions of the officers of the Forty-third Illinois appeared in the issue of January 29, 1862.

General Corcoran tendered a military escort from the Irish Legion, as a touching tribute from a fellow-Irish organization.[137]

A final act in the sad drama of camp and field was the disposition of the effects of a fallen soldier, a task which usually fell to his closest friend. A single illustration of the countless thousands will suffice. A Norwegian of Company A, Eighteenth Iowa, wrote from Springfield, Missouri, to "Honored but unknown Friend Johannes Johaneson," to inform him of the death of his son James in battle on January 8. Despite the fact that the son had been asked, on account of his illness, to remain in the fort, he had gone out to the field with his company, the friend wrote. He added the only possible words of comfort: "He was always loved and honored of his officers and the whole company." The writer then asked what disposition the father wished made of the son's clothing and promised that on payday the sum owing the son would be sent to his father.[138]

[137] New York *Irish-American*, October 4, 1862.

[138] Nels N. Olson to Johannes Johannessen, February 18, 1863, Manuscript Collection of Civil War Letters, Luther College Library. James would seem to be the same person as Johannes (see above, p. 370), but the writer cannot explain the discrepancy in names.

CHAPTER FOURTEEN

Eager Volunteers and War Immigrants

IN THE land and naval forces of the United States there are found not only some Canadians, some Englishmen, and some Irishmen, but also many subjects of continental European powers. All of these persons were voluntary immigrants into the United States. They enlisted after their arrival on our shores, of their own free accord, within our own limits and jurisdiction, and not in any foreign country. The Executive Government has no knowledge of the nature of the special inducements which led these volunteers to emigrate from their native countries, or of the purpose for which they emigrated. It has, however, neither directly nor indirectly invited their immigration by any offers of employment in the military or naval service. When such persons were found in the United States, exactly the same inducements to military service were open to them which by authority of law were offered at the same time to citizens of the United States."

Thus wrote Secretary of State Seward in reply to an inquiry by the Senate on June 25, 1864, in regard to enlistments abroad; he further declared that the government of the United States had "practiced the most scrupulous care in preventing and avoiding in Great Britain, and in all other foreign countries, any violation of international or municipal laws in regard to the enlistment of soldiers and seamen." [1]

Secretary Seward also stated that if any such recruits had been obtained in any foreign country, it had been by subjects of the country where the recruits were secured, answerable to the laws of that country and not within the reach of the laws of the United States, and that such persons acted without the authority and even without the knowledge of "this Government." In "two or three cases" violation of the Canadian frontier by recruiting agents had been reported, which action was promptly disavowed, the recruits at once returned, and the offending agents dismissed. He then pointed out as a "notorious fact" that a continual tide of emigration was flowing from Europe, especially from portions of the British

[1] *Official War Records*, Ser. 3, IV, p. 456.

Empire, Germany, and Sweden, to the United States, resulting from the "relative conditions of industrial and social life" in the countries on the two sides of the Atlantic. Most of the immigrants, he insisted, went immediately into industry. Those who were attracted to military life, however, "voluntarily" entered that service with inducements equal to those offered native citizens and from the same patriotic motives. "There is no law of nations and no principle of international comity which requires us to refuse their aid in the cause of the country and of humanity." This government frankly encouraged immigration from all countries, but only by "open, lawful, and honorable agencies." [2] It is the purpose of this chapter to test the exact accuracy of these statements made by Seward.

The European governments generally warned their respective subjects against participating in the war then in progress between the United States and the Confederate States of America, informing them clearly that if they did, it would be at their own peril, that their government would consider all such subjects outside the realm of protection, and that they would be liable to such punishment as might be inflicted upon them by those to whom they were opposed in arms.[3] England and France issued their proclamations to that effect promptly, some of the smaller countries more tardily.

That the outbreak of war would be followed in all countries, even those which were to prove friendly to the North, by a period of doubt and hesitation was inevitable until the diplomatic and consular representatives of the new Lincoln government reached their posts. Consul Henry Börnstein at Bremen reported on October 9, 1861, that the cause of the Union had been represented feebly abroad but that the arrival of the new Republican ministers and consuls at their respective posts had produced an effect. He thought that he noted a change even in the London *Times* (although this proved to be only temporary), as well as in the French and German newspapers.[4]

The number of officers in the Union army as compared with the number of privates was naturally limited; and the motive actuating a foreigner to offer himself as an officer was quite different from that actuating the common soldier or humbly placed civilian, who was thinking of the huge

[2] *Ibid.*

[3] It is interesting that a Confederate citizen suggested to President Davis early in the war that such foreigners assisting the United States be considered "interlopers," and not be treated as prisoners of war but be punished by death. D. G. McRae to President Davis, November 16, 1861, *ibid.*, Ser. 2, II, p. 1397.

[4] Henry Börnstein to Secretary Seward, Consular Dispatches, Bremen, XI, No. 6.

bounties and of the pay, which was large in comparison with that of the European soldier. As has been indicated, a few men, especially officers, began to make their way to the American consulates abroad fairly soon after the outbreak of the war; but it was not until the middle of the next year that word of the huge bounties procurable in America began to be disseminated among the masses. Hence, it was not until 1863 [5] and 1864 that the stream of would-be recruits poured through the various American consulates in most of the countries of Europe.

Evidently, the report of the monthly pay and bounties provided, in time, all the stimulus needed.[6] The consul at Hamburg, James H. Anderson, wrote Seward on August 5, 1863, that a rumor was circulating in that city that the United States government was finding difficulty in raising three hundred thousand men and that as a result he was being swamped by would-be emigrants: "Hundreds of applications have been made to me since the President's call for more troops, to enter our service, on one condition: a free passage to America. The applicants are large, strong, healthy, robust-looking men. I could send 10,000 soldiers for the Army, and 1,000 sailors for the Navy, to New York, without in any way compromising my country, or my standing." He evidently had a plan all worked out, for he added immediately, "There are generally in port, some American vessels, the masters of which, would from motives of patriotism, and on account of the difficulty of procuring cargoes, take such emigrants to the United States on very reasonable terms." A formal contract he held unnecessary, as ninety-nine out of every hundred would enter the service.[7] When one recalls the appalling number of desertions among foreigners recruited late in the war, this consul's optimism seems unbounded and unjustified.

A similar report had come from Bremen earlier, for in September, 1862, Consul Börnstein had reported to Seward that his consulate was daily crowded with men wishing to enlist in the Federal army. He had suggested the possibility of sending them over free of charge as emigrants and had

[5] Tantalizing hints of earlier offers are to be found. Secretary of War Simon Cameron wrote to M. C. Dupuis and others on July 5, 1861, thanking them for an offer made through our consul at Geneva but declining their services since we already had an army of three hundred thousand, "a number greater than we need for the actual crisis." *Official War Records*, Ser. 3, I, p. 322.

[6] For an instance of a naturalized German back in Germany on a visit who encouraged young men to enlist in the Union army, see L. W. Kölkenbeck to James H. Anderson, consul at Hamburg, Consular Dispatches, Hamburg, XXX, Nos. 1, 174. For Anderson's reply, February 12, 1863, see *ibid.*, No. 174.

[7] James H. Anderson to Seward, August 5, 1863, *ibid.*, XV, No. 125. He had reported on February 12, 1863, that he received letters on this subject every day. *Ibid.*, XVI, No. 174.

reported some as willing to have the travel expense deducted from the bounty. "I could have sent a few Brigades to the States already," he had written.[8]

About the same time, September 2, 1862, William Marsh, consul at Altona, openly urged that the United States seek enlistments abroad. He reported that a large number from Denmark and the two duchies (by which he doubtless meant Schleswig and Holstein) were eager to go to the United States. The men had not the means of paying their passage but declared that they wished to serve in the Army, Marsh said. He believed that they represented this as their object simply because they were without money and wanted to get to America. He stated that he had been informed that during the Crimean War, Great Britain had organized, clothed, and equipped a German legion. Why could not the United States do the same? He confessed that this was a question admitting of much doubt as to its propriety, but he thought that the battles the Union was fighting had for their object a greater amount of benefit to the human family at large than would be the result of preventing the partition of a weak and sickly power like that of Turkey, or of fighting to protect a government dying of inanition. "We are fighting for a principle of right, of justice. For liberty, for freedom to reestablish and perpetuate a Government based upon these two fundamental principles to the millions unborn not only of America but of all the nations of the earth." [9] Later that same month his faith in the idealism of the prospective German recruits was a bit exaggerated: "We have the best evidence also of the honest character of their sympathy in the fact that they manifest a desire to help us and this arises from love of our institutions—from a desire to see the right prevail. They are not like a [sic] many nations seeking to enlist under another banner to avenge injuries done to an old one but they are with us in the hour of our difficulty, ready to sacrifice our [their?] lives purely from a love of liberty, and a desire to perpetuate the institutions of freedom—this is pure patriotism. . . ." It is as if he were lamenting the three thousand Swedes and Norwegians he reported as embarking in late January for Utah—"poor deluded Mormons." [10]

More impressive is Marsh's report of August 14, 1863: ". . . my

[8] Börnstein to Seward, September 12, 1862, ibid., Bremen, XII, No. 67.

[9] Marsh to Seward, September 2, 1862, ibid., Altona, II, No. 16. It is of passing interest that Marsh had reported shortly before, on August 28, 1862: "Europe swarms with naturalized American citizens. They will seek protection at the hands of Consuls, if none is extended to them they will hurry home." Ibid., No. 15.

[10] Id. to id., September 18, 1862, ibid. For the reference to the Scandinavian Mormons, see ibid., No. 45. For Scandinavians who had embraced Mormonism see Chapter I of text.

consulate is besieged from morning to night by able-bodied men desirous of enlistment into the army of the United States." In obedience to orders, Marsh declined the offers, but he could not refrain from asking whether these men could not be assisted in emigrating: "Poor fellows they have a soul for the enterprise but have not the means for the journey." [11] The last communications from Marsh on this subject are dated March 19 and 31, 1864. The Hamburg newspapers had reported that an agent of the United States government had been engaging men in Hamburg to serve in the Union army and had already sent one hundred of these via England. Many in Altona were applying to go. As Marsh was ill, he wrote to Consul James H. Anderson in Hamburg to look into the matter.

His own opinion was that the agent must have been a Confederate or he would have made himself known to Anderson, the official representative of the Federal government. Marsh told Anderson that the report should be contradicted and the Hamburg government requested to inquire into the matter, as such reports hurt the reputation of the Union while the Confederacy benefited accordingly. Allusions to these reported enlistments appeared continually in the Hamburg press, and severe indictments were made against the United States.[12] Inquiries concerning the matter were frequently directed to Marsh after he recovered.

From poverty-stricken Ireland, as the reader would expect, came a flood of applications. Typical of the letters which poured in on the consuls is the following from I. E. Parker to William West, vice-consul at Dublin: "I am desirous of enlisting in the army of the United States, provided my passage was paid out to America. If you could put me in the way of getting out I could no doubt prevail upon one or two others to go with me who like myself are pretty well drilled and therefore would not require any preparations before going to join the army." [13] The bait of two or three additional soldiers did not tempt American authorities. "Every day," wrote Consul H. B. Hammond from Dublin on April 3, 1862, "numerous applications are made to me, for a free passage to America." The persons "doing so say they are informed that the Government of the United States is giving free passage to all desiring to emigrate." The consul desired to know the whereabouts of the agent for that purpose, if there were one,

---

[11] Id. to id., August 14, 1863, Consular Dispatches, Altona, II.

[12] Id. to id., March 19, 31, 1864, ibid., III, Nos. 122, 125. The statement regarding a hundred men sent via England appeared in Die Nessel (a weekly circulating in Schleswig-Holstein and Hamburg), March 30, 1864.

[13] Consular Dispatches, Dublin, IV, No. 54.

that he might direct to that person the "large numbers" coming to him.[14] His letters of July 31 and August 14 of the same year bore the same refrain, the one of August 14 stating that thousands would leave Ireland if passage were provided gratis.

That a heavy migration from Ireland was taking place, no one could question; for Edwin G. Eastman wrote Seward from the consulate at Cork on May 2, 1863, that emigration continued unabated, "no less than Fifteen hundred persons leaving the port this week for New York." Consul Hammond wrote from Dublin on April 23, 1863, that the spring had opened with such an emigration as had not been known for many years and that in Dublin incentives were being given to increase it.[15] By the beginning of 1864, West felt the need of great circumspection, as the British government had spies out in all directions. These spies, he said, made "several attempts in disguise, by letter, and otherwise to commit me to a breach of the enlistment act, and I learn, from a member of the Fenian Fraternity, that they (the spies) number in Ireland alone, 82,000." [16] By April 2, 1864, he was satisfied that fully one hundred thousand Irishmen would start tomorrow, even after reading a terrifying and "calumnious" article in an Irish paper against emigration to America and "even on the expressed terms of joining our army, if it were possible to make such a Contract."

An interesting variation of West's notes was his report of how he was frequently obliged to relieve the distress of Irish-American citizens who had been in the Union Army and had returned to Ireland to recover their health. There they suffered from a worse disease, starvation; and when they were ready again for active service, they lacked the means for the return passage to America. He cited, as an illustration, one of the officers of Grant's army, present at the surrender of Vicksburg, to whom he gave a gratuity of two pounds and six shillings.[17]

In general, in the last period of the war, West merely sang a variation of the old tune, insisting that visits from soldiers and police had convinced him that a free immigration scheme "would drain Ireland of its bone and

---

[14] *Ibid.*, III, No. 6. Hammond's letters carried accounts of Confederates in Dublin trying to induce certain officers to enter the service of the Confederacy and he reported citizens of Dublin as sympathizing with the secessionists. H. B. Hammond to Seward, December 3, 1862, *ibid.*

[15] *Ibid.*, Cork, V, No. 27; *ibid.*, Dublin, IV, No. 41.

[16] William West to Seward, March 26, 1864, *ibid.*, Dublin, IV, No. 53. The number of spies given seems, to say the least, a slight exaggeration.

[17] *Id.* to *id.*, April 2, 1864, *ibid.*, No. 54.

sinew," and that assisted transportation—with a side glance at enlistment
—was no more illegal than the sending of munitions of war.[18] As late as
March 11, 1865, West told of "many fine young men" presenting themselves at his consulate who would "undertake any conditions that may
be required for a passage to America." [19] The applications at Ballybay,
County Monaghan, seem to have been more spasmodic. The consul at
Cork, H. Keenan, reported in April, 1863, that he had had several requests
a year earlier and that recently the applications had been renewed in large
numbers. One offer by an old Irishman is so touching that it cannot be
omitted. Thomas Conroy, who was in an Irish poorhouse in October, 1862,
wrote to Vice-Consul West that he yearned to be in the fight again as he
had been in the Mexican War, in which General Scott had awarded him
a medal for saving the lives of two of his officers.[20]

By this time, however, there had begun to be opposition to the departure
of Irishmen from the country by the thousand, a migration greatly aggravated by the economic distress in the island. Agitation of the subject
in the Irish newspapers gave it great importance. As early as January, 1862,
the Liverpool *Reporter* observed that for several months young men loaded
with gold watches and large bounties had been leaving Ireland, ostensibly
to emigrate to America, but actually to serve in the Federal army, for
which they were engaged by Northern agents.[21] An extract from the
Ulster Observer of Belfast is typical of comments appearing in the opposition press: "We have more respect for our country and our countrymen
than to see them wearing the livery of a foreign State in a cause which
involves no principle with which they can be identified. Were America
engaged in a contest with a foreign invader there would be a glory in
sustaining her, and no country would more wildly leap to her assistance
than Ireland. But she cannot and should not, expect our countrymen to
be her mercenaries in the present fractricidal struggle. We therefore im-
plore our young men not to be cajoled into a course fraught with danger
and dishonour. Already the battlefields are white with the bones of their
brethren. Thousands of Irishmen have, thanklessly, it would appear, laid
down their lives for the North. . . . They have fully proved their fidelity
to their adopted country; their allegiance to the cause of freedom; and
if President Lincoln still stands in need of human hecatombs, he should

[18] *Id.* to *id.*, June 11, 1864, *ibid.*, No. 67.

[19] *Id.* to *id.*, March 11, 1865, *ibid.*, No. 102.

[20] II. Keenan to *id.*, April 11, 1863, *ibid.*, Cork, V, No. 23. The touching letter of Thomas
Conroy to West, October 20, 1862, is enclosed. *Ibid.*, Dublin, IV, No. 79.

[21] Consular Dispatches, Cork, January 31, 1862, V, No. 27.

look elsewhere than to the decimated home of Ireland for the victims." [22] In general, it can be stated that the public journals were loud in denouncing "Federal agents" and clamorous for their prosecution and punishment.

General Meagher had been greatly annoyed by the way in which the Irish demagogues and newspaper journalists had been consistently misinterpreting his attitude toward the American war to the people in his native land. Only one influential national journal, the *Irishman,* and only one of the leaders of the Confederation of '48 then in Ireland stood by the North in this crisis. The papers, both metropolitan and provincial, which liked to boast of themselves as liberal went as far as they dared in espousing the sentiments of the English Tory press and in reprinting the calumny against the North and circulating it among the Irish, who would naturally have sympathized with the Union side in the American conflict. Much of the printed attack, of course, found its way back to the loyal Irish in the United States. To stem this flood of innuendo, the Nationalists of Dublin invited Colonel Michael Doheny, one of the American delegation to deliver an address on the subject; Doheny did, in fact, give a lecture on November 18, 1861, in the large theater of Mechanics' Institute in the Irish metropolis.[23]

To emphasize the disapprobation of the British government toward the enlistment of Irish nationals on the Union side—placed before the public as a violation of the neutrality which Britain had declared—the government officially took two actions. The first was allowing a parliamentary debate early in 1864 on the enlistment of Irish in the United States service, specifically noting instances occurring at Boston and Portland in the spring of 1864. The remarks of the British foreign minister, Earl Russell, the sentiments of the president of the council, Earl Granville, and of other speakers, were suggestive, as they clearly established the fact that there was no law against the *free* emigration of bona fide laborers for industrial work in America. Sir Robert Peel announced during the debate on the "depopulation of Ireland" by emigration that another half million must leave the country before its progress could be arrested or any check be given to the exodus.[24]

[22] This excerpt has been taken from a clipping filed in the Consular Dispatches, *ibid*. The editor appeared to be sympathetic to the South. He pointed out that the Southern army was full of Irishmen and asked on what principle the Irish could leave their homeland to steep their hands in the blood of those who were their kith and kin—meaning, doubtless, Irishmen in the Confederate army.

[23] Cavanagh, *Memoirs of Gen. Meagher,* 422, 424.

[24] Thomas Curson Hansard (ed.), *Parliamentary Debates* (London, 1830–1891), Ser. 3, CLXXIII (1864), 1318–34.

The second action by the British government was the trial of four or five unfortunate Irishmen for violation of neutrality by serving for a short period on board the United States cruiser *Kearsarge*. The attorney general for Ireland appeared personally at the Cork assizes to prosecute, while Justice William Nicholas Keogh presided on the bench. Both took occasion to denounce the naval officers, the government of the United States, and the country generally. In the course of the trial the benignity of the British government and the tremendous power of the British flag were emphasized. No issue could be made with the United States government, as the captain of the *Kearsarge* had reported immediately that the men had concealed themselves aboard the vessel on the night of her departure from Queenstown, that he had refused to enlist them, and that he had set them ashore at Queenstown as soon as possible. The British government turned the full weight of its power against its nationals guilty of violating neutrality.[25]

Swedes and Norwegians were no whit behind Germans and Irishmen in eagerness to become soldiers for the preservation of the American Union —and probably for the same reasons. After the arrival in Stockholm of Charles A. Leas as United States consul had been announced in the Swedish papers sometime in March, 1862, he was solicited from almost all parts of the country for places in the United States army and navy. This action was vastly stimulated by the President's proclamation for three hundred thousand additional troops, which gained currency in the northern peninsula in mid-August, 1862. Leas reported that a large number of young men had visited his office and begged to be accepted by the Union as common soldiers. They had read of the bounties offered and imagined not only that acceptance was assured but that the bounty would be paid them on the European side in order to help them defray their expenses to America. Despite the consul's insistence that the President's call related only to citizens of the United States, some Swedes had, he understood, left on their own responsibility for New York in order to enlist.[26]

The Minister of the United States himself, Jacob S. Haldeman, reported in the fall of 1862 that he was the recipient of many letters from Norway from persons who wished to go to the United States: "Within the last seven months [I] might have sent from three to five thousand

[25] *Ibid.*, 1326–27.

[26] Charles A. Leas to Seward, July 1, 1862, Consular Dispatches, Stockholm, IV, No. 251; *id.* to *id.*, August 20, 1862, *ibid.*, No. 37.

able-bodied young men (and their example would have spread like prairie fire) to the U.S., I or others advancing passage money they entering into an agreement to enter the army of the United States giving an order on the proper authorities for the advance, or apprenticing themselves in any manner that might be suggested as security. The advances would not exceed $55–$65 per emigrant, extras included by the Hamburg Steamers. If N.Y., Phil. or Boston wish emigrants or substitutes on terms like the above, modified to such peculiar motives they can be had here." [27]

There seemed to exist on the part of the American consuls a strange desire to feed these eager recruits into the army, for Leas, like other consuls, dragged in an allusion to England's search for men in the Crimean War and reported as his statement to these volunteers, "I have no doubt that you will be permitted to enlist upon the same terms and conditions as citizens of the United States providing you shall comply in all respects with our laws and regulations." However, he was careful to tell them that he could not offer them the slightest inducement to migrate for military purposes and added that they "leave disponding." [28]

Even more striking is the statement of his successor, B. F. Tefft, to Seward on January 9, 1863, that he could send a thousand recruits each month for a year or two, if he had the means of sending them; that he had had sometimes from ten to twenty soldiers in their uniforms in his office at one time. In a burst of enthusiasm he declared, "I verily believe I could send half of the regular army, rank and file, with the consent of the Swedish government; for the King has expressed a great interest in the success of the Union Army." By April 4, 1863, he revealed that he had a record in his office of over two thousand applications in person and one hundred and twenty-nine written applications, from all parts of Sweden, Norway, and Finland, regarding enlistments.[29]

That some of these eager recruits were finding their way into the Northern army is apparent when we read from a Confederate source that the Fourteenth New York Metropolitan Cavalry Regiment had just reached

[27] Jacob S. Haldeman to *id.*, November 18, 1862, Diplomatic Dispatches, Sweden, X, No. 25.

[28] Leas to *id.*, August 22, 1862, Consular Dispatches, Stockholm, IV, No. 1. Leas said September 17, 1862, that he "feels desirous that our Country should have the benefit of their services during the War, and afterwards of their labor in either the Mechanic Arts or the Department of Agriculture." *Ibid.*, No. 43.

[29] B. F. Tefft to *id.*, January 9, 1863, *ibid.*, Nos. 52, 8. In Tefft's communication of June 30, 1863, he reported that the applicants offered to bind themselves by written contract to perform any service for the Government, or any other party by way of remuneration. *Ibid.*, No. 15.

General Banks's army via New Orleans and numbered over eight hundred men, most of these being Swedes, none of whom had been in the United States three months. In an engagement near Port Hudson, Louisiana, the Confederate officer declared, these Swedes were so demoralized that they practically "offered no resistance, throwing themselves face downward on the ground, many on their knees, begging for quarter or praying in a foreign tongue to be spared." [30]

In Sweden as in Ireland opposition arose in time to the migration of so many men to the United States. The Swedish government warned its citizens against acting with too great haste in emigrating. Foreign Minister Count Manderström advised the American Embassy in Stockholm that his government could not condone the solicitation of soldiers by United States consuls in Sweden.

Despite the sympathy of the British government and aristocracy for the Confederacy, the United States minister at the Court of St. James, Charles Francis Adams, reported as early as June 8, 1861, that he was constantly receiving offers of assistance for the Union.[31] The offer, on June 10, 1864, of their services by two members of the British army, stationed in Ireland, indicates not only restlessness and perhaps a desire to get into a land of opportunity but also, doubtless, an intention to desert the English service. These soldiers had heard the rumor about free passage to America, and so they declared their willingness to comply with any conditions "in reason." They were under "orders for the Cape [Cape Colony?]" for the seventh of July and so urged the need of prompt action.[32] However, the communications of the American consuls stationed in England certainly indicate no such zeal for entering the Union army on the part of Britishers as was exhibited in Germany, Ireland, and the Scandinavian peninsula.

From several countries came offers of considerable bodies of troops— all of which failed to materialize. Colonel Dom Francisco Valle, a Spaniard, came to the United States Embassy in Rome with the offer of a

[30] W. H. Pascoe, "Confederate Cavalry around Port Hudson: their Dashing Exploits," in *Southern Historical Society Papers*, XXXIII (1905), 88–89. These foreigners were hurriedly got together, disarmed, and sent under a guard back to the Confederate lines. The persons, through an interpreter, were given to understand that any one attempting to escape would meet with instant death.

[31] *Official War Records,* Ser. 3, I, p. 293. The offers of "all sorts of military implements," to which Adams alludes, and the desire for contracts do not concern us here.

[32] Consular Dispatches, Dublin, IV, No. 67. One of the soldiers wrote from Camp Curragh, County Kildare, June 10, 1864.

regiment of two thousand men, chiefly Catalans; but obviously the acceptance of this offer by the American military authorities was impossible. Otto von Corwin, a Forty-eighter who had come to the United States after many years in prison, and who though he held the title of colonel was acting as a war correspondent, worked out in 1863 a plan for recruiting twenty thousand soldiers in Germany for the Union. Lincoln found the plan attractive but dropped it after Secretary of War Stanton opposed it. If Schurz had proposed it, it might possibly have been approved, but Corwin killed the idea when he betrayed that he expected monetary profits for himself.[33]

Of course, a number of individual Canadians attempted to slip over the border to enlist in the Union army, sometimes swearing false oaths as to their ages; but it was also true that certain citizens of the United States—and even noncitizens, as will be detailed later—were engaged throughout the Canadian provinces in offering inducements to Canadians, both adults and minors, to cross the frontier to enlist. In passing, cognizance might also be taken of the fact that numbers of Canadians joined the Confederate army—as many as forty thousand according to Canadian claims.[34]

The zeal of foreigners to enter the military service of the United States brought, as we have seen, protests from foreign governments. The protests, in turn, called forth from Secretary Seward a circular to the ministers and consuls abroad, admonishing them to abstain from any encouragement to those applying for military service under the Union flag. He proudly stated that the Federal government had experienced no difficulty in recruiting armies from the ranks of the Union's own citizens, who had responded to all appeals made to them. Neither directly nor indirectly were agents abroad to be permitted to make any enlistments in foreign countries for the armies. The Department of State renewed the warning in July, 1864. On the twenty-fifth of that month, F. W. Seward, son of the Secretary of State, in charge of the correspondence with the consuls, wrote to J. E. Marx, consul at Amsterdam, "With reference to emigration,

[33] For the offer of Dom Valle, see *Official War Records,* Ser. 3, II, p. 551; for Corwin's plan, see Kaufmann, *Die Deutschen im Bürgerkriege,* 489–90. Princess Salm-Salm claimed for her husband part credit for the project. Corwin thought that Lincoln could avoid difficulties with foreign governments by giving him and Prince Salm-Salm authority simply to raise twenty thousand men; *where* they thought it expedient to raise them would be their responsibility and danger. Salm-Salm, *Ten Years of My Life,* I, 56–59.

[34] See Chicago *Illinois Staats-Zeitung,* April 20 and May 2, 1861, for rumors of bodies of volunteers from Canada; for the Canadian claim of thousands in the Confederate army, see Lonn, *Foreigners in the Confederacy,* 209.

at this time, to the United States, you are cautioned to be scrupulously careful to avoid any procedure which may be construed to be a violation of the rights of neutral states." [35]

But scrupulousness with regard to enlistments in the army by no means implied prohibition of immigration or, indeed, any cessation of efforts to encourage it. On the contrary, one might say that Seward did everything he could to encourage it. The point of departure was the Homestead Act of May, 1862, which provided free farms to all aliens who had filed declaration of intention to become citizens of the United States. It further provided that foreign-born residents might become full citizens after one year's residence on condition of honorable service in the army. By an act approved July 4, 1864, the office of Commissioner of Immigration was created under the Secretary of State; the duties imposed upon him were to gather information as to soil, climate, minerals, agricultural products, wages, transportation, and employment needs. This information was to be disseminated throughout the countries of Europe.[36]

In order to spread knowledge concerning the Homestead Act, Secretary of State Seward issued on August 8, 1862, his Circular No. 19 to the diplomatic and consular agents of the United States. "At no former period of our history," he declared, "have our agricultural, manufacturing, and mining interests been more prosperous than at this juncture. This fact may be deemed surprising in view of the enhanced price for labor occasioned by the demand for the rank and file of the armies of the United States. It may, therefore, be confidently asserted that, even now, nowhere else can the industrious laboring man, and artisan expect so liberal a recompense for his services as in the United States. You are authorized and directed to make these truths known in any quarter and in any way which may lead to the migration of such persons to this country.[37]

There are only two interpretations to be placed on Seward's bid for immigrants: either he hoped for European immigrants to release natives from the fields and factories for the army, or he hoped to gain enlistments from among these newcomers. The Secretary of State himself, in replying

[35] The first circular seems to have been No. 18, issued by Secretary Seward. For the admonition to J. E. Marx, see Instructions to Consuls, XXXVIII, No. 9.

[36] For the Homestead Act, see *United States Statutes at Large*, XII, 387; for the Act to Encourage Immigration, see *ibid.*, XIII (Washington, 1865), 385–87; for the creation of the office of Commissioner of Immigration, see *ibid.*, XIII, Sect. 1.

[37] This circular may be found in a number of places, but conveniently, in *Naval Records*, Ser. 2, III, p. 521. Seward added at the close of the circular, "The Government has no legal authority to offer any pecuniary inducements to the advent of industrious foreigners."

to Consul James H. Anderson, had this sound observation to make about German migration: "Nor do I sympathize with your fears of a diversion of German emigration. No man will leave his native land except upon a strong motive. Every emigrant decides his choice of a new home upon motives equally strong. Where else in the world will the German find a new home so prosperous, so free, so hospitable as the United States?" [38] His son was even more explicit in a reply to William Marsh at Altona, dated September 11, 1862: "Truths like these, fitted to stimulate wholesome influx of industrious foreigners, you are authorized and directed to make public, but the Government has no authority to enter into any pecuniary engagements to promote the advent hither of emigrants from abroad." [39] The circular from Secretary Seward appeared in a number of German and French newspapers in translation, the French translation being by John Bigelow, the minister at Paris. It caused considerable excitement in Germany and was attacked, in Prussia and Austria especially, as a "false pretense to enlist men for the army." An Austrian paper declared the Homestead Act "a common lie," and stormed that such an act had never been passed.[40]

Only six months later Secretary Seward followed up his earlier circular with Circular No. 32, issued on February 8, 1863. "The privileges of the law," as all could perceive, "are extended to every person who is the head of a family or who has arrived at the age of twenty-one years," he wrote, "and is a citizen of the United States, or has declared his intention of becoming such, and who has done no disloyal act, direct or indirect." An exception, however, to the foregoing requirement as to age was made in the sixth section of the act, in favor of any person who had served not less than fourteen days in the army or navy of the United States, either regular or volunteer service, during actual war, domestic or foreign. Any person coming within the foregoing requirements, from and after January 1, 1863, would have the right to enter one quarter section, or a smaller quantity, of unappropriated public land, upon which said person should have filed a pre-emption at $1.25 per acre; or eighty acres, or less, of such unappropriated lands within the reserved sections of railroad-land-grant zones at $2.50 per acre. He added that strong inducements were also held

[38] This is one of the rare occasions when Secretary Seward wrote the reply to a consul himself. It is signed William H. Seward and dated July 31, 1862. Instructions to Consuls, XXXI, 487.

[39] *Ibid.*, 523.

[40] "Seward's circular ist eine verdruckte Werbung für den Kriegsdienst." Börnstein to Seward, November 5, 1862, Consular Dispatches, Bremen, XII, No. 78.

out to settlers on unsurveyed lands west of the Mississippi River, had much to say in glowing terms of the mineral lands of the West, and concluded, "It is believed that in no country in the civilized world are such opportunities afforded as in the United States, to active, industrious and intelligent men, for the acquisition of abundant means of support, and comfortable homesteads for themselves and their families." He instructed the consuls to make the above facts known in such manner as they considered "most expedient and proper" within their respective districts.[41]

The consuls were eager to aid in stimulating emigration; they fairly leaped to the enterprise. John Young at Belfast replied on April 1, 1863, that it would afford him "great pleasure" to promote emigration from Ireland. He had already made known the inducements to the shipping officers, who had agreed to insert them on their bills; he also thought that he would issue placards.[42]

William B. West, vice-consul at Dublin, gave a letter of introduction to Seward to a "valued friend," Brother Jerome Ryan, the "president" of a monastery in Galway, who, being an ardent lover of the United States and its institutions, had done the Union much service, as he had aided and advised hundreds of persons to emigrate from Ireland. This monk was about to make a visit to America to collect money for religious and charitable purposes. West revealed clearly what was in his mind when he wrote Seward, ". . . if you gave him a *Carte blanche* to send any number and *class* of emigrants, you may designate, from his district in Galway, he could distribute your free tickets to hundreds and thousands, in a quiet, satisfactory and judicious manner, allowing him a small profit on each emigrant for his work of usefulness and charity. . . ."[43]

Consul Hammond was equally eager to promote emigration from Dublin and promised to do all in his power to encourage it. He did not feel, however, that scarcity of labor and high wages alone would induce a large number of Irishmen to emigrate to America, since the condition of the laboring class was so bad that they did not have the money necessary for the passage and outfit. Great numbers applied for free passage and appeared to Hammond to be fine young men who would be of great

[41] Instructions to Consuls, Great Britain, France, Russia, and the Netherlands, XXXIV, 48½.

[42] Consular Dispatches, Belfast, IV, No. 12, Marsh to Seward, January 30, *ibid.*, Altona, II, No. 45.

[43] West to *id.*, May 6, 1864, Consular Dispatches, Dublin, IV, No. 61. He expressed also his satisfaction at the adoption of a suggestion he had made long before of exempting from port duties all ships carrying immigrants.

service to the United States. He deplored the fact that a large number had been sent by emigrant societies to New Zealand and South America, and he suggested as a means of increasing emigration to America that societies be formed in the larger cities to charter ships to go directly from Irish ports in order to save the expense of the journey to Liverpool.[44] By the spring of 1863 he declared that he was obliged to use considerable care, for any marked effort on his part toward greater Irish emigration would be seized upon by the papers. He stated, however, that the Dublin *Freeman's Journal* had given the Homestead Act wide publicity.[45]

It is clear that meanwhile the press in Ireland was active and hostile, for West alluded to "envenomed articles to deter Irishmen from going to the United States on any terms, containing as many untruths as calumnies"; and Consul Eastman declared that the public press throughout the whole country "used every means to impress the poor and ignorant people that immediately after their arrival they were liable to be impressed into the Army."

Fostered by the hostile press, growing concern appeared among prospective Irish emigrants lest they be impressed into the Federal army upon their arrival in America. Eastman wrote from Queenstown that would-be emigrants were seeking from him a certificate to exempt them from the draft; he suggested a certificate something like a passport which would afford such exemption unless an immigrant was naturalized or had voted for a certain length of time. He thought such a measure would be an inducement to emigration and yet not prevent volunteering.[46] Consul John Young had encountered the same situation at Belfast as early as October, 1863, but had ameliorated his refusal to give the prospective emigrants a certificate of exemption by informing them that they could get a passport at a small expense from the agent of the British government in Belfast; although he assured them that this was unnecessary, they invariably armed themselves with a British passport. By the next April he reported that thousands, at the rate of as many as fifteen men a day, were coming to his office, begging to be sent to the United States. "I have known them to walk over 100 miles to reach me and when refused it would be discovered that they had neither food nor money to return home with." [47]

[44] Hammond to *id.*, August 28, 1862, *ibid.*, III, No. 24.

[45] *Id.* to *id.*, April 23, 1863, *ibid.*, IV, No. 41.

[46] Eastman to *id.*, August 27, 1864, *ibid.*, Cork, V, No. 53.

[47] John Young to *id.*, October 14, 1863, *ibid.*, Belfast, IV, No. 31; *Id.* to *id.*, April 20, 1864, *ibid.*, No. 12.

William Marsh had Circular No. 19 extensively circulated among the farmers throughout the provinces of Schleswig and Holstein, and he felt that it had aroused them to efforts at self-improvement. Despite opposing influences, including a subsidized press, these farmers still regarded America as the great labor mart of the world and retained their faith in the freedom of its laws. After Marsh had received copies of the rules regulating immigration from the commissioner of immigration in the fall of 1864, he sought permission to have them framed and hung in the emigrant boardinghouses in Altona, as nearly all the emigrants coming to Hamburg for embarkation stayed in Altona, where board was cheaper and where the law on sojourn of strangers was more leniently administered than it was in Hamburg.[48] Like the consuls in Ireland, Marsh found Germans concerned about the possibility of being conscripted after arrival in America, "one of the scarecrows of their inimical press which should be universally contradicted." In March, 1865, he was concerned about Mexican emigration agents at Hamburg seeking to divert emigration to that country, and his last communication of the war period, dated April 5, 1865, showed him busy distributing additional circulars on emigration.[49]

Consul Anderson at the neighboring city of Hamburg had been concerned as early as January, 1862, over a hostile press, which was, as he thought, taking its tone from the English press. To counteract the pernicious influence of the Hamburg newspapers with their wide circulation, he urged that at Hamburg an able German writer, personally acquainted with America, be appointed "to diffuse a wholesome sentiment in our favor." He especially urged this because Hamburg was the principal port of embarkation for America. He even recommended for this post a certain man who was then residing in Germany for his health and who was living in the family of the count who owned the Hamburg *Presse*. This consul deplored the fact that English papers and ideas were circulating freely while American ideas were being extirpated. In his communication he was careful to talk only of the value of emigration for the sake of labor.[50]

From one source, at least, came a friendly note favoring emigration, from the *Deutsche Auswanderungs-Zeitung,* published at Bremen. Con-

[48] Marsh to *id.*, January 30, 1863, *ibid.*, Altona, II, No. 45; *id.* to *id.*, October 11, 1864, *ibid.*, III, No. 165.

[49] *Ibid.*, III, Nos. 122, 189. He felt that the superintendent of immigration at New York should distribute the circulars all through Germany. *Id.* to *id.*, April 5, 1865, *ibid.*, No. 190.

[50] Anderson to *id.*, January 18, 1862, *ibid.*, Hamburg, XII, No. 174. Anderson stated in his letter that he had many ideas on how to increase the emigration but he did not divulge them.

sul Börnstein knew the editor of that paper and secured a promise of help. "We are now once again," wrote that editor, "the steadfast advocate of the belief that emigration is not only a good thing for our German Fatherland in a political as well as social aspect, but that it is to be regretted that many more of its children do not seek the West. . . . Under these circumstances [the widespread unemployment in France, England, and Ireland] it is certainly better for the working man to go abroad, and settle there, where, as for instance in the United States, a homestead farm is proffered him as a free gift, with very many guarantees of a future, free from care about subsistence. Nor should the existing civil war deter [men] from emigration to the United States, for we have always said, and hold to it, that the manufacturer and husbandman of East and West will not be directly affected by it, as not being in the slightest manner mixed up with it." [51] After the arrival of Seward's Circular No. 32, Börnstein told Seward that the chief obstacle to greater emigration was the lack of publicity for the Homestead Bill—a lack so complete that a Prague paper, *Die Morgen Post,* had declared that there was no such law and that the pretended bill was only a base lie invented by emigration agents to lure Austrian subjects to America, there to enroll them in the army. Börnstein promptly contradicted this charge through a friend but apparently to no avail.[52]

Then, oddly enough, an article appeared in the New York *Journal,* a German paper edited by a man bitterly hostile to the Lincoln administration, who was denounced by Börnstein as a "notorious copperhead hireling." "The Federal Government," it stated, "is consciously scheming to replace its subjects lost in the war by a strangely encouraged emigration from Europe. . . . the want of husbandmen is becoming sorely felt especially in the thinly peopled woodland districts of the West; the thinned ranks of the army require constant filling up. The highest bounties don't affect this because there are no men left, conscription becomes worse, and an end of war hopeless. Now Ireland and Germany are looked to for help, and they whom the boastful Yankees at an earlier day scorned and mocked as 'the scum of the earth' are now welcomed to be turned into hireling slaves and food for fodder." [53] The article greatly disturbed Consul Börnstein, especially as it had been published, he declared, by nearly all the papers in Germany with the largest circulation, "exagerated

---

[51] Börnstein to *id.,* September 10, 1862, *ibid.,* Bremen, XII, No. 65.

[52] *Id.* to *id.,* March 30, 1863, *ibid.,* X, No. 25.

[53] The article appeared in the New York *Journal* of April 15, 1864. This issue is not extant, but was quoted by Börnstein.

[*sic*] by comments and accompanied by frightful warnings," and great weight had been laid upon the circumstance that such an article had been published in a paper appearing *in the Northern states* and amounting therefore "to a confession of their own guilt." As the article had created a "great sensation throughout Germany," he suggested that the falsehoods be contradicted by an official publication, adding that, for his part, he had already taken such action in the *Universal Emigranten Gazette*.[54] The *Auswanderungs-Zeitung* of Bremen not unnaturally came to the rescue, probably urged on by Börnstein. Noting the untruths in the *Journal*'s article and declaring that in view of the paper's wide circulation the statements could not be ignored, the Bremen newspaper denounced the article as a lie, written by one who was manifestly opposed to the Union government and sympathetic to the South.[55]

The consul at Frankfurt, W. W. Murphy, evidently supported a suggestion that a special emigration agent be appointed at that city; but he was curtly informed that the State Deparment had no authority to make such an appointment in the absence of Congressional legislation on that subject.[56]

Meanwhile, some American agents had been busy recruiting laborers in Europe under contract for firms or contractors in the United States. A case in point is that of a hundred Irishmen who arrived at Portland, Maine, aboard the *Nova Scotian* shortly before March 14, 1864. They had signed a contract in Ireland, with an American agent named Finney, binding them to work at Boston for a certain monthly stipend and their board. As will be detailed in the next chapter, seven of these men were tempted into drinking until they became intoxicated and were entrapped into the military service. These Irishmen were brought out by a Mr. I. G. Kidder of Boston, who paid their passage through the agency of an Irish-American, the above-named Finney. Kidder attempted to lay documents on this subject before the American minister at the Court of St. James, Charles Francis Adams, in order to remove any suspicion of illegality in

[54] The above excerpt was copied and sent by Consul Börnstein with his communication of June 13, 1864. Consular Dispatches, Bremen, XIII, No. 104. Börnstein also called attention to a comment on Seward's circular in the Bremen *Handelsblatt* of June 11, 1864 (which, however, is not available in this country).

[55] The date of this denunciation in the *Auswanderungs-Zeitung* does not appear in Börnstein's dispatch No. 104, but it was clearly made before June 13, 1864, the date when the consul translated and commented on it.

[56] The suggestion came from one August Gläser and was contained in Murphy's dispatch No. 10. F. W. Seward's reply is in Instructions to Consuls, XXXVII, No. 123. Gläser's zeal may have arisen from hope of an appointment as special agent.

the contract, but Adams thought it imprudent to raise the question with the British foreign office or to satisfy the fears of the mail line that its boats might be seized for carrying immigrants. In consequence of the question not being settled, only one hundred, instead of the contemplated thousand, were brought over by Finney.[57] The consular officials at Dublin also tried to prevent difficulties by suggesting certain provisions in regard to the repayment of the passage money. It was proposed that the emigrant's agreement or note of repayment should be acknowledged before a consul in Ireland in order to qualify it to serve as legal evidence in an American court; furthermore, such advance handling of the agreement would serve as proof positive that the passage was to be repaid by industrial labor and not by a bounty from military enlistment.[58]

Also in Maine was formed a Foreign Immigration Society for the purpose of importing foreign laborers to fill the deficit created by the drainage of native laborers to the war. The Reverend B. F. Tefft, recently American consul in Stockholm,[59] became active as agent of the Foreign Immigration Association of Maine and of the Lake Superior Copper Mining Companies. Tefft advertised for nine thousand miners and artisans, offering a written contract from the company to pay passage and expenses; the sum thus advanced was to be repaid later by labor at the mines under certain conditions. He revealed to Minister Haldeman that he was employed at a salary of $6,000 a year and commissions and that since he expected to be engaged in that business for several years, any essential misstatement would defeat his object. The fact that he was an ordained clergyman would, he pointed out, heighten his scrupulousness in the exactness of his statements. The fact that he was willing to take entire families was a partial answer to the charge of enlistment of men for the American army. He chartered the *Ernest Merk,* the largest and best steamer ever built in Sweden for the iron trade, which sailed from

[57] West to Seward, April 2, 1864, Consular Dispatches, Dublin, IV, Nos. 54 and 57; J. H. Murphy, British consul at Portland, Maine, to the mayor of Portland, March 14, 1864, Notes from the British Legation, LXI. The question of explaining the matter to the British foreign office was laid before Minister Charles Francis Adams through W. B. West of Dublin. West to Seward, March 5, 1864, Consular Dispatches, Dublin, IV, No. 57.

[58] Consular Dispatches, Dublin, IV, No. 61.

[59] It is important to clear up the relation of the Tefft brothers to the office of American consul at Stockholm. Benjamin F. Tefft was appointed consul at that city in 1862 and so continued until early 1864. George W. Tefft was appointed consul at that city; but unfortunately his commission did not arrive at the legation before the middle of May, 1864, up to which period B. F. Tefft was (or at least served as) consul, G. W. Tefft acting as viceconsul for B. F. Tefft for that period. Haldeman to Seward, June 18, 1864, Diplomatic Dispatches, Norway and Sweden, X, No. 49.

Stockholm on July 15, 1864, with five hundred emigrants, for Portland, Maine. About three hundred of the number were to go to the Lake Superior copper mines; the remainder were under contract with the Foreign Immigration Association of Maine—a contract which was not contrary to Swedish law. By the time Tefft was back in Sweden the following October to contract for a fresh group of emigrant-laborers, Swedish authorities were disturbed lest the emigrants be forced to serve in the Northern army or be bound for life to cruel masters.[60]

Another of the agents sent to Sweden by the mining companies was the young Swedish engineer Axel Silfversparre, previously mentioned as the captain of an Illinois light artillery battery. He resigned and left the army shortly after March 3, 1863,[61] entering the service of the Michigan copper companies probably early the next year. Owners of these mines had become so desperate over the scarcity of labor at a time when there was a heavy demand for copper that they subscribed a large sum to defray the expenses of agents to be sent to Sweden in search of immigrants. Silfversparre brought back nearly 150 Swedish, Norwegian, and Finnish laborers, many of whom were accompanied by their families. On the boat from Detroit, which was bringing the party on the last leg of their journey, Silfversparre lost twenty or thirty men to a recruiting officer. Later disclosures revealed that he had even obtained from the Swedish government permission to take men from prison on condition that they not return to the country. A few of the immigrants finally reached the mines, but the mining companies could hardly have regarded the venture as profitable.[62]

Wisconsin had had a Commissioner of Immigration and agents in the chief European countries ever since 1852. The Western Immigration Agency of Chicago had established in Stockholm and Göteborg agencies seeking settlers, especially for Minnesota. Minnesota maintained an immigration agency in New York, at least during the late war years. Ohio had created the office of Commissioner of Immigration, as had also Michigan.

[60] Hokanson, *Swedish Immigrants*, 26 n. See also Haldeman to Seward, June 18, July 2, 1864, Diplomatic Dispatches, Norway and Sweden, X, Nos. 49, 50; George W. Tefft to *id.*, October 11, 1864, Consular Dispatches, Stockholm, V, No. 20. Oddly enough, Minister Haldeman was charged with being involved with B. F. Tefft in the immigration scheme; the latter wrote Seward from Hamburg under date of November 1, 1864, emphatically denying the charge. Consular Dispatches, Hamburg, V (unnumbered).

[61] It is clear that Silfversparre had resigned his commission before this date, but that the resignation had not yet been acted upon. *Official War Records,* Ser. 1, XXIV, Pt. 3, p. 82.

[62] The author owes this data on Silfversparre's work as immigration agent to Hokanson, *Swedish Immigrants*, 76.

Furthermore, foreign diplomats and consuls resident in the United States sent home favorable reports concerning conditions here. One striking illustration is the comment of C. E. Habicht, Swedish consul at New York, dated September 20, 1861: "I will make a humble attempt to throw some light upon the American situation, which seems to be entirely misunderstood in Europe. Some seem to think that the North is suffering from all the atrocities and hardships of a common civil war but it is not so. The population is rapidly growing in the North, commerce and trade are thriving, and the loss of the Southern market seems to be already repaired." [63]

In Sweden the reaction to what appeared to the Swedish government to be enlistment for the Northern armies under the guise of labor engagements was immediate and emphatic. Most of the officials had been disturbed over the voluntary exodus, of which we have already taken note; indeed, the stream of immigration which had been mounting during the forties and fifties and threatening to depopulate sections of certain European countries had already caused deep concern to the rulers. One of the early letters written to Secretary Seward by Minister Haldeman from Stockholm portrays clearly the attitude of the sovereign of the northern Scandinavian peninsula: "Although Sweden and Norway are but sparsely settled, many of the rich peasants are selling out to emigrate to the U.S. This government are opposed to this emigration and do all in their power to discourage and prevent this loss of their subjects by offering crown lands on better conditions than ever before. . . . It is well known that the King and his brother Prince Oscar are violently and bitterly hostile to all who recommend or encourage immigration, and I find if I wish to stand well with the King and his Ministers the less said for the present on this subject the better." [64]

The newspapers of that country expressed their views in strong, even

---

[63] For the Western Immigration Agency of Chicago, see *ibid.*, 26–27, n. 19; for the agency maintained by Minnesota officials in New York, see St. Paul *Press*, April 25, 1865; for the Ohio Commissioner, see Executive Correspondence of the Governors of Ohio, January–April, 1864.

Wisconsin had an elaborate agency distributing thousands of pamphlets in German, Norwegian, and Dutch; five thousand were sent abroad and the rest were passed out to incoming immigrants as they arrived in New York. In 1864 an office was opened in Quebec under a Norwegian-born director. See Qualey, *Norwegian Settlement*, 61–62. For the quotation, see Hokanson, *Swedish Immigrants*, 21.

[64] Haldeman had gathered the above facts, he reported, from frequent conversation with Count Manderström (minister for foreign affairs), with the diplomatic corps, and with others. Haldeman to Seward, July 4, 1861, Diplomatic Dispatches, Norway and Sweden, X, No. 3.

violent, language, denouncing the effort to recruit labor as a great fraud and stigmatizing Tefft as a recruiting officer for the United States Army. They made many references to the case of the Irishmen taken to Portland and printed excerpts from the speech of the Marquis Clanicarde on this subject to the British Parliament. As early as the fall of 1862 Haldeman reported that he was receiving from Norway many letters asking if emigrants on their arrival in the United States were drafted into the army without their consent. The reports which led to such queries, he felt, had a tendency to check emigration or to turn it into other channels.[65] In 1863, after the Homestead Act had been passed and Seward's circulars had been issued, Haldeman reported the activity of the United States consul at Bergen, Norway. Circular No. 32 was translated into Swedish and Danish and was given considerable publicity.[66]

Naturally, the zeal of Europeans to enter the Union armies, the large numbers passing through the consular offices of the United States representatives, the wide publicity given the Homestead Act, and the recruiting of laborers did not pass unnoticed by the Confederate agents abroad. To them this activity meant but one thing: enlargement of the Union army, whether by direct enlistment—and nothing could alter their conviction that a uniform and musket would be the ultimate fate of most of the departing emigrants—or by the release of native Americans from field and factory as replacement by European laborers made possible their departure for the front. No detailed scrutiny of the correspondence which poured into Richmond from Confederate representatives abroad is necessary, but a few citations will show how greatly concerned they were over any possibility of augmentation of the Union army as they saw their own numbers depleted. James Mason, Confederate commissioner to England, was especially disturbed over the alleged enlistments in Ireland. By June, 1863, he was reporting to Confederate Secretary of State Judah P. Benjamin that information had reached him concerning extensive shipments from Liverpool of Irish whose passages were paid and who had received bounties in advance, though the engagement was for work on railroads or on farms or "in some other evasive form." In order to uncover the purpose of the emigration, he had authorized a man at Liverpool to employ agents to procure evidence as a basis for a representation to the British government. A few days later Mason was writing to a

[65] *Id.* to *id.*, October 16, 1862, *ibid.*, No. 24.
[66] Haldeman's report is dated April 24, 1863. *Ibid.*, No. 28.

Confederate commercial agent at Cork, Robert Dowling by name, directing him to secure the desired evidence.[67]

It is probable that it was the visit of Archbishop Hughes of New York, an emissary of the United States government, to Ireland, where he spoke in Dublin on the American situation, which stimulated the Confederate government to send three agents to Ireland. These men, charged with arresting "these unlawful acts of the enemy" as far as they could, were James L. Capston, a cavalry officer detailed by the Confederate Department of War to the Confederate State Department for special service; Father John Bannon, an Irish Catholic priest serving as chaplain to Missouri troops; and a Captain Lalor, concerning whom there is a sad lack of information. Though the purpose of the mission of Bishop Patrick Niesen Lynch to the Pope is not clear, it is probable that it was designed to secure the intervention of the head of the Catholic Church to end the enlistment of Catholics in Ireland and Germany in the Union armies [68]—an enlistment which the Confederates were convinced was occurring. It is interesting that James Mason himself went to Ireland for a fortnight and was able to learn only that emigration was going on, chiefly to New York, under inducements held out by Northern agents—but "always under the guise that they were wanted for work." [69]

Other Confederate agents charged officials of the Union with recruiting in Ireland. James D. Bulloch, who was active in securing arms and ammunitions abroad, alluded in the fall of 1863 to recruitment in Ireland for the Federal army and the dispatch of Irishmen "by hundreds" from Liverpool as "notorious." [70] Henry Hotze, the Swiss-born commercial agent of the Confederacy in London, reported to Secretary of State Benjamin in 1863 that a detective, who had been employed in Liverpool, judged from the character of the emigrants, from the small proportion of females, and from the fact that the cost of passage was defrayed by a New York company that the emigration was really disguised recruitment;

[67] *Naval Records*, Ser. 2, III, p. 762. It is true that Secretary Benjamin had broached the subject to the Confederate representatives in England the preceding April with a view to a protest to England for violation of neutrality obligations. *Ibid.*, 753–54. For Mason's letter to Dowling, see *ibid.*, II, 436.

[68] For the statement of intention to send over several Irishmen, see *ibid.*, III, 636. For an account of the three missions and of the visit of Bishop Lynch, see Lonn, *Foreigners in the Confederacy*, 75–81.

[69] *Naval Records*, Ser. 2, III, p. 891.

[70] Communications from Bulloch to Secretary of the Navy S. R. Mallory, September 1 and October 20, 1863. *Ibid.*, II, 488–89.

and six months later Hotze sent what he termed "legal evidence" of Federal enlistment at Queenstown.[71]

A. Dudley Mann, Confederate commissioner to Belgium, contributed his share of information by reporting Union efforts to secure Belgian and German emigrants. To defeat the purpose of Seward's circular—the now-famous No. 32—was, he declared, "the object of my constant thoughts." He admitted that the right of expatriation, where no military service was due, was accepted by all the European nations. He regretted that Seward, "quick at unscrupulous shifts," had covertly asked for foreign recruits, and he thought it more than probable that Seward had numerous emissaries at work in Germany and Switzerland to get emigrants. The following November he felt belligerent, not only against the United States, but against the foreign mercenaries; he advocated "summary execution" of every such mercenary captured from the ranks of the foe, or "at least solitary confinement at hard labor for life." He was bitter against the "Red Republicans" of Europe, who, with Garibaldi as their champion, were, he found "just as hostile to us as have ever been the Black Republicans of the North."[72] Mann's famous interview with the Pope was clearly aimed at arousing the pontiff to action designed to halt the emigration, which was solicited ostensibly to supply laborers, "but in reality to fill up the constantly depleted ranks of our enemy." He pointed out that once in the service, immigrants were invariably placed in the most exposed posts of danger on the battlefield, and that but for these foreign recruits the North would most likely have failed months ago in the "absurd attempt to overpower the South."[73]

Mann, reverting to the role of a detective, sent his Italian servant to Antwerp in early July, 1864, to learn the methods of the Union agents.

---

[71] Hotze, in his communication to Secretary Benjamin of March 21, 1862, cited a report in the Liverpool *Albion* of Federal instigation of unrest in Ireland, though he would not pretend to say how much truth was in the report. *Ibid.*, III, 719. He expressed in his letter of June 6, 1863, little faith in, and "little taste" for, such detective means, but authorized the expenditure. *Ibid.*, 785. He wished to withhold the depositions from publication because he thought the most effective use of them would be by the Southern Independence Association, then being formed in Manchester on the model of the Corn Law Repeal movement of 1848. Unfortunately for him, they were published prematurely. *Ibid.*, 962.

[72] *Ibid.*, 521–22; for his letter of November 1, 1862, to Benjamin, see *ibid.*, 588.

[73] *Ibid.*, 954. Mann indulged in some sensationalism; the accuracy of some of his statements may be questioned. He reported himself as saying, "Their champions, and would your Holiness believe it unless it were authoritatively communicated to you, their pulpit champions have boldly asserted as a sentiment: 'Greek fire for the families and cities of the rebels and hell fire for their chiefs.' " This report to Secretary Benjamin is dated November 14, 1863. Mann exaggerated the value of the Pope's ambiguous letter to President Davis.

Posing as a would-be emigrant, this Italian was told that he could be engaged only as a laborer for a three-year term, but that after his arrival in New York, he could become a soldier if that was his desire. Upon signing the instrument, as all the "laborers" were required to do, he would receive free passage and two francs a day after arrival. He was assured of making his own choice between working on the railroad and working on a canal. Inquiry at the agency in Brussels met with exactly the same conditions. Obviously, the same practices were in effect in Germany and Ireland. Mann represented the agents as the "meanest of mercenaries." [74]

It is difficult to determine whether an article in *L'Independance Belge,* which Mann clipped and sent to Richmond on August 20, 1864, had been inspired by him or not, but it reflected the tone of many European papers: "We read in a journal of Mons that the Dis-United States use up so large a supply of men in their fratricidal war that they are forced to resort to every other country in search of 'food for powder!' " Continuing, the article stated that two days previously forty-five inmates of a house of correction at Mons had been liberated to embark at Antwerp for New York, where immediately after arrival they would be enrolled in the Northern army.[75] The writer of the article waxed indignant over an advertisement in the evening edition of the Brussels *L'Étoile Belge:* "A demand is made for healthy unmarried men from 21 to 40 years of age to emigrate to the United States of America. Useless to apply without a certificate of military service." In his opinion the war would have been over but for succor which the Federal armies clandestinely received from the other hemisphere.[76]

Mann also had much to say about Lincoln's having dispatched Bishop John B. Fitzpatrick of Boston to Brussels, there to use all his influence to enlist the sympathies of the Catholic clergy in particular, as well as of the population generally, for the cause of the abolitionists. Mann rejoiced to be able to report that though the bishop had been "diligent and vigilant" in the discharge of his trust, rarely absenting himself for even a day from the American legation, his mission had been entirely unsuccessful: "The

[74] *Ibid.,* 1165.

[75] The article appeared in an issue of *L'Independance Belge,* mid-August, 1864. No copy of this paper is available in the United States. Quoted by Mann in his letter to Benjamin, August 20, 1864. *Ibid.,* 1189.

[76] It appeared in the evening issue of *L'Étoile Belge,* July 4, 1864. This, also, is not to be found in the libraries in this country. Mann hastened to send this information to M. Charles Rogier, the Belgian minister for foreign affairs. *Naval Records,* Ser. 2, III, p. 1167.

clergy are almost to a man for us, and the Catholic press, at the head of which stand the *Journal de Bruxelles* and *L'Emancipation* earnestly and boldly advocate our cause and hold up the enormities of the North to the animadversion of continental Europe." [77] As a matter of fact, the number of Belgians who joined the Union army was small, probably not exceeding two hundred.

The Confederate agents abroad were equally disturbed over evidences of Federal activities in Germany. As early as September, 1862, Edwin De Leon, confidential agent of the Confederate State Department, reported emigration to the United States from Germany via Hamburg; and only a few months later L. Q. C. Lamar reported that the Lincoln government had its agents throughout Germany enlisting laborers. They were successful in finding men willing to emigrate under the conditions of free passage and high pay. Combined with other causes, these inducements had made the lower class and a majority of the middle class of Germany warm partisans of the North. The charge that many of the leading newspapers were in the pay of the United States is in sharp contrast with Consul Börnstein's concern over the hostility of the German press toward emigration. Hotze declared in September, 1864, that the Confederacy had allowed the Union "unopposed to use a population of forty millions [Germany] as a recruiting ground and to draw at will upon their accumulated savings. These are the last two props which have sustained his aggressive power; cut them and I verily believe that he will be prostrate." It was probably to cut them that Hotze made a trip to Germany. His plan was to discredit Federal obligations and to divert the emigration to Hungary, to the Danubian provinces, and even to Poland.[78]

Mann was much more active in Germany than the other Confederate representatives. He was planning in September, 1862, to send his son, "who has long been perfectly familiar with these countries," on an extensive trip through Germany and Switzerland to counteract Seward's schemes for aid from abroad "in support of the desperate fortunes of the Lincoln concern." At the very end of June, 1864, the steamer *Bellona*, with about five hundred workmen (chiefly Germans) aboard and believed to have been contracted for by a Pole, arrived in Antwerp, en route to New York. Since no passports were required in Belgium, Mann felt that no legal steps could be taken, but that did not debar him from re-

[77] Letter of July 7, 1864, *ibid.*, 1166.

[78] For De Leon, see *Official War Records*, Ser. 4, II, p. 103; for Lamar, see *Naval Records*, Ser. 2, III, p. 718; for Hotze, see *Naval Records*, Ser. 2, III, p. 1209.

garding it as his "imperative duty" to bring the presence of the vessel to the attention of the Belgian government, or from sending his son to mingle with the passengers and, by tales of the fate which awaited them in America, to induce some forty or fifty to desert.[79]

In turn, the representatives of the interests of the United States practiced what might be termed counterespionage. Henry Börnstein at Bremen worked valiantly to correct the "misstatements" of Confederate agents. Consul Eastman reported promptly in early 1864 the presence of "many persons in the employ of the Rebel Govt, now in Ireland for the purpose of checking or turning the emigration from our shores." He told of the presence of a Catholic clergyman, probably Father Bannon, with letters of introduction from many influential Southern men. He proposed that money be allotted to send several well-known Irish Catholic chaplains to revisit their homes to tell others in the clergy the true state of affairs in the United States. He was confident that it would be money well expended.[80] Finally, Union representatives abroad were eager to pass on to the Federal government information about the proposed securing of some fifteen thousand Polish exiles to fight for the Confederacy.[81]

All this zeal on the part of Irishmen, Scandinavians, and Germans to reach America would seem to suggest that emigration to the United States continued despite the war. The truth is that the war checked, but did not stop, it; indeed, one of the striking phenomena of the American Civil War was the increase of immigration from year to year, as will be detailed in a later chapter. Actual figures from the immigration office show that almost 650,000 foreigners poured into the country during this period. Unfortunately, no data are available for determining how many of this number found their way into the army. Scraps of information only can be presented. Loose statements were easily and naturally made from Confederate sources, as Bullock's assertion in the fall of 1863 that Irishmen had been shipped "by hundreds" from Liverpool. More precise figures record the forty-five Belgians from a house of correction embarking at Antwerp, and the five hundred "Germans chiefly" aboard the *Bellona* in June, 1864, en route to New York.[82]

Most striking is the testimony of ship sailings, as published in *Harper's*

[79] For accounts of the *Bellona*, see *Naval Records*, Ser. 2, III, pp. 1158–59, 1166, 1174. For the son's trip to Germany and Switzerland, see *ibid.*, 522.

[80] See Consular Dispatches, Bremen, X, No. 20, for Börnstein; see *ibid.*, Cork, VI, No. 77, for Eastman.

[81] For the story of these Polish exiles, see Lonn, *Foreigners in the Confederacy*, 223–28.

[82] See p. 574 of text.

Weekly: by the middle of 1863 seven steamers were leaving Cork each two weeks; the Cunard Line announced the dispatch of an extra steamer every second week; and the Inman Company also increased its sailings by one extra vessel fortnightly. *Harper's* quoted a local Irish paper which had said, "No less than a thousand emigrants passed through Dundalk last week on their way to America and Australia. . . ." By January 14, 1865, *Harper's* declared that "hundreds in the army cannot understand one word of English." [83]

More telling and trustworthy, though by no means comprehensive, are the admissions from the Union side. Mayor H. Alexander of Springfield, Massachusetts, wrote Governor Andrew on August 20, 1864, "I have, I think, a reasonable prospect of procuring 300 men (foreigners) to apply on our quota, but to get them here will require six or seven weeks. . . ." [84] Confirmatory of the actual entry of foreigners into the Union army is the admission by Senator Henry Wilson of Massachusetts, on the floor of the Senate, that his governor had recruited soldiers abroad. Of the 10,672 foreign-born soldiers supplied by Massachusetts in its total of 153,486 recruits, "907 were imported from Germany and put into four Massachusetts regiments." [85]

The conclusion to which the research points is that some recruiting agents, hoping to make a neat profit for themselves on the bounties, went to Canada and to Europe—Germany and Ireland especially—to decoy recruits, and that as agents of industrial associations they engaged emigrants to come over, expecting to lure them into the military service after they had landed, partly of their own free will, partly, as we shall see in the next chapter, by force. Some of these agents, such as Tefft, Finney, and Silfversparre, were bona fide agents of organizations seeking genuine laborers; others, of the type described by Mann, were indubitably of a low order, were interested only in their own profits, and "represented" fictitious firms or associations. That men high in the government of the United States, Lincoln and Seward in particular, were interested in securing laborers to relieve the pressure on farm and factory occasioned by the war, must obviously be true. That, after the eagerness to enter the military service manifested by foreigners early in the war and attested to in the reports of the consuls, they may have discerned among the sturdy emigrants some recruits for the army is probably true; however, Seward was

[83] *Harper's Weekly,* VII (1863), 355; IX (1865), 18.
[84] *Official War Records,* Ser. 3, IV, p. 631.
[85] *Congressional Globe,* 38 Cong., 2 Sess., 607.

careful to stay within the bounds of international law. That these administrators countenanced the practices to which some of the agents stooped is unthinkable.

Certain other important reasons for the heavy emigration must be clearly recognized. For more than a quarter of a century there had been numerous American agencies at Bremen, Hamburg, Rotterdam, Antwerp, and Le Havre for inducing emigration to the United States, especially to the western states. Immigrants were looked upon as desirable in order to develop these new areas. Industries could not be developed or acreage planted without labor; territories could not reach statehood without population. Hence, placarding European port cities with advertisements of the opportunities in the New World was nothing new; indeed, it was merely a continuance of old methods. Furthermore, the reader will have lost sight completely of a stark, stubborn factor in Irish emigration if he fails to take into reckoning the conditions in Ireland which would have promoted emigration without any outside stimulation by Federal agents. The poor crops in Ireland for several years, the withdrawal of large tracts of land from cultivation for purposes of pasturage, the abrupt cessation of remittances from prosperous relatives in America with the opening of the war, and the cotton embargo, which threw Irishmen out of work in British factories, would in any case have turned the faces of many Irishmen toward the "promised land." Certainly, however, the Federal government enlisted in its army nothing comparable to the foreign legion organized by England on the Continent for the Crimean War.

CHAPTER FIFTEEN

The Draft and Abuses in Recruitment

THE outpouring of volunteers in response to Lincoln's first call for seventy-five thousand men for three months, which was issued immediately after the attack on Fort Sumter, included far more men than the government could accept and was an inspiring manifestation of American patriotism. But the failure of the authorities to accept all the eager volunteers in April tended to dampen their ardor. On May 3 the President called for a modest addition to the Regular Army and Navy. The panic which followed the defeat of the militia at First Bull Run stirred the administration out of its delusion and lethargy, though it still lacked any real conception of the problems before it. The jolt of defeat revived the recruiting spirit in the North. On July 22, 1861, Congress passed an act calling for five hundred thousand volunteers for three years. Then came the call, on July 2, 1862, for three hundred thousand volunteers for three years, to replace the losses of the Peninsular campaign; this call was followed promptly by a new militia law of July 17, 1862, which set the maximum term of service at nine months. For those states without adequate militia laws, the Federal act constituted, by virtue of authority vested in the President, a draft, with exemptions and substitutes permitted by detailed regulations from the War Department. In order to encourage volunteering, the law offered a bounty of $25 to each of one hundred thousand volunteers for nine months, while previous legislation continued to grant a bounty of $100 to each volunteer for three years service. The draft was not intended as a real source of man power, but rather as a whip to stimulate volunteering, and to a degree it did so serve. While this law could not be regarded as a draft law, it clearly pointed to the Federal draft of the next year and met some of the resistance which the draft of 1863 evoked.[1]

[1] Shannon, *The Organization and Administration of the Union Army*, I, 35–36, 259, 271, 273–76, 277–80, 286–87; James Ford Rhodes, *History of the United States from the Compromise of 1850* (New York, 1903–1919), IV, 236–37.

A full discussion of this law and the call issued under its provisions on August 4, 1862, for 300,000 men in addition to the quota of July 2, is not regarded as necessary for this

The spirit of the times looked upon a draft as a disgrace, and consequently an extensive and demoralizing system of bounties was embarked upon in order to so stimulate enlisting that a draft would prove unnecessary. Undoubtedly, in the very beginning, the bounties were intended as an expression of appreciation by the citizens who remained at home to the soldiers for their sacrifices; [2] but—just as undoubtedly—they degenerated into a pernicious evil, besmirching all connected with them. Some discussion of the question in connection with this study is unavoidable. It must be recalled that bounties were paid in addition to the regular monthly pay, which in 1864 was increased from $11 to $16.

The amount of the local bounties differed in various parts of the country. In the agricultural districts, where every able-bodied man could find occupation during the harvesting season, it was no uncommon thing to find bounties of $1,200 to $1,500 offered for three-year recruits; even among the large floating population of unnaturalized foreigners in the seaboard cities, from which substitutes were mainly drawn, the prices demanded were unprecedented in the history of warfare. The Federal government, the states, the counties, and other political divisions were munificent in their offers of bounties. A striking example of the totals which could thus be piled up can be seen in an advertisement in New York County by the Volunteer Committee: thirty thousand volunteers were wanted, to each of whom was offered a county bounty of $300; a state bounty of $75; a United States bounty to volunteers of $302; and an extra bonus to veterans of $100—all of which summed up to a total of $677 to the new recruit and $777 to the veteran. The bounty in New York County was, it must be admitted, more than that generally offered. However, the average sum paid to a recruit in an Illinois district once rose to $1,055.95.[3]

---

study. For the law and the supplementary act of July 25, 1861, and the law of July 17, 1862, see *United States Statutes at Large*, XII, 268–69, 274; for the amendment of July 17, 1862, see *ibid.*, 597–600. The militia law amended the law of 1795 and later acts.

[2] It is difficult to realize in what a fine spirit the bounties originated. In Worcester, Massachusetts, a man, in behalf of his firm, offered $11 to each employee who enlisted and the guarantee of his position on his return. Marvin, *History of Worcester in the War of the Rebellion*, 25.

Another man said at the meeting at which the city was making provisions to meet its quota that he had great regard for the number 75, alluding to the $75 bounty provided for, but declared that he felt a greater thrill for the number 76 and pledged himself to add one dollar to the sum specified for each volunteer. *Ibid.*, 131. The sums involved here were not large, as the firm had comparatively few employees.

[3] For a fuller discussion of bounties and bounty jumping, see Shannon, *Organization and Ad-*

The system was thoroughly vicious, for it nurtured a class of substitute brokers who embarked on getting recruits as a business, a subject to be discussed later in the chapter. It also begot the evil of bounty jumping—which likewise became for a few a business. Thieves, pickpockets, and vagabonds would enlist, take that portion of the bounty which was paid in cash, desert at the first opportunity, go to another district, re-enlist under a different name, collect another bounty, desert again, and play the game until they were finally caught. The number of times that a man could make the trick work seems unbelievable, but the provost marshal–general of Illinois is authority for the statement that one man had jumped his bounty thirty-two times. It is some satisfaction to know that he was rewarded with a four-year sentence in the penitentiary. Sometimes, out of a detachment of new recruits dispatched to the front, hardly one half arrived.[4] The premium paid to any under officer, soldier, or civilian bringing in a recruit was officially fixed by the state or district. In Baltimore, for instance, it was fixed in May, 1864, at $25 for a veteran, and $15 for a new recruit. But such trifling returns for their efforts would hardly have appealed to the type of men who embarked in the business of bounty broker.[5]

Late in the war this was poor business for the government, as it might have invested $100 cash advance on the bounty and two suits of clothing costing $9 each only to find that the recruit had decamped with the clothing, haversack, knapsack, canteen, and rifle. If he were discovered and arrested, he might escape from confinement, in which case the government lost the additional $30 which had been paid for his apprehension; the records in the Descriptive Books show that this happened frequently.

In any case, the entire bounty system came far too high in cost for the government. A few gross figures will be illuminating. From the time of the draft of 1863 to the conclusion of the war, the states and localities paid over $286,000,000 in bounties, while during the entire war the Federal government paid more than $300,000,000. Add to these sums the amounts paid in substitute fees, and the grand total must mount to about $750,-

ministration of the Union Army, II, 79–96; Rhodes, History of the United States, IV, 430; Report of the Provost Marshal–General, Official War Records, Ser. 3, V, pp. 634, 671–78.

[4] Report of the Provost Marshal–General of Illinois, General James Oakes, Official War Records, Ser. 3, V, p. 831. (The entire report is printed here, ibid., 803–42.) For the sentence on the bounty jumper who had violated his oath thirty-two times, see ibid., 725. See also Baltimore Der Deutsche Correspondent, May 23, 1864.

[5] John Ely Briggs, "Enlistment of Iowa Troops During the Civil War," in Iowa Journal of History and Politics, XV (1917), 377.

000,000—in all likelihood, to even more. Hence, the average recruit cost about $300 regardless of whether or not he received a single dollar of bounty money. This bill was practically the equivalent of the total sum paid the army as wages for the four years of the war. Little wonder that the mercenary bill constituted one of the greatest drains of the war! [6] Lest it be thought that only Europeans or depraved natives participated in the bounty jumping, it must be recorded that many Canadians deliberately crossed the border (Windsor, Ontario, was a virtual hotbed of the traffic), collected their bounty of $500 to $600, went as far as Louisville, jumped the bounty, and returned to Canada. General H. B. Carrington of Ohio stated that on a single day he had had to shoot three men, each of whom had been shown in court-martial to have enlisted and deserted three times.[7]

In truth, however, the recruit who wished to follow this game must be a wily fellow. He needed to have some knowledge of the law and of the secret paths for escape in the area where he proposed to desert; and, above all, he must not be handicapped with errors of speech or with the characteristics of a special nationality. Otherwise he might easily betray himself when repeating the trick. Lack of "smartness" or wile, added to unfamiliarity with the locality, probably discouraged many would-be bounty jumpers. Before the end of the war the methods had been reduced to a system—indeed, to a profession. Combining in groups, the men traveled in gangs of from five to twenty or more, one half of the number enlisting in one city while the other half assisted the enlisted group to escape. They used disguises to avoid detection: civilian clothes, false beards, wigs, false eyebrows. In January, 1865, it was estimated that there were from three thousand to five thousand such bounty jumpers on Manhattan Island, organized in small gangs, reveling in good hotels. They did not always go scot free, however, for a government agent once captured almost six hundred in New York City in a raid.[8]

If recruiting was difficult in 1862 under the dismal outlook of McClellan's complete defeat on the Peninsula, it was almost desperate a year later after many men had been recruited for the old regiments and the territory had been thoroughly canvassed to fill the quotas. Discouragement over the defeats on the battlefield and general weariness over the prolonged character of the war, together with the opening of many new avenues of

---

[6] Shannon, *Organization and Administration of the Union Army,* II, 80–81.

[7] J. M. Callahan, "The Northern Lake Frontier during the Civil War," in *Annual Report of the American Historical Association,* 1896, p. 358.

[8] Shannon, *Organization and Administration of the Union Army,* II, 71–72.

well-paid employment, had conspired to bring volunteering practically to an end by the spring of 1863. Under such circumstances it seemed necessary for the Federal government to resort to a draft. Efforts at a draft by the states had not proved satisfactory; yet to fill the ranks some general measure of compulsion was clearly necessary.

The government was soon to have striking proof of the futility of depending on the volunteer militia. It will be remembered that when Maryland, Pennsylvania, West Virginia, and Ohio seemed in June, 1863, to be in danger of invasion, the President called on those four states to furnish one hundred thousand militia for six months for their own defense during the Gettysburg campaign. When the danger was over, it was found that barely twelve thousand volunteers had responded, of whom nearly one third had been provided by Indiana, which was not included in the call.[9]

Already the government had embarked upon a policy of conscription to secure the soldiers needed. The act signed on March 3, 1863, provided for direct action by the Federal government on the people of the nation instead of action through the medium of the states. It divided the country into enrollment districts, corresponding roughly to the Congressional districts; each of these was headed by a provost marshal, and all in turn were under a provost marshal–general at the head of a separate bureau in the War Department. All male citizens, and all male aliens who had declared on oath their intention of becoming citizens, who were physically fit and between the ages of twenty and forty-five must be enrolled and were liable to be drafted for the service for three years; but anyone drafted could furnish a substitute or gain exemption by payment of $300 to the government.[10] The amendment to the law enacted on February 24, 1864, retained the conscription feature and forbade exemption of persons of foreign birth who had at any time assumed the rights of a citizen by voting at any election or by holding office, such acts constituting a conclusive bar to claims of alienage. Commutation was abolished, but substitutes were still allowed. The last act of this character, passed on March 3, 1865, came so late that it had little effect on the last few weeks of the war and so requires no analysis here.[11]

[9] *Ibid.*, I, 296.

[10] *United States Statutes at Large*, XII, 731–37. While curtailing exemption of clergy and teachers, it still exempted the physically and mentally unfit, felons, and necessary administrative officers.

[11] The act of July 4, 1864, had no changes which related especially to the foreign-born. For the act of February, 1864, see *ibid.*, XIII (Washington, 1865), 6–11. The act of March, 1865, virtually reversed the law of the preceding year and practically nullified conscription.

The large number of aliens in the country vastly complicated the administration of the draft. Naturally, the question of exemption from military service on the ground of alienage had arisen before 1863. As early as May, 1862, the War Department required proof of the claim of foreign citizenship, which usually took the form of certificates of nationality from the consuls of the respective countries. In consequence, however, of the fear entertained by the Irish and other foreign residents of St. Louis of being forced into the militia service of that state, General John M. Schofield issued an order on July 25, 1862, providing that the subjects of foreign powers lawfully pursuing their vocations would be exempt from militia service. General Butler drew the line tighter at New Orleans by demanding that each citizen of a neutral power should present himself with the evidence of his nationality to the nearest provost marshal for due registration of himself and his family.[12] By August of that same year Secretary Seward felt it necessary to assure British subjects through their chargé d'affaires at Washington that none but American citizens were liable to military duty in this country. Already the efforts of military commanders to exact of resident aliens an oath of allegiance to the United States had produced such difficulties that an order had been issued by the War Department enjoining all commanders from imposing such an oath.[13]

President Lincoln, in order to avoid misapprehension concerning the obligations of foreigners under the law of 1863, issued a proclamation on May 8, 1863, declaring no alien exempt who had declared his intention of becoming a citizen of the United States or a state or had exercised other political franchise. Such an alien was allowed sixty-five days to leave the country if he so desired.[14]

Substitutes could be taken from among those subject to the draft. It marked a complete reaction against the sincere efforts during the preceding two years to construct an effective law. It was felt that the war was so nearly over that almost any concession should be made to avoid the necessity of another draft.

[12] The evidence demanded by General B. F. Butler included the country of birth, length of residence in the United States, names of all members of the family, place of residence, occupation, date of certificate of nationality, and date of registration of certificate with endorsement by passport clerk. For General Schofield's order, see Moore (ed.), *Rebellion Record,* V, 47; for Butler's order, see *ibid.,* V, 80.

[13] Halleck to Rosecrans, May 22, 1863, *Official War Records,* Ser. 3, III, p. 217.

[14] *Official War Records,* Ser. 3, III, pp. 198–99. The provision for exemption of Quakers and conscientious objectors in some state drafts of 1862 brought about some strange alignments among the naturalized citizens. For example, in Indiana and Ohio exemption of religious sects brought about an unsought revival among the Society of Friends. One of the singular results in New York was the remarkable increase of Quakers in the Sixth Ward—an Irish ward! "Even broad hats could not conceal the identity of the Celtic faces beneath the

There followed in rather rapid sequence from the office of the provost marshal a number of circulars intended to interpret or clarify the law and to facilitate its administration. Since these were numbered, they are fairly simple to follow. The procedure in regard to enrollment was the first issue and was provided for in Circular No. 17, dated June 2, 1863. The provost marshal–general directed boards of enrollment to instruct their officers to enroll all males of the stipulated age group, whether citizens of the United States or persons of foreign birth who had on oath made declaration of intention to become citizens. This amounted then simply to a mandatory census of the above groups of residents and granted no discretion for exemption to enrolling officers.[15] Six weeks later, on July 19, the provost marshal–general issued Circular No. 53, which prescribed the procedure for an alien claiming exemption: the alien must state his nationality, the date of his entry into this country, and his place of residence; he must affirm that he had never made a declaration of intention or voted in any election; and he must state that he claimed exemption as an alien—the affidavit to be supported by any proof he might wish to offer. If the Board of Enrollment was satisfied, it could discharge him from the draft; but if it was not satisfied, it must refer the case through the provost marshal–general to the State Department for decision, in the meantime suspending all action on the case.[16] On August 13, Circular No. 71 made a further demand of the boards of enrollment—that they forward with the claim to exemption "all evidence they might be able to secure to contravert the claim" or to show that the claimant had exercised the franchise.[17] A few days later, on August 19, another circular, No. 72, dealt with the status of minor children of citizens naturalized according to the law of 1802 or of persons who, prior to the passage of any Federal law on the subject, had become citizens of any state in the Union: if dwelling in the United States,

---

brim." By 1863, when such blanket immunity no longer prevailed, the Quaker revival was no longer pronounced. See the cartoon in *Harper's Weekly*, VI (1862), 560. Throughout the war, Congress wisely granted no complete exemption on the score of conscience. The law was soon interpreted to exclude any one who had made a Declaration of Intention or exercised the franchise. Shannon, *Organization and Administration of the Union Army*, II, 249.

[15] *Official War Records*, Ser. 3, III, p. 245. This was signed, of course, by James B. Fry, provost marshal–general.

[16] *Ibid.*, Ser. 3, III, p. 545. Seward stated in a letter to Dayton, ambassador to France, that "the law had been acquiesced in by all foreign powers." Instructions to Consuls, France, X, 409–11. Fry's Circular No. 65 of August 6 was merely a further elucidation, stating that where alienage was clearly established, exemption must be granted, but where "any" doubt existed, it must be referred to the State Department. *Official War Records*, Ser. 3, III, p. 632.

[17] *Official War Records*, Ser. 3, III, p. 675.

they must be held as citizens.[18] The procedure in practice, then, amounted to this: No names could be struck from the list on the ground of alienage until the persons concerned had been drafted, whereupon, after formal notice, the man drafted could go before the Board of Enrollment of his district and show cause for exemption.

It was, in truth, only when conscription attached onerous duties to the exercise of the privileges of American citizenship that residents who had enjoyed those privileges sought to discover irregularities in their naturalization papers. Emigrants who had left Europe without any intention of returning should, in all honesty, have been regarded as Americans, and the number of those who meant to preserve their original nationality unimpaired was insignificant. Thousands discovered immediately after passage of the conscription act of 1863 that their original nationality was inexpressibly dear to their hearts. This brought a flood of applicants to the various consular offices to secure the precious certificates of nationality to save them from the draft.

The enforcement of the draft brought, as is well known, resistance and riots, which do not demand lengthy treatment here. There were early evidences that actual drafting might encounter serious opposition. Arms were being brought in and distributed in a manner that implied intention to resist; the Irish in the larger cities were especially restive; from many of the rural areas came reports of military drill by members of secret orders and others hostile to conscription. Outbreaks of violence here and there pointed to an underlying current of passionate emotion which might take form in bloody violence. Conscription was contrary to the genius and habits of the people and could not be enforced unless backed by arms. Fortunately, because of volunteering and surpluses credited on previous calls, the draft proved unnecessary in Ohio, Indiana, and Illinois, in which states the portents had been most ominous.

On June 18, 1863, instructions were issued for the enrollment to go into effect. Despite the fact that this was only preliminary to the actual drafting, it encountered opposition in four of the seven states of the Middle West, reaching its worst manifestation in Milwaukee, where a turbulent population, largely German and Irish, seemed disposed to have a show-down with the whole question of conscription.[19] On July 7, the first draw-

---

[18] *Ibid.*, 692. It is superfluous to enter into the rules for aliens in regard to militia in beleaguered places, such as Memphis.

[19] An enrolling officer in Dodge County, Wisconsin, and a registration official in Milwaukee were badly injured. Gray, *The Hidden Civil War*, 139. Even in New York City several per-

ings under the actual draft occurred in Rhode Island; the next day drawings were held in other New England districts, where, outside of Boston, the draft proceeded quietly. On July 11, drafting began in New York City but was broken up by riots, which began on July 13 and lasted for about four days. The provision which admitted of commutation for $300 was the main grievance, as laborers felt it a device to enable the rich to escape the burden, which must then fall on the poor. In consequence, the draft there and in other parts of New York had to be suspended until August 19, when better means were at hand to enforce it. The riots of July 13–16 in New York were by far the most serious. So much did they overshadow in violence, bloodshed, and tenacity the lesser outbreaks elsewhere that the others have been largely forgotten. Ultimately the draft embraced twelve states—the New England states, New York, Pennsylvania, Delaware, Maryland, Michigan, and Wisconsin.

The story of the draft riots has been told in such detail [20] that no extended recapitulation should be undertaken here. We are concerned, however, with the resident foreigners and their reaction to the draft. The large proportion of unassimilated foreigners in New York furnished just the right kind of material for an outburst. The large Irish element constituted the prime factor in the revolt. Lacking American background, volatile by nature, deprived of their real leaders and better element by the volunteering of two years, the residue of the Irish population was occupied mainly with the mercenary aspect of the question, in which respect, as already stated, they felt aggrieved. In addition, they were bitterly opposed to being forced to fight to free the negro. Their prewar feeling toward the negroes as their chief competitors in the labor market had been aggravated during the war. Wages had been boosted by the war and they naturally wished to maintain them at that level; they feared that if the negroes were freed they might easily reverse the existing favorable situation by glutting

---

sons were arrested for giving false names or refusing to give any name. Shannon, *Organization and Administration of the Union Army*, II, 210.

[20] For the whole subject of the draft and riots, see Shannon, *Organization and Administration of the Union Army*, II, 205–37; Kirk, *Heavy Guns and Light*, 104 ff. Archbishop Hughes himself held in addressing a gathering that the blame was "justly laid on Irish Catholics." *Appletons' American Annual Cyclopaedia*, 1863, p. 816. It was reported that some of the residents of the Ninth District met secretly on Sunday, July 10, resolved to resist and, if necessary, to "proceed to extremities." At least five hundred of the mob were killed or died shortly afterwards while ten to twenty soldiers were killed and as many injured quelling the riot, Shannon, *Organization and Administration of the Union Army*, II, 213.

the market. The existence of this sentiment is attested by the antinegro demonstrations and by the fact that most of the eighteen persons murdered during the riots were negroes.

Natives should not, however, forget that the discontent was fanned by the acts of unscrupulous politicians, ready to resort to any measures to discredit the administration. Among this number must be reckoned the editors of certain of the large newspapers and two of the chief Democratic leaders, Governor Horatio Seymour and Mayor Fernando Wood, who, though perhaps not guilty of complicity, encouraged the mob by their denunciation of the draft as unconstitutional. Of course, the War Department made a serious and almost disastrous mistake in holding the draft at a moment when the city had been denuded both of the soldiers usually stationed in the forts about the harbor and of the militia in order to deal with the menace presented by the Gettysburg campaign.

The disorders other than in New York were also largely attributed to foreigners: in Vermont, to the Irishmen in the marble quarries at Rutland, where officials serving notices were driven away with stones and sticks; in Boston, to Irish men and women; in Troy, to Irishmen (the fact that a Catholic priest did the most to quell the riot by his influence over the Irish, argues Irish prominence in the riot); in Pennsylvania, to Irish and Welsh miners in the Pottsville region, a hard lot who confused labor grievances with the draft; and in Milwaukee, to the German and Irish elements, particularly the women and children.[21]

There can be no doubt that the local provost marshals and enrolling officers threw obstacles in the way of the aliens. Exemption was not the simple matter of producing a consular certificate. Sometimes even the procuring of such a certificate was not an easy matter. Take the case of Britishers who were working in Pennsylvania mines remote from a consular officer. They had difficulty in securing the certificates in time to

[21] For the disorders outside New York, see Shannon, *Organization and Administration of the Union Army*, II, 219–37. The Chicago *Times*, October 4, 1864, indicated that scarcely any except Germans were being drafted in Milwaukee and Illinois and tried to detect a political motive. "It seems strange that in a fair draft, nobody but Germans are called upon to do military duty. Is it because so many of them are turning democrats and going to McClellan that they are drafted. . . . Very few of the Germans in Woodford County are responding. They have sold out their farms, their homes, the products of all their labor since immigrating to this country, including money brought from the old country. Thus they have realized a thousand dollars and purchased substitutes and are now homeless. These things are telling strangely against the Lincoln Party." The reader must recall that there was a strong reaction against the administration after Chancellorsville.

prevent their being hurried into the service. The President suspended the habeas corpus so far as draft dodgers were concerned, so that appeals to the courts of justice were closed to them. The British consul at Philadelphia wrote British Minister Lyons on November 15, 1863, of how universal was the statement of all applicants for consular certificates that "the Provost-Marshals of their districts throw every possible difficulty in the way of making good their claims as aliens." They all complained of expense, personal fear, and contumely.[22]

The first ground of complaint seems to have been refusal to accept the consular certificate or other papers of identification. A Canadian complained from Louisville on July 12, 1863, that he had showed the captain of his company an affidavit sent him from Canada with the Canadian seal attached to prove his nationality; the captain had directed him to present his papers at headquarters, where he would be exempted. His reception by the major in command was an abrupt order to "go right straight, and pick up my musket" or he would put him in prison as he would any other British subject seeking exemption.[23] The provost marshal at Frankford, a suburb of Philadelphia, seems to have been even more peremptory. One Thomas Armrod, a British subject, took his consular certificate and one other document (the nature of which is not disclosed) to the provost marshal, Mahlon Yardley. The latter said the certificate was of no use whatever and added, "I don't want to see it." When Armrod said that he would go back to his consul, Yardley pointed to another room and said, "No you won't; go in there." Then, turning to an attendant, he said, "Guard, take charge of this man." After one hour's confinement Armrod was released to go to an alderman for an affidavit, but when he returned with it, Yardley rejected it because it was not accompanied by proof from every state in which he had resided. The draftee asserted that it would be impossible to obtain such proof. When Yardley insisted that he could not be exempted without it, Armrod left without any satisfaction as to his exemption.[24] Several Frenchmen, among them Jules Biette, clerk in chancery in the French consulate general in New York, found their consular certificates rejected without examination by a provost marshal in New York. Seward ordered the provost marshal to strike Biette's name

[22] British Consul at Philadelphia to Lord Lyons, November 15, 1863, Notes from the British Legation, LI.

[23] G. I. Shaw to id., July 12, 1863, ibid., LIII.

[24] Thomas Armrod to the British Consul at Philadelphia, undated, ibid. The writer infers from the placement of the letter in the bound volume of manuscripts that the date is probably about July.

from the rolls unless proof existed of his having exercised the rights of citizenship.[25]

The provost marshal Yardley seems to have imposed unjust financial burdens on draftees. Philip Quinn was required to prove the date of his arrival in the United States and to produce in person the vouchers before the Board of Enrollment. The draftee was poor, had been ill, and would have to pay witnesses for their loss of time from work in attending the Board. At times the provost marshal required the testimony of two witnesses. George Lee, a British subject, made the trip from Smyrna, Delaware, to Warwick, Maryland, to secure the affidavit of two acquaintances residing there, only to be told that the papers were not in due form. He then procured a certificate from his consul, but still he could not satisfy the provost marshal. His financial losses to no purpose were his wages for two weeks and $32 in travel expenses. Though Martin Taylor offered an affidavit drawn up in Philadelphia, where he had produced two witnesses to prove his alienage, the provost marshal at Smyrna refused to accept this paper because it had not been made out in Delaware—despite the fact that Taylor had been in Wilmington only two months and had no acquaintances there. A poor man, Taylor had lost eight days from work to produce proof which was unacceptable.[26] This situation bore especially hard on foreign laborers, who were notoriously migrant, moving from state to state and settling wherever they were able to find work.

Exemptions were refused on slight or frivolous pretexts. One Bernard Leddy's claim to exemption on the score of British citizenship was rejected by a Philadelphia Board on the ground of his father's American citizenship, though he held that he was of age at the time of his father's naturalization. A similar instance arose in connection with two Swedes drafted in Minnesota in 1863. Lewis Lorenson claimed that he had come to the United States in 1853 at the age of twelve years and to Minnesota two years later, where he had resided ever since. He had never voted or been naturalized, in proof of which fact he pointed to the absence of his name from the poll lists. Reference of his case to Washington was denied, so that he and his comrade, John Holmes, each paid $300 commutation

[25] Notes to the French Legation, VIII, 95, 96–97, 100. Charles Roussell and Pierre Pflaum were the other two Frenchmen whose certificates were rejected.

[26] Notes from the British Legation, LIV. The requirement of two witnesses is found in a note to the State Department, August 25, 1863. For George Lee, see an affidavit executed before George Crump for the Philadelphia consul, August 27, 1863, *ibid.*; for Taylor, see affidavit before George Crump. The boards of enrollment were regularly alluded to by the British consuls as boards of examiners.

money—under protest. Since Lorenson's father had declared intention to become a citizen before the son was of age, the Board of Enrollment decided against exemption. It is interesting that this decision was later reversed. Because Arthur J. King had been connected with a home-guard company in Cincinnati during the General Kirby Smith raid in 1862, serving during the thirty days of martial law as a lieutenant without commission or pay, his claim to exemption was rejected by an Enrolling Board in Kentucky; but his indignant remonstrances brought submission of his papers, with the adverse opinion of the Board, to the provost marshal general at Washington for confirmation. In the spring of 1864, under the call for one-hundred-day men, many British subjects in Cincinnati had been compelled—under the same pretext of their having enrolled in the militia corps organized in 1862 for home defense—to find substitutes or else serve.[27] A flagrant case was that of the Irishman John Walsh. Drafted in one of the Pennsylvania districts, he was ordered to report at Scranton in mid-November, 1863. He appeared, prepared to prove his alienage and also the enlistment of two brothers in the service. The Board of Enrollment refused to hear his witnesses and sent him under guard to Philadelphia and thence to South Carolina, where he was still held months later in the Fifty-second Pennsylvania Volunteers. The only reply to his father's petition for his discharge was that the case had been referred to the Board of Enrollment and reported on adversely.[28]

Very late in the war, in January, 1865, Provost Marshal W. G. Collins wrote from Alton, Illinois, in reply to an inquiry as to what constituted proper papers for exemption, that an alien draftee who had lived in the country more than five years should present to the Board of Enrollment a certificate by the county clerk that he had never voted and a second certificate from the clerk of the Circuit Court that he had never declared an intention of becoming a citizen, inasmuch as the experience of the Board rendered that course necessary to prevent imposition.[29]

With all due allowance for deliberate evasion of the draft, the statement

[27] For Leddy, see Lyons to Seward, January 2, 1864, *ibid.*, LVIII; for Lorenson, see Notes from the Swedish Legation, II. King had joined a home-guard company under rather unpleasant circumstances. He was stopped in the street by a squad of armed citizens and ordered to fall in. He explained his status as a noncombatant, but because his own home was endangered, he took a musket. Later the members of the company made him a lieutenant. See King to Lyons, June 18, 1864, Notes from the British Legation, LXV. Evidence that British subjects were compelled to serve or furnish a substitute appears in a note from Lyons to Seward, May 10, 1864, Notes from the British Legation, LXIII.

[28] Memorandum, February 13, 1864, Notes from the British Legation, LIX.

[29] Note dated January 23, 1865, *ibid.*, LXXVI.

made by William Stuart of the British embassy to Secretary Seward on September 23, 1863, pictures fairly the situation for many provosts. The British consul at Philadelphia had reported that one of the provost marshals continued to reject almost every claim to exemption, "often on most frivolous grounds." [30]

There can be no question that, in one way or another, many aliens were coerced into the army. One favorite device was to arrest a man on suspicion of draft evasion or desertion and then to apply pressure for enlistment. Thomas Maguire, who claimed British citizenship, is a case in point. Arrested in Vermont for trying to evade the draft, he was induced, by threats of rigorous treatment during his confinement, to enlist in Company D of the Tenth Vermont Regiment. W. P. Grant was arrested in Virginia and imprisoned for over a year; the only cause to which he could attribute such treatment was his refusal to enlist. However, it must in justice be recorded that he had been living in the United States continuously for fifteen years, so that his three visits to his native Ireland did not justify the assumption that his sojourn in America was merely temporary.[31] Alleged desertion could easily be—and was—used as a pretext for unjust coercion. Such coercion could verge on cruelty. Patrick Connaughton, whose nationality scarcely needs to be stated, asked for a furlough—evidently to prove his alienage—but his request was refused. He consequently declined to put on his uniform, whereupon he was sent to jail in irons and confined for eighteen hours. When threatened, however, he put on the uniform. Under guard he was allowed to go to see a lawyer; but while waiting in the lawyer's office, he was seized and taken away, to be escorted the same day to the cars and sent to the camp at Philadelphia. If he had had time to go to Baltimore, he insisted, he could have proved his British citizenship.[32]

It must be pointed out that there was much evasion of the draft by foreign-born, as well as by native-born, citizens. Hundreds of citizens of the West and of other parts of the North fled into Canada "like cravens" to escape the draft. The exodus through Detroit was especially large. An episode related by the Cincinnati *Gazette* shows the extremes to which draft dodgers would go. A deputy marshal of Coshocton County, Ohio, went to a house near Chillicothe with a squad of five men to arrest two

[30] *Ibid.*, LV.

[31] W. Stuart of the British Legation to Seward, November 3, 1862 (an early instance), *ibid.*, XLIII. Grant was imprisoned at Camp Chase. *Ibid.*, XLVI.

[32] Affidavit of Patrick Connaughton, *ibid.*, LIV. A later note shows that he was sent to the One Hundred and Eighteenth Pennsylvania Regiment.

Germans who had evaded the draft for many months. When they approached the barn, the two evaders came out and opened fire. In the melee which followed, the two Germans and one of the marshal's men were killed, while another of the marshal's men was severely wounded.[33] One feels considerable sympathy with the provost marshal who rejected the plea of Isaac Bradley that he was an alien, for Bradley had come to the United States in 1843 at the ripe age of three and so was claiming British citizenship under the technicality that his citizenship had never been altered.

The crime of desertion also plagued the army, until it became one of the major problems presented to the authorities during the war. The question has been the subject of special study and so it is unnecessary to devote space to it here; [34] however, it should be reiterated that the numbers of deserters, according to the statistics of the provost marshal–general, was far higher for the eastern states, with their large foreign population, than for the western states, where the native-born were in the majority. Furthermore, no one could examine the Descriptive Books for foreign regiments during the later years of the war without being struck by the number of desertions. It is little wonder that men suspected of being deserters were promptly arrested or that the procedure of arrest first and investigation later brought forth many injustices. Since a man's citizenship could not be determined by his appearance or speech, and since the protests of a possible deserter could not be accepted as necessarily truthful, wrongs were bound to occur. The historian deplores the abuses dealt out to some foreign subjects but has to recognize that under the pressure of a great civil war there was no time for nice discriminations. Probably, also, provost marshals who had had experience with foreign-born residents who had sought a refuge in the United States and enjoyed the benefits of the economic opportunities of a rich country in time of peace, but who now in time of war were seeking to evade a debt of gratitude, became bitter against "draft dodgers," as those who invoked foreign protection seemed to them.

Cases of maltreatment of alleged deserters were charged which, if true, were outrageous. William Rodgers, who was arrested in Baltimore on October 27, 1864, reported that a gag was forced into his mouth—a detail not mentioned in his first statement—and that he was subjected to such maltreatment that, to escape further torture, he admitted to being a deserter. The second case was worse. Luke Riley, who was arrested as a

---

[33] Cincinnati *Gazette*, August 25, 1862.
[34] Ella Lonn, *Desertion during the Civil War* (New York, 1928), especially Chap. XVI.

deserter, claimed that he was subjected to nine cold drenchings a day when the temperature was down to zero and was held in solitary confinement on hard bread. He further charged that when he was transferred to Alexandria, he was knocked senseless by a revolver, handcuffed, strung to a chain suspended from the ceiling with his back bent, and for three days swung up and down every half hour. He had been in the country only six months and took pride in the fact that he could not be forced into renouncing his allegiance to Queen Victoria. After being sent to the headquarters of various regiments for identification, he was finally dispatched to the Ninth New York Cavalry.[35]

Much more serious and morally culpable than the rejection of legal exemptions, the rigid regulations as to evidence of foreign citizenship, the financial burdens imposed by the necessity of producing proof and witnesses, or even the coercion was the actual impressment and kidnapping of unwary foreigners newly arrived in our port cities or of Canadians who had dared to cross the border. This was the worst scandal of the war period, and, indeed, it remains one of the darkest blots on the history of the United States.

Before such a traffic can be intelligible, a brief explanation of the type of men who engaged in it is necessary. The very names applied to these men are offensive—"runners," "crimps," "bounty brokers." These men monopolized the business of seeking out and presenting volunteers and substitutes to recruiting officers, pocketing a handsome profit on the transactions. The broker stood to gain not only his brokerage fee of approximately $15 for each new recruit or $25 for each veteran (the fees varied from state to state and from time to time) but also whatever proportion of the huge bounty he could appropriate from the victim, this often amounting to as much as three fourths of the whole, or perhaps $600. These men covered the country in so well contrived and adroitly handled a network that it was seldom that a recruit or substitute entered the service except through their hands. The worst aspect of the situation was that there was considerable wrongdoing and corruption among the subordinates in the provost marshals' offices.[36]

The methods of these bounty brokers were as vile as their business. They seized indiscriminately upon sailors, foreign visitors, or aliens long

[35] For these two cases of cruelty, see Joseph H. Burnley to Seward, November 25, 1864, Notes from the British Legation, LXXIII, and *id.* to *id.*, December 1, 1864, *ibid.*

[36] This charge of corruption was made by Governor John Brough of Ohio, February 6, 1865. He was satisfied "that there is more or less corruption in at least one-half of the subordinate provost-marshalships of the States." *Official War Records*, Ser. 3, IV, p. 1150.

resident and pressed them into the army or navy as best suited their purposes. The diplomatic correspondence between Seward and the ministers of the various countries is full of complaints and countless instances of this despicable business. A few striking cases will sufficiently illustrate the techniques. One method of kidnapping grown men for the Union army followed a set pattern: the "runner" hung about the docks and taverns of the cities, on the watch for some unwary man, a sailor off a ship or some other stranger to the city; under the friendly offer of a glass of liquor—for he was always a good friend of his victim—he managed to hand him a drugged potion, which stupified him. When the man awoke, he found himself in the United States army or navy uniform, was told he had enlisted, and sometimes found a portion of his bounty money in his pocket, though usually the larger portion had vanished with his erstwhile friend. The practice of kidnapping and coercing British subjects began shortly after the opening of the war, but cases of drugging began to appear in the records only by 1863. Noteworthy is the fact that the British minister, Richard B. P. Lyons, reported to Seward on February 3, 1863, that a "practise" of kidnapping British subjects and forcing them into the army had "prevailed for some months in New York."

The story of one McGinis was simply that he landed at New York on the twenty-eighth of April, 1863, on his way to New Haven to reach some friends; and as it was too late for him to catch the boat to that point, he was obliged to spend the night in New York, where he fell in with some men and got drunk. In that state he was kidnapped by some soldiers, who took him to a recruiting office, insisted when he became sober that he had enlisted with them, and finally forced him to allow himself to be sworn into the service of the state of New York. Before long he found himself at New Bern, North Carolina, in the Third Regiment of the New York Cavalry.[37]

The case of Clark King engaged the warm efforts of the British consul, E. M. Archibald, at New York. On February 9, 1863, King "fell in" with some men who induced him to drink until he was in a state of gross intoxication. The fact that he was ill from the effects of the drink as he never had been before from too much liquor suggests that it had been drugged. He was taken to a recruiting rendezvous, where he signed enlistment papers while he was not in a condition competent to enter into such a contract. As soon as he recovered from his inebriation, he returned openly

---

[37] The case of McGinis was described in Lord Lyons' note of June 9, 1863, to Seward. Notes from the British Legation, LII.

to his daily work at the place where he had been employed for double the pay he was to receive as a soldier. His bounty money had, according to a receipt for $54 signed by King and witnessed by a W. Blake, been given him in the form of a due bill and been invested in an outfit for a seaman. His arrest a fortnight later for failure to report back for service was his wife's first intimation of his enlistment.[38]

William Whitehead had left a wife and four children in Manchester, England, to visit a brother in Ohio, whom he had not seen in eleven years. Upon his return to New York after his visit he was accosted by a man terming himself a recruiting officer, who drugged him and then enlisted him in the Tomkins Cavalry. It was possibly his good fortune that the surgeon rejected him because of rupture and varicose veins, but that did not save him from arrest later as a deserter and from detention for three months without pay.[39]

In other instances the runners did no drugging but resorted to bold, ruthless force. The case of James S. Bassett well illustrates this technique, and, because it shows the contemptible connivance of others, it will be told through Bassett's own words. He and a companion were attacked by five men on a New York street: "They immediately drew pistols, saying we had either to go with them or *die*. We suspected what they wanted us for, and told them we were British subjects. . . . We then resisted for about a quarter of an hour, but three of the men had clubs and commenced beating us very severely. We called for a policeman and saw one coming toward us, when one of the men went up, and said something to him, whereupon the officer of the law turned away. They then began to push and drag us, and we were obliged to give up to them. They attempted to take us to Brooklyn, but we again resisted, and, while struggling, a decently dressed man came up and told us that rather than see us so ill-treated, he would let us go into his room near by. After talking together a little while, they consented to let us go there, but as soon as we entered they locked the door and remained in the next room all night. . . . They then told us not to give in our right names, that we would soon get out, that

---

[38] Archibald wrote lengthily to Minister Lyons on this case on April 28, 1864, pointing out many details which made a voluntary enlistment seem improbable. His very sharp comment on Lieutenant McLeod Murphy, who had evidently investigated and written Archibald about this case, is worth recording: "Lieut. Murphy with a ruthlessness which he has displayed on similar occasions heretofore pronounces King's statement 'entirely false,' a statement in which a responsible, though humble man, asserts facts of which he himself was more competent to speak than any one else." *Ibid.*, LXIV.

[39] Memorandum dated August 10, 1863, *ibid.*, LIV.

when we got on the cars to return to the city, they would give us some money." Of course, the victims never saw them again, did not receive any bounty money, and lost their clothes and wages.[40]

Sailors seem especially to have been regarded as fair game. On November 12, 1862, William Gibbon got shore leave for twenty-four hours from the British steamship *Great Eastern*. The next day a man offered to take him to see some Englishmen at a naval rendezvous but instead lodged him in the Debtor's Gaol in New York City and denied him permission to communicate with anyone. Gibbon was then conveyed by a transport to Newport News, where the military officers tried to swear him in as a soldier. He hoped to escape through the fact that he had never signed a document, taken an oath, or accepted bounty money.[41]

One of the cases which seems especially dastardly was that of three colored men in the British navy from the Bahamas. According to the master of the British schooner *Mary Harris* of Nassau, the three men were allowed, as usual, to leave the boat in New York Harbor at noon on July 3, 1863. On shore two strangers induced them to drink with them; when the Bahamians attempted to leave, however, the strangers locked the doors, overpowered them, and took them aboard the *North Carolina*, the receiving ship for recruits. These terrified victims of foul play succeeded in getting word to the master of their vessel, who visited them on July 6 and then made an affidavit before Consul Archibald, who promptly brought the matter to the attention of Admiral Paulding of the United States Navy.[42]

Especially telling is a general statement made by Consul Archibald on March 3, 1864, concerning the crew of the wrecked vessel *Antonica*, twenty-six of whom were British subjects and had been confined in the county jail since mid-January because of being captured on a blockade-runner. These men complained of being constantly pestered by men trying to make them enlist in the naval or military service of the United States

---

[40] James S. Bassett to Archibald, February 28, 1864, from Riker's Island, *ibid.*, LXI.

[41] Lyons to Seward, December 3, 1862, *ibid.*, XLVII. The statement says he went ashore the "12th instant," which must refer to a preceding month; it seems reasonable to think that that was the last month preceding.

[42] Archibald to Paulding, July 8, 1863, *ibid.*, LIV. There are several instances of such kidnapping of colored seamen. For an example of one such kidnapping from the *Bounding Billow* in New York in October, 1864, see J. T. Brown to the British consul in New York, October 23, 1864, *ibid.*, LXXII; for another example of kidnapping, from the *Phoenix*, see Archibald to General Dix, February 7, 1865, *ibid.*, LXXVI.

and reported that they were informed that that was the only way in which they would be able to obtain their liberty.[43]

In the interior of the country there were, of course, cases of kidnapping with a slightly different technique. James Brown, residing in Cincinnati in 1862, was assured after examination before the provost marshal that as an alien his name would be removed from the list; however, three soldiers came to his house subsequently, and, refusing to pay any heed to his protests, would have dragged him away, had he not had a sore arm, on account of which they allowed him a respite of a few days. This did not prevent them from carrying off by force another British subject who happened to be with him, one Andrew Hardie. While Andrew McMillan, also a British subject, was on his way from Wisconsin to fulfill an engagement in Canada, he was arrested and kept in prison for fifteen days at Cleveland; there he was coerced into enlisting by a captain, who told him he must do so or be sent to Columbus and put at hard labor. He chose service in the One Hundred and Third Ohio Regiment. From Prince Edward Island came complaint of the coercion of John Trowsdale, a Canadian employed on an Illinois farm, into the Kentucky Brigade; a recruiting officer had encountered him on a train and forced him to enlist, not even allowing him time to collect the wages due him—some $150.[44]

Similar complaints of kidnapping and browbeating came from the ministers of most of the European countries—of France, Prussia, Belgium, Italy, Denmark, and Sweden. The correspondence with the French diplomatic officials shows some cases of kidnapping and coercion, chiefly of French seamen, but also cases of desertion from the French sea service, probably because of the larger monetary returns in the American service. The Prussian minister, Baron Friedrich von Gerolt, also had countrymen to rescue. Among the more interesting of these were Dr. Ferdinand Schafer, Charles Spierling, and Consul C. Kirchoff. The first-named came to America intending to practice medicine in a western state, but after his arrival in New York he felt that he might have an opportunity to perfect himself by experience in a military hospital. He was "swindled" into the ranks of the Forty-first New York Regiment by a German innkeeper and runner and was serving at Folly Island, South Carolina, when

[43] Archibald to Lyons, *ibid.*, LX.

[44] For Brown and Hardie, see Marsh to Seward, September 6, 1862, *ibid.*, XLV; for MacMillan, see Stuart to *id.*, September 6, 1862, *ibid.*; for Trowsdale, see letter from the Governor of Prince Edward Island to Lyons, April 6, 1862, *ibid.*, XLIV.

Von Gerolt secured his dismissal. Spierling was a German who had been drugged and enlisted into the First Connecticut Cavalry; although he escaped, he was recaptured and condemned to imprisonment for three years at Fort McHenry. This created a serious situation, as under Prussian law he must return at once to fight in the threatening Austro-Prussian War of 1866. C. Kirchoff had landed in California in September, 1850; on December 3 he had made a declaration of intention to become a citizen but had taken no further steps and in fourteen years had never exercised the franchise. By 1853, Prussia, Hamburg, and the Grand Duchy of Oldenburg had appointed him consul at San Francisco for those three states, whereupon he had renewed his allegiance to Oldenburg by signing a paper sent out for the purpose. Later he left for South America, but he was drafted in Hoboken upon his return, as the draft law of 1863 withdrew his exemption.[45]

When Guido von Grabow, chargé at the Prussian embassy, learned that a number of German immigrants had been lured into the army by the promise of $100 in gold (paid, however, in paper), he visited Gallop Island in Boston Harbor, where they were being detained. He then dispatched a sharp note to Seward on September 11, 1864, threatening serious consequences if these Germans were enlisted "by means contrary to good faith." He did not want the act repeated and hoped for a friendly settlement.[46]

The chief consequences with Prussia came at the close of the war, for that country pressed insistently for indemnities to its wronged subjects. One Jacob Rübel, who had been arrested as a deserter in Washington, on January 21, 1865, and several times subjected to the cold-water treatment to make him confess, claimed thereafter to be unable to work and acted deranged, according to a United States surgeon. Another, Martin Drier, subjected to the same treatment about the same time, confessed to deserting from a gunboat but became so ill that he had to go to a hospital. For these men, Von Gerolt demanded indemnity to the amount of $1,000 for Rübel, $500 for Drier, and $500 for a Frederick Ruschke, imprisoned for alleged desertion, with a covert threat that more would be asked if the health of the last two were impaired. It should be recorded that the Federal government did pay indemnities to these three men.[47]

[45] For Dr. Schafer, see Von Gerolt to Seward, February 15, 1864, Notes from the Prussian Legation, IV; for Spierling, see *id.* to *id.*, August 2, 1864, *ibid.*; for Kirchoff, see *id.* to *id.*, June 17, 1864, *ibid.*

[46] *Id.* to *id.*, September 11, 1864, *ibid.*

[47] The above information was gleaned from a note from Johann Nooski to the Prussian

It is worthy of note that naturalized German citizens tried to help their countrymen. At least one German paper published the names of Germans drawn for the Fifth Congressional District of Maryland in the draft of May, 1864. In Baltimore County 37 of the 546 names drawn sounded German. After the arrival of the emigrant ship from Hamburg in the spring of 1864 with laborers aboard who were diverted to the army, the German residents of Boston published a protest against all contracts of that type.[48]

The complaints with regard to illegal drafting of Italian subjects were of the same tenor and were all proffered by the envoy extraordinary of that country, Count Joseph Bertinatti; but all date after the passage of the first Federal draft law. The same tales of drugging and coercion appear. Antonio Cutormini, a seaman, was arrested as a deserter, drugged, and put into the Thirty-ninth New York at Petersburg. His utter helplessness is set forth by the ambassador's remark that the man could not defend himself in English. The fact that foreign-born shared in the nefarious traffic is illustrated by the case of Antonio Ferrari, who was falsely enticed by one Polini, leader of the "military music (band)" at Hart's Island, to enlist as a musician, only to find himself a private in a New York regiment. Because of a confusion of identities, Dominico Cavagnaro was drafted for a John Bassio. The experience of Joachim Gafferalli was more serious. Seaman in the First Marines of the Italian Bersaglieri, he found himself in the same situation that so many foreign sailors fell into. Lured to drink some liquor while on shore leave, he awoke to find himself at Folly Island, enrolled in the Fifty-fourth New York. Carabino Polidrotti was a humble organ-grinder who was arrested in October, 1864, as a suspected rebel; he was still languishing at Camp Chase in January, 1865.[49]

Probably the case most offensive to the envoy was that of P. E. Benzi, an officer of the Italian army; resigning his Italian post nine months before his unhappy experience, he went first to London and then to New York

---

minister, January 8, 1865, *ibid.*, V, and affidavits of Ruschke and Drier, January 22, 1865, and January 30, 1865, respectively, *ibid.*

[48] Baltimore *Der Deutsche Correspondent*, May 23, 1864; the fact of the protest of German residents in Boston appears in the note from Johann Nooski to the Prussian minister, January 8, 1865. Notes from the Prussian Legation, V.

[49] For Cutormini, see Minister Bertinatti to Seward, August 11, 1864, Notes from the Italian Legation, III; for Ferrari, *id.* to *id.*, October 26, 1864, *ibid.*; for Cavagnaro, *id.* to *id.*, October 7, 1863, *ibid.*; for Gafferalli, *id.* to *id.*, April 13, 1864, *ibid.*; for Polidrotti, *id.* to *id.*, January 3, 1865, *ibid.*, IV. Note that all except one of these letters are dated within the last two years of the war.

in the hope of a commission in the United States Army but was prevented from obtaining one by his lack of command of English. He was preparing to return to Italy when two men offered to take him to Montreal to secure him a post as private secretary to a rich merchant. The usual drinking and drugging followed, with the result that he was soon Carlo Gianotti, by his own signature, in the First Connecticut Heavy Artillery. General Ferrero advised appeal to his ambassador.[50]

The cases complained of by the Scandinavian ministers, W. von Raasloff for Denmark and Count Piper for Sweden, add little that is new. Several of the men pressed into the Union service were Danish seamen coerced into the Union naval service. The search revealed very few complaints from Swedish subjects. Count Piper secured a permit for a vice-consul of Sweden and Norway at Boston to visit four Swedish subjects confined in Fort Warren; later the report made by the vice-consul was forwarded by Count Piper to Seward.[51]

The proximity of Canada to the United States led to violations of Canadian neutrality in various ways by the more vicious of the enrolling officers and bounty brokers. Canadians resident in the States became victims,[52] and just as there was disguised recruiting in European countries, so recruiting under one guise or another occurred in Canada. The questions of the abuse of the neutrality of Canadians within the United States and of the violation of the border are so interlocked that it seems wise to deal with the wile, force, and imposition practiced on Canadian citizens once and for all in this chapter.

The first cases of coercion and kidnapping of Canadians to come to light occurred in 1862, with the mistreatment of John Roge, who had come from Canada to the United States in 1862. At Portland, Maine, he met a party of men who asked him to enlist and on his refusal forced him to go to their camp. They kept him three days until the arrival of the com-

---

[50] Id. to id., February 20, 1865, ibid., IV.

[51] Illustrative cases are Johannes Ahlmann, seaman, Von Raasloff to Seward, November 5, 1861, Notes from the Danish Legation, III; and Jacob Johnson, seaman, captured on a blockade runner, id. to id., October 21, 1865, ibid. The data concerning the visit of the vice-consul to the Swedes confined at Fort Warren is found in Notes to the Swedish Legation, VI, 136–37, 138. The report of the vice-consul, forwarded by Count Piper, appears in Notes from the Swedish Legation, July 1, 1864, IV.

[52] Almost at once, the newspapers of Montreal complained of forced enlistments—even into the famous Sixth Massachusetts Militia. This is based on a statement in the New York Courrier des États-Unis, May 1, 1861. This can hardly be taken seriously, in view of the thousands of volunteers who had to be rejected in the first months of the war.

manding officer, who tried to swear him in. Upon his flat refusal, he was thrown into the guardhouse; after a month's confinement he was induced "through cold and misery" to enlist in the regiment, which proved to be the Seventh Maine Infantry. When transferal to Washington gave him an opportunity to escape, he deserted, only to be arrested and put in prison, where he had been languishing for nearly six months by the time the British embassy brought his case before Seward.[53]

There is no point in piling up instance after instance of drugging, kidnapping, and coercion. More is to be gained by discussion of the way in which the frontier was violated and the tactics boldly pursued on alien soil. Stated in the words of Governor General Monck of Canada to Lord Lyons, the enormity of the offense stands out in its nakedness: "These papers appear to establish the fact that a serious violation of British Territory was committed by a Party of United States soldiers who crossed the frontier armed and in uniform, entered a house in the township of Wolfe Island in Canada West and thence forcibly carried off a man named Ebenezer Tyler." On January 8, 1863, a party of four men in United States uniform crossed the frontier. On March 9, the Governor General reported that he had heard that Tyler had been seen confined as a deserter in Watertown, New York.[54] A similar case was reported by a Peter Needham who wrote to Lord Lyons from Irving Block Prison in Memphis, Tennessee, that he had been kidnapped from his own home in Canada on August 18, 1863, by Americans, who had gagged him and removed him during the night; that he had ever since been detained as a prisoner; and that at the time of his writing he was chained to the floor with a chain only two feet long.[55]

The greater number of complaints dealt, however, with the luring of Canadians across the border by false promises of work at high wages. A few of the many cases will suffice to point the fact. Richard Malone was represented as the victim of fraud by parties who engaged him, along with "many other young men of the city" of Montreal, to work as a laborer in the mines of Lake Superior. When the Canadians reached their supposed destination, they were told that there was no work for them in the mines

[53] Burnley to Seward, December 10, 1864, Notes from the British Legation, LXXIV.

[54] The affidavits which Governor Monck stated that he was sending in connection with his report seem to be missing.

[55] Lyons to Seward, December 31, 1863, *ibid.*, LVII. Although Needham was arrested on the charge of obtaining money from the Adams Express Company at Vicksburg, it is difficult to regard his case as other than a kidnapping.

and that their only recourse was to enlist in the United States Army.[56] In the fall of 1863, Clark E. Lloyd, a blacksmith by trade who had a wife and seven young children in Montreal, fell into company with a person representing himself as the agent of a railroad company in the United States, offering Lloyd steady employment with good wages, and promising that there was no danger of any British subject being "draughted" into the army. Lloyd was tempted into going to the States, where he was drugged by a recruiting agent and induced to enlist.[57]

French-Canadians speaking only their own patois were even more helpless. Two Canadians, whose real names were Dasité and Maxime Millette, were hired in Canada by an American to chop wood; but when they reached a point near Concord, New Hampshire, they were enlisted in the army under false names. On the same date that he reported the case of these two youths (April 2, 1864), Lyons reported to Seward that thirteen men, all with French names, had been brought over the border, ostensibly to cut wood but actually to be drugged and put into the Second New Hampshire Volunteers.[58]

The last case to be here cited is that of James Fitzgerald, who landed in Quebec from India on August 1, 1863, and wandered on to Montreal in search of work. There he signed a contract for six months labor on a railroad and accompanied his "employer" to Burlington, near which place he understood he was to be employed. His employer left him at a hotel, but when he returned it was with a man in uniform, to whom Fitzgerald was presented as a deserter. The defense given by the supposed employer for his use of such underhand tactics was that he was only doing his duty in getting a recruit out of Canada any way he could. When the victim produced a certificate proving his recent return from India, the provost marshal promised to help him out but left him in the charge of a guard, who threatened to shoot if he attempted to escape. That evening the provost marshal returned and, with fair words, proposed a drink "to kill the time." The victim accepted the drink from one he thought a friend, with the usual consequences—unconsciousness and awakening in a guardhouse in the American uniform. When he told his tale, the officer

[56] The petition of the father to Secretary of War Stanton for his son's release was dated August 7, 1863. A similar petition was sent by Francis Xavier Gunther for his son Joseph. See *ibid.*, LV.

[57] Lyons to Seward, November 18, 1863, *ibid.*, LVI.

[58] The affidavit of the father affirmed that the younger of the youths was not yet eighteen. *Id.* to *id.*, April 2, 1864, *ibid.*, LXII. The instance of the thirteen men appears in the same volume.

advised him to say no more about it, "if I did not want to get a hole in my jacket." When he could get no redress, he wrote to Ambassador Lyons, but the letter was opened and brought the threat that a second such letter would keep "him from writing for some time." He was then sent to a Maine regiment in the Army of the Potomac. Despairing of redress after repeated efforts, he deserted, "if it could be called such." He was rearrested, tried by court-martial, and, despite his written defense, dishonorably discharged from the army. He then was sent to Fort Delaware and told that he must go to Dry Tortugas for the period of the war.[59]

Complaints began to be heard as early as the fall of 1861, about a Lieutenant Colonel William C. Davies of the Second Michigan Cavalry— "If, indeed," one writer added, "he holds the rank in the service of the United States which he professes to do"—who was distributing handbills calling for five hundred "young men of good habits and character accustomed to farm labour and the care of Horses," to whom steady work at good wages was offered—"$13 a month and upwards, with good board and clothing," and traveling expenses to Detroit upon the duly certified statement of a railroad agent at the point of departure. The similarity of pecuniary returns to those offered at that time by the army could hardly escape Canadian authorities. The handbill was signed by J. N. Tillman and was being circulated broadcast by mail; eight hundred copies were distributed in Hamilton alone, and it did not pass unremarked that Lieutenant Colonel Davies had been seen in uniform in Hamilton (which is only seventy miles north of Buffalo) only a few days earlier. Furthermore, it was charged that he was there, "according to his own confession, to offer Capt. Villiers of the Field Battery, a major's rank and $200 a month." [60]

Naturally, the advertisements in the papers, the handbills, the tales of the kidnapping and the enticing of men to the United States, combined with the lure of high wages attracting labor from Canada, could not fail to disturb Canadian officials and editors. The Quebec *Daily News* did not mince words in mid-August, 1863:

[59] James Fitzgerald to Lord Lyons, Fort Jefferson, Florida, December, 1864, *ibid.*, LXXIV. Dry Tortugas, a barren isle south of Florida which was being used as a Federal military post, was to American prisoners a synonym of desolation.

[60] The above charge is made in a letter from Edmund Neal to Lord Lyons, October 10, 1861. He sent a copy of a letter from Lieutenant Colonel Bowder of the Canadian militia at Hamilton: "I shall be obliged if Your Lordship will call the attention of the United States Government to the conduct of the person calling himself Lt. Colonel Davies. . . ." The writer declared that Colonel Davies "made no secret of his purpose." *Ibid.*, XLII.

An advertisement appears in today's paper calling for 500 laborers to work on the Great Western Railway, Ohio. The wages offered is $1.25 per diem. We do not think that the party who brought this advertisement to our office would willingly lend himself as a recruiting sergeant in Canada for Uncle Sam, but we deem it our duty nevertheless to put the laboring classes on their guard against being caught in any such trap. There are plenty of laborers idle in the large cities of the Northern States who would be willing to work on the terms offered, and therefore we look upon the demand for laborers from this section as only a ruse to catch substitutes for unwilling conscripts. When those who may go are conveyed into the centre of the State of Ohio, they will be too far removed from home and friends to seek redress.

The newspaper then reminded its readers of the experience of some laborers from Ottawa who had been inveigled by a contractor named McDonnell into the States, drugged, and put into the Northern army uniform, and whose claims of British citizenship brought only ill usage. The editor then threatened to publish the name of the person inserting the advertisement in that day's issue.[61]

The Quebec *Chronicle* not a great deal later stated baldly with regard to items in the French papers, "It would appear from the statements of several of our French Canadian contemporaries, that the steady and continuous drain upon the rural population of Lower Canada has commenced to assume alarming proportions. The *Journal de St. Hyacinth* [a town near Montreal], in a recent issue, alludes to the fact of a very large number of active young men leaving that town and the surrounding parishes, in order to obtain, in the United States, a market for their labor." [62] The Montreal *Transcript* expressed alarm over the loss not only of the French element but also of the English-speaking population. The writer expressed, moreover, his belief that most men went to replace the American laborers who had been drained off to the war but frankly stated that he personally was not aware of emigration to such an extent as was claimed.[63]

---

[61] Quebec *Daily News*, August 18, 1863. This is found with Dispatch No. 73 from the United States consul at Quebec. Consular Dispatches, Quebec, I. This newspaper is not otherwise available in this country.

[62] It was impossible to determine the exact date of this clipping, sent by the consul at Quebec with his Dispatch No. 132 (undated), but it was obviously after August 20, 1863, the date of his Dispatch No. 73. It was also after December 13, as appears from Note 63. (Neither of these papers is available in this country.)

[63] Montreal *Transcript*, December 13, 1863. This clipping was sent with Consular Dispatch No. 132 from Quebec by Consul Charles Ogden. Consular Dispatches, Quebec, I.

The matter then received an airing in the lower house of the Canadian legislature on September 7, 1863, on the day when Lord Lyons on a visit attended a session. One member sought information from the government in relation to organized recruiting in Montreal for the United States Army. He held in his hand a placard, which he had been told had been widely circulated in Montreal, stating that two hundred men were wanted for government service in the United States, to whom $200 would be paid at once and who would ultimately receive $500 in addition to clothing and pay. Applicants were invited to apply at Ogdensburg, New York, where they would be inspected. Another speaker also reminded the house that Canadians had been offered work at high wages in the States, but, that the road to employment lay through New York, where the deluded workers had often in the past been forced to enlist in the army. Members were reminded that the Foreign Enlistment Act and the Queen's Proclamation of 1861 made it a misdemeanor to enter another country to enlist. The proper minister promised that care would be taken to detect and punish such infringements of the law.[64]

Charles Ogden, United States consul at Quebec, had already made on August 20, 1863, in regard to the advertisements for laborers which had so exercised the press of that city, a report worth quoting: "I deem it right to place upon record in the state department, my investigation relative to this and similar advertisements for laborers, farm hands, etc, that have appeared from time to time, as the necessities of the advertiser required; as the daily papers have often warned the people of Canada from engaging with said advertising parties, insinuating and in some instance, openly stating that they were federal recruiting agents in disguise. I have yet to find that any one party or parties, were in any way direct or remote, engaged with any recruiting service in any state of the union." In this particular case, he added, the principal contractor upon the railway under construction was a former member of Parliament; the subcontractor, chief engineer, and chief superintendent were all residents of Canada (except when engaged upon similar enterprises) and had no intention of renouncing their allegiance to the British realm.[65]

Meanwhile, however, a refutation of the charges of dishonest advertising—by the contractor who had inserted the advertisement for the labor-

[64] Consul Ogden, in reporting to Seward the situation in Canada, gave a résumé of the parliamentary session of September 7, with the substance of the speeches and names of the speakers. It was pointed out how difficult it was to trace persons placarding a city by stealth. Enclosure No. 1, Dispatch No. 82, September 10, 1863, *ibid.*

[65] Ogden to Seward, August 20, 1863, *ibid.*, No. 73.

ers for the Atlantic and Great Western Railroad Company of Ohio in the papers of August 18—had appeared in the daily journals: "I now offer to furnish a free ticket to the works and back, and also pay the parties' time, if any man in Quebec who is of standing will agree to go to the works and give a truthful statement of the whole matter on his return. I will deposit $100 in the hand of any gentlemen in Quebec to bind me in the above, provided any other person in that City will stake the same amount. I will also deposit a like amount if any British subject has been forced or drafted off the works or been induced by any person in the employ of the Company, to enlist in the Northern army. The last amount to be paid to any charitable institution in the City." [66]

Deplorable as were all of the instances of kidnapping, there were certain types of cases which were truly pitiable. Among these were a number of old British soldiers and sailors. It would seem that David Brooks, for twenty-one years in the British army, an outpensioner of Chelsea Hospital, was entrapped while en route to Canada and sent to the Forty-first New York at Folly Island off the South Carolina coast. The state of mind of these old soldiers still loyal to the British flag is well exemplified by Brooks's letter to Lord Lyons: "My Lord it is out of my power to give you an idea of my anxieties and trouble of mind during the four months I was on the island [Folly Island] without my Papers. A thousand times I conjured up the infamy that would be attached to me and my family when it should be reported at home that I deserted my flag after nearly twenty-two years faithful service in the field and camp as my discharge can certify." [67] John Crozier Lloyd was discharged on January 3, 1856, from the British army after eight years in the Eleventh Regiment of Hussars. About the end of January, 1863, while intoxicated, he was enlisted at Buffalo into the Ira Harris Cavalry and taken to Staten Island. Though he applied repeatedly to his superior officer for permission to see the British consul, he was insultingly refused. He was denied a discharge even though he held from a British regimental surgeon a certificate of disability caused by injury to his leg. On one occasion when he tried to escape to see his consul, he was, he asserted, tied by the thumbs for eleven hours. He also claimed certain knowledge that there were at least two hundred British

[66] This appeared in the *Journal de St. Hyacinthe*, September 4, 1863, and also in the *Canadian Journal and News*, presumably on the same date. Ogden does not state whether the latter paper was published at Quebec or elswhere.

[67] Lyons to Seward, June 5, 1864, Notes from the British Legation, LXIV.

subjects in the same regiment enlisted under similar circumstances.[68] Another case is that of Thomas C. Cannon, who had served in the Crimean War and was entrapped in Albany en route to Troy, where he meant to seek work as a stonemason. One glass with two soldiers proved his undoing, for he awoke in a police-station cell. Despite his protests that he was a British subject and still liable to military service if called up, he was examined by a doctor, escorted under guard to barracks, and finally sent to Newport News. Because he refused to perform any duty, ill-treatment was his portion.[69] The plight of Patrick McCann, another old soldier enlisted under the usual deplorable conditions, engaged the attention of such high British officials as the Secretary for Foreign Affairs and the Field Marshal Commander in Chief of the British Army.[70]

The entrapping of grown men by the various tricks of the runners is enough of a blot on our history; the entrapping of minors, sometimes mere lads, is something over which the historian must blush. The number so enlisted and brought to the attention of the State Department, when the enrollment of American sons under twenty-one except with the consent of their parents or guardians was illegal, is appalling. Of the hundreds of instances reported to Seward, a few of the most glaring will be presented. In the first place, it is necessary to know what legal basis foreign parents had on which to claim for their sons the right to discharge from the army. The point of departure was the Act of 1850, under which the Secretary of War was to order the discharge of any soldier under twenty-one years of age upon evidence of enlistment without the consent of parent or guardian. General War Order No. 14 of August 28, 1854, embodied the opinion of the Attorney General and would exclude minors whose parents or guardians were not domiciled in the United States.

The question arose early with Great Britain, for although the American

---

[68] Deposition of John Crozier Lloyd, *ibid.*, XLIX. The number may be an exaggeration, but that there were many Britishers in the regiment is amply testified to by the Descriptive Books of the Ira Harris Cavalry (There were three regiments of cavalry of this name—the Fifth, Sixth, and Twelfth New York Cavalry). Angus McDonald was one member of Company E whose physical qualifications left much to be desired: his one leg was lame, one arm was stiff from a broken bone, and he was suffering from tuberculosis! *Ibid.*

[69] Lyons to Seward, January 24, 1863, *ibid.*, LXVIII. He was put into Company B, Fourth Regiment (the One Hundred and Seventy-fifth) of Corcoran's legion. He was seized October 11, 1862.

[70] When Seward reported that the discharge of McCann was not recommended, Lyons intimated the interest which the case was arousing in England. *Id.* to *id.*, June 5, 1864, *ibid.*, LXIV.

Secretary of War refused to assent to the discharge of minors who had enlisted without due consent of parents or guardians, Lord Lyons held the belief that he was entitled to claim such discharges; by October 10, 1861, he had already made numerous applications for discharges, and by December 9 he had sent a list of nearly a hundred British minors enlisted in the Union army.[71] Some anxious parents besieged Lord Lyons with distressing letters, and others made long journeys to secure by their personal presence the discharge of their sons. Seward informed the British ambassador on December 11 that a discharge would be granted in each case where the proof was considered adequate. Lyons admitted later that discharges had, in general, been granted in all cases where sufficient evidence was adduced. However, Seward also stated that the President was about to ask for revision of the law; hence the Secretary of State would not take up any new cases until the legislation had been considered. In fact, Congress did on February 13, 1862, pass an act which relieved the Secretary of War from discharging minors. Lyons, however, continued to press for the release of minors who had enlisted before the new act had come into operation.[72] He accordingly pressed for the release of Richard Lambert, aged sixteen, who had been for more than three years at the Wesleyan Collegiate School at Dublin and, without the knowledge of his father, had left school in July, 1862, to join a ship at Liverpool for California. Before long the father learned that his son was serving as a common sailor aboard the United States frigate *Narragansett*—a post, as his father felt, utterly unsuited to his education and family status. Influence counted in this case, as it usually does; thus, when Lord Russell, Minister of Foreign Affairs, brought pressure to bear on the British ambassador, the United States acted promptly to release Richard Lambert.[73]

The respect which the British held for American law, however much they may secretly have disagreed with that law, did not extend to the kidnapping and coercion of British minors. The case of Richard Doherty from West Canada is interesting because of the extreme youth of the "soldier." He had entered Oberlin College and enlisted under "undue pressure," his father, Captain Doherty, felt. As the son was only fourteen

[71] See the communications of Lyons to *id.*, November 4, 1861, *ibid.*, XLII and December 9, 1861, *ibid.*, XLIII. See Volume XLIII for the amended list of British minors with the regiments in which they were serving.

[72] *Id.* to *id.*, May 24, 1862, *ibid.*, XLIV.

[73] *Id.* to *id.*, April 30, 1863, *ibid.* Seward had acted before May 5, 1863, for that is the date on which Lord Lyons thanked the Navy Department for the "obliging readiness in the discharge of Richard Lambert." *Ibid.*

years old, the father refused consent for his enrollment and sent the boy's mother to camp at Cleveland to bring him back home. The officers and men at the camp evaded her questions, denying any knowledge of the lad, so that it was by accident that she discovered him. Fearing efforts to detain him, she did not deliver the affidavits of his age, which she felt would be useless, but induced him to go off at once with her. The father wanted a regular discharge to obviate the possibility of the son's arrest as a deserter in the event of his ever returning to America.[74] The fact of such discharge does not appear, but obviously the son reached his home in Canada.

A particularly aggravated case was that of Michael Quinn, seventeen, who had in January, 1863, emigrated from Ireland with his sister-in-law to Portland, Maine, en route to San Francisco. As the sum advanced by a brother was not sufficient for the fare of both, they agreed that the sister-in-law should go on and Michael should remain in New York until more money arrived from the brother. Enticed by an offer of work from some runners, he accompanied them to a rendezvous, where he changed his clothes, evidently for a uniform, and was taken to the receiving ship *North Carolina* to serve as a seaman. He managed to get a note to his uncle, John Quinn, who visited him and brought the facts to the attention of the British consul on February 4, 1863; the consul wrote to Admiral Hiram Paulding, who in turn referred the matter to the Secretary of the Navy. An order from the Navy Department directing a thorough examination did not prevent Quinn's being conveyed to Cairo, Illinois, to join the Western Flotilla. Before arriving at that point, he leaped from the train while chained to another man and was seriously injured. An Illinois farmer and a physician gave him harborage and medical attention. After he recovered from his injuries, he returned to New York, where he made a full statement to the consul before he carried out his original plan to go to California. Consul Archibald's plea for an indemnity was supported by Lyons with an appeal to the "benevolence and compassion not less than to the justice of the government." [75]

[74] Captain Doherty to Lyons, November 20, 1862, *ibid.*, XLVII, and Lyons to Seward, November 7, 1862, *ibid.*

[75] The soldier to whom he was chained escaped injury because the handcuff was slipped over his hand. For the details of this case, see Deposition of John Quinn at New York, February 4, 1863, *ibid.*, XLIX; letter of Jeremiah Pittinger, Illinois farmer, to Henry Ward (the man with whom Quinn stayed while in New York), Salem, Illinois, February 25, 1863, *ibid.*; and Archibald to Lyons, March 12, 1863, *ibid.* See also letter of Archibald to Lyons, July 8, 1863, *ibid.*, LIII.

The case of Samuel Tillotson will serve to show how inadequate was the action of reviewing boards on these cases. A mother came all the way from Bowmansville, Canada, to Boston in search of her fifteen-year-old son. A resident of Boston had decoyed the boy from home by telling him that his uncle had found work for him in Buffalo and had arranged for his expenses to that point. In Buffalo there was, of course, no uncle; but the plot broke down when the youth refused the proffered drink. The man then threatened him with arrest if he did not at once repay the travel expenses. This inevitably led to the suggestion of enlistment as the alternative. The mother succeeded in getting an inquiry ordered at Fort Independence, but before the inquiry could be made, the lad had been sent on to the Army of the Potomac. The mother found her son at Fort Independence on October 4. Here more tricks were played. The lieutenant colonel, to vindicate the recruiting officer, secured from the lad an affidavit that he had been accompanied to Buffalo by his guardian, but the fact still remained that an oath under durance was void. When the Board finally met, its members found that Private Tillotson was, in their opinion, fully seventeen years of age. The examination was made without the knowledge of those acting for the mother, no witnesses were called, no testimony was introduced, and the proceeding did not, in the opinion of Hanson Hawley, who acted for the mother, "rise to the dignity of a decent farce." When Hawley asked a Board member on what evidence the Board had based its opinion, the member replied with a smile that they had judged only by the boy's appearance. To the credit of Hawley, it must be added that he wrote Governor Andrew and tried to get some redress for the lad and his mother.[76]

The number of cases of enlistment of French minors presented to the Department of State by the French minister at Washington amounted to only twenty-seven for enlistments dating from September 25, 1861.[77] Particularly touching, however, is the case of a French lad whose story has come to us from Confederate sources. An officer of the Southern army heard a lamenting cry, "O! Mon Dieu! Mon Dieu!" which proved to come from a French boy who did not appear to be over seventeen years of age. He had been inveigled into enlisting in the Northern army, had been put in the cavalry, and was in the front line with his captain when ordered to charge. He soon found that the rest of the company had been cut off,

[76] Hanson Hawley to Governor John Andrew, October 15, 1864, *ibid.*, LXXIII.
[77] Notes from the French Legation (scattered through Vol. VI).

so that he and the captain were surrounded by the enemy. Because he did not understand the demand to surrender he continued to slash with his saber until he received a serious scalp wound. One of his captors spoke enough French to understand the boy. The writer added, "I think the boy would have died of fright and grief or become insane if it had not been for us." [78]

The carelessness in impressing feeble-minded and insane persons was beyond belief. The case of Cornelius Garvin, whose British mother spent six weeks in a journey from camp to camp in Virginia in search of her only son, affords a striking illustration of the ills stemming from such wrongdoing. The boy was sold as a substitute in September, 1863, by the heartless keeper of the asylum at Troy, New York. Before the order for his release reached Riker's Island, he had been sent to Alexandria and thence to various stations; but no trace of him could be found after February 14, 1864, when he was being drilled in the Fifty-second New York Regiment. His case attracted the attention of General John A. Dix, who was anxious to discover the parties to the villainy, including the medical examiners. The mother testified that once before he had been induced to enter the military service but had been discharged. This was not the only case of insane persons being accepted in the army.[79]

The reader will be interested in knowing how many cases of kidnapping and coercion of one sort or another and how many cases of illegal drafting (drafting done on the basis of technicalities or by arbitrary action of draft boards) there were. The reader will recall that Lord Lyons sent in almost a hundred complaints in behalf of British nationals in the fall of 1861. A count of all the cases which were discussed in Seward's correspondence with the various diplomatic representatives does not yield unassailable figures, since there were cases of impressment which never came through to the ambassadors because of inability to make contact or despair of ever escaping from the net. For what the figures may be worth, it may be stated that the British legation presented some 235 cases; the French, 50; the Italian, 22; the Scandinavian, 11; and the German, a negligible number. On so large a scale did impressments occur that the careful reader of

[78] Frederick W. Wild, *Memoirs and History of Capt. F. W. Alexander's Baltimore Battery of Light Artillery, U.S.V.* (Baltimore, 1912), 92–93.

[79] Acting Consul Pierrepont Edwards, at New York, to Lyons, October 15, 1863, Notes from the British Legation, LV; Archibald to *id.*, March 28, 1864, *ibid.*, LXII; for the case of John S. Sturgis, see Lyons to Seward, May 19, 1864, *ibid.*, LXIV; for the case of Jeremiah Barrett, see Barrett to Lyons, March 30, 1864, *ibid.*, LXXIV.

Seward's correspondence, incoming and outgoing, on this one subject marvels that Seward had time to attend to any of the other duties incident to the secretaryship of state.

The vast majority of the United States officials were upright men, condemning such vile practices when they were brought to their attention. We have seen the attitude of General Dix in the case of the insane British subject. General N. J. Jackson wrote on January 28, 1864, concerning the treatment of the Britisher James Murphy, "This is a most aggravated case, [sic] the rascality it discloses among recruiting Parties is shameful." [80] A head surgeon of the Forty-seventh New York Regiment urged a British subject to lay his case before Lord Lyons and promised the Britisher to furnish additional information concerning his drugged condition upon arrival if it should be desired.[81] Likewise, the assistant surgeon at Camp Bradford near Baltimore reported to the British consul at New York fully on three colored men from St. Vincent's who had been kidnapped from the *Bounding Billow* and put in as substitutes. The commander of the receiving ship *Vermont,* at the Navy Yard in New York, wrote Admiral Paulding, suggesting that the Britisher Francis Ashton, who had been arrested aboard a British merchant schooner as a deserter and delivered to the *Vermont,* be discharged.[82] The difficulty almost always lay with the subordinate enrolling officers; with the low "crimps," who made the profits from delivering recruits and robbing them of a large part of the bounty; and with the police, against whom the evidence is overwhelming. Governor John Brough of Ohio was convinced that at least one half of the subordinate provost marshals were involved in the corrupt dealings, it will be recalled.

It is apparent that knowledge of the traffic had percolated through to high officials by the close of the war. Indicative of this fact is a letter from an assistant provost marshal to Colonel John Ely in relation to three colored men from the *Phoenix* who enlisted under false names: "As complaints of this kind had been made in several instances in the cases of colored men in filling a former draft, we have been very careful to question every colored man brought to this officer, and did so with these men. . . . I have ascertained the names of the runners who brought the men from

---

[80] General N. J. Jackson, quoted by Lyons in his letter to Seward, January 28, 1864, *ibid.,* LIX.

[81] Ebenezer East to Lyons, from Hilton Head, South Carolina, March 2, 1864, *ibid.,* LXI.

[82] J. T. Brown, assistant surgeon at Camp Bradford, October 23, 1864, to the British consul at New York, *ibid.,* LXXII; Commander of the *Vermont* to Admiral Paulding, *ibid.,* LXXVI (letter undated).

New York, and they can be arrested whenever an order is given to that effect." Colonel Ely had the colored men detained and also arrested the men concerned in the enlistment and held them to bail in the sum of $1,000. General Dix then sent all the papers in his office relating to the case to the Adjutant General and a report to Consul Archibald.[83] Even then there had been variation in the stories of the men to Archibald and in Colonel Ely's report from the provost marshal at Elizabeth, New Jersey. By the spring of 1864, reporters and editors of the daily metropolitan papers were alert to the situation and were printing frequent notices of the unlawful proceedings. General Dix sent a report on the outrage to the legislature of New York. It is a commentary on human nature that these contemptible men, relatively few in numbers, should add to the burdens of upright leaders at the head of the state.

There were, of course, some discharges of foreign subjects wrongfully impressed into the military service, though these occurred in smaller numbers than the modern citizen could wish. There were also, on the other hand, refusals to discharge foreign subjects and interminable delays and evasions, partly owing, no doubt, to the exigencies of war. Secretary Cameron set the example in the first October of the war by denying all of the requests for discharges, which were "daily pouring in from various quarters, and which multiply with the encouragement given by each fresh discharge." [84] The British ambassador received little satisfaction from the State Department. In the period from October 28, 1862, to April 23, 1864, there went from the British legation no less than twenty-two inquiries about British subjects, apparently without tangible results.[85] Delays occurred even after a discharge had been granted. For instance, Seward notified Lord Lyons of the discharge of a Canadian minor in the Third Wisconsin Regiment on March 7, 1863; almost six months later, on August 25, 1863, the father wrote Lord Lyons that an officer had informed his son that there was no order for his discharge.[86]

[83] Captain W. M. Shipman, assistant provost marshal at Elizabeth, to Colonel John Ely, January 17, 1865, ibid., LXXVI.

[84] Secretary of War Cameron to Seward, Official War Records, Ser. 3, I, p. 563. Cameron specifically refers to discharges requested by Lord Lyons, which, he regretted, "It is not in my power to accede to."

Seward used much more diplomatic language to Lord Lyons. He regretted "that in obedience to a rule which it was necessary to adopt, he [the Secretary of War] is unable to grant the discharge." Notes to the British Legation, IX, 13.

[85] Notes from the British Legation, XLVIII and XLIX.

[86] Chargé d'Affaires Stuart to Seward, September 7, 1863, ibid., XLV. The person in question was William Alexander Doyle, who had enlisted under the name of John Doyle.

Long and inexplicable periods elapsed without action being taken. Lord Lyons complained that three months had elapsed without action since he had made application for the release of Robert Cooper; that James Mac-Hugh was not free two months after the Military Commission had recommended his release; and that Richard S. Lee was not free one month after the Secretary of the Navy had sent the order for his discharge. Seward stated on May 18, 1864, that Charles Lamb had been discharged, but the British consul at Philadelphia reported on June 8, 1864, his capture in the battles in Virginia. His discharge came too late, for on December 21, the same consul reported his death at Andersonville on August 18.[87] Neal McMonigal and Michael King, who claimed the right to exemption as aliens, were sent to Morris Island and then to the rendezvous in Philadelphia, where they were detained in prison five weeks without action, awaiting Seward's decision. Where an order from the War Department for the return of men to headquarters was not followed up by an explicit order to proceed with an investigation, such men remained prisoners. McMonigal was finally released early in May, 1864, after detention since mid-January; however, King was still being detained on June 7, 1864.[88]

In view of the multitude of charges of drugging and swearing in of the victim without his knowledge, it is difficult to feel that the lower recruiting officers had always been as careful as two at the Cherry Street rendezvous in New York professed to have been: the surgeon declared that it was his invariable rule never to make examinations when the men were intoxicated; Henry Laler, acting master, wrote that he did not hesitate to say that the statement of a William Smith that he was shipped " 'without his knowledge or consent' was wholly and utterly untrue." [89] Certainly, there has been in these pages much evidence of connivance of the city police in New York with the "crimps."

Seward himself, in the face of the preoccupation of the Secretary of War with military problems and the lack of decisions on many cases, had to be noncommittal, merely stating that the case had been referred to the War or Navy Department, sometimes promising a prompt investigation,

---

[87] For Cooper, see Lyons to Seward, June 15, 1864, *ibid.*, LXV; for MacHugh, see *id.* to *id.*, April 28, June 5, 1864, *ibid.*, LXIV; for Lee, see *id.* to *id.*, June 4, 1864, *ibid.*, LXIV; for Lamb, see *id.* to *id.*, June 8, 1864, *ibid.*, LXIV; and Consul Charles E. Kortright to Burnley, December 9, 21, 1864, *ibid.*, LXXIV. Much correspondence followed as late as March 30, 1865, with regard to an allowance to the mother of Charles Lamb.

[88] Kortright to Lyons, February 26, 1864, *ibid.*, LX. For release of McMonigal, see *id.* to *id.*, June 7, 1864, *ibid.*, LXV.

[89] Report of Captain Oscar Bulles, Recruiting Officer at Cherry Street Rendezvous, *ibid.*, LXI.

sometimes saying that the case had been "submitted to the favorable consideration" of the Secretary of the Navy or of the War Department.

Sometimes the alien was guilty of neglecting to mention pertinent facts in his affidavit to his consul. John Jones, whom the consul had reported as kidnapped on January 21, 1864, into the De Kalb Regiment, failed to mention that he belonged to the British Fourth Regiment of Lancashire Militia and that it was his duty to present himself at the beginning of the next month for twenty-eight days of drill, in default of which action he would be considered a deserter; also he did not add that he had a wife and family in England entirely dependent upon him. Lord Lyons had to come trailing along with this information three months later.[90] Furthermore, the government had to be constantly alert to false representations by persons seeking to evade service.

Some exemptions, discharges, and even reparations remain to be noted. On the whole, as would be expected, it was in the matter of discharging minors that the government was the most co-operative.

On September 24, 1861, orders for the release of a British minor, Thomas Sinclair, from the Sixth New Jersey Regiment were issued. Three days later Seward sent notice of the discharge of two Irish lads. On April 18, 1862, he again notified Lord Lyons of the discharge of a number of British minors.[91] Likewise, record exists of the discharge of several French subjects who were minors.[92] The search revealed, of course, discharges of other aliens of various nationalities, but, as indicated by the diplomatic correspondence, they certainly were not numerous; in fact, there is a striking difference between the number of alien subjects represented as impressed into the service as compared with the number released. Only nine French subjects, in addition to those under age, have been noted as discharged. It is impossible to attempt to give any figures in connection with discharges of British subjects because of the indefiniteness of such statements as that made by Chargé d' Affaires Stuart when he acknowledged to Seward "the release of the *rest* of the British subjects who had been

[90] Letter to Seward, April 24, 1864, *ibid.*, LXIII.

[91] For these releases, see Seward to Lyons, September 24, 1861, Notes to the British Legation, IX, 8, 9; and Lyons to Seward, April 18, 1862, Notes from the British Legation, XLIV. In his letter Lyon calls attention to those who had not been released "through some error."

[92] This group was compiled by the author from communications of Seward to the French minister, Henri Mercier. They included the following: Alphonse Surgent, released October 21, 1862; Joseph Enderlin, released October 21, 1862; Gilbert Moise, applied for discharge January 30, 1863, released June 20, 1863; Émile Joseph Miget, discharged June 15, 1863; Leon Paul, applied July 14, 1863, discharged July, 1863; and Michel Weltz, discharged October 8, 1863. Notes to the French Legation, VII, 133, 231, 230, 236, 273, 216.

drafted in Pennsylvania." [93] Lyons, in writing to Seward about the kidnapping of Ebenezer Tyler from Canadian territory, said that the Governor General conveyed his cordial thanks through Lord Lyons "for the promptitude and for the ample redress made by the government of the United States." [94] The drafting of Alex Gau, chancellor of the Prussian legation, was an error and was promptly rectified. The discharge of John Icorokfalvi, a Hungarian who had been enrolled on April 12, 1862, for three years, came with unusual speed; for he was discharged on May 23, little more than five weeks later. The discharge of a lone Swede through Count Piper's protest is on record. [95]

After bounties reached astronomical proportions, they became a serious factor in the release of kidnapped persons. The War Department took the position that certain recruits would be released upon refund of the bounties and substitute money. Sometimes these were paid under protest by the father, who was anxious to release his son on any terms; it was rare indeed that the victim had received all the money to which as a recruit he was entitled. [96] Sometimes this condition created the greatest possible difficulty and distress, as when the parent was poor, which often proved to be the case. The mother of Samuel Tillotson, to take a single concrete instance, could not pay the expenses for the discharge, let alone return the bounties; for, as a matter of course, "it mostly went into the pockets of the men who decoyed him from his home by false pretenses. . . ." [97] The author feels that when everything is taken into consideration, it must in fairness be said that the diplomatic representatives of the foreign governments dealing with this harassing subject took a fair and reasonable attitude toward,

[93] Stuart to Seward, November 5, 1862, Notes from the British Legation, XLIII. A few discharges appear in Volume XLIX.

[94] Lyons to *id.*, May 9, 1863, *ibid.*, LI.

[95] For Gau, see Notes from the Prussian Legation, III; for the Hungarian, see Consular Dispatches, Altona, II, No. 56; for the Swede, Ole Michelson, see Notes to the Swedish Legation, VI, No. 107.

[96] Samuel Potter wrote Earl Russell, October 29, 1864, that Henry Delafield, Esq., of 269 Fifth Avenue, New York, had been instructed to pay the money and send it to Lord Lyons. Potter continued, "But as Y.L. will see by my declaration, my son only received a small portion of the bounties to which he was entitled." Quoted by Joseph H. Burnley to Seward in his letter of November 11, 1864. Notes from the British Legation, LXXIII.

[97] Hanson Hawley to Governor Andrew, October 15, 1864, *ibid.* The extreme hardship of such a demand is illustrated by the case of James Walsh. He was to be discharged when he refunded $450 to the United States, although he received only $100, which he had paid over to his brother and which the brother had transmitted to the mother. See John Walsh to Lowell, February 13, 1865, *ibid.*, LXXVI.

and manifested patient understanding of, the problems besetting a government at war.[98]

The protests against impressment of foreign subjects and against the practices of the kidnappers and bounty brokers poured into the files of the Department of State with undiminished frequency, becoming stronger as the enormity of the wrongs practiced became more clearly revealed. The British ambassador's views were necessarily largely colored by the reports sent him by the consuls of his country. The consul stationed at New York, where the largest number of foreign boats docked, where the largest immigrant population was congregated, and where a corrupt police force was in control, experienced the evil situation in its most aggravated form, and so from E. M. Archibald came the most vehement denunciations. As early as March, 1863, he suggested that the consul or someone appointed by him have in these cases access to the complainant in order to test the truth of the charges, a position later strongly supported by the ambassador. Lord Lyons pointed out that this method would prevent the submission of unfounded complaints and expedite redress of real grievances.[99] The consul revealed a judicial attitude of mind. A little later, on March 31, 1863, he wrote, "Making great allowances for exaggerated statements, there can be no doubt that the complaints of abuses which have been practised in recruiting in New York are to a great extent well-founded; and, further, that many of the aggrieved parties are prevented from preferring their complaints to me. . . . From what I can learn . . . the unfortunate men, after being detained for a week or ten days, yield to their fate and accept pay." Again, about a month later, he frankly admitted "that were it not for the present troubles, Mr. Finn like many others, who have lived from almost infancy in this country, have married and become permanently domiciled here,—would hardly have asserted their rights as British subjects, were it not for the perils to which they are liable during the existing Civil War." [100] Archibald was still restrained when he wrote in the spring of 1864, "I have complained merely of a want of vigilance on the part of the Recruiting officer. . . . I am constrained to repeat that complaint. . . . To hold him to service on an engagement

---

[98] It is possible, of course, to trace through the diplomatic correspondence the legal positions of the American government and the British government on this issue, but the legalistic question hardly concerns this study.

[99] Extract enclosed in a letter from Lyons to Seward, March 14, 1863, *ibid.*, XLIX.

[100] Letters from Archibald to Lyons, March 14, 1863, *ibid.*, LIX.

entered into under such circumstances, would, as it appears to me, be taking a most unfair and unjust advantage of him." [101] But already a sharper note had begun to creep into his communications, which reached a climax in a lengthy report on conditions to Lord Lyons on February 22, 1864. He detailed the nature of the traffic and then stated baldly, "The seperate [sic] and independent statements made to me by individual sufferers, only serve to confirm the notorious fact of their vile and detestable practice." His dealings with the recruiting officers had brought him to a low opinion of them.

When Archibald submitted to the officer commanding the Naval Station complaints of fraudulent enlistments, they were generally referred to the recruiting officers at the Naval Rendezvous, at which the men appeared in order to be enlisted. A report made there in reply to complaints was almost invariably in the same terms: it declared that the recruit had complied with rules and enlisted voluntarily and was therefore guilty of gross falsehood. Archibald pointed out that the officers of the Rendezvous held, in most cases, a merely temporary rank in the navy. He then reported personal visits to the *North Carolina* (the receiving ship) and an interview with Captain Richard Worsam Meade (commander of the ship), who had frankly stated his conviction that the complaints of the victims were true and that they ought to be discharged. Meade had said further that the Recruiting Rendezvous was not, in his judgment, conducted properly, had read copies of two letters he had written to Admiral Paulding, complaining of the two Rendezvous Acting Masters, and had stated belief that the Rendezvous should be suppressed. Archibald wrote, "The separate statements of similar facts and circumstances by so many complainants, furnish a cumulative testimony in proof of the abuses and deception practised upon them individually, which cannot be rejected without greatly disregarding the interests of truth and justice." The case of the man from the *Bounding Billow* in the fall of the year he declared "one of gross villany on the part of the 'substitute brokers.' " [102]

Archibald's report of February 22 spurred Lord Lyons to a firm, if temperate, demand shortly afterwards: "It is not for me to suggest any particular measures to the Government of the United States, but it is certainly my duty to make an appeal to the justice and humanity of that

---

[101] *Id.* to *id.*, April 28, 1864, *ibid.*, LXIV.

[102] This long report is found in Volume LXI, under date of March 2, 1864. For Archibald's comment on the men entrapped from the *Bounding Billow*, see Archibald to Lyons, October 26, 1864, *ibid.*, LXXII.

Government and earnestly to request that a stop be put to a system from which British Subjects appear to suffer so often and so severely." [103] About this time also the British representatives began to insist on punishment: Consul Archibald asked General Dix for the punishment of the brokers who had carried off the men of the *Bounding Billow;* Lord Lyons asked not only that "measures be taken to bring to justice the perpetrators" of another outrage but also, in another communication, for the "prevention of a recurrence of such acts of fraud and violence." [104] Similar complaints came from the British consuls at Philadelphia and Boston and from the attorney general of Bermuda.[105] It is perhaps a sufficient commentary on the entire situation that a foreign government felt obliged to suggest means to combat the evil: consideration of the advisability of abrogating the regulations under which payments were made as bounties or payments for bringing in recruits.[106]

While the suggestions as well as the complaints from other countries were almost negligible compared with those from Britain, a few were encountered. The Prussian envoy Von Gerolt protested against the Conscription Act of 1863 as authorizing conscription of any Prussians who had preserved their nationality according to Prussian law.[107] If the amount of correspondence is any gauge, the success which crowned the efforts of Ambassador Henri Mercier to secure the discharge of Frenchmen who were enlisted was out of proportion to the effort put forth at the French legation. Sweden was perhaps the most generous of all countries in her interpretation of continuing Swedish citizenship. The foreign minister wrote the Swedish minister at Washington that after a Swede had formally declared his intent to become a citizen of another country, he saw no reason for granting him a protection which he had voluntarily renounced. The Swedish government was unwilling to encourage a mixed position, under shelter of which individuals could screen themselves from the citizens' duties as well toward the country in which they were born as toward that

[103] Lyons to Seward, March 7, 1864, *ibid.,* LXIV.

[104] Archibald to Burnley (first secretary at the legation), on the matter of the *Bounding Billow,* October 26, 1864, LXXII; Lyons to Seward, March 7, 1864, *ibid.,* LXI; *id.* to *id.,* May 14, 1864, LXIV.

[105] Kortright to Lyons, Philadelphia, August 11, 1863, *ibid.,* LIV; Memorandum (undated), citing remarks of the British consul at Boston, *ibid.,* XLV; Attorney General Gray to the Governor General of the Bermudas, Hamilton, Bermuda, February 14, 1864, *ibid.,* LXI.

[106] Burnley to Seward, November 16, 1864, *ibid.,* LXXIII. The suggestion was made as a means to aid Governor General Monck to protect the frontier against violations of this character.

[107] Von Gerolt to *id.,* May 6, 1863, Notes from the Prussian Legation, III.

in which they had freely chosen their residence. He ordered, therefore, that Count Piper inform the Swedish consuls to grant protection only to those who intended to remain subjects of the King of Norway and Sweden and intended to return to establish their domicile in the land of their birth.[108]

It seems superfluous to devote more than a single paragraph to discussion of the effect on the quality of the military service of the presence of the conscripted foreigners—whether conscripted legally through the draft or forced by one trick or another into the Union army. The quality of the army had deteriorated during the two early years of the war. The kind of men who sprang forward to respond to the President's first calls were no longer enlisting; many of them were already in the ranks, or dead. Foreigners who were enticed, kidnapped, or bludgeoned into the army could hardly make good soldiers. Either they spent their time in prison, claiming exemption as aliens or refusing to render service, or they performed their service sullenly or indifferently. Despite all the strenuous efforts of the government and the bounty brokers, the conscripts were relatively few. The product secured was clearly not worth the enormous sums expended by the government.

[108] Minister of Foreign Affairs Manderström to Piper, May 31, 1863, Notes from the Swedish Legation, IV.

CHAPTER SIXTEEN

Service During Period of Defeat

GENERAL FRÉMONT was criticized for appointing so many foreign-born officers to his staff. He had the choice, in the main, of selecting his officers from green native civilians or from foreign-born civilians who had had military experience abroad. Later he might also have foreign knights-errant or adventurers added to his staff from Washington.

It seems unnecessary to analyze meticulously the contribution of each of the principal foreign-born generals, apart from what has already been said, for it is obvious that promotion and the bestowal of brevet rank was in itself a measure of success as evaluated by the superior officers and by the authorities at Washington. Furthermore, no matter how brilliant the strategy, no matter how able the execution of the strategy by the maneuvers of the men commanding on the field, no war can be won except by the fighting qualities of the rank and file. It is exactly in this way that the service of the foreign-born troops must be measured. Did the conduct of the German Division at Chancellorsville cost the Union the victory? Did the Eleventh Corps help win the battle of Gettysburg? What did the Irish valor at the storming of Marye's Heights at Fredericksburg accomplish, despite the fact that Fredericksburg had to be written down as a failure? What credit is due the Wisconsin Germans when we note that the presence of the Twenty-sixth Wisconsin on the field was felt as a good augury? Did the Scandinavians of the Fifteenth Wisconsin actually contribute toward ultimate victory by preservation of their morale after Chickamauga, though they had lost their colonel? Individual acts of bravery (as the capture of a Confederate flag or the recovery of a lost cannon), whether they received the recognition of a Congressional Medal or not, were inspiring—and some of them have merited our attention—but they seldom determined battles. The battles were won by good officers directing the work of good soldiers in companies and regiments.

LOSSES AND HARDSHIPS

The very losses in dead and wounded sustained by foreign units is a certain indication of their contribution, for poltroons did not ordinarily come under withering fire. The number of desertions recorded in the Descriptive Books is a further indication, for it is a self-evident fact that men who were thinking enough about escaping the service to seek opportunities to desert were not then rendering any aid to the cause. Captures by the enemy were not so clear a gauge, for they turned on a score of circumstances over which the soldier or officer had, frequently, little control. No one would dream of charging General Corcoran with lack of courage because he was taken prisoner at the First Battle of Bull Run. Sometimes we have bits of evidence as to how foreign-born captives bore their imprisonment; then we see whether they were a weakening influence or, by their patience, fortitude, and ingenuity, a sustaining factor to their fellow prisoners.

The Federal fatalities during the entire war were 359,528 men. Of this number, 110,070 were killed in battle or died of wounds; 249,458 died of disease or accident or succumbed to the hardships and lack of food in the Confederate prisons.[1] However, those who died or suffered wounds or spent the rest of their lives maimed or handicapped by illness [2] might all properly be counted as sacrifices to the Union cause and as thus serving their adopted country. Over 250,000 men were discharged for disabilities arising from wounds or disease rendering them unfit for service. Losses in the main battles of the Civil War ran high. A comparison of the casualties at Gettysburg with those sustained in some of the European conflicts might prove illuminating. The Third Westphalia Regiment lost at Marc La Tour 49.4 per cent in killed and wounded; the Garde-Schütze Regiment lost at Metz 46.1 per cent; the Light Brigade lost at Balaklava 36.7 per cent. These battles probably recorded the greatest losses in single engagements up to the time of the Civil War; yet it has been asserted "without fear of contradiction" that in the Union army at least 63 regiments lost more than 50 per cent in killed and wounded in single engagements. At

---

[1] Fox (author and comp.), *Regimental Losses in the Civil War*, 50, 531; Thomas L. Livermore, *Numbers and Losses in the Civil War in America, 1861–1865* (Boston and New York, 1900), 8, 47–48.

[2] The greatest scourge among Civil War veterans was rheumatism, derived from sleeping on the cold, and frequently damp, ground.

least 23 regiments lost more than one half in killed and wounded in the three bloody days of Gettysburg. Native regiments made splendid records there—and paid for it, the Iron Brigade losing almost exactly 50 per cent of its number—but so did units of foreign-born and some composed largely of foreign-born, notably some Pennsylvania regiments. The Fifth New York, Duryée's Zouaves, in which there were many foreigners, lost at the Second Battle of Bull Run over 60 per cent in killed and wounded, with none missing; the regiments went into battle with 490 men, but in less than ten minutes nearly 150 lay dead or mortally wounded. Though this regiment had only half of its complement when it faced four Confederate regiments supported by the Hampton Legion at Gettysburg, it never faltered but returned the fire of the enemy promptly and effectively. Though almost annihilated, it retired slowly, carrying off with it the flags and some of the wounded.[3]

Losses were always high among the Irish; consequently, statistics for the regiments composed of that nationality will be given first. The reader will recall without effort the death of Colonel Thomas Cass of the Ninth Massachusetts, before Richmond; of that fighter Colonel Patrick Kelly of the Eighty-eighth New York, who fell in the battles before Petersburg; of Colonel John Burke of the Sixty-third, who died as the result of a wound sustained at Malvern Hill; and of many captains of the Irish Brigade.[4] The service of the common soldier was equally honorable and tragic. As the eye travels down the column reserved for comments in the Descriptive Books of the Sixty-third New York, it meets frequently the notations "absent and wounded," "killed in action at Gettysburg," "killed at Antietam," "killed in the Wilderness," "missing in action," "absent wounded since June 6, 1864," "transferred to the invalid corps," "returned, escaped from prison," "died while prisoner of war." The Eighty-eighth New York lost 102 men at Antietam and 127 at Fredericksburg; the One Hundred and Sixty-fourth New York, another Irish regiment, it will be recalled, participated in the assault on Cold Harbor and carried the works, but at the cost of 127 men, including the colonel and 6 other officers. The One Hundred and Seventieth, a third Irish regiment, in Corcoran's Irish Legion, lost 99 men in the fight at the North Anna River in the summer

[3] These impressive figures are given in Mulholland, *The American Volunteer*, 26, 27, 67–68. In Fox's list of regiments sustaining heavy losses in various battles a number of foreign regiments appear, such as the Eighty-second Illinois, the Eighth, Ninth, Sixty-third, Sixty-ninth, Eighty-eighth New York, and the One Hundred and Sixteenth Pennsylvania. Fox (author and comp.), *Regimental Losses in the Civil War*, 28–34.

[4] These deaths were taken from the Descriptive Rolls.

of 1864 and 136 in the early assaults on Petersburg; in fact, this one regiment lost during the war a total in killed and wounded of almost half of the thousand men in the regiment.[5] Similar is the record of the One Hundred and Sixteenth Pennsylvania, fifth of the regiments which made up Meagher's Irish Brigade.

The ultimate of sacrifice was probably sustained by the Irish Brigade when it was hurled by General Pope against Marye's Heights in December, 1862, in a useless massacre. It may be said that the Brigade virtually ceased to exist, with an average loss in casualties per regiment of almost 41 per cent. Yet there fought at Gettysburg a remnant of the Brigade so reduced that each of the five regiments had been consolidated into a battalion of two companies; its men were armed still with the same old buck-and-ball muskets with which they had marched out to war. Nugent has summarized the losses of the Irish Brigade, including officers and men, as follows: in the Peninsular campaign, almost 500 men; at Antietam, 540; and at Fredericksburg, 545.[6] Seven thousand men in all were entered on the rolls of the Brigade; less than 1,000 returned to New York.

No less striking, both relatively and absolutely, was the record of the losses by the Germans. The Twenty-sixth Wisconsin lost, with those killed, those dying from their wounds, and those missing, 34 officers and 582 men, or 52.5 per cent. It is worthy of record that Fox placed this German regiment first in his list of "bravest regiments." [7] At Second Bull Run the Seventy-third Pennsylvania lost its leader, Colonel Koltes, and nearly half of its officers and men were killed or wounded. As a part of Buschbeck's division, it was the first to make a stand against Jackson's army at Chancellorsville. The heavy casualties from these two battles left the regiment without a field officer and every company sadly depleted

---

[5] For these statistics, see Rossiter Johnson and others (eds.), *Campfire and Battlefield*, 479–80. We are fortunate to have these compilations (which were made soon after the war), for the Company and Regimental Descriptive Books for the One Hundred and Sixty-fourth New York and the One Hundred and Seventieth New York are disappointing, with many blanks and little in the way of remarks to aid in the research. The exact number in the One Hundred and Seventieth during the entire war was 1,002. *Ibid.*, 480.

[6] Fox (comp.), *New York at Gettysburg*, I, 108; Nugent, "Historical Notes on the Irish Brigade," *ibid.*, II, 488; Fox (author and comp.), *Regimental Losses in the Civil War*, 35.

[7] Kaufmann, *Die Deutschen im Bürgerkriege*, 564–65; Rossiter Johnson and others (eds.), *Campfire and Battlefield*, 481, estimated the loss at about 50 per cent. Hense-Jensen, *Wisconsin's Deutsch-Amerikaner*, 194, differed slightly from Kaufmann's figures but reached the same per cent.

in numbers. The remnant of 333 men standing in Steinwehr's division at Gettysburg mustered strength to repel the Louisiana Tigers from the batteries on East Cemetery Hill.[8] The Sigel Rifles (Fifty-second New York Regiment), under Colonel Paul Frank, left New York City 700 strong to take part in McClellan's Peninsular campaign and were almost that strong on the eve of the Battle of Fair Oaks, but they emerged from that battle with less than 200 sound men.[9]

The tremendous losses of German regiments may be told in condensed form. The Fifty-second New York carried 2,800 names on the roll from first to last, but 200 only came back; the De Kalb Regiment, or the Forty-first, which had gone out with a full complement of 1,046 men, returned with 180; Blenker's Eighth New York Regiment lost at the single Battle of Cross Keys over a third of its number; the Seventh, Twentieth, and Forty-sixth New York regiments lost frightfully at Antietam and Fredericksburg and on the Peninsula; and the One Hundred and Third New York could muster only three companies at Appomattox.[10] Losses were as heavy in the western regiments. The heaviest loss at Wilson's Creek was suffered by Company J of the First Kansas Regiment, composed exclusively of members of the Turner Society in Leavenworth; this company lost one third of its strength. Over one third of Company A of the First Minnesota consisted of Germans; of this number only 3 men came back uninjured.[11]

Units representative of other nationalities suffered proportionately. The Seventy-ninth New York will be recalled as the regiment of Scotchmen; it lost almost 200 men at First Bull Run, among them its commander. At Chantilly some months later General Isaac Stevens, formerly its second colonel, seized the flag after the sixth color-bearer had been shot down and led the regiment to victory, though he himself was killed.[12] The research reveals that losses among the Swiss consisted chiefly of officers: Trepp, a Sharpshooter colonel, who fell at Mine Run; Mösch, of the One Hundred and Third New York; Frederick Zurflüh; Komli; Morelli; and Gerber. Many, like Captains Aschmann and Fellman, had, after the war, to limp

---

[8] "Oration of George T. R. Knorr," in Nicholson (comp.), *Pennsylvania at Gettysburg*, I, 423-36.

[9] Baltimore *Der Deutsche Correspondent*, June 10, 1862. There were actually only 190 survivors of the battle.

[10] Kaufmann, *Die Deutschen im Bürgerkriege*, 185, gives this summary.

[11] *Ibid.*, 234 n., 190.

[12] Rossiter Johnson and others (eds.), *Campfire and Battlefield*, 479.

through life on one leg.[13] Aschmann's company of Sharpshooters consisted of only 12 men by the end of 1864. The Scandinavians contributed their fair quota to the dead and wounded. The Bishop Hill Company under Captain Forsse, as a part of the Fifty-seventh Illinois Regiment, participated in the capture of Fort Donelson; at the Battle of Shiloh, 16 of the casualties of this regiment were from Company D. The long fighting record of the Scandinavian Regiment rendered it inevitable that there should be many casualties: in addition to their commander, Colonel Heg, 302, or over one third, were killed on the field or died of wounds.[14]

In the discharge of their duty, the foreign-born soldiers suffered all the discomforts and hardships incident to the war (from which, indeed, there was no escape for troops of any nationality). They knew all the weariness of plowing through the sticky, deep Virginia mud; of enduring intense cold; of being in driving, penetrating rain two thirds of the time; of suffering from lack of food, and—which was almost as bad—of trying to eat moldy hardtack and rancid meat; of undergoing homesickness and the bitter disappointment of receiving no letters from relatives, some of whom could not write. These hardships, however disagreeable, were slight compared with greater ills. Foreign-born flesh was just as susceptible as native flesh to fever and ague, neither of which was improved by sleeping on the ground. The foreign-born were baffled, just as were the natives, at being marched, thirty thousand strong, a long distance, only to be marched back again without striking a blow.[15] Some of the tales of suffering enlist sympathy as keenly as do any of the tales of suffering from either of the World Wars. Mrs. Hoge, a wartime nurse, has described poignantly the sufferings of a French lad. Hearing a moan, which was rare in a hospital, she saw a French boy quivering and crying for help. He had been driven, untended, several miles in an ambulance with his feet projecting from the rear; as a result they were so badly frozen that the surgeon had just decided on amputation, and the poor lad in his agony was begging for the operation.[16]

[13] Steinach, *Geschichte und Leben*, 43. The Christian names of most seem to have been lost.

[14] Hokanson, *Swedish Immigrants*, 115, 119.

[15] See letters of Knute Nelson to his parents, July 29, 1862, and to a brother, April 12, 1863. Knute Nelson Papers. Western soldiers seemed to find humor in referring to such maneuvers as "Potomac tactics." Frémont commiserated with his soldiers because they had had nothing but meat for four days! Frémont to his wife, October 30, 1861, in Frémont, *The Story of the Guard*, 180.

[16] Mrs. A. H. Hoge, *The Boys in Blue; or Heroes of the Rank and File* (New York, 1867), 354–55.

QUALITY OF THE SOLDIERS

Among soldiers of every nationality there were both good and bad. There were Germans who rendered splendid service, and there were Germans who were craven and lazy; there were Irishmen with the hearts of lions, and there were plenty of Irish who could and did desert the flag; the Scotch Highlanders could so forget military obedience as to mutiny, and yet they later redeemed their record and commanded respect. The Fourth New York Cavalry, a half-German regiment, bore an unenviable reputation, which, unfortunately, they sustained by their conduct at Hartwood Church on February 23, 1863. The Confederates were threatening the rear of the First Rhode Island Regiment at Chancellorsville when with the greatest alacrity one squadron of their German neighbors broke by individuals to the rear. The other two squadrons, which had never been under fire, after a few shots, instead of obeying the order to charge, followed the bad example of the first squadron and made good time to the rear.[17] Yet, it was another German regiment that partially retrieved the bad situation at New Market. After that disgraceful battle had been lost on May 15, 1864, General Sigel met the foe near Piedmont on June 5 in an entrenched position. Though four Union regiments were driven back, the Germans of the Twenty-eighth Ohio remained on the ground to prevent the foe from making a countercharge and held it at bay for three quarters of an hour, whereupon they were recalled to their place in the line of battle and complimented by General Hunter.[18]

The Southerners frequently charged the foreigners of the Union Army, especially the Germans, with pillage, arson, rape, and even the murder of civilians and prisoners of war in cold blood. In Missouri after the Battle of Pea Ridge, General Sigel denied such charges and brought countercharges of similar import.[19] Yet it was of the Ninth Connecticut, a foreign

[17] John Bigelow, Jr., *The Campaign of Chancellorsville. A Strategical and Tactical Study* (New Haven, 1910), 62.

[18] D. Cunningham and W. W. Miller (comps.), *Report of the Ohio Antietam Battlefield Commission* (Springfield, Ohio, 1904), 72–73.

[19] Duyckinck, *National History of the War for the Union*, II, 296. The depth of feeling of Southerners toward the foreign-born fighting on the Northern side is indicated by the following excerpt: "Why not hang every Dutchman captured? We will hereafter hang, or shoot, or imprison for life all white men taken in command of negroes, and enslave the negroes themselves. That is not too harsh. No human being will assert the contrary. Why, then, should we not hang a Dutchman, who deserves infinitely less of our sympathy than

contingent, even though Irish rather than German, that General Butler found occasion to speak as follows:

> After having been for months subjected to the privations necessarily incident to camp life upon this island, these well disciplined soldiers, although for many hours in full possession of the rebel villages, filled with what to them were most desirable luxuries, abstained from the least unauthorized interference with private property, and all molestations of peaceful citizens. This behavior is worthy of all praise. It robs war of half its horrors. It teaches our enemy how much they have been misinformed by their designing leaders as to the character of our soldiers and the intention of our Government.[20]

The record of the Irish Brigade has become almost a legend. To read the list of engagements in which it participated, and always with honor to the Irish race, is like a roll call of the battles of the Army of the Potomac —thirty-three engagements in all.[21] Likewise creditable is the record of participation in battle by Company D of the One Hundred and Twenty-fourth New York—to select a German unit at random. It shared in the fighting of eleven battles, including the great engagements of Manassas, Fredericksburg, Chancellorsville, Gettysburg, the Wilderness battles, and Spotsylvania.

The same contrasts of character appear in the highly illuminating comments recorded by officers on various privates and still to be read in the Descriptive Books. "His conduct was invariably good, and without shade of reproach," was the pronouncement on an Irishman. Of an Englishman the superior officer wrote, "This man, never during his three years service was absent from the command, except as prisoner of war—never skulked in battle—never was drunk, never was punished . . ."; of a German who had been recommended for a medal of honor, "A braver man than August Frey don't live"; of an Irishman, "An excellent soldier." However, there also occur the following disparaging remarks: after the names of a Canadian and a German, "A poor soldier"; of another foreigner who deserted, "Small loss to the U.S. service"; of a German who was wounded slightly, "Must have done it himself for he Did not go into action with

---

Sambo? The live masses of beer, kraut, tobacco, and rotten cheese, which on two legs and four, on foot and mounted, go prowling through the South, should be used to manure the sandy plains and barren hillsides of Alabama, Tennessee, and Georgia." Copied from Knoxville *Register*, June 12, 1863, by Moore (ed.), *Rebellion Record*, VII, Pt. 3, p. 83.

[20] New York *Irish-American*, June 21, 1862.

[21] See Nugent, "Historical Notes on the Irish Brigade," in Fox (comp.), *New York at Gettysburg*, II, 487.

the Co. and has Been absent since May 6, 64 and was considered a shirk." [22] By the names of men in Mattson's Swedish company there are often such comments as "of good character," "an excellent soldier," and "always performing his duty with pride and efficiency"; but a comment on this company by its leader sums up the situation well, revealing, as with all nationality groups, good and bad among the ranks. On one occasion the company had been placed in line for an expected attack and everyone was at his post with the exception of two, who had pleaded a bad headache; "I told them to go and lay down and sleep till the war was over if they wanted to—but many of those that were really sick I could not make them stay to home—they all were bound to go and we felt glad that we would soon have an opportunity to fight." [23]

MILITARY CONTRIBUTION

Defense of the Capital

Probably the most definite way to determine the amount and value of the service rendered to the war by the foreign element is to follow the various campaigns and, for the sake of clarity, to follow them roughly in their chronological sequence.[24] As a relatively unimportant point of departure, it might be remarked that the first volunteers in the service of the Union were the Turner Schützen of Washington, who at President Lincoln's inauguration formed the honor guard. Reinforced by the Baltimore Turners in April, after the fall of Fort Sumter, they probably gave the government the feeling that there was, at least, a pretense of armed defense. The news of the arrival of the Irishmen of the New York Sixty-ninth Militia at Annapolis on April 26 must have brought relief to the anxious mind of the President, since the capital had been for a week as good as cut off from the North. It meant, first, the protection of the easily accessible naval academy of the nation and, second, the protection of communication between that point and the capital, since the unit was instantly assigned the duty of guarding the railroad from Annapolis to the Junction and two days later was ordered to march to Washington via the railroad, guarding and re-

[22] These comments appear in the Company Books of Companies A, Fourth Minnesota; C, Fifteenth Missouri; G, Forty-fifth New York; and A, Fifth Wisconsin. For the poor soldiers, see Company Books of Companies I, Sixteenth Michigan; A, Twenty-seventh Michigan; and D, Third Minnesota.

[23] Mattson to his wife, May 9, 1862, Mattson Papers.

[24] There is no intention to treat every battle.

pairing the vital line of communication. Once in the capital, the Sixty-ninth set to work cutting timber and erecting the work which was christened Fort Corcoran. The fact that the President and several of the cabinet members visited the regiment to encourage the men by their presence is sufficient evidence that government leaders were relieved of some anxiety and that they appreciated the presence of the regiment in the capital.[25]

THE FIRST BATTLE OF BULL RUN naturally afforded no satisfaction to the North, and yet it must be recorded that the units which did well on the first testing ground between the North and the South were chiefly units of foreign-born citizens—Blenker's brigade, the Scotch Highlanders, and the Irish. Blenker's brigade, which was posted, together with the regulars and a portion of the reserves, at Centerville, was ordered to advance upon the road from Centerville to Warrenton—an order executed only with difficulty, as the road was choked with retreating baggage wagons and fleeing soldiers. Blenker's men were able to retain their organization, to take up a position despite the panic about them, and thus to prevent the advance of the enemy. In his brigade were the Eighth, Twenty-ninth, Thirty-ninth, and Forty-first New York, and the Twenty-seventh Pennsylvania. Although tired out by upwards of thirty hours of marching and fighting, these units covered the retreat until about midnight, when, under General McDowell's order to march to Washington, the brigade retired in perfect order, bringing back their own six guns and two stands of Union colors left on the field by other soldiers. These five regiments had withstood a force far larger and flushed with victory, but they had had only a brush with Stuart's cavalry. If the Confederates had had any thought of taking Washington, such a plan was shattered by the opposition of Blenker, who was hailed as the savior of the capital.[26]

The Irishmen of the Sixty-ninth New York Militia fought well at this first battle of the war, considering the fact that they felt keenly—as Irishmen always do any supposed grievance—that somehow they had been trifled with and defrauded by being precipitated into action when

[25] Cavanagh, Memoirs of Gen. Meagher, 377, 381.

[26] The story is told that Blenker had repeatedly asked to be allowed to remain in his position or to advance. When McDowell's courier brought the order to retreat, Blenker said, "Zurückfallen, bringen Sie mir lieber Order zum Vorwärtsgehen, mein Herr!" Harter, Erinnerungen aus dem amerikanischen Bürgerkriege, 29. See also Tomes, The Great Civil War, I, 408–409. McClellan praised Blenker and his German adjutants for this work. See also Kaufmann, Die Deutschen im Bürgerkriege, 166–68. The newspapers heaped praise on Blenker. See New York Herald, July 29, 1861, and New York Tribune and New York Times, July 26, 1861.

their term of service had expired on July 20. It should also be recalled that they had met their baptism of fire at the skirmish of Cub Run three days earlier, on July 18, and that they had borne themselves so well that they there first earned the title "The Gallant Sixty-ninth." After a stirring appeal from their leader, Colonel Corcoran, the entire regiment decided to see the engagement through and so entered the initial battle of the war enthusiastically, winning their general's approval for gallantry.

At Bull Run the Sixty-ninth and Seventy-ninth Highlanders formed a part of McDowell's desperate effort to form a line of battle at the center to move against the enemy's position in order to support Heintzelman's effort to capture some abandoned batteries. First the Highlanders twice tried desperately to mount the hill to the batteries and failed. Then it was the turn of the Irishmen. Nobly they held their ground for a time and even reached the batteries, but at last they had to fall back before the withering fire of the Confederate guns. Three times in the course of the desperate struggle the batteries had been taken, and three times they had been retaken. As the exhausted troops retired toward Sudley Ford, it was mainly by the exertions of Colonel Corcoran that an irregular square of infantry was formed to resist a threatened charge of Stuart's cavalry. In Meagher's terse phrase, "We beat their men—their batteries beat us." It was at this first battle, the reader is reminded, that Corcoran became separated from his men and was captured.[27]

The Struggle in Missouri

The first real field of action was in the West, and here the conduct of the Germans was decisive in preserving Missouri for the Union by tipping the scales in the struggle between Unionists and Secessionists. The St. Louis arsenal was held by pro-Southern troops, and the governor was hostile to the North. The Turners of St. Louis and many others of the excellent type of Germans who resided in that city and its neighboring counties quickly raised four regiments, as well as a regiment of artillery and a home guard of three thousand men. In May, 1861, General Lyon, with a few regulars to supplement the German regiments, seized Confederate Camp Jackson. The troops who carried out the subsequent ten months campaign to hold Missouri were almost entirely German. Many Germans distinguished themselves under General Sigel, although many

[27] See Meagher, *The Last Days of the 69th in Virginia*, 13; Logan, *The Great Conspiracy*, 325–30. For the skirmish near Cub Run, see J. E. Smith, *A Famous Battery and its Campaigns*, 17–18.

went home, it is true, after expiration of their three months enlistment.

BATTLE OF PEA RIDGE. Sigel lost the battle of Wilson's Creek on August 10, 1861. His command was completely broken up; five of his six pieces of artillery were captured; and many of his men were taken prisoner. He fully retrieved this defeat by his victory at Pea Ridge on March 8, 1862; for though he was only second in command on that occasion, the entire West attributed this first large decisive victory of the Southwest to his strategy and tactics. The Fifteenth Missouri, composed of Swiss and Germans, participated in the victory; and the Turners of the Seventeenth Missouri stormed a powerful position, thus contributing directly to the outcome. In addition, the almost wholly German Second, Third, and Twelfth Missouri Regiments were present, as were also the Twenty-fifth, Forty-fourth, and Thirty-sixth Illinois, all of which had a strong German admixture in units largely composed of second-generation Germans. One of the real advantages of the northern forces lay in artillery, three fourths of the personnel of which were Germans. Around 5,000 of the over 11,500 men engaged in the campaign to save Missouri were, according to Sigel's claim, Germans, found almost entirely in the Osterhaus and Asboth divisions. Thus one of the early significant victories of the Union was fought essentially by German troops and under the direction of German officers.

While certain papers, such as the New York *Times*, gave the Germans full credit for saving Missouri,[28] some Germans felt that Lyon and Blair had harvested the glory of what German bayonets had won. The government reaction to Frémont's proclamation freeing slaves of Confederates in arms was a further step in alienating certain Germans. In Teutonic eyes Frémont counted as the man who had understood how to give the war real meaning. The proclamation in their view required no justification; exceptional circumstances—the condition of war—amply justified an act long overdue. Apparently, the Germans were ignorant of Frémont's inefficiency, or preferred to ignore it; consequently, his removal from office angered the Germans not only in Missouri but also in the entire West.[29] It was probably owing to the protests of the German officers in

[28] New York *Times*, February 21, 1863. See also Raymond D. Thomas, "Study in Missouri Politics," in *Missouri Historical Review*, XXI (1926–1927), 450.

[29] See observations in Kaufmann, *Die Deutschen im Bürgerkriege*, 239–41, 244. To government officials Frémont's bid appeared to be a political bid for popularity with emancipators. Though Lincoln acted only after careful investigation, it was thought that Frémont was removed not for inefficiency but for his political interference.

Sigel's division and of German citizens in mass meetings that Lincoln gave Frémont a new command in the Army of the Potomac.[30]

BATTLE OF LEXINGTON AND SPRINGFIELD. The service of other nationality groups in Missouri must not pass unnoticed. Even though Colonel Mulligan and the brave Chicago Irishmen of the Twenty-third Illinois were obliged to capitulate to overwhelming numbers at Lexington, Missouri, on September 20, 1861, their heroic stand for an entire week despite the fact that for one whole day they did not have a drop of water, and their surrender only after fifty-two hours of continuous fighting, made them popular heroes. It has been said that at the capitulation, the colonel and many of his men shed tears of regret because they had not secured victory, and their friends shed tears of rage because the Twenty-third could easily have been relieved if the command had not been handled in such an indifferent manner by Frémont. It is almost incomprehensible that the latter did not send several thousand men by boat from St. Louis, since it was believed that they could easily have arrived in two days. Most of the prisoners were soon released on parole, and the gallant Mulligan was exchanged—to be hailed as a hero; but the fact still remains that there was a serious loss of matériel, as well as of the services of over 2,100 men, at a time when brave fighters were greatly needed.[31]

Before Sigel had wrung his victory from the hand of fate, one brilliant and spectacular victory had brightened Frémont's otherwise sad leadership. The often-ridiculed bodyguard, in concert with a troop of regular dragoons—altogether 300 swords—made an heroic attack upon Springfield and captured it on October 25, 1861, under the leadership of the Hungarian Zagonyi. A group of 150 cavalrymen routed in less than three minutes 2,000 Confederates formed in line of battle. "I have seen battles and cavalry charges before," wrote the commanding officer, "but I never imagined that a body of men could endure and accomplish so much in the face of such disadvantages. At the war cry of Frémont and Union! which was raised at every charge, they dashed forward repeatedly in

[30] *Ibid.*, 241–42. This hostility of his German friends in the West was said to have hurt Lincoln. He was at heart an abolitionist, but he felt that the country was not yet ready for emancipation. *Ibid.*, 242. The degree of anger on the part of the German citizens is indicated in a report by Corwin, November 15, 1862, to the *Augsburger Allgemeine Zeitung*, "The news of the anger against Lincoln, which appears in the demonstration of the Germans, especially in Chicago, comes close to madness." *Ibid.*, 241 n. There is no copy of this paper in this country.

[31] Seven cannon, an extraordinary amount of stores, and a war chest of $900,000 fell into the hands of the Confederates. *Ibid.*, 235. See also Tomes, *The Great Civil War*, I, 445–54.

perfect order and resistless energy. Many of my officers, non-commissioned officers, and privates had three or even four horses killed under them, capturing new ones from the enemy." [32] But around eighty Union saddles were empty after the victory. Because this was one of the early Northern victories and because of the tremendous disparity in numbers, this cavalry skirmish became a sensation throughout the country. General Frémont compared it with the famous death charge at Balaklava.

Battles for Kentucky and Tennessee

ROWLETTS STATION. Next to be considered is the service performed by the foreign-born volunteers in the western field of combat. The forward movement of General D. C. Buell against the secession states of the West did not begin until November, 1861. On December 17 at Rowletts Station near Munfordville (a small engagement, to be sure), four companies of the German Thirty-second Indiana under Lieutenant Colonel Henry von Trebra, on outpost duty with only about four hundred men, threw back a hostile force almost five times their number. They held the bridge over the Green River for an hour and a half for the passage of the Army of the Ohio—until the appearance of Colonel Von Willich with four more companies of his regiment, this being the signal for the Confederate withdrawal. An interesting detail is the fact that the Indiana Germans formed into squares when threatened with a cavalry charge and repulsed three such attacks. [33]

MILL SPRINGS, the main battle for Kentucky, whereby almost the entire state came into the hands of the Union, was fought on January 19, 1862. The Polish general Schoepf had been posted there with two Ohio regiments since September, 1861, opposed to the Confederate general Zollicoffer, but early encounters amounted only to clashes of outposts. When General Thomas learned that Zollicoffer had crossed the Cumberland at Mill Springs, he moved against the Confederate general and defeated him after a sharp battle. The death of Zollicoffer confused the Confederates, who rushed about wildly in a hand-to-hand encounter. To the Ninth Ohio Regiment of Germans belongs the credit for first causing the Con-

---

[32] *Official War Records*, Ser. 1, III, p. 251.

[33] For a fuller account of the skirmish, see Headley, *The Great Rebellion*, I, 220–21; Kaufmann, *Die Deutschen im Bürgerkriege*, 263. The command was handsomely complimented a few days later in an order from General Buell at headquarters and was ordered to inscribe the name of Rowletts Station on its regimental colors. Kaufmann, *Die Deutschen im Bürgerkriege*, 263. The fullest account of this action is to be found in "General August Willich," in *Der Deutsche Pionier*, IX (1877–1878), 489–90.

federates to yield. Its bayonet charge was the most striking incident of the conflict. Associated with it in the attack was the partly German Second Minnesota. Although Colonel McCook had had a horse shot under him and was wounded in the leg, he refused to leave his command but went boldly ahead on another charger. When he saw that the superior numbers of the foe must tell, he ordered a bayonet charge. The close formation and the fearless bearing of the Germans were too much for the Southerners, who, just before the final lunge, wavered, swayed backwards, and then broke in utter rout. The shout that went up from that hilltop was heard in every part of the field and was recognized as heralding victory. This was an important victory, as it opened the Cumberland Gap and East Tennessee to the Unionists; moreover, the moral effect produced by the rout no doubt helped to restore Union sentiment in the state. The Union soldiers indulged in the pleasantry of referring to this battle as the Western Bull Run.[34]

FORTS HENRY AND DONELSON. To the Western troops and to a Western general, U. S. Grant, fell the honor of the first great victories of the war, the capture on February 6 and 16, 1862, of Forts Henry and Donelson. But little special distinction attaches to any foreign unit for the seizure of these forts. The Fifty-eighth Ohio, recruited almost wholly among the Germans of Dayton, made the last decisive charge and claimed to have been the first to penetrate into Fort Donelson. One company of the Fifty-seventh Illinois, composed of Swedes, also participated in the capture of that point.[35]

The consequences of Grant's victory at these two points on the Tennessee and Cumberland rivers was immediately apparent; there was a general withdrawal southward by the Confederates. They renounced their first defensive position at Bowling Green; before the end of the month of February (the forts fell on February 6 and 16) they evacuated their strongest fortress on the Mississippi, Columbus; in not too swift succession fell New Madrid and Island No. 10; and not too long afterward Fort Pillow and Memphis capitulated.

---

[34] Mottelay and Campbell-Copeland (eds.), *The Soldier in Our Civil War*, I, 325; Headley, *The Great Rebellion*, I, 245–46. The reports of Generals Thomas and McCook appear in convenient form in Duyckinck, *National History of the War for the Union*, II, 204–208. For the report of Albin F. Schoepf, see *Official War Records*, Ser. 1, VII, pp. 7–9.

[35] There is some basis for the claim of the Ohio regiment, for it was, in recognition of its action, allowed four of the captured cannon. See Colonel Bausenwein to the Adjutant General of Ohio, in Moore (ed.), *Rebellion Record*, IV, Pt. 2, p. 160. Hokanson, *Swedish Immigrants*, 115, for Company D, Fifty-seventh Illinois.

SHILOH. Before Island No. 10 fell, the two Western armies were locked in the Battle of Shiloh. Grant's army moved south and in April lay encamped at Pittsburg Landing on the west bank of the Tennessee (then at flood stage), while General Albert Sidney Johnston's army lay at Corinth below the Tennessee border, about to move north before Buell could join Grant. The Confederate movement north brought the clash at Shiloh on April 6–7, a complete surprise to the scattered Northern army. Everyone knows how disastrous to the Union cause was the first day's battle.

Many German batteries fought at Shiloh. Münch's First Battery of the Minnesota Artillery especially distinguished itself; it was manned by Turners from New Ulm, and had joined the army very shortly before the battle. This battery forced the center of the "hornet's nest," which figures so prominently in the Confederate reports, and covered Sherman's retreat to his last defensive position. Indeed, these gunners conducted themselves bravely during the entire day and procured by their first fire time for the placing of General B. M. Prentiss' surprised division. Several cannons were disabled, but with the five remaining, Lieutenant Wilhelm Pfänder fought on until the rest of Prentiss' division had been taken prisoners. The battery then fought its way through to General Stephen A. Hurlbut's division, to share with it the last victorious struggle at the landing place. In the evening the battery moved into the strong position which Grant had chosen for the protection of his infantry on the plateau near the Tennessee River. This German battery won an honorable name, as did the German-American Hickenlooper battery from Cincinnati. Although Sherman complained of the flight of the German battery Behr of Indianapolis, Indiana, from a position which the Germans felt was untenable, it executed a fine deed that same evening. Covered by only two companies of infantry, this battery defended for hours the bridge over Owl Creek; and when the position finally had to be surrendered, the commander saved one more cannon. Edward Brotzmann, who commanded Mann's German Missouri battery, fought effectively on the evening of April 6 when the Confederates tried to take the landing but were thrown back by Hurlbut's division. Brotzmann lost so many horses that he could take off only three of his cannon. Several other German batteries were present in this battle—Friedrich Welker's and George Nispel's among others.[36]

---

[36] Kaufmann, Die Deutschen im Bürgerkriege, 283–85, 486–87. According to Heitman, Welker's was Battery H, First Missouri Artillery, and Nispel's was Battery E, Second Illinois Artillery.

Only one purely German infantry regiment, the Thirty-second Indiana, appeared at Shiloh, and that arrived on the field of conflict early on the morning of the second day, April 7, as an advance guard of Buell's army. General Lew Wallace has left a record of the performance of this regiment. At the last moment, before a forward rush by the foe was about to materialize, a regiment of bluecoats filed out of the forest; when the enemy became aware of this thrust, they halted, about-faced, and turned back into the safe forest covering, whence they poured out a strong fire on the Indiana regiment. When the Unionists showed signs of wavering, an officer rode swiftly around the left flank to the front, turned his back to the foe, and began to put the regiment through the manual of arms, even as many were falling in the ranks. This cool action of the officer worked like magic. The colonel went back to his post while, despite the frightful fire, the regiment went forward as if on parade and stormed the woods whence the firing came. Thus encouraged, General Wallace pressed the division forward, for he thought Buell's army had come up. The Indiana regiment distinguished itself twice in similar manner on this same day, while Von Willich, its colonel, was made a brigadier general on the field.[37]

Another officer of Swiss-German ancestry, Colonel Jacob Ammen, led the first troops from Buell's army up from the transports which had ferried them over to the cannon-crowned ridge—the forerunner of the succor which was to force withdrawal of Johnston's troops after a second day of obstinate fighting. The Twenty-fourth Indiana, a half-German regiment, was also present and lost its colonel, Gustav von Gerber, who fell as his men stormed a hostile battery. Of him Lew Wallace spoke the famous words "No one died more honorably than Gerber." The Fifty-eighth Ohio, under Colonel Valentine Bausenwein, was early called from the reserve into the line. Sherman sharply criticized Colonel Jesse J. Appler of the Fifty-third Ohio for twice ordering a retreat and later removed him. In addition, the Forty-third Illinois, that regiment from Belleville composed of second-generation Germans, and the half-German Ninth Illinois shared honorably in the Battle of Shiloh. A number of distinguished Germans appeared as officers on this battlefield: Julius Raith (who commanded a brigade and died of burns sustained in the woods after he was wounded), Major Hildebrand, Colonel Mersey (who was severely wounded), Colonel Engelmann, and General Laumann of Iowa.[38] In

[37] See Lewis Wallace, *Lew Wallace, An Autobiography* (New York, 1906), II, 561–63; Kaufmann, *Die Deutschen im Bürgerkriege*, 282–83. Wallace felt that that drill was the "most audacious thing that came under my observation during the war."

[38] Kaufmann, *Die Deutschen im Bürgerkriege*, 283–85, 486–87.

the terrific slaughter of Shiloh the regiments of foreign-born bore their full share of losses.

ISLAND NO. 10. On April 7, General John Pope with the aid of two gunboats took Island No. 10, a fortress below Columbus, Kentucky, commanding the Mississippi. The Scandinavian Fifteenth Wisconsin Regiment formed part of Pope's forces in the reduction of the island. On March 27 a part of that regiment and the Twenty-seventh Illinois under Colonel Napoleon B. Buford had started on an expedition against Union City, Tennessee, where was posted a Rebel force of fifteen hundred men. The Northerners completely surprised the town and camp on the morning of April 1, drove the Rebels in every direction, and captured a goodly booty of horses, mules, and camp equipage. On June 11, eight companies of the Scandinavian regiment left Island No. 10, which they had been guarding since its capture, for Corinth, and Jacinto, Mississippi, where they were attached to Colonel Carlin's brigade.

BATTLE OF PERRYVILLE. The Scandinavians of the Fifteenth Wisconsin endured all the hardships of the rapid march north to Louisville and participated in the Battle of Perryville on October 8, 1862, one of the companies of this regiment being the first to enter the village.[39] Owing to a combination of adverse circumstances, this battle was a disappointment to the North, but General Braxton Bragg fell back the next day. General Schoepf showed an initiative in the conflict which, if it had not been interfered with, might have altered the course of the battle. Sheridan's division, composed in greater part of Germans, brought the battle to a standstill. Toward evening Carlin's brigade joined the fray, fighting until nightfall put an end to the conflict. Under cover of darkness, Bragg withdrew south with his booty. Colonel Heg and his Scandinavians joined in the pursuit of Bragg's army; ineffective though this pursuit otherwise was, it again drove Bragg out of the state of Kentucky. When Rosecrans superseded Buell in command of the Army of the Cumberland, as it was now designated, the Scandinavians continued in his command—to the mutual satisfaction of commander and commanded, for the Norwegians greatly admired Rosecrans, and he, on his side, often praised the Fifteenth Wisconsin.[40]

---

[39] Fitch (comp.), *Annals of the Army of the Cumberland*, 229–30; Kaufmann, *Die Deutschen im Bürgerkriege*, 288–89.

[40] Fitch (comp.), *Annals of the Army of the Cumberland*, 230; Tenny, *The Military and Naval History of the Rebellion in the United States*, 767. General Rosecrans, in a special order of November 24, 1862, gave honorable mention to the Fifteenth Wisconsin and Thirty-eighth Illinois for the capture of forty-six prisoners and some equipment from guerrillas. Milwaukee

BATTLE OF MURFREESBORO. At this battle, which began on the last day of the year 1862, much the same foreign-born units were engaged. The Scandinavians passed through the bloody contest with coolness and courage, thus winning Carlin's praise; but they lost their lieutenant colonel and 120 of their men, one third of the number that went into the battle.

The work of the Germans under Von Willich requires special attention. Rosecrans had placed on the right wing McCook's corps, which was to feint early in the morning to divert the foe while the left wing made the main attack. Von Willich's brigade was stationed on the extreme end of the position and therefore formed the wing extending farthest to the right—hanging, as he said, in the air. Von Willich was not with his troops at the time when the Confederates struck in overwhelming force; he had ridden to the division headquarters, one and a quarter miles behind the front, to report that the right wing was hanging in the air. Although the enemy was not in sight when he rode off, he naturally should have dispatched an adjutant. Possibly he had reasoned that if he went himself there was more likelihood of his securing reinforcements. It is untrue, however, that his brigade was not fully in position when the storm broke. Nevertheless, within a few minutes nearly a third of his men lay dead or wounded, and an equal number had been taken prisoners. Meanwhile, as Von Willich galloped back to his brigade, his horse was killed and he was surrounded by a hundred Confederates; however, though captured, he was soon exchanged. Although he was clearly at fault in leaving his command, his presence would probably not have altered the outcome, since five brigades of McCook's divisions were quickly crushed.[41]

Two divisions of McCook's corps had been so disorganized at the first attack that only some remnants had found refuge with McCook's third division under Sheridan. Against this division the victorious Confederates stormed, but terrific musketry and artillery fire hurled back the gray ranks

---

Sentinel, December 4, 1862. On the other hand, Colonel Heg wrote to his wife, "I have just been up to Rosecrans' Headquarters, and had a shake of the old fellow's hand. . . . You do not know how pleased everybody is at the change of Buell for him." From undated letter, Blegen (ed.), *Civil War Letters of Colonel Heg*, 152. As one more instance of Rosecrans' enthusiasm for the Scandinavians, one might cite a passage from one of Colonel Heg's letters to his wife, that of March 27, 1863: "Rosecrans said when he reviewed the camp, 'There is a regiment that suits me. Col. Heg's old Regiment is in a fine condition.' " *Ibid.*, 198–99.

[41] Kaufmann, *Die Deutschen im Bürgerkriege*, 289–93. For the battle as a whole see James K. Hosmer, *The Appeal to Arms* (*The American Nation: A History*, XX, New York, 1907), 230–33. It is but just to Von Willich to state that his Germans drove two Confederate regiments completely over the river on January 2. B[ickham], *Rosecrans' Campaign with the Fourteenth Army Corps*, 316.

after they had come within pistol range. Sheridan was also attacked in the rear and threatened with envelopment. Since he was supported only by Negley's division, he could not maintain his position and had to withdraw to a hill, cutting his way through the enemy. Twice in the course of the battle he had to shift his position, fighting his way through the enemy each time; but his ranks remained closed and he saved some of his cannon, thus affording Rosecrans time to alter completely his original plan and to bring the divisions massed on the left wing and in the center gradually to the support of what was left of McCook's corps.

Sheridan lost 40 per cent of his division; these losses were in German regiments and bear comparison, it might be remarked, with those of the Irish at Fredericksburg. Officers fell so fast that the succession in command presented difficulties. Two brigades warded off attacks by the bayonet after their munition was exhausted, and Sheridan ordered these brigades to cover the final retreat with lowered bayonets, a task brilliantly discharged under the two German commanders Nikolas Greusel and Friedrich Schäfer, who lost his life. On the left wing the Ninth Ohio fought grimly beside the half-German Second Minnesota and the German regiments from Missouri which were not with Sherman. The attack was not renewed until January 2, only skirmishes occurring on January 1; but by that time Rosecrans had taken up a new position, which proved so strong that the enemy withdrew during the following night.[42]

It is apparent that here German soldiers contended mightily to save the battle from ending in complete defeat. Schäfer's second brigade contained the partly German Second and Fifteenth Missouri regiments, the half-German Seventy-third Illinois Regiment, and the German-American Forty-fourth.

Germans constituted one third of the four Illinois regiments, the Twenty-second, Twenty-seventh, Forty-second, and Fifty-first. The Twenty-fourth Wisconsin was more than one-half German. The Twenty-first Michigan and the Thirty-sixth and Eighty-eighth Illinois had large contingents of Germans. The composition of Sherman's artillery was very similar to that of these regiments of infantry.[43] Here fought also the men

---

[42] Kaufmann, *Die Deutschen im Bürgerkeriege*, 291–92. Schäfer's death is noted in *Official War Records*, Ser. 1, XX, Pt. 1, p. 367.

[43] Kaufmann, *Die Deutschen im Bürgerkriege*, 292. Some slight attempt was made to attribute blame to Von Willich, but enquiry showed that he had adjusted his picket lines properly and the commanders of his brigade insisted that his men were prepared. Indeed, it would have been out of character for him to have been caught unprepared. B[ickham], *Rosecrans' Campaign with the Fourteenth Army Corps*, 241–42.

of the Sixth Kentucky, about half of whom were Germans. It was the kind of fighting which these men did that enabled Rosecrans to hold the field after what seemed likely to be utter defeat, though credit should be freely given to the chief commander for the coolheadedness and energy which alone saved the day.

The eagerness of the Irish for combat is admirably illustrated by an episode in the Murfreesboro battle. The Michigan regiment of Mechanics and Engineers, a small force of less than four hundred men, had been posted at Lavergne, midway between Nashville and Murfreesboro, to protect communications. Behind a flimsy barricade it had to fight off Wheeler's cavalry of three thousand men on the afternoon of the first day of battle. The hard-pressed colonel, William Power Innis, sent a messenger to ask aid of Colonel Joseph W. Burke, who was stationed five miles away at Stewartsboro with his Tenth Ohio. Very shortly afterwards, Burke and some of his sturdy Irishmen (who were already known as the "Bloody Tenth") were racing up the road with eager energy. Since Carnifex Ferry and Perryville they had held their own post, had rescued captured trains, and had driven Wheeler's cavalry from the front; but they had not been able to get into a fight. "I never," said Colonel Burke, "saw fellows so disappointed. When we got to Lavergne, Innis had whipped the enemy and we had no fight." [44]

West Virginia

CARNIFEX FERRY. A glance at the campaign in West Virginia is in order before we follow General McClellan and the Army of the Potomac. Three Ohio regiments of foreign-born, two German and one Irish, distinguished themselves at Carnifex Ferry on September 10 of that same year in the West Virginia campaign. General Rosecrans learned that Confederate forces under General Floyd were stationed at that point and consequently determined to attack without delay, though General Floyd held a strongly entrenched position on a height. The Irish regiment which led the advance, under fire for the first time, engaged a Confederate battery on the parapet and drew the concentrated fire of the enemy's large supporting force. The entrenched Confederates were so strong that the Tenth had to fall back, their colonel replacing his earlier rallying cry of "Follow, Tenth!" with orders to retreat only after he himself had been wounded. To a man, the regiment distinguished itself—the officers steadily spurring

[44] B[ickham], *Rosecrans' Campaign with the Fourteenth Army Corps*, 301.

the men on while three color sergeants fell in succession. Every man was said to have stuck to his officer with unswerving fidelity.[45]

The Germans were equally eager and brave. Drawn up in line of battle on the crest of a hill, they were straining at the leash. The sun was sinking when orders came to Colonel Robert L. McCook, who was acting as commander of the German Brigade, consisting of his own Ninth, the Twenty-eighth, and the Third Ohio, to go forward to storm the entrenchments. The gallant colonel rose in his stirrups and, snatching his slouched hat from his head, roared out, "Forward my bully Dutch! We'll go over their entrenchments if every man dies on the other side." His men exploded into terrific cheers; old graybeards threw up their hats with frenzied excitement; and the brigade shot forward at the double-quick. As the intrepid McCook dashed furiously up and down the line, shouting to his men in trumpet tones above the din, all were sure that they could storm the works if given the opportunity. The opportunity was denied them, however, for at this juncture, when a part of the Ninth had charged almost up to the enemy's works, Rosecrans forbade the assault because night was about to close in. The attack was never made, for the dawn revealed that the foe had fled. The presence of these regiments helped ensure success, for the Ninth and the Twenty-eighth Ohio had shown their steadiness under galling fire. The third German regiment, the Forty-seventh Ohio, was detained in the rear and did not get into action at all, though its commander, Colonel Poschner, moved into the storm of bullets to see how the battle went.[46] No claim is made that these regiments won the victory (such as it was), for there were American regiments present; but the claim is made that these three units of foreign-born soldiers contributed richly.

[45] The courage of the color-bearers of the Tenth Ohio should be noted. Color Sergeant Fitzgibbons, who was behind Colonel Lytle when he fell, had his right hand shattered, but, gathering the flag in his left, he waved it enthusiastically, only to be torn to pieces by a round shot. O'Connor snatched the falling colors to hold them aloft once more, whereupon he, also, was struck by a ball in the left hand, but he dropped behind a log and kept the colors flying until he dropped them from sheer exhaustion. His captain, Stephen McGroarty, snatched the flag up again and, while rolling it up, ordered his men to retire to cover, but as he was bringing up the rear a ball struck him. Although the ball passed through him, it failed to disable him until he had succeeded in bringing the colors off the field. Tomes, *The Great Civil War*, I, 502. The Third Ohio was not, of course, a foreign unit.

[46] See Headley, *The Great Rebellion*, I, 144; Tomes, *The Great Civil War*, I, 500, 502–503; Mottelay and Campbell-Copeland (eds.), *The Soldier in Our Civil War*, I, 135; Cincinnati *Gazette*, September 11, 1861.

In the Eastern Theater

PENINSULAR CAMPAIGN. Obviously, the regiments raised among the foreign-born in New York and the eastern cities played an important part in the Peninsular campaign, as did also some units of foreign-born raised in the West. Some of these regiments figured definitely in McClellan's plans. A defensive campaign against Jackson in the Shenandoah Valley was necessary to protect Washington and also later to support McClellan's advance against Richmond. For this task the commander designated Blenker's division—recognizing, evidently, which troops had stood firm at Bull Run among the many runaways. The troops in the Valley, including Blenker's division (ten thousand strong) and General Banks's Fifth Corps, amounted to about thirty-five thousand men.[47] The Germans never ceased to recall the frightfully difficult march of two hundred miles from Warrenton through the mountains to Winchester.

Among the troops on the Peninsula were five purely German regiments, the Seventh, Twentieth, Forty-sixth, Fifty-second and One Hundred and Third New York regiments, scattered in various brigades. Some entered the campaign late, as they had been sent first to South Carolina. In fullest measure the Twentieth, the Forty-sixth, and the Fifty-second participated and suffered. The Irish Brigade went to the front in the fall of 1861, was assigned to the corps of General E. V. Sumner, whose complete confidence it soon won, and marched with that corps into the Peninsula. Though it did not participate in the siege at Yorktown, the old Revolutionary battleground, another Irish regiment, the Thirty-seventh New York (the Irish Rifles), was present at the battle of Williamsburg. Other units of foreign-born which fought on the Peninsula were the Scotch Highlanders of the Seventy-ninth New York and the French Fifty-fifth New York.

It was another Irish unit, the Ninth Massachusetts, which scattered the enemy at Hanover Courthouse on May 27 after the brigade commander had told Colonel Cass that he wanted that regiment to retake two pieces of battery—"which I know they will." A line of battle was formed, and with a loud, vigorous cheer the command made a bold dash into and through the brush and tangled brier of a Virginia swamp. They charged upon the enemy; then, pouring a hot fire from behind a fence,

[47] John C. Ropes, "Gen. McClellan's Plans," in *Campaigns in Virginia*, 1861–1862, Papers of the Military Historical Society of Massachusetts, I, 82–83.

they scattered and drove the Confederates a long distance in every direction and captured a large number of prisoners.[48]

It will be recalled that the situation at the Battle of Fair Oaks was serious. The French observer [49] recorded that General Hiram G. Berry's brigade of Michigan regiments, of which an Irish battalion was a part, advanced through the disordered masses on the field as firm as a stone wall and did more by their single example than the strongest reinforcements. But it was the Irish Brigade which really won the day. Meagher's men, with eighteen pieces of artillery, formed the third line on the second day, June 1. When the foe, strengthened by reinforcements, moved forward again to the attack, Meagher's brigade was sent forward. General Sumner told the men of the brigade that they were his last hope; but pointing to his shoulder straps, he added, "I'll go my stars on you. I want to see how Irishmen fight and when you run, I'll run too." Responding with their well-known battle cry, the men of the brigade advanced with ferocity, mowing the enemy down and refusing to yield an inch of ground. From that day General Sumner swore by the Irish Brigade. The timely arrival of Hooker, moving upon the Confederate rear, together with a bayonet charge along the whole line, ended the battle and drove the Confederates in retreat toward Richmond; however, it proved to be a barren victory, as it left the armies in the same relative positions.[50]

The Brigade again won distinction at Gaines's Mill,[51] where General Fitz-John Porter publicly thanked the Irishmen on the field for having saved his army from disaster when, by a bayonet charge, they stopped the fugitives, rallied them, and allowed Porter to cross the river. At Savage Station and at White Oak Swamp the courage and discipline of these Irishmen once more elicited the encomiums of General McClellan and General Heintzelman.[52] At Malvern Hill, the last of the Seven Days' battles, the Sixty-ninth and Eighty-eighth sustained each other as genuine brothers. After bearing their full share in the action all day on July 1, they were called upon by Sumner to undertake the brilliant charge which decided the day. Sumner told Meagher that he had called upon the Irish because

[48] New York *Irish-American*, June 28, 1862.

[49] De Joinville, *The Army of the Potomac*, 73–74.

[50] Cavanagh, *Memoirs of Gen. Meagher*, 440–47; Mottelay and Campbell-Copeland (eds.), *The Soldier in Our Civil War*, I, 353; Headley, *The Great Rebellion*, I, 434, 436; New York *Irish-American*, June 14, 1862.

[51] For an account of this battle, see Rhodes, *History of the United States*, IV, 40–43.

[52] For the Irish services at these battles, see Greeley, *The American Conflict*, II, 162; Fox (comp.), *New York at Gettysburg*, II, 478.

he wanted a decisive charge, adding, "I depend upon your men as I could upon no others in all the army." Though this was no ordinary praise, it had been fairly won by their feats on that day. When, from incessant firing, their guns became too hot to handle, they picked up the muskets of the nearest dead or wounded comrades. When, after darkness had fallen on the hilltop, the conflict became hand-to-hand for a few moments, with the Louisiana Tigers fighting with knives and pistols, the Northern Irish, after they had ruined their guns by using them as clubs, seized the Confederate Irish by the throat and flung them to the ground. It was reported that thereafter General Sumner said he thought he could whip Lee's army with the Irish Brigade and Pettit's battery.[53]

The contribution of the Ninth Massachusetts to the battle of Gaines's Mill on June 27, 1862, where, after eight consecutive hours of fighting without food, they still found strength to rally for nine desperate charges, and to the victory of Malvern Hill on July 1 should receive recognition. When the batteries on the plain at the latter battle were in imminent danger of seizure by General John B. Magruder's brave men, who advanced in the face of a fire which actually blew whole ranks to pieces, the officer in command ordered the Ninth "up and at them." At Colonel Cass's order to charge, the Irishmen dashed out in front of the cannon against the advancing foe to such effect that the enemy paused an instant and then fled to the woods. The enemy's artillery then opened fire, compelling the Ninth to retire; and the conflict that followed that charge was scarcely paralleled in the battles of the Civil War for the desperate ferocity of the charges and the countercharges. It was here that this Massachusetts regiment lost its colonel, after having sustained serious losses including six line officers and over two hundred men four days earlier when it was assaulted by Stonewall Jackson's troops at Turkey Run.[54]

[53] New York *Irish-American*, July 19, 1862. See the tremendously graphic description of the battle in the August 2, 1862, issue of that paper.

The morning after the battle, Meagher invited General Sumner to inspect a pile of broken muskets in order to secure his order for new ones; the sight of splintered stocks and twisted bayonets brought from Sumner an outburst of wrath, until he was made aware that the damage had resulted not because stragglers disgracefully abandoned their weapons but because the "biys went for the Ribs in the way they wor used to" and "licked them well." The General never forgot this nor failed to remind the "biys" of the incident. O'Grady, "88th Regiment Infantry," in Fox (comp.), *New York at Gettysburg*, II, 511. For the same story, see Cavanagh, *Memoirs of Gen. Meagher*, 451.

[54] MacNamara, *The Irish Ninth in Bivouac and Battle*, 99 n., 101–104, 106–107; Miller (ed.), *The Photographic History of the Civil War*, I, 343; New York *Irish-American*, June 21, 1862.

The story of the contribution of the French unit, the Fifty-fifth New York, to the Peninsular campaign may best be told in figures. When, after an illness, their colonel, De Trobriand, rejoined his men on July 10, 1862, they had been reduced by the battles of this campaign to less than four hundred men. The others, apart from a few deserters, were lying on four battlefields, in the prisons at Richmond, or in hospitals. Their most noteworthy service was at Fair Oaks, where Generals Erasmus D. Keyes and Henry M. Naglee, after repeated vain efforts to rally their troops, caught sight of a small battalion of French troops, the Gardes Lafayette, standing in good order. Instantly the two commanders rode up to them, and, putting themselves at their head, charged the enemy and retook a battery. The battalion lost a fourth of its numbers in the charge, but with Gallic wit its members cried, "They may call us *Gardes Lafourchette* now if they like," in allusion to an uncomplimentary nickname which had been given them.[55]

BATTLE OF CROSS KEYS. A quick glance at the work of foreign-born units in the Shenandoah Valley will suffice to indicate that there was no arena of the conflict in which they were not found. Here Frémont's troops were pitted against Jackson's stalwart Virginians, many of whom were of German descent as were their Northern antagonists. Separation from the Army of the Potomac came early. The Garibaldi Guard, assigned during the first winter to Stahel's brigade of Blenker's division, was withheld from embarkation with the Army of the Potomac for the Peninsula and ordered to join Frémont in West Virginia, where it arrived after a series of fatiguing marches without proper food or supplies, a fact touched on before. The De Kalb Regiment was likewise detached the following April from McClellan's army and ordered to the Shenandoah Valley to join Frémont; it arrived early in May without the first articles of necessity for service in the field. In fact, it is difficult to escape the conviction that the German regiments of Blenker's division had been neglected by the War Department, under which neglect they had been remarkably patient. These detachments had been sent, of course, to strengthen the Union forces against General Jackson.

It was not long before Frémont was advancing against the Confederates and hotly engaging in battle at Cross Keys against General Richard S. Ewell on June 8, 1862. Oddly enough, the battle occurred between two old German churches, a Lutheran church and a chapel of the United

[55] De Trobriand, *Quatre Ans de Campagnes*, I, 277; De Joinville, *The Army of the Potomac*, 73.

German Brethren. General Robert C. Schenck's Ohio brigade formed the right wing; General Robert H. Milroy's three West Virginia regiments with one Ohio unit and Cluseret's small brigade constituted the center; the Eighth, Forty-first, and Forty-fifth New York and the Twenty-seventh Pennsylvania, forming Stahel's brigade, constituted the left wing; and Von Steinwehr's brigade, the Twenty-ninth and Sixty-eighth New York, together with the Seventy-third Pennsylvania, served in the reserve. Eight batteries were ranged in the line, and two were held in reserve. On the flanks were stationed the half-German cavalry regiments of Karge and Christian F. Dickel. The Garibaldi Guard was in the advance in Cluseret's brigade, which had, in addition, two nonforeign units. Bravely this little brigade held its ground after being engaged by the foe. Stahel's brigade was in the hottest part of the fight and lost heavily, acquitting itself well in its first battle. The men under Kryzanowski (the members of the Fifty-eighth New York, with its several Polish companies) elicited praise for their conduct on their first battlefield; for by a bayonet charge they drove the enemy's line back about a hundred yards and supported admirably the guns of Schirmer's light artillery at one point in the battle. The fight was over before dark, and, in view of the heavy loss of nearly seven hundred killed and wounded, the Federals were ordered to retire at midnight toward the south branch of the Shenandoah. In the German newspapers of the time, Blenker was represented as the real hero of Cross Keys. At the critical moment he had brought on the reserve of Koltes' three regiments, had thus secured a distinct advantage, and was just about to turn the defeat of the left wing into a victory when he was called back by Frémont. Blenker and Frémont were no longer in service after this campaign, the latter being replaced (to the great satisfaction of the German soldiers) by General Franz Sigel, who commanded Frémont's men as the First and later as the Eleventh Corps under Generals McClellan, Pope, and Burnside. That the units under Sigel fought stubbornly in the Shenandoah campaign of that summer is borne out by the reports of Confederate commanders.[56]

SECOND BULL RUN is the next engagement which requires consideration. Lee's bold and entirely successful maneuvers are too well known to require more than the barest mention: Lee divided his army, keeping Longstreet but sending Jackson around the Union right and rear, accepting calmly the risk of Pope's falling upon either portion of the army while it was divided. Two days later Jackson's "foot cavalry" had covered fifty-

[56] Kaufmann, *Die Deutschen im Bürgerkriege*, 303–307. For the bayonet charge, see Fox (comp.), *New York at Gettysburg*, I, 305–29.

six miles and stood at Manassas Junction in the rear of the foe, squarely across his communications. While Pope thought to crush Jackson at Manassas, James Longstreet, following swiftly on Jackson's path, joined the latter so that on the morning of August 29 the Confederates with a reunited army opposed Pope's scattered forces.

Sigel rendered his best service of the war at the only large battle in which he participated. After a slight brush with Jackson's outposts on the afternoon of August 28, 1862, had revealed that general's position north-west of Groveton, Sigel, recognizing the uselessness of marching further to Centerville, disregarded orders and informed Pope that he would bivouac where he was, in order to attack the next morning. Sigel opened the battle of Groveton at five in the morning and disposed the troops of his division as follows: Schurz's division extended to the northwest; Kryzanowski's brigade extended to the left; Schimmelfennig's brigade was arrayed at the right; and Koltes' brigade was held in reserve. Fairly early it became necessary to send in from the reserve the Twenty-eighth New York and also the reserve artillery. Schurz, understanding that Philip Kearney's division, which had come up on his right, would advance, went forward without the expected support; but Schimmelfennig's brigade succeeded not only in storming the railroad embankment but in pressing forward to the Cushing farm. Against fresh troops the exhausted men of Schurz's division held the embankment. Sigel sent Stahel's brigade in to help Schurz but could not avail himself of General John F. Reynolds' support, as Longstreet came up at that moment from Gainesville, a moment which might otherwise have been critical for Jackson's right wing. Only in the early afternoon, after more than eight hours of combat, did relief come for Schurz's division from two of S. W. Kearney's brigades, whereupon Schurz could take his division to a protected position. Pope squandered his opportunity to strike at Jackson by sending four small divisions against him separately instead of making a mass attack, which might have upset, if not wholly prevented, the junction of Longstreet and Jackson.

On the second day of the battle, the struggle centered chiefly around Bald Hill and Henry Hill, though the battle had really been lost with the failure of Porter's attempt to storm the embankment at a point somewhat below that which Schurz had taken the day before. Maps show clearly that Longstreet had first to take Bald Hill if Pope's position were to be taken. Only Nathaniel C. McLean's and Stahel's brigades of Schenck's division stood on the hill when Longstreet's legions struck against it. They offered strong resistance, and it was chiefly as a result of the havoc wrought by Sigel's artillery that Longstreet's attack came to a halt. Against ever-new masses of the enemy the Northern soldiers could not maintain their positions. Schurz promptly recognized the danger and hastened up, first with Koltes' and Kryzanowski's brigades, and then with Schimmelfennig's—his last. Despite his superiority in numbers, Longstreet made no progress against the grapeshot of Dilger's batteries. The German infantry also covered itself with glory and even passed from defense to attack. When Koltes led his brigade against a heavy battery, he was killed by a shell; Major A. Brückner fell beside Koltes, and almost a third of his small brigade was wiped out in this attack. Sigel, perceiving that the Schurz division was in danger of being cut off, ordered the retreat; but the opposition had held Longstreet for half an hour, and it was probably this space of time which prevented Longstreet from encircling the army. There was offered at Henry Hill a further defense, in which Schimmelfennig's brigade, also bringing up Dilger's artillery, participated and, for three quarters of an hour, met furious attacks from the greater part of Longstreet's corps.[57]

A final service may justifiably be credited to Sigel. In the critical situation at the end of the battle it was his arrangements which warded off the worst evils; the retreat to Centerville might have become a wild flight if Sigel, who was in the reserve with his decimated corps, had not with cool-headed caution erected a fourfold chain of infantry and cavalry which supported the fugitives. Except for Sigel and the approaching darkness, hundreds of cannon would have been lost. Lee's genius showed up at its best in this conflict, whereas the Federal measures were so ill-conceived and unfortunate that the Union army was all but wrecked. The gloom of that day was lightened only by the dogged fighting of the privates and the wisdom of some of the officers.[58]

ANTIETAM. After Lee had defeated Pope at Second Bull Run, the way was open for his advance into Maryland. Encouraged by the capture of Harpers Ferry without a struggle, he drew up his host on a row of heights that stretched along the west side of Antietam Creek around the village of Sharpsburg. While the Irish played an important role in the subsequent battle, as we shall see, several German regiments and the Scotch High-

---

[57] The fullest account of German participation in this battle is found in Kaufmann, *Die Deutschen im Bürgerkriege*, 323-32. See also Gordon, *History of the Campaign of the Army of Virginia under John Pope*, 254-60.

[58] Harter, *Erinnerungen aus dem amerikanischen Bürgerkriege*, 89.

landers fought with credit. It was a German regiment, the Twenty-eighth Ohio, which was the first to cross the river and attack the strong Confederate position on the other side. The Twentieth Regiment of New York Turners, which had gone to pieces badly at Gaines's Mill and again at White Oak Swamp, was now under Colonel Von Vegesack and about eight hundred strong. Its men marched on the field, moving obliquely to the left, in such fine martial array that they drew the whole fire of the enemy upon themselves. Colonel Von Vegesack and his field officers were riding behind them and urging them on in the most spirited manner. Together with the Seventh Maine Regiment, they charged a body of the enemy near some barns on the left flank, tearing down the rail fences in their path, and soon driving off the foe. The Germans thus lost heavily, but they took their position for the battle lying on the ground. Though adjoining regiments were protected by numerous boulders, the open ground in front of the Germans made them more vulnerable, so that every few minutes some of them were struck. When Colonel Thomas W. Hyde of the Seventh Maine pointed out to Von Vegesack that the elevation of his colors was drawing the enemy's fire, the Swedish commander refused to have them lowered, saying, "They are our glory." Von Vegesack continued to ride back and forth behind his Turners, revolver in hand to shoot any skulkers, easily the most conspicuous object on the field.[59]

Under the able leadership of the German major Charles Brestel, the Steuben Regiment of New York advanced on a hostile battery, seized it, took about a thousand prisoners, and captured three Confederate flags, sustaining a loss of sixty-four dead and wounded out of a regiment already reduced to scarcely five hundred able-bodied men.[60]

In less than half an hour after taking its position, the Irish Brigade came into action, and here, too, it sustained its enviable reputation. When Sumner went to the relief of Hooker, the men advanced steadily through the famous cornfield against heavy fire with a cheer to be heard a mile, though the mangled corpses lay in heaps among the tall, bare stalks, shorn of their leaves by the bullets. The Irishmen advanced almost to the crest of the hill against a foe posted in a continuation of the sunken road, and here they opened a terrific fire, continuing until their ammunition was nearly gone and their commander had been disabled by the fall of his

[59] For bad behavior of the Twentieth New York at Gaines's Mill, see Hyde, *Following the Greek Cross*, 68; at White Oak Swamp, *ibid.*, 73–74. For their action at Antietam, *ibid.*, 95–96, 96–97.

[60] Kaufmann, *Die Deutschen im Bürgerkriege*, 486.

horse. Then the Irishmen were relieved by General John Curtis Caldwell's brigade, held until that time in reserve. General Israel B. Richardson declared later that the Irish Brigade, and particularly the Eighty-eighth Regiment, were the finest troops in the United States Army, and that the credit of driving the enemy from the formidable position they occupied on the hill opposite the center of the Union attack belonged of right to them.[61] The loss sustained by the Brigade was terrific—nearly 50 per cent in one regiment and over 30 per cent in another. The Confederates seemed to have a particular grudge against the green flag, for five color-bearers were shot down successively in a short period of time. This caused even these intrepid men to hesitate for a moment in a task which seemed to invite death, but "Big Gleason," a captain in the Sixty-third, snatched up the flag. When, in a matter of minutes, the staff was shattered, Gleason tore the flag from the staff, wrapped it about his body under his sword belt, and passed through the rest of the battle untouched.[62]

In the advance along the Sharpsburg road in the afternoon of this fall day, September 17, 1862, the Seventy-ninth New York, which had been held in the reserve, deployed as skirmishers. From orchards and cornfields and from behind fences and haystacks the Confederate sharpshooters opened upon them, but the Scots swept on, driving in a part of one division and capturing a battery just before General A. P. Hill's troops came on the scene. With these reinforcements, the Confederates drove back the brave Highlanders from the suburbs of Sharpsburg, which they had by this time reached. Sharp fighting occurred around the Sherrick house.[63]

Also to be noted in connection with this battle is the work of several artillery units manned by Germans. Major Charles von Kusserow was praised on the field; Major Albert Arndt of the First New York Light Artillery was killed. The batteries of William Hexamer and A. A. von Puttkamer, of New Jersey and New York respectively, distinguished themselves. Here also Max von Weber, as commander of a brigade, won

[61] With the aid of Caldwell's men the Irish Brigade crossed the enemy lines, breaking by companies to the rear, while Caldwell's men broke by companies to the front—both brigades breaking as steadily as if on drill. Fox (author and comp.), *Regimental Losses in the Civil War*, 118. For Richardson's praise, see New York *Irish-American*, October 11, 1862. For other accounts of the charge of the Irish, see Judd, *The Story of the Thirty-third N.Y.S. Vols.*, 198; *History of the Corn Exchange Regiment, 118th Pennsylvania Volunteers*, 43–46; Cavanagh, *Memoirs of Gen. Meagher*, 458–62.

[62] For these losses, see Cavanagh, *Memoirs of Gen. Meagher*, 460, 461–62; Fox (author and comp.), *Regimental Losses in the Civil War*, 432.

[63] Miller (ed.), *The Photographic History of the Civil War*, II, 73; Todd, *The Seventy-ninth Highlanders*, 242–43.

his greatest fame but was severely wounded in the shoulder. His brigade in Sumner's corps held its position in a murderous fire, throwing the enemy back repeatedly and yielding only after the Confederates brought four more batteries into action against it.[64]

FREDERICKSBURG. The glorious achievement of the Irish Brigade in the Battle of Fredericksburg, although it failed in its attempt to take Marye's Heights, has almost obscured from recognition the effort of any other troops in this conflict. The events scarcely need repetition except to emphasize the service rendered that day by the sons of the Emerald Isle. The great struggle came, of course, in the effort to take Marye's Heights, the crest just back of the town. The Confederate position on this line of partially wooded hills was very strong. South of the town between the hills and the Rappahannock lay a section of low ground. The guns of the Washington Artillery of New Orleans lined the crest, while about fifty heavy guns were so placed as to enfilade the columns (which must approach through the narrow road leading to the hills and, finally, to a deep ravine in front of Fredericksburg), all the guns being invisible from below. Behind a stone wall at the foot of the hill stood part of Longstreet's force. Nothing more desperate than the effort to scale Marye's Heights could have been attempted.[65]

As the men of each successive brigade moved along the narrow road, they came within range of the Confederate guns, which mowed them down, creating great gaps in every company. When the ranks closed up and moved to the foot of the hill, they were met from the sunken road behind the stone wall by murderous volleys, with which it was impossible to cope. After two futile attempts by Sumner's and Hancock's divisions, the Irish Brigade deployed into line. Resolutely the twelve hundred men breasted the slope; shoulder to shoulder under the green flag of the Twenty-eighth Massachusetts and the Union standard, they swept forward against the low wall at the base of the hill. It is a singular fact that the thin line of Irishmen who charged so boldly across the plain was opposed, behind the stone breastwork in General Howell Cobb's brigade, by Irishmen just as fearless.

On the morning of the battle, General Meagher had bidden his Irishmen to deck their caps with sprigs of evergreen to remind them "of the

---

[64] Kaufmann, *Die Deutschen im Bürgerkriege*, 338 n., 524, 479, 512, 539, 561–62. For Arndt's death, see *Official War Records*, Ser. 1, IX, Pt. 1, p. 206.

[65] For the lay of the land and plans for Fredericksburg see Hosmer, *The Appeal to Arms*, 238–44.

land of their birth," for the New York regiments had sent their tattered colors home for replacement. The evergreen as an Irish symbol was quickly recognized by their countrymen among the Confederates and evoked the cry "Oh, God, what a pity! Here come Meagher's fellows." Continuing to advance, Meagher's men reached a point only a hundred yards from their goal, where the gunners were unable to depress their pieces sufficiently to fire on them. A shout went up from the shattered ranks as victory seemed within their grasp, when suddenly a sheet of flame leaped from the parapet and a murderous fire struck the advancing line. Though scores fell in their tracks "like corn before the sickle," the ever-thinning ranks dashed on. The Confederates sent volley after volley at such short range that every bullet met its mark. Though the defiant Irish struggled on a bit further no mortal could long withstand the terrific fire and at length the broken file had to yield ground. Many fell back to fight no more. The Irish Brigade virtually ceased to exist. Twelve hundred started the charge; almost six hundred fell. Forty yards from the wall the dead and the dying lay in heaps, one man within fifteen yards of the parapet. Not more than twenty minutes had elapsed from the moment when the first brigade of Hancock's division deployed until that when the broken remnants of Meagher's and Caldwell's brigades reeled back.[66]

The casualties among the officers were unusually great. Both the Sixty-ninth New York Regiment and the One Hundred and Sixteenth Pennsylvania Regiment were brought off the field by the fourth in line of command, the first three in each instance having been killed or wounded. At the next inspection of the Irish Brigade by General Hancock, one company presented seven men! A solitary private standing at company distance in the column, when angrily accosted by the commander and asked why he did not parade with his company, replied, "This is all my company, Sir." Of the nineteen commissioned officers of the Sixty-ninth New York Regiment who went into the fight on that day with Colonel Nugent, sixteen were killed or wounded, the leader himself being badly wounded. The

[66] For details of the Irish assault, see Mottelay and Campbell-Copeland (eds.), *The Soldier in Our Civil War*, II, 9–12; G. F. R. Henderson, *The Campaign of Fredericksburg, November–December, 1862* (London, 1886), 80–83, and *passim*; Conyngham, *The Irish Brigade*, 337–54. It is difficult to say just which regiment carried its colors nearest to the stone wall, and it is of little moment, as all were close; but Mulholland says that the bodies found nearest to the wall were those of Major Horgan and Adjutant Young of the Eighty-eighth New York. *The American Volunteer*, 18. See also MacNamara, *The Irish Brigade in Bivouac and Battle*, 157–66; Mulholland, *The Story of the 116th Regiment Pennsylvania Infantry*, 61–75. In his report Meagher said that of the 1,200 men he had led into battle, 280 remained. *Official War Records*, Ser. 1, XXI, pp. 129, 240–46.

color sergeant and all the color guard were shot down close to the enemy's guns. The regiment lost 75 per cent of its enlisted men.

Probably the story of Irish bravery in this battle can best be concluded with the words of the correspondent of the London *Times:* "Never at Fontenoy, Albuera, or at Waterloo, was more undoubted courage displayed by the sons of Erin than during those six frantic dashes which they directed against the almost impregnable position of their foe. . . . But the bodies which lie in dense masses within 40 yards of the muzzles of Colonel Walton's guns are the best evidence what manner of men they were who pressed on to death with dauntlessness of a race which has gained glory on a thousand battlefields, and never more richly deserved it than at the foot of Marye's Heights on the 13th day of December, 1862." [67]

It must not be imagined that the Irish Brigade alone suffered on that winter day. Hancock's entire command, of which it was a part, sustained a loss of over 40 per cent, the second highest loss of any division in any one engagement in the war. After the battle it numbered only 2,800. The Germans of the Steuben Regiment suffered bad losses at Fredericksburg; they went in with 25 officers, 18 of whom were killed or wounded. [68] Fredericksburg was a Union defeat and left its gloom, but the verdict of history has been "What a defeat!"

CHANCELLORSVILLE. The name and the reputation of the German divisions of Schurz and Von Steinwehr are indissolubly linked with the fate of the Eleventh Corps at Chancellorsville. Volumes have been written vilifying and reproaching the Germans for the defeat; other volumes have been written in their defense. It is no part of the purpose of the author to enter deeply into the arguments pro and con, but rather to state as succinctly as possible her conclusions after a fresh study of the subject. However, since many German regiments were involved, it is but just to state such of the facts as seem to justify the conclusion. In the first place the facts have often been distorted. A candid examination into the nativity

[67] Mulholland, *The American Volunteer,* 17, 18, 19; O'Grady, "88th Regiment Infantry," in Fox (comp.), *New York at Gettysburg,* II, 513–14. The usual touching stories of the fidelity of the color sergeant are told. The colors of this regiment (Sixty-ninth New York) were missed; they were found tucked into the blouse of the color sergeant when the detail went back to bury the dead. Mulholland, *The American Volunteer,* 19. "Albuera" refers to a battle fought at Albuera, Spain, on May 16, 1811, when Britain and her allies defeated the French under Marshal Soult, under whom an Irish regiment was fighting. London *Times,* January 13, 1862. The quotation is imperfectly copied in Moore (ed.), *Rebellion Record,* VI, Pt. 2, p. 111.

[68] On Hancock's division, see Miller (ed.), *The Photographic History of the Civil War,* II, 93; on the Steuben Regiment, see Mulholland, *The American Volunteer,* 17.

of the personnel of the corps at that time, May, 1863, has disclosed undeniably that only somewhat more than half of those involved in the first
blow by Jackson were German or of foreign lineage.[69] Popular belief at
the time, based on captious reports, was that the corps was almost wholly
German; that it had become demoralized and vindictive because of the
withdrawal of its idol, General Sigel; [70] and had been posted as skillfully
as any other division and yet had collapsed en masse without urgent reason,
thus jeopardizing the national safety at a critical moment in the war. It
was asserted that the corps had rushed past Chancellor House with the
disorder of a blind stampede.

Careful investigation seems to show that not all the corps was involved
in the flight, that the advance of the routed part of the corps was much
exaggerated, and that the frantic and tumultuous crowd fired into by
Hooker's staff included none of the Eleventh Corps. On the contrary, this
historic rout was the result of the flight chiefly of men and camp followers
of the Third and Twelfth Corps, with only perhaps a few of the pickets
escaping from the Eleventh Corps. In fact, the retreating portion of the
"German Corps" had passed the Chancellor House some time before and
was being halted in the rear of that structure. It has been shown that of
the entire strength of the corps, then estimated at 11,500, some 7,000 or
more were not at the Chancellor House at this rout: they were standing
in battle line or on the right flank of General Berry; had been killed,
wounded, or made prisoners of war on the Dowdall fields; or were with
Francis C. Barlow's detached brigade in search of Lee. The fewer than
5,000 who were at the Chancellor House have been made to represent the
entire Eleventh Corps, and as a consequence the members of the corps

[69] The reader will certainly recall that the author has stressed the changing character of
the various units in the army. Regiments which entered the service in 1861 made up almost
entirely of a given nationality often changed their character markedly through new recruits.
Kaufmann, *Die Deutschen im Bürgerkriege*, 345, puts the number of the Eleventh Corps at
Chancellorsville at 8,500, of which 4,600 were German.

[70] Kaufmann points out that Sigel, by resigning just before this battle, missed a great
opportunity to distinguish himself, and Kaufmann ascribes the cause to his "Pechvogel (bad
luck)." *Die Deutschen im Bürgerkriege*, 453–55. The author is aware that Howard forwarded
to Hooker on May 21 a list of the German troops in the Eleventh Corps, from which it would
seem that the Germans in the corps numbered 5,282, or more than half the corps present
for duty. *Official War Records*, Ser. 1, XXV, Pt. 1, p. 660. But the list does not indicate
how the count was taken nor what was understood by "German Troops." A veteran of the
corps writes that there were fifteen so-called "foreign regiments," eleven of which were
"exclusively German" and numbered 4,500 men, the other four being of mixed nationalities.
Captain Hartwell Osborn, *Papers of Military Order of the Loyal Legion* (Illinois Commandery), IV, 174. This shows the difficulty in presenting exact figures.

have been excoriated as cowardly "Dutchmen" without any care being taken to separate the natives from the naturalized soldiers of foreign birth. The truth is that many Germans fought well at Chancellorsville and should have been praised.[71]

The fundamental difficulty lay in the unfortunate location of the Eleventh Corps; and for that, General Howard, officer in command of the corps, was clearly to blame. His corps held the right of the Federal army with Generals Charles Devens, Schurz, and Von Steinwehr in command of the three divisions—right, center, and left respectively. The works thrown up for protection faced southward and were parallel to the Plank and Turnpike roads. These were formed by a deepening of the ditch at the side of the road, and by earthworks hastily thrown up and then strengthened with timber from near-by out-buildings and rails from fences. Only a portion of one brigade on the extreme right was thrown across the pike and faced west; and those men were protected only by slight works, an abatis, and two pieces of artillery. These were the preparations to meet the flank movement soon to be made by Jackson.[72]

A little closer examination of the placement of the different brigades of the corps may prove helpful. At four o'clock on the afternoon of May 2, 1863, the corps, from which the most efficient brigade, Barlow's, had been withdrawn, stood alone with no supporting troops near. Howard's headquarters were at Dowdall's Tavern. In the fields a few rods south of the tavern stood Buschbeck's brigade. Half a mile west of the tavern was the Talley House, where Von Steinwehr had his headquarters. At this point the line turned sharply to the north through a tangled thicket to the Hawkins farm. On the north side of the pike a short distance from Dowdall's Tavern was the Wilderness Church, a small, plain building, around and beyond which was placed Schurz's division, stretching toward Hawkins' farm, while northwest of the church stood Devens' division. Holding the extreme right of the line within the timber and facing west stood Von Gilsa's brigade. Furthermore, Howard's corps was isolated three quarters of a mile from the nearest supports. Among Von Gilsa's men on

[71] Some of these facts are brought out in Augustus Choate Hamlin, *The Battle of Chancellorsville; The Attack of Stonewall Jackson and his Army upon the Right Flank of the Army of the Potomac* . . . (Bangor, Maine, 1896), 99–100.

[72] For the placement of the parts of the corps, the author is accepting Jedediah Hotchkiss and William Allan, *The Battle-Fields of Virginia. Chancellorsville, embracing the Operations of the Army of Northern Virginia* . . . (New York, 1867), 48, as accurate. On the Fifty-third Pennsylvania and Sixty-eighth New York, see Charles Carlton Coffin, *Marching to Victory* (New York, c. 1888), 137.

the extreme right were the One Hundred and Fifty-third Pennsylvania (a new regiment of nine months men, mostly American citizens by birth) and the Fifty-fourth New York, an old regiment, mostly Germans. One section of Julius Dieckmann's battery (the Thirteenth Independent New York Battery) occupied the salient in the road. Two brigades of Schurz's division, Schimmelfennig's and Kryzanowski's, in double lines and Buschbeck's brigade of Von Steinwehr's division, together with Dilger's battery in the interval of the Orange Road, all stretching to the east but facing south, completed the corps. Barlow's brigade of Von Steinwehr's division, which constituted the all-important general reserve in the attenuated formation, was detached from the corps when the disaster engulfed it. The knowledge of two facts is absolutely essential for understanding the situation: the right or northern wing was unprotected, and dense woods around the wing concealed the stealthy advance of the foe to within charging distance.[73]

Schurz happened to be at Howard's headquarters at half past nine o'clock in the morning when two couriers arrived, one after the other, from Hooker, who was at this time in supreme command, warning Howard to examine the ground and decide on a position to meet the contingency of the Confederates throwing themselves upon his flank. There was reason to suppose that the enemy was moving to the Federal right. "The right of your line does not appear strong enough," reported the couriers from Hooker. Schurz believed that his and Devens' divisions should be withdrawn from their present positions to be formed on the open space which they then occupied and in the adjacent woods at right angles to the Chancellorsville Road so as to present a good front to the threatened attack. Howard, however, insisted that his right flank was sufficiently protected by the two regiments of Devens' division formed at right angles to his line of battle. Schurz was so convinced of the importance of an entirely different formation to meet the probability of a flank attack that on returning to his division he withdrew all his regiments in the second line to form them on the open ground north of the Plank Road facing the west.[74]

Meanwhile twenty-six thousand Confederates were moving quietly to overwhelm the few thousand of the Eleventh Corps. Howard interpreted

[73] For a sketch of the battlefield and exact location of the brigade, see Coffin, *Marching to Victory*, 135; Rice, "Afield with the Eleventh Army Corps at Chancellorsville," in Hunter (ed.), *Sketches of War History*, I, 371–72.

[74] Samuel P. Bates, *The Battle of Chancellorsville* (Meadville, Pa., 1882), 96, gives Schurz's views and action.

the clouds of dust reported to him as indicating retreat of the foe. Schimmelfennig, who had reported observation of the dust, distrusted any such idea and, in obedience to Schurz's order, sent a hundred picked men on a reconnaissance to ascertain what was in front. These men found the enemy in force a mile and a half south and, though fired upon, retired swiftly to give the information to corps headquarters. Later in the afternoon, Schurz again ordered Schimmelfennig to make a reconnaissance; the Seventy-fourth Pennsylvania accordingly came upon the enemy in great force. The Pennsylvania general then ordered his adjutant general, Major Gustav Schleiter, to ride full speed to inform Howard of the facts; but the major was received by Howard with an incredulous smile and told to direct his superior to stop reconnoitering and to remain in the position assigned him. This was two hours before the blow fell.[75] Furthermore, Major John F. Frueauff, of the One Hundred and Fifty-third Pennsylvania, has stated that an hour before the attack came, two scouts of an Ohio regiment reported in his presence to General Howard, as that commander was riding along the line, that the rebels were massed and had stacked arms in an open field fronting the Union lines. After all these warnings Howard still discredited the report, insisting that the foe was retreating.[76]

The blow caught most of the Eleventh Corps entirely unaware while they were eating their supper or lying listlessly on the ground with their heads upon their knapsacks, their cartridge boxes unslung and their arms stacked. They heard guns; rabbits and squirrels came leaping over their breastworks; and then in came the pickets shouting that the Confederates were upon them. Barely two regiments were drawn up to face the horde, the One Hundred and Fifty-third Pennsylvania and the Fifty-fourth New York; and these were covering the front, not in regular formation, but standing three feet apart like a line of skirmishers, with no artillery and no earthworks. The other troops of Von Gilsa's command faced south on the Turnpike Road. When the extreme right heard the wild Rebel yell, as startling as an Indian war whoop, accompanied by the roll of musketry and the explosion of a shell in the midst of the men, they did what any other men, native or alien, would have done under like circumstances. A few, the stouthearted among them, grasped their guns and fired, but some of the two most advanced regiments ran like deer across the fields.

[75] *Ibid.*, 97.

[76] *Ibid.*, 97–98. For Major Frueauff as inspector general, see *Official War Records,* Ser. 1, XXV, Pt. 1, p. 635.

Less than a thousand men held the front, completely isolated; the south front slowly, and then more swiftly, crumbled upon and over Schurz's lines, sweeping all in a broadening rout. Soon many units were struggling in wild disorder. Baggage wagons, ambulances, ammunition trains, a herd of oxen, all the camp followers, and frightened soldiers went tearing down the Plank Road and streaming across the fields in panic. A general demoralization seemed to threaten most of the corps, against which the officers strove in vain. The Eleventh Corps had given way, and this precipitated a crisis in the entire battle.

Many German units, doomed from the moment that Jackson succeeded in reaching the right flank, valiantly fought a losing fight, and that notwithstanding the disadvantageous position in which they had been placed. Even the two regiments which had to meet the first onslaught at the extreme right in the woods were not without honor. The Fifty-fourth New York did not abandon its position until one fourth of its number had fallen. The One Hundred and Fifty-third Pennsylvania was able to stand as a unit until the order to retreat was given. At break of day the next morning it marched by the silent reserve battalions on its way to change position to the extreme left; it felt the daggers of reproach until the commander of a New York regiment asked what regiment it was. At the reply that it was the One Hundred and Fifty-third Pennsylvania, there promptly came the order "Battalion present arms!"—the recognition of comrades for soldierly demeanor.[77] Von Gilsa's brigade certainly could not have fought any longer, attacked in the rear and simply rolled up as it was.

For ten minutes the Seventy-fifth Pennsylvania, with a few rallied supporters, tried to breast the Confederate advance to afford opportunity for the division to deploy in its rear; but in this brief interval the regiment was utterly wrecked—the colonel killed, the adjutant wounded, and 150 of the privates struck down while firing three rounds. In thirty minutes Jackson had disabled Devens' division of nearly four thousand men.

The Confederates next reached the Twenty-sixth Wisconsin, the Eighty-second Illinois, and the Fifty-eighth New York of Schurz's command. The first-named regiment, flanked on both sides and exposed to a terrible fire, maintained the unequal contest for twenty minutes, falling back only when ordered to do so. According to Schurz, had it not been for the firmness of these men, the enemy would have taken the rifle pits from the rear and appeared on the Turnpike before the artillery could be with-

[77] Major Rice recounts this very significant episode, "Afield with the Eleventh Army Corps at Chancellorsville," in Hunter (ed.), *Sketches of War History*, I, 391.

drawn.[78] All of these regiments fought desperately, retreated in battle order north of the road, and halted in line of battle on the right of Berry's position. The next German regiment in Schurz's line, the Seventy-fourth Pennsylvania, one of the best regiments in the entire corps, was disabled in the rush of Devens' broken division and could not be collected, but it did about as well as the American regiment next to it, the Sixty-first Ohio. General Schimmelfennig commanded a brigade in the second line of the corps. When the troops of the first line came dashing through his regiments, he kept them steady, changed front in less than two minutes, and advanced to meet the foe. Seventy men went down in the Eighty-second Illinois, and the colonel of this regiment, Friedrich Hecker, was shot from his saddle while trying to rally it.

Buschbeck's brigade of three German regiments and one American regiment of Von Steinwehr's division on the south side of the road had had time to assemble and, by taking the opposite side of the entrenchments created for Barlow's brigade, could deliver an effective flanking fire as the dense masses of Confederates rushed madly on. Dilger's battery with its deadly canister was again brought into position here to deliver a flanking fire. For the space of nearly an hour, heedless of the wild race of men past and over them to the rear, the four thousand men of this brigade, to whom a number of Schurz's regiments attached themselves, and the artillery on the ridge east of the church checked the Confederates, who outnumbered them three to one. Night was settling down when, before twenty thousand of the enemy, the men of this brigade retreated sullenly down the road toward Chancellorsville in perfect order, a feat which won applause from everyone. This stubborn resistance took a heavy toll from Jackson's front line. Several of Schurz's regiments retired in good order into the woods north of the pike. Later Schurz and Buschbeck, with soldiers rallied from Devens' broken regiments, formed a line of battle before Chancellorsville. Buschbeck's fourth regiment, the Seventy-fifth Pennsylvania (an American regiment), was on picket duty south of Dowdall's Tavern with only 180 men; for ten minutes it tried to breast the Confederate advance, but it could not with its meager numbers be expected to resist the seventeen regiments turned loose upon it.[79]

[78] *Official War Records*, Ser. 1, XXV, Pt. 1, p. 655.

[79] For accounts of the way these regiments fought, see Coffin, *Marching to Victory*, 139–40; Rice, "Afield with the Eleventh Army Corps at Chancellorsville," in Hunter (ed.), *Sketches of War History*, I, 383–87; Hamlin, *The Battle of Chancellorsville*, 69–76; Bates, *The Battle of Chancellorsville*, 102; Kaufmann, *Die Deutschen im Bürgerkriege*, 358–63.

With the three German batteries, Dilger's, Dieckmann's, and Wiedrich's, no fault can justly be found. Dilger and Wiedrich stood to their guns as long as their positions were tenable. The two guns on picket from Dieckmann's battery were served as long as they could be worked, with a loss of thirteen men to each section. The other four guns at the Talley House were in a faulty position and had no opportunity to fight, as the enemy was completely in the rear.[80]

It is not pertinent to this narrative to recount the events of the second day of fighting other than to note that the Eleventh Corps, notwithstanding its disorganized condition, was so far reorganized during the night as to be fit for duty again. It was assigned to a position on the left, where it seemed probable that there would be little or no fighting. It is in order, however, to point out that in this day's conflict 120,000 Union troops were defeated by less than half that number of Confederates.

The conclusion seems inescapable that the Eleventh Corps, and more particularly the German contingent, was made the scapegoat for General Howard's persistent, stubborn neglect of the plainest precepts of military foresight (as manifested by his failure to put his corps in position to meet an attack from the west); for his utter disregard of even elementary principles of flank defense; and for his inexplicable contempt of reports which came to him from before midmorning until late afternoon. For the ultimate failure of the battle, General Hooker's more comprehensive errors in tactics must be held responsible (despite the fact that his brilliant strategy had previously brought a signal victory within the grasp of the Army of the Potomac [81]). Considering the disparity in numbers, forty-five hundred opposed to twenty-six thousand, and the fact that the Union forces were completely outflanked at the commencement of the attack, no more resolute resistance could have been offered. This seems to be the opinion of those in the best position to judge [82] and is the conclusion to which independent study has forced this writer. Large numbers of the Eleventh Corps were undoubtedly as brave as any troops in the army. The censure of the Germans as cowardly was most unjust and was partly

[80] Hamlin, *The Battle of Chancellorsville*, 166–67.

[81] Hooker did what was rarely done—he outgeneraled Lee.

[82] See the views of Marvin, *History of Worcester in the War of the Rebellion*, 320; Rice, "Afield with the Eleventh Army Corps at Chancellorsville," in Hunter (ed.), *Sketches of War History*, I, 358–59; Bates, *The Battle of Chancellorsville*, 181–82; William R. Hilyer, *Chancellorsville, May 2 and 3, 1863* (*Military Order of the Loyal Legion of the United States*, Commandery of the District of Columbia, *War Papers*, No. 55), 13; W. R. Livermore, *Story of the Civil War*, III, Bk. 1, p. 164; Hamlin, *The Battle of Chancellorsville*, 128.

attributable to ugly race prejudice. Probably the verdict of history can be put in no more trenchant words than those of Colonel T. A. Dodge, who was present in Schurz's command: "No division of the Army of the Potomac, not the old Guard of Napoleon, not Frederick the Great's automats, could have changed front under the staggering blow. . . . Rather wonder that the onset of Jackson was actually checked by this surprised and overmatched, this telescoped force, for more than an hour, at the loss of one-third its effective force. Could more have been expected?"[83]

Unfortunately, the calm verdict of history was not available at the time. In the bitterness of a disastrous defeat the nation accepted the excuses of the leaders and gave free rein to a prejudice willing to find a scapegoat in the foreign-born element in the army. The passion and prejudice which manifested themselves at the time did not reflect credit on the American people and brought some unfortunate results; but discussion of that subject belongs to a later chapter.[84]

The service rendered by the Irish at Chancellorsville came almost entirely on the second day of battle. Dilger, while retreating with his single gun on the evening of May 2, was supported, it is true, by two companies of Irishmen of the Sixty-first Ohio,[85] who kept the enemy at bay and the Turnpike free from active pursuit. This was one of the bright episodes of the ill-fated May 2. On this first day, the participation of Meagher's Irish Brigade was limited to halting the runaways at a ford called Scott's Mills; this was effected by Meagher's throwing across the road and into the wood a line of his men, who stood calmly with lowered

[83] Rice, "Afield with the Eleventh Army Corps at Chancellorsville," in Hunter (ed.), *Sketches of War History*, I, 382 n. It was said that Hooker disliked the Eleventh Corps, though his reason is not known, as the men of the corps were fond of him. He also wished to get rid of Schurz, then only in temporary command. Hamlin, *The Battle of Chancellorsville*, 158.

Hancock told an investigating committee of Congress that the Eleventh Corps had never been considered a part of the original Army of the Potomac, and that not much dependence had been placed upon it. Hooker in a letter to Lincoln of May 7, 1863, claims that a glorious victory would have crowned his efforts but for one corps. Hamlin, *The Battle of Chancellorsville*, 141. "It is quite certain that the composition of the corps had much to do with the fierce and unrelenting denunciation hurled upon it by those really at fault, who sought to escape censure by declaring the men of the Eleventh Corps as the scapegoats, and whose amazing self-conceit and shameless selfishness prevented them from exercising the common dictates of fairness and humanity." Hamlin, *The Battle of Chancellorsville*, Addenda, note 20, p. 165.

[84] See Chapter XVIII of text.

[85] This was not an Irish regiment, but it had two Irish companies. It is particularly pleasing to note that Irish and Germans supported each other in this way in battle.

bayonets in the scene of confusion.[86] Many of the wounded of Fredericksburg had returned to the ranks by this time; in a measure they had forgotten that bloody field and the morale was excellent, for they were glad to leave the winter camp.[87] Altogether the brigade numbered 1,150. By ten o'clock on the morning of May 3 an order arrived for the Irish Brigade to move out to Chancellorsville to join the rest of the division, which was engaged in beating back the Confederates, and especially to support the Fifth Maine Battery. The brigade started for the front, soon encountering evidence of the conflict as streams of wounded passed them. Despite the whirr of the canister and the whistle of the bullets, the men marched on quietly through the woods, many exchanging repartee.[88] After two hours they reached the battery, which was well worked and never ceased firing until all the men and horses were killed or wounded except one corporal and one private. The Irish Brigade arrived just in time to save the guns and possibly to save the army from another panic, as several regiments were giving way. Hancock put Meagher in command of the retreat, a task which engaged the brigade Sunday night and all day Monday and which was discharged at small cost—only fifty killed and wounded. As the men emerged from the woods, they met General Sickles, who called for three cheers for the regiment that had saved the guns.[89]

[86] See Hamlin, *The Battle of Chancellorsville*, 78, for the episode of Dilger's gun. For the line at Scott's Mills, see Cavanagh, *Memoirs of Gen. Meagher*, 483, and Mulholland, *The Story of the 116th Regiment Pennsylvania Infantry*, 107–13.

[87] With the usual Irish good nature they exchanged greetings with the Confederates as they were being stationed at the United States ford: "Hello, Yank," and "How are you, Rib?" *Ibid.*, 105.

[88] The irrepressible humor of the Celt merits recording. A sergeant, looking back, waved his hand to the earth and air, and in a ludicrous manner exclaimed, "Good-boi, wurrelld." Another said to a comrade, "What are we going in here for, Jimmy?" "To be after making history, Barney, to be sure." *Ibid.*, 109.

[89] *Ibid.*, 116–17; Cavanagh, *Memoirs of Gen. Meagher*, 484–85.

CHAPTER SEVENTEEN

The Rising Tide of Victory

THE second half of the war, roughly considered—for the war does not lend itself to any easy division between East and West or to precise chronology—was largely concerned with the period of mounting Union victory and declining Confederate strength. Since Gettysburg was the first decisive battle in the East and since, indeed, in the minds of most scholars it marks the turning point in the war, this chapter begins with this climactic struggle. The reader's attention is then directed to the war in the West, although chronologically some of the battles in that theater, occurring long before the opposing forces met at the little Pennsylvania town which the battle made famous, had been victories for the North. However, excluding the failures of Grant in the Wilderness and the defeat at Chickamauga, this chapter may not too illogically be considered as developing the period of Union successes and measuring the part of the foreigners in that victory.

SIGNIFICANT BATTLES AND MOVEMENTS

GETTYSBURG. All the various nationalities represented in the Army of the Potomac, reinforced by state militia summoned hastily from Pennsylvania and adjacent states, shared in the Battle of Gettysburg. The main body of the Eleventh Corps arrived on the field about half past one on the first afternoon of battle, July 1, fatigued by a forced march of ten miles or more under a hot July sun without a halt, from their encampment of the night before near Emmitsburg. General Howard held back Von Steinwehr's division and Wiedrich's battery to fortify Cemetery Hill but sent Schurz's and Barlow's divisions forward to assist General Abner Doubleday. Schurz on this occasion commanded the corps, as Howard by virtue of seniority had assumed temporary command of the entire field when General Reynolds fell; General Schimmelfennig succeeded to the command of Schurz's division. Schurz saw instantly the advantage of seizing

Oak Ridge in order to make connection with the right of the First Corps and thus prolong the Union line northward along the ridge. However, before his troops could reach the ridge, General R. E. Rodes's division of Ewell's Confederate corps, whose movement had been concealed by the woods, had occupied it. This forced Schurz to deploy his two divisions on the lower ground in the rear between Oak Ridge and Rock Creek.[1] Schimmelfennig, first on the field, deployed his two brigades in double lines to hold the right. The second brigade of Von Steinwehr's division of the corps under General Orlando Smith, which was placed in reserve, held Cemetery Hill from the time of Howard's arrival on the field and was not engaged in the fighting of the first day. Barlow's division, with the German Rifles (Fifty-fourth New York) was caught between two Confederate forces; after fighting desperately, it was finally withdrawn, leaving behind many dead and wounded. Among the latter was its commander, who was badly disabled. The Southern force turned at once against Schimmelfennig's division and with a brigade routed the entire division, which began a race rearward in competition with Barlow's men. General Early, profiting from the disorder and confusion among the Germans, especially in the town of Gettysburg, gathered in thousands of prisoners. Though the Eleventh Corps and the First Corps fought bravely against thirty thousand of Lee's men for six hours, by the close of this first day of battle both had been crushed and driven in disorder through the streets of Gettysburg. Both suffered from the lack of main direction which resulted from General Reynolds' death early in the first day's fight.[2]

Possibly because it was still suffering from the humiliation of the reproaches after Chancellorsville, the Eleventh Corps did not measure up to its best; but to leave the story at that point would be a grave injustice. Some of the brigades and regiments fought bravely and well. Adelbert Ames's brigade was the last of the corps to fall back and did not share in the panic. Some of the foreign regiments stood their ground stanchly, and these, after issuing from the town of Gettysburg, were promptly reorganized, as Schurz has pointed out.[3] The veteran Forty-first New York was absent from Von Gilsa's brigade on detached duty until evening; therefore, that brigade consisted that day of only three regiments to hold

[1] Fox (comp.), New York at Gettysburg, I, 15.

[2] [Pierce], The Battle of Gettysburg, 122–25; De Trobriand, Quatre Ans de Campagnes, II, 135–36. Schurz admitted defeat and retreat but denied a rout, for it had "no element of dissolution in it." Schurz, Reminiscences, III, 12.

[3] George A. Thayer, "Gettysburg, as We Men on the Right Saw It," in Hunter (ed.), Sketches of War History, II, 32.

a position at the base of a knoll. It was attacked by General John Brown Gordon's Georgia brigade, assisted by strong artillery fire, which enfiladed the entire line of the Eleventh Corps. These regiments were forced back over the knoll, but only after a prolonged resistance did the division retreat to a second position, where it formed anew. The striking down of the divisional commander, General Francis Barlow, who had been directing his troops with coolness and intrepidity, was certainly no contribution to morale.[4]

Meanwhile, Schimmelfennig's two brigades, arriving on the field earlier than the others of the Eleventh Corps, had come under heavy artillery fire from Early's batteries. The Forty-fifth New York under Lieutenant Colonel Adolphus Dopke, arriving at the double quick and taking position near the First Corps, delivered an effective fire. Even more honorable was the conduct of the One Hundred and Forty-seventh New York Regiment of Colonel George von Amsberg's brigade; for despite the severe fire that struck down over two hundred of its men along with six officers, it fought its way forward to the farthest point reached by any regiment on the line of the Eleventh Corps. Likewise, when the Second Brigade under Colonel Kryzanowski was ordered forward to support Barlow's division, the One Hundred and Nineteenth New York held its ground for a long time, though suffering severely from shot and shell.[5]

When the Eleventh Corps was given the order to retreat, the Seventy-fifth Pennsylvania Regiment, unconscious of the danger of being flanked, obeyed only reluctantly and not a moment too soon; but owing to the foresight of Major August Ledig, who as senior officer had succeeded to the command when Colonel Franz Mahler fell mortally wounded, the regiment retreated in good order. After passing through the town, the corps was assigned a new position on the plateau of Cemetery Hill, where it remained (with the exception of small sallies) during the rest of the battle and where it was joined by the Forty-first New York late on the night of the first day. Owing to its conduct during the first day's fight, the advance of the enemy was checked, thus enabling General von Steinwehr to post his batteries and fortify himself on Cemetery Hill. This hill proved the key for the Federal army in the further course of the battle. One writer claims, with some reason, that if the Eleventh Corps, along with the First, had done nothing else than maintain that position, it would

---

[4] Fox (comp.), *New York at Gettysburg*, I, 20.
[5] *Ibid.*, 21; "Address by Col. James C. Carmichael," *ibid.*, III, 1059.

have amply justified its claim to a share in the victory.[6] It should be noted that Von Steinwehr's division was on Cemetery Hill before General W. S. Hancock took charge of the field under General Meade's orders to succeed Reynolds.

Although then led not by its organizer, General Meagher,[7] but by Colonel Patrick Kelly, the Irish Brigade, its three New York regiments consolidated into a battalion of six companies, came to that battlefield on the late evening of July 1, in Hancock's command, footsore and weary but as ready for conflict as if its ranks had been full. Here it again won the plaudits of the country for its brilliant conduct and the desperate character of its fighting. When the Third Corps recoiled in the late afternoon of the second day during the advance on the peach orchard, the Irish Brigade was ordered to its aid.

Here there occurred one of the dramatic events which had been seen in connection with Catholic regiments on European battlefields but possibly had never before been witnessed in America. When the order was given on July 2 for the Irish Brigade to "fall in," it was formed in close columns by regiments, even though it had been sadly reduced in numbers. There was a short delay, during which the regiments stood at "Order Arms." Father William Corby, the chaplain of the brigade, stepped upon a large rock in front of the men, secured their attention, and announced his readiness to grant them, one and all, the rite of absolution before they entered battle. The war-worn veterans knelt upon the ground with bowed, uncovered heads while the priest with outstretched hands pronounced in Latin the solemn words of general absolution.[8] He urged them to perform their duty, reminded them of the sacred nature of their trust as soldiers and of the noble object for which they were battling, and ended by saying that

[6] Nachtigall, "Account of the Part Taken by the Seventy-fifth Regiment Pennsylvania Volunteers," in Nicholson (comp.), *Pennsylvania at Gettysburg*, I, 438–39; "Oration of Christian Böhm," in Fox (comp.), *New York at Gettysburg*, I, 375.

[7] Meagher resigned immediately after the Battle of Chancellorsville. As no reply had been given to his memorial to the Secretary of War asking for reinforcements for the Irish Brigade, he felt that he could not, in justice to himself or to his command, submit any longer to the treatment he was receiving from the government.

[8] Each could receive the benefit of absolution by making a sincere act of contrition and firmly resolving to embrace the first opportunity to confess his sins. See Fox (comp.), *New York at Gettysburg*, I, 51–52, 52 n. The words read: "Dominus noster Jesus Christus vos absolvat, et ego, auctoritate ipsius, vos absolvo ab omni vinculo ex communicationis et interdicti in quantum possum et vos indigetis, deinde ego absolvo vos a peccatis vestris in nomine Patris, et Filii, et Spiritus Sancti. Amen." *Ibid.*, 51–52. Father Dillon, it is said, also gave absolution to the Sixty-third Regiment at Savage Station. *Ibid.*, II, 498.

the Catholic Church refused Christian burial to the soldier who turned his back upon the foe or deserted his flag. Thus spiritually strengthened, the men moved forward.

The Irish Brigade engaged in battle late on July 2 in the woods on the west side of the wheat field near the foot of Little Round Top, sometimes in hand-to-hand fighting as it sought to surmount that hill. It lost fully a third of its men and captured a number of prisoners. When the sun went down on that day's fighting, the brigade still held the wheat field, but it was then ordered to Cemetery Ridge, where it formed to the left of the Second Corps on ground which it had occupied earlier in the day.

All the morning of July 3 the brigade sat around awaiting the result of the fight at Culp's Hill and joined in the cheer which announced about eleven o'clock the victory of the Twelfth Corps. The Confederate batteries in the artillery duel for Cemetery Ridge directed their fire largely on that part of the Ridge held by Hancock's corps. The Pennsylvania regiment of the Irish Brigade was in the center as George E. Pickett's men approached. During the two hours of the artillery duel preceding the charge, the men hugged the ground closely; and as they lay in front of their own guns, their own fire as well as that of the enemy passed over them. When the smoke cleared and the Irish could see Pickett's men advancing and falling by the hundreds and thousands, they felt grimly that this was Fredericksburg in reverse. And when the day closed on the victory of Gettysburg, the Irish could again feel that they had borne an honorable part in the victory.[9] The fact that New York cared to appropriate money for a monument to commemorate the services of the Irish Brigade on the battlefield of Gettysburg is sufficient testimony to the quality of that service. A Pennsylvania unit which stood with its countrymen from Ireland on Cemetery Ridge and helped to break Pickett's charge was the Sixty-ninth Regiment of the Keystone State.

As everyone knows, the artillery played an important role in this battle. Wiedrich's battery held a commanding position on East Cemetery Hill through the three days of battle. After dark on the second day, the enemy made an attack along the whole line of the Eleventh Corps to capture the batteries on the top of the hill. The Louisiana Tigers assaulted Wiedrich's battery but suffered near annihilation. The assault was so sudden that the infantry in front gave way and the enemy got within the battery. A Confederate soldier planted the Rebel colors on one of the lunettes of the

[9] Mulholland, *The Story of the 116th Regiment Pennsylvania Infantry*, 135–41.

left section and demanded surrender of the gun, but he was promptly knocked back and lost his flag. Schurz told how, after the guns became so hot that they could no longer be fired, the cannoneers defended themselves with sponge staffs, fence rails, hand spikes, and even stones; and how a Confederate officer brandished his sword and cried, "This battery is ours!" but a sturdy Teuton replied, "No, dis battery ist unser," felling the officer at the same time with a sponge staff.

Schurz had correctly interpreted the uproar near at hand and the danger to the ammunition trains parked between Cemetery Ridge and Culp's Hill; consequently, with the consent of Howard, he accompanied Kryzan-owski and two regiments, which went with fixed bayonets to the aid of the batteries, encountering stragglers from the already broken lines en route. The melee at the batteries was almost indescribable. The infantry rushed upon the invaders and after a spirited hand-to-hand scuffle hurled them down the embankment.[10] Dilger's cannoneers from Ohio also rendered good service.

The Fifteenth Independent Battery of New York, organized originally with the expectation of being attached to the Irish Brigade but later known as Patrick Hart's Battery, rendered, with its four brass Napoleons, valiant service here as a part of the reserve artillery. The battery entered battle only about half after four on the second day of battle. Stationed in the peach orchard, it repulsed an attack by J. B. Kershaw's South Carolina brigade. After repulsing a second charge, it found its munition exhausted except for some solid shot, and so it was obliged to withdraw after having been in action over two hours. On the third day, posted about halfway between Cemetery Hill and Little Round Top, it participated in the grand cannonade which preceded the famous charge by Pickett; likewise, it played its part in repulsing the Confederate advance after the artillery duel had ceased. During the artillery fire with which the foe sought to cover the retreat of Pickett's men, this New York battery succeeded in exploding two Confederate caissons and dismounting two guns by skill-fully placed shots.[11]

The Eleventh Corps had to bear a share of the terrific artillery barrage from the Confederates against Cemetery Hill and to endure the storm of missiles passing over their heads, though the loss of life was slight. As

[10] Frederick Smith, "Historical Sketch," in Fox (comp.), *New York at Gettysburg*, III, 1245–48; Schurz, *Reminiscences*, III, 24–25.

[11] Edward Knox, "Historical Notes," in Fox (comp.), *New York at Gettysburg*, III, 1327–29.

the Confederates approached close enough, they added the bullets of their muskets to the cannon.[12]

As a part of the Second Corps, the Thirty-ninth New York, or Garibaldi Guards, then numbering only four companies (322 men to be exact), had its share in the victory. It distinguished itself by charging the enemy, by retaking a battery of the Fifth United States Artillery, which, after great loss of men and horses, had been abandoned, and by conveying this battery safely to the rear. It was against the front of the Second Corps that Pickett made his charge. As indicative of the initiative of the minor officers of this regiment, it might be remarked that after the major was wounded each of the captains commanded independently.[13]

The Fifty-second New York, another German regiment, saw action in the Second Corps on the evening of the second day from five to eight o'clock. It lost a great many men in the woods between the wheat field and the peach orchard—perhaps half of the tiny number with which it had gone into battle; and when it was forced back, it left many wounded in the wheat field.[14]

An incident of that day which bears repetition is the deed of a young Irishman, Colonel Patrick O'Rorke, whose quick grasp of a critical situation was probably responsible for the saving of Little Round Top to the Union. This hill, which the Confederates had already begun to climb, commanded Meade's entire position. O'Rorke's regiment, the One Hundred and Fortieth New York, was marching with its division toward the front on the second day of battle and had reached the point in the ridge where the railroad now crosses the roadway when General G. K. Warren with several officers rode rapidly to the head of the regiment. In a manner showing unusual excitement, he called to O'Rorke to lead his regiment up the hill. Though O'Rorke demurred that his superior officer expected him to follow the division, he nevertheless accepted Warren's assumption of responsibility and led his men diagonally up the eastern slope to the summit of Little Round Top just as the Confederates were reaching the crest from the other side. Bullets greeted his leading company as it mounted the ridge, and consequently there was no time for tactical formation. Leaping from his horse O'Rorke drew his sword and shouted to his men, "This way, boys." The men grasped their weapons by the

[12] Schurz, *Reminiscences*, III, 27–33.

[13] "The Garibaldi Guard and its Service," in Fox (comp.), *New York at Gettysburg*, I, 282; see also introductory account, I, 57, in the same work.

[14] Charles H. Althans, "52d Regiment Infantry," *ibid.*, I, 394.

butts (not by the barrels, as has been stated elsewhere) and charged over the rocks and down the hillside till they came abreast of Colonel Strong Vincent's brigade, a Northern unit posted in the ravine to the left.

Among the rocks was soon formed an irregular line, which was extended toward the right as the other companies came upon the scene of action. It was only when O'Rorke's men came abreast of Vincent's men that they had time to load and return the fire of the enemy from the trees and underbrush. The foe pressed very close to the Union line; the steadiness of both sides made the result for some minutes doubtful, especially as the foe had almost enveloped Vincent and his Eighty-third Pennsylvania, who, though outnumbered and outflanked, had maintained the fight. A desperate and bloody struggle soon forced the Confederates back. By this time Charles Hazlett's battery, which had broken through O'Rorke's lines before they fully reached the top, had taken position on the crest and was sweeping the hostile lines. O'Rorke's regiment paid a stiff price for saving this crucial point, for in a few minutes not only were one hundred of its number killed and wounded but its young commander was lost and with him the further service which he could undoubtedly have rendered to the cause.[15]

SIEGE OF VICKSBURG—BATTLE OF CHAMPION'S HILL. With the details of the siege of Vicksburg this study has no concern. Naturally, there were in the Army of the West some of the same foreign-born regiments which have already been encountered. In the general premature storming of Vicksburg ordered by Grant on May 22, 1863, many German regiments participated: Osterhaus' old brigade, the Third, Twelfth, and Seventeenth Missouri. Colonel von Wangelin criticized sharply the insufficient preparations for the attack. The troops first had to march uphill and downhill for three miles before they reached their position. Then they had to run through three places where they were helplessly exposed to the fire of the enemy. Von Wangelin felt, most justifiably, that they could have passed these places at night without any loss in order to venture at dawn the chief attack upon the true defenses. The result might have been very different if the command had not exacted of troops already wearied by marching the running of three gauntlets and if, above all, it had not afforded the enemy opportunity to count in bright daylight almost

[15] The name also appeared as "O'Rourcke," but the writer has accepted Heitman's spelling as well as his number for the regiment, though Marshall [Pierce] refers to it as the One Hundred and Fiftieth. Heitman (comp.), *Historical Register and Dictionary*, I, 760. For the episode given in the text, see "Address by Captain Porter Farley," in Fox (comp.), *New York at Gettysburg*, III, 956–59. Hazlett was killed.

every man who was put into the assault. The Twelfth Missouri went out with 350 men, of whom almost one third were killed or wounded. A part of this regiment succeeded in climbing the slippery hill, pressing up to the front of the bastion, and coming within 400 yards of the last trench of the foe. Major Gustavus Leichtfuss fell as he was leading his men to storm the works. Most of the troops of the Third Missouri, the Seventeenth Missouri, and the Ninth Iowa, which were following him, remained stuck in the slippery sand, and only a few of them reached the plateau. The men of the Thirty-seventh Ohio, which the reader will recognize as a German regiment, distinguished themselves in this assault and suffered heavy losses. This frightful day's work cost the Union 2,500 dead and wounded.[16]

In the many battles fought to win the ground east of Vicksburg, Osterhaus was especially distinguished. Grant had summoned him from Missouri in the preceding January. It was his misfortune to have his division assigned to the corps of General John A. McClernand, a political appointee who committed many blunders. To deliver sturdy, even brilliant, blows under such a commander was indeed a feat; and Osterhaus achieved it, especially in the battles on the Big Black River, where he was wounded.[17]

CHICKAMAUGA. In the significant battles after Vicksburg fell (Chickamauga, Lookout Mountain, and Missionary Ridge), the foreign-born soldiers bore an honorable part, and for the first time some of the foreign-born units from the East fought in the West. Among the twenty thousand men from the Army of the Potomac who were under Burnside and Hooker were the men of the Eleventh Corps, which was reorganized after the losses of the Chancellorsville and Gettysburg campaigns and sent along with the Twelfth Corps to the relief of Rosecrans, though not until after his defeat at Chickamauga. Wiedrich's battery was here, of course, and it was while this battery was in Tennessee that its commander resigned in order to command the Fifteenth New York Heavy Artillery. The essentially German brigade of Colonel Laiboldt, the regiments of Germans from the West, and the Norwegians of the Fifteenth Wisconsin were also here—all to face soldiers as good as the Confederacy possessed.

Rosecrans began his Chickamauga campaign brilliantly; with excellent strategy, he marched South to threaten the Confederate communications.

---

[16] Kaufmann, *Die Deutschen im Bürgerkriege,* 387–88, and 526 n. (under "Leichtfuss"). The Major's name appeared as "Lightfoot" in *Official War Records,* Ser. 1, XXIV, Pt. 2, p. 252, where his death is recorded.

[17] Kaufmann, *Die Deutschen im Bürgerkriege,* 387 n.

He maneuvered General Bragg out of middle Tennessee; advanced through a difficult country; and, without even a battle, captured Chattanooga, one of the most important strategic points of the South. Just when his troops were widely separated (while crossing the mountains by gaps far apart), Bragg turned on his enemy and placed Rosecrans in deadly peril. Von Willich's brigade had distinguished itself by the capture of several strategic passes. The fierce encounters of the first day of the Battle of Chickamauga, September 19, 1863, settled nothing for either side. The disaster of the second day was saved from becoming a catastrophe only by General George H. Thomas' stand on the "rock of Chickamauga," a horseshoe-shaped, rocky hillock, against which the army of Bragg dashed itself in vain.[18] The terrain was unfavorable for the disposition of the artillery, in which Germans had played a large role, as the place was heavily forested, broken only by a few cotton fields out of which rose individual hills. Laiboldt's German brigade participated in the counterattack and practically perished; it attempted to hurl Longstreet's troops back as they found and stormed through a gap in the right wing and rolled up the entire right wing of the Union army. Those who were left of the German brigade became involved in the wild flight toward Chattanooga.

It should be noted that Von Willich's brigade and that of the Russian general Turchin covered the retreat of Thomas' army to Chattanooga, a retreat accomplished during the darkness of the ensuing night. These two brigades also captured five of the enemy's cannon, the bearing of both units commanding general admiration. The famous Thirty-second Indiana Regiment won especial glory in the fight at Horseshoe Ridge and on the retreat.[19] However, the Turners of the Ninth Ohio won the highest laurels as the only regiment which Thomas, ever parsimonious of praise, mentioned in his report. This regiment entered the battle with about five hundred men and emerged with only half that number. It stormed a battery under Colonel Gustav Kämmerling's direction, which the regular Union artillery had lost, and recaptured it, a feat recognized as one of the most brilliant single deeds of the war. It returned from this achievement to find the other regiments of the brigade in the greatest danger of being annihilated. Again the Turners were hurled forward and turned the defeat

[18] *Ibid.*, 393 n. It will be recalled that the Thirty-second Indiana moved, Prussian fashion, in response to trumpet signals. Von Willich used to say that the maneuvers were made with the precision of a parade, entirely according to trumpet signals. "General August Willich," in *Der Deutsche Pionier*, X (1878–1879), 116.

[19] For a general description of the battle, see James K. Hosmer, *Outcome of the Civil War* (*The American Nation: A History*, XXI, New York, 1907), 26–40.

of their brigade into a victory.[20] The Swiss and the Germans of the Fifteenth Missouri, along with the Germans of the Second Missouri, were among the men of their nationalities who suffered most heavily in this battle.

The Scandinavians in the Fifteenth Wisconsin naturally saw service as a part of Rosecrans' army at Chickamauga, where the regiment was torn to pieces and where, worst of all, it lost its beloved leader, Colonel Heg, who since April 29 had been in command of a brigade in McCook's army corps. Here it was left so depleted that it would probably have disappeared as a unit except for the opportune arrival of two of its companies, which had until then been garrisoned at Island No. 10.[21]

CHATTANOOGA—WAUHATCHIE. The encounters inevitable after an indecisive battle followed Chickamauga, but not instantly. Bragg naturally moved up to besiege Chattanooga, into which the Army of the Cumberland had withdrawn. Under the orders of General Grant, who had been placed in supreme command in the West, Rosecrans was replaced by Thomas, who entered the city on October 23 to lead soldiers whose confidence he commanded. Rations were short, of course, but the opening of a shorter route to the North soon removed that difficulty. During the night of October 28, Longstreet's veterans hurled themselves on J. W. Geary's division, which was lying encamped at Wauhatchie below Chattanooga and in the pitch blackness was shortly in danger of being driven into the Tennessee River. The troops of Schurz and Von Steinwehr, in near-by camps, hastened to Geary's aid and were able to drive Longstreet's forces back. The division of Von Steinwehr especially distinguished itself by making a bayonet attack up a steep and difficult hill and hurling the enemy out of his barricades—a feat which one of Grant's biographers has classified among the most valorous deeds of the war. Schurz's division enjoyed a bit of luck in this episode. The mules attached to this division became nervous at the noise and ran wild, several hundred animals pressing together. They ran into the midst of the enemy, who mistook their pres-

[20] For these details in regard to German units, see Kaufmann, *Die Deutschen im Bürgerkriege*, 395, 396. For the work of the Ninth Ohio, see *ibid.*, 585. This regiment sustained the heaviest losses of any at Chickamauga. For Thomas' praise, see *Official War Records*, Ser. 1, XXX, Pt. 1, p. 288.

[21] See Tenny, *The Military and Naval History of the Rebellion in the United States*, 767. This regiment in the Army of the Cumberland had taken part in all the movements of the Twentieth Corps, which resulted in the evacuation of Shelbyville, Tullahoma, and Chattanooga. See also Blegen (ed.), *Civil War Letters of Colonel Heg*, 38; for losses, see Fox (author and comp.), *Regimental Losses in the Civil War*, 515 n. Its morale was good even after that defeat. A soldier wrote, "The country must and shall be saved."

ence for a cavalry attack. General Hooker severely criticized Colonel Hecker, who led a brigade in this division, because instead of moving forward he had clung to a certain position; this was, of course, an indirect attack on Schurz. The latter promptly demanded an investigation and proved that Hecker had not advanced, upon the express command of Hooker.[22] This midnight battle had the fortunate result of opening completely the road to Chattanooga and thus provisioning the half-starved soldiers of General Thomas.

LOOKOUT MOUNTAIN AND MISSIONARY RIDGE. Since some German units had an important share in these battles, they must receive brief mention. It was not until late November that Grant felt strong enough to attack the positions which Bragg after Chickamauga had taken up before Chattanooga, the most important of which was Missionary Ridge. Orchard Knob, a spur of the ridge between Chattanooga and the main ridge, was stormed on November 23 by Union troops, among whom Von Willich's regiments had a prominent part. This height then became Grant's headquarters. Several of the German elite regiments of both eastern and western armies participated in this famous battle. Here were to be found Von Wangelin's brigade, the Forty-fifth New York under Major Charles Koch, the Twenty-sixth Wisconsin under Frederick C. Winkler, Hecker's Eighty-second Illinois under Edward Salomon, the Seventy-fifth Pennsylvania under Colonel Ledig, the Fifty-eighth and the Sixty-eighth New York, Buschbeck's old Twenty-seventh Pennsylvania, the Thirty-seventh Ohio under Von Blessing, Osterhaus' brigade (the Third, Twelfth, and Seventeenth Missouri regiments), the Second and Fifteenth Missouri units of Laiboldt's brigade, Kämmerling's Ninth Ohio, and Franz Erdelmeyer's Thirty-second Indiana.

Likewise, the number of well-known German artillery units is striking: Wiedrich's battery, or Battery I, First New York Light Artillery; Dilger's Battery I of the First Ohio Light Artillery; Battery K of Dayton under Captain "Nick" (Nicholas) Sahm; and the German batteries from Missouri, Ohio, Illinois, and Indiana.

In addition, there were many half-German regiments. Kaufmann estimates that one third of the troops who won this victory were Germans or of German descent. He admits, however, that there was only one purely German brigade, that of Von Wangelin under Osterhaus. Schurz com-

---

[22] This episode turned upon the ill will awakened by Schurz's criticism of Hooker's negligence at Chancellorsville. Kaufmann, *Die Deutschen im Bürgerkriege*, 397, 397 n. There were several New York troops in the divisions, among others the Fifty-eighth Regiment.

manded more non-German than German regiments, while in Von Steinwehr's entire division only the Twenty-seventh Pennsylvania was at this
time still wholly German. In Von Willich's brigade there were only a
few German regiments, but in all the regiments a strong percentage of
the men were Germans. Of six batteries of Sheridan's force, only two had
non-Germans as commanders. By one of those strange fortuities which
occur when commanders are separated from their commands by rivers,
Osterhaus, instead of being with his old brothers-in-arms of Sherman's
corps, was assigned to Hooker's corps, while Schurz and Von Steinwehn,
hitherto under Hooker, had to announce themselves to Sherman. To
Osterhaus this brought, as we shall see, the greatest opportunity of his
career.[23]

Osterhaus sought and received from Hooker permission to attack Lookout Mountain the next morning. The pioneer company of the Third Missouri Regiment, to Hooker's manifest astonishment, erected a bridge across
Lookout River during the night; over this there strode to the attack Osterhaus' division and later General William Grose's division. Geary's division
of the Twelfth Corps, crossing the stream in its upper course, constituted
the second attacking column, since the plan called for an attack from two
sides in order to overwhelm the enemy between them. Both columns were
successful; indeed, they encountered no strong opposition, for the enemy
had divided his strength when General Braxton Bragg sent Longstreet's
corps to Knoxville. Bragg could not determine the strength of the assault
through the clouds and mist and consequently fled down into the Chattanooga Valley, though the summit of the mountain could easily have been
held.

Early the next day the stormers of Lookout were in the valley of the
Chattanooga Creek, Osterhaus in the lead. After a delay of an hour and
a half to allow Herman Klostermann to build a new bridge over the
swollen stream, the assault troops began the second part of their task, the
surmounting of Missionary Ridge from the south. Part of the battle of
Missionary Ridge had already been won before Osterhaus assaulted. On
November 24, simultaneously with the attack on Lookout Mountain, the
attack on these heights had been begun (but only from the north side) by
Sherman's corps, which was charged to occupy the enemy in the north and
to try to win a good position for the main attack of November 25. A minor
incident shows how great events are often dependent on small factors. One

[23] For these important details the author is indebted to Kaufmann, *Die Deutschen im Bürgerkriege*, 401–402.

Major Karl Hipp, a German officer of the Thirty-seventh Ohio, made possible the passage of Sherman's corps over the rising Tennessee. He brought about a hundred barks, which had been assembled in Chickamauga Creek, into the Tennessee River, moved them upstream by night to a landing place, overran and captured the Confederate outposts, and then hunted up Sherman. With these barks he improvised a pontoon bridge for Sherman's corps. Hipp's was a bold deed in the face of great danger, as he had only a few men and must venture deep into the enemy's chain of outposts.[24] Sherman had, however, after quickly surmounting the ridge, found himself isolated by a gorge from the ridge proper and had been held in a bitter fight the entire day of the twenty-fourth by batteries hidden in a ravine on Tunnel Hill. Early the next morning Grant sent both Schurz's and Von Steinwehr's divisions to Sherman's support, but only Buschbeck's brigade got into the fight, in an attack which Sherman later praised enthusiastically. The battle raged around the ravine the entire morning, but it proved to be impossible to take the heights from that side.

To withstand Sherman and preserve his communications over a railroad bridge, Bragg had weakened the center of his six-mile-long line on the heights and almost abandoned the southern side, from which Osterhaus, Geary, and Thomas now advanced. The assault came from three sides—Sherman in the north, Osterhaus and J. W. Geary in the south, and Thomas in the center. Now came the attack which is famous in history for having been made contrary to orders. Grant had ordered Thomas' troops to take only the rifle pits at the foot of the mountain and there await further orders. Most of the Germans participating were in the foremost ranks in Sheridan's and Thomas J. Wood's divisions. The brigade commanded by Von Willich moved steadily through the open field despite the terrific fire from the rifle pits, to which it was the most exposed of all the brigades, and which left it no choice but to go forward or to retreat. Von Willich was reported as cogitating to himself, "Even if I am put before a court-martial, I am going on." A few minutes later Von Willich's regiments climbed up the almost precipitous ascent over the barren rocks. Neighboring brigades in Wood's and Sheridan's [25] divisions took exactly

[24] This episode of Major Hipp's exploit was told by Kaufmann, *Die Deutschen im Bürgerkriege*, 402–404, 404 n., and was told originally in *History of the 37th Regiment, O.V.V.I., Furnished by Comrades at the Ninth Reunion Held at St. Mary's, Ohio, Tuesday and Wednesday, September 10 and 11, 1889* (n.p., n.d.), 25–27.

[25] Generals Sheridan and Von Willich told exactly the same story of their men. It is possible that two such impetuous fighters should have felt simultaneously that that was

the same action without awaiting orders. Before the regimental commanders grasped the situation, their men all along the line were scrambling to
the summit. Watching through his glasses from Orchard Knob, Grant,
half irritated, asked Thomas if he had commanded the assault. "Not I,"
answered the latter, adding dryly, "This is surely a stroke of Old Willich,
at least is very like him." [26] A second line of rifle pits halfway up the
slope had offered even less of an obstacle than the first, and soon the pant-
ing bluecoats stood on the summit. There followed a short, frightful fight
in the woods; and then the Confederates, entirely broken, retreated over
the east slope of the ridge.

Among other German officers and regiments meriting special mention
for their conduct in these battles at Lookout and Missionary Ridge are
Arnold Sutermeister, who commanded an artillery brigade in which
fought five batteries composed of Germans; Francis C. Deimling, who,
after his superior officer was wounded, assumed command of the second
brigade of Smith's division; Ludwig von Blessing and his Thirty-seventh
Ohio; Gustav Kämmerling and his Ninth Ohio; Charles B. Seidel, who
led the Third Ohio Cavalry; Herbert von Hammerstein, the former
Austrian officer who commanded the native Seventy-eighth New York;
and Carl von Baumbach, in command of the non-German Twenty-fourth
Wisconsin. Brigadier General Karl Matthies of Iowa was severely
wounded. The Hungarian Géza Mihalotzy, who sustained a severe wound
at Chickamauga, made a glorious record with his Twenty-fourth Illinois
in all the important engagements in Tennessee.[27]

The Wisconsin Scandinavian Regiment—or what was left of it after
Chickamauga—was with the troops which stormed Missionary Ridge,
where, fortunately, its loss was negligible, only four of its men being
wounded. Its new commander, Major Wilson, took charge the day after
the Battle of Missionary Ridge and led it as it set out on November 28

---

not a time for hesitation, but a moment of which a leader must take advantage, regardless of
orders.

[26] Kaufmann tells this story in *Die Deutschen im Bürgerkriege*, 406. Von Willich's men
contested long with Sheridan's as to which unit had had the honor of reaching the summit
first. The defenses were broken at six points.

[27] *Ibid.*, 407 n., 555. Kaufmann gave other names which the author rejects because there
is no evidence from the sources that the owners of these names were born abroad or that the
regiments to which they belonged were composed of Germans. For Mihalotzy, see Piványi,
Hungarians in the American Civil War, 33.

on the chase after Longstreet. He was in command until Lieutenant Colonel Ole C. Johnson, captured at Chickamauga, made good his escape from Libby Prison and rejoined the regiment.[28]

BATTLE OF RINGGOLD. The pursuit of Bragg's army fell to Osterhaus and Geary, since Grant was obliged to dispatch Sherman's corps and Schurz's and Von Steinwehr's divisions to Knoxville to free Burnside from Longstreet's threat. At Ringgold, across the Georgia line, Osterhaus encountered the main portion of Bragg's army; he attacked at once, although his artillery was still far behind, as he counted on Geary's division for support. The latter was, however, tardy in arriving, and so Osterhaus was thrown back upon his own infantry. Von Wangelin's brigade of four German Missouri regiments and a native Ohio regiment had the honor of opening the attack in what was to prove a frightful battle. Colonel von Wangelin lost an arm, several officers fell, and the rank and file lost so heavily that after this battle there was general grief in St. Louis and Belleville. The foe had seized a pass between two hills and was driven out only when the German horse batteries of Clemens Landgräber and Captain Wölfle came up.[29]

As a result of the siege of Chattanooga and the battles just mentioned, the state of Tennessee had been fully regained by January 1, 1864. Except for Hood's later incursion into Tennessee, which was repulsed by Thomas, the great struggle for the West was over. No one will deny the significant contribution of German units to that victory.

The promotion of Grant to the command of all the Union armies East and West, Sherman's march to Atlanta and through Georgia, the Wilderness campaign, despite Grant's serious reverses—all pointed toward the end. What contribution did the contingents of foreign-born make to the efforts of the last year?

BATTLE OF NEW MARKET. Sigel's Shenandoah Valley campaign with its humiliating defeat at New Market was, it must be admitted, a disastrous failure. This German general had again been given a command, an action undoubtedly dictated partly by considerations of his popularity with the German-Americans. Primarily, the military objectives were to keep Confederate troops so occupied in the Valley that they could not be detached to strengthen Lee against the main army in Virginia under

---

[28] See letter from Major Wilson to the editor, December 26, 1863, in La Crosse (Wis.) *Faedrelandet,* January 14, 1864.

[29] Kaufmann, *Die Deutschen im Bürgerkriege,* 408.

Grant, and to prevent provisions and munitions from being sent to Lee from that fruitful region.[30]

But there are some facts which in all justice to Sigel should be set forth. An army computed on paper at thirty-two thousand men shrank in actuality to twenty-four thousand; then Grant took away the greater part of these troops and expected Sigel to perform with seven thousand men a task for which, after Sigel's failure, fifty thousand were made available for Sheridan. Sigel was further hampered by a long wagon train with which he was to supply two outlying armies in remote parts of the Valley.[31] The troops were reduced to the tempo of the train, which dragged through rivers of mud under torrents of rain, so that he was greatly hampered in reaching a state of readiness for battle. Furthermore, his troops had to enter battle after marching seven hours in the rain through mud knee-deep; under these conditions, to arrange battle lines from long marching columns was no slight task. The enemy had the advantage of knowing the terrain on which the fighting occurred—of which knowledge he made excellent use. Sigel might well have complained of the failure of his two Ohio German regiments, the Twenty-eighth and the One Hundred and Sixteenth, to come up to a point three quarters of a mile back of the battle line as he had ordered; instead they remained on a hill three miles distant. He himself ascribed his defeat to the absence of these twelve hundred veterans of long experience.

So much has been written of the 225 sixteen- and seventeen-year-old cadets from the Virginia Military Institute—and, indeed, these lads do deserve much credit for courageous conduct which would have reflected honor on men far older—that the reader sometimes tends to forget certain facts. The infantry of Generals John Breckenridge and J. D. Imboden consisted mainly of five thousand veterans who had been three years in the field, and Imboden's cavalry had been trained chiefly as infantry and was so used in this battle. Sigel's cavalry could not participate at all in the fight and so must be deducted entirely from his number, and, furthermore, almost half of his men were young recruits destined originally for the defense of the Baltimore and Ohio Railroad, here facing much better

---

[30] What Sigel was expected to do was set forth in Grant's letter to him, March 29, 1864, *Official War Records*, Ser. 1, XXXIII, pp. 765–66.

[31] The scattering of his army came about as follows: Grant ordered Sigel to send General George Crook with ten thousand men into the southwestern part of the Shenandoah Valley; General (brevet title) William W. Averell with two thousand to another remote part; five thousand he had to leave for the protection of the Baltimore and Ohio Railroad, for communications had to be preserved at all costs.

trained troops. Ready for actual combat he had, if we discount his cavalry, only about forty-one hundred men.[32] So much by way of justice to Sigel.

On the other hand, Sigel did not, even when all allowances are made, show off to advantage. The battle need not have been fought at New Market, where he could not use his cavalry. It would have been far better if, instead of trying to draw a battle line three quarters of a mile back of the town, he had tried to make a stand at Rude's Hill three miles away. Then he could have made his arrangements more quietly and with better preparation, and in addition he could have had the help of his two veteran Ohio regiments. This position would also have afforded him an additional hour for preparation before the Confederates could have come up. It is clear that he was surprised, for his own report shows that he had not had time to inspect the placing of his left wing, which he has mentioned merely to state that the battle was lost through the crushing of the left wing. It would hardly seem that he had command of his own men, for he himself has admitted that he ordered two companies of the Twelfth West Virginia regiment to advance from their position to support a battery but could not by threats or warnings move them from the spot. Among the nine regiments recorded as participating in this battle, only one, the Twenty-eighth Ohio, was wholly German and but one other, the One Hundred and Sixteenth Ohio, had a strong representation of Germans.[33] In the face of this showing, the removal of Sigel from high command was hardly an injustice.

As the historian progresses in his story of the war to the later battles, it becomes ever more difficult for him to distinguish the participation of units of the foreign-born in particular battles, because as the war progressed, death thinned the ranks of the regiments composed of foreign-born, military units were broken up and scattered, and consolidations merged various foreign regiments with native-born units. Furthermore, more and more of the new recruits drawn from recent arrivals from Europe proved to be of very different fiber from the Forty-eighters and the loyal Swedes and

[32] The regiments noted by Kaufmann as under Sigel at the time were, besides those named in the text, the Eighteenth Connecticut, One Hundred and Sixteenth Ohio, One Hundred and Twenty-third Ohio, Thirty-fourth Massachusetts, Twelfth West Virginia, First West Virginia, Fifty-fourth Pennsylvania, and Stahel's Cavalry. Kaufmann, *Die Deutschen im Bürgerkriege*, 419, 420, 421.

[33] The best account is to be found *ibid.*, 411–22. The best primary source is General Sigel's report, in Johnson and Buel (eds.), *Battles and Leaders*, IV, 487–91. It is not to be found, oddly enough, in *Official War Records*. Presumably, it is one of the reports which have been lost since the war.

Irish, Germans and Hungarians, Poles and Swiss, who had stepped forward out of loyalty and gratitude to succor the Union in its hour of distress. Only the more significant contributions of foreign-born officers and troops will henceforth be mentioned.

SHERMAN'S MARCH TO THE SEA. A goodly number of the foreign-born who survived the Chattanooga campaign accompanied Sherman on his famous march to the sea and were certainly to be reckoned as excellent, veteran material. Only one brigade could claim to be largely German, Von Wangelin's brigade, consisting of the Third, Twelfth, and Seventeenth Missouri and the Forty-fourth Illinois, to which the non-German Seventy-sixth Illinois was later added. The half-German One Hundred and Thirty-sixth Indiana shared in the march. The old leaders, however, had largely disappeared: Von Willich was so severely wounded in the first battle as to become incapable of service; Schurz had been drafted by Lincoln for the political campaign; even Von Steinwehr had withdrawn; a little while later Hecker was gone. The indefatigable Osterhaus still sat his steed as fresh as ever and commanded a division in the Fifteenth Corps until the army reached Atlanta, when he succeeded as commander of the entire corps. Buschbeck's brigade joined in the march and fought well at Peachtree Creek and Ezra Church on July 28, driving back a foe three times its size; though Von Wangelin now had only one arm, he withdrew only after the main battles. Wiedrich's battery shared in the siege of Atlanta and in the march to the sea; it then engaged a Confederate gunboat in the investment of Savannah and marched on to North Carolina. Dilger's battery fought under Sherman to the end of the war. Joseph Conrad and Bernhard Laiboldt led brigades; Winkler, colonel of the Twenty-sixth Wisconsin, was gone. Up to a third of Sherman's host consisted of Germans or descendants of Germans. The greatest number of Germans were to be found in the Fifteenth and Twentieth corps, the latter being created by the amalgamation of the Eleventh and Twelfth corps.[34]

We are little concerned here with battles or skirmishes, though there were many, for Sherman preferred wherever possible to envelop or flank the enemy and by this device forced the slow retreat of General Joseph E. Johnston. At the combat near Dallas during the Atlanta campaign, May 27–28, Osterhaus' division did brilliant work, though the result as a whole was indecisive and cost both sides dearly. Again at Marietta this division contributed materially to the success of Sherman's tactics. After

[34] Kaufmann, *Die Deutschen im Bürgerkriege*, 433–44. For Wiedrich's battery, see Frederick Smith, "Historical Sketch," in Fox (comp.), *New York at Gettysburg*, III, 1248.

Sherman had suffered the only defeat of his entire campaign in the mistaken effort to storm the heights of Kennesaw Mountain on June 27, he returned to the method of envelopment and thus obliged Johnston to evacuate the height. Osterhaus' men made this result possible by breaking through the Confederate line at Marietta.[35] A few more days elapsed, and Sherman stood before Atlanta. The Scandinavian Regiment also made this march with Sherman.[36]

Some foreign units were left behind for specific purposes or had to be sent back to meet new threatened dangers. The Fifty-eighth and Sixty-eighth New York regiments were stationed at Bridgeport, Tennessee, and along the Nashville and Chattanooga Railroad to guard the communications, a post which they held in the main for the remainder of the war. Little opportunity for distinction as this patrolling work afforded, the protection of the four-hundred-mile-long, single line of communication was of the utmost importance, and history records the work as well done.[37] Sherman had also to meet the possible threat of a new expedition into Tennessee by General John B. Hood after the evacuation of Atlanta. He, accordingly, sent one of his veteran corps under General J. M. Schofield back to Tennessee to aid Thomas. Here Schofield, in a strong position at Franklin, repelled the attack of Hood and joined Thomas in Nashville for the bloody battle near there on December 15–16. The German-Swiss group can be identified as sharing in these battles, for the Fifteenth Missouri fought splendidly in the two last important battles in the West, after having participated in the eleven actions between Chattanooga and Atlanta.[38]

EARLY'S RAID AGAINST WASHINGTON in early July, 1864, was a very real threat to the administrators of the nation and to the residents of the capital. Though he had been sent to the Shenandoah Valley ostensibly to protect Lynchburg, his adventurous soul saw his major undertaking in the command to make thrusts toward the North in case of a favorable opportunity. He believed he could surprise Washington, and certainly the swift march with his twelve thousand men threw the city into a panic.

[35] Kaufmann, *Die Deutschen im Bürgerkriege*, 435–36. For the campaign, see Rhodes, *History of the United States*, IV, 448.

[36] Blegen (ed.), *The Civil War Letters of Colonel Heg*, 392.

[37] Sherman declared this railroad to be the "delicate point of my game." Rachel Sherman Thorndike (ed.), *The Sherman Letters. Correspondence between Gen. and Sen. Sherman from 1837 to 1870* (London, 1894), 236. See also "58th Regiment Infantry," in Fox (comp.), *New York at Gettysburg*, I, 432; Arnold Kummer, "68th Regiment Infantry," in Fox (comp.), *New York at Gettysburg*, II, 570.

[38] Kaufmann, *Die Deutschen im Bürgerkriege*, 436–37, 489.

Every school child has read how General Lew Wallace's improvised army at the Monocacy near Frederick, Maryland, held Early one entire day and thus afforded time for the arrival of the Sixth and Nineteenth corps sent up hastily by Grant from the James River. The service of three German generals at the head of the Shenandoah Valley, which was just as real a service, has been utterly forgotten. Sigel was posted there with four thousand men; Max von Weber, with eight hundred; and Stahel, with fifteen hundred cavalrymen, whose horses, however, were exhausted. These weak forces could not, of course, fight Early; but they halted him for almost four days, and that was of immeasurable importance in view of the fact that the reinforcements which Grant had sent up arrived at the very moment that Early was about to storm the capital. Early had expected to swallow easily Sigel's little garrison at Martinsburg by encircling it, but the German commander after summoning Stahel and Weber to his aid, quickly fell back on Harpers Ferry, and took up a strong position on the heights near that place. Before this position Early hesitated; he did not care to expose himself to Sigel's cannon and found himself forced to hunt out the ford over the Potomac at Shepherdstown back of Harpers Ferry. His undertaking at Martinsburg and the delay there cost him four days, even though Sigel's troops had offered only an outpost skirmish at Leestown. Early, who would have had a much shorter way by Harpers Ferry, now had to move through the South Mountains in order to win the approach to Washington. When he faced the capital on July 11, he was checkmated by the newly arrived troops. To have the whole story, one must in all fairness add to the one day's delay by Wallace the almost four days' delay at the head of the Valley.[39] Otherwise Early would probably have gained a temporary victory over the capital, with important consequences of panic throughout the North and unfortunate encouragement to the South.

VARIOUS ISOLATED CONFLICTS involving foreign units remain to be studied. The Highlanders of the Seventy-ninth New York shared in the combined land and naval expedition against Port Royal in November, 1861. In the attack on James Island in front of Charleston on June 16, 1862 (a desperate, daring venture, in which the Seventy-ninth New York left half of its killed and wounded lying behind it), this group of Scotchmen failed to take Fort Johnson only because the regiments that were to support them failed to come up.[40] At the attack on Roanoke Island on February 8, 1862, Captain Thomas O'Neil's company of the Twenty-fifth

[39] Ibid., 430–31.
[40] Headley, The Great Rebellion, I, 480–82.

Massachusetts, consisting chiefly of naturalized Irishmen from Worcester, conducted themselves with the coolness and daring of veterans.[41] The De Kalb Regiment rendered service after Gettysburg on the South Carolina coast for one year, participating in the fight at St. John's Island on February 11, 1864. In August, 1864, the remainder proceeded from Hilton Head to Washington, where they were assigned to the Army of the Shenandoah under Sheridan, only to be again shifted to the Army of the James the following December.[42] At the capture of Charleston, late in the war, the Seventy-fourth Pennsylvania was the first regiment to enter the city.[43] Colonel Mattson's Third Minnesota was stationed all through 1864 and 1865 in Arkansas near Little Rock, where it saw some action in several scouts up the White River—necessary, if not significant, service.[44] Oddly enough, Knute Nelson, with the partly foreign Fourth Wisconsin, saw service also during 1864 in the southwest, defending New Orleans and Louisiana against recapture. Service here took the form of building extensive earthworks to make the position impregnable.[45] Aschmann's company of Swiss sharpshooters, that elite troop attached to the Army of the Potomac, certainly justified its claim to a record of distinguished service, for it participated in eighteen battles and skirmishes and was thereby reduced to twelve men.[46] All the sharpshooters under Colonel Trepp had a brilliant record.

Individual service can sometimes be measured by the number of battles in which a given person participated. Some Swedes from Chautauqua County in the Ninth New York Cavalry shared in eighteen battles. Another Swede, George F. Lindquist of the Fifth New York Volunteers, fought in thirty battles.[47]

FORT HELENA, ARKANSAS. One of the German-born citizens, General Friedrich Salomon, who attained the title of brigadier and even of titular major general, seems not to have received the credit which was justly his— credit for the victory at Fort Helena, Arkansas, on July 4, 1863, when he

[41] For Captain O'Neil's company, see Marvin, *History of Worcester in the War of the Rebellion*, 126–27.

[42] "Dedication of Monument 41st Regiment Infantry, De Kalb Regiment," in Fox (comp.), *New York at Gettysburg*, I, 307.

[43] Kaufmann, *Die Deutschen im Bürgerkriege*, 508.

[44] Mattson to his wife, April 16, 20, 1864, Mattson Papers; James H. Stevenson, "The First Cavalry," (originally published in the Philadelphia *Weekly News*) in M[cClure] (ed.), *The Annals of the War* (Philadelphia, 1879), 636, 640.

[45] Undated letter to his brother, William; the context leads the writer to conclude that it was written some time in 1864. Knute Nelson Papers.

[46] Kaufmann, *Die Deutschen im Bürgerkriege*, 479–80.

[47] Hokanson, *Swedish Immigrants*, 101.

brilliantly beat back an attack of twelve thousand Confederates. He commanded independently here and at the engagement at Jenkins Ferry. General Prentiss, Salomon's superior, later claimed the victory at Helena as his, although he was on a gunboat on the Mississippi during the fighting and appeared only after the enemy had been driven off. All the officers who participated in the battle signed a document stating that Salomon had conducted independently the defense of that point. It was claimed that Grant prevented this attested document from reaching Lincoln, as he cherished an old grudge against the Salomon brothers because of a defeat by Eberhard Salomon in his early days in an election for the office of land surveyor.[48]

REAMS STATION. What the cavalry can contribute when led by a fearless and resourceful leader is well demonstrated by an episode in which the German Kautz played the leading role and which occurred in an engagement at Reams Station in late August, 1864. Stung by the daring and destructive raids of Kautz, Lee is said to have declared his determination to crush the raiders, "if it cost him his army"; consequently, he sent General William Mahone's entire division to intercept General James H. Wilson's command of eight thousand men, including the Third Cavalry division under Kautz. As the last-named general approached Reams Station, he found the enemy drawn up in battle line. Kautz's division, which led the advance, and the Eleventh Pennsylvania, just behind, charged through the Confederate line, only to find themselves isolated and abandoned when General Wilson made a wide detour to avoid the enemy. Kautz was soon in a triangle, shut in on two sides by enemy forces in overwhelming numbers and on the third side by a railroad running through a deep cut. Rather than surrender, this indomitable cavalryman led his mounted men down a steep embankment, where the horses somehow contrived to slide down to the track without unseating their riders, scramble up the opposite bank, dash down the next declivity into a river, and wallow through the water and mire under a rain of shot and shell until they reached the opposite shore.[49]

BOURBON PRINCES ON RECONNAISSANCE

It may be not inappropriate to close this record of the service for which the United States was indebted to officers and soldiers born outside its

[48] Kaufmann, *Die Deutschen im Bürgerkriege*, 389 n., 545. See also, p. 198 above.

[49] Merrill, *The Campaigns with the First Maine and First District of Columbia Cavalry*, 268–70.

boundaries with mention of contributions, sometimes romantic, made by the Bourbon princes in their capacity of aides to General McClellan. They did the humdrum, routine tasks just as did any other aides and so contributed their mite just as did any other soldiers. It is almost amusing to find these princes of the blood royal very human—though why they should be immune to mortal discomforts is certainly not to be explained. One particularly disagreeable night, when the rain was descending in torrents, the Comte de Paris was aroused from his sleep to make a reconnaissance. Grumbling mentally and wondering why McClellan might not have selected some other of his many aides for the distasteful task, he wrapped himself in a rain cape and mounted his horse to ride through the pitch darkness—darkness so black that he had to let his horse pick his own way.

A more thrilling reconnaissance, because it was touched with real adventure, was that undertaken by the two princes together. Encountering on their route a locomotive, they calmly requisitioned it, climbed aboard, and thus were enabled to explore the country promptly and comfortably, bringing back in the space of a single morning an accurate report of the actions of the enemy for a distance of fifteen "leagues" from headquarters.[50]

No one knows better than the author that the procedure in these last two chapters for appraising the share of our foreign-born in the winning of the various battles is unsatisfactory. Their work is torn both from its setting and from its relationship to the contribution of the native regiments, which should also be evaluated for an entirely fair method of presentation. Short of writing again from this point of view a full, detailed history of all the battles of the war, a work which would require volumes, there seems no other method of procedure. Certainly, these chapters will serve to put into sharp focus the fact that the regiments of foreign-born played a large role in most of the great conflicts of the war. The reader will readily recognize that Grant's campaigns in the East, as well as the Wilderness campaign with the battles at Spotsylvania and Cold Harbor and the final duel with Lee before the surrender, are omitted, not because they were not of the highest importance, but because it is not possible to evaluate the contribution of the foreign-born in this decisive part of the struggle, so mixed had become the units in the Army of the Potomac.

[50] Ferdinand Lecomte, *The War in the United States* (New York, 1863), 76.

CHAPTER EIGHTEEN

Support of the War Effort by the Home Front

AFTER the reverberations of the guns on Fort Sumter had sent a tremor through every true heart in the North and had crystallized the sentiment of patriotism, men, women, and children, native and foreign-born alike, sought some means of expressing this newly aroused passion, which overwhelmed every other interest and emotion. Native Americans set the example of patriotic acts. Worcester, in the Old Bay State, appropriated $4,000 to provide uniforms and supplies for two companies. Sometimes friends of a regiment paid for the instruments of a band. Friends of the Twelfth Massachusetts organized a committee of leading citizens, who assumed responsibility for the sum of $70,000 in case contributions were not sufficient to arm, uniform, and equip the Webster Regiment. When that unit left Boston with twenty baggage wagons, two hospital wagons, five ambulances, one powder wagon, and ninety-six horses, it was the best equipped organization that ever left Massachusetts.[1] The generous raising of money for the soldiers and their families, regardless of nationality, clearly impressed the foreign groups; for one of the foreign-language newspapers noted the fact that 159 cities and towns of New York had given from $1,000 to $3,000,000, New York City raising $2,173,000. The total sum raised throughout the Union was estimated at $23,277,000.[2]

Everywhere, from metropolitan New York to the smallest Iowa town, from Boston to St. Paul, mass meetings to promote enlistments or collect money were held. It is not strange that New York staged its mass meeting, called without distinction of party, for April 20, 1861, in Union Square. It proved one of the largest and most enthusiastic meetings ever held in

---

[1] Marvin, *History of Worcester in the War of the Rebellion*, 20; Cook, *History of the Twelfth Massachusetts Volunteers*, 10–11.

[2] Chicago *Illinois Staats-Zeitung*, May 21, 1861. The Ninth Massachusetts (Irish) presented an elegant flag captured from the Confederates to the city of Boston as a mark of appreciation for their kindness to the regiment. New York *Irish-American*, June 14, 1862.

that famous square. The speakers included, along with former Governor Washington Hunt, Mayor Fernando Wood, and other distinguished Americans, a number of Irish and German citizens, such as Friedrich Kapp and Oswald Ottendorfer, all breathing the one sentiment of patriotism and all ignoring differences in political opinions to stand by the government. All the speakers pledged the fortunes and lives of the citizens to that great goal.

With equal unanimity of sentiment, leaders of all parties in St. Paul acted even more promptly, calling a mass meeting for Thursday evening, April 16. People of all classes and races began to stream through the streets to the capitol, and when the Hall of Representatives could not accommodate the crowd, they adjourned to the enormous open space in front of the building. One speaker, the defeated Douglas candidate for Congress, struck at the very heart of the issue by declaring that if the North won, the war could end only in the freeing of the slaves. "The North is the defender of the great idea, on which the Union rests," he declared, "the defender of the inheritance of the Revolution, the defender of the Nation, united in battle for the republic." One speaker gave the Germans their full meed of acknowledgment, "which," the *Minnesota Staats-Zeitung* said, "was very much in place," by speaking of the loyalty of the Germans in Texas.[3]

Some of the foreign groups scarcely required the impetus of the fervor of the Americans, the example of young sons of the finest men in the community marching up to sign the muster roll, the constant parading of new companies, or the flutterings of flags on all the public buildings and on many homes.[4]

A great gathering of Germans on a splendid imposing scale occurred in Cincinnati in the *Turnhalle* very early in May. Perhaps the most impressive speech there came from the lips of Friederich Hassaurek; this was certainly the more impressive because he had just resigned his high post as minister to Ecuador to enter the Second Ohio Regiment. When he declared, "Freedom or submission is now the watchword; words avail no more, only deeds," the emotions of the audience reached a climax. Probably the most exalted sentiment uttered anywhere came from a Cincinnati German at this time: "Brave Germans! let us, untroubled concerning praise or censure on the part of the other nationalities, show

[3] St. Paul *Minnesota Staats-Zeitung*, April 20, 1861; New York *Courrier des États-Unis*, April 22, 1861.

[4] Frost, *The Rebellion in the United States*, I, 141–42, 143–44.

that we are Germans and are ready in German faithfulness to defend our American home as the blessed land of freedom."

At St. Paul a separate meeting of Germans was held on the evening of April 23, at which the necessity of creating without delay a German company was urged. The speaker was a man not only of words but also of action, for he put down his name as one of the members. Others followed his example so promptly that that very evening a German company seemed assured, and, indeed, by April 27 it was drilling. The resolutions adopted breathed understanding of the issues of the war, for they declared that the St. Paul citizens of German birth were prepared for every sacrifice to preserve the Constitution unchanged, affirmed full confidence in the patriotism and ability of the existing government, pledged support without regard to party, and adopted as their motto "Freedom and the Union, now and always, one and inseparable." [5]

A number of French residents of New York held a meeting on April 29 for the purpose of taking measures with reference to the existing condition of the country. A committee of three was created to concert the proper measures. One of the members stated the object of the meeting and proposed that it should be preliminary to a general meeting of French citizens for their organization and participation in the conflict. It was presented to them as their duty to support the government in a strife of liberty and freedom against slavery and feudal oppression. Resolutions tendered the support of French citizens to the Union; and the chairman of the committee, in presenting the resolutions, expressed the hope that if the war were carried to extremes the government would extinguish slavery. Swedish societies in New York City passed resolutions urging their members to do their duty in support of the Union. [6]

A mass meeting in Madison, Wisconsin, in the large assembly room of the capitol, which was packed to suffocation, was obviously attended by people of all nationalities, for the *Emigranten* so reported and further declared that never "have we in America seen such an inspired mass of people." That newspaper noted that in a city of only about 6,600 inhabitants $7,490 was donated in an hour. From the *Illinois Staats-Zeitung* we learn that just about that time the Norwegians of Chicago held a large meeting in the West Market Hall, where various brief, patriotic speeches were made. Though it was determined to organize a company of

---

[5] St. Paul *Minnesota Staats-Zeitung*, April 27, 1861.

[6] New York *Daily News*, April 29, 1861; Hokanson, *Swedish Immigrants*, 68. See p. 58 of text.

Norwegians, the writer has found no evidence that the company materialized.[7]

The different nationality groups were prompt with measures to succor the families of their absent soldiers. The first of these efforts in Chicago was probably premature, as it did not evoke an even fair response. Only two dozen persons were present, the German newspaper of that city sadly reported; it then quipped grimly, in the words of the chairman, "I see so many who are not here." Among the Germans, it declared, there was much chatter of war within the four walls of home, but when it came to activity for a purposeful goal the Germans had much, very much, to learn from the Americans—this, though the Germans knew that already they had about five full regiments in the field in Missouri alone! [8] Toward the close of August in the first year of the war an enormous meeting of the Irish friends of the Sixty-ninth New York Regiment took place in New York in support of a fund for the widows and orphans of soldiers who had died in the war. Nearly fifty thousand people were present to listen to a stirring address by Colonel Thomas Meagher.[9]

Meetings were frequent for promoting the enlistment of new recruits. On July 25, 1862, a meeting of Irish residents of St. Louis was held for the purpose of denouncing as "cowardly, base, and infamous" the conduct of those among their countrymen who had tried to avoid the call of the governor for troops by appealing to the British consul for protection. The Irish of New York staged a meeting on the same date for recruiting the ranks of the Irish Brigade to replace the losses of the Peninsular campaign.[10]

Even more marked was the participation of the Germans in the mass assembly of citizens of New York City at Union Square on July 15, 1862, to support Lincoln's second call for three hundred thousand men. Programs were arranged at four stands, one of which was planned for the German citizens. Here the chairman was the renowned Francis Lieber, who had won great acclaim when his hostility to slavery forced him from his professorship at South Carolina College in 1857—to find, however, a

---

[7] See Madison *Emigranten*, April 20, 1861, for the Madison meeting; Chicago *Illinois Staats-Zeitung*, April 20, 1861, for the Chicago meeting.

[8] Chicago *Illinois Staats-Zeitung*, May 7, 1861. This paper probably based its statements as to numbers on figures coming out in the St. Louis *Anzeiger des Westens*. On May 8, 1861, that paper reported four overfull regiments, a fifth one nearly completed, and hundreds registered for a sixth. It had also published figures fourteen days earlier.

[9] Moore (ed.), *Rebellion Record*, III, Pt. 1, p. 9.

[10] *Ibid.*, V, Pt. 1, p. 48; New York *Irish-American*, August 2, 1862.

welcome at Columbia College, New York. Music was furnished by Helmsmüller's Grand Band, and a large chorus of German men sang for the first time the song composed by Lieber himself, "Our Country and Her Flag." As was fitting, Lieber contributed to the success of the meeting still further by an address.[11]

The warm welcome accorded to returning heroes or officers on leave to recruit for their regiments was not merely a personal tribute to the officers but also a means of demonstrating support by the home front of the cause which these men represented. The dinner tendered General Corcoran when he returned to Washington after ten months in a Confederate prison was largely of a personal nature. On this occasion the Thirty-fourth Massachusetts, in which there were a number of Irish, formed in front of the Willard Hotel to salute him. The demonstrations which Meagher's visit to New York in July, 1862, evoked were clearly staged to support and aid his efforts to secure recruits. On July 24 he attended a theater illuminated in front with red, white, and blue lanterns and decorated with banners for his visit. His box was draped with Irish and American flags. His entry was greeted with uproarious applause; and at the end of the first selections, calls arose from the audience for a speech—which opportunity he embraced by appointing every "lady" present a recruiting officer. More clearly directed toward the Irish population of New York was his appearance with his staff at Niblos' Theatre on August 2 for a performance of *The Colleen Bawn,* on which occasion Collins, the popular chief actor, was ready with a song, "The Irish Brigade." Again Meagher responded to calls from a crowded house with a patriotic speech. When the Steuben Regiment returned at the end of its term of enlistment, the entire regiment was entertained by two Germans, and the day ended with a ball and a supper in the evening.[12]

Irish clergy, sharing in the emotions of their parishioners, did not hesitate to reveal their sentiments and to guide their flocks in what they held to be the right path of loyalty to the Union cause. Soon after Lincoln's first call, Father Creedon of Auburn, New York, preached a sermon which might almost be termed a recruitment speech: "This is the first country the Irishman ever had that he could call his own country. The flag of the

[11] *Proceedings at the Union Meeting of Loyal Citizens in Union Square, New York.*

[12] See New York *Irish-American,* August 23, 1862, for the welcome to Corcoran; *ibid.,* August 2, 9, 1862, for the demonstration for Meagher; Salm-Salm, *Ten Years of My Life,* 50–51, for the welcome to the Steuben Regiment.

Stars and Stripes is the only flag he can fight under and defend as his own flag. . . . There are two classes whom I most despise—cowards and traitors; and those who can enlist and do not, are either one or the other." The Reverend Thomas F. Hendricken of Waterbury, Connecticut, later bishop of Providence diocese, called a meeting of his parishioners in the basement of his church and thus helped organize a company.[13] The support of a more prominent prelate, Archbishop John Hughes, was sought and valued by the government. To the first mass meeting of the war period in Union Square, he sent a letter in which he said: "It is now forty years since, a foreigner by birth, I took the oath of allegiance to this country. . . . Still desirous of peace, when the Providence of God shall have brought it, I may say that since the period of my naturalization I have known but one country. . . . This has been my flag, and shall be to the end." [14] After his return from a government mission in Europe, he delivered on August 17, 1862, an important and patriotic sermon in St. Patrick's Cathedral. After reporting on his course of action in Europe, he called upon the entire North to come out in its strength, for "volunteering to continue and for a draft to be made." He said that if three hundred thousand men were not enough, the President should call out another three hundred thousand. The people should insist on being drafted in order to bring the unnatural strife to a close.[15]

Foreign-born men and women gave strong support to their "boys" at the front, just as did the native-born, and in much the same ways. Among the Germans the women's associations for aiding soldiers were early at work. In Chicago, for instance, a group of about twenty women began to meet daily as early as May 16 in the dining room of the *Deutsches Haus* to make necessary clothes for the German volunteers. It must be understood that there was a wide field for their activity with needle and thread, for at that time underwear and shirts were not purchased from the most convenient men's clothing store but were made in the home by wife and sister. Bandages were made; lint was scraped; knapsacks and havelocks [16]

---

[13] Moore (ed.), *Anecdotes, Poetry and Incidents of the War*, 460–61; Murray, *History of the Ninth Regiment, Connecticut Volunteer Infantry*, 28; for Bishop Hendricken, see *The National Cyclopaedia of American Biography*, V, 165. C. F. Dunham, *The Attitude of the Northern Clergy toward the South* (Toledo, 1942), 139, places Father Creedon in Albany.

[14] Duyckinck, *National History of the War for the Union*, I, 139–40; Moore (ed.), *Rebellion Record*, V, Pt. 1, p. 61.

[15] Moore (ed.), *Rebellion Record*, V, Pt. 1, p. 61.

[16] It will be remembered that the havelock was a small piece of cloth, fashioned to protect the neck of the soldier. See Chapter XIII, note 85.

were made. In the earliest period of the war, before uniformity was established for the dress of the soldiers, women sometimes made even the uniforms and the caps for their men.

The group of Chicago women, seeking to equip Captain Gustav Kowald's company, wisely consulted him in advance and were instructed precisely as to what was most pressingly needed and what should be first completed. Every woman owning a sewing machine was urged to place it at the disposal of the group for work for the soldiers. Captain Kowald urged that bandages find a place in each knapsack. The leaders of this group suggested that each woman take ten cents a week from her house money to hire some sewing done if she could not herself participate. They besought German dry-goods stores to give pieces of shirting and arranged for packages to be left at a certain store in La Salle Street. By May 22 this group was ready to send two chests containing two dozen shoes which they had purchased and one hundred bandages which they had made to the German soldiers at Camp Yates. As a further demonstration of their patriotism this group of women made an American flag to fly over *Deutsches Haus,* but unfortunately it was torn to shreds by a high wind the very first day it was unfurled.[17] As early as June 7, Captain Mihalotzy of Hecker's regiment was thanking the German women for caps and havelocks. Turner Sisters, as the relatives of the German men in the Turner societies were termed, busied themselves also in all parts of the country with making underclothing and providing the linen bandages needed by their "brothers" for the campaign. An allusion to their activity appears especially in connection with Max Weber's Turner regiment, the Twentieth New York Volunteers.[18]

Of course, the same tales of self-sacrificing devotion to their sons have been recorded of the German women as of the American mothers. One such tale is sufficient for the record. An old German mother came from Wisconsin to a hospital tent at Gettysburg to bring a patchwork bedquilt for her wounded son, whom she feared might have lost his blanket; sitting beside her son as he lay wrapped up in the quilt this old mother professed herself content with the care taken of the soldiers and sipped her tea happily from a barrelhead serving as a table. Of the three sons whom she had given to the service, one was dead and this one was wounded; but

[17] For the data covering this group, the writer is indebted to the Chicago *Illinois Staats-Zeitung,* May 7, 15, 21, 23, 1861.

[18] New York *Courrier des États-Unis,* May 19, 1861.

she nevertheless declared that if she were a man, she would enlist at once.[19]

Scandinavian women were just as ready to do their share of war work; but, like the German women, they worked for their own Swedish or Norwegian or Danish soldiers, and did not (as was done later in World Wars I and II) volunteer for war work for soldiers of every nationality in the army. Captain Hans Mattson, in a letter to his wife, dated January 27, 1862, acknowledged receipt of a box of clothing which had been sent by the Swedish women of Minnesota and conveyed his thanks in behalf of his men. He had immediately taken some of the sheets, quilts, and morning gowns to certain of the men who were in the hospital; and he assured the donors that if they could have seen the tears of joy and gratitude, they would have felt abundantly rewarded. He suggested as further donations shirts for the sick and oilcloth capes for the well soldiers as a safeguard while they were on guard duty.[20] In about a month another box of linen, sheets, shirts, and stockings arrived from the Scandinavian women of Red Wing, Minnesota, for the men of Companies D and E, Third Minnesota, the former being Mattson's own company. This time we learn of the gift through Mattson's gracious letter of thanks, dated February 28, 1862 (the day of its arrival), which was published in the *Hemlandet*. The articles were intrinsically of great material value, of course, but they were of even higher value as testimonials to the "solicitude with which we are remembered by our dear friends at home." [21]

Likewise, the Swedish women of Galesburg sent to Cape Girardeau, Missouri, in the winter of 1862 a barrel filled with stockings and gloves to be distributed to their compatriots in the Seventeenth Illinois; but it seems that the sergeants and corporals took advantage of the opportunity afforded by their rank to appropriate these first, with the result that the men got nothing—though a private nevertheless thanked the women politely in August for "their kind intentions." [22] Usually items of food— hams, glasses of jelly, and homemade wine—constituted the most highly prized articles in the boxes.

The Norwegian and Swedish women also organized their soldiers' aid societies. The Soldier's Aid Society in Norway and Raymond townships

---

[19] Frank Moore (author and comp.), *Women of the War: Their Heroism and Self Sacrifice* (Hartford, 1866), 144–45.

[20] Mattson to his wife, January 27, 1862, Mattson Papers.

[21] Chicago *Hemlandet*, March 12, 1862.

[22] A letter by C. Augustus Levine, published in the Chicago *Hemlandet*, August 13, 1862, gives the above facts.

in Wisconsin, Colonel Heg's own community, was especially solicitous for the Scandinavian Regiment. What those societies meant to the soldiers was well expressed by Colonel Heg in one of his letters of appreciation: "Your kindness speaks to the heart of every soldier in the Army," he wrote.[23] The money contributions of the Norwegians (of all the Scandinavian citizens, for that matter) represented real sacrifice. The money came in small sums—fifty cents, one dollar, two dollars, even ten or twenty-five cents—but all tried to give something out of their usually humble means. Gifts of books were solicited by a Danish chaplain for a library for the soldiers, as has been reported more fully in an earlier chapter, and the suggestion won a warm response.[24]

Probably the richest contribution made by the Scandinavian and German women—indeed, by the womenfolk of any of our foreign-born citizens—was made on the farms as those women took up the heavy tasks of their absent menfolk in the fields. They ran the farms and attended to the business affairs of their husbands, meanwhile anxiously following through the columns of the *Emigranten, Hemlandet,* or some German *Zeitung* the movements of the regiment in which they knew their absent ones to be enrolled and treasuring the letters from homesick soldiers at the front. Not infrequently the letters had to be carried to a neighbor or, more often, to a neighbor's child to be read, and replies had to be written vicariously to their husbands or sons through an intermediary.[25]

The warmhearted Irish naturally tried to give aid to their soldiers and to the families of the absent soldiers. A committee of some of the best-known of their number in New York was appointed to collect "monies" and receive subscriptions for the well-being of the men of the Irish Legion and their families. This was primarily an undertaking of Irish men and was said to be a source of gratification to General Corcoran. The contribution of a very humble Irish woman to this fund won the notice of the committee and of the editor of the chief organ of the Irish in New York. Having no son to give to the service and a husband too old to shoulder a musket, she handed her modest ten dollars to swell the fund and won the following encomium in the *Irish-American:* "Mrs. McKenna is very poor in this world's goods and what she possesses is the product of steady, honest

[23] Blegen (ed.), *Civil War Letters of Colonel Heg,* Introduction, 32, 219.

[24] Madison *Emigranten,* September 13, 1862. See p. 367 of text.

[25] Knute Nelson, having received a badly written letter from his mother, had to carry it about to many Scandinavians in his company until he finally found a Dane who could make out the badly formed letters, though the recipient was better educated than most of the Norwegian soldiers.

industry, but she is rich indeed in instincts of gratitude and generosity." [26]

Festivals and fairs to raise money for the relief of the soldiers were the order of the day and were by no means confined to the Sanitary Commission. The activity on the part of our foreign sisters began early in the war. On May 26, 1861, the Germans in Chicago gave an opera in the German Opera House to raise money with which to equip the Hecker regiment. "The German ladies' aid societies," the New York *Tribune* reported, "gave numerous concerts and entertainments to raise funds for the troops." The Chicago *Tribune* revealed the zeal of the Scandinavian women for raising funds for the Chicago company of the Scandinavian Regiment: "The Scandinavian ladies of this city are arranging the preliminaries for the grand festival at West Market Hall on Thursday, the 27th instant [of October, 1861,] for the benefit of the *Orcus Rifles,* Captain Andrew Torkildsen." Then it added, as a pat on the back, "The descendants of the old War Gods are coming up bravely to the defense of their adopted country." [27]

What one small town populated almost entirely by Norwegians could do to support its soldiers by bounties was illustrated by Pleasant Springs, Wisconsin. On August 12, 1862, it held a meeting at which the citizens present decided to give each volunteer of the town's contingent a bounty of fifty dollars and to contribute five dollars monthly to the support of each family concerned. Undoubtedly this was done partly in order to secure the town's quota of soldiers, but that fact does not alter the rather remarkable outpouring of money from a humble community with a population of only about 1,100. The effort was not in vain; to the seven or eight who had already enrolled sixteen volunteers added themselves at once—which number filled out the town's contingent. In money, this meant the direct payment of $1,200 and a yearly toll of $1,440 paid to the soldiers' families. In the Norwegian town of Vermont in Dane County, Wisconsin, a war meeting was held a few days later, on August 18, in order to recruit the town's contingent of eighteen men from its population of less than a thousand. Of the thirteen volunteers who came forward, almost all were Norwegians—which fact can be interpreted as convincing evidence of Norwegian support of the war meetings and of the war. [28]

[26] New York *Irish-American,* August 13, 1861.

[27] Chicago *Illinois Staats-Zeitung,* May 25, 1861; New York *Tribune,* October 16, 1861; Chicago *Tribune,* October 20, 1861. Rather oddly, the author usually searched in vain for comments in the nationality newspapers on this phase of activity among the foreign-born.

[28] Madison *Emigranten,* August 18, 1862. The volunteers in Pleasant Springs were com-

The constant presentation of flags to the companies and regiments has already been described. As among the Americans, zeal for furnishing the regiments with flags, the officers with swords, and the separate companies with equipment appeared among the nationality groups. The *Illinois Staats-Zeitung* of April 20, 1861, announced in the very issue which urged formation of a Chicago regiment of Germans that a costly flag was already being made for the first German company in Chicago to be fully organized and accepted by the governor. The flag was described as of silk with the thirty-four stars embroidered in silver on the blue field, the staff being adorned with a streamer of red, black, and gold. Of the $100 which the flag was to cost, $80 had already been subscribed.

Without doubt the largest gift made by any single German and probably the costliest presented to a single regiment was that of Rudolph A. Witthaus to the De Kalb Regiment of New York City. Witthaus manifested great interest in the welfare and the full equipment of this regiment, to a degree which endeared him to the hearts not only of his fellow countrymen but of all who were concerned for the welfare of the land. Whatever the regiment seemed to need this German benefactor provided, and whatever the Union Defense Committee did not furnish he purchased from his private fortune. The regiment expressed gratitude by electing him its honorary chief. It was a proud moment for Witthaus when the regiment, a thousand stalwart men, fully uniformed and equipped in six weeks by his unflagging perseverance, drew up on June 19, 1861, before their patron's residence on West Thirty-fourth Street to receive the flags which his bounty had provided—a handsome regimental flag, an American ensign, and a set of guidons.

The ceremony there enacted in the presence of a group of distinguished guests, including Governor Morgan and General Dix, is worth recounting. With a speech, Mrs. Witthaus, an American, presented to Colonel von Gilsa an American flag. After the *Liederkranz* had sung "The Star-Spangled Banner," the president of that organization, Frederick Kapp, presented to the colonel a superb cavalry sword, a belt, and a cartridge box of gilt material, with a speech eulogizing De Kalb, to which the colonel responded briefly. Then followed the presentation of the regimental flag by Pauline Witthaus in behalf of her father, who then delivered a patriotic address. The two guidons were presented by Witthaus' young son. The regimental standard had a dark-blue satin ground and was trimmed with

puted at the higher figure, twenty-four. For the population in each case, see *Eighth Census,
1860. The Statistics of the Population*, 533.

heavy, yellow silk fringe. On the front was worked on drab-colored silk a lifelike portrait of De Kalb; above it appeared the American shield, and underneath were the intermingled American and German flags. Around the edges was embroidered the suitable inscription:

The generous stranger who left his home
To water with his blood the tree of our liberty.

On the reverse side appeared the star-spangled banner, across which were embroidered the implements of warfare, while around the edges appeared two lines of the national anthem.[29]

This presentation of flags was almost incessant. The German Turner Sisters presented to Colonel Max von Weber for the Turner Regiment shortly before it left New York a regimental flag and the German colors of black, red, and gold after an elaborate procession and a review of the regiment by the City Council in front of City Hall. In the background was a display of society banners, badges, and mottoes such as had not often been assembled in New York; the most common were those of Turner societies, which exhibited an ogling owl with a torch in one claw and a sword in the other.[30] Blenker's regiment received flags in the governor's room on May 17, 1861; the next day the Steuben Regiment received a magnificent flag from the hands of the little niece of General Stephen Steuben. Still earlier in the month, on May 9, the Gardes Lafayette had received a banner at the hands of a Mlle. Doubet. The Jewish women of Chicago, many of them German Jews, dispatched a committee to Springfield with a handsome flag to be given to Hecker's regiment. The Chicago Norwegian Society, Nora Lodge, caused a long march and delay for the Fifteenth Wisconsin as it passed through that city early in March, 1862, in order to present it a flag. This was a handsome banner of silk with gold fringe, bearing on one side the stars and stripes and on the other on a blue field the united American and Norwegian coats of arms with the inscription "For Gud og vort Land (For God and our land)." [31]

This was one way in which the people behind the front could demonstrate their pride in their home regiments, their appreciation of the sacri-

[29] New York Herald, June 20, 1861.

[30] Ibid., June 14, 1861; Moore (ed.), Rebellion Record, I, Pt. 2, pp. 364–66.

[31] For the flag to Blenker's regiment, see New York Herald, May 18, 1861; for the flag to the Steuben Regiment, see New York Courrier des États-Unis, May 18, 1861; for the flag to the Gardes Lafayette, see ibid., May 13, 1861; for the flag given by the Jewish women, see Chicago Illinois Staats-Zeitung, September 16, 1862; for the flag to the Scandinavian Regiment, see Madison Emigranten, March 17, 1862.

fices of these men, and their determination to support the cause and the
men fighting to sustain it. Civilians could not pour out their blood; they
could pour out their financial resources.

A form of moral support which was not present to any strong degree
in World War I and was practically absent in World War II was the outpouring of the population to see a regiment depart, the escorting by an
organized body of a regiment from station to station or from station to
boat, or the formal welcome given to a returning minor officer (who under
the circumstances usually appeared to be a hero). The reader has already
had a picture of the dramatic, spectacular scene staged by the Irish to send
off the Sixty-ninth Regiment with a consciousness of the support of their
fellow countrymen. More staid and restrained, but no less heartfelt, was
the send-off which the Scandinavians gave their Fifteenth Wisconsin.
When on March 2, 1862, the men marched out of Camp Randall to the
train by companies, crowds of their countrymen from the surrounding
settlements had gathered at the camp to bid them farewell and to send
them off with waving of hats and handkerchiefs and with cheers. At many
points along the route from Madison to Chicago crowds, chiefly of Norse,
gathered to cheer them on their way; at Stoughton, Clinton Junction, and
Harvard, the people even offered them warm cheer in the form of hot
coffee. The usual waving of hats by farmers in the fields and of aprons by
farmers' wives from the farmhouse doors greeted the troop-laden trains
as they passed. The meals provided by the citizens in Philadelphia and
Chicago and many other places awaited the foreign soldiers just as they
did the native Americans, but this service was not a special activity of the
foreigners. It should be stated that committees of foreign-born did meet
departing and returning troops in order to aid soldiers of their respective
nationalities.

The reader need not think that as the officers and men reached the field,
the women were all left behind. Just as many of the wives in World Wars
I and II felt constrained to follow their husbands to the camps and live in
the near-by cities until the departure abroad, so the wives of the Civil War
period followed their husbands to the camp; but there was a great difference. Since the front was overseas in both the World Wars, wives were
debarred from the front (possibly nothing but the pressure on transportation kept them home); but in the Civil War, where the camp might be
very near the front, women were practically—and occasionally actually—
at the front. Men craved the companionship of their wives. Foreign-born
officers saw the wives and children of native Americans in camp and

naturally began to plan for theirs to join them. Even such a timid woman as Hans Mattson's wife, who had probably never been farther away from home than St. Paul, made the long trip to her husband's camp in Arkansas with her two children. The physician, the quartermaster, and one of the captains of the Scandinavian Regiment had their wives with them in camp at the beginning of their life at the front. Mrs. Heg accompanied the Colonel only to Chicago; but by the time he had reached Island No. 10 and noted the many wives in camp he began to write to his wife that he hoped for a place the following winter where he could have her and the children with him.[32]

If Scandinavian women could muster the courage to accompany their husbands to the field, it was to be expected that the wives of hard-fighting Irishmen would manifest the same spirit. The wife of an officer of the Sixty-third Regiment in the Irish Brigade set forth bravely for the Peninsular campaign with a fine parade of Irish loyalty in her dress, for she wore a dark-green riding habit and an enormous green feather in her hat. Neither her finery nor her spirit could survive the drenching rains of Virginia, however, and so she promptly returned to New York.[33]

The presence of women in camps and in hospitals as nurses or in other useful service is, however, another story. Dr. Sören J. Hansen, a physician in Colonel Heg's regiment, took his wife with him as a war nurse. Wives of the foreign-born volunteers supplemented the work of the men nurses. Comparatively few of these are known by name. An Ida Johnson among the Swedish women was appointed nurse by the Western Sanitary Commission.[34] The lists of nuns who went out on the battlefields to succor the wounded assembled by Ellen Ryan Jolly in the appendices to her work *Nuns of the Battlefield* testify how overwhelming was the number of these who had been born in Ireland or Germany, though there were representatives of many nationalities among them.[35] One woman, English by

[32] Blegen (ed.), *Civil War Letters of Colonel Heg*, 57, 60, 63 n., 69. Heg wrote March 9, 1862, "I see a great many women along with the soldiers, and even small children, but the poor things suffer awfully." *Ibid.*, 60. Princess Salm-Salm said, "The whole camp was teeming with women and children." *Ten Years of My Life*, I, 38.

[33] Dwyer, "63rd Regiment Infantry," in Fox (comp.), *New York at Gettysburg*, II, 493.

[34] Blegen (ed.), *Civil War Letters of Colonel Heg*, 63 n., for Mrs. Hansen; for Ida Johnson, see Hokanson, *Swedish Immigrants*, 75. The writer does not admit Mrs. H. Holstein, as she was a descendant of the Delaware Swedes of colonial days and not born in Sweden. Ida Johnson's name, on the other hand, occurs in Linus Pierpont Brockett and Mary C. Vaughan (comps.), *Woman's Work in the Civil War. A Record of Heroism, Patriotism, and Patience.* (Philadelphia, 1867), 790. It is possible that she also was Swedish only by descent.

[35] The following table to show nativity has been compiled from the lists of nuns which

birth though she had come to the United States while a mere child, labored in the hospitals from 1862 till after the war. Mary W. Lee, who had a son of her own in the service, was persistent, thorough, and obedient to the orders of the surgeons. Her wards were always in perfect order and well supplied. For a great part of the time she was in charge of the light-diet and special-diet department, where her duties and responsibilities were vexatious and laborious.[36]

Mary A. Brady, born in Ireland and married to an English lawyer, had lived in this country twelve years when the outbreak of war brought her to the hospitals to aid the soldiers. She had no personal incentive at first, as had so many others, since she had no son, husband, or brother in the armed forces; but she forsook her family of five children and her comfortable home in Philadelphia to push her way through the army lines and sometimes, despite general orders, to the very front or to those advanced hospitals where the men were brought fresh from the battlefield. She spent weeks at the field hospitals just to the rear of the great battlefields and returned home only to restore her wasted energies. In July, 1862, she met with a few others to deliberate on how the pitiable condition of the wounded soldiers, then being brought from the James River after McClellan's Peninsular campaign to various hospitals in and near Philadelphia, could be ameliorated. In one hospital near her home, over three thousand soldiers were then languishing, after the hard fights of that terrible campaign, with the low, dull fever to which many succumbed, while others were looking at their mutilated bodies with despair. In the summer of 1864, as she was planning new fields of service, she died from overexertion and exposure.[37]

Closely allied to the bona fide nurses attached to hospitals were those men and women who visited the sick and wounded soldiers hospitalized in their cities. A striking instance of this kind of support is afforded by John

follow each chapter in the book by Ellen Ryan Jolly, *Nuns of the Battlefield* (Providence, 1927):

Ireland	289	England	4
United States	189	Belgium	2
Germany	40	Switzerland	1
France	12	Scotland	1
Canada	5	Cuba	1
TOTAL			544

Records of two Polish Sisters of Charity were found in the search. See the New York *Times*, March 26, 1930.

[36] Moore (author and comp.), *Women of the War*, 156.

[37] *Ibid.*, 37-39.

Hitz, the Swiss consul resident in Washington, and his wife, Ann Hitz. The fact that they spoke several of the languages of central Europe and so could appreciate the feelings of those born in Europe and could address them in their native tongues made them particularly valuable, especially to the German soldiers. From the very first arrival of volunteers in Washington, Mr. and Mrs. Hitz threw open their doors to soldiers (they were located near a camp); and thus they rendered a great service, especially on occasions when no preparations had been made to receive the weary, and often drenched, soldiers. They filled all the boilers they could find with coffee, collected bread by begging and buying, and fed the hungry. Mrs. Hitz often played the role of mother to little German drummer boys. Mr. Hitz joined a German aid society and visited the hospitals almost daily. As the Hitzes became known among the patients, they were frequently sent for when a patient arrived whose language could not be understood. The effect of a few words in his own tongue to a German who could not make his needs known was often electrical. Furthermore, the comfort Mrs. Hitz could bring to a dying German, when she was able to bring a Catholic priest so that the soldier might die in peace, can readily be imagined. To hundreds, as she sat beside their cots, she became a mother confessor.[38]

To a somewhat different category belonged Mme. Turchin, the wife of the colonel of the Nineteenth Illinois, as she was nurse and mother confessor rolled into one. The daughter of a Russian officer, she had been born and reared in foreign camps and was a favorite with the men of her father's command. She likewise shared the fortunes of her soldier husband in the war of the American republic, accompanying him to the field and first of all to the camp at Springfield, Illinois. Fine-looking but unmistakably foreign in appearance and manner, she was intensely loyal to the military regime and American in her sympathies. She proved as popular among the men of her husband's American regiment as she had been with the Russian soldiers. They made their way to her with their illnesses and troubles and were invariably received with kindness, with considerable badinage, and with skillful nursing when that was the treatment indicated. On one occasion the regimental train crashed through a trestle in crossing Beaver Creek about forty-six miles east of Vincennes, Indiana, killing or injuring 130 men. Mme. Turchin was instant with her aid, tearing her skirt into bandages in order to be able to bind up the injuries of these men. She improvised beds with the car cushions and made the suffering men as com-

[38] *Ibid.*, 473-77.

fortable as possible. The men respected and later loved her for her bravery, gentleness, and constant care of the sick and wounded.[39]

A field of service which was dangerous, thrilling, and valuable all at the same time, that of acting as spy, has been abundantly exploited by writers on Civil War history. No one up to the present time has, however, taken the trouble to determine whether there were any foreign-born among the Union spies. Certainly no one would pretend that the number was anything but exceedingly small. While not to be regarded as records of professional spies, the tales of women who undertook daring exploits to convey valuable information to Union forces certainly evidence secret-service missions. One bona fide case of a spy from among the foreign-born turned up in the search. Miss S. E. E. Edmonds, a Canadian from New Brunswick, desiring an education in order to become a missionary, came to the "States," as she doubtless said, in 1859 or 1860 and sold books to support herself. When the war came, she resolved to devote herself to nursing the sick soldiers in the hospital and went to Washington to secure an appointment. After eight or nine months in this labor of love, she learned that one of the spies in General McClellan's service had been captured by the Rebels and executed. A determined and daring woman, able to sustain great fatigue, skilled in horsemanship and capable of shooting straight, and commanding in addition quick perception and unrivaled power of impersonation, she was readily accepted when she applied for the dangerous post. Many are the tales of her adventures which have been preserved. She assumed the role of orderly to General Kearney and was repeatedly under fire in the retreat across the Peninsula while acting as orderly or on detached duty with the wounded. Under an assumed name, that of Frank Thompson, she took part in most of the battles of the retreat. She penetrated three times into the enemy's camp under different disguises during the last days of Pope's campaign. She even dared to penetrate to the headquarters of the enemy and succeeded in bringing back information of intended movements and even valuable papers. After the Battle of Antietam, a body of cavalry with which she was traveling on detached service was attacked by Confederate guerrillas, in consequence of which her horse was killed and she herself was seriously injured. At Fredericksburg, as aide-de-camp to General Hancock, she was under fire during the entire battle. After Hooker assumed command of the Army of the Potomac, she went to the Western army, where she was soon playing her old role; but after she had wounded a Confederate captain who had tried

[39] Mary Livermore, *My Story of the War*, 114–15; Haynie, *The Nineteenth Illinois*, 144–45.

to conscript her while she was within the Southern lines, her work as a spy became too hazardous to pursue within the enemy lines, though as a detective in Louisville she located several Rebel spies in the city.[40]

Women went even beyond becoming spies and nurses; a few turned soldier and supported the fighting front. Some enlisted, as did Mme. Loreta Velasquez in the Confederate army, in Union companies and escaped detection for a longer or shorter period. Sometimes women went out with the soldiers informally, to rescue the injured, or on picket duty. Bridget Divers, or "Irish Biddy," as the soldiers called her, sometimes went out with the men on picket duty and remained on watch all night. Occasionally, when sickness or hard service had depleted the ranks of the regiment, she would take the place of a soldier in the ranks and go out scouting or on a raiding expedition, rendering the full duty of a soldier. At other times, she conducted herself even more fearlessly by taking the place of an officer. Once, when the brigade had been engaged in a skirmish with the object of completing the investment of Richmond, a captain of the regiment to which she was attached had fallen in a skirmish and his body had been left within the lines of the foe. Knowing that the body had been abandoned in the retreat, Bridget rode into the enemy lines boldly, unchallenged by the foe, who either failed to see her or respected her sex for the nature of her mission. Lifting the lifeless body and laying it over her horse, she rode alone twelve miles before she found the regiment. During the ride she came upon a small wagon train with which she rode for some distance and which afforded her another opportunity to display her bravery. A hostile demonstration against the train occurred, whereupon the badly armed teamsters were about to abandon their train in flight; but Bridget rode among them and rallied them with the reproach that they should not abandon their wagons before the Confederates were within a mile of them. Recalled to their senses by a woman, they brought the train into camp. It was also asserted that at the battle of Fair Oaks, as they were advancing to the fight, she rallied the Seventh Massachusetts when General Silas Casey's division gave way.[41]

It was with the First Michigan Cavalry, in which her husband was

[40] Linus Pierpont Brockett (comp.), *Battlefield and Hospital; or Lights and Shadows of the Great Rebellion* (Philadelphia [?], n.d.), 66–72.

[41] Moore (author and comp.), *Women of the War*, 533–35. This book also tells the story that as the Seventh Massachusetts was advancing slowly at Fair Oaks, it passed Irish Biddy, leading her wounded husband from the field. Swinging her cap over her head, she shouted, "Arrah! go in, boys, and bate the bloody spalpeens, and revenge me husband, and God be wid ye." *Ibid.*, 535.

a private, that this Irishwoman had gone out to the field; and she served through the entire war. Her acquaintance with the men extended from the First Michigan to the entire brigade, and even to the division. So well did she know every man in the regiment that she could estimate his character, his sufferings, his needs, and the value of his military record. She took it upon herself to look after not only his health but also his moral and religious needs. In the absence of the chaplain, she would visit the Christian Commission to obtain books and papers for the men, asserting that she was "acting chaplain." She was a sort of composite vivandière, nurse, hospital steward, and sometimes even surgeon. Yet she was no jack-of-all-trades, for she seemed expert in each role that she assumed. Long practice with disease and wounds had brought her such perfection that in practical skill she was often said to rival a physician. Her judgment in seeking supplies from the Sanitary Commission or the Christian Commission prevented waste or reckless use of what the country poured out. If inquiries came concerning a private, Bridget was the person to whom the Commission first turned for the desired information; if the man was in the division, she was more likely to know him than was the commanding officer. She shared with the brigade all the actual dangers of active service and had two or three horses shot under her. At the battle of Cedar Creek, though at one time surrounded by the enemy, she still effected her escape.

Her personal appearance was what one, under the circumstances, should expect—unattractive. Her figure had grown heavy and athletic by constant overexercise, her hair was bleached and unkempt, her skin from exposure to the burning sun and roughening winds had turned brown and weather-beaten; but many a soldier knew that under her simple, plain exterior her heart never lost its tenderness.[42] She was ever fearless and daring. Her love of army life was really remarkable, for even after the war she, with her husband, joined a regiment of the Regular Army and was stationed on the western plains.

Mme. Turchin not only filled in her husband's regiment the role of nurse and mother confessor to whom the men came with their illnesses and troubles, but she could—and did at least once—actually take the field. In the spring of 1862, when the regiment was actively engaged in Tennessee, Colonel Turchin fell seriously ill and had to be transported for days in an ambulance. Mme. Turchin, besides nursing her husband, took his place at the head of the regiment, gaining cheerful obedience from the

---

[42] *Ibid.*, 109–12; Mary Livermore, *My Story of the War*, 115–17. Mrs. Livermore spelled the Irishwoman's name "Devens," not "Divers," but it is clear that the same woman is meant.

privates and subordinate officers. Some declared her the equal of her husband in courage and military skill, for she manifested perfect indifference to shot and shell and Minié ball even when they rained thickly about her. She led the troops into battle, facing hot fire and fighting stanchly at their head.[43]

Mrs. Kady Brownell was perhaps the most widely known woman warrior in the Union army. Born, like Mme. Turchin, in camp, as her Scotch father was at the time of her birth serving in the British army on the African coast, she was at home in camp. Domiciled in Providence, Rhode Island, in 1861, she first accompanied the First Rhode Island Regiment to the field for the three months service and then accompanied the Fifth Rhode Island Infantry, in which her husband was a noncommissioned officer. She became, not the color-bearer of her husband's company, as in the earlier period of service, but nurse and daughter of the Fifth Rhode Island Regiment; moreover, she was skillful with a gun and expert at swordsmanship. She marched with the men, asked no favors, and, on occasion, bore the brunt of battle as fearlessly as any soldier. She shared in General Burnside's expedition to Roanoke Island and New Bern, in which battle her husband was so severely wounded that he had to be discharged. This ended her military career, as she retired with him to domestic life and private obscurity.[44]

A Norwegian girl who had ambitions to serve her country and also a turn for adventure was not able to get very far with her plan. About sixteen years old, she presented an attractive appearance as a boy, though not as a girl—"pretty" was the word used in the newspaper account—and she certainly secured in three weeks more adventure than is usually a woman's lot in a lifetime. She ran away from home, cut her hair, donned boy's clothes, drifted about in different characters for a time, enrolled in the army, and eventually tried to drown herself. After this last experience she returned home, but not to stay, for in a few days she was again found in boy's clothes among the Zouave company of the Nineteenth Illinois Regiment. She did not, the account states, accept the warning of the police judge with especial humility or acknowledge her military career as ended when her elderly father came to take her home.[45]

The writer has encountered two instances in which a commission was

[43] Ibid., 115.

[44] Ibid., 119; Moore (author and comp.), Women of the War, 54–64.

[45] This was Company F of the Nineteenth Illinois. The account appeared in the Chicago Hemlandet, July 17, 1861, and seems well substantiated, for it gives the name of the girl, Caroline Olson, and says that the facts were acknowledged by her father.

actually issued to a woman, in both cases by the same official. The first case is that of Princess Agnes Salm-Salm. The story of her activities to secure for her husband a colonelcy and finally a brigadier-generalcy has been told—activities which secured for her the acquaintance of several influential figures, including Governor Richard Yates of Illinois. She accompanied her husband to the war, was admired as a bold rider, and had many adventures in the field. She possessed, it was said, great beauty, excellent gifts, and a nimble brain; and she also undeniably (judging by the facility with which she handled public characters) possessed great charm. She refused to reveal her origin in her book, but it was commonly believed that she came of a French-Canadian officer's family. In the process of trying to secure her husband's promotion she was accorded a captain's commission for herself along with the pay of an army captain—in acknowledgment, Governor Yates said, of her services to the sick soldiers. Certain it is that she concerned herself actively with the hospital at Bridgeport, Tennessee. To her credit it should be stated that she used her charm not only to advance her husband's interests but also to secure needed supplies for hospitals.

A brief résumé of her life after the Civil War should be given in order to show how much of a "soldieress" of fortune she herself was. After her husband's service in the Union army was ended, she accompanied him to Mexico and won by eloquent pleading postponement of the execution of Emperor Maximilian; it was probably owing to her efforts that Prince Salm-Salm was spared and permitted to depart from Mexico after he had been captured with Emperor Maximilian and condemned to death in May, 1867. The pair then went back to Germany, where she was summoned to Berlin and Vienna to give the sovereigns an eye-witness account of the tragedy which had befallen Maximilian. In the Franco-Prussian War, in which her husband fell, she managed a Prussian field hospital and performed heroic deeds in the service of the Red Cross.[46]

The other commission to a foreign woman from the hand of Governor Yates was given to Frau Reynolds, wife of the German Lieutenant Reynolds of the Seventeenth Illinois Regiment. She, like Mme. Turchin and Princess Salm-Salm, followed her husband to the war and nursed the

[46] Salm-Salm, *Ten Years of My Life*, I, 84, and *passim*; Kaufmann, *Die Deutschen im Bürgerkriege*, 546–47. James R. Joy records that Princess Salm-Salm was born on a farm in Quebec Province or in Vermont and that she had married Prince zu Salm-Salm under the name of Agnes Leclerq. Johnson and Malone (eds.), *Dictionary of American Biography*, XVI, 310.

wounded after the Battle of Shiloh with such devotion that as a reward Governor Yates sent her a patent as major.[47]

Finally, we come to the most colorful of the group, though not the most dramatic. The reader of books on the Confederate army has probably not been surprised to find vivandières among the Louisiana regiments, where French traditions might be expected to linger, but such figures as female sutlers seem alien to the practices of the North. It is just to call them alien, for they have been encountered only among the regiments of foreign-born. The *Illinois Staats-Zeitung* reported that a Miss Seraphin Tandey of Indianapolis accompanied the Eleventh Indiana Zouaves, a three months regiment, as *Wärterin* and *Marketenderin* (nurse and sutler), the German equivalent for vivandière.[48] Only the Garibaldi Guards and the Gardes Lafayette, adhering to French traditions, carried with them vivandières. Even if at its departure "the *Gardes di Garibaldi* lacked guns," declared the *Courrier des États-Unis,* "it was rich in vivandières." The paper went on to relate the misadventure of two of these women, who, escaping the parental roof without permission, were stopped in their romantic adventure and brought to Jersey City; there one, a Mme. Edelstein, was shut up by her father, presumably until her enthusiasm had waned.[49] The vivandière who accompanied the Gardes Lafayette was presumably of somewhat more mature years; though alluded to as "a blooming young lady," she was evidently married, for her name is given as Mme. Susenal. This regiment apparently eschewed women cooks, native or foreign, and as *bons vivants* took with them a recognized New York chef, a fact to be deduced from the newspaper statement ". . . and an important fact to be mentioned is that M. Soyer is cook." [50]

Only in one single regiment—the Eleventh New York State Militia, composed chiefly of musicians—was there the position of "cantière" (doubtless a mispelling for *"cantinière"*) ; it was as a "cantière" that the wife of a singer from the Bowery enrolled herself.[51] The reader can guess as readily as the writer at her nationality, but her duties seem clear—those of a sutler.

In the Civil War, as in our World Wars, the heavy enlistments pro-

[47] Kaufmann, *Die Deutschen im Bürgerkriege,* 542.

[48] Chicago *Illinois Staats-Zeitung*, August 25, 1861. For vivandières in the Southern army, see Lonn, *Foreigners in the Confederacy,* 379–80.

[49] New York *Courrier des États-Unis,* June 6, 1861.

[50] New York *Tribune,* September 1, 1861.

[51] New York *Courrier des États-Unis,* April 24, 1861.

duced a scarcity of labor. Unquestionably, much of the labor for the munition plants was drawn from the more skilled of our foreign-born laborers; and as more and more men were drawn off to the battlefields, there was an increasing demand for foreign labor to supply the deficiency of workers in every field of industry—especially in agriculture and in the mines. To supply the need, strenuous efforts were made to import foreign laborers. Echoes run through all the consular reports, as we have seen, especially those from the German and Swedish ports. One effort in particular, an effort distinct from recruitment for the army, was that made by the owners of some copper mines in northern Michigan, who subscribed a large sum to send representatives to Sweden to recruit immigrant laborers. This was the venture of Axel Silfversparre which has already been detailed. Another agent brought over one hundred Scandinavian laborers, who were put to work behind the Union lines near Chattanooga as horseshoers, repairmen, and bridgebuilders. Their pay was fourteen dollars a month and expenses. It is impossible, of course, to measure the contribution thus made by foreign-born laborers to the war effort.[52]

Probably the strongest support from the foreign element on the home front was the almost unswerving support which the foreign-nationality press gave to the war. The *Emigranten* in its issue of April 27, 1861, took comfort in the absence of a Confederate navy, an augury of the optimistic attitude which it would assume on many later occasions. This paper, in common with much of the native American press, was unduly hopeful of an early peace, representing conditions in the South in June, 1861—far too soon—as unduly grave for the Confederates. It reported that in the South, according to a man just arrived from New Orleans, business was at a standstill, hunger prices were prevailing, and the blockade was effective from Norfolk to New Orleans.[53]

The comments of the nationality newspapers on the first Union defeat, First Bull Run, were generally understanding. The Columbus (Ohio) *Westbote* admitted that it was a disastrous defeat and that it would prolong the war by months but declared that this one defeat gave no reason for despairing of ultimate victory. It quoted the proverb "One swallow does not make a summer" and drew the obvious analogy that a single battle

[52] Hokanson, *Swedish Immigrants*, 76–77. This is based on the personal testimony of one of the number. See above, p. 426.

[53] Madison *Emigranten*, June 8, 1861. The only prediction which was verified was that which it made in common with an officer who said that the United States would be in New Orleans by July 4, 1862.

seldom decides a war.[54] The *Emigranten* took the defeat well, thus helping the Norwegians of the central West to take it well: "All the powers
of the government have been set in motion again to have the army ready
to march and when the word of command sounds the next time, it will
be delivered to such huge masses of troops that victory will be certain.
There streams already a throng of new troops to Washington. Within one
week New York will have eight new regiments in Washington . . .
Connecticut one regiment, and Vermont one regiment. The governor of
Illinois has offered thirteen new regiments." Already this Norwegian
editor had turned his back on Bull Run and was facing forward.[55]

Hemlandet rejoiced over Grant's victories in the West—over the fall
of Fort Donelson, over the taking of Island No. 10, over the entry of Union
troops into Memphis. It, naturally, took great pride in John Ericsson for
his invention of the *Monitor,* printing crude pictures of the strange craft
in the issue of March 26, 1862. It gave little space to McClellan's campaign in Virginia except to the Seven Days' Battles around Richmond and
commented but briefly when that general was replaced by Burnside.[56]
The *Emigranten* was patient and tolerant rather than indifferent about
the Peninsular campaign: "In the absence of other news, it is therefore
fairly clear that McClellan planned badly to go the roundabout way on
the James River. . . . But there is not in and of itself any evidence of
incapacity; such circumstances arise, and we have therefore no grounds
to doubt what the telegram of the 11th relates; namely, that President
Lincoln, who has been at the James River, has said in a speech to the
Potomac Army, that he 'had confidence in it and in its general.' " [57] This
partiality in interest toward the western campaigns was only natural because the West was where most of the Scandinavian soldiers were fighting.
Hemlandet did not hesitate, however, to criticize the Union officers "for
the unforgivable neglect" at Shiloh which was the "cause of Sunday's

[54] "Immerhin ist es eine verderbliche Schleppe Für uns, die das Ende des Krieges wieder um
Monate hinausrückt. Keinesweges aber giebt sie uns Grund, an dem endlichen Siege des
Sternenbanners zu zweifeln! Eine Schwalbe macht keinen Sommer und eine einzige Schlacht
entscheidet selten einen Krieg. Im Kriege muss sich der beste Feldherr zuweilen auf Niederlage
gefasst machen." Columbus *Westbote,* July 25, 1861.

[55] Madison *Emigranten,* July 27, 1861. This paper followed closely the reports of the
English reporter William Howard Russell and passed his hostile comments on to its readers. See
issues of May 10, June 1, 1861.

[56] Chicago *Hemlandet,* February 19, April 9, March 26, June 11, June 25, November 12,
1862.

[57] Madison *Emigranten,* July 14, 1862.

severe defeat." Again, "All accounts agree that the rebels completely surprised our troops on Sunday morning. Through neglect to place necessary
picket guards, our commander was unaware of the presence of the foe."
The same paper noted that Grant did not arrive at the battlefield until
after nine o'clock; that even he was utterly unprepared and without a
plan, for "each division and brigade fought the whole day for itself according to its best judgment." [58]

Both of these Scandinavian papers tried to find some grain of comfort
after Antietam and even after Fredericksburg. Of the former battle the
editor of the Swedish paper wrote, "Does not the fact that they [the Con-
federates] have paid a high price for the invasion [into Maryland] fore-
shadow the ominous outlook? Our victory consists solely in the enormous
loss the rebels suffered." He conceded that the enemy secured great stores
of food. He concluded, however, that the victory leaned toward the Union
side. The Norwegian paper measured the gains of each side at Antietam
and left—properly—the impression of a drawn victory.[59] The editor of
Hemlandet headed his comment on Fredericksburg with the query
"Whose fault is all this Misfortune?" but was generous toward Burnside.
The editor of *Emigranten* could even find some comfort several weeks
later: "In the Potomac Army all seem to lie in a death-swoon since the
great battle of Fredericksburg, of which the Rebel chieftain speaks with
such unusual bitterness in his report, which was communicated in the
Emigranten last week, that there is no ground to believe that the enemy
regards it as any brilliant victory." [60]

The attitude of the German press was correctly stated by one of the German editors: "With the conviction that the co-operation of all good citizens
was necessary in order to overcome the danger threatening the land and
our freedom, with the cessation of all previous party differences, all remaining rudeness and hatreds disappeared; and as the members of the different
hostile parties marched courageously together to meet death under the
same flag, so also the press laid aside earlier contentious issues and worked
for the one great and exalted goal, the saving of freedom and the Constitution." [61] German editors, however, did not hesitate to criticize and to

[58] Chicago *Hemlandet*, April 23, 1862.
[59] Chicago *Hemlandet*, September 24, 1862; Madison *Emigranten*, September 29, 1862.
[60] Chicago *Hemlandet*, December 21, 1862; Madison *Emigranten*, January 12, 1863. The
editor of the latter reported a rumor that "the noble, but according to his own confession
not frightfully able, Burnside," had long since offered his resignation. Madison *Emigranten*,
January 12, 1863.
[61] Chicago *Illinois Staats-Zeitung*, June 23, 1862.

indulge in heavy sarcasm. After the battle of Corinth the editor of the Chicago German sheet declared that the army chiefs were following the old story of Manassas and Yorktown in a new western edition. Just as at Manassas and Yorktown so now at Corinth the Confederates under Joe Johnston had retreated without the "great" Halleck's noticing it. In all three cases the retreating Rebel army could have "at least been 'struck in the pan' if our generals had been informed at the right moment of the retreat." This newspaper also declared "quite simply" that the lack of information was owing to the neglect "of the truest and most dependable" sources of information—the slaves.[62]

It goes without saying that all the foreign-language newspapers—German, Swedish, Norwegian, and French—rejoiced over the double victory of Gettysburg and Vicksburg. After Chancellorsville, however, when the Germans of the Eleventh Corps were made the scapegoat for the great disaster—unjustly, as they then felt and as history has since justified them in thinking—the tone of the German press changed. The editors did not thereafter give the same unswerving, enthusiastic support to the war, though they continued to support it as a matter of principle.

The Irish press was likewise steadfast. Even though it resented the needless slaughter of its countrymen at Fredericksburg and the refusal to allow the Irish Brigade to be properly recruited, the *Irish-American* and the *Pilot* continued to support the cause.

The Scandinavian press gave its finest support, however, in stanchly standing by the government and in encouraging a war-weary folk during the depressing months of 1864, when the Union leaders knew that the war was won but had yet to prove it to a people who not only had grown dreadfully tired of the fighting but also had in considerable numbers begun to doubt the possibility of victory. No American editor with Revolutionary ancestors could have answered the cries for peace better than an editor born on the soil of Sweden did in these words: "This country's condition has manifestly approached its crisis. We stand in the grip of a war for the preservation of the Union. The Union is not yet restored, and yet we hear cries for 'peace.' The desire for peace does not belong to any particular political party. We all yearn for it with all our hearts. But what is peace and how can it best be restored? That is a question that the people must take into consideration in November. On this question rests everything else." The editor then proceeded to examine the terms on which the Rebels offered peace, especially the acknowledgment of the Confederacy;

[62] *Ibid.*, June 2, 1862.

he next examined the possibility of peace on those terms and the question of whether such a peace was desirable. He closed with a ringing challenge to continue the war: "The restoration of the Union is a manifest and absolute necessity and since we are convinced of it, what conclusion follows. War must, in case we concluded such a peace, be again renewed." [63]

[63] Chicago *Hemlandet*, November 2, 1864.

CHAPTER NINETEEN

Numbers and Rewards

By THIS time the reader is well prepared for definite and tremendous figures for the number of foreigners and foreign-born in the Union army, more particularly for the number of these of two nationalities—the German and the Irish. The most pertinent question in connection with the size of the foreign contingent as it relates to this study is the number of white males of foreign birth of military age (military age as it was construed at the time—that is, between the ages of eighteen and forty-five). In Europe, and in any settled population, one fifth of the total population represents very nearly the number of males between these two ages. On the other hand, since older persons rarely migrate, and thus over 90 per cent of all male immigrants are under forty years of age, the ages of immigrants coming into a new country usually correspond very closely to the military ages. In addition, for every three male immigrants to America between 1800 and 1865 there were only two female immigrants, and immigrant children numbered only 22 per cent of the immigrant horde. These are simple facts, which are confirmed by the history of the 19,500,000 Europeans who came to America during the nineteenth century.

All of this means, with respect to the question at hand, that the proportion of men of fighting age was greater in the newly settled states of the West than in the Atlantic states. The way in which the proportion rose from East to West in the following selected states is striking: in Maine the white men of military age constituted 19.5 per cent of the entire white population; in Illinois, 22.1 per cent; in Minnesota, 23.8 per cent; and in California, 47.1 per cent.[1]

The fact that the foreign-born could furnish more soldiers proportionately for the Union army than could the native-born has, therefore, a simple, natural explanation. For the reasons outlined above, there were many more young men in the immigrant stock than in the native population, with its many women, children, and older men.

[1] *Eighth Census, 1860. The Statistics of the Population,* xvii.

The population of the states which adhered to the Union was upwards of 23,000,000 people, of whom less than 500,000 were slaves.[2] The males of fighting age constituted one fifth of the population and amounted to 4,600,000, the number with which comparisons must be made.

The thoughtless person might easily and falsely assume that a civil war would automatically end all immigration on the presumption that no one safely outside the zone of war dangers and discomforts would deliberately run his head into the noose. The assumption that immigration to the Confederate States of America ceased automatically is very near the truth. Not so with the Northern states. The field of combat impinged upon the North only twice and then briefly; moreover, the war increased the demand for immigrant labor, since it not only increased the demand for production of all types of war materials but also, by draining off a vast amount of man power for the battlefield, reduced the available supply of labor to work the machines in the factories and to till the fields in the agricultural areas. Some of the potential immigrants doubtless had the wit to know this; but others were not long left in doubt, for the fact of the great demand for laborers was in various ways quickly disseminated through European countries.

The records reveal that the number of arrivals from foreign countries in 1861 was 112,705. This represents a tremendous decline from the year of greatest immigration to our shores prior to the Civil War, 1854, when the total number of immigrants reached 256,177. In 1862 the number of immigrants rose slightly, to 114,475; in 1863 it increased to 199,811; in 1864, under the stimulus of encouragement from our consuls abroad, it increased again, this time to 221,525. To attempt to estimate exactly the number of foreigners of military age entering the United States during each of the war years is difficult, and to estimate the number among them who enlisted is even more difficult. By an intricate process of calculation, into which it is unnecessary to enter here, Benjamin Gould, the statistician of the Sanitary Commission, arrived at the following figures as the increase to the volunteer army from the immigrant military population for each of the war years: 31,879 in 1861; 32,380 in 1862; 56,518 in 1863; and 62,663 in 1864, making a total of 183,440 by the close of the year 1864.[3]

From consular reports we glean details of numbers from particular

[2] *Ibid.*, 597.

[3] For his method of arriving at these figures, see Benjamin A. Gould, *Investigations in the Military and Anthropological Statistics of American Soldiers* (New York, 1869), 5.

countries and ports. From Hamburg 9,370 left for the United States in 1861; 14,287, in 1862. Consul Börnstein reported the emigration through the port of Bremen as rising steadily after the decline in 1861, when it sank to 12,048. It rose only slightly in 1862; but in 1863 it increased markedly—to 16,428—and in 1864 it mounted to 24,133. It is striking that from 1861 to 1864 immigration from Germany doubled. Consul James Anderson has recorded the following figures for 1862: from Sweden and Norway, 878; from Denmark, 2,812; from Austria, 520; from Russia, 232; and from Switzerland, 163. The number from Ireland in 1863 was 175,000 (double the figure for 1861); and it rose in 1864 to 193,000. There is no evidence that the Norwegian immigration to Minnesota declined; in fact, the influx, most of which entered by way of Quebec, tended constantly to increase. The decline in 1863 is explicable as the result of the outbreak of the Sioux Indians the preceding fall.

Certainly the predominance of males of military age, and especially among the German part of the population, is strikingly illustrated in Missouri. Note the comment of one of the German papers on May 23, 1861: "One of the most surprising manifestations for an attentive observer is the astonishing mass of German men in St. Louis capable of bearing arms. At this moment there are around ten thousand Germans, if not more, under arms. Just go on a Sunday from camp to camp and look around at the spectators at the drill. We do not exaggerate—but around the ranks of German soldiers there stand just as many German men of military age in the best, most active age. If the need for manpower should arise, twenty thousand Germans could be mustered for the Union in this county alone. We are fully convinced that the last census of St. Louis, which gave around 60,000 Germans, has erroneously Americanized more than 10,000 Germans, so that the essential character of St. Louis, in that which concerns the national origin of its inhabitants, is obviously more German than Anglo-Saxon or Irish, indeed outweighs both." [4] Four fifths of the unconditionally Union men of St. Louis were either foreign-born citizens or their offspring—most of them Germans.

The actual numbers and proportions of foreign-born in the Union

[4] Quoted by the Chicago *Illinois Staats-Zeitung* in its issue of May 30, 1861, from the St. Louis *Anzeiger des Westens*. It has proved impossible, despite a careful search by a member of the staff of the St. Louis Public Library, for which grateful acknowledgment is made, to identify the issue of the *Anzeiger* which carried this statement. It is possible that the Chicago editor misnamed the paper from which it was taken. In any case, we know that some German paper printed a statement which has so much value that the author has allowed it to remain in the text.

army has been a matter of almost as much dispute as the relative numbers of the Federal and Confederate armies. The figures which seem to be regarded as authoritative, those of Thomas L. Livermore, placed the total number of enlistments in the Union army at 2,898,304, including militia and emergency men. This number must, however, be reduced by perhaps 400,000 to allow for repeated re-enlistments by individuals, thus leaving about 2,500,000 as the figure for the total number of individuals (native and foreign-born) who actually at some time during the war years stood in the ranks of the United States army. In this study we are interested in determining what proportion the foreign-born soldiers sustained to the native white soldiers; hence the 186,000 negro soldiers must be subtracted. The basic number of enlistments, therefore, stands at around 2,312,000. Reducing the numbers to a three-year standard, Livermore has computed the services on the Union side as 1,556,678.[5] This would give what might be termed the average size of the army.

It has been repeatedly asserted that the Federal army consisted mainly of foreign-born soldiers. The Confederates, civilians and soldiers alike, were firmly convinced that except for the host of foreign mercenaries in the Union army, the outcome of the war would have been quite different.[6] These assertions will bear investigation. It should not be forgotten that though the population of the Northern states embraced a large number of persons who had migrated from Europe, a great many of these had established themselves in the country and had secured by naturalization the rights of citizenship—and its obligations. In the states that remained loyal to the Union, the total number of foreign-born was 3,903,672, nearly one sixth of the total population. No data are available from which can be determined what proportion of this number had become naturalized citizens, but unquestionably a large proportion had, since naturalization

[5] T. L. Livermore, *Numbers and Losses in the Civil War in America*, 50. The number of negro soldiers is that given by Shannon, *The Organization and Administration of the Union Army*, II, 160.

[6] It is unnecessary to quote at length the multitudinous remarks to this effect by Confederates. One example is found in the following: "While it cannot be expected that they [negroes] will ever fight with the bravery or gallantry of our own men, we are disposed to believe that they will be as soldiers but little inferior to the riff-raff of Germany and Ireland, which enters so largely into the composition of the Northern army." Richmond *Daily Examiner*, April 3, 1864. Another example is the remark made by a South Carolina woman to an officer of the One Hundred and Seventeenth New York: "Yankees indeed! Your whole army is made up of Irish, Dutch, and negroes." J. A. Mowris, *A History of the One Hundred and Seventeenth Regiment N.Y. Volunteers (Fourth Oneida) from the Date of its Organization, August, 1862, to that of its Muster Out, June, 1865* (Hartford, 1866), 196.

was very easy in the United States. It would seem only natural to suppose that the effective strength of the army showed almost as great a porportion of foreign-born soldiers as the general population showed of the foreign-born.

Naturally, the author cannot attempt to present precise figures for the various nationality groups in the Union army. That would have called for an enormous piece of research in itself. Furthermore, the person attempting it should be trained in the handling of statistics. On the other hand, the reader has a right to expect to be given some rough figures for the larger nationality groups. What the author has attempted to do is to study carefully the figures of students of the question and arrive at a reasonable figure.

The census figures give 1,276,075 as the total number of German-born living in the United States in 1860, from which number must be deducted the 72,000 resident in the states which seceded; this yields the official figure of 1,204,075 (or somewhat over 1,000,000) Germans in the Northern states, about 200,000 of whom were resident in the border states. If one adds the 100,000 Germans estimated by Kaufmann to have entered the United States during the war years, one arrives at a reservoir of over 1,300,000 among the German-born for recruits. Gould has estimated, on the basis of the total number of Germans in the population, that approximately 118,402 Germans were subject to service in the Union army; the number of this nationality who actually enrolled in the ranks he has given as 176,817.[7] On this basis the German element in the population furnished many more Union soldiers than could fairly have been expected of them, exceeding by 58,415 the hypothetical quota herein established for their nationality. If we accept as the number of this nationality who actually enrolled Kaufmann's more generous figure of 216,000, the excess beyond their fair quota mounts by almost an additional 40,000. Of the total number of Germans, 36,000 were, according to Kaufmann's count, in purely German regiments or batteries under the leadership of German officers and, in most cases, heard German as the speech of command. The other 180,000 were in mixed regiments alongside Anglo-Americans, Irishmen, and the descendants of immigrants of these two nationalities. It is

[7] Gould, *Investigations in Military and Anthropological Statistics*, 27, 28 (tables). These figures properly do not include those of Teutonic stock who came from Switzerland, Austria, or some of the areas bordering on the German states, nor do they deal with second-generation German-Americans. Also, some volunteers from certain western states and territories such as Utah, Nevada, Nebraska, etc., were not considered. It is unfortunate that some more recent writer has not compiled figures on these national quotas.

true that many of them remained to a degree isolated, as they often formed purely German companies or, occasionally, battalions scattered in mixed regiments; but such nationality units were too small to count as nationality factors in battles.

Albert B. Faust felt that an estimate of over 200,000 Germans in the Northern armies was not at all exaggerated.[8] The writer is inclined to accept a figure approximating Faust's, for Kaufmann's objections to the methods by which Gould established his figures are certainly well founded. In addition, this research proves conclusively that Germans were enlisted from the states and territories omitted by Gould, who also failed to take into account the large number of German immigrants who entered the United States during the war. Furthermore, Gould did not attempt to compute the number of Germans who escaped from the Confederacy (especially from Texas) and entered the Union army; these were numerous in Missouri regiments and certainly amounted to several thousand in the entire Union army. On the other hand, Kaufmann avowedly treated as German all the foreign-born of Germanic stock, thus including Poles, Swiss, Dutch, Hungarians, and Austrians. It is worthy of note that there were 300,000 Germans of the first generation born in this country and 234,000 of German descent in the ranks. Furthermore, of those raised under the conscript law, 36,740, or slightly over 10 per cent, had been born in Germany.

A scrutiny of the number of Irishmen in the civilian population reveals that there were slightly over a million and a half (1,502,267, to be exact) resident in the Northern states of the Union at the last census before the war; 139,052 of these were of military age. The Irish actually furnished 144,221 soldiers—5,169 above their fair share.[9] Canadians yielded abnormally high figures in relation to the census of 1860, which records 22,695 as within the age limits for normal military service. When we recall that Canadians migrated across the border in summer, returning home in winter, and that they were as a nation hospitable to the secessionist views, their showing of 53,532 actually enlisted in the Unionist cause is rather remarkable, and perhaps unreliable, since it more than doubles the national quota to be reasonably expected.[10] How deeply Canada was

---

[8] Faust, The German Element in the United States, I, 524 ff.; Kaufmann, Die Deutschen im Bürgerkriege, 111, 118–28, 181–82.

[9] See Gould, Investigations in Military and Anthropological Statistics, 27, 28 (tables). Figures for the loyal states are taken from the Eighth Census, 1860. The Statistics of the Population, xxix.

[10] Eighth Census, 1860. The Statistics of the Population, xxix. In view of the number of

affected by the war is evidenced by the fact that she furnished, it was claimed, 40,000 soldiers to the Confederate army.[11] The English, likewise, with a census enrollment of well over 400,000 to more than justify the computation of 38,250 as residents capable of duty according to the age limits, actually sent to the camps 54,508, or far more than their fair share.[12]

Though the Swedes were almost negligible in number in the ranks, it is interesting to compare their civilian numbers with their military showing. Their total number in the population by 1862 was only 20,925, while it is estimated that they supplied to the army and the navy in all some 3,000 men (not including Swedes who served as home guards in Illinois, New York, and Minnesota), a number slightly under the legitimate quota to be expected. As could be surmised, the larger numbers were drawn from the midwestern states of Illinois, Minnesota, Iowa, and Wisconsin, where some 14,000 Swedes were congregated. From the Swedish element of 6,470 in Illinois were drawn about 1,300 volunteers and from Minnesota's 3,178 Swedes came 600 volunteers, the number of volunteers from each of these states corresponding closely to what might justly be expected from the size of its population; from the smaller settlements in Iowa and Wisconsin came proportionately smaller contingents of soldiers; from the other midwestern states only a small number volunteered; and, finally, from the eastern states perhaps some 160 enlisted in eastern regiments.[13]

---

residents, the author cannot explain how Gould arrived at his figures. The census gives the number of Canadian-born residents in the United States in 1860 as 249,970, from which a negligible deduction of 3,130 must be made for those residing in the Confederate states. The author arrives at a far larger figure as the reasonable quota, using as the basis of calculation the proportion of one fifth of the entire number of resident Canadians to obtain the probable number of males of military age. See p. 573 of text. *Eighth Census, 1860. The Statistics of the Population,* xxviii. It is clear that Gould did not use 20 per cent for his basis.

[11] Lonn, *Foreigners in the Confederacy,* 209 n.

[12] Gould, *Investigations in Military and Anthropological Statistics,* 27, 28 (tables). The *Eighth Census* gave the number of Englishmen in the population as 431,692; as modified by the author to subtract those resident in the seceded states (17,929), the number amounted to exactly 413,763. Again, one fifth would yield over 80,000, or more than twice the number cited by Gould. *Eighth Census, 1860. The Statistics of the Population,* xxix.

[13] Hokanson, *Swedish Immigrants,* 23, 70–71, 111–12. On the basis of one fifth as the accepted proportion of the male population within the military ages, the Swedish element should have furnished 4,185 men, but, since young males constitute a larger proportion in an immigrant stock than in an old, settled society, a slightly larger number would be reasonable. The problem is rendered more difficult because the three Scandinavian groups were not handled separately in the census of 1860. Hokanson gives the following figures for Swedes in Minnesota regiments:

When it comes to the Norwegians, precise figures are difficult to secure. According to the reports of the adjutant generals of Minnesota and Iowa, 800 and 400 Norwegians were enlisted from those two states respectively. The largest contingent came from Wisconsin; this numbered 3,000 in all and included those in the Scandinavian Regiment. There is wide discrepancy between the figures of O. N. Nelson, which are cited above, and those of Waldemar Ager, who rather loosely placed the total Norwegian enlistments at 6,000 to 7,000 (a figure again including the numbers from Wisconsin, which he placed at 4,000).[14] Nelson's more conservative figure of 4,200 from these states is probably the safer to accept.

It is unlikely that the exact number of Hungarians who fought in the Civil War will ever be definitely established. Piványy has stated that there were approximately 800 Hungarians in the war. However, he has made a number of other loose statements, such as the assertion that half the Garibaldi Guard were Hungarians, a statement in sharp contrast with the declaration of Vasvary, a later writer, that he could find only seven Hungarians in that famous regiment. Perhaps the most that can be said is that not more than 800 Hungarians shared in the American war.[15]

A spokesman for Polish history, Miecislaus Haiman, attempted to give figures as to the participation of his countrymen in the Civil War. He believed that about 4,000 Poles fought in the Union armies, which

First Minnesota Regiment	18	Eighth Minnesota	11
Second Minnesota	56	Ninth Minnesota	41
Fourth Minnesota	84	Eleventh Minnesota	21
Fifth Minnesota	8	Co. I, Minnesota Heavy Artillery	50
Sixth Minnesota	34	Co. M, Minnesota Heavy Artillery	23
Seventh Minnesota	69		

TOTAL   415

Ibid., 115–16. Since the classification is probably based largely on names, numbers may not indicate men born in Sweden.

[14] Nelson, *History of the Scandinavians and Successful Scandinavians in the United States,* I, 303, 304; II, 65–68, 119–21. Nelson used the unpublished records in the Adjutant General's offices, but seems to have depended on names as a certain index of nationality. This is not satisfactory, since such a procedure included many who had been born of Norwegian parents in this country. Furthermore, names can be no certain index of nationality, for many foreigners, especially Scandinavians, often changed their names, as has been pointed out.

The writer has been unable to have access directly to Waldemar Ager's book, *Norge i Amerika,* but has had to depend on the citation in Blegen, *Norwegian Migration to America, 1825–1860,* II, 389. The edition which Blegen used was one published in Christiania in 1915, but it must be a reprint of a much earlier edition. It has merely the value of an estimate by a man who lived at the time and was deeply interested in the subject.

[15] Piványy, *Hungarians in the American Civil War,* 13; Vasvary, *Lincoln's Hungarian Heroes,* 36–38. The Descriptive Books do not sustain Piványy's claim.

number, added to the 1,000 in the Confederate army, comprises, as he pointed out, rather more than 16 per cent of the estimated 30,000 Poles in the entire population of the United States in 1860. He further noted with justifiable pride that this record is better than that of the native population, as only about 14 per cent of the native population participated directly in the fighting. The Poles were most numerous in New York regiments, especially in the Thirty-ninth (the Garibaldi Guards, in which fought many Polish veterans of the Hungarian insurrection of 1848), the Fifty-second, the Fifty-fourth, the Fifty-fifth, and the Fifty-eighth. In addition, there were many Poles in the First New York Cavalry (the special organization of Carl Schurz) and the Fourth New York Cavalry. Poles were also present in the first ten Missouri regiments in sufficient numbers to constitute 2 per cent of the entire Polish contingent.[16]

One compiler has figured out that 23 of every 100 soldiers were foreign-born, an estimate which comes close to one fourth of the army. Another compiler after listing the figures for the Germans, the Irish, the Canadians, and the British, brought all other nationalities together in the considerable number of 74,000. This latter compiler computed the total foreign contingent in the Union army at 494,900, or not far from a half-million men.[17] In order to compute percentages for the number of enlistments of the various nationalities, it has been necessary to depend largely upon Gould, as no other statistics have been compiled—with the exception of those for the Germans, for which the estimate of Faust has been used. Comparison has been made in each case with the total number of enlistments, according to Livermore, modified by deductions for re-enlistments but not for negro troops, who are counted as part of the native population. On this basis, the native Americans constituted almost 80 per cent.[18] It would undoubtedly be more satisfactory if one could reduce all figures to the three-year basis (as Livermore has reduced the total enlistments), for one could then offer an estimate of the average number of foreigners in the army at any given time. This being impossible, how-

---

[16] Haiman, *Polish Past in America*, 109–10, 110–12. There is no way for the writer to check on these figures, as the Poles were not listed separately in the census of 1860 or in the Descriptive Books, except by accident. The other regiments which contained the largest percentage of Poles were the Seventh, Eighth, Twentieth, Twenty-ninth, Forty-first, Forty-fifth, Forty-sixth, and Fifty-fifth New York Regiments; the Fourth New York Cavalry, already noted; the Twenty-fourth Illinois; the Sixteenth Illinois Cavalry; and the Ninth and Twenty-sixth Wisconsin. *Ibid.*, 110–12. Obviously, the largest number of Poles was in New York.

[17] Rosengarten, *The German Soldier in the Wars of the United States*, 88, 92.

[18] John William Draper, *History of the American Civil War* (New York, 1867–1870), III, 646, calculates 7 per cent Irish, 9 per cent German.

ever, the author is obliged reluctantly to conclude this statistical portion
of the study with the generalization that her rough calculation of the total
number of enlistments of foreign-born is 518,161, a figure which, when
compared with Livermore's estimate of the total number of enlistments,
2,312,304, shows the foreign element as amounting to between one fourth
and one fifth of the total number of enlistments—nearer one fifth.

In addition to arriving at these approximate fractions, it is necessary
to note the variations in the composition of regiments from one part of
the country to another and from one year to another. In regard to the
first point, it is sufficient to stress again the fact that foreigners were much
more numerous in the regiments from the eastern states than in those from
the western states because of the much larger proportion of foreigners long
settled on the Atlantic seaboard. Statements as to the composition of
various regiments can be made with less assurance for the first year of the
war than for the later years, when nativity was recorded—owing to the
fact that the writer has been forced to rely for information concerning
the first year on statements of participants, which cannot be authoritative
but should be given for what they may be worth. It was the observation of
the Comte de Paris, a careful, disinterested observer, that in the first year of
the war only 10 per cent of the men in the Union army were foreigners; two thirds of the 90 per cent remaining had been born in the United
States; and less than one fourth were naturalized citizens.[19] According
to that writer, the proportion of Europeans in the army, especially in
eastern regiments, was smaller in 1864 when partial conscription was in
effect, for the reason that only a small number of the new recruits had
settled in the East, and thus the proportion of natives was relatively higher,
reaching as high as 80 per cent. However, the Comte de Paris failed entirely to take into account the forced, fraudulent enlistments, which
were almost entirely among foreigners, and the large number of laborers
recruited abroad, a part of whom were diverted to the army. All other testimony tends to show that the proportion of foreigners increased with the
war years. It is interesting that this Frenchman reached much the same
conclusion arrived at through the statistics of some later writers: the
reasonable quota for the foreign-born, according to their numbers, would
have been considerably more than one third, while their contribution was

---

[19] De Paris, *History of the Civil War in America*, I, 180–81. It would be interesting to
know on what he based his figures for naturalization, as he frankly stated that he had not
examined the documents to ascertain how many had become naturalized. However, his book
seems to argue that practically all had taken the necessary steps.

exactly one third,[20] if we use Livermore's figure for the army reduced to a three-year basis. In this writer's judgment this estimate is too high.

Now the reader approaches the crux of the matter—the number of native-born soldiers and the degree to which they measured up to their responsibility. There were some 23,000,000 inhabitants scattered over the states trying to preserve the Union, of whom 19,377,757 were natives. Of this entire number, men who were Americans by birth and ancestry, 1,660,068 were within the military age limits. The statement that 1,523,267 responded to the nation's call to arms would seem to indicate that the native-born were slightly below their proper quota and were therefore less loyal than the Germans or Irish. However, before judgment is passed on the native Americans, several factors should be taken into consideration. In the first place, the figures ignore some 186,000 negro troops, who logically should be classed as native-born Americans and were definitely so counted in the census of 1860. However, that point is waived, as this study is confined to a comparison of whites, native and foreign-born. Secondly, from all the evidence—chiefly from the belligerent, not to say disloyal, tones of many newspapers and from the votes at elections—it is safe to deduce that at least a fourth of the population of the North opposed the war. It is certain that this element furnished no soldiers to the Union armies, but, on the contrary, devoted itself to creating as much trouble for the government as possible. The loyal three fourths had to divert strength to keep down the machinations of disloyal foes in the rear and at the same time had to muster enough strength to suppress the organized revolt in the front. Soldiers who should have been in the field against the open enemy had to be detained at home to guard prisons against a possible uprising and to suppress riots incited by these home disloyalists, who discouraged enlistments and opposed in every way they could the war effort. So numerous and so bold were they that they dared to rejoice over Confederate successes and to glory in the name which should have been a term of bitter reproach, "Copperhead." Their motto might have been "No more men and no more money for this nefarious war." [21] In other words, the battle for the Union was fought by volunteers from only the loyal portion of the loyal states, not from the entire population of the North. Justice demands that this fourth be deducted from the

[20] *Ibid.*, 181–82. It is difficult to feel that impressions, as far as statistics are concerned, are worth much.

[21] Thomas Speed, *Who Fought the Battle. Strength of Union and Confederate Forces Compared* (Louisville, 1904), 9.

19,377,757 inhabitants, whereupon it becomes apparent that the burden of the war fell upon less than 15,000,000 of the population. If we now measure the actual enlistments of the native-born, 1,523,267 according to Gould, against the number of military age, 1,660,068, reduced, as it should be to allow for the disloyal, by a fourth, or even a fifth, as the most vocal of oppositionists are usually of greater years, or to 1,328,056, the native Americans will appear to have done fully their fair share and more.[22] These considerations do not indicate that soldiers of foreign birth bore more than their share of the burden of fighting.

Disloyal sentiment was not entirely confined to the native element but existed also to a degree among the Irish. Some of them took part in the Copperhead movement because they were opposed at the outset to the purposes of the war and were even more strongly opposed after the abolition of slavery. The Irish, and in lesser numbers the Germans, violently feared the negro as an economic and social competitor; some of them hugged to their bosoms the bitter party warfare of the period, which in some respects approached in bitterness the religious controversy of the seventeenth century and the economic controversy of the twentieth century. Manifestations of the existence of such feelings appeared in the form of undercover depredations in southern Illinois and in the strongly Democratic Irish mining section around Dubuque, Iowa, where the houses of recruits for the Union army were burned. In some communities open expressions of Confederate sympathy were uttered. In Chicago, for instance, it will be recalled that the Roman Catholic bishop James Duggan offered little support for the Union cause, evidently voicing the sentiment of his Irish parishioners. It is asserted that if the Confederates had pursued a bolder policy and had inaugurated it earlier in Missouri, many Irish would have followed their old Democratic and Southern leaders.[23]

In the light of the splendid support of the Union cause by the German element, it seems difficult to credit Copperheadism among that group, but the testimony of one of their own newspapers is not lightly to be swept aside. The *Illinois Staats-Zeitung* stated, "There are Germans who are not only secessionist-minded but openly support the traitors." It refused to give names but carried a covert threat that such persons would do well to keep such sympathies to themselves: "While patriotic citizens offer their lives for the Union and freedom, it cannot and will not be tolerated that

---

[22] De Paris, *History of the Civil War in America*, I, 181; Gould, *Investigations in Military and Anthropological Statistics*, 27, 28 (tables).

[23] Gray, *The Hidden Civil War*, 71, 211.

behind their backs aid shall be given to high treason, if only by word." [24]

Probably the greatest surprise is to find treason lifting its head in north-eastern Iowa at Ossian in Winneshiek County; however, the account of this disloyalty does not make clear that it appeared among the Scandinavians who were numerous there. A large body of secessionists demonstrated at Ossian about mid-June, 1861, even daring to raise over a shop a Confederate flag; Union men promptly pulled it down and replaced it with a Union flag, whereupon the secessionists burned both the store and the Union flag.[25]

Impressions cannot, of course, be compared with cold figures, but it is certainly of passing interest that the Comte de Paris was convinced that American-born soldiers were more numerous in the army than would have been the case if it had been recruited by a draft bearing equally upon all residents of the country. With regard to the late period in the war, when bounties were bringing in inferior recruits and unfair methods of impressment by corrupt crimps were dragging in innocent foreigners as victims, the charge of foreign mercenaries is a just one.

Certainly, the response by the foreigners to the first call for three months troops was immediate and generous. New England, the home of abolitionism, sent only 11,987 men. From New York came 12,357; from Pennsylvania, 20,175; from Ohio, 12,357; and from Missouri, 10,591. These last four states, where the German element was strongest, furnished over half the number called for. By September a Norwegian paper was copying a letter sent in to the Madison *Argus and Democrat,* which claimed 58,600 German troops under arms by September 19 and dared to predict in the near future as many as 70,000 Germans in the field. In Missouri, where there was prompt resistance to hostile armies traversing the homeland, Germans and those of German descent furnished 80 per cent of the troops and produced 10,000 troops in St. Louis almost overnight; French, Irish, Bohemians, and other groups produced only 8 per cent; Americans furnished the other 12 per cent from the state.[26]

Before we can properly discuss the rewards accorded to the foreign-born, it is proper, indeed necessary, to learn how meagerly rewards were passed

[24] Chicago *Illinois Staats-Zeitung,* June 24, 1861.

[25] About four hundred men in Decorah, Castalia, and other places in that part of Iowa armed themselves and marched to Ossian to crush the movement. Madison *Emigranten,* June 22, 1861.

[26] For the claim of 58,000 Germans in the field, see Madison *Emigranten,* September 21, 1861; for the claim of 80 per cent Germans in the St. Louis uprising, see Robert Rombauer, *The Union Cause in St. Louis,* 349.

out to foreign-born citizens during the war and to discuss frankly the degree to which prejudice entered into the matter.

Prejudice, in the North as in the Confederacy, played its ugly role. It appeared, furthermore, not only on the part of the native Americans, but also on the part of the foreign-born in the form of prejudice of one nationality group against another. If rivalry and intense jealousy could exist among native-born officers, as we know full well they did,[27] there is little wonder that strong prejudice existed against attainment of high office by aliens, as many felt that the foreign-born citizens still were. Such a competition arose between General de Trobriand and an American. In the early fall of 1863 the French Gardes Lafayette, which had been consolidated with the Thirty-eighth New York Regiment and then transferred to the Fortieth New York, was disbanded. De Trobriand found himself in rivalry with an American for the colonelcy of the consolidated regiment; from this situation the Frenchman was neatly extricated by a promotion to a brigadiership.[28]

That native soldiers should prefer to be under an American commander is understandable and was smoothly phrased by Seward: "The volunteers naturally prefer the command of one who speaks their language to that of a stranger who had that language yet to learn." [29] Seward's word "prefer" was much too mild to describe the state of the soldiers' feeling, for they frequently objected strenuously to a foreign officer over them. A striking case was the opposition of the commissioned officers of the Fifty-eighth Ohio to the appointment of one J. Andregg to office in that regi-

[27] The bitter jealousy between Generals David Hunter and John Gray Foster is a case in point. The comment of W. W. H. Davis apropos of those two officers may be cited: "The old sore was reopened at a later period, when a spicy correspondence took place between Naglee [who had taken up the cudgels for his chief, General Foster] and Hunter, which resulted in the former's being sent to New York, with orders to report from there to the adjutant general of the army. This is a sample of the quarrels which interfered with the efficiency of the army during the war. In this case the army lost one of its most gallant officers, without cause." Davis means, of course, Henry M. Naglee. W. W. H. Davis, History of the 104th Pennsylvania Regiment, 188. Note also the comment of Augustus Hamlin on this subject: "The feeling of discontent and jealousy among the higher officers of the army at this time [May, 1863] was disgraceful, and the fact of such a condition is well established by many observers." The Battle of Chancellorsville, 140.

[28] His superior officers had asked the promotion of Régis de Trobriand five times in a year. As the President had adjourned all promotions until Congress should reconvene, several weeks elapsed between his mustering out and the issuance of his commission as brigadier general, during which time he was without a command—and the country was without his services. De Trobriand, Quatre Ans de Campagnes, II, 49, 194-95.

[29] Seward to Minister William L. Dayton at Paris, September 20, 1862, Diplomatic Instructions, France, XVI, 257-58.

ment. Their reasons are so typical of the feeling that they may well be quoted: "1st. He is a foreigner who cannot speak our language that he can be understood. 2d. Has no claims on the Regt except his personal acquaintance with Col. Bausenwein and 3rd. There are enough men in our companies whom the *men* would *wish* for officers, and who deserve such position not only from *personal merit,* but who have fairly earned them by their endurance of privations and suffering in camp and on the battlefield in common with us all." [30] Andregg had been appointed by the colonel of the regiment without consultation with the other officers; when this created much dissatisfaction, the adjutant wrote Governor David Tod, requesting that executive to make no appointments on Bausenwein's recommendation.[31] About this same time the filling of a vacancy in the captaincy of Company F of that regiment created deep feeling, since in a tie election the German candidate was selected rather than the American Lieutenant Stiers, who was preferred by the Americans in the company. The petition sent Governor Tod by the Americans of the regiment was strongly worded: "But there is a disposition manifested upon the part of the German officers in the Regiment to have matters so arranged that all promotions shall be among themselves and to their own advantage regardless of the interests of the Regiment or of the service." [32]

Meanwhile, General Halleck had removed Colonel Bausenwein; Governor Tod seems subsequently to have restored him, however, as he rejoined the regiment on April 21, 1862, to the discomfiture of Lieutenant Colonel Ferdinand F. Rempel, a political appointee and apparently a center of intrigue in the regiment.[33]

At the beginning of the war there was a commendable desire on the part of officers as well as enlisted men in many regiments to ask for young but

[30] Protest of Commissioned Officers, Headquarters of the Fifty-eighth Ohio Regiment, Shiloh Church, Tennessee. Executive Correspondence of the Governors of Ohio, January–May, 1862.

[31] Adjutant M. P. Chrisen to Governor Tod. Although the letter is undated, the context shows that it was written before April 22, 1862. Executive Correspondence of the Governors of Ohio, January–May, 1862.

[32] It is difficult to understand why, if the claim that "the greater part of the company are Americans" is correct, the election did not result in a clear majority for Stiers over the German Bohls. The petition also pointed to the Ohio law which required promotion from the company in which a vacancy occurred. Evidently, Bohls was from another company.

[33] For a long complaint by Bausenwein against his lieutenant colonel, F. F. Rempel, see Bausenwein to Governor Tod, Camp Monterey, May 28, 1862; Bausenwein charged his subordinate not only with intrigue but also with cowardice at the Battle of Shiloh. Executive Correspondence of the Governors of Ohio, January–May, 1862.

experienced officers of the Regular Army or cavalry, or even for the appointment of civilians who had served in European armies. Officers so selected were from the first encouraged by the hearty spirit in which officers and privates entered into the training.[34] This was not, however, the attitude toward soldiers of fortune. A letter to the New York *Times* probably accurately conveys the feeling of the average native:

> We hear often of military men from European countries, especially from Germany, who have come to our shores with the intention of offering themselves and their swords to the Government. . . . It is a matter susceptible of discussion, whether these men are, on the whole, a valuable acquisition to us or not. That an educated Artillerist or Engineer would be so, we do not doubt. But certainly it is unwise to accept foreign birth and inability to speak the English tongue as prima facie evidence of military education and experience. There are many German officers now on their way to America, or forming their plans for coming, because they have not the ability necessary to do well at home.

American vanity came out apropos of German adventurers: "There is not a military school in all of Germany like those of America or France. They are unfitted to command American troops, because they have only had a rude peasantry to deal with and do not know what it is to treat a soldier like a man." The writer was careful to add that these remarks did not apply to "brother Germans" who were fighting by the side of natives for a common country.[35]

Almost always there was a strong feeling on the part of officers who were graduates of West Point that high-ranking positions should be reserved for them; and they excluded from their intimate circle, as outsiders, both civilian and foreign appointees who had attained high rank. This West Point exclusiveness was especially manifest in the Army of the Potomac and was thought by Germans to have been directed with great force against General Sigel. It must be admitted, on the other hand, that there was justification for the feeling that foreigners, trained in the rigid caste rules and discipline of the European systems, were little adapted to deal with American civilians, who retained in the army the feeling, which they paraded as democratic, that each was "as good as anybody else."

Not all foreign officers had the adaptability of Colonel de Trobriand.

[34] D. M'M. Gregg, "The Union Cavalry at Gettysburg," in M[cClure] (comp.), *The Annals of the War*, 373.
[35] New York *Times*, August 15, 1861.

When General D. N. Couch came to congratulate him on the conduct of his Gardes Lafayette at the battle of Williamsburg, De Trobriand thanked him but declared his intention to ask a court-martial for eight or ten of his officers who had acted as cowards. General Couch urged him to do nothing. He pointed out that when the officers came under fire for the first time they were unprepared to guard themselves against the effect of actual warfare but at the second test they would bear themselves as bravely as the others. The Frenchman wrote later: "General Couch was right. He judged the affair sanely as was proved shortly by the fine conduct of the entire regiment at Fair Oaks." [36]

The mildest form in which prejudice against the foreign-born expressed itself was amusement at strange ways and at the distortion of the native language in the mouths of foreigners. A member of an artillery company declared that it was an unfailing source of amusement to watch the maneuvers of the New York Germans every morning when they started out of camp for cavalry drill. Many were unskilled in the handling of horses; the horses were also green and sometimes vicious. While the horses balked, kicked, or reared, the men whipped them to the accompaniment of German oaths, some of the men often measuring their length on the ground. The language was almost inevitably a perplexing barrier between a foreign officer and his command and between the foreign-born privates and the native recruits. The Germans had been trained under a severe system of discipline to some semblance of "frozen military Proprieties" which struck their American comrades not as excellent military form but as ludicrous and which they greeted with levity and often with "Sportive affront." [37] It did not help in the least that some foreign-trained officers did not cavil to reveal their contempt for American form and material; their attitude was soon ascribed to lack of capacity for adjustment.

A few of the foreign officers, it must be admitted, were unworthy. Justifiable contempt and prejudice are probably mingled in the following description of the conduct of a German general in the battle of the Wilderness: "He was a whisky-pickled, lately-arrived, blusterous German, and when he reached MacAlister on the left of the line, he wanted to burst right through, saying his orders were, 'To find the enemy wherever he could find him and *whip him!!*' " But he was soon sending back to Mac-

[36] De Trobriand, *Quatre Ans de Campagnes*, I, 203, 204.

[37] Owen Rice, "Afield with the Eleventh Army Corps at Chancellorsville," in *Sketches of War History* (Ohio Commandery of the Military Order of the Loyal Legion of the United States), I, 360.

Alister for relief, and when it was denied, he came running back with part of his brigade for ammunition to be had apparently only "away back in the rear." That was the last MacAlister saw of him.[38]

From tolerant amusement the transition is not far to biting criticism: "We were conducted to this position [near Edinburg in the Shenandoah Valley] by a foreign officer of Banks's staff, who spoke English so well that one could almost understand him. It was in reference to these European adventurers as a class, some of whom set up for experienced cavalry officers on the strength of having kept a livery stable in Germany, that I once heard that stout old fighter, General Nathan Kimball, remark, that when he could not find American officers competent to serve on his staff he would take them from the ranks, as he knew he had them there." [39]

Remarks made to some of the foreign-born citizens who rendered the country great service were sometimes so derogatory that they were actually insulting. Two examples are quite sufficient. The Hawkins' Zouaves cherished ill will toward General Corcoran because of the unfortunate shooting of their lieutenant colonel, Edgar A. Kimball, as a result of a misunderstanding over action of a sentry, so that a member of the Ninth New York Regiment could say disparagingly, "Corcoran was then, and subsequently remained until, the breaking out of the Rebellion, the keeper of what was known in the vernacular of the day as a 'three-cent grog shop,' Hibernia Hall, in Prince Street, New York City." [40] Worse was the treatment of General Osterhaus, who was in command of an army corps. As he was passing the One Hundred and Third Illinois Regiment, a few scamps, weary of the army beef on which they had been living for a month, called out "Sowbelly." Endeavoring to accept this as a bit of fun, the general smiled, but when someone cried "Kraut" and another responded with "Kraut by the barrel," he wheeled and with face tense and white asked, "Vat Regiment ish dis?" Awed, no one replied until he repeated the question. When a soldier gave the information without bothering to rise, Osterhaus demanded, "Vy don't you git up?" The soldier then rose and answered respectfully. "Vare is your Colonel?" asked Osterhaus. Upon receiving a reply, he rode up to Colonel Wright and "gave him the devil."

[38] Morris Schaff, *The Battle of the Wilderness* (Boston and New York, 1910), 260–61. It would have been better if Schaff had given the officer's name so that it could be determined if this were a single instance of cowardice on his part.

[39] James F. Huntington, "Operations in the Shenandoah Valley, from Winchester to Port Republic. 1862," in *Campaigns in Virginia, 1861–1862* (*Papers of the Military Historical Society of Massachusetts*) (Boston and New York, 1895–1902), I, 307.

[40] Graham, *The Ninth Regiment New York Volunteers*, 418.

The majority of the regiment had the grace to regret the incident, as almost all of them really thought a great deal of Osterhaus.[41]

Naturally, the Germans and all other racial elements resented such invidious remarks and discrimination against "foreigners." At the very beginning of the war, the editor of the St. Paul *Minnesota Staats-Zeitung* complained bitterly of the neglect of the foreign element by their American "fellow-citizens" which was evident in the manner in which the preparations for war were being conducted. Proceedings at a meeting on April 25, when a committee of thirteen was created to draw up resolutions, brought forth from the same editor, "Also on this committee no German!" The same demand for recognition appeared in regard to the surgeons in the army when a Medical Board of three American physicians was set up for Illinois in early May: "Why is there no German physician on the commission? Are there no physicians trained and tested at the German Universities? Is not Dr. Trapp of Springfield whom Governor Bissell of Belleville took with him as his personal physician a capable man, as good as one of the three members of this examining commission?" [42] On May 11, 1861, the editor of the *Illinois Staats-Zeitung* pointed out that more than half of the troops already raised were Germans.

The Germans were quick to sense discrimination where conceivably it might not have been intentional. When Captain Frederick Schambeck found his Illinois cavalry company after a long stay at Springfield still without pistols or a cent of pay, though an American company at Cairo was fully equipped, he declared positively that his men would not march until they had received weapons and pay. In a few days they had received both.[43] The German press was likewise quick to defend the Steuben Regiment of New York when an unfortunate affair occurred at Little Bethel: the men of that regiment and those of Colonel Frederick Townsend's

---

[41] *Reminiscences of the Civil War from Diaries of Members of the 103rd Illinois Volunteer Infantry* (Chicago, n.d.), 136.

[42] St. Paul *Minnesota Staats-Zeitung*, April 20, May 2, 1861. William Henry Bissell was governor of Illinois, 1857–1860.

[43] In the issue of June 21, 1861, the Chicago *Post*, which seems not to have been too friendly to Germans, spoke of the "disgrace" with which Schambeck's company had covered itself and reported the incorrect news that an order had been telegraphed by the governor to dissolve the company and to take away their horses and uniforms, in which the *Post* could imagine "full-blooded" natives decked. The Chicago *Illinois Staats-Zeitung*, June 22, 1861, defended Schambeck warmly, stating that Home Guards were armed with muskets, while authorities wished to send German troops against the foe without a revolver and without affording them the opportunity to accustom their horses to the noise of gunfire. It rejoiced that Illinois had found a man who could impress the authorities and that he was a German.

Third New York Regiment fired at each other in the gathering dusk. The Chicago editor retained the suspicion that General Butler and an officer named Pierce had tried to throw the blame on the German regiment.[44] The nativism of the Know-Nothing party had struck so deep that some Germans began the war with resentment, as is evidenced by a letter signed "C.R." in the Sunday edition of the *Illinois Staats-Zeitung:* "It is truly a pity that so many strong, capable, and patriotic Germans go to the war, when one reflects how much vileness is already turned against the Germans, how the Know-Nothing papers grin and say, 'You Germans, you understand no English. You cannot even pronounce Boston.' " [45]

Naturally, men who had had military experience in Europe hoped, at a time when America was in dire need of trained officers, to secure commissions; when they were rejected, they were disappointed and often bitter. One C. Knobelsdorff of the Chicago Reserve Jäger Corps went to Springfield to offer his service to the state as an experienced officer; but in spite of the best of recommendations his efforts remained without result, as the pressure for commissions was so great that "even military talents like Napoleon's or Garibaldi's could command no consideration." His disappointment probably sharpened his criticism of conditions at the camp.[46] The French observer Auguste Laugel told of a German officer whom he encountered on the Potomac, a leader in a Hesse-Darmstadt revolt, who complained bitterly of the jealousy of the Americans: "When they need us, they flatter us; when we have finished, we are only the damned Dutchmen." [47]

While Teutons were bitter over any discrimination against Germans, they sought recognition for Germans as Germans. The nationality press fumed that no American paper mentioned the fact that the credit for Lyon's victory at Springfield belonged to an Iowa regiment composed in large part of Germans from Davenport and its neighborhood. One editor saw here another argument for exclusively German regiments, for, otherwise, German units would be under American commanders and regarded as American contingents. The credit, if possible, must go to Germans! [48] This press also supported formation of a German division, declaring that this would be of great advantage to the *Deutschtum*. It was thoroughly

[44] Chicago *Illinois Staats-Zeitung,* July 1, 1861.

[45] *Ibid.,* June 23, 1861.

[46] *Ibid.,* May 7, 1861. Probably this was the Knobelsdorff who later commanded the Forty-fourth Illinois Regiment.

[47] Auguste Laugel, *Les États-Unis pendant la Guerre* (Paris, 1866), 241.

[48] Chicago *Illinois Staats-Zeitung,* August 23, 1861.

awake to the political advantages which might result from such a strong aggregation. Germans could make massive migrations to the West after the war. They would certainly find that more agreeable than to live under fixed conditions no longer to be influenced by them: "What this must result in in the way of wider consequences needs scarcely to be mentioned." [49]

The German press of the West could be prejudiced for one of its leaders as against a German of the East. This appears strikingly in connection with Sigel versus Blenker. Early in January, 1862, the *Illinois Staats-Zeitung* was boosting its favorite: "General Blenker is more clever than Sigel: He has torch parades, makes addresses, gets 'puffs' in the papers and makes visits to all the persons in high authority; his ambition has raised him over the citizen's level so that he moves only in the circle of princes, counts, and barons upon his staff; also the influence of all these men from afar has been effective on the European ambassadors in favor of Blenker. Still he does not become a division general. The Congressional Committee of Inquiry is still busy with the swindling in his division." [50] Probably the ridicule poured out by the Illinois paper over the enthusiasm for titles manifest in the German regiments of the East was an indirect defense of Sigel against another German or against a Hungarian: "D'Utassy says that he had received a certificate of nobility from Kossuth. He and von Steinwehr both want the position of a brigadier for the same brigade and puff themselves in the papers . . . he [D'Utassy] charges his rival with physical incapacity. Thereupon von Steinwehr goes to the editor and has his body examined; the editor puffs him as eminently of military fitness. The mania to be of the nobility has so taken the upper hand, that people greet each other only as Herr von. . . ." [51] By April this same paper was printing, "Already '*Nativismus*' is stirring against Sigel and the Germans." But what the editor did not understand was that the chicaneries against Sigel arose almost exclusively from General Halleck. That Halleck was the main obstacle to Sigel's promotion was grasped only vaguely by Sigel's friends, and so the view gained currency in the German press that his nativity was the chief reason for his persecution by the military authorities. Unfortunately this resentment against what they regarded as pure prejudice blinded the German population to the potent fact that Sigel was

[49] *Ibid.*, August 13, 1861.

[50] *Ibid.*, January 11, 1862. The reader will recall the charges of swindling made against General Blenker.

[51] *Ibid.*

personally utterly unsuited to penetrate into the closed circle of West Pointers in the Army of the Potomac.[52]

Great protest meetings were staged in January, 1862, after Sigel had resigned, notably the one at Cooper Institute, when ten thousand of the most solid citizens of German birth assembled to give expression to their feelings of indignation and to emphasize their demand for his appointment to a new post of honor. Undoubtedly, they wanted to see his "eminent talents" retained in the service; but they also wanted to see a German holding the high office of a major general. Likewise, the Irish in St. Louis acted promptly upon receipt of word of the removal of General Frémont, popular with all nationalities for his known liberality toward foreigners, by closing their recruiting rendezvous for an Irish regiment.

The defeat at Chancellorsville brought to a climax the American prejudice against foreigners. Unfortunately, the calm verdict of history was not available at the time. Instead, in the excitement and worry of the moment, when Lee was again preparing to invade the North, the denunciation of foreigners became extreme and even passed the bounds of decency. Some Northern papers talked of shooting the entire corps; the Germans were condemned as a worthless lot, coming from the scum of a vicious population. Officers, speaking some years after the war, of the conduct of the Germans at Chancellorsville, were guilty not only of injustice but of outrageous falsehoods. Witness the words of Captain Henry N. Blake: "[In the attack] a spectacle of shameful cowardice was witnessed, which can be rarely paralleled in the history of civilized warfare. The corps, composed mainly of Germans, was stationed behind strong earthworks and broke a few minutes after four P.M. . . ." De Trobriand, more unbiased, stated correctly the feelings of the army when he said, "The Eleventh Corps was the object of a general hue and cry, nobody stopping to ask if there were not some extenuating circumstances—so quickly does injustice germinate in adversity."[53]

The abused men demanded an opportunity to present their defense, but they were refused it. The morale of the Eleventh Corps was seriously affected by the virulent invectives in the press and the indifference of the government. Nowhere were heard words of comfort and understanding—to say nothing of indignation at injustice to fellow citizens. It was pointed

---

[52] See *ibid.*, April 12, 1862, for the remark on nativism; for comment on Sigel's personality, see Kaufmann, *Die Deutschen im Bürgerkriege*, 462.

[53] Henry M. Blake, *Three Years in the Army of the Potomac* (Boston, 1865), 178; De Trobriand, *Quatre Ans de Campagnes*, II, 130.

out in vain that Von Gilsa with one thousand men and two guns withstood the assault of two Confederate divisions as long as General Berry's division withstood it the next morning with an entire brigade; that it took Jackson's men one hour and a half to march one mile and a quarter after the attack began! Schimmelfennig presented to General Schurz on May 10 a letter in which he voiced in burning language his righteous indignation after the men of his brigade had come with newspapers in their hands to ask if such was their reward for their bravery and suffering. He wrote: "General, I am an old soldier, to this hour I have been proud to command the brave men of this brigade; but I am sure that unless these infamous falsehoods be retracted and reparation made, their good will and soldierly spirit will be broken. . . . In the name of truth and common honesty, in the name of the good cause of our country, I ask, therefore, for satisfaction." Schurz's reply is found at the end of his studiously correct report: "I am far from saying that on May 2d everybody did his duty to the best of his power. But one thing I will say, because I know it; these men are not cowards, I have seen most of them fight before this, and they fought as bravely as any." He asked that his report be published.[54]

The loyal Germans of New York City, under the inspiration of the German leader Friedrich Kapp, held a great mass meeting at the Cooper Institute a month later to protest in vigorous language against the unjust treatment of the German soldiers. General Meagher, who was provost marshal at White House in the rear of Chancellorsville and stopped the fugitives at that point, made a speech in defense of the Germans, stating that he saw few Germans among the men arrested by his troops. At the mention of the name of Colonel Buschbeck the entire vast audience rose spontaneously and stood in silence in tribute.[55] The government paid no attention to this meeting or to its demands, with the result that voluntary enlistments of the better class of Germans, and indeed of other foreign nationalities, almost entirely ceased. The whole Eleventh Corps was embraced in the general denunciation; French, Italians, Hungarians, and Swiss were all stigmatized indiscriminately as cowardly and lumped as "Dutchmen," with the result that resentment rose in many groups. Some Germans so resented the ingratitude of the Americans that they resigned. Though many officers and men continued in the war, there was never, it was declared, the same spontaneous enthusiasm from the Germans as a group that had prevailed before Chancellorsville.

[54] Hamlin, *The Battle of Chancellorsville*, 172; Schurz, *Reminiscences*, II, 434–35.
[55] Kaufmann, *Die Deutschen im Bürgerkriege*, 368.

Justice came only tardily. Howard stated, at a midnight conference of his corps officers called by General Hooker on the night of the first day of battle at Chancellorsville, that the situation was due "to the bad conduct of his corps"; this assignment of responsibility was accepted by Hooker, repeated by him at the inquiry into the conduct of the war two years later, and long accepted as the official verdict. It was not until the late eighties and nineties—when Dr. A. C. Hamlin, Medical Inspector of the Eleventh Corps, Colonel T. A. Dodge, and Owen Rice, major in the One Hundred and Fifty-third Pennsylvania, lifted their voices in behalf of the truth—that "Chancellorsville" ceased to be a term of disgrace to the Germans.[56] The responsibility for the collapse of the Eleventh Corps must rest on Howard for having placed it in its unfortunate position; the responsibility for the ultimate defeat must rest on Hooker, who, after displaying excellent strategy which should have destroyed Lee's army, failed utterly in tactics, as stated in an earlier chapter.

The Irish, with a slightly larger population than the Germans but with a distinctly weaker nationality press (there were but two outstanding Irish papers, the New York *Irish-American* and the Boston *Pilot*), felt as strongly as the Germans that prejudice was unjust; but they were not so vociferous. Because of the volatile nature of the Irish, their papers sometimes made extravagant claims. A case in point was the assertion made by the famous Irishman John Mitchell, printed by the *Irish-American* in its issue of June 7, 1862, concerning the seizure of the Confederate commissioners Mason and Slidell from the British vessel the *Trent*. Mitchell assured Irishmen in America that England would never go to war against the North and had never had the least intention of doing so.

Of course, the Irish were belligerent in trying to win recognition for the outstanding general of their nationality. The action of the Senate in refusing to confirm a major-generalship for James Shields brought forth a characteristic outburst from Irishmen throughout the country. The *Irish-American* led off with the following: "We believe there is not an unbiased person in the loyal states of this Union, who is capable of judging the circumstances of the case, that will not share the indignation felt by every Irish-American at the manner in which the brave and patriotic General Shields has been treated by the party that now, by the accident of a fictitious majority, controls the actions of the United States Senate." [57]

---

[56] The works of Hamlin and Rice have been referred to in the discussion of this subject in Chapter XVI.

[57] New York *Irish-American*, July 5, 1862.

With the enthusiastic ardor characteristic of his race, an Irishman wrote the following from Ohio to the editor of the *Irish-American:* "A more general favorite amongst his countrymen never lived than he [Shields]; never did a brighter history adorn the name of a patriot or soldier. The heart, hopes, and pride of Irishmen are centered in him, and grandly has he vindicated his position as a representative of all that is noble in our race. We believed he had attained his merited rank some months ago; but the announcement of this base ingratitude has almost paralyzed our confidence and enthusiasm, and suffused every Irish cheek of Iowa and the nation with a flush of indignant disgust. None have contributed more towards the number and efficiency of the Union army than the countrymen and admirers of General James Shields." [58]

A correspondent from Boston contributed, "We have been in the most feverish excitement on this matter for some days past, and a public meeting is talked of and will soon be held, to give utterance to the views of the adopted citizens of the capital of Puritanism, upon the gross injustice of the Senate towards our gallant countrymen." [59] A few weeks later a voice came from the West to rebuke those in authority for daring to slight the "great military representative of our race. We in the West feel that his first appointment was an insult, while these civilian politicians who had never smelt powder were placed over the veteran soldiers; nevertheless we were slow to cavil at any action of the government so long as they gave our soldiers a fair chance." The same newspaper flatly expressed the belief that Shields had been rejected because of his Irish associations—meaning, possibly, his religious faith. It further declared its awareness of the injustice inherent in the fact that 150,000 Irish volunteers were represented by only two brigadiers while Irish privates constituted one fourth of the army—a gross exaggeration, as the reader knows. This Irishman, airing the grievances of his race, for good measure called attention to the disproportion of Catholic chaplains to the entire number of chaplains and to the refusal to admit into the lines clergy who were willing to administer the rites without charge, as had happened at Camp Douglas in Chicago. To a Catholic it seemed an outrage that Catholic soldiers should die without the ministrations of a priest. [60]

[58] *Ibid.*, July 12, 1862.   [59] *Ibid.*

[60] Thomas M. Halpin to "Friend Cole," Chicago, July 11, 1862, printed *ibid.*, July 26, 1862. Halpin quite frankly stated that it was the duty of every Irishman to say aloud that the sacrifices, the indomitable courage, and the lives lavishly offered up on the altar of American constitutional freedom had not been and never would be appreciated until the voices of the friends of the soldiers were lifted in thunderous tones.

With the example of a German division before them it was inevitable that Irish voices should be lifted for an Irish division. The idea was heralded through the press and proposed to the Secretary of War early in 1862, but it seems to have died with a "pert and somewhat tart answer from Adjutant General Thomas." The rather plaintive cry was uttered, "Not only are we not to have an Irish Division, but the honor of having an Irish Major-General is not allowed us." [61]

Naturally, General Meagher's indignation and protest at what he considered rank injustice to the Irish Brigade—the refusal to allow the brigade to return to recruit after the losses at Fredericksburg—could not be allowed to pass without vehement support from the always volatile Irish: "Just imagine the condition of some companies on entering the battle field: two men to a company commanded by an officer. Can the history of the world show anything to equal it in barbarity and downright butchery? Besides they seem not to recollect the fact that they are doing all in their power to demoralize the remnant of a magnificent brigade. It is miserable to see this small band of heroes going up boldly for the last time for the slaughter. . . ." [62]

It is possible to find cases of individual dissatisfaction with rank accorded among the Scandinavians, but no evidence exists of racial dissatisfaction (dissatisfaction arising from the feeling that Scandinavians were not being recognized in proportion to the sacrifices made by them for the war) such as was so abundantly expressed by the Germans and the Irish. Hans Mattson and Hans Christian Heg both wrote to their wives, in moments of discouragement, threats that they would resign unless they were accorded more recognition; [63] but the reader of these letters feels sure that when the sun shone again and things looked brighter, they quickly changed their minds. Colonel Vegesack brought pressure for promotion to a brigadiership through the highest possible source, Count Piper [64]—but in vain. Complaints found currency among the Swedes as among all the troops. The difficulties in securing a commission which beset the path of a Swede who finally found a place as cavalry chief with General Frémont are detailed at length in *Emigranten*.[65] Swedes resented (probably with

---

[61] *Ibid.*, July 12, 1862.   [62] *Ibid.*, January 17, 1863.

[63] On April 26, Heg wrote that he would go home in the fall unless made a brigadier. Blegen (ed.), *Civil War Letters of Colonel Heg*, 206.

[64] See memorandum from Count Piper to Seward, May 14, 1863, Notes from the Swedish Legation, IV, in which he stated that he understood that General Hooker had recommended Vegesack for promotion. If occasion offered, a favorable word by Seward could not but assure the success of Baron Vegesack.   [65] Madison *Emigranten*, October 19, 1861.

the more vigor because they had so little money) the sale of commissions. Carl F. Grevellius, for instance, has told of arousing the ill will of his major, who was reported as making a handsome profit of $100 on each officer introduced into the regiment, when he obtained a commission without the major's recommendation.[66] Finally, there was the usual grouching among soldiers of this nationality over politically appointed generals and over being assigned to guard railroads without having any prospect of actually fighting. One officer wrote, "I believe we have too many political 'humbug' gen. in our army . . . We are impatient to be led against the foe, but until now we have not received weapons that are worth anything." Like all other captains, he took pride in his Scandinavian Guards as "an adornment to the service." [67]

Occasionally one catches echoes of bitterness from the French. The editor of the *Courrier des États-Unis* remarked early in the war, "There is prompt flattery and encouragement for those who have sacrificed their position in Europe in order to place their swords at the disposition of what they thought the cause of liberty." Then he added pointedly that they were not the only ones for whom recompense should be provided in the future—a reference, no doubt, to the French residents of the United States in the service. The same race prejudice was reflected in *L'Opinion Nationale* of the Paris press, which expressed the conviction that it was not the millionaire bankers of Philadelphia and New York who were filling the ranks.[68]

As suggested earlier, native Americans had no monopoly on prejudice. There had always been rivalry and some resentment between Germans and Irishmen in the country; as might be supposed, that rivalry sprang up afresh between German and Irish regiments—a rivalry so well known that the point does not need to be labored. And if native Americans resented having German or foreign officers over them, foreign-born just as often resented the action of American officers. A case in point is revealed by a letter from First Lieutenant Anton von Brabender of the Fifty-eighth Ohio written from Camp Chase in the fall of 1861. Overcoats had just arrived and Von Brabender started to assist the quartermaster to distribute them in the presence of Major Peter Dister and Lieutenants Barentzen and Deweg. Von Brabender remarked innocently that he thought the men

[66] Hokanson, *Swedish Immigrants*, 72.

[67] Letter from the captain, Mattson, Camp Dana, Kentucky, January 20, 1862, printed in the Chicago *Hemlandet*, January 29, 1862. Mattson Papers.

[68] Paris *L'Opinion Nationale*, August 16, 1861; the excerpt from this paper was copied by New York *Courrier des États-Unis* on September 6, 1861.

should try them on to avoid later exchanges, but the quartermaster rudely forbade him to interrupt and called out in English to a guard to "take that man away." When Major Dister, a German, objected that the guard had no right to make the arrest, Quartermaster Bishop himself "took the liberty to take hold" of Von Brabender, who protested in vehement language. To emphasize the difficulties of language in mixed regiments, it should be recorded that the German seemed to resent the fact that Bishop used English exclusively, although he knew that the other "was not much conversant in the English language." The German, deeply offended, as any nobleman of his tradition would be, asked Governor William Dennison to transfer him to another German regiment, as he had "no inclination to be exposed another time to such ungentlemanly treatment." [69]

On the other hand, one sometimes finds illustrations of warm respect and even affection between soldiers of different nationalities. The Germans at times bestowed high praise on the fighting qualities of the Irishmen. One would assume that there were tributes of praise after Fredericksburg, but an acknowledgement in a German paper as early as May, 1861, is more meaningful as a considered judgment severed from any emotion: "The Irishmen are as brave soldiers as there can be, and the brigade of this place [Mulligan's Illinois Brigade] would in any case have brought honor to the state troops of Illinois." [70] If the opinion of Hans Mattson can be accepted as authoritative for Swedish opinion early in 1862, his countrymen entertained a high regard for German leadership. He wondered "how

[69] Von Brabender to Governor Dennison, November 27, 1861, Executive Correspondence of the Governors of Ohio, November 16–30, 1861. Dister later rose to be lieutenant colonel of the regiment.

The case of Patrick McKerney is hardly typical enough to be included in the text, but its queer combination of a sense of personal dignity and crude language is too rare a specimen not to be incorporated in a note. After hoping the governor would pardon "an ignoramus Irishman" for troubling him, he asked to be transferred from the Sixty-seventh Ohio Regiment, "where nothing but misrule and irregularity *prevail.*" He had many reasons for the request but gave only the more simple ones from a desire not to harm the reputation of the regiment. The first was that a "soldier who has been in service before do not like to be handed over to men who are quite ignorant of everything that appertains to military rules and discipline. I petitioned the Col but was threatened with punishment for having the audacity to write an humble petition to any person endowed with the principles of Monarchy." He was then in prison because he refused to go with this regiment and "of late gave up drilling." He asked the governor to "do one of the corporal works of Mercy," and hoped that the executive would "see to this immediately on receipt of this rustic note." He would sooner go in the regulars for life than be under the officers in whom he had lost confidence. He signed the letter "Your humble high private in the rear rank." McKerney to Governor Dennison, Camp Olive, Toledo, December 18, 1861, *ibid.*, December 16–31, 1861.

[70] Chicago *Illinois Staats-Zeitung*, May 7, 1861.

many victories the union troops could have counted in this war if it had not been for those much despised dutchmen. . . . the great American political officers are a perfect Humbug—if the President would leave the job to some of these dutch—Sigel—Blenker—Shoeps [Schoepf?] or Willich or Hecken—they would have cleaned out secession long ago—but no—political favorites must have a chance to get big salaries, and stealings." [71]

Personal friendships crossed the line of racial origin. A story of warm affection between an Irishman and a Swede is worthy of preservation. The Swede had wandered off from the picket line and appeared, therefore, to be a deserter; he even admitted the facts. The Irishman pleaded for him, a chaplain said, as he had never heard one man plead for another of a different nationality. It was evident that here was one of those Damon-Pythias friendships. "For the love of God, Misther Chaplain, save him ev you can! For God's sake spake to the Giner'l! O God! I'll die ev they shoot im! And I know he was niver afther maning it." Then the Irish friend recounted the "attractive ways on him," his linguistic ability with three languages (though he could write only his native Swedish), and his skill in writing songs and in plotting out a course on the sea. "Nothin' was a mystery to him." To relieve the reader's mind, it might be added that the Swede escaped the threatened penalty, not because of the Irishman's eloquent pleading, but because of the termination of the war. [72]

Many rewards were apportioned to the knights-errant, the soldiers of fortune, and especially to our fellow American citizens of foreign birth. First among these were the promotions and honors accorded during the war for meritorious service on the field. We have already noted the men who succeeded in attaining the highest military rank (save that of lieutenant general, which was bestowed on Grant alone). Here we are concerned only with numbers. Among those reaching the highest rank, that of major general, were only six, the reader is reminded, born outside the United States; and that scanty number included General Sheridan, whose place of birth is in doubt. Small indeed was the foreign representation in this exalted rank. It is noteworthy that three of the number, Sigel, Schurz, and Osterhaus, were German-born, and their appointment was partly intended as recognition and expression of appreciation for the abundant outpouring of help from the German element of the population. The fourth was the Hungarian Stahel, whose appointment could certainly not have been

[71] Mattson to his wife, Camp Dana, January 12, 1862, Mattson Papers.
[72] H. Clay Turnbull, *War Memoirs of an Army Chaplain* (New York, 1898), 63–64.

intended as a tribute to the handful of Hungarians in the country at the time. It is a conspicuous fact that despite the strength of the Irish in the population and the devotion which they had shown in enlisting, no Irishman attained this rank in recognition of the valuable service of the Irish.

The number of brigadier generals who had been born under another flag (fourteen in all) was more generous but could scarcely have satisfied the foreign element. However, the brigadier generals were more widely representative of different racial elements, embracing the German, French, Hungarian, Swedish, Polish, and Russian nationalities. Perhaps the best way to give a real gauge of the degree of representation is by bald figures. In all there were no less than 2,533 men among the volunteers who could boast of the title of generals—counting both major generals and brigadier generals [73] and including those holding brevet rank—of whom only 72 or only slightly more than 3 per cent were foreign-born.

The number of colonels was far larger, and here the ratios as distributed among the various racial elements are all out of balance, for the rank of colonel had been allotted to the Germans with a far more lavish hand than to other nationalities, as if partially to make up for the niggardliness with which the two higher ranks had been passed out. Altogether the writer has located 147 foreign-born men on whom the rank of colonel was bestowed; all except 16 were Germans. The actual number of lieutenant colonels ascertainable is smaller, only 56, though logic would suggest that the number in reality probably approached more nearly that of the colonels, as most of these officers were found in foreign regiments and would, therefore, presumably be of the same nationality as that of most of the members of the regiment.

Likewise, when it comes to calculating the proportion of majors, the number 76 probably does not embrace all, and again includes a handful of other nationalities than German—an Austrian, a Hungarian, several Swedes, and several Swiss. The total of foreign-born captains, including chiefs of batteries who rank as captains, who are identifiable is 96 and must come far short of reality; in this group, also, less than a handful are other than German.[74] The reason why the author could identify a larger

[73] Frederick Phisterer (author and comp.), *Statistical Records of the Armies of the United States* (New York, 1883), 251, 256, 267. The figures are established by actual count, checked against Heitman's work.

[74] These figures are compiled from the various books used in this study: Hokanson, *Swedish Immigrants;* Vasvary, *Lincoln's Hungarian Heroes;* Pivány, *Hungarians in the American Civil War;* Haiman, *Polish Past in America;* and Kaufmann, *Die Deutschen im Bürgerkriege.*

number of colonels than of the lesser officers is simple: compilers of lists of officers, with which more or less biographical material is usually associated, were interested in the important military figures, but their interest often did not extend below the colonels. As has been stated earlier, the chief deterrent to satisfactory statistics is the failure to record nativity for commissioned officers in the Descriptive Books. Statistics for lieutenants are too scanty to make possible any effort to establish numbers.

It might be worth while to note briefly the total number of officers from the different racial groups. The chief student of the subject for the Germans, Wilhelm Kaufmann, collected a list of around 500 German officers of all ranks. A Polish writer claimed for the Poles 166 commissioned officers, in which number were 3 brigadier generals and 4 colonels. According to the best count of which the author is capable, 74 Swedes (knights-errant from the mother country and Swedes resident in the United States) received commissions to serve in the Union army. The most recent writer on the Hungarian contribution to the war claimed for this nationality the astonishing number of 74 commissioned officers. The author has checked these individuals by the *Official War Records* for officers not recorded by Heitman.[75]

The way of showing appreciation for valiant service which was the cheapest of all was the awarding of brevet titles and words of praise. There seems to be no way of determining whether in bestowing brevet rank to avoid granting higher pay and lineal rank the government was proportionately more generous to foreign-born officers than it was to American officers. The preceding chapters dealing with officers certainly gave abundant evidence that there was much use of the brevet title. Words were cheap but could give much satisfaction, partially making up for the lack of more substantial rewards. It is conspicuous that such praise was not awarded solely by the high-ranking foreign-born officer who wished to call attention to one of his own nationality. It is true that General Schurz praised Colonel August Otto, his chief of staff, for his skillful handling

---

The figures presented in these books have been checked against Heitman (comp.), *Historical Register and Dictionary*, the Descriptive Books, *Official War Records*, and the *Volunteer Army Register.*

[75] Kaufmann, *Die Deutschen im Bürgerkriege*, 445–575; Hokanson, *Swedish Immigrants, passim*, checked by the writer's own research; Vasvary, *Lincoln's Hungarian Heroes*, 43–89. To the number of Germans given by Kaufmann the author would add a few, but since she would subtract Poles, Austrians, Hungarians, and Swiss—all of which he listed as German— the number may stand as approximately correct.

of the operations at Gettysburg; likewise, Osterhaus held Colonel Friedrich Schäfer one of the best regimental leaders of the entire Western army.[76] The highest-ranking Americans also bestowed enthusiastic praise on subordinate officers who had been trained abroad. General Hurlbut, for instance, acknowledged warmly the services of the artillery officer Edward Brotzmann on the field at Shiloh; Sherman in a circle of higher officers named Colonel Edward Siber as the most accomplished officer in his army; Sheridan declared Major Francis Mochardt of his staff an extraordinarily able topographer.[77] Sometimes the praise took the form of a speech of formal thanks, as when McClellan thanked the Irish Brigade on July 4, 1862, for their "superb conduct in the field" and expressed the wish for twenty thousand more of them. Governor Charles S. Olden of New Jersey thanked Colonel Joseph Karge in a special letter which declared that his services would be ever remembered by the people of New Jersey and of the country. Shortly after the war Karge was recognized with a commission in the Regular Army and command of two important military reservations in Nevada, but he resigned in 1870 for a professorship in modern language at Princeton College.[78]

Medals and honors were bestowed on a goodly number of our foreign-born. Colonel Mindil, the Hungarian on McClellan's staff during the Peninsular Campaign, was distinguished by two medals for bravery: the first for directing, as adjutant, the attack of a regiment which broke through the center of the enemy and silenced the artillery of the Confederates at the battle of Williamsburg; the second for bravery on the march through Georgia. Congress awarded the Congressional Medal of Honor to Theodor Schwan, who had been in the Regular Army since he was sixteen, and to Frederick Phisterer, also of the Regular Army infantry, for a heroic ride behind the rear of the enemy at Murfreesboro, though he was destined to become far better known for his statistical study of the war, cited previously. Captain William Grebe of the Fourth Missouri Cavalry and Captain Franz Irsch of the Forty-fifth New York both became possessors of the Congressional Medal, the former for heroic conduct at the Battle of Jonesboro in August, 1864, the latter for his glorious defense

[76] For Otto, see *Official War Records*, Ser. 1, XXVII, Pt. 1, p. 731; for Schäfer, see *ibid.*, Ser. 1, VIII, Pt. 1, p. 221; and Kaufmann, *Die Deutschen im Bürgerkriege*, 548.

[77] For Brotzmann, see *Official War Records*, Ser. 1, X, Pt. 1, p. 207; for Siber, see Kaufmann, *Die Deutschen im Bürgerkriege*, 553; for Mochardt, see *ibid.*, 534. Kaufmann claimed certain distinctions for others which it has proved impossible to verify. Mochardt appeared as "Mohrhardt" in *Official War Records*, Ser. 1, XX, Pt. 1, p. 351.

[78] Haiman, *Polish Past in America*, 126, 128.

of a part of the town of Gettysburg while the Eleventh Corps gathered at Cemetery Hill. Irsch received this medal after the Cross of the Loyal Legion had already been accorded him for the same courageous conduct.[79]

The Congressional Medal, highest honor in the gift of the Union, was awarded to at least eleven noncommissioned officers and privates for deeds of valor, some of which merit description. Sergeant Fritz Fuger, after all the officers of his battery had been killed or wounded and five of the cannon rendered useless by Pickett's charge at Gettysburg, took over the command and fought on heroically with the last cannon. Leopold Karpeles, flag-bearer of the Fifty-seventh Massachusetts, so gathered his fleeing comrades about the flag on May 6, 1864, at the battle of the Wilderness that they took a stand and hurled back the foe. Julius Langbein, a German drummer boy, saved a wounded officer at Camden, North Carolina, by carrying him out of the fire.[80] General Howard had a special medal struck for two companies of the German Eighth New York, who acted as his bodyguard or Headquarters Guard and served throughout the entire war. Iowa prepared a special honor for a distinguished son—an adopted son, let it be noted—General Karl Matthies, for he had led a brigade and then a division of the Seventeenth Corps: a medallion relief of this German-American adorns the war memorial in Des Moines.[81]

Several posts of the Grand Army of the Republic were named for out-standing Germans of war fame—one in New York for Von Gilsa; one in St. Louis for Hassendeubel; and another in Philadelphia for Koltes. The fourth person so honored was Colonel Theodor Meumann, whose name is so little known that we must hasten to add that he commanded Sigel's old regiment, the Third Missouri. Charles Demmy, although he reached no higher rank than a captaincy in the Twelfth Missouri, was so honored—probably because he fell in the assault on Vicksburg. In each of these instances a large number of the members of the post were doubtless German veterans. The highest possible honor was shown the adopted citizens

[79] Kaufmann, *Die Deutschen im Bürgerkriege*, 533–34, 538, 551–52, 504, 516. Grebe's war record was checkered; he was cashiered for fighting a duel with a German comrade, but the act was revoked by special act of Congress twenty years later. *Ibid.*, 505.

[80] The other recipients were Ignatz Gresser, for bravery at Antietam in carrying a wounded comrade to safety under a storm of bullets; John Schiller, for pressing into the enemy's redoubt at Chaffin's Farm; Jacob E. Schwap, for achieving distinction in the Wilderness; Martin Wambagen, for saving the regimental flag at Cedar Creek; Benjamin Levy, for saving the flag after the regular bearer had fallen; Charles Schambach, for capturing a Confederate flag; Fred F. Rohm, for saving a wounded officer at great personal self-sacrifice; and Sergeant Konrad Schmidt, for saving his wounded captain, Rodenbaugh. *Ibid.*, 555–56.

[81] *Ibid.*, 526, 531.

by this association when its central organization chose Major Leo Rassieur to head the Grand Army of the Republic—the only foreigner so distinguished.[82] Since he had attained no higher rank than major, the honor probably became his for zeal in the work of the association.

Another way in which honors were passed out was to bestow the name of a fallen hero on a battery. After the battle of Roanoke Island, to give a concrete instance, where De Monteil (French officer of the D'Epineuil Zouaves) fell, General Burnside issued an order of the day in which, "desiring to express his deep respect for the memory of a gallant soldier," he bestowed the name of De Monteil on one of the batteries which had been captured in the action. Again, the honor might take a more tangible form. General Edward L. Molineux, while in command at Savannah, had been instrumental in saving the ship *Lawrence;* in recognition of this service the New York Board of Underwriters voted him a service of plate.

Tribute paid to the dead yielded the fallen hero slight comfort, but the great public funerals which were the order of the day were undoubtedly one way of expressing gratitude to the officer himself and to the nationality group which he represented. Let one illustration suffice. When the body of Colonel Thomas Cass came back to Boston for burial, it was escorted by a large group of civic and military organizations, a band, and a number of state and city authorities. Resolutions were passed in Cass's honor by the Boston City Council as well as by numerous Irish societies.[83]

To claim that some of the adopted sons attained high political office as a reward for their war contribution would be false; but, in the psychology which prevailed during the seventies and eighties, a war record was manifestly no disadvantage, while we may be certain that it was exploited in all campaign speeches for any candidate, native or alien-born. The most striking Civil War foreign-born officer to reach high civilian office was Carl Schurz, who soon after the war added to his high military title that of Senator from Missouri. The mission which Johnson asked of him very shortly after the close of the war may not have been an honor which Schurz desired, but there can be little doubt that Johnson's selection of him was prompted by the fact that he had been born abroad and might therefore be fairly expected to present a more objective report on conditions in the South than a native whose views had been colored from birth by the

[82] *Ibid.*, 491, 504, 508, 521, 532, 541.

[83] Duyckinck, *National History of the War for the Union,* II, 251; Mottelay and Campbell-Copeland (eds.), *The Soldier in Our Civil War,* II, 314; New York *Irish-American,* July 26, 1862.

heated political controversies which had torn this country since 1820. The fact that James Shields, after his resignation from the United States Army at the close of March, 1863, became a member of the Missouri state legislature and was elected to fill an unexpired term in the Federal Senate from January to March, 1879, should be noted for the completeness of the record rather than for any relation existing between his war service and his selection for high political office. Colonel William Joyce Sewell progressed from the New Jersey senate, where he had occupied a seat for nine years, to the United States Senate, in which he held a seat from 1881 to 1887.[84]

The post of secretary of the Territory of Montana fell to General Thomas Meagher, probably in recognition of his war services; however, he filled temporarily an even higher post, for in the absence of the governor, he served for a year in the capacity of chief territorial executive, encountering many obstacles in the administration of his office. He did not long enjoy tenure in the post of secretary, for in July, 1867, while on a reconnaissance on the Missouri River near Fort Benton he fell from the deck of a steamer and was drowned.[85] Colonel Edward Salomon became governor of Washington Territory; Gustav Finkelnburg, who had an inconspicuous war record as adjutant in the Third Missouri, was several times elected to Congress from St. Louis and was finally appointed a Federal judge in Missouri. President Lincoln was probably rewarding the politician in Arnold Krekel as much as the lieutenant colonel of the First Cavalry Battalion of Missouri when he appointed him a Federal judge, for in 1864 he had presided over the Missouri state convention which abolished slavery in that state before the Thirteenth Amendment became effective.[86]

The richest plums for adopted citizens in the gift of the Federal government were probably in the diplomatic and consular services. Two officers who had served the country on the field of battle received their rewards by being allowed to represent the United States abroad. The Hungarian General Asboth was confirmed by the Senate, without the usual bickering, as minister to Argentina, where his handling of the diplomatic negotiations in the war of that country with Paraguay were so eminently satisfactory that the government made him minister to Uruguay also. This post he held until his death two years later from a wound sustained in the

[84] For Shields, see Johnson and Malone (eds.), *Dictionary of American Biography*, XVII, 106–107; for Sewall, see *ibid.*, 1–2.

[85] *Ibid.*, XII, 482.

[86] See Kaufmann, *Die Deutschen im Bürgerkriege*, 546, for Salomon; for Finkelnburg, see *ibid.*, 497; for Krekel, see *ibid.*, 522.

Civil War. The second adopted citizen to receive a diplomatic post was Colonel Leopold Markbreit, an Austrian, who was appointed Minister Resident of the United States to Bolivia by President Grant.[87]

The appointments to the consular service were more generous. After the war, Wilhelm Heine was rewarded for his valuable service in the Engineer Corps during the war by being made consul general in Paris, from which post he returned to Germany for the last few years of his life. Brigadier General Max von Weber, closely identified with the Turner Regiment of New York, served as consul at Nantes; and the French officer General Alfred Duffié went to Spain to serve as United States consul at Cadiz, a post which he held until his death a decade later.[88] Osterhaus, after the dubious honor of serving as military governor of Mississippi, embarked for France to discharge the duties of consul at Lyons, where his helpful attitude toward German citizens during the Franco-Prussian War won him the thanks of the German government. After eleven years as consul at that post and after more than twenty years back in the United States, he returned to his native Germany to take over the consulate at Mannheim.[89]

Lincoln had offered the Italian knight-errant Luigi di Cesnola the post of consul at Cyprus if he would become a citizen of the United States. The Italian accepted the offer before the close of 1865 and assumed the responsibilities of the position, which he discharged until 1877. President Johnson appointed George Pomutz consul at St. Petersburg in 1866. He later became consul general for Russia, from which post he was not recalled until 1878. Oskar Malmroos, a Swede by birth, who as adjutant general in Minnesota during the war had organized 22,000 troops, received the appointment of consul at several French and Spanish ports. In 1868 Grant, with a soldier's partiality for wounded soldiers, appointed Hugh Hillebrandt, a Hungarian who had been wounded at Gettysburg, American consul on the island of Crete, where he remained until the consulate was

---

[87] Piványi, *The Hungarians in the American Civil War*, 30–31. Kaufmann is in error in saying that Asboth became consul. *Die Deutschen im Bürgerkriege*, 479. The best account of Asboth's diplomatic work is in Vasvary, *Lincoln's Hungarian Heroes*, 46–47; this writer told of how Asboth, after his appointment, went to Paris for an operation to have the bullet removed from his face by a celebrated surgeon who had performed a similar operation on Garibaldi. Asboth died in January, 1868, at the relatively young age of fifty-seven.

For Markbreit, see *The National Cyclopaedia of American Biography*, XII, 467–68. Both of these men appear in the official diplomatic lists.

[88] For Heine, see Rosengarten, *The German Soldier in the Wars of the United States*, 71; for Weber, see *The National Cyclopaedia of American Biography*, XII, 264; for Duffié, see Wilson and Fiske (eds.), *Appletons' Cyclopaedia of American Biography*, II, 247–48.

[89] Kaufmann, *Die Deutschen im Bürgerkriege*, 448; Johnson and Malone (eds.), *Dictionary of American Biography*, XIV, 88.

discontinued in 1874 at his suggestion.[90] Since Secretary of State Seward in all likelihood was somewhat responsible for Philip Figyelmessy's coming to America, he probably felt some responsibility for his future after the war. In any case he offered him a consulship, and the Hungarian chose that at Demerara in British Guiana, which he continued to hold, under several administrations, from 1865 to 1888. One of his consular reports on the evils of coolie labor commanded wide attention in Britain, with the result that the situation was considerably improved.[91]

The consulates in the Far East assigned to former soldiers of the war are particularly interesting. General Stahel had gained the confidence of his superiors so fully that Secretary of State Seward selected him for the task of reorganizing the consulate at Yokohama, then in great need of overhauling. Altogether the period of his foreign service spanned nineteen years, though he resigned for a part of that time. He first entered into arrangements with Japan for opening new ports, with the result that he became consul general with direction over Osaka and Hiogo as well as Yokohama. He left Japan in 1884 to become consul general in Shanghai for Chinese ports. He sent the State Department lengthy reports containing recommendations for reorganization of the service in the Far East which became the basis for several reforms.[92] The Frenchman Charles W. Le Gendre received appointment as consul at Amoy, China, in 1866 and continued in the service until 1872, when his diplomatic skill and acquaintance with the Far East led to his being employed by the Japanese government as a diplomatic officer. The Swiss Major A. G. Studer, who served in the war with an Iowa regiment, ultimately functioned as consul in Singapore. Finally, one notes that Hans Mattson was rewarded by the Federal government with a consul general's post in India and served from 1881 to 1883, between his two periods of service as secretary of state for Minnesota.[93]

The adopted citizens were liberally sprinkled about in many branches

[90] See *The National Cyclopaedia of American Biography*, I, 422, for Di Cesnola; for Pomutz, see Vasvary, *Lincoln's Hungarian Heroes*, 74; for Malmroos, see Hokanson, *Swedish Immigrants*, 116; for Hillebrandt, see Vasvary, *Lincoln's Hungarian Heroes*, 57.

[91] For Figyelmessy, see Vasvary, *Lincoln's Hungarian Heroes*, 53. Although he yearned to see Hungary once more, he refused to set foot on her soil until it was free from the Hapsburgs.

[92] *Ibid.*, 82–83; Piványi, *Hungarians in the American Civil War*, 41.

[93] It is an interesting fact that in *The National Cyclopaedia of American Biography*, XXV, 79, the writer of Le Gendre's biography attributed to him encouragement of Japan's awakening ambition for ascendancy in Asiatic affairs. For Studer, see Kaufmann, *Die Deutschen im Bürgerkriege*, 555; for Mattson, see Explanatory Note with the Mattson Papers, prepared by the Minnesota Historical Society.

of the Federal civil service and represented many nationalities. The only Pole who seems to have been rewarded with appointment to the civil service (though he was unquestionably one of the three most outstanding Poles) was General Krzyzanowski, who, after holding several offices in the Department of the Treasury and serving as customs inspector at Panama, settled down in the custom office at New York. Adolf von Steinwehr, after a professorship in military science at Yale, became an engineer for the Federal government and gave to that department a better standard for beauty, accuracy, and finish in its cartography.[94] In proportion to their numbers, the Hungarians appeared in surprising profusion. To Eugene Arthur Kozlay was assigned a position in the customs at New York, which he exchanged only a few years before his death for an engineer's post in the waterworks of that city; to Charles Semsey, a post in the customs and then the position of chairman of the Board of Special Inquiry in the Immigration Service at Ellis Island; and to Emeric Szabad, a post as assistant collector at the port of Galveston. In this same customs service were Colonel Denis Burke, familiar to the reader from his association with the Irish Brigade; and the Swiss Johann Rudolf Fellman, who was stationed at Baltimore as an appraiser from 1865 to his death in 1886.

Foreigners were not confined to the customs service. Another Swiss, A. Martin Tanner, passed from Trepp's company of sharpshooters to a position in the Treasury Department. Two Hungarians served in the Bureau of Internal Revenue, Robert Rombauer and Anselm Albert, the latter as a district assessor. General Alvin Schoepf can hardly be said to have been rewarded by appointment to the Patent Office, for he merely returned to an old post, but he rose to be chief examiner.[95] We find several Hungarian officers, Alexander Jekelfalussy and Francis Langenfeld, in the Chicago post office; two Germans appear in the same service—Lieutenant Karl Schurig and General Hugo von Wangelin, who was named postmaster at Bellevue by Lincoln. To the Bureau of Pensions were appointed Frederick Knefler, the popular Hungarian, who was named chief of the pension office by President Hayes; Colonel E. F. M. Fähtz, who

[94] Haiman, *Polish Past in America*, 122; Fox (comp.), *New York at Gettysburg*, III, 1345–46.

[95] For Kozlay, see "Deutsch-amerikanische Nekrologie," in *Der Deutsche Pionier*, XV (1883–1884), 421; for Semsey, see Vasvary, *Lincoln's Hungarian Heroes*, 81; for Szabad, see Vasvary, *Lincoln's Hungarian Heroes*, 83; for Burke, see Powell (comp.), *Officers of the Army and Navy (Volunteer)*, 294; for Fellman and Tanner, see Steinach, *Geschichte und Leben*, 117, 143–44, respectively; for Rombauer, Albert, and Schoepf, see Vasvary, *Lincoln's Hungarian Heroes*, 77, 44, and 80, respectively.

served in the Bureau of Pensions as well as in several other minor government jobs; the Irish colonel St. Clair Mulholland, who, after serving Philadelphia as chief of police, accepted appointment by Cleveland as pension agent in the same city.[96] Ernst M. Roszafy, another of the handful of Hungarian soldiers, found a source of bread and butter in the Bureau of the Census. The Chilean Louis Beirel held a position under the Commissioners for Immigration; and the Canadian John McNeil became an inspector in the Indian service.[97] More humble soldiers were not neglected: Joseph McCoy of the Second United States Cavalry secured appointment to a clerical post in the adjutant general's office.

States and cities rewarded some loyal adopted citizens, probably not only for their prominence in their respective groups but also with an eye to the votes they might garner for the ticket as a whole. In such cases, prominence and leadership among the nationality group undoubtedly were partly owing to prominence in the war. Loyalties bred in the camp are known to be about the strongest in the world; former soldiers of the Union army were no exception and could be counted on to vote for a beloved captain or colonel. Hans Mattson had already dabbled in politics before the war, having been elected to the modest post of city clerk in the town of Red Wing in 1859 after a residence of only six years in Goodhue County, and having been chairman of the branch of the Republican party in Red Wing in 1860. His appointment as secretary to the State Board of Immigration in 1867 was natural enough. His election as secretary of state, however, in 1870 for a term of two years was a distinct recognition of his importance in the state. After his return from a consular post in India, he won a second election to the office of secretary of state for Minnesota, filling that post from 1887 to 1891.[98]

Several of the alien-born who had been connected with the army in one way or another won election as mayors of their respective cities. Two Germans who were thus elected in cities with large German populations were Colonel Gustav Tafel, who after commanding an Ohio regiment in the

[96] Vasvary, *Lincoln's Hungarian Heroes*, 57, for Jekelfalussy and Langenfeld; for Schurig, see "Deutsch Nekrologie," in *Der Deutsche Pionier*, XVI (1884–1885), 166; for Von Wangelin, see "General Hugo Wangelin," in *Der Deutsche Pionier*, XV (1883–1884), 410; for Knefler, see Vasvary, *Lincoln's Hungarian Heroes*, 59; for Fähtz, see "Deutsch-amerikanische Nekrologie," in *Der Deutsche Pionier*, XIV (1882–1883), 115; for Mulholland, see Johnson and Fiske (eds.), *Appletons' Cyclopaedia of American Biography*, IV, 154.

[97] For Roszafy, see Pivány, *Hungarians in the Civil War*, 58; for Beirel, Mottelay and Campbell-Copeland (eds.), *The Soldier in Our Civil War*, II, 383; for McNeil, see Wilson and Malone (eds.), *Dictionary of American Biography*, XIII, 319.

[98] Explanatory Biographical Note with the Mattson Papers.

war later won election to the mayoralty of Cincinnati; and Colonel Karl Zollinger, who after leading an Indiana regiment, later served for twelve years as mayor of Fort Wayne. Dr. Alexander Fekete, who had served as surgeon in the Thirteenth Missouri Cavalry (in which it is doubtful that there were any of his fellow-Hungarians) was elected mayor of East St. Louis.[99] General Sigel, after several years as pension agent and collector of internal revenue, was elected to the modest post of registrar in New York City in 1871. Heinrich Sontag served as secretary in the state assessor's office of Missouri from 1865–1871. Two of the Rombauer family received minor positions in Missouri: Robert served as president of the Board of Assessors; Roderick became a municipal judge and then judge of the Missouri Circuit Court and Court of Appeals. Georg Hillgärtner evidently fell upon evil days, for in his last years the governor of Missouri bestowed on him the office of state claim agent for widows and orphans with claims on the Bureau of Pensions.[100]

The generosity of the United States in the payment of back pay and bounties to the relatives of deceased soldiers and the prodigal liberality in the granting of pensions calls for no extended discussion. The consular dispatches are full of claims from widows or parents of soldiers who had died on the battlefields, for arrears of pay or money due the soldiers at the time of death. These claims were most numerous for Irishmen, as would be expected from the impecunious condition of many relatives in the homeland. Under the law, such money due to any soldier was paid to his next of kin, whether residing in the United States or not. Some conception of the extent of these claims in 1864 was suggested by William B. West, consul at Dublin, who stated that he had prepared nearly two hundred claims for relatives in Ireland. This demand began before the close of the war and was handled by the consuls in co-operation with the magistrates of Ireland, before whom the claimants had to swear to their statements, through whom the consul made the payments, and by whom the receipts were witnessed. Some of the consuls shrewdly took advantage of this opportunity to distribute literature to counteract erroneous opinions.[101]

[99] For Zollinger and Tafel, see Kaufmann, *Die Deutschen im Bürgerkriege*, 566, 557; for Fekete, see Vasvary, *Lincoln's Hungarian Heroes*, 51.

[100] On Sigel, see Johnson and Malone (eds.), *Dictionary of American Biography*, XVII, 153; on Sontag, see *Der Deutsche Pionier*, XIV (1882–1883), 157; for the Rombauer brothers, see Vasvary, *Lincoln's Hungarian Heroes*, 76, 77; on Hillgärtner, see "Georg Hillgärtner," in *Der Deutsche Pionier*, XIV (1882–1883), 468–69.

[101] West to Seward, July 7, 1864, Consular Dispatches, Dublin, January 7, 1865–March 3, 1866, IV (dispatches in this volume not numbered). West distributed such documents as

The consideration of the State Department for the limited finances of the applicants reflects credit on the American government. Evidence of this consideration is contained in a letter from Secretary of State Seward to the consul at Manchester. It had evidently been brought to the Secretary's attention that the applications for arrears of pay and bounty were bulky and entailed considerable postage. Seward's letter authorized the consuls by October, 1864, in cases where this charge bore hard upon the applicants, to transmit the applications to London so that they might be forwarded in the diplomatic pouches without expense to the applicants.[102] Some hint of the work which was piling up on this subject for the period after the war is given in a note from Consul W. Marsh to Seward from Altona, dated February 7, 1863, in which he says that there were "thousands of natives of Holstein-Schleswig serving in our armies."[103]

Without attempting to go into the extensive subject of pensions, it might be added that soldiers of foreign birth shared fully in this reward for their sacrifices. No reader could follow the sketches of the Hungarian soldiers without noting that pensions went regularly to a number who had returned to their native land; one striking illustration was the pension paid to the mother of Nicholas Dunka in Rumania until her death.[104]

Charles Sumner's "Foreign Relations" and Alexander Stephens' "Speech on the outbreak of the Rebellion." See West to Seward, November 26, 1864, *ibid.*, 183.

[102] Seward to H. W. Lord at Manchester October 5, 1864, Instructions to Consuls, XXXVIII, 280–81, for the direction to transmit applications in diplomatic pouches.

[103] Marsh to Seward, February 7, 1863, Consular Dispatches, Altona, II, No. 46. Sometimes, certificate of death was necessary to secure English advantages; for example, such a certificate for William Edward Atkinson, a corporal of the Twelfth Michigan Regiment, was necessary in order to administer property to which he would have been entitled if he had lived. In another case, proof of the death of an Englishman was necessary to permit the admission of some of his nine children into an orphan asylum. Lord Lyons to Seward, December 31, 1863, Notes from the British Legation, LVII.

[104] Some recipients were Andrew Gálfy-Gállik, Henrik Lang, Emery Radnich. See Vasvary, *Lincoln's Hungarian Heroes*, 55, 64, 75. For the case of Dunka, see *ibid.*, 51.

CHAPTER TWENTY

Foreign-Born in the Navy

THE United States Navy was as important a factor as the Army in winning the victory in the Civil War. Without the strong support of the navy, it is not certain what the outcome might have been at Forts Henry and Donelson, along the inland waterways, and on the Atlantic and Gulf coasts. It is certainly questionable whether the North could have been successful had it not been able to disrupt the commerce and the European contacts of the Confederacy by the blockade and the occupancy of the Mississippi River. This seems a considered statement in view of the opinion of military experts. To maintain the blockade was the primary function of the navy, though it had other important duties. The Atlantic Squadrons kept watch over the blockade as far as Cape Canaveral, Florida; the East Gulf Squadron stood guard over the stretch from Key West to Pensacola; and the West Gulf Squadron, from Pensacola to the Rio Grande. Although the line was extended three thousand miles, the harbors practicable for ocean commerce were relatively few. By 1864 the only ports that ships could still enter were Wilmington, Charleston, Mobile, and Galveston.

There were no such general fleet engagements in the Civil War as in World Wars I and II because of the absence of a real Confederate navy. The nearest approach to such an engagement was the naval conflict in the summer of 1864 for Mobile Bay, which gave access to the only Gulf port then available to blockade runners. New Orleans had fallen early in 1862; the ports of the Texan coast, since they were cut off by Federal control of the Mississippi, could afford little further service; and the Federal garrison at Fort Pickens barred entrance to the chief port of the Florida coast, Pensacola. The Confederate navy lacked ships, marines, machines, plants, and sailors; therefore, except in a few instances, it remained on the defensive.

On the eve of the outbreak of war, the condition of the Union navy, like that of the army, was bad. The navy was not in a condition to render the assistance for the defense of the Union that the occasion demanded. The larger number of vessels were employed on foreign stations, and the government did not have a class of ships which could enter the Southern ports to take offensive action. If a proper naval force had been in existence at the time of secession and if the spirit for prompt, firm action had existed, the task of suppressing the secession would have been much easier. The North could have seized quickly every Southern port; then the Confederacy could have secured supplies from Europe only on the open coast, and these must necessarily have been scanty. The bald fact was that the United States had no navy of any account. Many of its war vessels were too large for entry into the shoal Southern ports. Many were sailing frigates and sloops of war quite unsuitable for the work required. The consequence was that, once the Confederacy had secured belligerent rights from the two chief European powers, the North had no alternative but to declare and make effective a blockade on such a scale as was never before known in the world's history. To sustain such a blockade was held by European statesmen to be an utter impossibility. It would require at least 600 ships, and these were not at hand and not promptly to be secured. However, in twelve months the efficiency of the blockade began to be felt.

When the war actually broke, the North had 90 ships available—on paper—but 50 of these were so old as to be obsolescent and could be used only as store vessels. What was more serious than the limited number was the fact that they were widely scattered. The Home Squadron comprised 12 vessels, only 7 of which were steamers; of these 12 the 3 in Northern waters constituted the only trustworthy force.[1] It was not enough that many of the vessels were abroad; they were painfully slow in returning. Although orders recalling them from their stations were drafted as soon as possible after March 4, 1861, they began to arrive only some months later.[2]

The situation with regard to naval construction during the decade before the war should be brought out. In March, 1861, the available ships of war at sea or in the yards numbered 61. Thirty-four were sailing vessels and such were practically worthless. Since commerce was still chiefly conducted by sailing craft, they were of some service against blockade-runners; but for the most part they were, according to the condemnation of one

---

[1] Hosmer, *Appeal to Arms*, 35.

[2] Since a number of the cruisers were under the command of Southern officers, the assertion was repeatedly made that those officers would run their vessels into Confederate ports and turn them over to the Confederacy. In justice to those naval officers it should be recorded that no attempt of this kind was made. Edgar Stanton Maclay, *A History of the United States Navy from 1775 to 1894* . . . (New York, 1894), II, 236.

competent authority, "scarecrows, if even respected as such." [3] There were 27 steamers, all but 6 built in the latter half of the decade just before the war.[4] In noting the paucity of ships, the reader should keep in mind the fact that some vessels moored at the navy yard at Norfolk and nearly ready for service were lost when the Federals, before evacuation, burned the navy yard, together with a large quantity of ammunition.[5]

Naturally, the situation called for prompt efforts to enlarge the navy. The Navy Department recognized that ships must be provided for the blockade, craft found for the inland streams, cruisers provided to pursue the Confederate commerce destroyers, and heavy ships built to deal with Confederate forts. The government went into action. It purchased every merchant craft available that could be adapted to war purposes, as either transport or fighting vessel, and thus secured a large and fairly effective fleet of this type of converted vessel. It began construction of 8 additional sloops of war and entered into contracts with shipbuilders for the smaller, heavily armed boats, suitable for use on the inland waters and for operation against heavy land batteries, which were to become famous as the ninety-day gunboats. It pushed to rapid completion 39 double-end, side-wheel steamers for river service, known colloquially as "double-enders" because they were built to be propelled in either direction. It gathered up early in January, 1862, a promiscuous assortment of ferryboats, riverboats, and tugboats; these were armed with guns but in no way adapted to war purposes, for they were easily disabled by a single shot. Even the firing of their own guns strained them seriously. It was a motley array of ships that sailed from Hampton Roads on the night of January 11, 1862, for Roanoke Island in order to secure for the Union navy control of Albemarle Sound. To those who knew the character of the boats it must have been no surprise that a number of them were lost in that expedition.[6] Armaments for the

---

[3] A. T. Mahan, *From Sail to Steam. Recollections of Naval Life* (New York and London, 1907), 34.

[4] For a table constructed from the explanations given by Maclay (*A History of the United States Navy*), see Appendix, Section I.

[5] Conspicuous were 1,200 fine guns, some of them new Dahlgrens, soon in use by the Confederates. David D. Porter, *The Naval History of the Civil War* (New York, 1866), 32. Among the vessels lost were the steam frigate *Merrimac*, soon to be converted by the Confederates into the ironclad *Virginia* (to avoid confusion, the author refers to this vessel throughout by its name as a Federal vessel); the sloops of war *Germantown* and *Plymouth*; the brig *Dolphin*; the unfinished ship of war *New York*; and a group of old ships valued by the country for their historical associations. *Ibid.*, 28.

[6] While entering the sound, the little steamer *Picket*, with General Burnside aboard, was almost crushed between two big vessels. On the way to Hatteras Inlet the old *Pocahontas* was

gunboats consisted of such cannon as could be picked up at the moment. Seven vessels mounting thirteen guns and constituting the gunboat fleet had been begun in August, 1861; by dint of constant labor day and night, seven days in the week, they had been launched and ready for their armament within less than a hundred days—hence the name "ninety-day gunboats." [7] In addition there were 38 mortar boats or rafts, each mounting one thirteen-inch mortar.

The greatest change in the navy, it is obvious, lay in the ironclads. France and England had long been experimenting with vessels clad with armor. The United States Navy Department in August, 1861, issued an advertisement for the construction of one or more ironclad steam vessels to carry an armament of eight 120-pounder guns and stores for a personnel varying from 185 to 300 persons. Discussion of the ironclads belongs to a later part of our story. [8]

This fleet was clearly designed mainly for blockade service, since weak vessels could blockade a Confederacy without a navy, but the paper blockade had to be backed up by actual ships. Speed was obviously the greatest factor against blockade-runners. At this point the South began to build a powerful ram to break up the blockade. Northern officers, in turn, urged construction of a ram and thus introduced another powerful feature, a naval battering ram. In March, 1862, after the converted *Merrimac* had demonstrated the efficacy of the ram, the government directed Colonel Charles Ellet, Jr., a civil engineer, to buy a number of river steamers and fit them out as rams. Ellet secured 7 side-wheelers and stern-wheelers; he strengthened their hulls with solid timber bulwarks and iron rods run through the hulls from side to side. Fitted out with light arms, their engines protected by bulkheads and cotton bales, these vessels in six weeks (by May 25) joined the squadron on the Mississippi under Captain Charles Henry Davis, who was in command of the gunboat fleet above

---

so injured that it had to be run ashore and, with its cargo of 113 horses, was lost. The *City of New York*, with valuable stores aboard, became a total wreck; the gunboat *Zouave* sank after crossing the bar. Maclay, *A History of the United States Navy*, II, 265–67.

[7] The vessels in the original gunboat fleet were the *De Kalb*, the *Carondolet*, the *Cincinnati*, the *Louisville*, the *Mound City*, the *Cairo*, and the *Pittsburgh*. Before their completion the snag boat *Benton* (of about one thousand tons) was converted into a formidable gunboat; the *Essex*, named after the famous vessel of the War of 1812, armed with seven guns, was also added to the group. *Ibid.*, 327–29. The *Essex* was commanded by David Porter, son of the Porter who later became admiral. *Ibid.*, 327.

Promptness in getting these vessels into service did much toward keeping alive the spirit of loyalty to the Union cause in the border state of Kentucky.

[8] This will be discussed in connection with the work of John Ericsson.

Fort Pillow.[9] Confederate and Union rams tilted against each other like knights of old, as their beaks drove into wooden hulls.

Gradually the few ships stationed at Union points in April, 1862, grew into a fleet of 300 to guard the thousands of miles of coast; the Union navy grew steadily year by year until by the close of 1864 the fleet totaled over 600 vessels.[10] In the course of the entire war 208 vessels were begun (most of which were completed), and well over 400 were purchased. The total sum spent by the Navy Department was over $314,000,000, or an annual average of $78,500,000. By the end of 1864, when the work of the navy during the Civil War had been substantially accomplished, the North had 671 vessels, with a few still under construction.[11]

The question of securing seamen to man the ships was just as grave a problem as securing the vessels themselves, a fact which becomes apparent with the simple statement that the number available at all the Union naval stations in April, 1861, totaled only 200. It is, perhaps, not too much to say that the personnel was moribund: one captain in command was nearly seventy years of age; the commandant at the Norfolk Navy Yard was sixty-eight.[12] The expansion in personnel was as rapid as that in vessels. In 1862 the average increase was 1,529 a month; by July, 1863, the number of seamen in service, including those on the Mississippi flotilla, was about 34,000, and during that year the increase averaged over 2,000 a month. Despite this marked increase, the demand for trained and experienced seamen was greatly in excess of the supply. The men enlisted were for the most part landsmen with little or no knowledge of seafaring

[9] Maclay, *A History of the United States Navy*, II, 360. As an antidote to too-great pride, someone should have pointed out to the Unionists of 1862—and possibly someone did—that Rome once fitted out an immense fleet ninety days after the timbers were trees standing in the forest. The city of Pisa built and equipped in forty-five days a fleet of 220 vessels to sail against the King of Syracuse. J. T. Headley, *Farragut and Our Naval Commanders* (New York, 1867), 35.

[10] Headley, *Farragut and Our Naval Commanders*, 45. The increase of United States ships year by year was impressive:

Date	No. vessels
July 4, 1861	82
December 1, 1861	264
December 1, 1862	427
December 7, 1863	588
December 1, 1864	671

Charles B. Boynton, *The History of the Navy during the Rebellion* (New York, 1867–1868), I, 139.

[11] Hosmer, *Outcome of the Civil War*, 185.

[12] French E. Chadwick, *Causes of the Civil War* (*The American Nation: A History*, XIX, New York, 1906), 164.

life, steamboat hands, or even soldiers transferred from the army. The chief cause for the deficiency of navy personnel was the high bounties paid for enlistment in the army, which tempted into the army many sailors whose service would have been much more valuable on the sea. Congress took steps to meet this situation by authorizing bounties for sailors and by providing for the transfer to the naval service of sailors who had enlisted in the army. As a result, the receiving ships were soon filled to overflowing.[13]

Fortunately some of the records of enlistments in the navy during the early weeks of the war have been preserved. Enlistments were regularly heavier at New York or in its immediate vicinity than elsewhere. For the week ending April 20, 1861, the record shows 145 men enlisted at Boston; [14] but, unfortunately, the figures for that date for New York and Philadelphia, cities which were comparable in size, are missing. The record for the following weeks shows a decided jump: 169 enlisted at Boston for the week ending April 27; [15] by the close of the second week in May, New York had rolled up a total of 355, the majority of these being old sailors with several years of experience; a slight drop in the number enrolling at the recruiting stations in the chief port brought the number down to 300 for the week ending June 1.[16] As early as April 23 a letter to H. B. Carrington, Adjutant General of Ohio, revealed an interesting situation within that state: "It may have escaped the notice of officers at Columbus, Ohio, that there are a number of well-drilled seamen scattered over the state who are mechanics and willing to leave their shops at a minute's warning if they can only know that they may surely enter in the actual service as seamen in the United States Navy immediately all they ask is to be conveyed to the seaboard and placed on board a Man of War Vessel without expense to themselves." [17]

[13] Tenny, *The Military and Naval History of the Rebellion in the United States*, 441. Secretary of the Navy Welles seems not to have been too enthusiastic over these transfers. On July 31, 1862, he wrote Commodore Wilkes, "If Gen. McClellan has any good men in his army whom he is willing to transfer to the navy, you can receive and ship them. The Department would, however, state that the Navy has not been particularly fortunate in receiving men from the Army. They are generally not of very good character and of little benefit to the service." *Naval Records*, Ser. 1, VII, p. 606.

[14] Enlistments—Rendezvous (Boston), for the week ending April 20, 1861 (Navy Branch, War Records Office, The National Archives).

[15] *Ibid.*, for the week ending April 27, 1861.

[16] New York *Courrier des États-Unis*, May 15, 1861.

[17] The writer then cites one case of an Englishman, Edward Fern, who had had three years of experience in the British navy in China. Executive Correspondence of the Governors of Ohio, April 16–24, 1861.

In his first call President Lincoln asked for 18,000 sailors. Officers of the navy were resigning in such numbers that the department was demoralized; 322 left to enter the Confederate navy, of which number 243 were officers of the line. To meet the need for officers, upperclassmen at Annapolis were assigned to active service. From along the coast and among the rivermen recruits hastened to the ships. To all competent men there readily came commissions to command and direct the ships which the government was chartering everywhere.[18] The total number of officers of all grades in the navy on August 1, 1861, was 1,457, a number manifestly inadequate; volunteer officers to the number of 7,500 enrolled before the close of the year. The expansion may perhaps be best grasped by noting the sharp contrast between 7,600 sailors at the opening of hostilities and 51,500 officers and sailors at the close of the war.[19]

The artisans and laborers, foreigners and natives, in navy yards and private establishments, increased in like proportion and were driven day and night. Men were not secured for the navy without effort. Witness the statement of Secretary of the Navy Gideon Welles to Flag Officer Louis M. Goldsborough on June 23, 1862: "Every exertion is being made to enlist men for the naval service. It is probable some time may elapse before the Department can comply with your requisition of the 20th instant." [20] As in the army, recruitment became more difficult as the war dragged on.

The question of enlisting sailors abroad arose fairly soon. Secretary of State Seward wrote Secretary Welles no later than December 12, 1862, as follows: "A dispatch has been received from Thomas Advance, Jr., Esquire, United States consul at Pernambuco, in which he states that he has frequent applications from able-bodied Seamen to enlist in the United States Naval Service—that he does not consider himself authorized to do so but will be very happy to receive and obey any instructions with which he may be charged.

"If his services can be properly so employed and it is your wish that

---

[18] An order of the Secretary of the Navy shows the need of officers. It related to the admission of volunteer line officers into the navy for temporary service. *Naval Records*, Ser. 1, VII, p. 592.

[19] Maclay, *A History of the United States Navy*, II, 226–27, gives 51,500, but Hosmer, *Outcome of the Civil War*, 185, gives 51,000. The Secretary of the Navy, in his report of December, 1865, gives the larger figure, which should be authoritative. *House Documents*, 39 Cong., 1 Sess., V, xiii.

[20] *Naval Records*, Ser. 1, VII, p. 498.

they should be, I will be pleased to instruct him to obey such directions as you may desire to give upon the subject." [21]

By 1863 many of the difficulties already noted in connection with alleged recruitments abroad for the Union army arose in connection with charges of enlisting Irishmen and Belgians for the navy.[22] Britain also complained that pressure was being exerted by United States officers on British seamen captured on blockade-runners—that in an effort to induce them to join the Federal navy, the United States officers were threatening them with imprisonment for the duration of the war.[23]

Despite the splendid and timely improvements in armaments by John A. Dahlgren, which will be noted later, few excellent guns of large caliber had been produced by the opening of the war. The paucity of efficient cannon in the possession of the Northern government in April, 1861, is surprising: on hand were 2,468 heavy guns (1,872 of which were 32-pounders of an obsolete pattern) and 557 light guns, also of an old pattern. There were only 305 nine-inch Dahlgrens and 32 eleven-inch guns of the same type. Unfortunately, many of the Dahlgren pieces were at Norfolk and hence were seized by the Confederates, while others were aboard the cruisers scattered in distant seas. The Navy Department actually had at its disposal about 50 efficient guns. Therefore, the government had not only to create ships but also to provide armaments and personnel with which to man the ships.[24]

Although none of the great naval commanders were born abroad, three of them were so directly descended from foreign-born Americans that the reader would scarcely pardon failure to indicate how great was the contribution of foreign blood to the naval record of the Civil War on the highest level—by Admirals Farragut, Dahlgren, and Du Pont.

Though Vice-Admiral David Glasgow Farragut, usually acclaimed the foremost naval hero of the war, was born near Knoxville, Tennessee, he was the son of a full-blooded Spaniard born in Minorca under the British flag in 1755. Farragut's father was, in addition, one of that list of knights-errant, which included Lafayette, Koskiusko, and Pulaski, who came to America in 1776 to espouse the cause of the infant republic. Later, early

[21] Instructions to Consuls, XXXIII, 15.

[22] See letters from the Confederate agent, Henry Hotze, to Secretary of State Benjamin of the Confederacy, *Naval Records*, Ser. 2, III, pp. 890, 965; for complaints of Belgian enlistments, see *ibid.*, 1159.

[23] Lyons to Seward, April 26, 1864, Notes from the British Legation, LXIII.

[24] Boynton, *The History of the Navy during the Rebellion*, I, 286–87.

in the nineteenth century, he entered the naval service of the United States; and subsequently he accompanied his friend, General Andrew Jackson, on his Indian campaign of 1813–1814.

Though the flag is the symbol of his country to every American citizen, the layman can probably never fully grasp the emotional attachment of the military officer to his flag. David Farragut had taken personal pride in the exploits of the *Essex* in the War of 1812, in which, for his years, he bore a distinguished part. He had seen the flag to which he bore allegiance emerge triumphant over the British jack; he had seen it float high and respected in many foreign ports. He had seen his comrades of the *Essex* give their lives at Valparaiso, in an engagement with two British ships, that Old Glory might not be hauled down. He had been aboard the man-of-war ordered to South Carolina by President Jackson during the Nullification controversy, and had, therefore, in a sense already taken sides on the issue of secession.

Half Spanish and half Southern (for Farragut's father had married a daughter of North Carolina), the great admiral was wholly Southern by family environment and had spent his early boyhood in the far South at New Orleans. Both of his wives came from Virginia, and he made his home at Norfolk. Yet this officer, high in rank and social status, immediately at the outbreak of war went North and applied for a position with the Union fleet.[25]

An analogous situation must be presented for Rear Admiral John Adolphus Dahlgren. He was born in Philadelphia in 1809, son of the Swedish-born Bernard Dahlgren, a graduate of the University of Upsala who had been driven from Sweden because of his effort to disseminate his republican principles and had settled in Philadelphia. The son received an appointment as midshipman in the navy, and his dream of a naval career was thus realized. In the course of the war, in response to his own request for active service, he was ordered to relieve Du Pont of the command of the South Atlantic Squadron and in that responsible position co-operated with the land forces in attacks on the Charleston defenses and in the capture of Savannah. However, Dahlgren's great service to the war was not in winning battles but in designing, casting, and improving arma-

[25] In view of Farragut's American nativity, no discussion of his service during the Civil War is regarded as necessary. Accounts of his career may be found in William Wood, *Captains of the Civil War* (*The Chronicles of America*, XXXI, New Haven, 1921), 94–96; Johnson and Malone (eds.), *Dictionary of American Biography*, VI, 286–91. The cruise of the *Essex* ended March 28, 1814, in the harbor of Valparaiso in an engagement with two British ships— the bloodiest engagement of Farragut's career.

ment. He developed the famous system of heavy ordnance. It was fortunate for the Union that his work began before the actual outbreak of war. Coldly received at first by the commandant at the Washington Navy Yard in 1847, he soon gained the confidence of his superior officer and within a few months was in charge of all ordnance matters at the yard. For sixteen years he gave to this work his inventive genius and extraordinary energy, with results which won him world recognition.[26] At that time there was no ordnance establishment; his suggestion introduced a workshop which became the foundation for an ordnance establishment to prove of tremendous importance to the country. The next few years saw the development of his "boat howitzer," a type of gun suited to both field and naval service; of several large guns of his own design, of solid cast iron, thick at the breach, and with smooth bores, which received the name of "Dahlgrens"; of rifled cannon adapted from the British guns; and, finally, of a bold and original plan of arming steam vessels of war. His plans were the practical application of results obtained by experiment. He introduced innovations which completely revolutionized the armament of the navy, annihilating by demonstration on a cruise the objection that eleven-inch guns were too heavy for use at sea. It is not too much to claim that Dahlgren during the decade preceding hostilities was laying the foundations for Union victory in the Civil War. By his inventive genius in the construction of ordnance and by his plan for arming steam vessels of war he did more for the navy probably than any other single person. He increased the destructive power of cannon fourfold.[27]

Rear Admiral Samuel F. Du Pont was, as his name suggests, of French

[26] When Franklin Buchanan, captain in command of the Washington Navy Yard, resigned to enter the Confederate service, Dahlgren was in command, although the law required the man holding this position to have the rank of captain. President Lincoln refused to place anyone over Dahlgren, basing his refusal on the eminent services of the inventor of our best cannon. Since this navy yard, because of its resources and strategic location, was the key to the defenses of Washington, this attitude was a measure of Lincoln's confidence in Dahlgren. The latter became captain on August 5, 1862 (the promotion to date from July 16), and reached the rank of rear admiral in February, 1863. Johnson and Malone (eds.), *Dictionary of American Biography*, V, 29–31.

[27] For further data on Dahlgren, see *ibid.* and Headley, *Farragut and our Naval Commanders*, 456–95, for a semiscientific discussion of his work.

Dahlgren's success is the more remarkable in that up to the time he went to the Washington Navy Yard he had never seen a gun cast or finished or even drafted, in that he had only the most primitive equipment with which to work, and in that he had to also devise a new, peculiar carriage for the gun. He achieved nothing less than the overthrow of the whole system of naval armament. He penetrated into the weaknesses of the British and French systems, which we had copied, and revealed to the world a system of his own.

extraction, his father and grandfather having migrated to this country at different dates. He himself was born in New Jersey in 1803, though he was taken at an early age by his parents first to New York State and then to Delaware. With public recollection of the French aid in the American Revolution still vivid, it was easy for the grandfather to obtain a midshipman's warrant for his grandson when Samuel had reached the ripe age of twelve. This was especially easy because this applicant for a favor to his grandson was a distinguished statesman and author. When young Du Pont was confronted with a choice between the navy and the army (for, owing to the influence of his grandfather's friend Jefferson with Madison, the President sent him also an appointment to West Point), he selected that branch which was most popular by virtue of the victories recently won over England on the sea. Shortly after the outbreak of the Civil War he was made senior member of a Commission of Conference to prepare plans for naval operations and to devise means for an effective blockade; one of the reports made by this commission recommended a naval base on the Carolina or the Florida coast. Relieved of his navy-yard appointment at Philadelphia and assigned to the command of the South Atlantic Blockading Squadron, the most important post in the gift of the Navy Department, he justified the confidence placed in him by quickly capturing Port Royal. This victory, after which Du Pont was rewarded with a rear admiral's commission, was followed by a series of continued successes along the coast. In addition, Du Pont maintained the blockade with a vigor not before manifested. The insistence by the Secretary of the Navy on the capture of Charleston (for this official held an exaggerated view of the efficacy of the monitors and assembled a fleet of them for Du Pont) wrecked the admiral's career,[28] as he suffered in his attack on Fort Sumter the worst naval defeat of the war. Having anticipated a brilliant victory, the North felt a great disappointment at his failure. The appraisal of experts seems to be that the average officer under similar circumstances would probably have failed; an officer with the audacity of a Farragut might conceivably have succeeded. It should be recalled that Dahlgren was unable to do what was expected of him when he succeeded Du Pont, and he concurred in the latter's views. The responsibility for the defeat

[28] Du Pont, sensitive because of the President's explicit order to hold his position off Charleston (issued April 3 and repeated April 14) requested Secretary Welles not to hesitate to relieve him with an officer more able to execute the service desired. This episode terminated not only Du Pont's active service for the remainder of the war, but also the active part of his naval career.

should undoubtedly have been shared by the Navy Department and not have been thrust wholly on Du Pont.

Du Pont's contribution to the Civil War came earlier, in the ten years preceding hostilities. In his tour of shore duty, 1848–1858, he was responsible for some of the most important improvements of the period in naval and marine affairs. He served on a board which recommended development of a naval academy, the first fruit of which was a group of trained officers for the impending war; and he discussed ably in a report on national defenses the effect of the application of steam to naval vessels.[29]

It is singular that the Northern navy should have been so indebted to Sweden for the great changes that were effected during, and just prior to, the war. It has been noted that a Swede of the second generation entirely revolutionized the armament of warships; John Ericsson, born in Sweden, gave his adopted country the monitors. Inevitably the man who made possible the defeat of the *Merrimac,* by fashioning for the Union in its hour of peril an instrument to shield its navy, must enter this story. The son of a mineowner, his earliest impressions were derived from the engines and machinery of the mines. Before 1814 (that is, at about the age of ten) he invented a miniature sawmill, and soon after, a novel pumping engine; these inventions undoubtedly helped his father win for him a cadetship in the Corps of Mechanical Engineers. After six months of study in the corps he was employed in the construction of the Gotha Canal, and laid out, when fourteen years old, the work for a section employing six hundred soldiers. In 1820 he entered the army, winning a lieutenant's commission through his skill in drawing. In London, on leave from the army, from which he severed his connection several years later, he entered upon his period of invention.[30] In 1839 he was induced by a captain of the United States Navy to come to this country to continue his experiments. Before 1861 he had a number of significant inventions to his credit, among others a screw steamer which in some respects foreshadowed his famous monitor.[31]

[29] A satisfactory article on Du Pont is found in Johnson and Malone (eds.), *Dictionary of American Biography,* V, 529–33; a more technical discussion is to be had in Headley, *Farragut and Our Naval Commanders,* 123–50.

[30] He became so absorbed in his work in England that he allowed his leave to expire without renewal, thus becoming technically a deserter; but friends cleared his record and even procured for him a promotion to a captaincy. Johnson and Malone (eds.), *Dictionary of American Biography,* VI, 173.

[31] Brown (ed.), *Lamb's Biographical Dictionary,* III, 1–2.

The monitor form of warship was an original invention, the embodiment of a fresh idea belonging to a high order of genius. Since battles, especially on the sea, are usually decided by the use of scientific machinery, the man who invents a weapon superior to those known before, shapes the character of an age. The idea of the monitor had been simmering in Ericsson's mind for nearly half a century. The concept had been suggested to him by the motions of the lumber rafts on the lakes in Sweden. "I found," he wrote in 1875, "that while the raftsman in his elevated cabin experienced very little motion, the seas breaking over his nearly submerged craft, these seas at the same time worked the sailing vessels nearly on their beam ends." [32] The inventor's enmity for Russia, the old-time foe of his native land, seems to have been his principal motive in developing this raft idea of naval warfare; and on the outbreak of the Crimean War he sent his plan of a monitor to Napoleon III. The emperor rejected the plan but adopted the idea of armor defense and built five ironclads. From that time both England and France looked toward the development of armored ships.

The idea of armored ships had taken stronger root in the South than in the North, with the result that the partially burned and sunk *Merrimac,* which the Confederates had raised from the Norfolk Navy Yard was converted into an ironclad and renamed the *Virginia.* The reports concerning this Confederate armored ship caused Federal authorities much anxiety. A board appointed to study the type of vessel best suited to meet the Confederate dreadnought recommended construction of three armored vessels, of which the *Monitor* was one.[33] Ericsson had already sent Lincoln

[32] Stated in a letter to Gustavus Vasa Fox, Assistant Secretary of the Navy, October 5, 1875, and quoted by Maclay, *A History of the United States Navy,* II, 300–301. Maclay must have had access to the unpublished correspondence of Fox, only portions of which appear in the two volumes published by the Naval History Society. It is possible that this letter may be in the Blair Papers, now preserved in the Manuscript Division of the Library of Congress, but not yet arranged or classified when this book was written, as the Fox Papers were turned over to the children of Francis Blair before the publication of the two volumes by the Naval History Society.

[33] The three members of the Naval Board appointed by President Lincoln to examine plans for ironclads showed rare courage, for the weight of professional experience and prejudice was against them. Furthermore, Ericsson had invented some notable failures, from a practical point of view, and had been unjustly associated with the bursting of the twelve-inch gun on the *Princeton,* which had caused the death of several prominent members of the government in 1844. If the vessels they endorsed proved failures, the odium would fall on the members of the Board. Two members agreed to sign a report advising the building of one trial battery on Ericsson's model if Captain Charles F. Davis (also a member of the Board) would join them. Davis' answer is a gem: He told C. S. Bucknell, who, as Ericsson's representative, had brought the plan to Washington, that he "might take the little thing home and worship it, as it

a memorandum, offering to construct a vessel "for the destruction of the rebel fleet" at Norfolk. With the aid of private capital, within the space of a hundred days from the laying of the keel, Ericsson built and equipped the *Monitor* at a cost of $275,000, to be paid by the government only after the boat had proved effective in battle with the *Merrimac*. The *Monitor* was small, an iron-plated raft only 172 feet in length by 41½ feet in beam, with less than 2 feet of the hull above the water, the target surface thus being reduced to a minimum. A distinctive feature was the circular, revolving turret, a heavily armored and protected gun position, not conceived by Ericsson but vindicated by his adoption. The guns were few but large, more powerful than anything aboard the *Merrimac;* the power was steam, applied through the screw propeller. Ericsson chose the name, which became the name for an entire class of vessels, because, as he said,

> The impregnable and aggressive character of this structure will admonish the leaders of the Southern rebellion that the batteries on the banks of their rivers will no longer prevent the entrance of Union forces. The ironclad intruder will thus prove a severe monitor to those leaders. But there are other leaders who will also be startled and admonished by the booming of the guns from the impregnable iron turret. "Downing Street" will hardly view with indifference this last "Yankee notion," this monitor. To the Lords of the Admiralty the new craft will be a monitor, suggesting doubts as to the propriety of completing those four steel-clad ships at three and a half millions apiece.[34]

The story of the battle of the ironclads, or the test of Ericsson's idea versus the Confederate idea, does not need to be retold here. There are no revisions to be made of the account, no new details to be added. Due allowance may be made for the fact that the *Merrimac* withdrew on the evening of March 9 undefeated and with the expectation of renewing the battle the next day, and yet the victory remains with Ericsson's small craft, as is pointed out in Maclay's keen analysis.

The *Merrimac,* which went into battle with the avowed purpose of destroying the remaining ships in Hampton Roads (having destroyed the *Cumberland* and the *Congress* on March 8), assumed the offensive;

---

would not be idolatry, because it was in the image of nothing in the heavens above, or on the earth beneath, or in the waters under the earth." Maclay, *A History of the United States Navy*, II, 301–302. However, Davis did sign the recommendation.

[34] *Ibid.*, II, 305–306. Stated in a letter to Assistant Secretary Fox. This original also may be in the Blair Papers.

the *Monitor,* on the contrary, assumed a defensive position, entering the Roads with the purpose of preventing the destruction of the rest of the Union ships. At evening the *Merrimac* withdrew, foiled in her purpose, while the *Monitor* had achieved hers. On the morning of March 9 the *Merrimac* was mistress of the situation; at eve the *Monitor* was mistress. Furthermore, the *Merrimac* was so badly damaged that she had to remain in dock for repairs, whereas her antagonist was practically uninjured. The above statements seem sound, even though we admit all the weaknesses of the *Monitor* and recall the fact that she foundered the following December in a gale off Cape Hatteras.[35] The *Minnesota* had been saved on March 8 only by the great draught of the *Merrimac* and the setting-in of ebb tide. The *Monitor* could play around her opponent and maneuver all over the surrounding shallows. The giant put her last ounce of steam into an effort to ram the pigmy foe, but with a touch of the pilot's hand the helm of the *Monitor* swung around in time to make the blow harmless. The *Merrimac* barged into her foe but only grated harmlessly against her iron sides and then sheared off, foiled.

The actual conflict may be called a drawn battle, and yet it had all the effect of a great Union victory. March 8, which witnessed the sinking of the *Cumberland* and the *Congress,* was probably the darkest day of the war for the Union, since all hope of McClellan's success in his Peninsular campaign turned on command of Hampton Roads by the navy. To supply the army on the Peninsula without control of the adjacent waters would have been impossible. The Confederacy won no other victory with such brilliant hopes of ultimate victory as that of the *Merrimac* on March 8. The entire destruction of the Union navy, defeat of the army movement against Richmond, raising of the blockade, recognition of the Confederacy in Europe—all seemed within reach. Nothing stood between the Confederacy and her hopes except the gigantic "cheese-box." The *Monitor,* one-fourth the size of her antagonist and equipped with only two guns,

---

[35] These disadvantages are pointed out in Wood, *Captains of the Civil War,* 88. Some of the disadvantages of the *Monitor* were that the sailors had to be stowed away for days in an iron box under water with artificial light and ventilation and without opportunity for exercise, that the accumulated smells of kitchen and engine room were insufferable, and that the superstructure was open to criticism. One recalls instantly the complaints against the submarine in its early days. Maclay, *History of the United States Navy,* II, 304–306.

Porter believed that if Lieutenant Worden, in command of the *Monitor,* had not been forbidden to use double charges of the steel shot because the eleven-inch guns might burst with more than fifteen pounds of powder, he could have pierced the *Merrimac's* armor and forced her surrender. It was proved later that the Dahlgrens could stand twenty-five pounds of powder. Porter, *The Naval History of the War,* 130, 133.

wrought on March 9 a revolution in naval warfare. The Confederacy could not convert its unwieldy ironclads in time to meet the fleet of monitors soon ready. That day settled for the period of the Civil War the question of broadside ironclads as decisively as the preceding day had settled the question of wooden ships.

To Ericsson goes the credit for designing the ship with all its parts; but to her commanders, Lieutenant John L. Worden and (after Worden's injury) Lieutenant Samuel D. Greene, to First Assistant Engineer Isaac Newton, and to her picked crew of volunteers must go full credit for knightly courage in embarking on what must have seemed on the morning of March 9 a forlorn hope. The success of the *Monitor* brought a significant change in position to Ericsson, whose relations with the Navy Department had often been strained. He was now hailed as a public benefactor. The name of Swede became highly honorable. Ericsson and his associates during the remainder of the war were busy designing and constructing a considerable fleet of monitors, larger units incorporating the changes dictated by experience. He received the thanks of Congress and of the New York legislature, was made a member of the American Philosophical Society, and was the recipient of honorary degrees, medals, and decorations from many countries to a degree that has seldom been accorded to anyone in his field.[36]

We have seen that the Federal government was chary in bestowing the highest ranks in the army on foreigners; it was perhaps even more so with the highest rank in the navy. It is true that a few of the admirals, Farragut, Dahlgren, and Du Pont, represented foreign blood of only the second generation; still the statement must stand that the rank of admiral, created during the war, was accorded only to the native-born with but one exception— Rear Admiral Stephen C. Rowan. Born near Dublin in Ireland, Rowan had while still a child accompanied his parents to the United States and settled with them in Ohio. He was given an appointment as midshipman in 1826 and attached to the first United States ship of war to encircle the globe in a four-year cruise. He came up the hard way. He saw service in the naval operations of the Seminole War and shared actively in the naval engagements of the Mexican War, in one of which he was

[36] In addition to Johnson and Malone (eds.), *Dictionary of American Biography*, V, 173–76, and Brown (ed.), *Lamb's Biographical Dictionary*, III, 1–2, the following may be consulted with profit: Boynton, *The History of the Navy during the Rebellion*, I, 374–76; Wood, *Captains of the Civil War*, 85–91; and Maclay, *A History of the United States Navy*, II, 300–307. Porter, *The Naval History of the War*, 119–33, presents a contemporaneous view, which lacks the perspective of the present.

wounded. By 1855 he had attained the rank of commander. In January, before the outbreak of war, he applied for active service, as he was then on ordnance duty and was assigned to the *Pawnee*, a ship which afforded the chief naval protection to Washington. In the first naval engagement of the war, he had a brush with Confederate forces erecting a battery at Aquia Creek. He commanded a flotilla in the expedition to the Sounds of North Carolina and received the thanks of Congress for distinguished service in the reduction of the Carolina coast. Rowan was for a period in command of the North Atlantic fleet. By July, 1862, he had reached a captaincy, undoubtedly as a reward for his work off North Carolina. The next year he was assigned to the command of the *New Ironsides* in the South Atlantic Squadron, with which he participated in the capture of Morris Island and repeatedly engaged the forts in Charleston Harbor. The rank of commodore followed in July, 1863, dating back to 1862; that of rear admiral came only in 1866, but so soon after the conclusion of the war and so clearly as a result of his war activity as to justify his classification as admiral in this discussion.[37]

The research revealed only one foreign-born commodore; he also hailed from Ireland but had entered the service from Maryland in 1815. T. Aloysius Dornin was thus a seaman of forty-five years experience when the Civil War began, and he commanded the steamer *San Jacinto* as captain. The next year he appeared on the rolls with the rank of commodore, but with advancing age he was relegated to the command of the naval station at Baltimore, which post he was still filling in 1865, though he was then on the retired list.[38] The rank of captain was held by no one of foreign birth other than, as earlier noted, as a steppingstone to higher rank. Even the list of commanders is a short one. Probably the most interesting of these to the modern reader is George M. Colvocoressis, as Greek as his name, who attained this rank only after many years in lower position, having entered the navy in 1832 from Vermont. The second commander was Benjamin J. Totten (an Englishman by descent, judging from his

[37] See Johnson and Malone (eds.), *Dictionary of American Biography*, XVI, 196–97; *The National Cyclopaedia of American Biography*, II, 101; W. H. Powell and Edward Shippen (comps.), *Officers of the Army and Navy (Regular) Who Served in the Civil War* (Philadelphia, 1892), 35; Headley, *Farragut and Our Naval Commanders*, 401–15. The New York *Irish-American* naturally noticed an Irish commander. See issue of April 5, 1862.

[38] *Appletons' American Annual Cyclopaedia*, 1865, p. 91; *Register of the Commissioned and Warrant Officers of the Navy of the United States, Including Officers of the Marine Corps and Others*, for the years 1861–1865 (Washington, 1861–1865), 1861, p. 16; 1863, p. 14; 1865, p. 14. This work is referred to hereinafter as *Navy Register*. There seems not to have been sufficient interest in Dornin to secure his inclusion in Powell and Shippen's compilation.

name), whose family had wandered to the West Indies. He had appeared in New York in time to enlist in the navy by 1823, so that in his last years of service he was assigned to the relatively easy post of commandant of the receiving ship at Norfolk and then of the Naval Rendezvous at New Bedford.[39]

The two men listed as lieutenant commander present a problem. The fact that Reigart B. Lowry was born at the consulate at La Guayra in Venezuela leads the researcher to deduce the fact that he was the son of an American citizen and hence himself an American citizen. This deduction is strengthened by the ease with which he made a career for himself in the navy. Entering the navy as midshipman in 1840, he rose by July, 1862, to the post of lieutenant commander, in which rank he served through the remainder of the war.

The other lieutenant commander, George A. Bigelow, also bears an American name, though he had been born in France; he was not, as might readily be surmised from the similarity of their names, a son of the American minister to France.

When we reach the rank of lieutenant, we find, from first to last, four foreign-born recorded, and in addition fifteen officers entered as acting volunteer lieutenants—four Englishmen, two West Indians, two Canadians, one German, one Hollander, one Scotchman, one South American, one Irishman, one Austrian, and one Sicilian. Since there was great demand for volunteer officers during the war, it is logical to assume that these men listed during 1865 were added to the rolls while the war was still in progress.

The four lieutenants of the regular navy merit closer attention. George Worthington Wood, an Irishman from Dublin, was appointed a midshipman from Pennsylvania at the age of sixteen. Remaining at the naval academy until the outbreak of war, he was sent to the frigate *St. Lawrence* with the North Atlantic Squadron. In 1862 he was attached to the steam sloop *Oneida,* a ship which on several occasions was detailed to draw the fire of the forts and batteries below New Orleans from the mortar vessels which were then blockading the forts. He was with the fleet when it passed the forts, at the destruction of the Confederate flotilla, and at the capture of the Chalmette batteries. He participated in the capture of Natchez, in an engagement at Vicksburg, in the battle with the ironclad *Arkansas,* and

[39] For Colvocoressis, see *Navy Register,* 1862, p. 15; 1863, p. 20; 1864, p. 20. For Totten, see *ibid.,* 1861, p. 20; 1862, p. 15. Totten's birthplace is recorded as having been the West Indies.

later in the attack on the Vicksburg batteries when the Union fleet passed down the river. He served in the North Atlantic Squadron as ensign until February, 1864, when he was commissioned lieutenant.[40] George W. Harrison, born in the West Indies, was appointed to the navy in 1828; Samuel W. Preston, a Canadian who enlisted in 1859, became a prisoner of war in 1864; and John W. Kelly, ten years a sailor before the mast before he became a commissioned officer, was another of the many Irishmen who served the Union flag. To give some conception of relative numbers it might be stated that among the 331 lieutenants in 1861, only three were not natives.[41]

Worthy of special comment among the fifteen acting volunteer lieutenants of the war period was Henry H. Gorringe, son of a Church of England clergyman in Barbados. He came to the United States at an early age and entered the merchant marine, but in 1862 he enlisted as a common sailor. He was sent to the Mississippi, there to remain during the entire war and to participate in nearly all the important battles of the Mississippi Squadron. For gallantry in battle and able seamanship he won remarkable advancement, so that he ranked by 1865 as acting volunteer lieutenant.[42] A second person worthy of mention is Charles O'Neil, one of the many Englishmen who entered the navy in a lowly position and rose to a post of some rank. He entered as master's mate in July, 1861, aboard the *Cumberland,* to which vessel he was attached during the disastrous engagement with the ironclad *Merrimac* on March 8, 1862. To his credit is recorded the rescue of Lieutenant George U. Morris from drowning on that occasion. This, naturally, brought him the favorable notice of his superior officer, and as a result he won promotion to the position of acting master. From the close of 1862 to July, 1864, he was attached to the gunboat *Tioga,* and cruised with a special West Indian squadron. He shared in both attacks on Fort Fisher and attracted attention, so that

[40] Powell and Shippen (comps.), *Officers of the Army and Navy (Regular)*, 472.

[41] George Harrison appears in the *Navy Register*, 1861, p. 26; for Kelly, see *ibid.*, 1861, p. 52; 1862, p. 21; 1863, p. 32; and 1864, p. 32; for Preston, see *ibid.*, 1863, p. 34; and 1865, p. 34; Wood appears only in the *Register* for 1865, p. 34.

[42] For Gorringe, see Powell and Shippen (comps.), *Officers of the Army and Navy (Regular)*, 171; *The National Cyclopaedia of American Biography*, VI, 439. His chief claim to public notice was his connection with the transportation and erection of the Egyptian obelisk in Central Park, New York, presented to the United States by Khedive Ismail. The *Navy Register* records his place of birth as New York, but in the light of all other statements this would appear in error. He received his appointment to this rank promptly after the close of the war in July, 1865.

just after the close of hostilities he was promoted to the rank of acting volunteer lieutenant.[43]

For the rank of master or acting master the records show no proportional increase in the number of foreign-born comparable with the increase in the total number of this rank. In 1861 there appear to have been three of the rank of master who had been born under another flag. The proportion to the native-born is what is important; since there were, in all, 46 of this rank, the 3 foreign-born constituted about 7 per cent. It is disappointing that the *Navy Register* offers no lists of masters for 1862 or 1863 which show nativity.[44] For the year 1864, moreover, it contains only a list of acting volunteer masters, but a goodly number of foreign-born are recorded thereon. Including those in the Mississippi Squadron, there were 34 alien-born in a total of 510, or, again, about 7 per cent. For 1865 the number remains almost constant, with many of the same names recurring; but since the war ended early in that year, the record for the preceding year seems the more desirable as a standard. Of the names thereon, two are sufficiently interesting to single out for mention. James M. Forsyth was born in the Bahamas but came to Philadelphia when only eleven years old. At the age of fifteen he went to sea in the merchant service; in August, 1861, at nineteen he entered the navy as a volunteer, becoming a pilot for the Hatteras expedition. By September he was already acting master's mate; and he served through the war in various grades in the blockading squadrons, was present in engagements under Farragut, and emerged from the war as acting master. Although the name of Abraham Christian occurs in none of the compilations, he is interesting as typical of the class of faithful Norwegians to whom promotion could not be denied. He first appeared on the rolls in 1863 as acting master, but the next year he was in command of the schooner *Sarah Bruen*. Though he attained the rank of acting volunteer lieutenant, the appointment was revoked in 1865 after the need for officers had passed.[45]

[43] For O'Neil, see *Navy Register* and Lewis R. Hamersly (comp.), *The Records of Living Officers of the U.S. Navy and Marine Corps* (3d ed.; Philadelphia, 1878), 195–96. The other acting volunteer lieutenants, with place of birth, were Charles H. Brown (South America), Howard Cavendy (England), William L. Cheesman (England), Henry J. Coop (Sicily), Martin Freeman (Germany), H. A. Glassford (Canada), Thomas B. Gregory (Canada), John Mc-Dearmid (Scotland), William McGloin (Ireland), John Pearce (England), Thomas Pickering (West Indies), John Rogers (England), and Gustave Vassalo (Austria).

[44] For 1863 there is printed a long list of acting masters with the ship on which each was serving, but there is no hint of place of birth.

[45] For Forsyth, in addition to the *Navy Register*, 1864, p. 128, see Powell and Shippen

There remain to be considered in this group only the ensigns and the midshipmen. Since most men in these two lowest ranks of commissioned officers were graduates of the naval academy or students ordered into active service, the foreign-born were represented only by the occasional child of foreign parents who somehow had won an appointment to Annapolis—an occasional Englishman, German, or Irishman. By far the most interesting in this group was Ensign Pierre d'Orleans, otherwise known as the Duke of Penthièvre (a scion of the D'Orleans branch of the Bourbon line, though a British citizen), who had entered the naval academy in October, 1861, graduated in 1863, and been commissioned as ensign. D'Orleans resigned, however, in May, 1864.[46] In addition to regular ensigns there were volunteer acting ensigns created by the dozen—until in 1864 the *Navy Register* showed 96 foreign-born of many climes in a total of 725, or less than 13 per cent. In the Mississippi Squadron alone there were 20 of foreign birth in this classification in a group of 167, or 12.5 per cent.[47]

Among the engineers of all classes (chief engineers and first, second, and third assistant engineers) a goodly number of foreign-born might be expected. It is conspicuous that there were throughout the war years nine chief engineers, including acting engineers, of foreign birth, all but one, a negligible percentage of the entire number, being from the British Isles. Moreover, the proportion of foreign-born assistant engineers, without regard to classification, was less than 5 per cent in 1861. The total number of assistant engineers rose sharply in the second year of the war to over 1,000; the number of foreign-born rose, however, only slightly, so that the proportion sank to slightly over 2 per cent. By 1864 the total had declined but the proportion of foreigners had risen to about 7 per cent. If the acting engineers were to be added to the record for 1864, the total would mount to over 1,300, but the representation of nonnatives would fall to just over one per cent.[48] A few names in this group should be rescued from oblivion in view of the tremendous importance of their jobs in the

(comps.), *Officers of the Army and Navy (Volunteer)*, 153; for the revoking of Christian's appointment, see *Navy Register*, 1865, p. 221.

[46] *Ibid.*, 1863, p. 78; 1864, p. 36, for his rank of ensign; and 1865, p. 116, for his resignation. For a brief sketch, see *Appletons' Cyclopaedia of American Biography*, IV, 590. See also Chapter XI of text.

[47] *Navy Register*, 1864, pp. 128–29; for the Mississippi Squadron, *ibid.*, 139–42.

[48] The rank of paymaster is passed over because the number of foreign-born paymasters was negligible. This is not surprising, as it was entirely natural that for this position, which would carry relatively high rank—even that of commander—the Navy Department should seek native Americans.

fleet. Joseph Trilley, another son of the Emerald Isle, who served from 1860 through the war, experienced a tremendous amount of danger in the hold of the *Pawnee* on the Potomac and from Hatteras Inlet to Fernandino; on the *Monongahela* in the West Gulf Blockading Squadron, where his vessel was engaged in constant fighting to keep open communications to New Orleans; in convoying General Banks's expedition to the Rio Grande; and in the capture of forts on Mobile Bay. Cipriano Andrade, born in Tampico, Mexico, gained his experience as engineer in one of the ships in the Pacific Squadron, protecting the Isthmus of Panama and cruising in search of Confederate privateers; in the Atlantic Squadron in an attack on a Charleston battery; and on the Savannah River in co-operation with the Georgia campaign of General Sherman. John Lowe, from Liverpool originally, was distinguished for serving both in the army (with the Second Ohio Regiment at the First Battle of Bull Run) and in the navy (on several gunboats). A Prussian, Eugene H. C. Leutze, entered the naval academy in 1863 and during the summer of 1864, while on leave, volunteered for active service on the *Monticello* in the North Atlantic Squadron.[49]

Among the warrant officers (not requiring confirmation by the Senate and corresponding to the noncommissioned officers of the army), investigation has revealed that the number born in foreign lands was larger than it was among the commissioned officers. Of boatswains one notes during the war years 11 foreign-born, their proportion to natives varying roughly from 11 to 16 per cent, the smaller proportion being in 1864; of gunners, roughly a proportion of one tenth to one eighth were made up of various nationalities. The number of foreigners employed in the navy as carpenters or sailmakers was negligible. One carpenter from Prince Edward Island was listed in 1861; and an Irishman, in 1862; 2 aliens, a Frenchman and a Canadian, served as sailmakers during the war years.[50] The record is changed only slightly, and not at all proportionately, when the acting gunners, the carpenters, and the sailmakers are added.

To make complete the record of the armed forces serving the Union, attention should be drawn to the fact that not one single officer of the Marine Corps during the Civil War years appears to have been foreign-born. This is the more striking in view of the fact that the Marine Corps

[49] For Trilley, see Hamersly (comp.), *The Records of Living Officers of the U.S. Navy and Marine Corps* (7th ed.; Philadelphia, 1902), 62; for Leutze, *ibid.*, 134; for Lowe, *ibid.* (3d ed., 1878), 306; for Andrade, *ibid.* (3d ed.), 90. After the war Andrade reached the rank of captain, Lowe, the rank of rear admiral.

[50] The data on warrant officers has been compiled from the *Navy Registers*.

before the war was composed largely of Southern men and consequently lost its full quota of officers by resignation or dismissal at the opening of hostilities, so that replacements were badly needed.

The chaplains and the surgeons would be entitled by their rank to consideration before the warrant officers and, indeed, before some of the commissioned officers. However, they are such a distinctive group that it seems desirable to set them apart.[51] Two chaplains call for comment: one, a Greek named Photius Fisk, was appointed from New York as early as 1842 and served throughout the war; the second, Charles W. Thomas, was a Welshman who entered the service seven years before the guns resounded at Fort Sumter. The former was not an adherent of the Greek Orthodox faith but a Congregational clergyman; as to the religion of the latter, the guess that a Welshman was a Baptist or a Methodist might prove well founded.[52] If the number of foreigners among chaplains seems limited, the same was not true of surgeons after the first year of war. It is true that the record shows only 2 in a total of 79 in 1861, but by 1864 the total number had increased to 174, of whom 18 (or about 11 per cent) were foreign-born. It is possible to compute 36 alien-born who served as naval surgeons during the entire war period; the list of such surgeons remained remarkably stable through 1862–1863, and a few alien-born surgeons served throughout the war.[53]

Typical of the kind of service rendered by these surgeons was the record of Dr. Christopher J. Cleborne. Though born in Scotland, he was graduated from the University of Pennsylvania in 1860. In May, 1861, he was appointed assistant surgeon with rank of master and assigned to a sloop of war in the North Atlantic Squadron. He saw service on several ships of war; he was present at the destruction of a Confederate vessel at the batteries of Fernandina; and he served in the expedition to Stone River and in the engagements on the South Edisto, at the operations of Mobile in 1863, and at both battles of Fort Fisher in December, 1864, where his vessel, the *Ticonderoga,* was lost by the bursting of her Parrott gun.

[51] No distinction between surgeons and assistant surgeons is felt necessary here.

[52] The reader need not be left in doubt about Photius Fisk. His Greek name, Kavasales, was legally changed in 1840 to that of his benefactor, the Reverend Photius Fisk, through whose influence he was educated, brought to the United States, and graduated from Auburn Theological Seminary into the Congregational ministry. He received appointment as chaplain in the United States Navy in 1842. Oddly enough, he accumulated a fortune and filled the role of philanthropist to the poor of Boston. Brown (ed.), *Lamb's Biographical Dictionary of the United States,* III, 103.

[53] The *Navy Register* had to be depended upon chiefly for the data on the chaplains and surgeons.

Finally, he was on duty at the bombardment and capture of Fort Fisher in early 1865. His presence aboard ship in so many engagements attests his service to the wounded.[54]

Finally comes consideration of the crews on the vessels, the rank and file of the navy. Naturally, no attempt has been made to examine the personnel on each of the war vessels, but selections have been made carefully so as to include samples of various types of naval craft. Conspicuous among the steam sloops of war was the *Hartford,* Farragut's flagship. In a crew of 324 no less than 216, or more than two thirds, were foreign-born as of March 31, 1863. Although Ireland, with 84 sailors, and England, with 36, provided a considerable proportion of the crew, the researcher was impressed by the widespread representation of many countries. While the size of the crew varied relatively little during 1864, the proportion of foreigners decreased early in that year to one third. The representation on the steam sloop *Brooklyn,* a warship of over 2,000 tons burden, was very similar.[55] It should be remarked that these totals include petty officers, seamen, ordinary seamen, apprentices, firemen, and coal heavers, and musicians—where the vessel had them. Du Pont's flagship, the *Wabash,* though classified as a steam frigate, along with its sister ship, the *Colorado,* was larger than the *Hartford* or the *Brooklyn* and was regarded as too large for coastal waters. Its size was reflected in the unusually large number of the crew—575; of this number, 224, or about 42 per cent, were foreign-born as of October 1, 1862. In December, one year later, the proportion had risen to over one half, but by October, 1864, it had sunk to nearer one third. On March 1, 1863, the crew actually numbered 775.[56] Other steam frigates sampled were the *Niagara* and the *Minnesota.* The first-named vessel in June, 1864, carried a crew of 559, of whom 278 (or almost exactly half) were alien-born, this being the largest number of aliens recorded at any time on her muster roll; the crew of the *Minnesota* numbered 628, of whom 226 (or over one third) had originally come from foreign lands.[57]

The crews aboard some of the ironclads should be noted: the crew of the *New Ironsides* varied only slightly in number from 400 during 1863

[54] Hamersly (comp.), *The Records of Living Officers* (3d ed.), 351; Powell and Shippen (comps.), *Officers of the Army and Navy* (*Regular*), 86.

[55] See Muster Roll H, for the *Hartford,* and Muster Roll B, for the *Brooklyn.* Muster Rolls, I, Navy Branch, War Records Office.

[56] For the *Wabash,* see Muster Roll W, *ibid.,* I; for the *Colorado,* see Muster Roll C, *ibid.,* I.

[57] For the *Niagara,* see Muster Roll N, *ibid.,* VII; for the *Minnesota,* see Muster Roll M, *ibid.,* VII.

and 1864, the proportion of foreigners ranging from one seventh to one half—often one third.[58] Scrutiny of the *Galena* and the *Weehawken* yielded similar results. Though the total number of the crew on each of these ships was smaller, an average of about 140 for the former and 70 for the latter, the number of the foreign-born varied from one fourth to more than one half.[59] Study of the gunboats *Wissahickon, Conestoga* (a wooden gunboat), *Sassacus, Aroostook,* and *Unadilla* indicates small crews, averaging only 84 or 86 men, except on the *Sassacus,* a double-ender which carried an average of around 146 men. With the exception of the *Wissahickon* and the *Sassacus,* on each of which the proportion of foreigners mounted to two thirds at one period, the relation approached more nearly one half than one third. On the *Powhatan,* an early side-wheeler, the proportion ran usually between one third and one half.[60] A quick glance at the crews of the brig *Bainbridge* and the bark *Brazileira* only produces more evidence of the same proportion on these two types of vessels.[61] Special interest attaches to the crew of the *Kearsarge,* which destroyed the Confederate privateer *Alabama* off Cherbourg on June 19, 1864; on the former rather more than one fourth of the crew had been born under an alien flag. The action was distinguished on the part of the *Kearsarge* for excellent gunnery.[62]

The comments in an earlier chapter on the vast variety of nationalities represented in the army could be repeated here for the navy. Nearly every country on the face of the globe was represented. Some nationalities were present in larger numbers than others. The presence of Englishmen and Irishmen is hardly surprising in view of Great Britain's dominance of the sea. The Scandinavian countries were well represented, considering their numbers in the homelands. Germans were present in goodly, even striking, numbers, as on the *Wabash,* but in no such overwhelming dominance

[58] The record was computed for January 1, April 1, July 1, and December 1, 1863; for April 1 and October 16, 1864; and for January 1, 1865. See Muster Roll N, *ibid.,* VI.

[59] See Muster Roll G, *ibid.,* I, for the *Galena;* Muster Roll W, *ibid.,* V, for the *Weehawken.* On March 31, 1863, the record showed forty alien-born in a crew of sixty-nine on the *Weehawken.*

[60] See Muster Roll W, *ibid.,* V, for the *Wissahickon;* Muster Roll C, *ibid.,* XV, for the *Conestoga;* Muster Roll A, *ibid.,* XV, for the *Aroostook;* Muster Roll U, *ibid.,* I, for the *Unadilla;* Muster Roll S, *ibid.,* XI, for the *Sassacus;* Muster Roll P, *ibid.,* XVI, for the *Powhatan.*

[61] On the *Bainbridge,* both in November, 1862, and in May, 1863, the proportion hovered around one third. Muster Roll B, *ibid.,* I. For the *Brazileira,* sampled for March, 1863, and December, 1864, the proportion showed one fourth and one third, respectively. Muster Roll B, *ibid.,* IV.

[62] See Muster Roll K, *ibid.,* II, for the *Kearsarge.*

as in the army. On the whole, France, Spain, and Italy were meagerly represented. Names of remote or obscure bits of land appear, as they do on the army muster rolls. One striking fact was that even if there was a considerable aggregation of one of two nationalities on a particular vessel, there was also always a wide diversity. On the *Colorado,* twenty-nine different nationalities rubbed elbows; on the *Hartford,* twenty-five; and on the *Minnesota,* twenty-six.

Great variation in age existed among these foreign-born seamen—from the sixteen-year-old lads to the fifty-year-old-men, the latter usually men who had grown gray in the service. While one finds a generous sprinkling of men in their forties, the greater number were in their twenties or thirties. Members of the crews, while occasionally recording farming as their occupation, were usually, as in the army, drawn from the humbler trades. Not infrequently a recruit recorded himself as "marriner," indicating that he had followed the sea from his youth.[63]

Not the least interesting of the occupational groups in the Union navy was the handful of musicians to be found on some of the vessels. The largest number of these encountered was that on the *Brooklyn,* where there were no fewer than 19 musicians on April 6, 1863; none appear on the roll from May 10 to December 1, 1864, when they reappear 27 strong. The *Niagara* boasted 5 musicians in November, 1863, and only 4 in June, 1864, but of this group, for whom nationality is given, only one had been born abroad—a Frenchman. Oddly enough, there is a record of 6 musicians on the smaller sloop *Powhatan.*[64]

Cognizance should be taken of another group of foreigners who served the fleet, though they were in no sense a part of it—a group of German woodchoppers. Nikolas Rusch, one of the ablest Germans of the West, who rose to be lieutenant governor of Iowa, gathered a group of German immigrants who were incapable of military service and welded them into a corps of woodchoppers. They felled and transported the wood for the Union fleet on the Mississippi but were under sufficient military discipline that they could with their weapons ward off the guerrilla bands of the foe. Providing the cannon boats with the requisite fuel was obviously of the greatest importance; themselves incapable of combat, they made it possible for combatants to fight and win victories.[65]

[63] The data with regard to age are drawn from the Muster Rolls of the various vessels; those with regard to occupation, from the descriptive lists in the Muster Rolls.

[64] Muster Roll B (the *Brooklyn*) and Muster Roll N (the *Niagara*), Muster Rolls, VII, for the indicated dates; Muster Roll P (the *Powhatan*), *ibid.,* XVI.

[65] Kaufmann, *Die Deutschen im Bürgerkriege,* 544.

The great service of the navy and of the men who served aboard the fleet in helping to win the war for the Union has been given full recognition only slowly by the layman. It was possible to evaluate the contribution of alien elements in many battles fought by the army, as the foreign-born —at least, the Germans and Irish—were there organized in battalions, regiments, and even divisions. This cannot be done for the navy, as the foreign sailors formed an integral part of the entire crew on each vessel. It can only be said that since foreign elements constituted from one fourth to one half or more of the crew, they contributed proportionally to the work and the victories of the navy. There is, therefore, no profit in following the battles on the water. It does seem worth while, however, to emphasize again the importance of the navy and hence of the foreign-born in the crews in winning some of the conflicts.

The capture of Hatteras and Ocracoke inlets on the North Carolina coast in August, 1861, which put under Federal control Albemarle and Pamlico sounds, and the more important capture of Port Royal farther south, affording a port of call and a base within Confederate territory, are well recognized as feats of the navy. The capture of New Orleans, effected by forcing passage of Forts Jackson and St. Philip from the mouth of the Mississippi with Farragut's powerful fleet, was acknowledged as an operation in which the navy played the larger part. The role of the gunboats in forcing the surrender of Forts Henry and Donelson and of Island No. 10 has been often and fully told, but their importance in holding the inland waters may well require emphasis. After the surrender of the points just named, the presence of the gunboats was necessary on the smaller inland rivers because Confederate guerrillas were a constant menace to the lines of communication of the western armies. These small armed boats even cut off Morgan's retreat from Ohio. On July 19, 1863, the little gunboat *Moose* prevented the Confederates from crossing the Ohio River and forced them to scatter in headlong flight. These boats were a factor in many small skirmishes which scarcely enter into our formal histories. On October 28, 1863, the *Conestoga* broke up a Confederate camp on the Cumberland, inflicting also a loss of matériel. Though these operations were relatively unimportant, they offered practice for green crews and accustomed them to the handling of this strange new craft.[66]

The great value of the Union fleet lay, however, in the blockading service on the Atlantic and Gulf coasts. The blockade was maintained with increasing vigor and efficiency under the triple stimulus of patriotism,

[66] Maclay, *A History of the United States Navy*, II, 331, 347–48.

duty, and personal gain. The profits of blockade-running were enormous, but so were the risks; it has been asserted that a balance sheet would show no profits in the aggregate for the foreign blockade-runners. The Confederates and the aliens who sought to run the blockade manifested great ingenuity, but experience developed in the Union blockaders resources and skill to cope with those who would outwit them. The blockaded Southerners kept pace with equal skill, ever devising new methods of evasion. They soon designed vessels built especially for the purpose—long, narrow boats in which everything was sacrificed to speed. Gray in color, to match the often-gray sea, these boats were invisible at a distance of a few hundred yards against the mist or the sandy shore and were fairly numerous: some 200 runners were engaged in the traffic. They dashed by night at full speed through the blockading line, the sound of their engines deadened by the breakers on the shore. Like swift-moving shadows, they baffled the keenest eye. Even in the early months of 1864 about two of every three blockade-runners evaded capture; but the moves of the Yankee pursuer drew the noose steadily tighter and the story was quite different by the close of that year: 40 out of 66 were captured while they were trying to enter a given port. During the war 1,149 prizes were taken, in addition to which 355 vessels were burned, sunk, driven on shore, or otherwise destroyed, and a few were wrecked without the knowledge of the Union officers until after the encounter. The total loss has been computed at 1,504 ships of all classes. At Wilmington alone 65 vessels were intercepted. The gross value of the cargo condemned in prize courts before November 1, 1865, totaled nearly $22,000,000, a sum subsequently enlarged by fresh condemnations. The value of the vessels captured and destroyed amounted to about $7,000,000, so that the ultimate total loss to owners of the ships and cargoes mounted to at least $31,000,000, a low estimate.[67] Quite aside from the prize money, the navy achieved on the blockaded coast, inland waters, and high seas much which cannot be measured by statistics. The blockaders slowly throttled the commerce of the Confederacy, preventing the passage of both imports and exports, destroying any possibility of a sound financial structure, and effectually preventing recognition, beyond belligerent rights, of the new state by foreign powers.

[67] Authorities agree fairly well on these figures. See Porter, *The Naval History of the Civil War*, 18; Hosmer, *Outcome of the Civil War*, 164–65; James Russell Soley, *The Blockade and the Cruisers* (New York, 1895), 44. For the figures on Wilmington, see Maclay, *A History of the United States Navy*, II, 540.

When the reader recalls that from one third to one half of the crews, to strike a fair average, on the war vessels of the United States navy had been born abroad, he will recognize what a large share the foreign-born had in securing these results. The task of the men on the blockade was tedious and annoying rather than thrilling and glamorous, as fighting sometimes appears to be. The enemy did them little harm; consequently, sailors in stanch, well-equipped, and well-armed vessels soon took their stations with steady nerves, dreading only the storms off Cape Hatteras. But the long months of monotonous watching, broken only by the occasional excitement of a sharp chase not always crowned by a capture, became filled with deadly ennui. The sailor had to be ready on the instant to spring into action. When darkness fell, instead of relaxing his vigilance, he had to increase his alertness, for night afforded what opportunity there was for slipping through the triple line of blockaders. Small, open patrol boats, close to the bar and the surf, were more likely to afford excitement than the comfortable, larger vessels on the outer blockade lines.[68]

There were many good gunners in the fleet, among them a full quota of foreign-born. The good gunnery of the fighting vessels of the Union was recognized by Confederates as well as Unionists. The "terribly accurate" aim of gunners on the *Kearsarge* has already been noted.[69]

Except on blockade vessels, the price paid by the sailors in suffering was equally as great as, if indeed not greater than that paid by the soldiers. To the perils of wounds from ammunition, cold, discomfort, and lack of food, there were added the dangers of drowning after the ship was blown up, of being pinned down and burned with the ship, and of being scalded to death by escaping steam if a shell struck the engine, which, we know only too well, unfortunately did occur. Nonnatives shared equally with natives in paying the supreme price, whether on land or on water. War raised all alike to the honorable status of American citizens.

[68] Hosmer, *Outcome of the War*, 164.

[69] Maclay, *A History of the United States Navy*, II, 57–71. One shell entered the port of the *Alabama*, sweeping off part of the gun crew; another heavy shell entered the wardroom, sweeping away the table on which a surgeon was operating, and blew out the side of the ship.

CHAPTER TWENTY-ONE

Some Conclusions

A GENERALIZATION with regard to the fighting quality of the Union army as a whole is in order as a point of departure. After the defeat on the field of Manassas had shaken the citizens of the North out of their delusion that a mere display of force could drive the South back into the Union, and especially after the failure of the Peninsular campaign had revealed the magnitude of the task before them, a different class of men from the three months militia came forward. That group had looked upon their term of enlistment as an excursion or a mere military demonstration in a war which would soon be ended gloriously. The middle and working classes now recognized the duty of leaving their respective occupations for the battlefield. The men who enlisted for three years were aware of the sort of life they were entering upon and of the perils they would have to face. The object of the great majority was not adventure nor fear of conscription nor pecuniary inducements, but conviction of right. They were not good soldiers, but they were honest in their desire to become good soldiers.

This was the period when whole regiments almost to a man were determined to "see it out," when the scenes in camp were heartening to officers as well as thrilling to spectators, when companies paraded on the company street in rapid succession as the dramatic way of announcing that a company had "veteranized" by re-enlistment. In one Ohio regiment there were only fifteen men in ten companies who did not sign the new roll, and they were almost all physically disabled. These scenes occurred in the closing weeks of 1861 at a time when the men were suffering from lack of food, shoes, and clothing.[1] From this time until the early spring of 1863 the quality of the Union troops was very high. By the latter date two years of strenuous fighting had weeded out those whose hearts were not in the war, and the subsequent feelings of disgust and weariness had

---

[1] When a company re-enlisted, it had the right to be called a veteran unit, and it also secured a month's furlough. See the vivid description in Cox, *Military Reminiscences of the Civil War*, II, 92–93.

not yet supervened to check the steady supply of recruits necessary to re-place the enormous wastage of the armies at the front. Loyalty to the state, the regiment, the division, and the corps was high.

After the Union had introduced bounties on a scale which vitiated the entire conception of reward, after the draft had been introduced, and after the slaughter of the campaign of 1864 had brought home the horrors of war, the caliber of the army declined. The supply of superior patriots had dried up—many of them were dead; bounty brokers and kidnappers were demoralizing the army by infiltrating an inferior foreign element. The increasing amount of the bounties was directly reflected in the de-clining caliber of the recruits. Later recruits were, on the whole, physically, morally, and intellectually inferior to those who had enlisted during the first two years. They became a part of the army, but they never fused with the veterans who had survived Antietam, Fredericksburg, and Gettysburg and whose attitude toward them is evidenced by the oft-expressed sentiment, "They are not Americans, they are not volunteers; they are the offscouring of Europe. They disgrace our uni-form." [2]

It is true that some of the pillaging which disgraced the conduct of Northern troops was done by foreign units, but several factors are to be recognized. Not all the offscourings of the Eastern cities, whose departure caused rejoicing in the hearts of police chiefs, were foreigners. The Sixth New York (Wilson's Zouaves), for instance, was composed of men of low morality, many of them criminals and drunkards and few of them worth knowing, and yet it was largely a native unit.[3] In the second place, the traditional conception of pillaging as synonymous with warfare was ingrained in the thought of the Europeans. They stole and plundered indiscriminately. The Germans were bad at this game, though they en-joyed no monopoly. William H. Russell commented early on this pro-pensity: "It is strange that this great free and civilized Union should be supported by Germans, . . . who plunder and destroy as if they were living in the days of Agricola. . . ." [4] Finally, the Federal army was operating in enemy country, where all property was held to be legitimate booty.

The value of the military training of all Europeans who joined the

[2] G. W. Redway, *Fredericksburg. A Study in War* (London and New York, 1906), 166.

[3] W. M. Babcock, Jr. (ed. and author), *Selections from the Letters and Diaries of Brevet Brigadier Gen. Willoughby Babcock of the Seventy-fifth New York Volunteers: A Study of Camp Life in the Union Armies during the War* (New York, 1922), 79.

[4] Russell, *My Diary North and South,* 571.

army, whether in the ranks or with commissions, must again receive acknowledgment. The well-disciplined private was a benefit to the entire company by his example of military bearing and submission to discipline; and the officers, from corporal and sergeant up to general, were of inestimable value in whipping a raw army into shape. Again, the reader must be reminded that the United States Army was utterly unprepared for war and had few trained officers or soldiers and only a handful of men with combat experience, while the country was full of experienced men who had had an active part in the Hungarian, German, Polish, Crimean, and Italian wars—some having seen service in more than one country. Their presence in the Union as exiles was a fortunate circumstance for the North. At the beginning of the war, while Americans were learning the game, they were especially helpful in relieving the confusion inevitable in so great an undertaking. Russell noted that few of the officers at Cairo, Illinois, except the foreigners and some of the staff, commanded the respect of the privates even to the degree of receiving salutes from them.[5] The paramount importance of good officers in an army can be no better stated than it was by the officer who said, "I needed not this experience to convince me that man is not a cowardly animal, for all history teaches that, no matter what his nationality, if he be well led, he is usually only too ready to accept the wager of battle." [6]

Of course, the question of the adaptability of European-trained officers to the American-bred soldier posed a problem. De Trobriand, afer considering court-martial for those of his officers who had played the poltroon at the Battle of Williamsburg, proved amenable to the advice of General Couch, as has been related.[7] Some German officers adhered too closely to the ideals of Rossbach; some, when they did not make themselves ridiculous by trying to introduce monocle-and-spat manners into their regiments, adjusted to American ways enough to work with American superiors.

The characteristics of the various nationality elements in the heterogeneous army will bear close scrutiny. The Irish will be considered first. The way the commanding generals felt about the fighting quality of the Irish has been mentioned several times.[8] Sumner often asked, "Are the

[5] McClellan's attitude is cited in Piványi, *The Hungarians in the American Civil War*, 15; Russell, *My Diary North and South*, 340.

[6] George F. Noyes, *The Bivouac and the Battlefield; or, Campaign Sketches in Virginia and Maryland* (New York, 1863), 93.

[7] See Chapter VII of text.

[8] Recklessness did not vitiate their ability as fighters in combat. General Dick Taylor of

green flags ready?" Fitz-John Porter "kindled into rapture" at Malvern Hill as the Irish hurrah came sweeping through the flame and roar of the battle from the rear.[9] Dr. Thomas Ellis cleaved to the heart of their ability to fight when he wrote, "Other men go into fights finely, sternly, or indifferently, but the only man that really loves it, after all, is the green, immortal Irishman. So there the brave lads from the old sod, with the chosen Meagher at their head, laughed and fought, and joked as if it were the finest fun in the world." [10] Sometimes courage took the form of utter recklessness,[11] but again it could rise to sublime heights, as when an Irish youth, told that he must lose an arm, replied promptly, "I'm *willing* to give an arm to my country." [12]

The excellent health of the Irish among unhealthful conditions, which amazed the physicians; their remarkable endurance, which enabled the Irish Brigade to march fifty-four miles in about twenty-one hours marching time; [13] and, most of all, their sense of humor and quick wit testified to their nativity in this war just as these traits characterize Irishmen in every age the world over. From Yorktown to Appomattox the Irishman was full of fun as well as full of fight. He was always cheerful and never disobeyed an order in battle. The buoyancy and optimism of his temperament enabled him to extract the maximum of satisfaction even from camp life and the march, while his ready quip and often clever repartee gave a lift to the spirits of everyone with whom he came in contact.[14] Thanks to

the Confederate army declared that if he could select men with which to make a reputation, he would choose the same men he had had in the war—the Irish. Maguire, *The Irish in America*, 576–77.

[9] New York *Irish-American*, August 2, 1862.

[10] Ellis, *Leaves from the Diary of an Army Surgeon*, 54.

[11] Corporal O'Neil of Company D in the Sixty-third New York, while waiting in the bloody angle at Spotsylvania for a Confederate charge, became so impatient that he leaped on the breastwork, yelling defiance above the noise: "We have licked you before, you ———— ———— Rebels, and we can do it again. Come on! We are ready for you." When a bullet from a sharpshooter struck him down and he had to be borne to the rear, he managed, despite the fact that his mouth was filled with gore, to yell, "I'll pay you for that some day." Dwyer, "63rd Regt. Infantry," in Fox (comp.), *New York at Gettysburg*, II, 503–504.

[12] Frazar Kirkland (comp.), *The Pictorial Book of Anecdotes and Incidents of the War of the Rebellion* (Hartford, 1866), 322.

[13] MacNamara, *The Irish Brigade in Bivouac and Battle*, 176–77.

[14] General John B. Floyd, on the retreat from Fort Donelson to Chattanooga, declared in a speech that he would never be taken alive by the Yankees, that he had a long settlement to make, which they might settle in h–l. As an officer was repeating the story to a soldier, an Irishman interrupted, "Thot's all right—we'll be ripresented thar too." H. V. Redfield, "Characteristics of the Armies," in M[cClure] (ed.), *The Annals of the War*, 370.

Sometimes the humor was quite unconscious. An Irishman from Michigan had the fingers

the Irish, every fight seemed to have a ludicrous feature, which evoked laughs as the incidents of the battles made the round of the camps.

More important than the Irishman's zeal for combat was his poise and steadiness, his watchfulness, his patience in impending battle; coolly, in- See p. 644 differently, even lazily, he met the dread intimations that death had commenced its havoc. Not a pulse seemed to quicken, not a mirthful word to falter—so inured did he become to war. These were qualities on which a commander could rely.[15] The Irishman's loyalty and pride in his regiment, his brigade, his race is notorious. "Colonel, your honor, them boys'll niver stand forninst the Irish brigade again. If they'd known it was us, sur, begorra they'ud ha' brought coffins wid 'em" was the common sentiment in the brigade.[16] The loyalty which forbade the Irishman to desert a fallen comrade produced in him ingenuity and resourcefulness in rescuing that comrade and also spurred him to greater ferocity to avenge his friend's death.[17] He responded quickly to praise or blame. He did his best when pitted against another regiment and was better in offense than in defense, once his fighting spirit was aroused.

The Irishman had traits which made for a good officer. He knew how to manage people; hence, on the whole, more Irish than Germans rose to low-ranking office. The Irish officer put his best foot forward, and his nimble mind stood him in good stead on the battlefield and enabled him to make quick thrusts and parries. A gift for oratory, so often present in the leaders of the period, together with a certain vivacity, gave him a hold over his men.

On the other hand, the race had certain qualities which were trying to the commanders. Irish soldiers were improvident, throwing away their knapsacks and blankets as they dashed to the scene of action. It was not in their nature to fight with four or five pounds of rations hanging at their

---

of one hand broken by a spent bullet at the First Battle of Bull Run. Naturally, he yelled with pain. "Blasht your soul, you ould woman, shtop cryin'; you make more noise about it thin the man that losht his hade!" Moore (ed.), *Rebellion Record*, III, Pt. 3, p. 62.

[15] This was the appraisal of Meagher himself. Meagher, *The Last Days of the 69th In Virginia*, 8–9.

[16] Townsend, *Campaign of a Non-Combatant*, 135, tells this story. These remarks were made by a burial detachment as they were burying some of their foes.

[17] One rescue of a man with a fractured leg was effected by a comrade who lay down on the ground, holding the injured man on his body while the other comrades dragged him by the feet for many yards. The rescue was achieved at the expense of a lacerated back, but the fallen soldier died of exhaustion. Mulholland, *The Story of the 116th Regiment, Pennsylvania Infantry*, 74.

hips; they preferred to go supperless to bed.[18] Their impetuosity sometimes led to attacks on other Union regiments, with resulting waste of
human life. Intemperance was one of their vices, and when they were
intoxicated, there was constant brawling and fighting among themselves
and with other groups; indeed, so contentious were they that inebriation
was not necessary to start a fight. At first they refused to accept discipline;
when stationed in New York they climbed the gate at the Battery and
disappeared into the city: on some occasions near the front they became
unruly when furloughs were denied them. Their natural vengefulness led
occasionally to outrages on officers.[19] Slovenliness was one of their unpleasant traits, and stains were almost always apparent on their clothing
until they were hidden by the smoke and powder of battle—and then they
did not matter. Nobly they stood by the Republic at that crisis in its
history, and gladly did Americans of all classes and sections acknowledge
the fact at the time. Undeniably the Irish added a picturesque and dramatic
quality beyond that of other races to the motley array of the Union army.

Quite different were the virtues and faults of the Teutons in the army.
At the top of the list of qualities to be approved stands the German loyalty
to the Union; with the Forty-eighters and the better class of these citizens,
loyalty was a genuine and profound sentiment. The average German
private could probably not have phrased his feeling so well as it was put
for him at the dedication of a Pennsylvania monument at Gettysburg:
"We love this land; it is the land of our children and children's children.
We may differ politically, but in the love of our country and its institutions, we are one. Henceforth your country is our country, your people
our people, your destiny our destiny, your flag our flag and your God our
God." Even though beautiful expressions did not come to his lips, a
humble German who lay wounded two nights on the battlefield of
Antietam uttered the fervent hope that he might have one more shot at
the enemy.[20]

The mass of the German soldiers were patient, philosophical, plodding
men, who came from the shop and farm and were withal industrious and

---

[18] Meagher, *The Last Days of the 69th in Virginia*, 10.

[19] For instances, see the attack of one Thomas McNillis against the Bucktails, another
Pennsylvania regiment near by. Hyde, *Following the Greek Cross*, 33. For an attack on an
officer who made a surly, lazy Irishman work, see Joel and Stegman (authors and comps.),
Rifle Shots and Bugle Notes, 320. See also the New York *Tribune*, September 25, August
15, 21, 29, 1861.

[20] "Address of Captain Paul F. Rohrbacker," in Nicholson (comp.), *Pennsylvania at Gettysburg*, II, 405; for the soldier at Antietam, see Noyes, *Bivouac and Battlefield*, 206.

thrifty. They yielded respect to authority and were, therefore, well disciplined, persevering, and inspired by some idealism. They were somewhat slow in response but were stable and solid in battle; they learned, in fact, to do some skillful fighting. Leisurely in their mental processes, they had a passion for thoroughness in the details of warfare as in everything else. If the Comte de Paris was correct in saying that the most important attribute of the volunteer is amenability to discipline, the Germans rated high. They were especially valuable because so many had had military training of an exacting type and because so many were scattered in mixed regiments as privates and noncommissioned officers. Strongest was their influence in that arm of the service in which the North surpassed its foe from the beginning, the artillery. The many well-trained artillerists from Germany served as substitutes for the artillerists lacking in the Regular Army. As drillmasters, these artillerists and their kin in the infantry and cavalry were of immeasurable worth. Likewise, among the engineers the German names stand out, as Lieutenant Hassendeubel, who planned the defenses at St. Louis, and Lieutenants Hoffman, Ulffers, and Von Schrader.[21] Their losses and the careful analysis of their services set forth in several preceding chapters prove their great courage. Furthermore, their conduct in Missouri in the very first months of the war stamps them as possessed of courage of a high order, for they knew perfectly well that if the Confederates ever felt themselves strong enough, a war of annihilation against the Germans would be conducted—so bitter was the hatred of the Southerners toward the Teutons.[22]

The list of German officers of the rank of colonel and general is a long one, including in many cases brilliant, educated, cultivated men such as Schurz, Osterhaus, Von Willich, Sigel, Hassendeubel, Von Wangelin, Von Gilsa, Von Schimmelfennig, Dilger, Wiedrich, and Kautz, to name only a few of the distinguished array. Many a cultured German scholar found his way into the ranks, as did a certain Corporal Philbert, who was heralded as the literary man of a New York regiment and who proved brave, cheerful, and modest even while suffering from a painful wound.[23] His motive was simply to serve his adopted country. Many of the Germans who served as trained officers passed acute criticisms on army discipline and strategy; and, after all due allowances have been made for their inflexibility

---

[21] For the artillerists, see Kaufmann, *Die Deutschen im Bürgerkriege*, 131–32, 134.

[22] Chicago *Illinois Staats-Zeitung*, May 8, 1861.

[23] He was in a New York regiment and was wounded at Port Hudson. Hosmer, *The Color Guard*, 176.

of mind in applying Prussian standards to America, it becomes apparent that many of their criticisms were just and valuable. The incompetent officers and inefficient privates of that nationality who crept in at first were weeded out, so that the Germans in due course of time contributed largely to final success.

Of course, the German afforded many opportunities for amusement, from the "Fritz" in the ranks who sampled some apple brandy so that if it didn't kill him the others might drink it, to high-ranking officers like Von Gilsa, whose barracks oaths vastly entertained those who heard them.[24]

Among the faults of the Germans which troubled the Americans were a Prussian arrogance in the demeanor of some of the officers; an insistence on the Prussian severity in drill, to which Americanized Germans refused to conform; and an idolatry, asserted with "all the vehemence of the Teutonic character," of Prussian "martinetism" and servility—all of which were obnoxious not only to Americans but to American-Germans.[25] As compared with the Irish troops, the Germans usually lacked dash and verve; as compared with the American units, they lacked tact. They fought in masses, with little individuality; but they were persistent and, most important, they put their hearts into the cause. The Germans gave to the army a conservative, stabilizing force.

In the light of primary evidence, the common impression of the Scandinavians as phlegmatic and slow will have to be revised, at least in relation to their fighting in the Civil War. When Mattson tells us that two of his Swedish officers wept when they were ordered to surrender, a third cursed, and all swore that they would never serve again under Colonel Henry C. Lester, we can hardly call them stolid. Heg represents his Norwegians as eager to get a chance to fight before the fighting was over.[26] They had the endurance for hard, forced marches for as much as twenty miles a day for ten days that we expect of the hardy Norsemen. The unmatched obstinacy and persistence of the Northmen made them tenacious fighters. The outstanding qualities of the Scandinavians, steadfast-

[24] Moore (ed.), *Rebellion Record*, IV, Pt. 3, p. 75.

[25] This is the observation of Owen Rice, who, from service with the Eleventh Corps, had had an excellent opportunity to see both the good and the bad in the German officers. See "Afield with the Eleventh Army Corps at Chancellorsville," in Hunter (comp.), *Sketches of War History*, I, 360.

It was reported that Colonel John E. Bendix, who was more American than German, resigned because he refused to drill his regiment in the fashion approved by his superior officer.

[26] Chicago *Illinois Staats-Zeitung*, August 7, 1861.

ness, persistence, patience, obedience, and endurance, were displayed on many fields and in many camps.

While no claim to superiority as fighters may be made for them, they certainly equaled the other companies in ability; moreover, several wholly Scandinavian companies and the Scandinavian Regiment proved themselves outstanding. As would be expected from their temperament, they were cool in times of excitement and were able to act with deliberation in danger. The youthful Knute Nelson, from his superiority of being a veteran and a corporal at the ripe age of eighteen, looked with scorn on all his "young friends who think more of their useless skins than of the country's weal." He did not wish to know or see them any more: "They are not friends of the land and therefore they are not mine. O how I wish to have these worthless fellows here for but one month to show them what it is to talk of war and be at war." [27] Both the hearts and the minds of the Scandinavians were in the war, for most of them were convinced Unionists and abolitionists. They, like the Irish, drew much solace and strength from their religion. The appraisal of John Fitch may well sum up the Scandinavian soldiers: "Temperate and virtuous, obedient and well-disciplined, they are in every respect model soldiers, and challenge the admiration and respect of all whose good fortune it is to mingle with them." [28]

In view of the tendency of each nationality group to exalt its own soldiers and national traits, a tendency amply manifested by the *Courrier des États-Unis,* it is refreshing to find the commander of the Gardes Lafayette quite objective in his appraisal. He declared that the men in the six companies which were largely French were guilty of the same faults in America that they had fallen into in France, except that they were slightly less well disciplined here, and that their punctuality at service arose less from a sense of duty than from national vanity: "At reviews and drills where they attracted attention, they made a fine figure and manoeuvred with unity and precision. At those drills where no one was watching them, they did neither better nor worse than their comrades." [29]

[27] On the surrender of the Third Minnesota, see Mattson to his wife, July 25, 30, 1862, Mattson Papers; for the Fifteenth Wisconsin, see Blegen (ed.), *Civil War Letters of Colonel Heg,* 135, 127, 130, 132.

[28] Fitch (comp.), *Annals of the Army of the Cumberland,* 231.

[29] "L'experience militaire des anciens soldats qu'il compte dans son sein a été mis à profit et lorsque viendra l'entrée du campagne, les Gardes Lafayette de New York seront prêts à affronter toutes les eventualitées, dans les conditions qui en feront un des corps les plus efficaces de l'armée." New York *Courrier des États-Unis,* May 14, 1861. See also De Trobriand, *Quatre Ans de Campagnes,* I, 83.

It seems unnecessary to pursue in detail this analysis of nationality traits for each of the other groups which have figured in these pages. However, it would be ungrateful not to note the particular *élan* and whirlwind vigor which distinguished the few Hungarians; the readiness and idealism of the Poles in coming forward promptly; the pertinacity and loyalty of the English, who fought for a country which most of them had not adopted; the stern steadfastness of the Scotch; and the quiet courage of the Swiss, who contributed their special skill in marksmanship.

The actual contribution of the individual military units of the various nationality groups in the winning of the different battles has been evaluated, as far as that seems possible. There remains, however, to make acknowledgment here of the response of the Germans. Spontaneous as it seemed, there was leadership in giving it direction, without which it would not have been so effective at just the critical moment. Recognition should be made of the fact that the Germans of this country never have had a more brilliant leadership than they did during the Civil War. Then lived the three men who probably deserve to be rated as the three greatest German-Americans—Francis Lieber, Carl Schurz, and Johann Bernhard Stallo. They rendered a valuable contribution to the spiritual arming of the German element of the population for the mighty struggle. At their head stood the surviving leader of the pre–Forty-eighters, Gustav Körner. The vast majority of the Forty-eighters, even the oldsters among these firebrands, moved to the field, for they had found a new avenue for their idealism. They were among the most energetic recruiters in the country and steadily fanned the flame of war inspiration among the phlegmatic of their countrymen. At the outbreak of the war, the German citizenry throughout the North rallied promptly and almost unanimously to the support of the Union. In New York City thousands of Germans offered their service at the firing of the first gun on Fort Sumter.

There can be no doubt that it was the Germans of St. Louis and Missouri who saved that state to the Union. When from every section of the state came reports of suspicious movements, the government and General William S. Harney made only weak efforts to stem the Confederate tide. The latter, indeed, signed an agreement virtually to respect the neutrality of the state.[30] The Germans sensed the danger to the nation and were

[30] Harney signed with General Price an agreement that meetings for the Union and for disunion were to be avoided; that gatherings of the people be styled mobs to be dispersed; that the United States regulars would serve practically as a *posse comitatus* for order when required by the state government. James Peckham, *Gen. Nathaniel Lyon and Missouri in 1861. A Monograph of the Great Rebellion* (New York, 1866), 202–203.

the first to prepare to meet it. They had the courage to stand up for the Union when no other groups in that state seemed to dare to show their loyalty. Without the Germans who fought under Sigel, Governor Jackson would probably have succeeded in wrenching Missouri from the Union and taking it into the Confederacy. Among the fifty thousand loyalists in Kentucky were many Germans who helped to keep a second border state in the Union. By the service of hundreds of able officers, by the service of about two hundred thousand soldiers, and by the sacrifice of the lives of thousands for the preservation of the Union, the Germans paid their debt to the Republic and to the patriots of 1776 who shed their blood to found it.

Rather more tardily the Irish, through the Irish Brigade and Corcoran's Irish Legion and by the thousands scattered through many mixed and native regiments, repaid their debt to the country which had offered the Irish a haven of refuge and economic opportunity—and repaid it richly during the four years of civil strife by some of the finest fighting and some of the heaviest loss of life of the war. The other nationalities brought their contributions in proportion to their numbers to the country which had welcomed and received them, but space is allotted to the two elements which were able to contribute the largest numbers and hence, necessarily, gave the greatest measure of aid.

The special services rendered by foreigners must be recognized as numerous and deeply significant. The reader is reminded of what the Catholic priest of his own nationality meant to the Irishman and of what the lone Polish priest encountered by the writer in her research must have meant in the confessional to the Polish companies in the Fifty-eighth New York. The comfort which religious people like the Swedes and the Norwegians drew from hearing the Lutheran service in their own tongue is obvious. For the preservation of the army in a fighting condition and the restoration of the wounded to their regiments in the shortest possible space of time the surgeons were of the greatest importance. What was owed to the surgeons, both British and, especially, German, is abundantly clear from an earlier chapter. Not only did these men bring a superior medical training (for American medical schools did not then rank with the best, those in Heidelberg, Vienna, and London) but the language and na-

---

Germans were thoroughly aware of their part in the saving of Missouri for the Union, for as early as May 10, 1861, the Chicago *Illinois Staats-Zeitung* was saying, "Ohne die Deutschen wäre Missouri längst aus der Union, ohne die Deutschen wäre St. Louis ein Waffenplatz fur die Secessionisten."

tionality factors entered. Soldiers could make their difficulties known, and they placed in men of their own country a confidence which was often lacking when the language barrier existed. What the Union owed these men is indicated in the long list of foreign-born surgeons given earlier, among whom were some of national and international reputation. When these men combined with professional skill an attractive personality and literary gifts, as did Dr. Reynolds of the Irish Brigade, they could mix with their potions and ministrations a certain magic, which redounded to the benefit of Uncle Sam. The foreigners trained in the special fields of engineering and cartography were particularly helpful and valuable in the army. It is almost a work of supererogation once more to call attention to the contribution which the German love of music made to the army through bands, choral singing, and even impromptu singing in the camp and on the march.

The women of the foreign element rose nobly to their opportunity, giving material support in the form of uniforms, bandages, flags, and food, and moral support in helping to maintain the morale of their "men." Now and then there was a weakling, to whom the absent husband had to give moral support, but in the main the foreign-born women accepted well the sacrifices demanded of them—even when the supreme sacrifice was exacted of their husbands.

Many of our foreign-born officers, Irish and Scandinavian as well as German, resented the treatment accorded their nationality and themselves. In the personal equation the trouble was usually owing to failure to accord them the rank to which they felt themselves entitled. Undoubtedly, titles were not always awarded with an eye single to merit but often with a view to political considerations. There were additional factors: Washington controlled relatively few of the appointments; these rested with the governors of the various states; and all important appointments had to be made only after considering the reaction of West Point officers. That many German officers in the East, among them the most gifted and capable, became discontented with their subordinate posts was natural. Many brave, able Germans remained during the entire four years only company officials, while such capable colonels as Von Gilsa and Buschbeck never won even one promotion. On the other hand, to the disgust of the faithful officers some comparatively poor fighters reached higher rank without having rendered genuine service. Promotion became often enough a mere lottery. There was not the same irritation in the western army, because the West Point attitude never attained such influence there as in the

East and because the western army was essentially a people's army; even when the generals were West Point men, like Grant, Sherman, and Rosecrans, they had been away from the Regular Army long enough to lose the sense of caste.

The sense of outrage among the Germans was the greater because they knew that many native Americans in the ranks had come to respect them. A certain soldier who had complained about the German officers, took it back in his next letter: "They are splendid fighters; in fact, all the foreigners are who are with us. . . . These Germans will fight and they care as much for this country as we Yankees do." [31]

That the graduates of West Point had first claim to the highest commands can hardly be challenged, a preference being accorded them by public opinion. No self-respecting nation would have entrusted a volunteer army to an untried foreign officer so long as there were available native officers. In addition, a certain odium attached to every former officer of a foreign nationality. How could errors be avoided when unknown foreign officers were being fed into the army with great haste to meet the demand for officers for the vast, new army? The officers in Blenker's division were largely German career officers who had been driven out of the army in Germany; for these men the United States had become a sort of overseas orphanage. These officers were usually not dishonorable; often they had found themselves to be misfits in the military profession in the homeland too late to enter another calling or had fallen victims to obliging usurers. Their lives were a tragedy in America, where their countrymen looked at them askance and where they found it difficult to find suitable work and often sank to the status of servants. Mingled with these unfortunates were scamps and frauds. Washington, because of the credulity of the authorities, became the gathering place of a band of international swindlers, streaming from all lands. Many imposed on the government through forged papers and confident approach. The pseudo count "Von Schweinitz-Crain" proved ultimately to be an ex-convict of Austria. He produced falsified recommendations and a forged letter, purportedly from the Archduke Maximilian, which gave him an entree with the Austrian and Prussian ambassadors and with Carl Schurz. He received a colonelcy at once, swindled in a shameless fashion, and then disappeared—to, it was thought, the Confederate scene.[32] Such scamps impaired the opportunities of the reputable foreigners, for after a few such experiences the authorities

[31] Livermore, *My Story of the War*, 669–70.
[32] Kaufmann, *Die Deutschen im Bürgerkriege*, 176 n.

were wary of bestowing high rank on any of the foreign-born, and to some extent the exploits of the scamps lessened the respect accorded the reputable foreign-born officers.

One area in which the Union army reaped great benefit from the presence of foreigners in the ranks was that of the handicrafts. Sooner or later the army had need of masons, millers, druggists, typesetters, carpenters, clerks, engravers, butchers, and barbers. While there were, of course, Americans from all these lines of work in the army, there were also many foreigners representing the trades. Men having such skills were most essential to the success of the army.

If stress has been laid upon the contribution of the foreign-born to the Union army and to winning the victory, it has not been done to belittle the contribution of the native American. The desire is to make the picture complete—to set each representative of the various foreign elements in proper perspective alongside the Vermonter, the New Yorker, the man from Ohio or Iowa or Michigan—to "render . . . unto Caesar the things which are Caesar's." In order that the picture shall not be drawn out of focus, it is here necessary to bring in the native element. The proportion of American-born was larger than the reader might feel after these many pages on what the foreign element did. Let it never be forgotten that the foreign-born constituted only from one fifth to one fourth of the army, which means that nearly three fourths of the army was drawn from native sons and that the chief command of the armies was always in American hands.

If the great majority of the Union armies consisted of "Yankees," then the responsibility for the length of the war and the many defeats cannot be ascribed to the foreign element. What then was the cause of the many defeats? In addition to the utter unpreparedness and inexperience of officers and soldiers, there were a thousand difficulties in the way of the organization of the armies, their armament, their equipment, and even their subsistence. It required months of assiduous labor to introduce order and method into this vast administrative machinery. There was constant occasion to regret that a general staff, such as was found at the time in all the European armies, was not available to serve as a medium between the chief and all subordinate agents placed under his command and thus to enable him to enforce at all times the execution of his wishes.[33] The general

[33] It is significant that both De Paris, *History of the Civil War in America*, I, 265, and Turchin, *Chickamauga*, 168, commented on the absence of a general staff as a great defect in the American military system.

situation during the first year of conflict shows that the Confederate army was well drilled and commanded by competent officers, who were fighting on their own terrain. With control of the railroad and the telegraph, the Confederate officers could concentrate a large body of men at a given position in a short time. The Union army, on the other hand, composed largely of new recruits and commanded by inexperienced and incompetent officers, was no match for the Confederate army, which quickly acquired the qualities of a veteran army. There were periods of deep gloom—as after Second Bull Run, Fredericksburg, and Chancellorsville; during the Wilderness campaign; and, most of all, during Early's raid on Washington in July, 1864. At such times the cause was felt to be a failing one.[34]

The writer was brought by her study of Confederate campaigns and problems to marvel that the Confederacy could sustain the struggle for four long years. Now she is ready to marvel that the *North* was able against its serious problems to sustain the war for four long years to the point of victory. There pass through the mind in review the serious Copperhead opposition in the rear; the opposition to the draft with consequent riots and serious setback to the Union cause; the many almost-disastrous mistakes in the long search for a supreme commander; the profound discouragement (despite the enormous advantages of the North in man power and resources) among leaders who clamored for peace when the North was on the verge of victory but her citizenry were unable to see it; and, finally, the miracle that the people could be held to see the war through.

Both North and South should fully grasp the fact of the relative equality of the forces engaged in many of the conflicts. Francis Marshall [Pierce] has computed that, on account of the heavy Federal detachments needed to protect the rear against treason at home and to serve on the frontier, the forces *actually* engaged in fifty important battles were almost equal. Rarely, he declares, did Federal superiority of numbers more than offset the physical advantages of the Confederates. The North could not fully avail itself of its superior man power and resources because a war too remote from home for the Northern citizen to feel that it was vitally his did not knit the people closely in a common cause.[35]

Therefore, we are driven to the conclusion that the miracle was achieved by the fighting part of the army (of which mercenaries and bounty jump-

[34] Hyde, *Following the Greek Cross*, 228.

[35] [Pierce], *The Battle of Gettysburg*, 38, 39. He claims that the two opposing forces at these fifty battles were within 2 per cent of being equal.

ers were not a part, of course), and this includes the fighting foreigners along with the fighting Americans. That portion was a fine army; if it had not been, it could never have survived the incompetent hands that at times directed it. At core, in all that was essential, its units, including the native ones, were well disciplined. Jacob Cox put his finger on the very essential of discipline when he wrote that his heart swelled with pride at the sight of his Ohio troops going forward under their first fire more steadily than they had ever done at drill and comprehending fully under danger the advantage of unity in the shock of battle. Thus his men became good soldiers at the moment of battle, though he had often deplored their reluctance to submit to discipline as fully as did the neighboring German regiments.[36] We do not need to accept the boasts of the native soldier or officer; it was a Swiss who declared that the battles of the Civil War were the most severe the world had ever seen up to that time. The Swiss Aschmann declared, "Even the Crimean or Italian campaigns cannot be compared with ours; for even such brave souls as made those [campaigns] and then also served with us, were astonished that it was possible to endure so much that was super-human." [37] In the units where intelligence was high, the morale was always high.

Thus we come to the last question of all: What was the effect of the war on the foreign-born soldier in his relation to the United States as an American citizen? Incontestably, the Forty-eighter and the average German of the type who came to America from 1830 to 1860 had a great love for freedom. Unquestionably, they entered the war with a strong impulse to fight under German direction. The German soldier, perhaps unconsciously, felt that at the same time that he was fighting for preservation of the Union he was fighting for the honor of the German people, a fact which explains, of course, his desire to serve in a German unit.[38] The war, however, did something to the German soldier. No experience had struck so deep into the life of German-Americans, and never before had there existed such unity among them; for the Germans both North and South, in contrast with the Irish and the English, found themselves in heart arrayed in the main only on one side. For the first time since they had come to America—perhaps for the first time in their lives—they felt a national consciousness, felt their descent from one race. The old par-

---

[36] Cox, *Military Reminiscences of the Civil War*, I, 266–87.

[37] Aschmann, *Drei Jahre in der Potomac Armee*, iv.

[38] This view was voiced by Carl Schurz in a speech cited by Kaufmann, *Die Deutschen im Bürgerkriege*, 464–65.

ticularism, which had been a curse to Germany and which they had brought over with them to separate them here as Bavarians, Saxons, or Prussians, fell before the common effort to defend the unity of America, their new home. Furthermore, they felt the burden of a double responsibility: to the old and to the new homeland. They must prove that their loyalty to the Union was as great as that of the native sons, but they must also in the eyes of the Germans do honor to the German name. Certainly, they impressed foreign visitors by their sincerity; for the Frenchman Auguste Laugel declared that it was "among the Germans that one could find the most exalted defenders of the Union, the most resolute enemies of slavery. Having grasped from the beginning the character and the object of the civil war, they have espoused the cause of the Union and of emancipation with an ardor and a passion, the influence of which has been felt even in Europe by the population beyond the Rhine." [39]

With the Irish, loyalty to America did not diminish loyalty to Ireland. Every Irishman felt, nevertheless, that he was a member of an expatriated race fighting for the unity of the nation that had extended to his countrymen liberty and citizenship; and that if he failed to maintain the reputation formerly gained for the Irish, the standing of the Irish race would be seriously affected.[40] Irishmen never ceased to try to use America to forward Irish independence. Hence they organized "circles" in the army and the navy with the object of taking advantage of the strained relations between the United States and England to launch at the close of the war a movement for Irish freedom. It eventuated in the so-called "Fenian Invasion of Canada." [41]

The war marked a new step in the identification of the Scandinavian immigrants with the fortunes and ideals of their adopted country. In the case of these nationality groups the war, with all its suffering and death, helped to effect the transition from immigrant to American. Each group had suffered for its country and emerged with deepened patriotism.

The word "Americanization" was probably not in common usage by 1865, and yet that process is exactly what happened, in greater or less

[39] Laugel, *Les États-Unis pendant la Guerre,* 195.

[40] Based on "Oration of Denis F. Burke," in Fox (comp.), *New York at Gettysburg,* II, 479.

[41] The plan eventually adopted was to invade Canada. Irish veterans of the American Civil War were eager to put their military training to further use. A convention at Cincinnati created on paper an Irish republic, and began to sell bonds to prepare for a Canadian invasion. They expected Canadians to join the movement and the United States quickly to recognize the new republic set up in Canada. Wittke, *We Who Built America,* 177.

degree, to each foreign-born participant in the war. Friendships between men of differing European races and of foreign-born with Americans were cemented. Phil Kearney, who had spent two years at the Samur École and who had won the cross of the Legion of Honor as aide to the Duc d'Orleans in Algeria, came sometimes to De Trobriand's tent to talk of Paris and the thousand other subjects which interest a man of the world. Hans Mattson struck up a warm friendship with Colonel Foster—one so close that the two men arranged for their wives to come down the Mississippi together to visit them. The Swede also exchanged visits with several American officers from Wisconsin. Heg met both Grant and Rosecrans and had close relations with several officers of his own rank, including colonels Harrison C. Hobart and John C. Starkweather.[42]

The war was a liberal education for many of these men who had not left their farms or provincial towns since they had come, or, as often was the case, had been brought as young children, to America. Their physical horizon, and by the same token their mental horizon, was vastly enlarged. The shock of seeing a slave auction changed slavery for many of them from an abstraction, against which they had certain moral prejudices, to an ugly reality. As one follows Knute Nelson from Madison, Wisconsin, to Baltimore, then by boat to New Orleans, and up to Baton Rouge, and then to the battles at Port Hudson and other skirmishes in Louisiana, he realizes that the mere lad would return home a man with a different conception of his country and that the speeches made to the soldiers and the talk in the camp had had their effect upon him, when he spoke of the United States as having the best government "to be had." [43]

Even the woman who did not participate in the war as spy, nurse, woman soldier, or vivandière but who was merely the wife or the mother of a soldier could not escape the broadening influence which forced its

[42] For De Trobriand, see *Quatre Ans de Campagnes*, I, 290–91, 293; for Mattson, see Mattson Papers; for Colonel Heg, see Blegen (ed.), *Civil War Letters of Colonel Heg*, 231–32.

[43] For reaction to the slave mart, see Mattson to his wife, January 1, 1862, Mattson Papers; for praise of the government, see Knute Nelson to "Good Friend Lars," Bardtown, Maryland, October 12, 1861, Knute Nelson Papers; for criticism of Colonel Heg for delivering a runaway slave to his master after one of the companies had tried to protect the slave, see letter (unsigned) from Camp Clear Creek, Mississippi, July 11, 1862, to the editor of the Madison *Emigranten*, July 28, 1862.

That Nelson appreciated his own growth is seen in a letter to his parents from the arsenal at Baton Rouge, June 10, 1862: "He [referring to himself] has learned that the world is not the school house nor the narrow limit of the little farm. In short he has learnt to respect the rights of his fellow creatures and regard them as equal to his own." Knute Nelson Papers.

way into the home through the letters of her husband or son, through her work for the soldiers in the Ladies' Aid, or through witnessing the ceremony of presenting a flag. The mere obligation to write frequent letters and the reception of thrilling letters from the front would perforce stimulate her to wish in some degree to live up to her husband's example of service. If, as sometimes happened, the wife accompanied or followed her husband to camp, the trip from Muskego, Wisconsin, to Tennessee, or from Minnesota to Arkansas, was an enriching experience. America must have meant to her something new and bigger than before, of which she felt herself and her family a part.

The experience of facing death, of looking it straight in the face, of thinking, really thinking, while on guard in the black silence of the night or on a lonely advanced post far from camp, made warfare a deepening and maturing experience.[44]

There were voices raised occasionally against the formation of companies and regiments based on racial origins lest such organization might contribute to the perpetuation of immigrant stocks as separate, segregated elements. The editor of *Emigranten* showed appreciation of the fact that his Scandinavians should fight as Americans and not as Scandinavians; but since the other nationalities had their regiments, he thought it desirable for the people of the far northern peninsula to be able to point to their unit as evidence that they had done their duty.[45]

The really remarkable result is that despite the fact that the army was composed in such a way that it seemed based on racial origins, it impressed foreign observers as a national army, both in sentiment and in the material of which it was composed. The foreign-born soldiers and sailors in large part shared the natives' sincere desire to serve the national cause, and the military forces accurately represented the whole American nation.[46] Without regard to nationality, soldiers of one regiment shared their rations with those of another who were in need of food. The American element seemed to absorb the foreign elements. In World War I and World War II the

---

[44] "The most leisurely hour to think is when we stand guard. When the sun goes down with its gleaming rays, moon and stars begin to shine from the clear heaven down on this dale of misery, when all work is ended and all at peace—in such an hour as I paced along on my beat, my thoughts began to race around the world, came back and struck me in the heart, with thoughts about my past life, my youth that I am throwing away. . . ." Chicago *Hemlandet*, September 25, 1861.

[45] Madison *Emigranten*, September 30, 1861.

[46] De Paris, *History of the Civil War in America*, I, 179; Laugel, *Les États-Unis pendant la Guerre*, 276.

army was organized in total disregard of the land of origin, with the result that Americanization proceeded even more rapidly and completely than it had in the Civil War; but it must be remembered that the people were not in the earlier period prepared to accept a draft. Under the necessary condition of dependence upon a volunteer army, perhaps no better plan for stimulating enlistments could have been devised than the spontaneous plan of nationality units, which produced of itself rivalry among the groups of adopted sons to show their gratitude and devotion.

Probably the finest result that flowed from this heterogeneous assemblage of various nationalities, this colorful, dramatic, fantastic, almost bizarre collection of men from all parts of the world, was the creation of a truly American army, composed of native sons and adopted sons, representing all nationalities, just as America itself was composed of all nationalities, all animated by a genuine devotion to the ideals for which the Union stood and hence constituting from its divergent parts a unity. All the various racial groups in the population of the North presented to the world a striking and thrilling example of devotion and loyalty to the government which had welcomed the exiles of the world, as well as of fidelity to political principles which they had embraced. The Tricolor, the British jack, the green flag of Ireland, the Garibaldi flag, and the Swedish-Norwegian flag could all float beside the Stars and Stripes as token of adherence to ideals represented by each of them and token of their conviction of the unity that must be preserved in the United States.

Appendix

A. FOREIGN-BORN POPULATION IN THE NORTH IN 1860 *

1. Population of the United States and of the North by Nativities in 1860 †

	ENTIRE UNITED STATES	STATES ADHERING TO THE UNION
Ireland	1,611,304	1,526,541
Germany	1,301,136	1,229,174
England	431,692	414,582
British America	249,970	246,940
France	109,870	89,718
Scotland	108,518	101,409
Switzerland	53,327	50,727
Wales	45,763	44,813
Norway	43,995	43,481
China	35,565	35,539
Holland	28,281	27,669
Mexico	27,466	14,649
Sweden	18,625	17,870
Italy	10,518	8,159
Other Countries	60,145	51,801
Total	4,136,175	3,903,672

* *Eighth Census, 1860. The Statistics of the Population,* xxix.

† *Eighth Census, 1860. The Statistics of the Population,* xxviii. The figures for Column 2 have been compiled by deducting the number of foreigners as given for each of the seceded states in Table No. 5, "Nativities of the Free Population," pp. 10 (Alabama), 20 (Arizona), 56 (Florida), 76 (Georgia), 196 (Louisiana), 272 (Mississippi), 362 (North Carolina), 453 (South Carolina), 470 (Tennessee), 490 (Texas), and 523 (Virginia).

2. *Chief Foreign Strains in Each of the States Adhering to the Union*

STATE	ENGLAND	IRELAND	SCOTLAND	BRITISH AMERICA	GERMAN STATES
California	12,227	33,147	3,670	5,437	21,646
Connecticut	8,875	55,445	2,546	3,145	8,525
Delaware	1,581	5,832	200	39	1,263
Illinois	41,745	87,573	10,540	20,132	130,804
Indiana	9,304	24,495	2,093	3,166	66,705
Iowa	11,522	28,072	2,895	8,313	38,555
Kansas	1,400	3,888	377	986	4,318
Kentucky	4,503	22,249	1,111	618	27,227
Maine	2,677	15,290	759	17,540	384
Maryland	4,235	24,872	1,583	333	43,884
Massachusetts	23,848	185,434	6,855	27,069	9,961
Michigan	25,743	30,049	5,705	36,482	38,787
Minnesota	3,462	12,831	1,079	8,023	18,400
Missouri	10,009	43,464	2,021	2,814	88,487
New Hampshire	2,291	12,737	741	4,468	412
New Jersey	15,852	62,006	3,556	1,144	33,772
New York	106,011	498,072	27,041	55,273	256,252
Ohio	32,700	76,826	6,535	7,082	168,210
Oregon	690	1,266	217	663	1,078
Pennsylvania	46,546	201,939	10,137	3,484	138,244
Rhode Island	6,356	25,285	1,517	2,830	815
Vermont	1,632	13,480	1,078	15,776	219
Wisconsin	30,543	49,961	6,902	18,146	123,879
District of Columbia	1,030	7,258	258	59	3,254
Territories	9,800	5,070	1,993	3,918	4,093
Totals	414,582	1,526,541	101,409	246,940	1,229,174

B. CALL ISSUED TO THE SCANDINAVIANS
BY SILFVERSPARRE'S COMPANY *

Have you forgotten the heroes who fought for your religious freedom and fell on Lützen's bloody field? Has the blood in your veins become so thin that without shame you allow apostles of treason to appear among you?

Swedes! have you forgotten that in the course of mankind's progress, enlightenment, and freedom the Swedish people were always found among the zealous defenders? Norsemen! Have you forgotten how stanchly and heroically you defended your free constitution in dear old Norway? It used to be our pride to say: among Scandinavians were found no traitors. Countrymen who have been misled, wake up! and bethink yourselves before you go too far. Consider carefully before you take the decisive step and place yourselves in the ranks of the traitors, for, know that thereby you lose irrevocably the most precious Scandinavian inheritance—a Norseman's honor! Fellow-Countrymen, how shall posterity judge such an inscription on a fallen comrade's grave: "Murdered by his fellow-countryman's treason," since this touches the honor of the old Northland and its freedom-loving people. Do not believe that former friendly and brotherly ties will prevent us from carrying out the law of justice—on the contrary, in order to erase a stain of disgrace you will become the first sacrifice.

Scandinavians! Countrymen! Do not let our warning be in vain! Be true to your inherited honor. Never disgrace your dear old native land. Never forget your fellow-countrymen in the army who courageously and patiently on many bloody battlefields have defended your freedom, your life, and your home! With joy and pride we should stretch out our hands to meet in brotherly affection when after having won the victory and an honorable peace, we turn again to the peaceful cares of the home.

* Chicago *Hemlandet.* The issue in which this call appeared was incorrectly dated March 6, 1863, by the printer, but it should have been dated May 6, 1863. (In order to confine the call to one page, the first paragraph and the list of signatures have been omitted here.)

C. COMPANIES AND REGIMENTS OF FOREIGN-BORN IN THE UNION ARMY *

1. German Units

NEW YORK

Infantry

Fifth New York Militia
Seventh New York Regiment, Steuben Rifles
Eighth New York Infantry, First German Rifles
Twentieth New York Infantry, United Turner Regiment
Twenty-ninth New York Regiment, Astor Rifles
Forty-first New York Regiment, De Kalb Regiment
Forty-fifth New York Regiment, German Rifles No. 5 or Platt Deutsch
    Regiment
Forty-sixth New York Regiment, Frémont Regiment
Fifty-second New York Regiment, Sigel Rifles
Fifty-fourth New York Regiment, Schwarze Jäger
Fifty-eighth New York Regiment, First Morgan Rifles (part German)
Sixty-eighth New York Volunteers, Cameron Rifles (part German)
One Hundred and Third New York Regiment, German Rifles No. 3 (one
    elite company composed entirely of former German officers)
One Hundred and Nineteenth New York Regiment (one-third German)
One Hundred and Forty-ninth New York Regiment (part German)
One Hundred and Ninetieth New York Regiment (part German)

Artillery

Brickel's artillery, First New York Independent Battalion Light Artillery
Battery Sigel in the Forty-sixth New York Regiment (composed of ex-
    perienced Germans)
Fifteenth New York Heavy Artillery
Schirmer's battery, Second Independent New York Battery
Von Sturmfel's battery, Light Artillery Company A, later Thirteenth
    Independent Battery
Wiedrich's battery, First Regiment Light Artillery, Battery I

Cavalry

Dickel's mounted rifles, Fourth Regiment Cavalry (largely German)
First Regiment New York Cavalry (four companies German)

* The sources from which this list has been compiled appear in the notes to Chapters V and VI. In general they are Kaufmann, *Die Deutschen im Bürgerkriege*; Haiman, *Polish Past in America*; Hokanson, *Swedish Immigrants*. All of these have been checked by *Official War Records*; Heitman (comp.), *Historical Register and Dictionary*; and *Official Army Register of the Volunteer Forces*.

NEW ENGLAND

Infantry

First Regiment Connecticut Volunteer Infantry, Company B

Sixth Regiment Connecticut Volunteer Infantry, Company H (from Bridgeport, Meriden, and New York. There was also Company B from New Haven, Norwich, and Waterbury under Captain Klein.)

Eleventh Connecticut Regiment, company under Captain Mögling

Seventeenth Massachusetts Regiment, one company recruited in Boston (one-third German)

Twenty-ninth Massachusetts Regiment, one company (one-third German)

PENNSYLVANIA

Infantry

Twenty-seventh Pennsylvania Regiment

Seventy-third Regiment, Pennsylvania Troops

Seventy-fourth Pennsylvania Regiment

Seventy-fifth Pennsylvania Regiment

Ninety-eighth Pennsylvania Regiment, originally the Twenty-first Männerchor Rifle Guards (Home guards)

NEW JERSEY

Cavalry

Third New Jersey Cavalry, from Hoboken

Artillery

Battery A, First New Jersey Artillery

Batteries B and C, First New Jersey Artillery (largely German)

OHIO

Infantry

Ninth Ohio Regiment, Ohio Turners, first German regiment, from Cincinnati

Twenty-eighth Ohio Regiment, second German regiment, from Cincinnati

Thirty-seventh Ohio Regiment, third German regiment, from northern Ohio

Forty-seventh Ohio Regiment (over one-half German)

Fifty-eighth Ohio Regiment (over one-half German)

Seventy-fourth Ohio Regiment (over one-half German)

One Hundred and Sixth Ohio Regiment, fourth German regiment

One Hundred and Seventh Ohio Regiment, fifth German regiment
One Hundred and Eighth Ohio Regiment, sixth German regiment
One Hundred and Sixty-fifth Ohio Regiment (over one-half German)

Cavalry

Third Ohio Cavalry (partly German)

Artillery

Dilger's battery, Battery I, First Light Artillery, originally Von Dammert's battery from Cincinnati
Hofman's battery, Fourth Ohio Battery, from Cincinnati
Markgraf's battery, Eighth Independent Battery, from Cincinnati (half German)
Twentieth Ohio Independent Battery, from Cleveland (about half German)

INDIANA

Infantry

Fourteenth Indiana Regiment (half German; Company E, wholly German)
Twenty-fourth Indiana Regiment (half German)
Thirty-second Indiana Regiment
One Hundred and Thirty-sixth Indiana Regiment, from Evansville (half German)

Artillery

Behr's battery, Sixth Independent Indiana Battery, from Indianapolis
Klaus's battery, First Independent Indiana Battery, from Evansville

ILLINOIS

Infantry

Ninth Illinois Regiment, a three months regiment (half German)
Twenty-fourth Illinois Regiment, Hecker's Jäger (largely but not wholly German)
Twenty-seventh Illinois Regiment (half German)
Thirty-sixth Illinois Regiment (half German)
Forty-third Illinois Regiment (second-generation Germans from Belleville)
Forty-fourth Illinois Regiment (half German)
Forty-fifth Illinois Regiment (half German)
Fifty-seventh Illinois Regiment (half German)

Fifty-eighth Illinois Regiment (half German)
Eighty-second Illinois Regiment, second Hecker regiment

Artillery

Battery E, Second Illinois Light Artillery (almost wholly German)

Cavalry

Twelfth Illinois Cavalry, Company B
Thirteenth Illinois Cavalry (half German)
Thielemann's battalion of dragoons, Company A, Sixteenth Illinois
   Cavalry
Schambeck's independent cavalry company, or Washington Light Cav-
   alry; later, Company B, First Regiment Dragoons; then Company C,
   Sixteenth Illinois Cavalry (half German)

Artillery

Gumbert's battery of artillery, Battery E, Second Light Artillery (half
   German)
D'Osband's battery of artillery (half German)
Stollemann's battery of artillery (half German)

MISSOURI

Infantry

First Missouri Volunteers including three Turner companies of St. Louis
   and one Irish company, after the three months service, an artillery
   regiment (half German)
Second Missouri Regiment (Germans and German-Americans)
Third Missouri Regiment, Sigel's regiment
Fourth Missouri Regiment, Black Jägers (including a few native Ameri-
   cans and a number of Bohemians)
Fifth Missouri Regiment, from southern portion of St. Louis and adjacent
   counties
Seventh Missouri Regiment, Company I
Twelfth Missouri Regiment, Osterhaus' regiment until he became briga-
   dier general
Seventeenth Missouri Regiment, Western Turner Rifles, composed of
   Turners drawn from a wide area
Eighteenth Missouri Regiment, Company K
Thirty-ninth Missouri Regiment (half German)
Fortieth Missouri Regiment (half German)
Forty-first Missouri Regiment (half German)
Home guards, five regiments

Artillery

Backhoff's independent battalion light artillery, Batteries B and C, First Missouri Light Artillery
Essig's, Landgräber's, Mann's, Neustadter's, and Wölfe's batteries
  Essig's, Battery A, Franz Backhoff's independent battalion light artillery, three months service
  Neustädter's, Battery C, Franz Backhoff's independent battalion light artillery
  Mann's, Battery B, Franz Backhoff's independent battalion light artillery, later Battery C, First Missouri Regiment Light Artillery
  Landgräber's, Battery F, First Independent Battery Flying Artillery, later Second Regiment Missouri Light Artillery
Pioneer Company, created by Sigel

Cavalry

First Missouri Cavalry, Company A
Fourth Missouri Cavalry, Frémont Hussars (almost wholly German)

Infantry

Fifth Wisconsin Militia (overwhelmingly German)
Sixth Wisconsin Regiment, Company F (more than half German)
Ninth Wisconsin Regiment, called Salomon Guards, in honor of the governor
Eighteenth Wisconsin Regiment (more than half German)
Twentieth Wisconsin Regiment (more than half German)
Twenty-third Wisconsin Regiment (more than half German)
Twenty-sixth Wisconsin Regiment
Twenty-seventh Wisconsin Regiment (more than half German)
Thirty-fourth Wisconsin Regiment (more than half German)
Thirty-fifth Wisconsin Regiment (more than half German)
Forty-fifth Wisconsin Regiment (one-half German)

Artillery

Second Wisconsin Independent Battery Light Artillery
Twelfth Wisconsin Battery, Platt Deutsch Battery, from Sheboygan

Sixteenth Iowa Infantry, Companies B, G, K (half German)
Fifth Iowa Cavalry, Company F (two-thirds German), from Dubuque and Burlington

(The First Iowa Regiment contained many Germans, but it was not, strictly speaking, a German unit.)

MARYLAND

Color Company, Public Guard Regiment, Fifth Maryland Infantry
Several companies organized just before Gettysburg

NEBRASKA

First Veteran Nebraska Cavalry (half German)

MINNESOTA

Infantry

First Minnesota Regiment (more than one-third German; Company A almost one-half German)
Second, Fourth, and Sixth Minnesota Regiments (one-third German)

Artillery

Münch's battery or Pfänder's battery, First Independent Battery (a Turner unit)

Cavalry

Brackett's cavalry, Third Independent Battalion Cavalry

KANSAS

First Kansas Regiment (Company A about one-half German)
Second Kansas Regiment (about one-half German)

WEST VIRGINIA

Dilger's Mountain Howitzer Battery, Company E, First Battalion Light Artillery

KENTUCKY

Infantry

Fifth Kentucky Regiment, from Louisville (half German)
Sixth Kentucky Regiment, from Louisville, considered the best regiment of the state (half German)

Cavalry

Second Kentucky Cavalry (many Germans)

Artillery

(Stone's Battery, Battery A, First Regiment Light Artillery, independent, contained many Germans, though it was not, strictly speaking, a German unit.)

TEXAS

First United States Regiment (almost all of the six hundred men were German)

2. *Irish Units*

NEW ENGLAND

Ninth Massachusetts Regiment, Irish Ninth, from Boston and environs
Twenty-eighth Massachusetts Regiment, part of the Irish Brigade
Fifteenth Maine Regiment, from Aroostook and Washington counties
Ninth Connecticut Regiment (Irish predominating in every company)
Tenth New Hampshire Infantry (hardly an Irish unit, though it was so regarded)
Thirteenth Vermont Regiment, Company A, Emmett Guards, from Burlington
Nineteenth Massachusetts, Company E

NEW YORK

Infantry

Sixty-ninth Militia
Irish Brigade
    Sixty-third New York Regiment
    Sixty-ninth New York Regiment
    Eighty-eighth New York, Connaught Rangers or *Faugh-a-Ballagh* or Mrs. Meagher's Own
Irish Legion or Corcoran's Legion
    One Hundred and Fifty-fifth New York Regiment
    One Hundred and Sixty-fourth New York Regiment
    One Hundred and Seventieth New York Regiment
    One Hundred and Seventy-fifth New York Regiment
    One Hundred and Eighty-second New York Regiment
Eleventh New York Regiment, First Fire Zouaves (decidedly, but not wholly, Irish)
Twentieth New York State Militia, Ulster Guard, recruited among Irish miners
Thirty-seventh New York Regiment, Irish Rifles
One Hundred and Fifth New York Regiment, Companies G, H, and I,

Western Irish Regiment (by 1862 only Companies G, H, and I remained Irish)

Artillery

Second Independent Battalion Light Artillery, Batteries A and B, later Fourteenth and Fifteenth New York Independent Batteries

PENNSYLVANIA

Infantry

Second Regiment Pennsylvania Reserves, Company C, Hibernian Target Company
Thirteenth Pennsylvania Reserves, Company F
Twenty-fourth Pennsylvania Infantry, three months service
Sixty-ninth Pennsylvania Infantry
One Hundred and Sixteenth Pennsylvania Regiment, a part of the Irish Brigade, called the Cameron Dragoons

Cavalry

Galligher's Battalion Irish Brigade, Irish Dragoons, part of the One Hundred and Sixteenth Pennsylvania Regiment, later the Thirteenth Pennsylvania Cavalry

CENTRAL WEST

Infantry

Eighth Ohio Regiment, Company B, Hibernian Guards
Tenth Ohio Regiment
Sixty-first Ohio Regiment (two companies Irish)
Thirty-fifth Indiana Regiment (First Irish Regiment)
Sixty-first Indiana Regiment, later merged with the Thirty-fifth Indiana Regiment
Twenty-third Illinois Infantry, Mulligan's Brigade, recruited in several western states
Ninetieth Illinois Regiment, Irish Legion
Seventh Missouri Infantry
Eleventh Wisconsin Regiment (largely Irish)
Seventeenth Wisconsin Regiment (Wisconsin Irish Brigade)
Twenty-seventh Michigan Regiment (partly Irish)

Artillery

Artillery Company, Twenty-third Illinois Regiment, Oconto (Wisconsin) Irish Guards; later Battery L, First Illinois Light Artillery

Eleventh Wisconsin Independent, Rourke's battery, in Twenty-third Illinois Infantry; later Battery L, First Illinois Light Artillery

3. French Units

Fifty-fifth New York Regiment, Gardes Lafayette (French majority found in over half of the companies); later absorbed into the Thirty-eighth, and still later into the Fortieth New York Regiment (Company H, German; Company K, Irish; Company I, native American)

Sixty-second New York Regiment, one company, Anderson Zouaves

4. Scotch Unit

Seventy-ninth New York Regiment, Cameron's Highlanders (Scotch and men of Scotch ancestry were at first in the majority but were later outnumbered by the Irish.)

5. Scandinavian Units

Infantry

Fifteenth Wisconsin Regiment, Scandinavian Regiment (chiefly Norwegians with some Swedes and a very few Danes)

Third Wisconsin Regiment, Company K, Dane County Guards

Third Minnesota, Company D, Scandinavian Guards, Hans Mattson's company (Swedes and some Norwegians)

Thirty-third Illinois Regiment, Companies E and G (Swedes)

Thirty-sixth Illinois Regiment, Company F, from Fox River Norwegian Colony (Norwegian-Americans)

Forty-third Illinois, Companies C and E (Swedes almost exclusively)

Fifty-seventh Illinois Regiment, Company D, Swedish Union Guards

Swedish Home Guard companies in New York City, Chicago, and Minnesota, during the draft

  Svea Garde, Second New York Militia Regiment

  Svea Guards, Thirtieth Illinois Militia

  Scandinavian Guards of Nicollet County, Minnesota, to protect against the Indian uprising (entirely of Swedes); Company D, Third Minnesota Regiment

  Scandinavian Company, First New York Volunteers

Artillery

First Illinois Light Artillery, Battery H, Silfversparre's Battery

Second Illinois Light Artillery, Battery G (largely Swedes with some Danes and Norwegians), Stohlbrand's Battery

6. Swiss Units

Fifteenth Missouri Infantry, Swiss Rifles (regularly called a Swiss regiment but soon composed of more Germans than Swiss)
Ninth New York Militia, one company
Eighty-second Illinois Volunteers, Frey's company of Swiss from Tell City, Indiana
First Regiment United States Sharpshooters, Company G from Wisconsin

7. Mexican Units

Infantry

Alarid's company militia infantry, Gaspar Ortiz y Alarid's Independent Company New Mexico Militia, three months service
Gonzales' company militia infantry, Nestor Gonzales Independent Company Militia, three months service
Martinez' company militia, José I. Martinez' Company, Mora County Militia; later First Regiment New Mexico Infantry, Company A
Francisco Perea's Battalion Militia, Independent Militia Infantry, three months service
Luis Tafolla's Company Militia, Independent Militia Infantry, three months service

Cavalry

Antonio Maria Vigil's Independent Company Cavalry, three months service

8. Dutch Unit

Second Michigan Cavalry, Company D

9. Welsh Unit

Ninety-seventh New York Regiment, Company E

10. Mixed Units

Enfants Perdus, independent regiment without numerical designation
Thirty-first New York Regiment (some companies almost entirely of Poles)
Thirty-ninth New York Regiment, Garibaldi Guard
Fifty-third New York Regiment, D'Epineuil Zouaves (many French officers and men but an intermixture including one company of Indians from the Tuscarora Reservation)
Fifty-eighth New York Regiment, Polish Legion
Ninety-seventh New York Regiment, Company H

First New York Cavalry Regiment, Company E

Eighty-ninth Illinois, the Railroad Regiment, Company D (fifty-six foreign-born in a company of fifty-seven)

D. CAPTAINS OF SWEDISH BIRTH IN THE UNION SERVICE *

Ahlström, J. V., captain, Company G, Fourteenth New Jersey Infantry; rose to major, Third New Jersey Cavalry

Anderson, Daniel, captain, First Iowa Cavalry; rose to colonel

Arosenius, Carl, captain, Company C, Forty-third Illinois Infantry

Balling, O. P. H., captain, Company I (Scandinavian Corps), First New York Regiment; rose to lieutenant colonel, One Hundred and Forty-fifth New York Infantry

Bergland, Eric, first lieutenant, Fifty-seventh Illinois Regiment; captain in 1862; stayed on in the service after the war after attendance at West Point

Broady, Knut Oskar, captain in the Sixty-first New York Infantry; rose to lieutenant colonel and was brevetted colonel

Brydolf, Fabian, captain, Company I, Sixth Iowa Regiment; rose to lieutenant colonel of the Twenty-fifth Iowa and then of the Second Regiment, Iowa Veteran Reserve Corps

Danielson, John A., captain, Company H, Fifteenth Iowa; wounded at Shiloh

Eckström, Axel P., captain, Sixty-fifth Illinois; killed in battle

Edvall, Olof S., captain, Company C, Forty-third Illinois Infantry; fatally wounded at Shiloh

Forsse, Eric, captain, Company D, Fifty-seventh Illinois Infantry; rose to major of regiment

Gustafson, Charles, captain, Company F, Fifteenth Wisconsin; killed at Chickamauga

Gustafson, John G., entered as sergeant, Company D, Third Minnesota; rose to lieutenant colonel, One Hundred and Twelfth United States Colored Regiment

Helleday, Gustaf Blidstein, entered as private, Ninety-ninth New York Regiment (Union Coast Guard); became captain; rose to lieutenant colonel of regiment; died of disease in August, 1862

* Compiled from all sources available, checked against *Volunteer Army Register*; *Official War Records*; Heitman (comp.), *Historical Register and Dictionary*; Henry (comp.), *Military Record of Civilian Appointments*; the Descriptive Books; etc. Dependence has been placed on Hokanson for correct spellings of the Swedish named. This writer gives names of other captains (*Swedish Immigrants in Lincoln's Time*, 194) which the author has not been able to identify in the official sources and has not, therefore, accepted.

Holmstedt, Ernest W., commissioned at once, owing to Mexican War service; rose to lieutenant colonel, Forty-first New York Regiment; then colonel of Seventy-fourth United States Colored Infantry

Hultman, Elof Oscar, captain in Fifty-eighth New York Infantry; soon became major on General Blenker's staff; resigned in 1862

Jocknick, George F., captain, Company I, Third New York Cavalry

Johnson, Adolphus J., captain in First New Jersey Regiment; rose to colonel, Eighth New Jersey Volunteers; disabled at Yorktown in May, 1862

Johnson, Charles L., captain, Company M, Minnesota First Heavy Artillery

Johnson, Eric, captain, Company D, Fifty-seventh Illinois Infantry; resigned in September, 1862

Landström, C. E., captain, Company B, Fifteenth Iowa Volunteers; rose from second lieutenant to captain

Leatz, Axel, captain of Company E, Fifth United States Veteran Regiment; rose to lieutenant colonel

Lembke, Jonas ("James" in *Official War Records*) Frederick, captain, Battery E, Second United States Colored Light Artillery; killed at Big Creek, Arkansas, in July, 1864

Lindquist, G. F., captain, Fifth New York Volunteers; participated in thirty battles

Lund, Herman, captain in Sixteenth Illinois Infantry

Mattson, Hans, captain, Company D, Third Minnesota Regiment; rose to colonel of the regiment

Nelson, John A., captain, Company E, Thirteenth Connecticut Volunteer Infantry; transferred to Thirtieth Massachusetts

Nelson, T. A., captain, Svea Guards, Second New York Militia, organized in 1863 to maintain order during the draft

Nordenstrohl, Thomas J. B., lieutenant in the Ninety-ninth New York Volunteers; topographical engineer with rank of captain for the third division, Eighteenth Army Corps; honorably discharged in July, 1864, but remained in the army

Silfversparre, Axel (soldier of fortune), captain and organizer of Battery H, First Illinois Light Artillery

Sparreström, Frederick, captain, Battery G, Second Illinois Light Artillery; resigned August, 1864

Stack, Gustaf A., captain, Scandinavian Guards (Home Guards organized in 1862 in Nicollet County, Minnesota, during the Indian uprising)

Stenbeck, Andrew, captain, Battery H, Second Illinois Light Artillery; resigned May, 1863

Stohlbrand, Charles John, captain, Battery G, Second Illinois Light Artillery; rose to rank of brigadier general; had been transferred in 1863 to command of the artillery brigade of the Fifteenth Army Corps with virtually the duties of a brigadier general

Wickstrum (or "Wickström"), Peter M., last captain of the three who headed Company D, Fifty-seventh Illinois Infantry

E. POLISH OFFICERS IN THE UNION ARMY *

Brigadier General

Shoepf, Albin (born near Cracow of an Austrian father and a Polish mother), commissioned brigadier general at outbreak of war

Colonels

Karge, Joseph, Second New Jersey Cavalry, transferred from First New Jersey Cavalry

Kryzanowski, Wladimir, Fifty-eighth New York Infantry

Sokalski, George O. (Pole of the second generation), lieutenant colonel, Second United States Cavalry

Majors

Koniuszewski, Ladislaus E., Twenty-sixth Missouri Regiment

Raszewski, Alexander, Thirty-first New York Infantry

Captains

Antoniewski, Edward, Company A, Fifty-eighth New York Regiment; died of wounds received at Gettysburg

Barwicki, Charles, Company G, Fifty-eighth New York Infantry (Polish Legion)

Bielaski, Alexander, aide-de-camp to General McClernand with the rank of captain; killed at Belmont in November, 1861

Blandowski, Constantin (soldier of fortune) in Third Missouri Infantry; wounded mortally

Galeski, Ludwig, Company H, Fifty-eighth New York Infantry; resigned in January, 1865

Gloskowski, Joseph, Twenty-ninth New York Infantry, in the Signal Service

* Individuals who merited a place in this list may have been omitted, as no one was admitted unless he could be verified from *Volunteer Army Register, Official War Records,* or the Descriptive Books. It seemed preferable possibly to omit some person rather than to print names which might prove incorrect, even though it may be conceded that the official lists are not infallible. Haiman, *Polish Past in America,* has been depended upon for spellings of these names.

Hulanicki, Edmund T., Twelfth United States Heavy Artillery

Hulanicki, Thaddeus C. (brother of Edmund), Battery L, Second Illinois Light Artillery

Kiolbassa, Peter, Sixth United States Colored Cavalry

Kossak, William, engineer with the rank of captain on the staff of General Grant

Kraszynski, Maurice ("Morris" in the *Official War Records* and the *Volunteer Army Register*), Eleventh Connecticut Infantry

Krzywoszynski, Julius C., pioneer in the Signal Corps; later captain, Company C, Twenty-second United States Colored Infantry ·

Leski, Baron Wladislaus, aide-de-camp to General McDowell with rank of captain

Magnicki (or "Magnitzki"), Gustav, Twentieth Massachusetts Regiment and Veteran Reserve Corps

Mlotkowski, Stanislaus, Battery A, Independent Pennsylvania Light Artillery

Morozowicz, Adelbert, Ninth Independent New York Light Artillery; dismissed in November, 1862

Radecki, Gustav H., Third Massachusetts Cavalry, First Texas Cavalry

Soboleski, Lucas, Independent Company of Missouri Lancers

Stampoffski (or "Stempowski"), Bernard A., Company F, Ninth Illinois Cavalry

Wesolowski, Maurice, Company T, Twenty-eighth Ohio Volunteer Infantry; resigned in 1862

Lieutenants

Boruski, Charles, One Hundred and Sixteenth New York Infantry; fatally wounded at Plain Shore, Louisiana, May 27, 1863

Michalowski, von, Theophilus B., First United States Artillery, Batteries H and I

Smolinski, Joseph, Jr., second lieutenant, Company C, United States Lancers; later in Ninth New York Cavalry (youngest commissioned officer in the United States Cavalry)

Wrotnowski, I. A., topographical engineer under General Weitzel; killed during the siege of Port Hudson, 1863

Zalinski, Edmund L. G., aide-de-camp to General Miles; second lieutenant, Second New York Cavalry, February, 1865; stayed on in the service and rose to distinction after the war

F. SWEDISH KNIGHTS-ERRANT AND
SOLDIERS OF FORTUNE *

Ackerström, John C., joined the Fifteenth Kentucky Cavalry; fell at Fort
Pillow

Anderson, Hjälmar Harold Christian

Asker, John, served in Royal Military Academy; in Forty-eighth New
York Volunteers

Banforth, Herman and Frederick (brothers), in Fifty-sixth Massachusetts

Bergquist, Pehr Gustaf, private; died of a wound

Berlin, Carl Ludvig Theodor, artillerist, in Ninth New York Cavalry

Blomberg, Carl Olof Oscar, in Swedish militia; in First New York Regiment; rose to major

Carlstein, John August, of Skara Institute; wounded and discharged
honorably from the United States Army

Cederström, von, Baron Jakob

Edgren, August Hjälmar, of Royal Värmland Regiment; staff engineer
in charge of battery construction

Engelbloom, Oscar, sergeant in Göta Artillery; captain in the United
States service; recommended for major

Grevellius, Carl Frederick, quartermaster sergeant and lieutenant in the
Swedish army; lieutenant in Fifty-second New York Volunteers

Gründström, Axel Henry, private in the Eighteenth New York; aide to
General Kearney; reached lieutenancy

Grunfelt, ———— (under assumed name of Roche), sergeant of Swedish
cavalry; captain in Twelfth New York Cavalry

Hamberg, Charles Nicolaus Conrad, lieutenant in Gotland militia; topographical officer; lieutenant; rose to captain in October of 1865

Holstein, von, Baron Corfitz Ludvig Joakin Stael, cadet, Royal Academy;
enlisted in the United States as "Charles Holstein"; lieutenant colonel
of a colored regiment

Hultman, Elof Oscar, Royal Militia; with French and Mexican armies;
major on Blenker's staff

Källstrom, Herman, Karlberg Military School; drillmaster at Washington dockyard; aide to General Cox

---

* This list is based on names found in the Consular Dispatches and Notes to and from
the Swedish Legation and on a list of Swedish officers in the Union service published in
the Chicago *Hemlandet*, December 4, 1861. The author has accepted the spelling adopted
by Hokanson, *Swedish Immigrants*, as correct. The more prominent officers appear in
Official War Records and can be there verified.

Knorring, von, Carl Gustaf, lieutenant in Swedish army; lieutenant colonel on staff of United States Commander in Chief

Leatz, Axel Arfvid, sergeant in Sweden; private in Fifth New York; lieutenant; wounded at Bethesda Church

Lindbergh, Mans Olsson, in Swedish and British service; captain in Eighty-second Illinois

Lindström, Anders August, lieutenant in Royal Militia Life Regiment; enlisted in the United States Army as a private

Ljunggren, Edward, Swedish officer; enlisted in the United States Army as a private

Nerman, Carl Ulrik Oscar, lieutenant in Royal Militia Life Guards; lieutenant in Forty-first New York Regiment; rose to captain

Peterson, Christian

Rosencrantz, Frederick Anton Ulrik, sergeant in Royal Life Guards; lieutenant in Twentieth New York; adjutant to several generals; rose to lieutenant colonel (brevet rank)

Rosencrantz, Palle, lieutenant in Skåne Dragoons; in Danish, French, and British service; major in fourth New York Cavalry

Rosenstjerna, Nils, Swedish officer; entered the United States Army as a private in the Third Rhode Island Infantry

Rossander, Carl August, Swedish officer; entered the United States Army; rose to lieutenant colonel in the Regular Army in the Sixth Cavalry after the war

Silfversparre, Axel, lieutenant in Swedish army; first under General Frémont; organized and commanded Battery H, First Illinois Light Artillery

Torslow, Otto L., in Royal Svea Regiment; artillerist, lieutenant in Battery G, First Rhode Island Light Artillery; retired in 1864

Uggla, C. N., Swedish officer; entered the United States Army as a private (Uggla's name does not occur in American records)

Vegesack, von, Ernst Mattais Peter, captain in Dalarne Regiment; major on General Wool's staff; enlisted as a private; became colonel of Twentieth New York; resigned in 1863; received the Congressional Medal of Honor

Warberg, Adolph Carlsson, lieutenant colonel in Alfsborg Regiment in Sweden; aide to General Frémont; April, 1862—March, 1863, major; October, 1864—March, 1865, lieutenant colonel, First Regiment United States Colored Cavalry; resigned, August, 1865

Weinberg, Carl Rudolph Constantine, Swedish officer in Helsinge Regiment; enlisted as a private in the United States Army

G. GERMAN SURGEONS IN THE UNION SERVICE *

Adolphus, Dr. Philipp, serving in the hospitals in Maryland; with the Fourth United States Artillery, 1862

Alter, Dr. Henry H., Fifty-second Kentucky Regiment

Axt, Dr. Gottfried, hospital steward in the Twentieth New York Regiment; acting assistant surgeon, 1864–1865

Bachman, Dr. J. P., assistant surgeon, Fourth Kentucky Regiment; resigned in December, 1864

Börner, Dr. Charles E., first assistant surgeon, Eighty-second Illinois Infantry

Borck, Dr. Edward, Tenth Maryland Infantry and Third Maryland Cavalry; later of Buschbeck's brigade; discharged in December, 1864

Bruckner, Dr. Karl, assistant surgeon, Seventeenth Missouri Regiment

Gross, Dr. Ferdinand H., medical director in the Fourteenth Army Corps; on General Thomas' staff

Hammer, Dr. Adam, Lieutenant Colonel of Fourth Missouri in 1862; Fourth Missouri Volunteers; devoted himself to surgical work at various military hospitals during the greater part of the war

Häring, Dr. Theodore, assistant regimental staff physician in the Ninth Wisconsin Regiment

Hartmann, Dr. Karl S., One Hundred and Seventh Ohio Regiment; killed at Chancellorsville

Hass, Dr. Emil, Fifth Missouri Militia Regiment; later chief surgeon in Boonville with the title of major (according to Kaufmann, but unsupported by official records)

Hausen, von, Dr. Julius H. (Austrian), regimental and then brigade physician in the Army of the Potomac

Heiland, Dr. Charles, assistant regimental physician in the Twentieth New York Turner Regiment; dismissed in 1862

Hovet, Dr. Henry, regimental physician in the German Forty-sixth New York Regiment; left in December, 1863

Hoffmeister, Dr. Augustus W., surgeon of the Eighth Iowa Regiment; resigned in August, 1864

Hübschmann, Dr. Franz, regimental physician, first of the Twenty-sixth

---

* This list had to be compiled largely from secondary sources, since the sources used for officers yielded little data on surgeons. The writer leaned heavily on Kaufmann, *Die Deutschen im Bürgerkriege*, 478–566. The most valuable primary source by which to check the service was *Volunteer Army Register*. The Jackets in the National Archives have been useful for some of the medical directors of corps. Each name admitted to the list has found confirmation from at least one source other than Kaufmann.

Wisconsin, later of a brigade, and then of a division; supervised the hospitals at a number of battles—Chancellorsville, Gettysburg, Chickamauga, etc.; head of an army corps at Gettysburg

Körper, Dr. Egon A., staff physician of the German Seventy-fifth Pennsylvania Regiment

Löhr, Dr. Louis, regimental physician of the Ninth Wisconsin Regiment; mustered out on December 9, 1864

Meyer, Dr. Louis G., staff physician of the Twenty-fifth Ohio Regiment; then chief medical director of the Eleventh Corps

Moschzisker, Dr. Franz A. (Austrian), physician in the hospitals of Washington

Neuhaus, Dr. Rudolf, regimental physician and then medical director in Sigel's corps (given by Kaufmann, but not in official records)

Reichenbach, Dr. Hugo, serving as surgeon with the First Iowa Regiment

Reuss, Dr. Peter Joseph, regimental physician of the Twenty-ninth New York Regiment; regarded as one of the best surgeons in the Army of the Potomac

Schenck, Dr. Julius C. (son of Dr. Konrad Schenck), assistant surgeon in the Twenty-first Ohio Regiment

Schenck, Dr. Konrad, of Cleveland, regimental physician of the Thirty-seventh Ohio Regiment; resigned in June, 1862

Schlötzer, Dr. George, Eighty-second Infantry, mustered in during September, 1862; discharged in January, 1864

Schmidt, Dr. Ernst, medical director of the Sixteenth Army Corps; one of the most distinguished of the German physicians

Söllheim, Dr. Konrad, of Cincinnati, served for more than a year in the Ninth Ohio Regiment

Spiegelhalter, Dr. Joseph, important surgeon of St. Louis; staff surgeon in the Twelfth Missouri Regiment

Starkloff, Dr. Hugo M., regimental physician for the greater part of the war in the Twelfth Missouri Regiment

Stumberg, Dr. John H., assistant physician of the Twenty-ninth Missouri Regiment; transferred to the German Third Missouri Regiment after June of 1864

Trau, Dr. Johannes P., surgeon in Blenker's division, though not listed in the *Official War Records*

Weber, Dr. Gustav C. A., surgeon of the One Hundred and Twenty-ninth Ohio Regiment; general medical director of Ohio troops; one of the most famous of German surgeons; rendered great service in the organization of medical care for the army in the West, especially in the appointment of able surgeons

Zipperlen, Dr. Adolf, regimental physician of the One Hundred and

Eighth Ohio, serving throughout most of the war; especially distinguished as a surgeon

The following served, but designation of regiment is impossible:

Doctors Basch, Stummer, and Welcher (possibly Rudolf Welker, surgeon of the Eighteenth New York Regiment), in some capacity with Blenker's regiment

Doctors Ballade, Steele, and William Wagner, with Illinois regiments at Camp Yates

H. HUNGARIAN OFFICERS OF HIGH RANK *

Major General

Stahel-Szamwald, Julius H., brigadier general, November, 1861; major general, March, 1863

Brigadier General

Asboth, Alexander, on the staffs of Generals Frémont, Hunter, and Curtis; brevetted major general

Colonels and Lieutenant Colonels

Albert, Anzelm, colonel, adjutant, and then chief of staff to Frémont

Amsberg, George (German-born, Hungarian by adoption), colonel, Forty-fifth New York Infantry

Dobozy, Peter Paul, lieutenant colonel, Fourth Colored Heavy Artillery

Fiala, John A., colonel, on General Frémont's staff, topographical engineer

Figyelmessy, Philip, colonel, on General Frémont's staff; inspector general at Wheeling

Fornet, Cornelius, colonel, Twenty-second New Jersey Volunteers (never served because of an accident and, naturally, not in official records)

Knefler, Frederick, colonel, Seventy-ninth Indiana Regiment; brevetted brigadier general in 1865

Korponay, Gabriel, lieutenant colonel, Seventh New York Regiment; was offered the rank of colonel, but rejected it because of health (not in official records)

Kozlay, Eugene A., colonel, Fifty-fourth New York Regiment (Black Jägers); brevetted brigadier general in 1865

* All names have been checked in *Official War Records*, Heitman, and *Volunteer Army Register*. For spellings, Vasvary, *Lincoln's Hungarian Heroes*, was followed because it was the source most likely to give the names correctly.

Mihalotzy, Géza, colonel, Twenty-fourth Illinois Regiment; killed in Tennessee

Nemeth, Joseph (soldier of fortune), colonel, Fifth Missouri Cavalry (Benton Hussars); discharged when his unit was consolidated with another

Perczel, Nicholas, colonel, Tenth Iowa Regiment; resigned in November, 1862

Pokorny, Anthony, lieutenant colonel of Seventh New York Volunteers in November, 1864

Pomutz, George, lieutenant colonel, Fifteenth Iowa Regiment; brevetted brigadier general in March, 1865

Rombauer, Robert J., colonel, First Missouri Reserve Corps

Szabad, Emery (soldier of fortune), brevet colonel, adjutant on staff of General Ayres

Utassy, George F., colonel, organized and commanded the Garibaldi Guard; court-martialed and dismissed from the service in May, 1863

Vandor, Joseph, colonel, Seventh Wisconsin Volunteers; resigned in January, 1862

Waagner, Gustav, colonel, commander of Second New York Heavy Artillery; discharged in August, 1863

Zagonyi, Charles, major in Frémont body guard; aide-de-camp to General Frémont, colonel

Zsulavszky, Ladislaus, colonel of the Eighty-second Colored Regiment

Majors

Czermelyi, Joseph, brevet major with titular rank of captain, Eighty-second Colored Infantry

Esti, William M., enlisted as lieutenant and rose to rank of major, Twenty-sixth Ohio Regiment

Gálfy-Gállik ("Gallfy" in American records), Andrew, Fifty-eighth Ohio Infantry

Haraszthy, Géza, Eighteenth New York Regiment

Hillebrandt, Hugo (soldier of fortune), lieutenant and adjutant, rising to major, Thirty-ninth New York Regiment; after being discharged for ill health, he became a captain in the Veteran Corps

Kuné, Julius, Twenty-fourth Illinois Infantry, May–October 31, 1861

Lülley, Emmanuel, a secret agent of the Department of Justice (pensioned as such, though there is no official evidence of military service on his part during the war)

Mészaros, Emerie, major, Fourth Missouri Cavalry; served in Florida under General Asboth

Mundee-Mándy, Charles, assistant adjutant general with rank of major, 1862; brevet colonel and brevet brigadier general, April, 1865

Ruttkay, Albert, First Florida Cavalry

Semsey, Charles, major in Forty-fifth New York Regiment; mustered out in June, 1862

Vekey, Anthony, Garibaldi Guard; killed in the Battle of Winchester, September, 1864 (cannot be identified in official records)

I. VESSELS OF THE UNITED STATES
CLASSIFICATION AND LOCATION IN APRIL, 1861 *

SCREW FRIGATES

Niagara, returning from Japan

FIRST-CLASS SCREW SLOOPS OF WAR

Brooklyn, at Pensacola
Hartford, in the East Indies
Lancaster, in the Pacific
Richmond, in the Mediterranean
San Jacinto, off Africa

SECOND-CLASS SCREW SLOOPS OF WAR

Dakota, in the East Indies
Iroquois, in the Mediterranean
Mohican, on coast of Africa
Narragansett, in the Pacific
Pawnee, in Washington
Pocahontas, returning from Vera Cruz
Seminole, at Brazil
Wyandotte, at Pensacola
Wyoming, in the Pacific

THIRD-CLASS SCREW STEAMERS

Crusader, at New York
Mohawk, at New York
Mystic, on coast of Africa
Sumter, on coast of Africa

SIDE-WHEEL STEAMERS

Michigan, on Lake Erie
Powhatan, returning from Vera Cruz

* Compiled from Maclay, *A History of the United States Navy,* II, 225–26.

Pulaski, off Brazil
Saginaw, in the East Indies
Saranac, in the Pacific
Susquehanna (sloop of war), in the Mediterranean

SAILING FRIGATES

Congress, off Brazil
Sabine, at Pensacola

SAILING SLOOPS OF WAR

Constellation, on coast of Africa
Cumberland, returning from Vera Cruz
Cyane, in the Pacific
John Adams, in the East Indies
Levant, in the Pacific
Macedonian, at Vera Cruz
Portsmouth, on coast of Africa
St. Louis, at Pensacola
St. Mary's, in the Pacific
Saratoga, on coast of Africa
Vandalia, in the East Indies

STORESHIPS

Release, supply ship in New York
Relief, off Africa
Supply, supply ship in New York

STEAM TENDER

Anacostia (propeller with two guns), at Washington

Bibliography

MANUSCRIPTS

Lists and Descriptive Books in the
War Records Office, The National Archives

Company Descriptive Books of the various companies of the Union Army.
  Variously combined with other military records as
    Clothing, Company, or Order Book
    Court-Martials, Company Descriptive Book, Clothing Book
    Clothing, Letter, Order, Descriptive, and Morning Report Book
    Muster and Descriptive Roll
    Muster Rolls of the Navy in the Navy Branch
    (Muster Rolls of the various vessels in the navy)
Regimental Descriptive Books. Variously combined with other military
  records as
    Regimental Descriptive, Order and Casualty Book
    Regimental Letters Received, Endorsements, Clothing Book, Non
      Com'd Staff, and Band
    Regimental Descriptive and Letter Book
    Register of Enlistments, United States Army (Regular) October,
      1857–1859
    Enlistments—Naval Rendezvous, Navy Branch
Jackets for Individual Officers and Privates.
    Folders into which have been gathered all available data on a given
    officer or soldier—his record from Muster Rolls, letters to or by him,
    comments concerning him, the bed ticket which was tied to the head
    of his hospital bed for identification, etc.

Diplomatic and Consular Manuscripts in the
Division of State Department Archives,
The National Archives

Diplomatic Dispatches.
Diplomatic Dispatches, Norway and Sweden, X.

Notes from the British Legation, XLII–LXXVII.
Notes from the Danish Legation, III, LVI.
Notes from the French Legation, VI.
Notes from the Italian Legation, III, IV.
Notes from the Prussian Legation, III–V.
Notes from the Swedish Legation, II, IV, VI.
Notes to the British Legation, IX.
Notes to the French Legation, VII, VIII, XLIX.
Notes to the Swedish Legation, VI.
Diplomatic Instructions, France, XVI.
Consular Dispatches and Letters.
    Instructions to Consuls, XXXI, XXXII, XXXIII, XXXVI, XXXVII, XXXVIII
    Instructions to Consuls, Great Britain, France, Russia, Netherlands, X
    Consular Dispatches—Ireland
        Consular Dispatches, Belfast, IV
        Consular Dispatches, Cork, V, VI
        Consular Dispatches, Dublin, III, IV
    Consular Dispatches—Germany
        Consular Dispatches, Altona, II, III, XXXVII
        Consular Dispatches, Bremen, X, XI, XII, XIII
        Consular Dispatches, Frankfurt, X
        Consular Dispatches, Hamburg, III, V, XII, XV, XVI, XXX, XXXIX
    Consular Dispatches—Other Countries
        Consular Dispatches [Odd Volume]—Spain, Portugal, Belgium, Denmark, Germany, Italian States, Turkey, Great Britain, and China
    Consular Dispatches, Quebec, I, III, VI
    Consular Dispatches, Stockholm, IV, V
The Reminiscences of General Julius Stahel-Szamvald on His Military Career in America.
    (General's Report of Service, War of the Rebellion, XI)
    Manuscript (105 pages) dated San Francisco, October, 1874

Other Manuscripts

Allotments, Minnesota State Treasurer's Archives, Minnesota Historical Society, St. Paul.
Connecticut Records, Adjutant General's Office (Muster Rolls of Sixth Connecticut Regiment), Hartford.

Esbjörn Collection of Letters, Augustana College Library, Rock Island, Illinois.

Executive Correspondence of the Governors of Ohio, 1861–1865, Ohio Historical Society, Columbus.

Hasselquist Collection, Augustana College Library, Rock Island, Illinois.

"History of the Nineteenth Regiment, Ohio Volunteer Infantry," Ohio Historical Society, Columbus.

Manuscript Collection of Civil War Letters, Luther College Library, Decorah, Iowa.

Massachusetts Records, Massachusetts Military Archives Division (records of certain individuals of Massachusetts who participated in the Civil War), Adjutant General's Office, Boston.

Mattson, Hans, Papers, Minnesota Historical Society. Some selected letters have been published in the *Year Book* of the Swedish Historical Society of America, IX, 1923–1924.

Muster Rolls and Records of the Civil War of the State of New York, Bureau of War Records.

Muster Roll, Fifty-third New York Volunteer Regiment.

Muster Roll, Company D, Third Minnesota Regiment, Minnesota Historical Society, St. Paul.

Nelson, Knute, Papers, Minnesota Historical Society, St. Paul.

Weidner, Peter, Papers, Ohio State Historical Society, Columbus.

PRINTED PUBLIC DOCUMENTS

Annual Report of the Adjutant General, Missouri, 1863. Jefferson City, 1864.

Annual Report of the Commissioner General of Immigration, 1920. Washington, 1921.

Congressional Globe. 46 vols. Washington, 1834–1873.

Eighth Census, 1860. The Statistics of the Population of the United States. 4 vols. Washington, 1864–1866.

Hansard, Thomas Curson (ed.) *Parliamentary Debates.* Ser. 3, CLXXIII (1864). London, 1830–1891.

McClellan, George B. *Report on the Organization and Campaigns of the Army of the Potomac; to which is added an Account of the Campaign in West Virginia with Plans of Battlefields.* New York, 1864.

Messages and Documents, 1860. Abridged, Washington, 1860.

Ninth Census, 1870. The Statistics of the Population of the United States. 3 vols. Washington, 1872.

Official Army Register of the Volunteer Forces of the United States Army for the Years 1861, '62, '63, '64, '65. 8 vols. Washington, 1865–1867.

Official Records of the Union and Confederate Navies in the War of the Rebellion. 31 vols. Washington, 1894–1927.

Register of the Commissioned and Warrant Officers of the Navy of the United States, including Officers of the Marine Corps and Others, for the years 1861–1865. Washington, 1861–1865.

"Report of the Joint Committee on the Conduct of the War," in *Senate Reports,* 37 Cong., 3 Sess., No. 108. 3 vols. Washington, 1863.

"Reports of the Secretary of War," 1860, 1861, 1865.

For 1860, in *Senate Executive Documents,* 36 Cong., 2 Sess., No. 1.

For 1861, in *Senate Executive Documents,* 37 Cong., 2 Sess., No. 1.

For 1865, in *House Executive Documents,* 39 Cong., 1 Sess., No. 1.

The Statutes at Large of the United States of America, XII (1863), XIII (1865), and XIV (1868). 61 vols. Boston and Washington, 1845–1919.

The War of the Rebellion: A Compilation of the Official Records of the Union and Confederate Armies. 130 vols. Washington, 1880–1901.

NEWSPAPERS AND MAGAZINES

Baltimore *Der Deutsche Correspondent,* 1860–1865 (broken file), and *Sontagsblatt.*

Baltimore *Patriot and Commercial Gazeteer,* April, 1841.

Baltimore *Wecker,* 1860–1862.

Boston *Daily Courrier,* May, 1861.

Boston *Pilot,* July, October, November, 1852; August, 1854; November, 1855; July–October, 1860; March, 1861; June, 1862—December, 1864.

Boston *Transcript,* July, 1856; December, 1863.

Boston *Traveller,* January, April, 1857.

Chicago *Hemlandet,* October, 1860—March, 1865. Published in Galesburg, Illinois, before 1858; removed to Chicago, then to Rock Island.

Chicago *Illinois Staats-Zeitung,* 1860–1865.

Chicago *Post,* June, 1861.

Chicago *Times,* October, 1864.

Chicago *Tribune,* 1861, 1864.

Cimbrishammbladet, June 17, 1855, November 18, 1867. Photostats in Minnesota Historical Society.

Cincinnati *Commercial,* April, August, 1851.

Cincinnati *Enquirer,* March, July, November, 1859.

Cincinnati *Gazette,* October, 1858; September, 1861; August, 1862.
Cincinnati *Volksblatt,* May, 1846.
Cincinnati *Volksfreund,* January, April, 1861.
Columbus (Ohio) *Westbote,* 1861–1864.
Harper's Weekly, VII (1863); IX (1865).
La Crosse (Wis.) *Faedrelandet,* January 14, 1864—January, 1865.
London *Times,* January, 1863.
Madison *Emigranten,* August, 1858; April, 1861—March, 1865.
Milwaukee *Sentinel,* December, 1862.
New York *Courrier des États-Unis,* April, 1861—January, 1865.
New York *Daily News,* April, 1861.
New Yorker Demokrat, 1861.
New York *Evening Post,* July, 1861–1862.
New York *Franco-American Advertiser,* May, 1861 (a few issues extant).
New York *Herald,* May, 1861–1864.
New York *Irish-American,* November, 1860—March, 1865.
New York *Sontagsblatt* (of the *New Yorker Staats-Zeitung*), January–
    December, 1864.
New York *Times,* April, June, 1850; April, 1861—January, 1865;
    March, 1930.
New York *Tribune,* April–June, 1850; September, 1861—December,
    1864.
New York *Weekly News,* December, 1845.
Nyeste Öresundsposten, November 13, 1868. Photostat in Minnesota
    Historical Society.
Philadelphia *North American,* December, 1912.
Richmond *Daily Examiner,* November, 1861—March, 1864.
St. Louis *Anzeiger des Westens,* 1861.
St. Paul *Minnesota Staats-Zeitung,* January, 1861—March, 1865. Almost
    a complete file at the Minnesota Historical Society.
St. Paul *Press,* January–April, 1865.
Toronto *Globe,* August, 1859.
Washington (D.C.) *Tägliche Metropole,* October, 1860—January,
    1861; April, 1861—March, 1865.

NONOFFICIAL COLLECTIONS AND COMPILATIONS

Ager, Waldemar (ed.), *Oberst Heg og hans Gutter ved Waldemar Ager.*
    Eau Claire, Wis., 1916.
Appletons' *The American Annual Cyclopaedia and Register of Important
    Events.* Ser. 1 (1861–1875), 15 vols. New York, 1862–1876.

Brockett, Linus Pierpont (comp.), *Battlefield and Hospital; or Lights and Shadows of the Great Rebellion.* Philadelphia[?], n. d.

—————— and Vaughan, Mary C. (comps.), *Woman's Work in the Civil War. A Record of Heroism, Patriotism, and Patience.* Philadelphia, 1867.

Brown, John Howard (ed.), *Lamb's Biographical Dictionary of the United States.* 7 vols. Boston, 1900–1903.

Cunningham, D., and Miller, W. W. (comps.), *Report of the Ohio Antietam Battlefield Commission.* Springfield, Ohio, 1904.

Fairchild, C. B. (comp.), *History of the 27th Regiment N.Y. Vols.* Binghamton, N.Y., 1888.

Fallon, John T., *List of Synonyms of Organizations in the Volunteer Service of the United States during the Years 1861, '62, '63, '64 and '65.* Washington, 1885.

Fitch, John (comp.), *Annals of the Army of the Cumberland.* Philadelphia, 1864.

Fox, William F. (comp.), *New York [State] Monuments Commission for the Battlefields of Gettysburg and Chattanooga. Final Report on the Battlefield of Gettysburg.* 3 vols. Albany, 1900.

—————— (author and comp.), *Regimental Losses in the American Civil War.* Albany, 1889.

Germain, Dom Aidan Henry (comp.), *Catholic Military and Naval Chaplains 1776–1917.* Washington, D.C., 1929. A brief abstract has been printed in the *Catholic Historical Review,* IX (1923–1924), 171–78.

Gerrish, Theodore, and Hutchinson, John S. (authors and comps.), *The Blue and the Gray. A Graphic History of the Army of the Potomac and that of Northern Virginia, including the Brilliant Engagements of these Forces from 1861 to 1865.* . . . Portland, 1883.

Hamersly, Lewis Randolph (comp.), *The Records of Living Officers of the U.S. Navy and Marine Corps.* 3d ed.; Philadelphia, 1878. 6th ed.; New York, 1902.

Hatcher, Edmund N. (comp.), *The Last Four Weeks of the War.* Columbus, Ohio, 1892.

Heitman, Francis B. (comp.), *Historical Register and Dictionary of the United States Army from its Organization, September 29, 1789 to March 2, 1903.* 2 vols. Washington, D.C., 1903.

Henry, Guy Vernor (comp.), *Military Record of Civilian Appointments in the United States Army.* 2 vols. New York, 1869–1873.

Herbermann, Charles G., and others (eds.), *The Catholic Encyclopaedia.* 17 vols. New York, 1907–1922.

Hunter, R. (ed.), *Sketches of War History, 1860–1865.* 3 vols. Cincinnati, 1880–1890. Papers read before the Ohio Commandery of the Military Order of the Loyal Legion of the United States.

Joel, Joseph, and Stegman, Lewis R. (authors and comps.), *Rifle Shots and Bugle Notes*. New York, 1884.

Johnson, Allen, and Malone, Dumas (eds.), *Dictionary of American Biography*. 21 vols. New York, 1928–1944.

Johnson, Robert Underwood, and Buel, Clarence Clough (eds.), *Battles and Leaders of the Civil War; being for the Most Part Contributions by Union and Confederate Officers*. Based upon "Century War Series." 4 vols. New York, 1887–1888.

Johnson, Rossiter, and others (eds.), *Campfire and Battlefield*. New York, 1894.

Kirkland, Frazar (comp.), *The Pictorial Book of Anecdotes and Incidents of the War of the Rebellion, Civil, Military, Naval, and Domestic. . . .* 2 vols. Hartford, 1866.

M[cClure], A. K. (ed.), *The Annals of the War written by Leading Participants North and South*. Philadelphia, 1879. Published originally in the Philadelphia *Weekly Times*.

Maddocks, Elden B. (comp.), *History of the Twenty-sixth Maine Regiment. . . .* Bangor, Maine, 1899.

Mann, Albert W. (comp.), *History of the Forty-fifth Regiment, Massachusetts Volunteer Militia, "The Cadet Regiment."* Jamaica Plains, N.Y., 1908.

Miller, Francis Trevelyan (ed.), *The Photographic History of the Civil War*. 10 vols. New York, 1911.

Moore, Frank (ed.), *The Rebellion Record: A Diary of American Events, with Documents, Narrative, Illustrative Incidents, Poetry, etc.* 12 vols. New York, 1861–1868.

——— (ed.), *Anecdotes, Poetry, and Incidents of the War: North and South, 1860–1865*. New York, 1866.

——— (author and comp.), *Women of the War: Their Heroism and Self Sacrifice*. Hartford, 1866.

Mottelay, P. F., and Campbell-Copeland, T. (eds.), *The Soldier in Our Civil War: A Pictorial History of the Conflict, 1861–1865*. 2 vols. New York, 1890.

Nason, George Warren (comp. and ed.), *History and Complete Roster of the Massachusetts Regiments, Minute Men of '61 . . . , and Biographical Sketches of Minute Men of Massachusetts*. Boston, 1913.

National Cyclopaedia of American Biography, The. 32 vols. New York, 1893–1947.

Nicolson, John P. (comp.), *Pennsylvania at Gettysburg. Ceremonies at the Dedication of the Monuments Erected by the Commonwealth of Pennsylvania.* 2 vols. Harrisburg, Pa., 1891–1893.

Phisterer, Frederick (author and comp.), *Statistical Record of the Armies of the United States.* New York, 1883.

———, *New York in the War of the Rebellion.* Albany, 1890.

Powell, William H. (comp.), *Officers of the Army and Navy (Volunteer) Who Served in the Civil War.* New York, 1893.

———, and Shippen, Edward (comps.), *Officers of the Army and Navy (Regular) Who Served in the Civil War.* Philadelphia, 1892.

Smith, Edward P. (author and comp.), *Incidents among Shot and Shell.* New York, 1866.

Strong, William, and others (authors and comps.), *History of the 121st Regiment Pennsylvania Volunteers.* Philadelphia, 1892.

Vernon, George W. F., and others (comps.), *History and Roster of Maryland Volunteers, War of 1861–5.* 2 vols. Baltimore, 1898.

Victor, O. J. (ed.), *Incidents and Anecdotes of the War: with Narratives of Great Battles, Great Marches, Great Events and a Record of Heroic Deeds and Daring Personal Achievements which Characterized the Great Conflict for the Union.* New York, 1866.

Wilson, James Grant, and Fiske, John (eds.), *Appletons' Cyclopaedia of American Biography.* 10 vols. New York, 1887–1924.

MILITARY AUTOBIOGRAPHIES, REMINISCENCES, DIARIES, AND LETTERS

Allan, William, *History of the Campaign of General T. J. (Stonewall) Jackson in the Shenandoah Valley of Virginia from November 4, 1861 —June 7, 1862.* Philadelphia, 1862. Printed also in the *Southern Historical Society Papers,* XLIII (August, 1920), 113–94.

Aschmann, Rudolf, *Drei Jahre in der Potomac Armee, oder Eine Schweizer Schutzen-Compagnie in nordamerikanischen Kriege.* Richtersweil, Switzerland, 1865.

Babcock, W. M., Jr. (author and ed.), *Selections from the Letters and Diaries of Brevet-Brigadier General Willoughby Babcock of the Seventy-fifth New York Volunteers: A Study of Camp Life in the Union Armies during the War.* New York, 1922.

Bardeen, C. W., *A Little Fifer's War Diary.* Syracuse, N.Y., 1910.

Blake, Henry M., *Three Years in the Army of the Potomac.* Boston, 1865.

Blegen, Theodore C. (ed.), *The Civil War Letters of Colonel Hans Christian Heg*. Northfield, Minn., 1936.

Brinton, John H., *Personal Memoirs of John H. Brinton*. New York, 1914.

Britton, Wiley, *Memoirs of the Rebellion on the Border, 1863*. Chicago, 1882.

Butts, J. T. (comp.), *A Gallant Captain of the Civil War* (a biography of F. Otto von Fritsch, compiled from his private papers and Washington records). London, 1902.

Chamberlain, Joshua Lawrence, *The Passing of the Armies*. New York, 1915.

Conyngham, David Powers, *The Irish Brigade and its Campaigns*. New York, 1867.

————, *Sherman's March through the South with Sketches and Incidents of the Campaign*. New York, 1865.

Cook, Benjamin F., *History of the Twelfth Massachusetts Volunteers. (Webster Regiment)*. Boston, 1882.

Cox, Jacob Dolson, *Military Reminiscences of the Civil War*. 2 vols. New York, 1900.

Cuffel, Charles A., *Durrell's Battery in the Civil War (Independent Battery D, Pennsylvania Volunteer Artillery)*. . . . Philadelphia, 1900.

Davis, Charles E., *Three Years in the Army. The Story of the Thirteenth Massachusetts Volunteers from July 16, 1861 to August 1, 1864*. Boston, 1894.

Davis, W. W. H., *History of the 104th Pennsylvania Regiment from August 22nd, 1861, to September 30th, 1864*. Philadelphia, 1866.

De Trobriand, Régis, *Quatre Ans de Campagnes à l'Armée de Potomac*. 2 vols. Paris, 1868.

Eldredge, Daniel, *The Third New Hampshire and All About It*. Boston, 1893.

"English Combatant, An" (T.E.C.), *Battlefields of the South, from Bull Run to Fredericksburg; with Sketches of Confederate Commands, and Gossip of the Camps*. 2 vols. London, 1863.

Ewer, James K., *The Third Massachusetts Cavalry in the War for the Union*. n.p., 1903.

Fout, Frederick W., *Die schwersten Tage des Bürgerkrieges von 1864 und 1865*. n.p., 1902.

Gates, Theodore B., *The "Ulster Guard" (20 N.Y. State Militia) and the War of the Rebellion*. New York, 1879.

Gibbon, John, *Personal Recollections of the Civil War*. New York, 1928.

Glazier, Willard, *Battles for the Union: Comprising Descriptions of Many of the Most Stubbornly Contested Battles in the War of the Great Rebellion together with Incidents and Reminiscences of the Camp, the March, and the Skirmish Line.* Hartford, 1875.

Gordon, George H., *Brook Farm to Cedar Mountain in the War of the Great Rebellion 1861–62.* Boston, 1863.

———, *History of the Campaign of the Army of Virginia under John Pope, Brigadier General, U.S.A.; Later Major General U.S. Volunteers from Cedar Mountain to Alexandria, 1862.* Boston, 1880.

Graham, Matthew J., *The Ninth Regiment New York Volunteers (Hawkins Zouaves). Being a History of the Regiment and Veteran Association from 1860 to 1900.* New York, 1900.

Harter, F. A., *Errinerungen aus dem amerikanischen Bürgerkriege.* Chicago, 1895.

Haynie, J. Henry, *The Nineteenth Illinois.* Chicago, 1912.

Heusinger, Otto, *Amerikanische Kriegsbilder.* Leipzig, 1869.

Hinton, Richard J., *Rebel Invasion of Missouri and Kansas and the Campaign of the Army of the Border against General Sterling Price in October and November, 1864.* Chicago, 1865.

History of the Corn Exchange Regiment, 118th Pennsylvania Volunteers from its First Engagement at Antietam to Appomattox. Philadelphia, 1888.

Hosmer, James K., *The Color Guard: Being a Corporal's Notes of Military Service in the Nineteenth Army Corps.* Boston, 1864.

Hough, Franklin B., *History of Duryée's Brigade during the Campaign in Virginia under Gen. Pope, and in Maryland under Gen. McClellan in the Summer and Autumn of 1862.* Albany, 1864.

Hyde, Thomas W., *Following the Greek Cross; or Memories of the Sixth Army Corps.* Boston, 1894.

Johnson, Charles B., *Muskets and Medicine: Or Army Life in the Sixties.* Philadelphia, 1917.

Johnson, Charles Frederick, *The Long Roll.* Aurora, N.Y., 1911.

Jones, Evan R., *Four Years in the Army of the Potomac. A Soldier's Recollections.* London, 1881.

Kidd, J. H., *Personal Recollections of a Cavalryman with Custer's Michigan Cavalry Brigade in the Civil War.* Ionia, Mich., 1908.

Kirk, Hyland C., *Heavy Guns and Light: A History of the 4th New York Heavy Artillery.* New York, 1890.

McClellan, George B., *McClellan's Own Story. The War for the Union, the Soldiers Who Fought it, the Civilians who Directed it, and his Relation to It and Them.* New York, 1887.

MacNamara, Michael H., *The Irish Brigade in Bivouac and Battle in Virginia and Maryland Campaigns*. Boston, 1867.

Marshall, James Ames (ed.), *Private and Official Correspondence of Gen. Benjamin F. Butler during the Period of the Civil War*. 5 vols. Norwood, Mass. 1917.

Mulholland, St. Clair A., *The Story of the 116th Regiment Pennsylvania Infantry. War of Secession, 1862–1865*. Philadelphia, 1899.

———, *The American Volunteer, the Most Heroic Soldier the World has Ever Known*. Philadelphia, 1909.

Newcomer, Armour, *Cole's Cavalry; or Three Years in the Saddle in the Shenandoah Valley*. Baltimore, 1895.

Nichols, George Ward, *The Story of the Great March. From the Diary of a Staff Officer*. New York, 1866.

Noyes, George F., *The Bivouac and the Battlefield; or, Campaign Sketches in Virginia and Maryland*. New York, 1863.

Palmer, Abraham J., *The History of the Forty-eighth Regiment New York State Volunteers in the War for the Union 1861–1865*. Brooklyn, 1885.

Parker, Thomas H., *History of the 51st Regiment of the P.V. and V.V. (Pennsylvania Volunteers and Pennsylvania Veteran Volunteers)*. Philadelphia, 1869.

Peckham, James, *Gen. Nathaniel Lyon and Missouri in 1861. A Monograph of the Great Rebellion*. New York, 1866.

Pellet, Elias P., *History of the 114th Regiment New York State Volunteers. Containing a Perfect Record of the Services, Embracing all its Marches, Campaigns, Battles, Sieges, and Sea-Voyages with a Biographical Sketch of Each Officer and a Complete Register of the Regiment. . . .* Norwich, N.Y., 1866.

Porter, David D., *The Naval History of the Civil War*. New York, 1886.

Price, Isaiah, *History of the Ninety-seventh Regiment Pennsylvania Volunteer Infantry during the War of the Rebellion*. Philadelphia, 1875.

Reminiscences of the Civil War from the Diaries of Members of the 103d Illinois Volunteer Infantry. Chicago, n.d.

Rhodes, Charles D., *History of the Cavalry of the Army of the Potomac*. Kansas City, 1900.

Schaff, Morris, *The Battle of the Wilderness*. Boston and New York, 1910.

Schurz, Carl, *The Reminiscences of Carl Schurz*. 3 vols. New York, 1907–1908.

Scott, Samuel W., and Angel, Samuel P., *History of the Thirteenth Regi-*

ment, *Tennessee Volunteer Cavalry, U.S.A., including a Narrative of the Bridge Burning.* . . . Philadelphia, [1903].

Sheridan, Philip H., *Personal Memoirs of P. H. Sheridan.* 2 vols. New York, 1888.

Smith, James E., *A Famous Battery and its Campaigns, 1861–'64.* Washington, 1892.

Snead, Thomas L., *The Fight for Missouri from the Election of Lincoln to the Death of Lyon.* New York, 1866.

Sprenger, George F., *Concise History of the Camp and Field Life of the 122d Regiment, Penn'a Volunteers. Compiled from Notes, Sketches, Facts and Incidents, as recorded in the Diary of George F. Sprenger.* Lancaster, Pa., 1885.

Stevens, Charles Augustus, *Berdan's United States Sharpshooters in the Army of the Potomac 1861–1865.* St. Paul, 1892.

Surby, R. W., *Grierson Raids and Hatch's Sixty-four Days March with Biographical Sketches, also the Life and Adventures of Chickasaw, the Scout.* Chicago, 1865.

Tafel, Oberst Gustav, *"Die Neuner," Eine Schilderung der Kriegsjahre des 9ten Regiments Ohio Vol. Infanterie, vom 17 April 1861 bis 7 Juni 1864.* Cincinnati, 1897.

Thatcher, Marshall P., *A Hundred Battles in the West, St. Louis to Atlanta. The Second Michigan Cavalry with the Armies of the Mississippi, Ohio, Kentucky, and Cumberland.* Detroit, 1884.

Thorndike, Rachael Sherman (ed.), *The Sherman Letters. Correspondence between Gen. and Sen. Sherman from 1837 to 1870.* London, 1894.

Todd, William, *The Seventy-ninth Highlanders, New York Volunteers in the War of the Rebellion. 1861–1865.* Albany, 1886.

Turchin, John B., *Chickamauga.* Chicago, 1888.

Vale, Joseph G., *Minty and the Cavalry. A History of Cavalry Campaigns in the Western Armies.* Harrisburg, 1886.

Wallace, Lewis, *Lew Wallace, An Autobiography.* 2 vols. New York, 1906.

Waring, G. E., *Whip and Spur.* Boston, 1875.

Wild, Frederick W., *Memoirs and History of Capt. F. W. Alexander's Baltimore Battery of Light Artillery, U.S.A.* Baltimore, 1912.

Wilson, James H., *Under the Old Flag. Recollections of Military Operations in the West for the Union, the Spanish War, the Boxer Rebellion, etc.* 2 vols. New York, 1912.

MEMOIRS AND RECORDS OF CIVILIAN OBSERVERS

Balme, Joshua P., *Synopsis of the American War*. London, 1863.

B[ickham], W. D., *Rosecrans' Campaign with the Fourteenth Army Corps or the Army of the Cumberland: A Narrative of Personal Observations, with an Appendix consisting of Official Reports of the Battle of Stone River*. Cincinnati, 1863.

Bremer, Fredrika, *The Homes of the New World. Impressions of America*. 3 vols. London, 1853.

Bullock, James D., *The Secret Service of the Confederate States in Europe; or how the Confederate Cruisers were Equipped*. 2 vols. New York, 1884.

Cavanagh, Michael, *Memoirs of Gen. Thomas Francis Meagher . . . , with Selections from his Speeches, Letters and Miscellaneous Writings. . . .* Worcester, Mass., 1892.

Coffin, Charles Carlton, *Four Years of Fighting: A Volume of Personal Observation with the Army and Navy, from the First Battle of Bull Run to the Fall of Richmond*. Boston, 1886.

————, *Following the Flag*. Boston, 1864.

————, *Marching to Victory*. New York, c. 1888.

Cook, Joel, *Siege of Richmond. A Narrative of the Military Operations of Maj. Gen. G. B. McClellan*. Philadelphia, 1862.

Corby, William, *Memoirs of Chaplain Life*. Notre Dame, Ind., 1894.

Dana, Malcolm McGregor, *The Norwich Memorial; The Annals of Norwich, New London County, Connecticut, in the Great Rebellion of 1861–65*. Norwich, 1873.

De Chanal, François Victor Adolph, *The American Army in the War of Secession*. Leavenworth, Kans., 1894.

Dicey, Edward, *Six Months in the Federal States*. London, 1863.

Eddy, F. M., *The Patriotism of Illinois. A Record of the Civil and Military History of the State in the War of the Union*. 2 vols. Chicago, 1866.

Ellis, Thomas T., *Leaves from the Diary of an Army Surgeon*. New York, 1863.

Frémont, Jessie Benton, *The Story of the Guard: A Chronicle of the War*. Boston, 1863.

Frost, Mrs. J. Blakeslee, *The Rebellion in the United States; or, the War of 1861; Being a Complete History of its Rise and Progress, Commencing with the Presidential Election. . . .* 2 vols. Hartford, 1862–1864.

Greeley, Horace, *The American Conflict: A History of the Great Rebellion in the United States of America, 1861–'64*. 2 vols. Hartford, 1867.

Gregg, Chandler, *Life in the Army, in the Departments of Virginia and the Gulf including Observations in New Orleans with an Account of the Author's Life and Experience in the Ministry*. Philadelphia, 1866.

Hoge, Mrs. A. H., *The Boys in Blue; or Heroes of the Rank and File*. New York, 1867.

Judd, David W., *The Story of the Thirty-third N.Y.S. Vols.; or Two Years Campaigning in Virginia and Maryland*. Rochester, 1864.

Körner, Gustav, *Das Deutsche Element in den Vereinigten Staaten in Nordamerika, 1818–1848*. Cincinnati, 1880.

Kuné, Julian, *Reminiscences of an Octogenarian Hungarian Exile*. Chicago, 1911.

Laugel, Auguste, *Les États-Unis pendant la Guerre*. Paris, 1866.

Lecomte, Ferdinand, *The War in the United States*. New York, 1863.

Livermore, Mary A., *My Story of the War: A Woman's Narrative of Four Years Personal Experience as Nurse in the Union Army and in Relief Work at Home. . . .* Hartford, 1887.

Logan, James A., *The Great Conspiracy: Its Origin and History*. New York, 1866.

McDonald, Cornelia, *A Diary with Reminiscences of the War and Refugee Life in the Shenandoah Valley, 1860–1865*, annot. Hunter McDonald. Nashville, 1934.

Mackay, Charles, *Life and Liberty in America*. 2 vols. 2d ed.; London, 1859.

Marks, J. J., *The Peninsular Campaign in Virginia; or Incidents and Scenes on the Battle-Fields and in Richmond*. Philadelphia, 1864.

Marvin, Abijah P., *History of Worcester in the War of the Rebellion*. Worcester, Mass., 1880.

Mattson, Hans, *Reminiscences: The Story of an Emigrant*. St. Paul, 1891.

Merrill, Samuel H., *The Campaigns with the First Maine and First District of Columbia Cavalry*. Portland, 1866.

Mowris, J. A., *A History of the One Hundred and Seventeenth Regiment N.Y. Volunteers (Fourth Oneida) from the Date of its Organization, August, 1862, to that of its Muster Out, June, 1865*. Hartford, 1866.

Olmsted, Frederick Law, *A Journey in the Seaboard Slave States with Remarks on their Economy*. New York, 1864.

Rombauer, Roderick, *The History of a Life*. St. Louis, [1903].

Russell, William Howard, *My Diary North and South*. London, 1863.

Salm-Salm, Princess Agnes, *Ten Years of My Life*. 2 vols. London, 1875.

Simons, Ezra D., *A Regimental History. The One Hundred and Twenty-fifth New York State Volunteers*. New York, 1888.

Stonebaker, J. Clarence, *The Unwritten South*. Hagerstown, Md., 1903.

Swisshelm, Jane Grey, *Half a Century*. Chicago, 1880.

Taylor, Benjamin P., *Mission Ridge and Lookout Mountain with Pictures of Life in Camp and Field*. Chicago, 1872.

Townsend, George Alfred, *Campaigns of a Non-Combatant, and his Romaunt Abroad during the War*. New York, 1866.

Turnbull, H. Clay, *War Memoirs of an Army Chaplain*. New York, 1898.

Woodbury, Augustus, *A Narrative of the Campaign of the First Rhode Island Regiment in the Spring and Summer of 1861*. Providence, 1862.

MILITARY AND CIVILIAN PAMPHLETS

Barnard, Frederick Augustus, *Letter to the President of the United States by a Refugee*. New York, 1863.

Benham, Henry W., *Recollections of the West Virginia Campaign with "The Three Months Troops," May, June, and July, 1861*. Boston, 1873.

Burt, Silas W., *My Memoirs of the Military History of the State of New York during the War for the Union, 1861–65* (New York State, *War of the Rebellion* Series, Bulletin No. 1). Albany, 1902.

Crossby, William J., "Extracts from my Crossby Diary," in *Personal Narratives of Events in the War of the Rebellion*. Soldiers and Sailors Historical Society of Rhode Island, Sixth Series, No. 4.

[De Joinville, Prince], *The Army of the Potomac: Its Organization, Its Commander, and Its Campaign*. New York, 1862. (Reprint of A. Trognon, "Campagne de l'Armée du Potomac, Mars-Juillet, 1862," in *Revue des Deux Mondes*, 2d ser., XL (October 15, 1862), 798–867. Translated by W. H. Hurlbert, who identifies "Trognon" as the Prince de Joinville.)

Dietrichson, P. G., *En Kortfattet Skildering af det Femtende Regiments Historie og Virksomhed under Borgerkrigen*. . . . Chicago, 1884.

Fritsch, William A., *German Settlers and German Settlements in Indiana; A Memorial for the State Centennial, 1916*. Evansville, 1915.

History of the 37th Regiment, O.V.V.I., Furnished by Comrades at the Ninth Reunion Held at St. Mary's, Ohio, Tuesday and Wednesday, September 10 and 11, 1889. n.p., n.d.

Johnson, John A., *Det Skandinaviske Regiments Historie*. . . . La Crosse, Wisconsin, 1869.

Meagher, Thomas Francis, *The Last Days of the 69th in Virginia. A Narrative in Three Parts.* New York, 1861.

Proceedings at the Mass Meeting of Loyal Citizens in Union Square, New York, on the 15th Day of July, 1862. New York, 1862.

Speed, Thomas, *Who Fought the Battle. Strength of the Union and Confederate Forces Compared.* Louisville, 1904. Address before the Army Corps Society of Louisville, January 26, 1904.

ARTICLES IN MAGAZINES AND PUBLISHED ADDRESSES

Berghold, Alex. "Geschichte von Neu Ulm, Minnesota," in *Der Deutsche Pionier,* III (1871–1872), VIII (1876–1877), IX (1877–1878), *passim.* (The portion in Volume III, "Die deutsche Ansiedlung von New Ulm," is anonymous.)

Briggs, John E., "The Enlistment of Iowa Troops During the Civil War," in *Iowa Journal of History and Politics,* XV (1917), 323–92.

Bruncken, Ernst, "The Political Activity of Wisconsin Germans, 1854–60," in *Proceedings of the Wisconsin State Historical Society,* 1901, pp. 190–211.

"General Adolph Buschbeck," in *Der Deutsche Pionier,* XVI (1884–1885), 213–16.

Callahan, J. M., "The Northern Lake Frontier during the Civil War," in *Annual Report of the American Historical Association,* 1896, I, 337–59.

Clark, James Albert, "The Making of a Volunteer Cavalryman," in *Military Order of the Loyal Legion of the United States,* Commandery of the District of Columbia, *War Papers,* No. 70.

Copeland, Louis A., "The Cornish in Southwest Wisconsin," in *Wisconsin Historical Society Collections,* XIV (1898), 301–34.

———, "Why the Men of '61 fought for the Union," in *Atlantic Monthly,* LXIX (1892), 382–94.

Dister, Cunz, "The Maryland Germans in the Civil War," in *Maryland Historical Magazine,* XXXVI (1941), 394–419.

Dodd, William E., "The Fight for the Northwest, 1860," in *American Historical Review,* XVI (1910–1911), 774–88.

"Major C. M. Degenfeld," in *Der Deutsche Pionier,* X (1878–1879), 223–24.

Frey, Emil, "My American Experiences," in *North American Review,* CLVIII (1894), 129–39.

"General Joseph Gerhardt," in *Der Deutsche Pionier*, XIII (1881–1882), 282.

"Dr. Adam Hammer," in *Der Deutsche Pionier*, X (1878–1879), 242–44.

Herriott, F. I., "Iowa and the First Nomination of Lincoln," in *Annals of Iowa*, 3d ser., VIII (1907), 51–115.

———, "The Germans of Chicago and Stephen A. Douglas," in *Jahrbuch der Deutsch-amerikanischen historischen Gesellschaft von Illinois*, XII (1912).

"Georg Hillgärtner," in *Der Deutsche Pionier*, XIV (1882–1883), 468–69.

Kargan, E. D., "Missouri's German Immigration," in *Missouri Historical Society Collections*, II (1904), No. 1, pp. 23–24.

"Adolph Krebs," in *Der Deutsche Pionier*, XVI (1884–1885), 513–17.

Kuhns, Luther M., "An Army Surgeon's Letters to his Wife," *Proceedings of the Mississippi Valley Historical Association*, VII (1913–1914), 306–20.

Lucas, Henry S., "The Beginnings of Dutch Immigration to Iowa, 1845–1847," in *Iowa Journal of History and Politics*, XXII (1924), 483–531.

McAvoy, Thomas, "The War Letters of Father Peter Paul Cooney of the Congregation of the Holy Cross," in *Records of the American Catholic Historical Society*, Philadelphia, XLIV (1923), Nos. 1, 2, and 3.

"General August Moor," in *Der Deutsche Pionier*, XVI (1884–1885), 340–49, 405–14, 438–54, 482–512.

"Nekrologie," in *Der Deutsche Pionier*, XIV (1882–1883), XV (1883–1884), XVI (1884–1885). Many unsigned biographical notices of various headings appear in the necrologies in these volumes.

Onahan, W. J., "Irish Settlements in Illinois," in *Catholic World*, XXXIII (April–September, 1881), 157–62.

Packard, William A., "Professor Joseph Karge," in *Princeton College Bulletin*, April, 1893, pp. 25–34.

Pascoe, W. H., "Confederate Cavalry around Port Hudson; their Dashing Exploits," in *Southern Historical Society Papers*, XXXIII (1905), 83–96.

Rederus, S. F., "The Dutch Settlements of Sheboygan County," in *Wisconsin Magazine of History*, I (1917–1918), 256–65.

Schafer, Joseph, "The Yankee and the Teuton in Wisconsin," in *Wisconsin Magazine of History*, VI (1922–1923), 125–45, 261–79, 386–402; VII (1923–1924), 3–19, 148–71.

———, "Who Elected Lincoln?" in *The American Historical Review*, XLVII (1941–1942), 51–63.

Schnake, Friedrich, "Der Ausbruch des Bürgerkrieges in Missouri," in *Der Deutsche Pionier,* XI (1879–1880) and XII (1880–1881), *passim.*

Smith, Donnell V., "The Influence of the Foreign-Born in the Northwest in the Election of 1860," in *Mississippi Valley Historical Review,* XIX (1932–1933), 192–204.

"Stanley, Henry M.," in *Confederate Veteran,* II (1894), 332.

"General Adolph Steinwehr," in *Der Deutsche Pionier,* IX (1877–1878), 17–29, 94–103, 160–66.

Szabad, Emery, "Diary in Libby Prison," in *Every Saturday,* V (1868), 421–32.

Thomas, Raymond D., "Study in Missouri Politics," in *Missouri Historical Review,* XXI (1926–1927), 438–54.

"Hermann Ulffers," in *Der Deutsche Pionier,* XI (1879–1880), 395–96.

"General Hugo Wangelin," in *Der Deutsche Pionier,* XV (1883–1884), 408–10.

"General August Willich," in *Der Deutsche Pionier,* IX (1877–1878), 488–95; X (1878–1879), 114–17.

Wilson, Lilian M., "Some Hungarian Patriots in Iowa," in *Iowa Journal of History and Politics,* XI (1913), 479–516.

Wittke, Carl, "The Ninth Ohio Volunteers," in *Ohio Archaeological and Historical Quarterly,* XXXV (1915), 402–17.

WORKS WITH SPECIAL REFERENCE TO THE WAR

Baltz, John D., *Hon. Edward D. Baker.* Lancaster, Pa., 1886.

Bates, Samuel P., *The Battle of Chancellorsville.* Meadville, Pa., 1882.

Bigelow, John, Jr., *The Campaign of Chancellorsville. A Strategical and Tactical Study.* New Haven, 1910.

Boynton, Charles B., *The History of the Navy during the Rebellion.* 2 vols. New York, 1867–1868.

Bruce, George A., *The Twentieth Regiment of Massachusetts Volunteer Infantry.* New York, 1906.

Bussey, Cyrus, *The Pea Ridge Campaign Considered (Military Order of the Loyal Legion of the United States,* Commandery of the District of Columbia, *War Papers,* No. 60).

Chadwick, French E., *Causes of the Civil War.* New York, 1906. Vol. XIX of *The American Nation: A History.*

Clark, James Albert, *The Making of a Volunteer Cavalryman (Military Order of the Loyal Legion of the United States,* Commandery of the District of Columbia, *War Papers,* No. 70).

Cole, Arthur C., *The Irrepressible Conflict, 1850–65*. New York, 1934. Vol. VII of *A History of American Life*.

Condon, W. H., *Life of Major-General James Shields, Hero of Three Wars and Senator from Three States*. Chicago, 1900.

Conyngham, David Powell. "Heroism of the Cross or Nuns and Priests on the Battlefield." Manuscript in the archives of the University of Notre Dame.

Coppée, Henry A. M., *Grant and His Campaigns: A Military Biography*. New York, 1866.

Dalbiac, P. H., *The American War of Secession, 1863. Chancellorsville and Gettysburg*. London, 1911.

De Paris, Louis-Philippe-Albert d'Orleans, Comte, *History of the Civil War in America*, tr., Louis F. Tasistro. 4 vols. Philadelphia, 1875–1888.

Draper, John William, *History of the American Civil War*. 3 vols. New York, 1867–1870.

Duyckinck, Evart A., *National History of the War for the Union, Civil, Military, and Naval, Founded on Official and Other Authentic Documents*. 3 vols. New York, 1861–1865.

Estabrook, Charles E., *Wisconsin Losses in the Civil War*. Madison, 1915.

Fletcher, Henry Charles, *History of the American Civil War*. 3 vols. London, 1865–1866.

Gould, Benjamin A., *Investigations in the Military and Anthropological Statistics of American Soldiers*. New York, 1869.

Gray, Wood, *The Hidden Civil War. The Story of the Copperheads*. New York, 1942.

Hamlin, Augustus Choate, *The Battle of Chancellorsville; the Attack of Stonewall Jackson and his Army upon the Right Flank of the Army of the Potomac at Chancellorsville. . . .* Bangor, Maine, 1896.

Haydon, F. Stansbury, *Aeronautics in the Union and Confederate Armies*. 2 vols. projected. Baltimore, 1941.

Headley, J. T., *The Great Rebellion. A History of the Civil War in the United States*. 2 vols. in one. Hartford, 1866.

———, *Farragut and Our Naval Commanders*. New York, 1867.

Henderson, G. F. R., *The Campaign of Fredericksburg, November–December, 1862*. London, 1886.

———, *Stonewall Jackson and the American Civil War*. London and New York, 1898.

Hergesheimer, Joseph, *Sheridan, A Military Narrative*. New York, 1931.

Heysinger, Isaac W., *Antietam and the Maryland and Virginia Campaigns of 1862*. New York, 1912.

Hilyer, William R., *Chancellorsville, May 2 and 3, 1863* (*Military Order of the Loyal Legion of the United States*, Commandery of the District of Columbia, *War Papers*, No. 55).

Hokanson, Nels, *Swedish Immigrants in Lincoln's Time*. 2d ed.; London and New York, 1942.

Horton, Charles F., *Virginia Campaigns of 1862 under General Pope* (*Papers of the Military Historical Society of Massachusetts*, No. 2). Boston and New York, 1895.

Hosmer, James K., *The Appeal to Arms*. New York, 1907. Vol. XX of *The American Nation: A History*.

————, *Outcome of the Civil War*. New York, 1907. Vol. XXI of *The American Nation: A History*.

Hotchkiss, Jedediah, and Allan, William, *The Battle-Fields of Virginia. Chancellorsville, embracing the Operations of the Army of Northern Virginia, from the First Battle of Fredericksburg to the Death of Lieutenant-General Jackson*. New York, 1867.

Huntington, James F., "Operations in the Shenandoah Valley, from Winchester to Port Republic. 1862," in *Campaigns in Virginia, 1861–1862* (*Papers of the Military Historical Society of Massachusetts*). Boston and New York, 1895–1902.

Johnson, Rossiter, *The Fight for the Republic*. New York, 1917.

Jolly, Ellen Ryan, *Nuns of the Battlefield*. Providence, 1927.

Kaufmann, Wilhelm, *Die Deutschen im amerikanischen Bürgerkriege*. 3d ed.; München and Berlin, 1910.

Kettell, Thomas P., *History of the Great Rebellion from the Commencement to its Close, giving an Account of its Origin, the Secession of the Southern States and the Formation of the Confederate Government, the Concentration of the Military and Financial Resources of the Federal Government*. Hartford, 1886.

Livermore, Thomas L., *Numbers and Losses in the Civil War in America, 1861–65*. Boston and New York, 1900.

Livermore, W. R., *The Story of the Civil War*. New York, 1894–1913. Vols. III and IV of four-volume work.

Lonn, Ella, *Foreigners in the Confederacy*. Chapel Hill, 1940.

————, *Desertion during the Civil War*. New York, 1928.

Lossing, Benson J., *Pictorial History of the Civil War in the United States of America*. 3 vols. Hartford, 1866–1868.

Maclay, Edgar Stanton, *A History of the United States Navy from 1775 to 1894. With Technical Revision by Lt. R. C. Smith*. 2 vols. New York, 1894.

Maguire, Thomas Miller, *The Campaign in Virginia May and June, 1864*. London, 1908.

Mahan, A. T., *From Sail to Steam. Recollections of Naval Life*. New York and London, 1907.

Murray, Thomas Hamilton, *History of the Ninth Regiment, Connecticut, Volunteer Infantry, "The Irish Regiment," in the War of the Rebellion, 1861–65*. New Haven, 1903.

[Pierce], Francis Marshall, *The Battle of Gettysburg. The Crest-Wave of the American Civil War*. New York, 1914.

Pivány, Eugene, *Hungarians in the American Civil War*. Cleveland, 1913.

Powell, William H., *The Fifth Army Corps (Army of the Potomac). A Record of Operations during the Civil War in the United States of America, 1861–1865*. New York, 1896.

Redway, G. W., *Fredericksburg. A Study in War*. Special Campaign Series No. 3. London and New York, 1906.

Rhodes, James Ford, *History of the Civil War 1861–1865*. New York, 1917.

Rombauer, Robert, *The Union Cause in St. Louis in 1861*. St. Louis, 1900.

Ropes, John Codman, *The Story of the Civil War*. 4 vols. New York, 1894–1913. Vols. I and II of four-volume work.

Shannon, Fred Albert, *The Organization and Administration of the Union Army*. 2 vols. Cleveland, 1928.

Soley, James Russell, *The Blockade and the Cruisers*. New York, 1895.

Tenny, W. J., *The Military and Naval History of the Rebellion in the United States with Biographical Sketches of Deceased Officers*. New York, 1866.

Tomes, Robert, *The Great Civil War. A History of the Late Rebellion with Biographical Sketches of Leading Statesmen and Distinguished Naval and Military Commanders*. 3 vols. New York, 1862–1867. Continued from the beginning of the year 1864 to the end of the war by Benjamin G. Smith.

Toombs, Samuel, *New Jersey Troops in the Gettysburg Campaign from June 5 to July 31, 1863*. Orange, N.J., 1888.

Vasvary, Edmund, *Lincoln's Hungarian Heroes; The Participation of Hungarians in the Civil War, 1861–1865*. Washington, 1939.

Wood, William, *Captains of the Civil War*, New Haven, 1921. Vol. XXXI of *The Chronicles of America*.

Woodbury, Augustus, *The Second Rhode Island Regiment. A Narrative of Military Operations in which the Regiment was engaged from the Beginning to the End of the War for the Union*. Providence, 1875.

WORKS OF BROADER SCOPE

Anderson, Rasmus B., *The First Chapter of Norwegian Immigration, Its Causes and Results*. Madison, 1907.

Bek, William G., *The German Settlement Society of Philadelphia and its Colony, Hermann, Missouri*. Philadelphia, 1907.

Blegen, Theodore C., *Norwegian Migration to America, 1825–1860*. 2 vols. Northfield, Minn., 1931.

Capěk, Thomas, *The Czechs in America*. Boston, 1920.

Dufour, Perret, *Swiss Settlement of Switzerland County, Indiana*. Indianapolis, 1925.

Emmett, Thomas A., *The Emmett Family*. New York, 1898.

Faust, Albert Bernhardt, *The German Element in the United States*. New York, 1909.

Gates, Paul W., *The Illinois Central Railroad and its Colonization Work*. Cambridge, 1934.

Haiman, Miecislaus, *Polish Past in America, 1608–1865*. Chicago, 1939.

Harlow, Alvin Fay, *Old Bowery Days*. New York, 1931.

Hense-Jensen, Wilhelm, *Wisconsin's Deutsch-Amerikaner bis zum Schluss des neunzehnten Jahrhunderts*. 2 vols. Milwaukee, 1910.

Holmes, Frank P. (ed.), *Minnesota in Three Centuries*. 4 vols. Semi-centennial edition. Mankato, Minn., 1908.

Körner, Gustav, *Das deutsche Element in den Vereinigten Staaten von Nord-Amerika*. Cincinnati, 1880.

Maguire, John Francis, *The Irish in America*. New York, 1869.

Nelson, O. N., *History of the Scandinavians and Successful Scandinavians in the United States*. 2 vols. Minneapolis, 1893–1897.

O'Callighan, John Cornelius, *History of the Irish Brigade in the Service of France from the Revolution in Great Britain and Ireland under James II to the Revolution in France under Louis XVI*. Glasgow, 1870.

Owens, John Algernon, *Sword and Pen, Ventures and Adventures of Willard Glazier*. Philadelphia, 1883.

Pieters, Aleida J., *A Dutch Settlement in Michigan*. Grand Rapids, 1913.

Qualey, Carlton C., *Norwegian Settlement in the United States*. Northfield, Minn., 1938.

Rhodes, James Ford, *History of the United States from the Compromise of 1850*. 8 vols. New York, 1903–1919.

Rosengarten, Joseph, *The German Soldier in the Wars of the United States*. Philadelphia, 1886.

Schafer, Joseph, *Four Wisconsin Counties, Prairie and Forest* (*Wisconsin Doomsday Book,* Vol. II [Wisconsin State Historical Society, Madison, 1927]).

————, *Wisconsin Lead Region.* Madison, 1932.

Schiavo, Giovanni, *The Italians in America before the Civil War.* New York, 1934.

Shambaugh, Bertha M. H., *Amana That Was and Amana That Is.* Iowa City, 1932.

Skelton, Isabelle Murphy, *The Life of Thomas D'Arcy McGee.* Gardinvale, Canada, 1925.

Steinach, Severin Alderich, *Geschichte und Leben der schweizer Kolonie in den Vereinigten Staaten von Nord Amerika.* New York, 1889.

Thompson, Charles Willis, *The Fiery Epoch, 1830–1877.* Indianapolis, 1931.

Tomes, Robert, *Battles of America by Sea and Land with Biographies of Naval and Military Commanders . . . ,* 3 vols. New York, 1878. (The volume dealing with the Civil War was written by John Laird Wilson.)

Van Der Zee, Jacob, *The Hollanders of Iowa.* Iowa City, 1912.

Wabeka, Bartus H., *Dutch Emigration to North America, 1624–1860. A Short History.* New York, 1944.

Wittke, Carl, *We Who Built America.* New York, 1940.

Index